Apogee of Empire

Stanley J. Stein & Barbara H. Stein

Apogee of Empire

Spain and New Spain in the Age of Charles III, 1759–1789

The Johns Hopkins University Press • Baltimore and London

This book has been brought to publication with the generous assistance of the University Committee on Research in the Humanities and Social Sciences, Princeton University.

The Johns Hopkins University Press
2715 North Charles Street, Baltimore, Maryland 21218-4363
www.press.jhu.edu

Library of Congress Cataloging-in-Publication Data

Stein, Stanley J.
    Apogee of empire : Spain and New Spain in the age of Charles III, 1759–1789 / Stanley J. Stein and Barbara H. Stein.
        p.   cm.
Includes bibliographical references and index.
    ISBN 0-8018-7339-8 (hardcover : alk. paper)
    1. Spain—Commerce—America—History—18th century. 2. Spain—Colonies—America—Commerce—History—18th century. 3. America—Commerce—Spain—History—18th century. 4. Spain—Commercial policy—History—18th century. 5. Spain—Economic conditions—18th century. I. Stein, Barbara H. II. Title.
    HF3685 .S737 2003
    382′.0946′08—dc21   2002013940

A catalog record for this book is available from the British Library.

Contents

Preface

In our historiography [i.e., that of Spain's American possessions], there is a kind of inferiority complex, a mélange of vapidity and a certain historical vision . . . [the idea] that the Indies were a divine gift to spread the faith rather than a source of profit.
                    Antonio-Miguel Bernal, *La financiación de la carrera de Indias*

By the middle of the eighteenth century, three established European empires were on a collision course in the western Atlantic, with each determined either to preserve its territory or enlarge it at the expense of its competitors. Spain, France, and England each had to renovate old or apply new fiscal measures to deal with real, envisioned, or imagined threats. Unrelieved competition thwarted efforts to achieve an equilibrium of power, an aspiration repeatedly aborted by interimperial conflict after the settlements of 1713–14 that concluded the War of the Spanish Succession, which had pitted France and Spain against England, the Netherlands, and the Holy Roman Empire. That competition would end, at least in the western Atlantic, at the Congress of Vienna in 1814, with England the clear hegemon in the Atlantic system.

After its seventeenth-century crisis, England had succeeded in mustering the financial resources to confront its competitors by mobilizing aristocracy and merchant bourgeoisie alike in support of its imperial aims. Eighteenth-century France, however, was unable to overcome late medieval institutions, interests, and mind-sets sufficiently to pay for an adequate army and navy. Spain managed to postpone the crisis by using the economic surpluses of its American colonies, especially the most populous of them, silver-mining Mexico, then called New Spain, to finance both its metropolitan and colonial needs.

When Charles III came to Madrid in 1759, after a quarter-century as ruler of the Spanish Bourbon Kingdom of the Two Sicilies (Naples and Sicily), Spain and its colonial empire in America were nonetheless seriously at risk. Madrid hoped to maintain its neutrality in the Seven Years' War (1756–63) between England and France for hegemony in the Atlantic. Without a confirmed ally, Spain had reasons to fear inevitable English operations—conducted by the world's most powerful navy—against Havana, the hub of its communications with New Spain and South America. Its maritime lifeline across the Caribbean to Veracruz was indispensable: without flows of colonial specie, there was little hope of rebuilding Spain's Atlantic defenses.

After two hundred years of Hapsburg rule in Spain, followed by a half-century of Bourbon "reform" projects that had gone nowhere, Charles and his Neapolitan staff, notably his Sicilian close collaborator Leopoldo di Gregorio, marqués de Esquilache (Squillace), who became secretary of Spain's Exchequer, or Treasury Department, the Consejo de Hacienda, had to come to grips with persisting political, social, economic, and intellectual Hapsburg institutions in both the Iberian Peninsula and the colonies. Part One of this book traces the attempt under Esquilache's direction to renovate those institutions, initially concentrating on the metropole. In essence, "traditionalists" and "reformers" wrestled with a persistent preoccupation: what adjustments were feasible in metropole and colonies to confront Spain's imperialist challengers without radically altering the Hapsburg inheritance?

The Esquilache-directed essay at domestic housecleaning was uncommonly ambitious and comprehensive for Spain, with many targets attacked simultaneously. Seven years after Charles arrived, however, a combination of privileged interests and factions fostered under the Hapsburgs engineered a coup at Madrid that forced Charles to send Esquilache, the architect of so many government initiatives, back to Italy. In Spain, renewal was stalled. But there remained, however, the possibility of revamping the colonial administration and the essential economic links between the metropole and its colonies.

Before the March 1766 rioting (*motín*) at Madrid that unseated him, Esquilache had launched what was tantamount to a colonial review. After recovering Havana, which had been taken in 1762 by an English amphibious assault, Esquilache dispatched military officers to survey the situation of Cuba and Puerto Rico. Subsequently, in 1765, he appointed José de Gálvez, a young career bureaucrat, as high commissioner (*visitador general*) and authorized him to conduct a broad investigation of New Spain, Spain's most important trading partner. With renovation ostensibly stalled in the metropole, Madrid now emphasized change in colonial affairs.

In Part Two of the book, we trace how Madrid moved to modify the persistent Hapsburg transatlantic trading system linking the metropole to its American colonies. No doubt Gálvez's years investigating New Spain's fiscal condition must be factored into Madrid's insistence after 1779 that Mexico City's Treasury transfer surplus to Madrid *and* Havana. "Bourbon reform" would prove to be a suction pump of decapitalization in Spain's richest colony. Although a successful fiscal mechanism, it brought no social benefit, nor was it intended to do so. Part Two concludes with promulgation of the last of three *reglamentos* deregulating what still remained a closed imperial trading system and an assessment of their impact upon Spain and New Spain, as well as of the decline in French exports to the Spanish colonies through the port of Cadiz.

Had Madrid's strategic decision to shift the focus from the metropole to the American colonies and to promote renovation incrementally and narrowly been correct? What precisely was "Bourbon reform" in Spain and New Spain? Were there fundamental changes in the imperial system, or was it merely a case of meliorist initiatives with indifferent outcomes, leaving both colonies and metropole ill-prepared for the decades of deepening crisis that were soon to follow? In this analysis of how an old colonial empire in the Atlantic survived intact the pressures applied by Europe's two hegemons, England and France, in the last phase of commercial capitalism and the initial decades of what became the Industrial Revolution, we have sought to address these issues, even if they remain ultimately as unresolved as they were on the eve of the French Revolution.

This is a study of incremental response by an old imperial order to challenges at home and abroad: of the capacity of tradition to "retard what we cannot repel," as Samuel Johnson once put it, and to "palliate what we cannot cure."

Acknowledgments

In the course of research we have benefited from the cooperation of many people and institutions. In Mexico, José Ignacio Rúbio Mañé and Beatriz Arteaga (Archivo General de la Nación), Ernesto de la Torre Villar (Biblioteca Nacional), Luís González y González, and Luís Muro (El Colegio de México), and historian, nationalist, and public servant Luís Chávez Orozco, who provided access to his documentary collections. In Spain, Antonia Heredia Herrero and Rosario Parra (Archivo de Indias) and the personnel of the Archivo Histórico Nacional, Real Academia de la Historia, and the Biblioteca del Real Palacio. In France, the staff of the Salle de Lecture of the Archives Nationales, the Quai d'Orsay, and, in England, the Public Record Office.

We are most appreciative of the assistance of the staff of Princeton University's Firestone Library (Circulation, Reference, Inter-Library Loan, and Rare Books and Manuscripts) and Peter T. Johnson, bibliographer for Latin American and Iberian Acquisitions. The university's Committee on Research and the Committee on Regional Studies financed research trips abroad, which were supplemented by the National Endowment for the Humanities. Chairmen, department managers, and secretaries of the History Department have patiently aided on innumerable occasions. Our colleagues Jeremy Adelman, Michael Mahoney, Arno Mayer, and Robert Tignor have, as always, been unsparing in encouragement, criticism, and technical support.

Finally, with pleasure we acknowledge the demanding copyediting of Peter Dreyer, the patience of Pamela Long, the editorial oversight of Michael Lonegro, Lee Campbell Sioles, and Tom Roche of the Johns Hopkins University Press, and the assistance of David Myhre (Ford Foundation–Mexico) in obtaining authorization for the jacket design.

Monetary Equivalents

marco = 68 reales de plata, or 8.5 pesos
peso sencillo = 15 reales de vellón
peso fuerte = 20 reales de vellón, or 8 reales de plata
medio real = half real
cuartilla = quarter real (trade money)
tlaco = one-eighth real
pilón = one-sixteenth real

Part One

Stalemate in
the Metropole

1. From Naples to Madrid

His [Charles III's] political benevolence comes down to little more than the appearance of reform, widely proclaimed, which resulted in hypocritical illusion.
Gaetano Garofalo, *La monarchía borbónica a Napoli*

Many are already convinced that it is necessary to change things.
Queen María Amalia of Spain to Minister of Justice Bernardo Tanucci

A change of leadership at the highest political level in the eighteenth century often brought opportunity for policy changes, the introduction of new personnel, and renewed hope for the resolution of long-standing problems. Fernando VI's death in August 1759 and the accession of his half-brother to the Spanish throne as Charles III promised new initiatives, not only in contrast to the drift associated with Fernando's last years, but above all because of the political and economic activism of Charles's twenty-five-year rule in Naples as king of the Two Sicilies. And, indeed, although Charles's Neapolitan achievements may be open to question, they prefigured many of the objectives, as well as the political style, pursued during his thirty-year reign in Spain.

On his arrival at Naples in 1734 at the head of an army of occupation, the eighteen-year-old Spanish *infante* had found a country of about three million controlled by great landowners and a structure of government complicated by ecclesiastical privilege to the point where only 20 percent of the population remained under direct royal jurisdiction.[1] The capital, Naples, was an eighteenth-century megalopolis absorbing wealth and income, a financial, commercial, and administrative center to which the underemployed of the surrounding countryside flowed seeking jobs or charity. Like Madrid, it was the place of residence of landlords, church dignitaries, high government officials, and lumpen proletarians—the latter always on the edge of starvation and mob violence. To stabilize his young son's government, Philip V immediately transferred 1.8 million pesos of colonial receipts in silver to Naples, not the last of such external financing from Spain.[2]

The financial condition of the Neapolitan state reflected the limitations of a backward, underdeveloped agrarian economy. Its fundamental problems were skewed land tenure and land utilization patterns, high taxes on production, whether for local consumption or export, commercial monopolies, and the omnipresence of ecclesiastical property. Eighty percent of rural properties (excluding those of the crown) were owned or controlled by the church. More than 70 percent of the combined annual income of the church and the landed aristocracy accrued to the church; and jurisdictional immunities permitted church authorities to supplement this income by smuggling salt, tobacco, and raw silk. Manufacture was virtually nonexistent; even cloth for the local armed forces had to be imported, and silk manufacture was confined by law to Naples and its immediate locale.[3]

These elements should not be viewed in isolation, for just as it is today, the syndrome of underdevelopment or stagnation in the eighteenth century was more than the sum of its parts. In the kingdom of Naples on the accession of Charles, the generalized symptoms of stagnation suggest a common pattern of vested interests in a status quo that satisfied most influential interest groups. There were, first of all, the large landlords (*barone*), who had acquired jurisdiction over their tenants during the breakdown of Hapsburg control in the seventeenth century. Their properties, which produced exports such as oil, silk, and to a lesser extent wool, were relatively lightly taxed; output was controlled by commission houses in Naples and other ports through the *contratto della liquidazione* regulating the storage and sale of such exportables, for which merchants collected a sales percentage.[4] Landlords and merchants were linked to the third vested interest, the ecclesiastical establishment, since landlords often registered their properties as church holdings to avoid taxation, and the large export houses also handled the production of church estates. As a whole, the church constituted a dominant group, consisting of about 75,000 wealthy, prestigious, powerful clergy, and its influence was enhanced by the fact that it represented papal interests.[5]

Wealthy merchants functioned as an essential part of the state apparatus: they farmed taxes and thereby employed an army of underpaid petty officials in the cities and countryside, who used and abused the complex of excise and customs duties to supplement their salaries. Under such conditions, smuggling and corruption were institutionalized at all levels. Fifth and last among those niched into the status quo were thousands of bureaucrats, exposed to pressures from landlords, merchant bankers, and, of course, the church.[6]

Neatly enmeshed in a functioning system, the dominance of these elements would undoubtedly have long gone unchallenged had it not been for new dynamic factors resulting from Charles's seizure of the kingdom from the Austrians. Some factors were the Italian dynastic territorial interests of the Spanish Bourbons, heirs to the state-building ambitions of Charles's great-grandfather, Louis XIV, and the dynastic preoccupations of his mother, Isabel Farnese of Parma. Undoubtedly, too, it was the determination of Charles and his Spanish supporters to create a model state administration for Naples in order to demonstrate his aptitude to succeed Fernando, if and when occasion should arise, as ruler of Spain, still one of western Europe's imperial powers.

Even before the expulsion of the Austrians from Sicily was completed by José Carrillo de Albornoz, duque de Montemar, the formation of a new state apparatus was undertaken. Selection of competent top bureaucrats and their immediate subordinates was crucial to reforming the existing underpaid bureaucracy, estimated at 26,000, a "natural adversary of any change for the better . . . in the public spirit, prime cause of social divisions and rivalry, principal cause of the elimination of any sound economic principle."[7]

Charles's initial appointments indicated an affinity with reform-minded elements in Madrid, as well as with the Neapolitan elite, who saw in the protection of the Spanish Bourbons an opportunity to revitalize their backward country. As virtual prime minister, the conde di Santostefano dominated Charles's government in its early years, aided by José Joaquín de Montealegre, a Sevillan who had risen under Philip V's minister José Patiño and had accompanied Santostefano from Spain, who became secretary of state with jurisdiction over war, navy, finance, and ecclesiastical affairs. Under him as intendant-general of revenues was Giovanni Brancaccio, whose reputation as a tax expert had also been acquired under Patiño, who had arranged his transfer to Naples.[8] Other protégés of Patiño's later to play important roles in Spain as innovators served in Naples during Charles's early years there: José del Campillo y Cosío as intendant in 1734 and Zenón de Somodevila (later marqués de la Ensenada) who did two years' service in Naples (1734–36).[9] Charles's third major appointee in 1734 was his minister of justice, Bernardo Tanucci, a former law professor at Pisa, prominent jurist, and hispanophile, notable for criticizing ecclesiastical privilege and the omnipotent Neapolitan nobility.[10]

In drawing from the pool of prominent bureaucrats in Neapolitan government linked to Spain and its ruling Bourbon dynasty in the struggle against Austrian hegemony and papal authority in Italy, Charles's selections displayed an inclination on his part to assign responsibility to talent rather than birth. A Sicilian of modest background (like Charles's other key economic administrator in Naples, Brancaccio), Leopoldo di Gregorio (subsequently marqués de Esquilache) had left Messina for Naples, where he became an accountant in a commercial firm. Although little is known of his early career, apparently his involvement in military procurement opened the way to appointment in the Naples customs service, where his competence was quickly recognized and he rose to be administrator-general (1746). Marriage to a Catalan cemented his link to Spain.[11] In 1755, in a political reorganization by Charles—perhaps in response to the unexpected ouster of Ensenada at Madrid—Esquilache was assigned the multiple portfolios of finance, war, the navy, and commerce, while Tanucci moved from the justice ministry to become secretary of state and minister of foreign affairs.[12]

The careers of Esquilache and Tanucci exemplify Charles's commitment to transforming his backward kingdom into a viable independent state, perhaps with a certain prestige. This required revenues capable of supporting a competent army and bureaucracy, along with the cultural prerequisites of a European-class court. Councils, or *juntas,* were created to confront old issues (e.g., the Giunta d'Infidenza to ensure state security) and above all to formulate new policies, particularly economic policies. The objective was not merely to reorganize tax collection to enhance income from the existing volume of goods produced but also to expand the tax base, the production of exportables—mainly olive oil, but also raw silk and wool—for which demand was rising in established as well as new foreign markets in England, France, the Low Countries, and the Baltic region. One fairly reliable indicator of economic expansion following Charles's arrival at Naples was the rise in receipts of export taxes on olive oil: between 1726–29 and 1737–40, these rose slightly more than 50 percent.[13]

In other words, fiscal reform accompanied by economic growth were essential underpinnings for an effective and enlightened state capable of achieving prosperity and national prestige. Charles's ministers hoped to reduce obstacles to growth: the tax-exempt status of church properties and income, prohibitively high export duties, inadequate customs revenues and widespread smuggling, the low output of manufactures and what was then called "passive" (that is, commission) trade, which involved external borrowing. The Giunta del Commerzio called for suggestions for improvement, and the *progettisti* responded. One of the most prolific, Jean-Baptiste de Vaucoulleur, then residing at Naples, supplied memorials on expanding

Neapolitan foreign trade, establishing an overseas trading corporation, and, most important, developing agriculture and manufacturing.[14]

One of this Giunta's first steps, following one of Vaucoulleur's proposals, was to create a Supremo Magistratto del Commerzio, which was given broad directives to "revive" manufacture, develop the transportation infrastructure, and simplify commercial procedures. It quickly established a Consolato di Terra e di Mare to handle commercial disputes and *consolati di Regno* in twenty urban centers. Early in Charles's reign, the most prominent agricultural interests, the major producers of olive oil for export, took their complaints about the malpractice of Neapolitan export merchants to the Supremo Magistratto. Under the mechanism of the *contratto a liquidazione*, oil producers shipped their output to the refining and storage tanks of exporters. For this service, including storage until the time of sale, merchants had been setting rates varying between 10 to 48 percent of export prices; the Supremo Magistratto ordered a ceiling of 6 percent, favoring producers over intermediaries. Given the expansion of oil exports throughout the eighteenth century, a key element in economic change in the Two Sicilies and a major source of government income, there is reason to believe that the legal maximum rate stimulated the proliferation of large estates, while indirectly contributing to the impoverishment of small landholders and the peasantry, whose *contratto alla voce* with exporters proved unfavorable.[15]

Revamping the bureaucracy, creating new councils, and simplifying excise and customs collection represented an effort to provide a climate for economic change, to stimulate the economy, and ultimately to generate government revenues. In a sense, they also laid the groundwork for a frontal attack upon the privileges and property of the church. The Neapolitan clergy were numerous, influential, and controlled a high percentage of landed properties. Worse, such properties were largely tax-exempt, sharply cutting into the tax base of a state whose major economic sector was agriculture. To a modern observer embedded in a generally secular Western culture, it is difficult to envision a society and economy in which the established church pressed upon the individual and the state in so many ways. The stagnation of the Neapolitan economy and society was traceable to an unholy alliance of what Tanucci labeled the "feudal tyranny" of the nobility with the "Italian slavery" imposed by the Roman curia.[16]

The Concordat of 1741 was an effort to bring the omnipresent church under some state control. It circumscribed the use of ecclesiastical asylum and the variety of cases subject to ecclesiastical courts. Jurisdictional conflict aside, the sections treating the tax liability of the church were essential to state finance. It was agreed that church property acquired prior to 1741 would now pay one-half the normal rate; it excluded, however, the property of seminaries, hospitals, the *sacro patrimonio* of the papacy, and, until 1751, 80 percent of the raw silk produced on church land, the "principal cause of all the considerable contraband [in silk]." As a concession to the papacy, the Neapolitan government accepted episcopal participation in reviewing church accounts and the formation of cadasters of church property; indeed, bishops would have to furnish written permission to royal collectors seeking to try clerics for falsification of accounts. Finally, the Concordat excluded foreigners from appointment to local benefices.[17]

Once in possession of authority to extend its powers of taxation over church real estate, the Neapolitan government undertook a national survey of wealth and income, the *catasto generale*. Despite numerous exemptions, the regressive nature of the incidence of taxation, and the ability of the wealthy to escape full liability, the cadaster facilitated the disentanglement of lay from ecclesiastical property and improved fiscal returns. It led logically to further extension of royal fiscal control when, in 1751, the government nationalized major tax farms and assigned royal intendants to tax collection. Whether the cadaster augmented state revenues appreciably—as some have argued—is moot. Like the Concordat, the cadaster nonetheless symbolized the exercise of regalism at Naples and may have inspired Ensenada at Madrid to initiate a comparable national survey in Madrid as the basis of a projected single tax, or *única contribución,* on income.[18]

Charles at Naples: A Balance Sheet

From the perspective of Charles's subsequent role in Spain, his Italian reign is illuminating. In Naples, he and his ministers set about creating an adequately salaried and efficient administration, the lack of which was the most immediate obstacle to forging a viable independent state and economy. His instruments of power were a small army, a loyal bureaucracy staffed by competent men at the top, and a climate of intellectual toleration that attracted Italian *iluministi.* And, one must add, Charles's readiness to placate, cajole, temporize, and often compromise, realizing that it was impossible, and perhaps even undesirable, radically to transform the basic structures of the society he found in the Two Sicilies. At one point, Tanucci reminded Charles with some bitterness that "neither Germany nor Poland has an aristocracy as powerful as that of Naples."[19] Charles's achievements were nonetheless impressive. Expansion of the Neapolitan export economy and an increase in revenues for defense and public works provided an opportunity for merchants and financiers to grow in numbers and influence. While this was hardly a transformed society, it now offered social mobility to many and attracted intellectuals of the caliber of Bernardo Tanucci, Giambattista Vico, and Antonio Genovesi. One suspects that Charles's supporters were drawn from among the large landed proprietors, the merchant and banking community, and the liberal professions and intellectuals.[20]

But if Charles and his ministers approached the limits of the possible in the area of domestic reform and growth, the ongoing conflict between France and England and its impact on lesser powers was a matter of growing concern. Not only because of his close association with Spain, but also because the growth of English naval and economic power in the Mediterranean threatened the sovereignty of the Two Sicilies, Charles inevitably became involved in the conflict. The limits of a small state were made dramatically clear in 1742 when an English naval squadron sailed into the Bay of Naples to demand an immediate declaration of Neapolitan neutrality in the War of the Austrian Succession, then going on, and threatening naval bombardment were it not forthcoming.[21] The government promised neutrality, but Charles and his ministers never forgot this example of English gunboat diplomacy wreaked upon a weak state. Nor would they overlook the English assault upon Cartagena de Indias and George Anson's capture of the *nao* (and its cargo of silver pesos) crossing the Pacific from Manila to Acapulco in the same war.

It is easy to exaggerate the improvement of the Neapolitan economy, society, and polity under Charles and to see in his bureaucratic appointments and legislation more gains than in fact were achieved. Spanish historians of the nineteenth century tended uncritically to accept his Neapolitan achievements, just as they tended to praise his subsequent thirty-year reign in Spain.[22] Twentieth-century Italian historians have been more critical, emphasizing the plasticity and resilience of the vested interests engaged.[23] Not to be overlooked was the fear, always lurking, that fiscal changes pushed too tenaciously might bring a decline in revenues and, in the volatile urban center of Naples, provoke civil conflict.

But to nationalistically inclined Spanish contemporaries who saw Spain and its American possessions in the 1750s as dangerously exposed, even adrift, under Fernando VI, Charles's performance at Naples inspired hope of change in Spain. Contacts between Madrid and Naples increased after the death of Philip V (1746) and became even closer once it was clear that Charles would succeed his now mentally unstable brother. In April 1754, when Ensenada was ousted in a quiet palace coup, Charles wrote his mother requesting that in the event of his brother's death, she rule with full powers until his arrival at Madrid.[24] Thereafter, through correspondence with Spain's prime minister, Ricardo Wall, and via Wall's reports to Tanucci, Charles kept abreast of the situation in Spain and its empire. From the onset of Fernando's self-destructive madness in September 1758 until his death the following August, Charles was au courant with the spreading administrative paralysis, breakdown of responsibility, and delays in making key decisions.[25] In addition, there loomed the threat that in 1759 Europe's two major imperialist powers, England and France, might even settle their differences by dividing Spain's colonial possessions.[26] Charles thus left Naples only too cognizant of imminent crisis in Spain and its colonies, and, one may presume, prepared to draw upon his Neapolitan experience.

Was Charles in fact prepared to deal with the complex problems of Spain and its far-flung empire? Undoubtedly, the Neapolitan experience was a major asset, giving him a measure of self-confidence in going to Madrid. In retrospect, it is significant that Charles, unlike many of his predecessors, had spent his formative years far from the Madrid court, with its obsessive ceremonial, factional rivalries, and intrigues. Charles II had been ill in body and mind; Philip V, unprepared to cope with his role as Spanish monarch and ever nostalgic for France, had retreated into intermittent depression; and for the well-meaning but temperamentally weak Fernando VI, the demands of office were a burden from which, it seems, the distractions of music (he subsidized Boccherini) and domesticity seemed the only escape. In contrast, by the time Charles became king of Spain, he had acquired through a natural constitution and experience the self-confidence, strength, and not least the patience to withstand the pressures that had debilitated so many of his predecessors. His rigid daily schedule of bureaucratic consultation in the morning and hunting in the afternoon undoubtedly helped him endure the vicissitudes of his three decades as king of Spain. A similar schedule would not be enough to save his son, Charles IV, who, although no less well intentioned, was less prepared by aptitude, upbringing, education, and experience to confront the far more difficult decades after Charles III's death.

In response to the question of Charles's preparedness to deal with the problems of Spain and its empire, however, there is a major caveat. In exchanging Naples for Madrid, he moved from a small, relatively homogeneous kingdom to the land-locked capital of continental Spain and its distant multi-ethnic colonies. Spain's possession of a vast empire in America brought Charles from the Mediterranean periphery of the Anglo-French conflict to its vortex. Furthermore, in undertaking the renovation of Spain, Charles was to confront not only external constraints but the complex webs of interest, practice, and privilege, sanctified by law and tradition, whose often invisible taproots penetrated the social and economic transformations (or deformations) brought about by the heritage of more than 250 years of conquest, colonization, and colonial exploitation, of wars and internal vicissitudes. To say that Charles was not fully aware of the resilience of the internal and external constraints upon his determination to remold Spain is only to assert that he was a man of his time and place. Although in the early twenty-first century, in an era of triumphant economic and political liberalism and critical postmodernism, there is a temptation to view Charles III as insufficiently "enlightened" and overly "absolutist," the historian must examine him in the context of the conditions and momentum of that time and place. This insight, appropriately enough, was articulated by the Neapolitan philosopher and jurist Giambattista Vico, whom Charles named royal historian of Naples in 1735.

War, the *Consulado* at Cadiz, and the Atlantic Complex

When Charles debarked at Barcelona in late 1759 accompanied by an experienced fiscal technocrat, Esquilache, his readiness to meet the challenge of ruling Spain seemed unquestionable. Now, as reigning monarch, he faced Spain's second major foreign policy crisis in the century, the imminent victory of England in its long struggle with France over colonies, trade, and sea power. At Zaragoza, en route to Madrid, he learned of Quebec's loss to English forces and the predictable elimination of the French from North America, including the Mississippi valley and the adjacent rim of the Gulf of Mexico. Along with English commercial and allied naval operations in the Caribbean—Martinique was seized in the 1759 campaign— the projection of English power renewed the threat to Spain's most valuable colony, New Spain ("the precious keystone of Spain's colonies"), then the world's principal source of silver.[27]

On news of Quebec's loss to the English, Charles ordered Esquilache to inform London of his concern that further territorial acquisitions in the Western Hemisphere would upset the balance of power set in place by the Peace of Utrecht, which in 1713 had stipulated that no European power would acquire further dominion in that area of the world. William Pitt had long supported English penetration of Central America through the logwood ("Campeachy") trade, and he responded that England recognized no balance of power in America established by the Treaty of Utrecht and would exploit recent victories over the French.[28] To French commercial interests, English military success spelled the loss to them of the market of New Spain, which the English would now "furnish exclusively with their own manufactures which would occasion a loss of trade worth 20,000,000 *livres* annually to France, and in consequence ruin to the greater part of our industry."[29] London's affirmation of its expansionist policy soon led to another defensive Franco-Spanish arrangement, the so-called Tercer pacto de familia, or Third Family Pact, in 1761, and then to war between Spain and England in 1762. For both France and Spain, it was an alliance based upon "fear and impotence."[30]

The dramatic impact of the Seven Years' War was the most immediate and serious problem that Spain faced on the eve of Charles's arrival at Madrid at the end of 1759. But it was scarcely a surprise. Colonial issues had long preoccupied Charles and his immediate entourage at Naples, as well as Madrid's bureaucrats. At the capital were personnel trained and advanced by José Patiño, chief architect of Bourbon colonial policy in the immediate post-Utrecht era. Two of these—José del Campillo and the marqués de la Ensenada—had, after service in Italy, attained prominent posts in Spain, where they recognized the centrality of colonial and related metropolitan issues and toyed with structural changes that would receive serious consideration or partial implementation only under Charles III. In the same middle decades of the century, through continuous contact with Madrid, Charles and his cadre at Naples kept abreast of the worsening imperial crisis and the associated financial and political ramifications. Ensenada's ouster in 1754, joined to the indecisive policies of Carvajal and then Wall, convinced Charles on the eve of his arrival in Spain that the situation of the empire was indeed precarious.

Since the end of the War of the Austrian Succession (1748), it had been clear that the Treaty of Utrecht had not resolved the problem of Spanish security in America. France was now unable to compete with English naval and commercial power without Spain's assistance. For Spanish interests, the vital theater of intra-European rivalry was not Europe but America, and the major threat was England—and so it remained over the next half-century. An anonymous mémoire drafted sometime after 1747 for circulation among Spanish bureaucrats depicted the situation of the Spanish colonies at mid-century, which "have induced great changes in the European system." Particularly significant was the Spanish colonial component of English and French trade, and "consequently the American trade of Spain and Portugal is so important and necessary to every trading country."

Nor did this author ignore the political repercussions of the changing economic situation. No longer was there the possibility of one "universal monarchy." However, what could not be discounted was "the wide influence of wealth . . . if one state would manage to become the absolute master of all the trade of America." In a three-cornered competition for empire in America, that threat came from England, whose policy alternated between peace and belligerency, striving to "expand its trade by hindering that of other powers and invading their possessions." England's predictable path to Spain's American colonies lay via French-occupied Louisiana; were the English to seize that colony, "they will not delay expanding into Mexico."[31] This was only another expression of Spain's fear of the domino effect of England's aggressive policies. Moreover the threat to the colonies in America had an internal as well as an external dimension; throughout the 1750s and early 1760s, there were rumors and the reality of insurrectionary ideas and activities, with the expectation of foreign intervention.[32]

On renewed warfare between England and France, Spanish and French Caribbean colonies braced for the inevitable confrontation with English amphibious forces; it was hardly a matter of where but of when an attack would occur. In April 1759, when Charles was still at Naples, Paris urged him to dispatch troops and equipment to the Caribbean, and he indicated that he would comply.[33] Meanwhile, French representatives at Madrid were encouraged by the unequivocal language of Colonial Secretary Julián de Arriaga (who had served in Venezuela) and of the (first) conde de Revillagigedo (formerly captain-general of Cuba and then viceroy of New Spain). In November 1759, according to French sources, Revillagigedo warned Arriaga that "if Spain fails to prevent the advance of the English, its American domains will soon be exposed to the greed of a country that wars against France only to prepare the way to a richer and easier conquest." Charles, who had followed Revillagigedo's career attentively and was impressed by his efficient transfer of New Spain's lucrative *alcabala* (sales tax) from private to direct state administration, despite the opposition of the influential merchant guild of Mexico City, its *consulado*, reportedly deferred to "every proposal concerning America by M. de Horcasitas."[34] Charles's promise made at Naples bore fruit in June 1760 with the dispatch to Havana of a naval squadron carrying troops and a new governor with orders to ready Havana's defenses.[35]

To Charles and his close advisers, the threat to Spain's American colonies was only the most serious and recent manifestation of Spain's perennial colonial problem. More disturbing to Spain's mid-century crisis managers and projectors was the failure of a half-century of Bourbon rule to render the colonial economy a source of growth and development for the metropole. The conviction of the budding bureaucrat José de Gálvez in the late 1750s that "the main object of this monarchy is the increase of its trade and navigation to the Indies" was, of course, not new.[36] That perception had underlain the programs of bureaucrats since the beginning of Philip V's reign, when a French technical adviser had advocated an imperial trading system opening direct contact between Spain's major metropolitan and colonial ports.[37] Spanish colonial policy-makers from Patiño through Campillo, Ensenada, Carvajal, and Wall never underestimated the importance of colonial trade and silver flows. Following contemporary mercantilist tenets and the views of recent projectors, they concluded that a more rational management of the economy of Spain and its empire could stimulate peninsular agriculture, commerce, and manufacturing. Spain's colonial commerce could be transformed from "passive" exploitation by foreign interests into an "active" instrument of economic development. Spain, "restored" to its former independence and prosperity, would be able to survive the mounting competition for overseas empire that had proven fundamental to the development of western European economies. In this new approach, the "old," or Spanish Hapsburg, empire, nominally managed by the state and in reality exploited by a narrow coalition of interests, might be adapted to new imperial arrangements to serve the broader interests of the Bourbon state, based upon a wider participation in its benefits.

For more than two centuries, the southwestern tip of Andalusia had been the sole authorized terminal of trade and communication between Spain and its colonies. In that long period, a system of infrequent convoys of merchant vessels, departing from a single port, whose monopoly position was exploited by the Andalusian merchant guild, Sevilla's *consulado,* had been legitimated by legal privilege and practice. The consequence was mainly a commission ("passive") trade based on the exchange of impressive quantities of colonial silver for low-volume, high-priced merchandise supplied largely from non-Spanish sources in Europe. After the Peace of Utrecht, however, the Andalusian port monopoly shifted from Sevilla to Cadiz, probably in consequence of Cadiz's contributions to the tune of 660,000 pesos to finance Philip V's insecure government between 1701 and 1710.[38]

Cadiz burgeoned into a major urban center of the Iberian Peninsula over the first half of the eighteenth century. Its population expanded by 50 percent, from 41,000 to 62,000, between 1700 and 1765. As in the Hapsburg centuries at Sevilla, resident foreigners at Cadiz employed Spaniards as intermediaries—straw men, agents, and factors on the fleets to the colonies—in the "passive" trade. A census of Cadiz's merchant community in 1762 showed a total of 379 traders; almost two-thirds were Spanish (220), 61 were French, and the remainder were Italians, Anglo-Irish, Flemings, and Germans. Migrants from Cantabrian and Basque peasant communities to the new imperial trade center increasingly sought, however, to shoulder aside and supplant these foreigners.

Foreign resident merchants' importance far exceeded their number at Cadiz, however, and the "French nation" constituted the most influential mercantile group.[39] French traders had begun arriving at the end of the seventeenth century, and their numbers increased rapidly during the War of the Austrian Succession (1740–48), when merchants and shipping from Saint-Malo in Brittany kept Spain in contact with its American colonies. Equally notable in their rise to prominence was Philip V's accession: by ordering his wardrobe from Paris, he set fashion in fine textile imports and style, quickly picked up by Madrid's elite and spreading to other classes. By 1743, French fashion "was fully implanted."[40] Ten years later, thirty French firms at Cadiz had aggregate incomes virtually six times those of ninety-seven Spanish counterparts. "The wealthiest firms [which] controlled the exchange rates" included a number established early in the century: Masson, Verduc y Vincent y Cia; Cayla, Solier Hermanos; Magon; Lefer Hermanos, and the Lecouteulx.[41]

Cadiz's expanding volume of colonial trade drew immigrants. For Spaniards from Cantabria and the Basque country, it was a magnet of opportunity, "the center for all the fortunes of the kingdom"; for foreigners, it was "a speculative center par excellence" but invariably risky.[42] As over the previous two centuries, foreigners furnished the bulk of the imported manufactures for reexport to the colonies, providing goods for export on credit, if cash were unavailable, and loans *a riesgo de mar* and in the form of *cambio marítimo*.[43] Through foreign residents' participation as investors, importers, and lenders, Spain's colonial trades at Cadiz (as formerly at Sevilla) were thus maintained in the absence of domestic manufacturing and adequate investment. The curious symbiosis of Spanish penny capitalists with more developed foreign merchant houses has been categorized as typifying "a stale archaism"; Cadiz was literally years behind commercial and financial centers like Amsterdam and London.[44]

A small number of native-born merchants purchased imports from western Europe's producing centers from resident foreigners, then reexported them to the colonies. Usually, they borrowed to purchase their cargoes and cover insurance and maritime shipping costs, which were comparatively high. The majority, however, as earlier at Sevilla, operated as dependents or front men for well-supplied, well-financed foreign residents. The Spaniards' greatest source of income derived from commissions earned as intermediaries, agents (*encomenderos, factores*) accompanying shipments aboard the convoyed fleets—*flotas* and *galeones*—to the main Spanish ports in the Caribbean—unlike the *comprador bourgeois* whom European traders encountered (or helped form) in Southeast and East Asia. This dependence upon foreign merchant houses for goods and finance persisted well into the eighteenth century; as late as 1742, the *consulado* of Cadiz itself had to confess that for "the maintenance of our current unsatisfactory condition, necessary deference and remedy depend upon foreigners."[45]

Despite these conditions, unique in the Atlantic economy, Cadiz's small-scale Spanish merchants sought to present to the rest of Europe an illusion of economic independence to match imperial Spain's regulations for monopolizing its colonial trade, which expressly denied non-Spaniards' participation in Spain's "managed" transatlantic trade system, either by shipping reexports under their names or employing non-Spaniards as factors. This façade obfuscated what the president of the Casa de Contratación, José Patiño, described explicitly in 1722 as "Spain's disheartening situation and weakness visible in lack of capital and poor trade performance." Decades later, the situation was unchanged. Beholden to foreign residents for goods, credit, and loans, members of the Cadiz merchant guild portrayed themselves in 1771 as "unos cargadores, otros navegantes," as well as others "who have made overseas trips without earning the hoped-for fruit of their labors."[46] In Cadiz's highly speculative world of transatlantic trading, a few were enriched, while the majority of hopefuls failed to attain wealth and status. When merchants did prosper in colonial trading, they tended to disinvest, to move their earnings into urban and rural properties, into mortgages (*censos*), and the purchase of ennoblement. In Andalusia, as elsewhere in the Peninsula, the values of an aristocratic-noble landowning class were hegemonic. By contrast, the influence of French commercial firms in eighteenth-century Cadiz was continuous; "French is as common as Spanish" there, it was noted in 1765.[47]

The way in which immigrants who had grown rich in Andalusia passed from merchant into gentry or aristocratic status is exemplified by the career of Pedro Colarte in late seventeenth-century Sevilla. This Flemish immigrant merchant left an estate that dwarfed those of Andalusian landed magnates by a factor of 14. He had arrived with letters of introduction to a Flemish merchant, Juan de Vint, and probably sailed to America as Vint's *encomendero-factor*. On returning, he served at Cadiz primarily as a commission agent for Flemish, French, and Dutch exporters, receiving and warehousing goods, then remitting colonial staples and, most important, silver pesos. Colarte filled multiple roles as commission agent, investment counselor, and exchange dealer. An efficient intermediary who grasped the essence of the Spanish system of colonial trade, Colarte earned a high credit rating, which translated into a flow of textile imports and funds from "the north," principally Antwerp and Amsterdam. Given Spain's prohibitory legislation, Colarte employed Spaniards to cover his colonial operations—"hombres de la carrera de Indias" ranging from crew to flag officers of *flotas* and *galeones* (*funcionarios de alta clase*).[48] Overseas at colonial ports, Colarte's straw men sold fine woolens, silks, and embroidered linens to administrators and clerics (one of them the bishop of Huamanga, Peru) for resale to discriminating consumers. Following Andalusian practice, Colarte invested his earnings from trade in Sevilla's privatized *alcabala* farm and a special charge (*uno por ciento*) collected by Cadiz's customs.[49]

As a successful businessman, Colarte found Andalusian society accessible to wealthy, upwardly mobile merchants. He married Vint's Spanish sister-in-law, was accepted into the prestigious military Orden de Santiago, bought a post on Sevilla's town council, followed this with the purchase of a seigniorial jurisdiction sold by the impoverished *monarquía,* then the title of marqués, all capped with the establishment of an entailed estate (*mayorazgo*). In the last half of the seventeenth century, while Spain's economy stagnated, Colarte's net worth rose by a factor of 15 (from 60,000 to 900,000 *pesos escudos*). In the process, he became an aristocrat, although a biographer claims that his values remained bourgeois. His estate records no investment in any local manufacturing; his son's commercial operations failed; his grandson was an Andalusian aristocrat with no appetite for either peninsular or colonial trading ventures.[50]

Colarte's success as an intermediary at Sevilla was an exception. In the next century at Cadiz, omitting a handful of long-lived firms, mainly French, success in colonial trading could be illusory, no matter how earnestly pursued, as Antoine Granjean's experience proves.[51] Granjean left Lyon and its silk factories in the late 1740s for Bordeaux, France's major colonial trading center, where he clerked briefly for a textile merchant. Somewhat later, in 1752, he was among hopeful French immigrants at Cadiz armed with letters of introduction to a solidly established French house.

His ties to Lyon remained strong. He began a long and often rocky business as a commission agent for, among other merchants at Lyon, a brother-in-law, Antoine Lenossier, a dealer in silk trimmings, who had initiated him into the silk trade. He sold consignments, managed to forward others to America under suitable Spanish cover, and kept his French correspondents abreast of economic conditions at "ce balcon privilégié de l'Europe." Unlike Colarte, who drew upon the resources of prosperous Flemish and Dutch exporters, Granjean was always hobbled by two shortages. Lenossier and other correspondents failed to forward a spectrum of textile products suitable for the changing tastes of Spain's colonial consumers, and neither—a more serious shortcoming—did they entrust Granjean with sufficient funds when competitively priced English, Italian, and German silks and other textiles were pushing French firms at Cadiz to emphasize financing Cadiz's colonial trade. Sensing Granjean's disappointment, Lenossier proposed that he return to Lyon and join his firm. Ever optimistic, Granjean turned down the proposition; at Cadiz, he said, "You can still make a fortune."[52] Sixteen years passed, and a now much disillusioned Granjean bitterly summarized his evanescent illusions: "When I came to this country, I thought I could make my fortune, like so many others. I merely hoped to build up a small capital to use back in France, but I've learned since that, without backing and some funds, [making] a fortune here is impossible."[53] His correspondence ends in 1774. By then a few well-capitalized French firms were heavily committed to financing Cadiz's colonial exchanges.[54]

When Cadiz assumed Sevilla's role in colonial trading, the "monopoly" inherited was structured upon a multitude of overlapping, repetitive, and often misleading regulations, codified and published in 1672 by Veitia Linaje, a bureaucrat of the Casa de Contratación. In point of fact, Sevilla never effectively "monopolized" its transatlantic trade, which goes a long way to explaining the careers of immigrants like Colarte and later of dozens of his would-be successors, like Granjean.

For Cadiz's Spanish community, represented by their merchant guild, the goal always remained to become self-financed, independent export merchants.[55] This meant acquiring expertise in colonial trade, infiltrating customs and fleet systems at all levels, and calculating colonial demand (discounting the inroads of English, French, and Dutch smuggling) and price levels. It also required eliminating long-resident foreigners and their Spanish-born sons (*genízaros*) as competitors, whether as merchants or as agents aboard *flotas* and *galeones*. The members of the Spanish community at Cadiz hoped to "nationalize" their port monopoly. This process began early when in the 1720s, the Cadiz *consulado* urged the Consejo de Indias to block the participation of foreign resident merchants and *genízaros;* to convince the central government of the validity of its aims, it provided it with loans and monetary "gifts."[56]

Viewed from Madrid, however, Cadiz's lobbying obliged the colonial secretary and the Consejo de Indias alike to balance nationalism against the demands of foreign groups, especially the French. Both Cadiz and Madrid understood that the state had to maintain the semblance of "absolute" authority, despite the reality of effective local resistance. This backdrop makes comprehensible the contradictory, repetitive, and often confusing labyrinth of statutes and counterstatutes issued by the central authorities to restrain *genízaros*' activity at Cadiz over the four decades between 1720 and 1760.

Cadiz's Spanish merchants aimed to elbow aside foreign competitors. For example, foreigners and *genízaros* acting as agents accounted for 80 percent by value of cargo on the *flota* to Veracruz in 1720, causing the *consulado* to complain that "none of the earnings or profits are retained in our country"—which was accurate.[57] In 1722, the Consejo de Indias (but not Contratación) responded by prohibiting *genízaro* participation. Matters took a different turn four years later; under Cadiz lobbying, Madrid reversed itself in a *real ejecutoria* of 1726, defining *genízaros* as full Spanish subjects (*naturales y originarios del país*) qualified to participate in the colonial trade. In 1729, however, probably as a result of the lobbying of the influential colonial secretary José Patiño, Cadiz was enjoined to form a Nuevo Cuerpo de Comercio empowered to exclude *genízaros* from its registry (*matrícula*). This exclusionary measure was broadened in 1730 by another statute specifically excluding foreigners' sons or grandsons from the proposed registry.[58] The *ejecutoria* of 1726 was thus undone; more relevant, however, neither the new commercial body nor a *matrícula* materialized. The central government was indecisive and Cadiz satisfied.

Cadiz had its way over the following thirteen years, until the outbreak of conflict with England in 1739. Then the sheer necessity of recourse to neutral shipping to supply the American colonies pushed Madrid to resuscitate its *ejecutoria* of 1726; once again, *genízaros* could enter into colonial trade on a plane equal with Spaniards, provided they were on the *matrícula* of the consulado and licensed by the Casa de Contratación.[59] Madrid's ambiguous ruling put *genízaros* at risk, as Guillermo Mace and his two sons found out. Over six decades of trading at Cadiz, Mace had established his own merchant house; at one point, he had hosted the royal family at the Isla de León when it visited Cadiz. When *consulado* officials denied them registry and the possibility of elective office in the guild, Mace and his sons turned to what was ultimate authority for redress. "How is it that Your Majesty has no influence at Cadiz without its *consulado*'s writ and consent?" Mace asked sarcastically in a letter to the crown. Only then did *consulado* officials commence registering *genízaros*, listing 39 between 1743 and the arrival of Charles III in 1759. The *consulado* continued, however, to prevent *genízaros* from office-holding and thereby from wielding influence.[60]

Consistent with the unrelenting strategy of displacing foreign residents and *genízaros* in Spain's transatlantic trade was the action of Cadiz's *consulado* and city council (*ayuntamiento*) in depriving the central government—

hence, too, the interested public—of details of individual merchants' incomes. Such data would shatter the fiction of Spaniards' monopoly of colonial trade and their capacity to achieve it. In 1749, Ensenada's administration initiated a statistical inquiry into national income to underpin a proposed single tax (*única contribución*) to replace multiple provincial imposts on consumers. Four years would pass before a reference appeared in the Cadiz *ayuntamiento*'s minutes to Madrid's request for income data. What collusion between *consulado* and *ayuntamiento* ultimately generated, a tabulation of aggregate income by sectors (Cadiz's *respuesta general*), provided no individual incomes and thereby no data about the relative wealth of native and foreign traders at the port. Cadiz did nothing further apropos of the *única contribución* until Charles III's regime reopened the issue in 1760.[61] Cadiz's resistance to any indication of the wide income gap between Spanish and foreign merchant communities justifies the recent observation that "[o]nce again the improperly titled 'Absolute Monarchy' could not act in a fashion matching its name."[62]

In point of fact, a review of state policy for Spain's transatlantic "managed" trade after the Peace of Utrecht, notably restoration of *flotas* and *galeones* and the fixing of a site for a trade fair at Jalapa in New Spain, leads to the conclusion that Madrid was reinforcing a Hapsburg economic legacy: the privilege of monopoly trade at one peninsular port. This strategy also met the objectives of the new *consulado* at Cadiz. Other government measures for the registering of *genízaros* and provision of income data for the planned *única contribución* were designed to mollify foreign governments and raise national revenues via fiscal reform. They were never intended as anti-Cadiz measures.

For its part, through its networks linking domestic and foreign trading houses, secular and religious corporate bodies, and state and local bureaucrats, Cadiz insulated its official monopoly on transatlantic exchange from competition by ports in Galicia, Cantabria, the Basque provinces, Catalonia, and Valencia, which low and inelastic internal demand, poor infrastructure, and trade barriers drove to enter external markets. Pressure to penetrate the lucrative colonial trading complex accelerated after the 1750s, when incorporation of tax farms by the state led former tax farmers (*asentistas*) and their collaborators to seek fresh investment opportunities. The largest such investment complex, Madrid's Cinco Gremios Mayores, proposed to charter a Philippine company in the 1750s, for example, and when this failed to gain approval, established a company for trade with the American colonies. Other ports, such as Barcelona, Málaga, La Coruña, Santander, and Bilbao, also aspired to bypass Cadiz and establish direct contact with the colonies.[63] Discerning officials detected that even at Cadiz, some merchants chafed at the unwillingness or incapacity (or both) of groups there to amplify trade contacts with suppliers at major European ports, or with colonial ports other than those primarily serving the mining zones of New Spain and Peru.

In fact, through the mechanism of colonial trade, some bureaucrats envisioned a linkage between Spanish regional development and that of neglected colonies in the Caribbean, along the Venezuelan coast, and in the La Plata basin. These peripheral zones of agricultural and ranching exports were now responding to the opportunities of constant, if illegal, contact with French, Dutch, and especially English island ports and shipping; the English-controlled slave supply contract (*asiento*) had been a tacit recognition of the inevitability of such communication. Ending the *asiento* in 1739 failed, however, to solve the problem. Trade abhorred a vacuum, and if Spanish shippers refused to expand operations from Cadiz, collusion between colonial officials, merchants, estate owners, and elements of the church, on the one hand, and foreign smugglers, on the other, would fill it.[64] Capuchin missions in the Orinoco valley and Jesuit enclaves along the Paraguay and Paraná river systems feeding into the La Plata basin, it was understood, maintained regular contact with English merchants and their intermediaries. The Jesuits had bitterly opposed transferring their missions to the Portuguese when Spain reoccupied the contraband center at Colonia del Sacramento in La Plata; and when complaints and intensive lobbying had failed, they mobilized their Indian wards to fight the colonial military forces of both Spain and Portugal.[65] Furthermore, in Spain, their adherents could be found at the upper levels of Madrid's administration and among some metropolitan bishops. English and French pressure for access to Spanish colonial raw materials and markets thus proved uncontainable. War with England when Spain withdrew its *asiento* (1739–48) and again in 1761 was seen by Madrid as a critical contest for hegemony in America. In response, innovative bureaucrats and some merchants now contemplated opening the trade of the Caribbean and Atlantic littoral of South America to the Peninsula's peripheral ports, hitherto barred from colonial trade except through a few largely unsuccessful privileged companies. This, it was reasoned, might reduce smuggling and stimulate peninsular manufactures.

The foregoing suggests that at mid-century, some Spanish policy-makers, reacting to foreign inroads in America, the ever-growing financial needs of the metropole's military, and the diffusion of physiocratic concepts of the sources of national wealth, were beginning to analyze the shortcomings of the Spanish economy, and particularly its colonial sector, in a fresh light.

The problem of Spain and its "vast dominions," many pragmatic administrators were coming to perceive (if in inchoate fashion), consisted of three major subsets of factors, all integrated as sometimes dependent (internal) and sometimes independent (external) variables. One such subset involved the traditional core of the imperial system, namely, the economic axis centered on Cadiz and extending across the Atlantic to the mining zones of New Spain and Peru, which was based upon the structures and relationships of the one-port monopoly at Cadiz, increasingly viewed as obsolescent and antithetical to the interests of the *monarquía* as a whole. Another involved the underdeveloped peripheries of both Peninsula and colonies, each with widely variant realities, but with common problems in their relations with the imperial core. Antagonism between Spain's peripheries and core would become critical in the second half of the eighteenth century.

A third subset of problems, and an independent variable in Spain's imperial syndrome, was the role of the advanced European economies and their stake in Spain and its colonial world. Between 1701 and 1713, England and France had converted the problem of Hapsburg versus Bourbon administration of Spain and its overseas possessions from civil, or internal, into international war. The treaties terminating that bitter struggle signed at Utrecht and Rastatt in 1713–14 promised to stabilize positions, not eliminate the causes of conflict. As Spain gradually attempted to reconstruct ("renovate") itself under a Bourbon dynasty, open conflict with England shifted to the colonial periphery in America. This should not blind us to the less obvious debate at Madrid and Cadiz, where policy was shaped, executed, or thwarted, as the case might be.

England's Spanish policy required holding on to the concessions yielded by Spain at Utrecht: customs privileges at Cadiz, the *asiento* in America, and British possession of Gibraltar, which (among other advantages) facilitated surveillance of Spanish naval forces.[66] The English had cultivated collaborators within the Spanish interest constellation nurtured under the Hapsburgs in the seventeenth century and subsisting into the eighteenth: sheepmen and wool exporters; Andalusian estate owners whose properties produced olive oil, wine, dried fruits, and almonds, which the English consumed or reexported; customs and port officials stationed at Cadiz; and members of the upper bureaucracy at Madrid whom they could suborn. Not for nothing did the British government for decades maintain Benjamin Keen as ambassador at Madrid; his expertise, contacts, and intelligence networks were well-honed instruments of English diplomacy. When diplomacy failed, the Royal Navy was there to dominate the skeletal naval forces that Spain had painfully assembled. It will be recalled that at Naples in 1742, Charles had had the experience of being menaced by English naval artillery. The English knew, the French commercial agent, the abbé Béliardi, observed, how to "pursue and have punished each and every intendant, administrator, or judicial officer who crossed them."[67]

The Utrecht settlement did not satisfy all London commercial interests, some of whom characterized it as a sellout. Others preferred, if necessary, to bypass Cadiz—its import and export duties, commissions to Spanish merchant intermediaries, unreliable convoy system, and the costs of collaborators in collusion—for direct contact with colonial producers and buyers through smuggling.[68] It follows, then, that a major constraint on policy-making during Charles III's administration was the predictable, forceful English reaction to Spanish attempts at protectionism in both metropole and colonies.

Another constraint was the complex of French interests in Bourbon Spain. The flow of French manufactures into Spain and via Cadiz to the colonies and the return inflow of silver were as vital to the French as to the English economy. French interests accepted the Utrecht settlement on the premise that French products and investment would be channeled to the Spanish colonies indirectly via Cadiz. There, like the English, they benefited from tariff concessions on linens, woolens, and silks—luxury items; at Cadiz, they employed Spaniards as agents or straw men (*prestanombres*), necessary collaborators in their American operations, since Spanish commercial regulations excluded direct foreign participation. Indirect commercial contact with the Spanish colonies was expensive, always fragile, often very profitable. But direct participation by the French through straw men flourished with official toleration.

There is reason to believe, moreover, that in the two decades after the Spanish government terminated the *asiento* contract in 1739, French trade with the colonies via Cadiz peaked in volume, value, and profitability. French diplomacy and influence at Madrid and Cadiz were effective and supple; French grasp of Spain's administrative structures and personnel and of the metropolitan and colonial economies was excellent, judging by the quality of memoirs and documents in French foreign office files.[69] In a curious way, the French more than the English were locked into the Utrecht system. Without a navy capable of offsetting English naval forces and a comparable merchant marine, it was only with difficulty that the French were able to trade directly with the Spanish colonies. Under the Bourbons, however, French business interests found Spanish collaborators to defend their interests, particularly in the somewhat anglophobic administration that Charles began to assemble, which reflected the Bourbon entente maturing during the second half of the century. Of course, a new economic policy to promote Spanish textile manufactures in competitive product lines might inevitably reduce the outflow of French manufactures into Spanish metropolitan and colonial markets, as well as returns in silver. As a consequence, French interest in Spain's continued underdevelopment constituted a further constraint on Madrid's new policy-makers.

It was therefore obvious to Charles's new cadres of Spanish administrators that if Spain were to sever the strands of underdevelopment imbedded in the unequal treaty system, reaffirmed at Utrecht, policies had to be formulated in secret, executed incrementally, justified by legal prescription, and always dissimulated. Many high Spanish bureaucrats in 1759 were neither committed anglophiles nor anglophobes, neither francophiles nor francophobes—simply pragmatic nationalists administering a fragile (nominally "absolutist") state and porous empire. They realized that foreign participation in the Spanish transatlantic trading system discouraged development of national manufactures; they saw that the commissions of Spanish *cargadores* at Cadiz, mostly *prestanombres* of resident foreign merchants who supplied the credits, capital, and merchandise, were invested in real estate (both urban and rural), government annuities (*censos*), and conspicuous consumption, rather than industrial enterprise. This syndrome of underdevelopment, to be sure, also gave low priority to the agricultural and ranching resources in the overseas empire.

Behind the broad spectrum of bureaucratic initiatives in the Esquilache years at Madrid, a pattern of initial priorities is discernible. There was a break with the drift characteristic of the previous regimes of Philip V and Fernando VI, Charles's father and brother. Renovation of the metropolitan economy would receive a priority higher than that accorded the colonial world. Second, whatever the forces impelling change, a few of Madrid's high officials assumed the obligation of state economic and administrative innovation in both metropole and colonies—an obligation involving challenge, reward, and great hazards.

Bureaucratic Cadres: Recruitment and Internal Divisions

Generally speaking, the problems confronting Charles III's administrators reflected the idiosyncratic development of a Spanish nation-state, its relations with its overseas colonies, with papal and papal-associated interests, and, of course, with England and France. Until recently and with few exceptions, historians have analyzed facets of these problems in geographical segments: those of Spain, of its colonies, those involving relations with

Europe and the papacy. In fact, these facets were intermeshed; they were often national as well as regional, international as well as national, and imperial as well as colonial. To be sure, elements of the Spanish political class were interested in the experience of other European states: Poland was an example to avoid, since it was in the process of being dismembered; Prussia was a model of military power and centralizing government. Spain, however, was a colonial power competing with England and France, many of whose institutions and interests were closely identified with national and imperial growth.

Many in Spain's political class were convinced that to restore Spain to an influential European and imperial role, they must accelerate population growth, maximize the resources of agriculture, trade, and industry, enlarge the sphere of state intervention, and supply it with revenues and effective armed forces.[70] To proceed further than earlier renovators, whose efforts had so often terminated in reports, consultations, and bureaucratic oblivion—paralysis by analysis—they had to come to grips with what were still late medieval institutions, curb the privileges and influence of the ecclesiastical establishment, and—neither necessarily last nor least—reorient and restaff the state bureaucracy.

Reorganizing the bureaucracy—the state servants, the bureaucratic instruments of change upon whom Charles and Esquilache might rely to review options, make decisions, and implement them—had the highest priority. Besides the handful brought from Naples (Esquilache and others), it is evident that Charles had the empathy of many among Madrid's high officials, and that he was familiar with the records of others, such as Pedro Rodríguez Campomanes, José Moñino, and (lesser-known today) Francisco Carrasco, whose careers he would later advance.[71]

In initial appointments, Charles proceeded cautiously. "I abandon no one and no one abandons me," he was quoted as saying. Among cabinet secretaries inherited from his late brother's circle, at first he replaced only one, Finance Minister Juan de Gaona y Portocorrero, conde de Valdeparaíso, whose ministry was assigned to Esquilache.[72] With this exception, Fernando's ministers were initially retained: the Irish-born Ricardo Wall at Estado y Guerra until 1763, when Esquilache took over the portfolio of Guerra, while another Italian, the marqués de Grimaldi, was shifted to Estado; Julian de Arriaga at Marina e Indias; and Alfonso de Muñiz at Gracia y Justicia. Evidently, from the outset, Esquilache coordinated innovations and in particular reorganization of the crucial Consejo de Hacienda, or Treasury Department. He assembled a cadre of like-minded bureaucrats, Campomanes, Carrasco, Moñino, and military men like the first conde de

Revillagigedo and Alexandro O'Reilly, all of whom would play prominent roles in planning and executing change. Charles, it appeared to French observers, encouraged civil servants to propose fresh solutions, often "so totally novel they were arresting," for old problems.[73] Upon the quality and loyalty of Esquilache's collaborators ultimately depended the renovation of the structures of Spain's old regime; in a prerepresentative or preconstitutional monarchy, the instruments of change were public functionaries, not apparently unrepresented interest groups. Charles III had to surround himself with competent and loyal public servants, otherwise, French observers warned with reason, the bureaucratic establishment would "never abandon their system."[74]

Assessing the thrust of the policy-makers' intentions is fundamental in seeking a pattern in the role of Madrid's new officeholders in the first decade of Charles III's reign. This is not to claim that what later became fashionable as enlightened despotism was purely the product of the bureaucratic mind. Bureaucrats of whatever kind responded to a variety of pressures applied by the society's interest groups—high, middle, and low—and the bureaucratic function was to satisfy or mediate demands according to an ordering of social and economic desiderata. Their intent was to eliminate friction among social and economic segments of a society and polity stratified by access to privilege; their function, to serve the interests of hegemonic social sectors by updating (or modernizing) them to preserve them. On occasion, the chief ministers of state called upon the services of experienced idea men and consultants; but the ministers themselves rarely contemplated innovation. They were not "reform-mongers" or *novadores*—to employ labels applied to advocates of change in that century and ours. Nor was the bureaucratic outlook oriented toward creating a new society; rather, it looked to an imagined time past when the machinery of state and society had presumably functioned more effectively. Hence the references to *renovation* of the body politic, *revival* of commerce and industry, and to the concept of *restoration*. Hence allusions to the state as a temporarily dysfunctional machine whose parts required only repair and readjustment—tinkering; hence the recurrent appeal, not for innovation in law, but for elimination of the abuses of law. The question remained: could adjustments be introduced quickly or was it unavoidable that "years must pass; certain public servants depart, to be replaced by others, better trained, dedicated rather than partisan"?[75] And hence, finally, the prominence among influential bureaucrats of outstanding lawyers who combined competence in jurisprudence with historical insight, indispensable in exposing fraudulent claims to privilege and other unwarranted, if time-hallowed, precedents that justified private rights to public office and wealth. As Richard Cantillon phrased it, under certain conditions, states like Spain might return to prominence "through sound administrative practice."[76] Then as now, the legal profession appeared preoccupied with devising legitimate processes to modify structures without undermining them and their values.

The term *reform,* or *reformation,* rarely appears in the discourse of eighteenth-century Spanish analysts, although modern Spanish usage defines *reforma, reformismo,* and *reformación* in the very terms (restoration, renovation, and the like) used at that time to describe the Bourbon paradigm. Spanish and other historians have, however, generally adopted *reform* to describe changes sought by Spanish Bourbon governments, particularly under Charles III. At the risk of indulging in Vico's "scholar's conceit," attributing to the "ancients" concepts that emerged at a later time, it seems appropriate to incorporate the term *reform* in Spanish discourse in assaying the achievements of the reign of Charles III. Reform meant calibrated adjustment, methodical incrementalism, never radical change or restructuring.

Since formulation of national and imperial policy occurred at the highest bureaucratic levels, appointments at the ministerial and proximate lower levels were the weathervane of new directions in state policy. In the structure of the eighteenth-century Spanish monarchy, interest groups—corporative, regional, and colonial—lacked a frequently convened legislative body to represent them in public debate designed to resolve conflict. And while political mechanisms for blunting, misinterpreting, and ignoring royal legislation were manifold, surreptitious, and usually legitimated by tradition, it was more efficient to abort adverse policy by controlling or shaping legislation at the source—at the level of ministers and consultative bodies, especially the *consejos,* chief among them the Consejo de Castilla and Consejo de Indias. Political leaders reckoned no doubt on the psychological impact of major appointments in creating a suitable climate for policy changes and execution. The appointment of Esquilache and the evolution of his ministry into the dynamic core of policy-making made clear to Madrid's political class—if Charles's role at Naples had not already alerted it—that policy changes, and perhaps even more important, changes in the bureaucratic personnel instrumenting change, would follow. Like many structures of traditional Spain, however, the bureaucratic establishment would prove as scheming, tenacious, and resilient as the interests it aggregated. Metropolitan and colonial bureaucracies mirrored society, economy, and polity; they were part of the problem facing the new regime.

The bureaucracy inherited by the Esquilache administration was a formidable state apparatus nourished by more than two and a half centuries of imperial rule, staffed at the highest levels by personnel (many *colegiales*) recruited for the most part from three university graduate schools (*colegios mayores*). These, in turn, by self-screening, chose, groomed, and supported their graduates for the main administrative posts in either the civil or ecclesiastical bureaucracies. Dominated by a preoccupation with maintaining the status quo, they had long stifled change.

To meet metropolitan and colonial demand for public servants, the universities of Alcalá, Salamanca, and Valladolid had expanded in the sixteenth century, drawing students from nobility and gentry, the bureaucratic middle class, and (rarely) the commercial bourgeoisie.[77] To educate poor students at the graduate level for the civil and ecclesiastical bureaucracies, patrons placed endowment funds at the disposition of the graduate schools of the major universities. Non-scholarship students (*manteístas*) had to finance tuition and residence. Reflecting the increased sensitivity to status of an aristocratically structured society with an agrarian base and small commercial bourgeoisie, the *colegios mayores* tended to allocate endowment funds to sons of the nobility and sons and relatives of the civil and ecclesiastical elites—in other words, to elite reproduction. Thus the *colegios mayores* became the main filter for leaders of the *letrado* hierarchy.

Once placed, *colegiales* worked long-established *colegial* networks and connections of birth and marriage to obtain preferment as they moved up the bureaucratic ladder to audiencias, chancelleries, and, it was hoped, the premier councils, those of Castille and the Indies. Well into the eighteenth century, bureaucratic and secular elites elaborated patterns of recruitment and advancement, established under the Hapsburg monarchy, that reinforced regional bureaucratic "dynasties" closely attuned to local interest groups. Charles III's bureaucratic inheritance exemplifies the fractured territorial entity that was Spain in the eighteenth century.

In the last half of that century, however, *colegial* domination of the bureaucratic elite would provoke widespread criticism. First, the university curriculum, expounded by teachers or pursued by students often known more for their extracurricular performance than for their application to the study of canon and Roman law, proved inadequate for changing times. Second, under the Bourbon monarchy, greater reliance was placed on the appointment and promotion of *manteístas,* who had acquired legal training as lawyers' apprentices. Melchor Macanaz, a *manteísta* and a forceful articulator of the Bourbon paradigm of reform in early eighteenth-century Spain, had tried to curb *colegial* influence in government, and particularly in the influential Consejo de Castilla, and failed. Persecuted by the Inquisition,

Macanaz took refuge in France. Nevertheless, less abrasive *manteístas* began slowly to ascend to important posts in the hierarchy.

And the *colegial* elite was threatened by another relatively new type of government functionary. In many positions not requiring a legal background, promotion of civil servants of unusual administrative capacity became frequent. Outstanding state servants such as José de Campillo, Miguel de Múzquiz, and Cenon de Somodevila—not to mention Esquilache himself—who had begun in modest administrative or even nongovernmental employments attained key positions.

But far more threatening to *colegial* elites was the appointment of bureaucrats drawn from the military establishment. Following the formation at mid-century of intendancies charged with provincial financial and military responsibilities, military officers began to emerge as key personnel in peninsular (and later, colonial) administration. Through the gradual penetration of *manteísta* and military appointees (many of Aragonese, Navarrese, and Basque origin), Castilian domination of the bureaucracy began to recede. These trends, which were already under way before 1759, accelerated under the impetus of the new regime's emphasis on modernizing the armed forces, upgrading the training of its cadres, and deploying officers to overhaul military installations and fill new administrative posts in both the Peninsula and the colonies. The military emerged as a kind of parallel official bureaucracy.

Bureaucratic cadres drawn from *manteístas* and the military contributed to the comprehensiveness and simultaneity that were salient characteristics of the Esquilache phase of Charles III's reign, those seven years (1759–66) when bureaucratic personnel scrutinized sector after sector in government, from finance to the customs, from international relations to metropolitan and colonial issues. The Esquilache era would be aborted not so much for what it accomplished as for what it threatened to accomplish. Nor is it devoid of significance that the coup ending this phase targeted the bureaucrat who personified relentless probing for information and advice and was emblematic of a kind of national *renovación:* Esquilache.

With Charles's backing, Esquilache galvanized a bureaucratic cadre impatient with those reluctant to undertake long-delayed change. In no small measure, they were responding to the pace and direction of economic change in the Atlantic economy of the eighteenth century—the transition from merchant to industrial capitalism, the source of Anglo-French imperialist conflicts mainly over colonies in America. Internal and external factors were so intertwined that it is difficult to assign clear priorities.

One detects, broadly speaking, a shift from the focus of seventeenth-century *arbitristas* to that of their logical successors, the *proyectistas,* or projectors, of the eighteenth. *Arbitristas* had proposed to augment state funds by exercising more efficient controls over revenue collection. On the other hand, while *proyectistas* shared a preoccupation with state finance, they introduced a new note: the search for fresh sources of revenue fomented by state intervention in basic economic sectors such as agriculture, manufacturing, and domestic and foreign trade in order to diversify and augment output. The *proyectista* is closer to the modern political economist than the earlier *arbitrista:* as a specialist in "political arithmetic," the *proyectista* looked for fresh income-generating instruments to support policy. Charles's administrators believed that a successful program of national renewal should begin with discreet committees of inquiry drawing upon reliable data and the advice of knowledgeable in-house critics, followed by rapid-fire legislation. As had been tried at Naples, so in Spain, the established instruments of the prerepresentative state—councils, tribunals, *juntas*—would be mobilized and reinvigorated, restaffed, and reoriented with broad directives to augment the fiscal power and income of the more complicated Bourbon state of the second half of the century.

Critics and rivals of conservative "old boy" *colegial* networks, joined by those anticipating greater opportunities under the new regime, felt empowered after Charles's arrival. Whatever ambivalence they may have felt about a foreigner, Leopoldo di Gregorio, marqués de Esquilache, being entrusted with multiple portfolios, as had been his predecessors Patiño, Campillo, and Ensenada, was outweighed by Charles's commitment to the goals they had long envisioned. One can confidently say that upon entering Madrid, Charles enjoyed broad consensus within the higher bureaucratic echelons. Even *colegial* elites occupying the bureaucratic summits—Julián de Arriaga (the colonial secretary), José de Rojas y Contreras (president of the Consejo de Castilla), and others—recognized the crisis that Spain confronted by late 1759 both in Europe and America. While cognizant of Charles's critical view of their virtual monopoly of major government posts, the *colegiales* at the same time remained confident that their networks of power and links to the religious establishment and the aristocracy of the court and provinces would preserve their hegemony over the state apparatus.

Integrated Elites: *Grandeza,* Nobility, Gentry, Church

Although a half-century of Bourbon rule had eroded the political power of the aristocratic elites that had dominated Hapsburg Spain, grandees still retained disproportionate influence through geographically distributed, often huge, entailed estates (*mayorazgos*), seignorial jurisdictions, and prominence at court. The War of the Spanish Succession, in which many grandees had collaborated with Anglo-Austrians against the Bourbons, justified their exclusion from high state office, even stripping them of some of their properties. The Bourbons had no intention of destroying the aristocracy, however. Besides granting titles to prominent supporters, once securely established, Philip V permitted defectors among the aristocracy to reclaim their former possessions and status. As an estate, however, the *grandeza* never recovered the political status it had enjoyed under the Hapsburgs.

To be sure, grandees continued to dominate the social life of the court and royal household, holding important posts in military and state service as diplomats, viceroys, and, occasionally, prominent ecclesiastics. But such appointments were rather tokens of loyalty or demonstrated capacity than recognition of inherent right. Throughout the eighteenth century, the *grandeza* in general nursed resentment of their being deprived of political influence and the promotion of a parallel aristocracy of state service based upon merit and non-landed wealth. Meanwhile, on their dispersed properties and in provincial government, grandees exercised disproportionate power in conjunction with the provincial nobility, to whom they were often closely related. Nowhere was this more evident than in Andalusia, where their wealth, based on great landed estates (*cortijos*), usually leased to commercial entrepreneurs producing oil, wine, grain, and wool, gave them the status of magnates. Wealth, income, and a large clientele enhanced their positions at court and advantages in consolidating status through marriage with the aristocrats of other regions.

If the wealth of many grandees provided clout and clientele at court and in the provinces, the lesser, often allied, nobility played a key role in the provinces. Often descendants of mercantile and bureaucratic families that in the seventeenth century had transformed the profits of office-holding or trade into real estate, annuities (*censos*), and then titles, they dominated municipal government and shaped local affairs through membership in the prestigious *maestranzas* of southern Spain and patronage of religious corporations. Their younger sons entered the bureaucracy, the armed forces, and the church, facilitated by connections to the court aristocracy and *colegios mayores*.

While the *grandeza* and provincial aristocracy of Andalusia enjoyed marked social influence in the eighteenth century, gentry from the northern provinces supplied personnel entering church and state service in the Peninsula and colonies. Less favored by wealth and often indistinguishable from the upper peasantry, they usually claimed *hidalguía* (often because an ancestor had occupied a local office conferring such status). They pursued careers in trade at Madrid, in Andalusia, or in America, as well as in government service. With success and wealth, many manipulated money and influence to acquire seignorial jurisdictions (*señoríos*) and titles for themselves, their direct descendents, and collateral relatives, who then conveniently forgot the circumstances of their acquisition.

United by privilege, the aristocracy and nobility thus presented a complex of problems for those devoted to the social, economic, and political development of Spain. For those born to high status and entailed properties, as for the lesser provincial aristocracy, gentry, and aspiring peasantry, social reproduction demanded stability in ongoing social and political structures. The integrated bureaucratic and religious elites, pillars of the Spanish state, presented a different obstacle to reform under the Bourbons. Ties between civil servants and clergy forged in the universities and graduate schools were only one set of constraints imposed on the Bourbon paradigm of change by the ecclesiastical establishment. Ecclesiastical immunities, increase in mortmain, and tax exemptions limited both the fiscal reach and authority of the Bourbon state, which also contested the ideological hegemony and local partisans of the papacy. This complex of conflicting interests also existed elsewhere in western Europe. In Spain, however, centuries of symbiosis of church and state, going back at least to the Catholic recovery of Muslim Spain, and reinforced by the occupation of America, magnified these issues. Disengagement of the state from religious structures and ideology was thus more difficult in Spain than in other states of western Europe.

Unlike in France, where gallicanism had buttressed the state in handling both the national church and Rome, and where bishops enjoyed latitude in matters of faith, regalism in Spain curbed papal influence by exercising powers conferred upon the state by Rome itself. By papal concession, Spanish monarchs could select key church dignitaries and share certain church incomes. Spain, however, proposed neither to separate the national from the international Catholic establishment nor to recognize episcopal authority in matters of conscience in the French manner. In Spain, that responsibility had been delegated at the end of the fifteenth century to the Inquisition, which ever since—although operating with some autonomy—had exercised its authority in tandem with the state, in the process forming a semi-official bureaucracy, membership in which was prized.

The ambiguity of Spain's regalism had its roots in particular historical circumstances. Reconquest in Spain and conquest in America had enhanced the role of the Catholic establishment in the metropole and created a lasting, if increasingly uneasy, partnership with Rome, from which the papacy received substantial financial benefits. This relationship successive Spanish Bourbon regimes aimed to redefine, although they neither wanted nor could afford to abandon it. Catholic evangelicalism had legitimated the reunification of Spain by rendering conquest a crusade, a jihad; the spiritual salvation of Amerindians rationalized the whole operation, including the latter's colonial subordination. In return for Spain's role in rolling back the Islamic tide, in Christianizing Amerindians, and in financing and leading the Counter-Reformation in western Europe, the papacy had given Spanish monarchs the right of patronage, namely, the right to appoint bishops in newly occupied Granada and subsequently in America. There, patronage inevitably involved the slowly evolving Spanish state in the organizational, spiritual, and economic aspects of the church establishment. In the eighteenth century, Bourbon regimes tried to extend and formalize their authority over ecclesiastical activity in the colonies and to enforce claims to sharing revenues with the church. This they tried to do by broadening the concept of the *patronato real* to include the *vicariato regio,* which appointed the king the pope's virtual surrogate in Spain's colonies, with extensive jurisdiction over economic, spiritual, and organizational aspects of the church.

The papacy resisted the claims of the Spanish state in the eighteenth century to an enlarged role in religious affairs although buffeted by the recession of ultramontanism in Europe and the expulsion of the Jesuit order from France and Portugal. Spain and its colonies, after all, constituted the largest single bloc of nominal Catholics in the Roman Catholic church and supplied a sizeable percentage of papal revenue. In 1753, a concordat extended the *patronato* to cover all church positions in the Peninsula and Spain's American colonies. Then, in 1765, Charles's government unilaterally extended its colonial jurisdiction, laying claim to the "spiritual governance of the Indies . . . as well as in economic, ecclesiastic, jurisdictional, and contentious matters."[78]

In the Peninsula, however, the state's authority over the religious establishment via the *patronato real* was less extensive, and the power and prestige of the church far greater than in the colonies, because of its seignorial jurisdiction over a large percentage of Spain's towns, multiple immunities, and close association with aristocracy and bureaucracy. In many ways, the Spanish religious establishment was a state within a state.

Central to the influence of the ecclesiastical establishment was, of course, its landed property, only matched by that of the aristocracy. Entailed estates in metropole and colonies had increased in the seventeenth century through bequests and purchases, stimulated by laymen's hopes for the security of sheltered income for themselves and their descendants. To be sure, land was not the sole economic resource of the religious establishment. Church capital came in large measure from tithe collections; although the state received a share in the form of the *tercias reales* and the *excusado,* controversy persisted over net receipts and the state's share. The religious corporations—convents, monasteries, *cofradías,* and sodalities, as well as the orders—generated loan capital (usually lightly taxed) borrowed by landowners, merchants, mine owners (in the colonies), and the state in periods of financial crisis. Naturally, religious corporations and lay borrowers alike resisted efforts to broaden the fiscal intervention of the Bourbon state, especially in the area of real estate acquisitions by religious corporations.

The problem of ecclesiastical mortmain and tax exemptions had been addressed at the end of the seventeenth century and periodically under the early Bourbons. In the 1750s, Ensenada's cadaster revealed that the church absorbed roughly 15 percent of aggregate national income from agriculture, ranching, and manufacture. On a per capita basis, clergymen had incomes averaging five times those of laymen, while surplus church income flowed in part into further land purchases. The Treasury *fiscal,* Francisco Carrasco, was led to two conclusions: first, "the affliction and licentiousness of the Spanish clergy are increasing markedly," and, second, after the 1740s, mortmain had increased "more than in the previous half-century, many properties [are] exempt from all payment because recently acquired, while the remainder . . . [are] protected from the most burdensome taxes and obligations."[79]

At mid-century, the state's policy of terminating the farming of taxes such as *alcabalas* and the customs had diverted investible funds into rural properties of rising profitability. Agricultural and ranching output was responding to population growth and to European and colonial demand for olive oil, grain, dried fruit, wine, and brandy. An expanding pool of funds among private investors, lay corporations like Madrid's Cinco Gremios Mayores, and ecclesiastical institutions strengthened demand for real estate. The result of competitive bidding was exhibited in the sale of one royal property, the Dehesa de la Serena, of which church corporations bought up more than 75 percent.[80] By 1759, many civil servants were convinced that ecclesiastical mortmain had to be controlled, that ecclesiastical revenue collection required closer state supervision, and that in times of urban food shortages affecting the moral economy of the country, the state must intervene to stabilize prices, if necessary by importing grain. On the other hand, influenced by physiocracy, many (among them, Campomanes) envisioned the ultimate goal as lifting outmoded price constraints—official pricing, monopolies, the extent of church-owned agricultural properties—to allow private entrepreneurs operating in an open market to respond to demand.

Bureaucrats recognized not only their inability to halt what seemed the inexorable spread of mortmain and consequent loss of partly or fully tax-able property but noted the wealth and income of the overseas Spanish ecclesiastical bureaucracies flowing across the Atlantic from colonial tithes, rents, interest, and other sources. These entered ecclesiastical institutions throughout Europe. The Vatican's bureau, the Dataria, issued *cédulas* or *pensiones bancarias* drawn on the income of vacant bishoprics, often using Spaniards as pseudo-pensioners. The Jesuit order, for example, had long maintained a bureau at Sevilla for distributing income generated in the American colonies and in southern Spain to Jesuit agencies in Spain, Portugal, France, and Italy. Around 1700, such annual outflow may have totaled 500,000 (Roman) escudos.[81]

Of course, the Jesuits were only one organization linked to wealthy estate owners, merchants, miners, and bureaucrats in metropole and colonies. But size, organization, and efficiency joined to the national and international ramifications of the Society of Jesus had by the mid 1750s transformed it into a formidable para-state entity. In the seventeenth century, its operations in New Spain had led to a celebrated critique by Bishop (and at one point viceroy of New Spain) Juan de Palafox y Mendoza; and in 1735, the Mexico City *ayuntamiento* had publicized its critique of the virtually tax-exempt status of the Society. In their Paraguayan missions, the Jesuits produced yerba mate, cotton, and minerals for export via the Rio de la Plata and Buenos Aires through legal transactions, and illegally via the Portuguese in Brazil and their English allies. They resisted execution of the Treaty of Madrid (1750) that transferred certain Paraguayan missions to Portuguese control; Jesuit missions in Brazil were equally conspicuous and politically influential. Through their prestigious schools, they placed their disciples—many of the nobility—in the upper ranks of the bureaucracy and competed with the secular clergy and other orders in recruiting or patronizing confraternities in other social strata.[82]

By origin, theology, and discipline, the Jesuits cultivated what can only be termed a spirit of Catholic capitalism that facilitated their expansion in the colonies in the eighteenth century. A census of the Jesuit order circa 1767 yielded a total of roughly 22,635 members, with 2,091 in America and 2,943 in the Iberian Peninsula, together constituting more than one-fifth of the order.[83] Established by Basques in a region of traditional involvement in commerce, the Society of Jesus did not prohibit material acquisitions and was peculiarly suited to forming a kind of "trade technocracy" in the colonies. Aware of the expansion of Atlantic trade in the eighteenth century, Jesuits recognized the export potential of cotton and cotton manufactures, tobacco, and yerba mate. One may postulate that their interests conflicted with the private sector, the secular clergy, other orders and, above all, with state bureaucrats preoccupied with the Jesuits' international financial networks. On his arrival in Spain, Charles III did not hide his support for the beatification of Palafox, who as bishop of Puebla and viceroy in New Spain had publicly attacked the Jesuit order, and whose writings it had, in turn, recently attempted to have placed on the Index.[84] Well before the Madrid rioting of 1766, there was a widespread anti-Jesuit undercurrent of dangerous proportions.

2. Renovation under Esquilache

Here he [Esquilache] tried to do what he did at Naples: curb disorder, apply rules, review public accounts long overlooked, correct faults, root out useless state employees who stole from those who worked the land, and maintain useful measures for handling public revenues.
"Carta . . . por un caballero de Madrid a otro en Cádiz" (1766)

We regret that Spain has more difficulty than other powers in abandoning the path it has followed for two centuries, in order to form a completely new system.
Anne-Robert-Jacques Turgot, baron de l'Aulne, "Mémoire" (1779)

In the broad spectrum of reforms in the early years of Charles III's regime, the historian detects the new bureaucratic cadres' sensitivity to challenge and the possible rewards of loyal state service, as well as their uncommon (and potentially dangerous) disregard of the dangers of a rigorously pursued policy of renovation. Convinced of the accuracy of their diagnoses, trusting the sincerity and commitment of consultants and advisers, confident of their sagacity and capacity to act on a broad front, first metropolitan, then colonial, Esquilache and his Spanish collaborators initiated programs whose very intensity and breadth promised success.

Although Esquilache's colleagues shared his commitment to renovating outworn structures and practices, however, many disagreed with his pace and scope. Where he was impatient, subordinates were cautious. They were imbedded in a larger imperial system consisting of many interests that were not readily budged; the recent experience of Ensenada, who had been removed by coup d'état in 1754, was a warning. Buoyed, however, by royal backing and hope of support from newly emergent business groups, mainly in Spain's peripheral provinces and Madrid, they banked upon their skill in overcoming opposition among supporters of the traditional structures that they proposed to adapt to changing conditions. Like most would-be innovating public servants in eighteenth-century Spain, they would discover too late that besieged, integrated interest groups, failing in customary paths of resistance, would coalesce, rather than disintegrate, and magnify any controversial government move to the point of distorting it in order to stage a counteroffensive, the *motín de Esquilache* of 1766, which José Navarro Latorre has described as "a real uprising comparable to a possible coup d'état."[1]

Overview

With good reason, the opposition focused its attack in 1766 on Esquilache, Charles's most prominent, foreign-born minister for over six years. On arriving in Barcelona, Esquilache had plunged into affairs of state with representatives of key ministries, and when illness detained the royal family at Zaragoza en route to Madrid, he hurried on to begin making changes in administration.[2] French diplomats, who had agonized over the lack of direction in Fernando VI's last months, sensed a deep sea change when Esquilache arrived and immediately (9 December 1759) took over the conde de Valdeparaíso's Hacienda post. They also warmed to the appointment of a protégé, José de Gálvez (a lawyer for the French embassy), as a *fiscal* of the *millones* tax, in whose administration he collaborated with a hard-driving regalist of the Consejo de Hacienda, Francisco Carrasco.

Carrasco typifies the bureaucrat drawn to a reform-minded minister like Esquilache, whose readiness for administrative and policy innovation he shared. He made his long career in the Hacienda, a ministry that became widely respected for the quality of its staff in the eighteenth century. Carrasco's career had begun under Philip V's minister José Patiño, who sponsored young public servants of promise and whose lifestyle was spartan, admirably so to Carrasco. Esquilache (and Charles III) quickly recognized Carrasco's abilities, and in turn Carrasco considered Esquilache his mentor, "amigo y bienhechor." Like Esquilache (and Campomanes), Carrasco worried about the privileges of the Spanish ecclesiastical establishment; as an officer of the Hacienda, he early on recognized the threat to government revenues of accelerating amortization of rural properties by church authorities. With Campomanes, he was commissioned to analyze the situation and probably prepared a substantial share of what ultimately appeared as Campomanes's *Tratado de la regalía de amortización*. More important, in 1764, Carrasco would be appointed by Esquilache to a *junta* reviewing colonial economic policy and finance. (He had a low opinion of colonial officers: "I have never seen a bureaucrat return from the Indies poor," he said.) He claimed to have drafted the instructions given to José de Gálvez as *visitador general* to New Spain. In his thirty-year career at the Hacienda, Carrasco exemplified that handful of nationalistic bureaucrats—competent (sometimes aggressively so), self-assured, and critical—who aimed at more than merely cosmetic adjustments in the government of Spain and its overseas empire.[3]

The abbé Béliardi, who knew his way around Madrid's bureaucratic labyrinth, wrote of Esquilache's dynamic program that he hoped to "reorganize royal finance, to achieve an accurate grasp of those branches of Spain's trade that might be improved. Twice weekly, he presided over a *junta* convened for this purpose; among the issues was how to encourage linen manufacturing in Leon and Galicia."[4] A principal objective of Esquilache and his group, Béliardi feared, was to produce textiles competitive with Norman and Breton linens, a major French export to Spain.

Béliardi faithfully chronicled the comprehensive quality of Esquilache's first year in office for the French foreign minister, the duc de Choiseul. In February 1760, an edict was promulgated against wide-brimmed hats and long capes in order to improve public order and prevent smuggling in Madrid, and management of the state-subsidized woolen mills at San Fernando, Brihuega, and Guadalajara was transferred by decree from the businessmen of Madrid's Cinco Gremios Mayores to the state's Junta de Comercio—a form of nationalization. In March, Esquilache offered to pay off most of the outstanding debts of Philip V's reign to Spanish and foreign (mostly French) creditors in cash, providing they accepted a 66 percent reduction in principal. In April, Esquilache announced that he would preside over meetings of the Junta de Comercio (the state economic planning board), which would henceforth hold public sessions. In June, he authorized a period of six months each year when raw silk could be legally exported *after* Spanish manufacturers had satisfied their requirements. Complaining of high prices, he cancelled the contract of the publicly held Compañía de la Habana as exclusive supplier of Cuban leaf tobacco to the state tobacco factory at Sevilla, then asserted state authority to tax the church. In July, he secretly advised the president of the Casa de Contratación at Cadiz that it was illegal for foreign-built shipping to participate in convoys to the colonies and announced that the state intended ultimately to incorporate all outstanding tax farms (notably *alcabala* collection) to achieve higher yields (he had already, according to Béliardi, saved the state over 6 million *livres tournois*).[5] In September, anxious about rising bread prices in the capital, Esquilache sought to prevent daily fluctuations in the price of bread. By October, he had directed the Junta de Comercio to overhaul the categories of privileged foreign residents, leading Béliardi to conclude that he was seeking "to strip foreigners of those prerogatives and exemptions Spain had to grant under pressure." In November, Esquilache planned to expand Cuban tobacco production by arranging shipments of African slaves to the island; in December, he removed duties on raw cotton imports in order to favor Catalonia's infant textile manufacture. And in January 1761, he contemplated a general revision of customs rates and related regulations at Cadiz and other ports to reduce incentives to smugglers. Eighteen months after Esquilache's arrival in Madrid, French observers detected the capstone of the government's policy, finance. Great historical perspective is not needed to conclude that no Spanish minister of the eighteenth century undertook as broad and far-reaching a program of accelerated reform as did Esquilache from the moment of his arrival at Madrid.

Primary to the program was reordering government finance as a prerequisite to further reform along lines reminiscent of Ensenada's administration—"the whole new system of government finance is designed to improve customs revenues," it was noted.[6] An initial promise to honor the domestic and foreign obligations of previous regimes was followed by painstaking review of current budgeting practices and income flows. The accounts of peninsular and colonial treasuries came under scrutiny and offices and archives were reorganized when signs of neglect, malfeasance, and incompetence accumulated. Royal household expenditures were cut, salaries were reduced, and redundant employees were either transferred or forced to retire. Plans for further budgetary reductions included elimination of liens on specific state revenues (many of them vestigial *juros* issued under the Hapsburgs). Existing tax legislation was now enforced vigorously and new legislation taxed selected ecclesiastical entails and limited secular entails by barring any but direct descendants from the benefits of entail-creating legacies. An understandably especially controversial move sought to reduce widespread customs fraud and the climate of corruption at Spain's principal port, Cadiz, and—far more threatening to those involved there in the transatlantic trade—to implement postponed modifications in colonial trade structures. If not perhaps the soul of colonial trade reform, Esquilache was clearly a firm supporter. This summary of a year's activity merely hints at how determined Charles, Esquilache, and their officials were about rationalizing Spain's finances.

To undertake these initiatives and, more important, ensure compliance with the new directives, fresh bureaucratic personnel were essential. While Charles and Esquilache moved cautiously to remove redundant upper-level bureaucrats, they early on revealed their intention to reinvigorate the civil service by appointing personnel unaffiliated with the established graduate schools (*colegios mayores*) of the universities, whose *colegiales* predominated in the high councils and tribunals. Appointees now drawn from non-*colegiales* (*manteístas*) proceeded to review university curricula and limit the *colegiales'* political influence, the product of their networks. New personnel were also responsible for changes at the provincial and municipal levels, insisting on periodic review of the performance of judges, clerks, and other office-holders, as well as of the managers of the municipal granaries (*pósitos*) upon which the urban population depended during shortfalls. In addition, to restore the financial independence of municipalities whose income from land (*propios*) and taxes (*arbitrios*) was managed and manipulated by local magnates, they insisted on more uniform accounting procedures.

Esquilache's attempts to transform Madrid from a city disparaged by foreigners into a more presentable European capital were immediately obvious. Prohibition of disposing of garbage by dumping it in the streets (where hogs foraged) and new investment in paving, municipal lighting, and the construction of public buildings and private residences began to improve the aspect of the city center. Military veterans were added to the police force, joining members of the city's guilds assigned to night watches. Madrid's municipal authorities were now required to prepare daily intelligence reports on events in the *barrios* for the capital's security agencies and royal review. To handle rural in-migrants, vagrants, place-seekers, and the dependents of aristocratic and religious households, measures were adopted to control the homeless and jobless, to expel clergy "without mission" from the capital, and to confiscate weapons and insist on public dress that would no longer provide cover for concealing smuggled goods. Above all, ever mindful of his Neapolitan experience, Esquilache insisted on adequate grain supplies at controlled prices to dampen the volatility of the urban population. Inevitably, these measures affected the growing numbers of immigrants from many places.

Needless to say, Esquilache had critics as well as supporters, and among the former was his former colleague Bernardo Tanucci, whom Charles had left behind at Naples. From the outset, and particularly when Esquilache began probing into the ultrasensitive operations of the Cadiz customshouse, Tanucci foresaw a backlash by disaffected civil servants resentful of Esquilache's broad powers and fearful of the consequences for their careers. Esquilache's power would last, Tanucci presciently warned, only until "hatred of him spreads among the populace."[7]

The comprehensiveness and simultaneity of Esquilache's reforms led France's agents at Madrid constantly to temper their admiration with defense of their privileges in Spain's metropolitan and colonial economies.

They sensed that Esquilache's housecleaning might impinge on foreign enclaves of commercial preferment. Spain's entry into France's war against England in 1761 postponed Esquilache's effort at radical customs reform; by December 1762 and news of peace, however, the French heard of revived discussions in Esquilache's residence of simplifying tax collection. Béliardi promptly passed along the rumor that at one of the sessions, someone had proposed shifting the terminus of colonial trade from Cadiz to the northern ports of El Ferrol and La Coruña as a way to "bypass the treaties Spain had made with foreign powers, applicable solely at Cadiz," a proposal potentially threatening to agricultural exporters in Andalusia—"Spain's wealthiest province"—and to lower Andalusia's commercial capital, Cadiz.[8] On the one hand, French exports to Spain, largely destined for reexport to the Spanish colonies, might benefit by entry via the peninsula's closer northern ports. On the other, if Spanish authorities at last had a free hand to formulate a nationwide tariff system, they might implement the Junta de Comercio's plan to raise import duties to a general level of 10 percent. This would expose French linens—France's main export item by value to Spain and America—to vigorous competition from Silesian producers. French agents reported that many in the Hacienda "constantly urge Esquilache to stand firm and carry out his program." They concluded that nationalistic civil servants cooperating with Esquilache aimed to destroy foreigners' trade, but took comfort in the thought that no previous finance minister had succeeded at tariff reform. As allies of Spain, however, they had to rely on diplomatic dissuasion ("conversations familières et amicales") to stall impending action.[9]

Here surfaced the characteristically schizoid attitude of representatives of French manufacturing and export groups toward what they considered a new breed of Spanish public servants. Although they admired the Spanish authorities' willingness to undertake a general housecleaning and tackle an entrenched, inefficient bureaucracy, they nonetheless feared that overhaul of the system might adversely affect the advantages French interests derived from inefficiency, influence-peddling, and corruption in Spain.

Reviewing Domestic Policy

The state of public finances was clearly central to Esquilache's strategy, as it had been to that of Ensenada two decades earlier. Moreover, it was critical to Spain's support of France against England. The perennial illiquidity of the Treasury permitted the dominance of private over public interests, of provincial over national aspirations, and of foreign influence in the Spanish state and empire. In theory, the sovereignty, structures, and power of the monarchy were "absolute" (presumably unlimited), but in practice, well-funded private interest groups farmed taxes, lobbied the bureaucracy, courted the nobility and clergy, and manipulated the powers of the state to satisfy personal and regional interests. The standard of living of common people in both Spain and the colonies was wretched, but the elite was notable for conspicuous consumption rather than economy. Vested interests had long ago staked out claims, cemented alliances, and ensured profits by access to privilege. The existence side by side of poverty and plenty was as easily rationalized in the eighteenth century as it is today.

By 1759, some Spaniards realized that many private interests were endangered by an anemic state incapable of defending the metropole or preventing loss of its colonies in America, a major (if not the principal) source of national wealth and income. One cure for this anemia was a well-financed state able to fund defense in an era of heightening tension in the Atlantic world: a navy both to patrol colonial waters and the approaches to Spain's ports, and an army led by officers who were dedicated and disciplined servants of the state. In addition, greater state revenues could amplify the royal family's civil list to subsidize allegiance through access to privileges, titles, charities, pensions, and royal construction on an impressively lavish scale. Adequate salaries, promotions, and pensions might attenuate the ties between underpaid bureaucrats and moneyed interests at home and especially in the colonies, where officeholders were a byword for malfeasance and corruption. A refashioned bureaucracy could also gather reliable statistical data for planning and priorities that previous administrations had repeatedly requested but rarely received.

Investigation of public finance disclosed what was anticipated: debts carried over from the War of the Spanish Succession, a lack of statistical data so glaring as to suggest connivance, widespread smuggling, illicit diversion of imports of colonial bullion and specie, skewed tariff schedules, and, at Cadiz, foreign enclaves of commercial privilege, the French being the most prominent.

In the early 1750s, one French calculation put the national debt at 50 million *livres tournois* (roughly 12.5 million pesos) carrying a high 20 percent annual interest charge. Little effort had been made to reduce the principal, leading Ensenada understandably to suspect "scandalous collusions." Another estimate put the debt incurred under Philip V and still outstanding at two and a half times that figure (127 million *livres tournois*) and provided details on French pensioners and creditors: 14–15 million pesos owed to the duc d'Orléans (a descendant of the widow of Philip V's son Luís) and to the French company that had formerly held the slave *asiento,* plus an equal amount to French officers and military suppliers during the War of the Spanish Succession. Offsetting these debits, an inventory of the estate of the deceased Fernando VI and his wife turned up about 15 million pesos, 80 percent of it banked abroad. This constituted the bulk of the Hacienda's resources; other windfalls were expected—for example, "gifts" (*donativos*), which were frequently provided by the Consulado de Cadiz, among other "donors."[10]

Successive finance ministers of eighteenth-century Spain had invariably encountered disordered data collection and accounts typical of a system relying upon merchant financiers (*asentistas*) to farm taxes. Esquilache's experience was no exception. To quote an exasperated investigator: "The documents in the Hacienda ministry are scattered and unprotected, bedding and nesting for mice; after seeing where they were stored, I wept on finding that they had for the most part disappeared." Piecing together bits of information, he calculated annual state revenues at 50 million pesos, of which the costs of tax collection absorbed an extraordinary 70 percent. "As long as no one in Spain is willing to give Caesar his due," he concluded, "this monarchy will not prosper."[11]

Still, there were hopeful trends. Earlier, under Ensenada, some major tax farms had been taken over by the state to improve yields and diminish *asentistas'* domination of state fiscal and financial policies. The state also took over the colonial mercury monopoly and collection of the *toneladas* fee on shipping and silver transfers abroad. Ensenada's administration endeavored to simplify taxation by instituting a broad-based income tax (the *única contribución*), too, but was able to get no further than the collection of data via a remarkably detailed cadaster (today of use to historians). Despite its episodic nature, Ensenada's economies and emphasis on Hacienda receipts nonetheless gave ground for optimism: a report of net revenue from *rentas generales* (of which customs alone supplied a third) showed an increase of roughly 53 percent between 1745–49 and 1755–59. Finally, it was always possible to tax precious metals transfers abroad (of which France alone may have received about 60–80 million *livres tournois* annually between 1755 and 1781) more effectively.[12]

It was symptomatic of Spain's Hacienda record-keeping that more than two centuries after the conquest of Spanish America, metropolitan administrators still found it difficult to establish net government income from the American colonies adequately. Colonial treasury bureaus lacked organization and appropriate regulations, and the available data on staffing, appointments, and salaries could not be depended on. At mid-century, France's colonies in America were reported to send home 40 million pesos annually, while Spain's more extensive American possessions unsurprisingly remitted only a quarter as much.

Customs revenues, which the spike in wartime expenditures in 1761–63, estimated at about 42 million pesos, made all the more important, also attracted the attention of Esquilache's men. Despite a large corps of customs officials, the data available to Madrid were unreliable. Official valuations had in many cases remained unchanged since the 1690s, notwithstanding changes in prices and quality, and customs duties were not uniform but varied from port to port. Unsurprisingly, the most flagrant abuses and the locus of greatest potential revenue improvement were at Cadiz, which handled the largest volume of trade, enjoyed the lowest duties, and in 1759 was the sole Spanish port authorized to trade with the American colonies. Small wonder, then, that Esquilache proposed to optimize customs operations there.[13]

A number of factors explain a further preoccupation of the Esquilache administration, the low tax rates on agricultural properties and the high proportion of tax-exempt ecclesiastical holdings. Raising excise taxes put an extra, highly visible burden upon low-income consumers, the domestic basis of any policy of industrial expansion. Second, the growth of church holdings by mortmain accelerated in the eighteenth century, reducing the tax base; it rendered the state, in a fashion vexing to regalist-minded functionaries protective of state sovereignty, client to the religious establishment. In the third place, a combination of population growth, demand for food grains, and inelasticity in supplying urban centers pushed physiocratic-minded Spaniards both within and outside the government to conclude that market forces rather than state intervention might be the better stimulus to agricultural output. Yet to be proven is the belief that land in religious mortmain was inefficiently farmed; to many, however, the church's landed wealth in Aragon, for example, seemed inordinately great. A cadaster of the city of Zaragoza in 1725 had revealed, for example, that annual per capita income from the real estate holdings of 3,699 ecclesiastics was sixteen times greater than that accruing to 24,042 laymen—this in a province where "no one enforces the law prohibiting entailment."[14] In 1759, it was not strange that high-level civil servants were convinced that ecclesiastical mortmain had to be halted, that tax collection by the church required close state supervision, and that during food shortages, the state needed to intervene to contract for grain imports. Meanwhile, Madrid's immediate objective was removal of the traditional economic constraints on foodstuffs—official pricing and supply monopolies—and enforcement of limits on religious mortmain to provide the private sector with the resources in cultivable land to be able to respond better to demand.

It was during the six-year period of Esquilache's leadership that pressure from the private sector in agriculture, along with the state's fiscal needs and a series of poor harvests, precipitated a confrontation between the state and the Spanish ecclesiastical establishment. At Charles's accession, ecclesiastical subordination was largely nominal, a result of the fragility of the Hapsburg state at the end of the seventeenth century and an accumulation of landed property unbroken since the early sixteenth century. This structure had pumped wealth and income into the religious establishment in both metropole and colonies. To be sure, the issue of taxing church property had come up in the Concordat of 1737, but the Spanish government had garnered less than had been hoped for. The church retained many tax exemptions; the papacy agreed to limit its tax liability, but only to post-1737 acquisitions; and supervision of tax collections on church holdings was reserved to episcopal authority. The main source of conflict was the fact that the state considered church exemptions "temporary," whereas the bishops insisted on treating payments to the state as discretionary "gifts." When Esquilache took over the Hacienda, the stalemate remained, and he found records of church property acquisitions after 1737 seriously defective.[15]

Consequently, there was renewed pressure from Esquilache's Hacienda on church properties, and in June 1760, it was not the Consejo de Castilla but the Hacienda that insisted upon the state's authority to tax the church under the 1737 Concordat. Acquisitions made after 1737 would be taxed; if ecclesiastical authorities resisted, treasury agents assisted by local officials (*alcaldes ordinarios*) would institute judicial proceedings. The influential bishop of Cuenca, Diego Rojas y Contreras, thereupon intervened, petitioning the Consejo de Castilla to create *alcaldes ordinarios* in his diocese subject to his nomination. On balance, these pressures signaled the state's preoccupation with regalian rights, but hardly a new direction. In fact, public officials skirted the principal phenomenon, unbroken growth of ecclesiastical mortmain fed partly by large inflows of income earned by Spaniards in the colonies and placed by them or relatives in so-called pious works. "The riches of America, however acquired by those who emigrate to those distant regions, arrive every day for investment in every type of pious fund."[16]

Obviously, fiscal control by ecclesiastical and secular bureaucrats had proven ineffective. The aggressive Esquilache administration proposed to attack the problem at its root. In 1763, ecclesiastical petitions from Valencia and Majorca for property acquisitions were denied by the Consejo de Castilla; in 1764, Francisco Carrasco, joined by Campomanes, urged the Hacienda to adopt a similar policy for Castille; and in 1765, the Consejo de

Castilla ordered formal papers on the subject from Carrasco and its two *fiscales*, Campomanes and Lope de Sierra y Cienfuegos. Their position papers would constitute the basis of the Consejo's resolution. Campomanes's paper of July 1765 urged vigorous state control over new religious mortmain; and, presumably to publicize the issue then before the Consejo de Castilla and to prepare the political class for a new direction, he was permitted to publish a much-expanded version of his often-cited *Tratado de la regalía de amortización,* a position paper drafted in its preliminary form by Carrasco, the new minister of Gracia y Justicia, Manuel de Roda, and Charles's confessor, Padre Eleta—a very select trio. The *Tratado* in substance reaffirmed the state's right to regulate religious mortmain without papal approval and collect taxes on church property directly rather than through the religious bureaucracy. But it accepted illegal acquisitions by the church after the Concordat of 1737. Despite all the marks of approbation by state and church, the *Tratado* appeared anonymously.

In retrospect, the resort to anonymity reflected bitterly divergent views within the Consejo de Castilla and—one may infer—unwillingness to commit the Spanish Bourbon state to moving decisively against all the interests that the religious establishment in Spain and its colonies integrated, or even inability to do so. In the fall of 1765, when the *fiscal* of the Consejo de Castilla, Lope de Sierra, was preparing his rebuttal of the Campomanes-Carrasco position, it was known that many *consejo* members shared his viewpoint. By early March 1766, after Carrasco and Campomanes had presented their refutation of Lope de Sierra's rebuttal, the *consejo* was moving slowly toward its decision.[17]

There were, to be sure, other factors behind the Consejo de Castilla's delaying tactics. Understandably, its members were sensitized to the implications of tax enforcement at a time when an unbroken succession of poor harvests beginning in 1761 was solidifying taxpayer resistance. Prior to Esquilache's arrival in 1759, the Hacienda had customarily granted tax collectors wide discretion, but their often rough-shod tactics, continued under Esquilache, prompted the Consejo de Castilla to reprimand them in November 1765. This was not the only instance in which the Consejo de Castilla tried to curb action by Esquilache's Hacienda. In 1764, mindful of food riots at Naples, Esquilache began importing grain from Marseilles through the port of Alicante in order to provision Madrid, where price-fixing and profiteering were notorious when local supplies ran low. Wheat prices rose 60 percent in 1761–65. At this point, Campomanes advocated a liberalizing policy (proposed in 1756 but not implemented) barring the participation of grain wholesalers' *cofradías* and *gremios,* insisting their accounts be reviewed by local officials (*corregidores*), and lifting government controls provided that the maximum price was not surpassed.[18]

Adopted in 1765, this policy, plus massive government imports, promised to limit the windfall profits anticipated during shortages by large-scale grain merchants, as well as by secular and religious intermediaries. Esquilache contracted with a French firm to handle grain imports on the government's account, but it misused the state funds put at its disposal for private speculation. Almost as serious were reactions to the Hacienda's abrupt mobilization of carters and muleteers to transport grain imports from Alicante to Madrid. Churchmen now challenged the state's demands, which included payment of a special tax levied to pay for the cartage. However, the clergy of the diocese of the bishop of Cuenca, Rojas y Contreras, were again exempted at his insistence. Aristocratic, influential, and emblematic of the malleability of the aristocracy and the church in the hands of disaffected interests, the elderly Bishop Rojas became a symbol of respected and respectable resistance to administrative fiat, so much so that Padre Yecla, who preached against Esquilache in Madrid's plazas, was affectionately dubbed "Padre Cuenca."

By early March 1766, unrelenting pressure from Esquilache's cadre on the religious establishment led Madrid's political elite to sense that a critical, possibly epoch-making decision by the Consejo de Castilla on ecclesiastical properties was imminent. Further deepening the sense that policy changes were imminent were other rumors (not without foundation) about the multiple activities of Esquilache's Hacienda, which reinforced anxieties at Cadiz and among merchants overseas that major innovations in colonial trade policy might now be imposed with uncharacteristic rigor. Postwar state finances would inescapably oblige the Esquilache administration to modify imperial transatlantic commercial structures, despite resistance, "because not all the nation's classes were duly sensitive to these issues."[19]

Imperiled Colonies and Spain's Response

"Renovation" or "regeneration" in the era of Charles III had both metropolitan and imperial colonial components, an interface usually overlooked. At the end of the War of the Austrian Succession (1748), the Spanish government had realized that the Peace of Utrecht had in no way resolved Spanish insecurity in America about the integrity of the empire. Neither were French colonial interests sanguine about their capacity to compete unassisted against England's well-financed, wide-ranging navy and impressive merchant marine. For Madrid, the major geographical focus of intra-European rivalry was America, not Europe, and the major threat, England, not France. An anonymous mémoire prepared after 1747 for circulation among Spanish bureaucrats had explicitly marked out the locus of future conflict, as well as the potential aggressor. Spain's American colonies were a "fountain of wealth in gold and silver, as well as the products traded," it noted, and the colonial trade of Spain and Portugal was "important, even essential, to all trading nations"—in particular, England and France. The "general effect on precious metals . . . were one nation to monopolize the trades of America" could not be ignored. In the three-cornered struggle in the Atlantic over empire in America, Spaniards saw England as the aggressor state. Its policies, the anonymous author concluded, alternated pragmatically between peace and belligerency, peace "as long as it increased its power and trade, if not, then war." England's unequivocal goal was to "expand its trade, oppose that of other powers, and then invade their colonies." Its pathway into Spain's possessions in America ran through French-occupied Louisiana.[20] At the same time, threats to the Spanish empire in America were internal as well as external; throughout the 1750s and early 1760s, there were not only rumors but disturbing instances of colonial insurrection in expectation of England's intervention—rioting at Quito in Ecuador in 1765, for example.[21]

On resumption of international warfare in 1757, Spanish and French interests braced for the inevitable confrontation with English forces overseas; it was hardly a matter of where but of when the attack would come. In April 1759, the French urged Charles, still at Naples, to dispatch troops and equipment to the Caribbean; later, en route from Barcelona to Madrid in November 1759, Charles and his entourage voiced regret at French losses in Canada. Sensitized to Cuba's strategic role in the West Indies and New Spain, in June 1760 the Esquilache administration dispatched a new governor, Mariscal de Campo Juan de Prado y Portocarrero, to Havana, with troop reinforcements and a fleet under the marqués de Real Transporte, who had convoyed Charles from Naples to Barcelona a few months earlier. The new cadre of Madrid bureaucrats could not be faulted for indecision.

The first conde de Revillagigedo (Güemes y Horcasitas), who had served in Cuba as captain-general (1733–46), then in New Spain as viceroy (1746–55), played a significant role as informal adviser on colonial affairs to Esquilache's team in Madrid. Revillagigedo was not only an experienced colonial administrator but represented a new element in the Spanish military, the product of wider intra-European military contacts of Spanish officers under the Bourbons, first with their French and later with their Prussian counterparts, and, equally important, of recruitment patterns emphasizing talent, as long as a minimum of acceptable gentry birth (*hidalguía*) was evident. One must disentangle the bureaucrat from the military officer, mindful that Anglo-French imperialist tensions, which were both frequent and intense in the eighteenth century, led the Spanish authorities to turn to military technicians to fill colonial posts and to put a premium on administrative skills and reliability—in other words, to favor talent over lineage.[22]

Revillagigedo was typical of the military officer of gentry background whose competence emerged in the course of colonial service. There were others of the same type, such as Felipe Nicolás Ricardos, born the son of an Irish merchant at Cadiz in 1689. Ricardos entered the Spanish military service, married the daughter of the conde-duque de Montemar, Charles's military strategist in Italy, and in 1748, as *mariscal de campo* (field marshal), commanded Spanish troops shipped to Venezuela to suppress English smugglers. When Julián de Arriaga left Venezuela to become colonial secretary in 1757, Ricardos replaced him at Caracas as captain-general. Revillagigedo, Ricardos, and their sons exemplify the ascendancy in Spain and its empire of military bureaucrats promoted on the basis of competence, because prominent officials of Charles's administration believed that they were less tempted than civilians by the rewards of bribery, smuggling, and administrative corruption, and identified with the higher interests of the emerging nation-state and its colonies. Which is not to say that they shunned investment opportunities in the colonies wherever they happened to serve.

It is difficult to divide the Spanish military at the accession of Charles III into well-defined categories. Some were the heirs of generations of military aristocrats; others, although of only acceptable noble birth, were familiar with the French and Prussian military models or had useful business connections. After 1759, however, senior officers esteemed primarily for their talents and for their commitment to bureaucratic housecleaning, such as the condes Aranda and Alejandro O'Reilly, began to move to the fore. Even so, in 1760, Madrid chose the aristocrat Juan de Prado y Portocarrero to command at Havana, and in 1762, Nicolás de Carbajal y Lancaster, marqués de Sarriá and brother of the recently deceased prime minister José de Carbajal y Lancaster, was initially appointed to lead the Spanish army that invaded Portugal. At the same time, however, army reforms were made with Esquilache's full backing, even perhaps at his instigation (he was assigned an additional portfolio, Guerra, in 1763): a pension fund (*montepío*) for veterans' widows and orphans was established, a more equitable system of conscription (*reemplazo*) was introduced, and an elite artillery academy was founded (under Aranda).

Perhaps it is in the nature of government that changes in policy and shifts in the most salient administrative posts mainly materialize (or at least are suggested or rumored) in response to crises. Once any confusing cross-currents have receded, the main trend then surges into view. It was amid the tension of international conflict, the military campaign in nearby Portugal and the defense of Havana and Manila in 1762, that the new military cadres linked to the Aragonese grandee Aranda surfaced as reliable instruments of renovation or change. Charles quickly lost confidence in the competence of his field commander in Portugal, Sarriá, and when he requested relief for "reasons of health," Aranda replaced him, bringing along as trusted subordinates among others the conde de Ricla (Ambrosio Funes Villalpando) and Alejandro O'Reilly. Esquilache himself went to Portugal to reorganize Aranda's logistical support. In Spain's colonial world in 1762, the loss of Havana (August) followed by the collapse of Manila (October) to widely ranging English amphibious forces were shocking and demoralizing. Rumors circulated of the incompetence of Havana's new commanding officer, Prado y Portocarrero, who had refused to cooperate with the nearby French fleet. "News of the taking of Havana," reported a troubled Béliardi on 18 October, "has gravely upset the Spanish nation. . . . There is no consolation for the irreparable loss of one-third of Spain's naval forces, surrendered without a cannon-shot."[23] The Aragonese nobility promptly petitioned Charles to ship overseas half of Aragon's regional forces to fight the English without pay. As a military gesture, this was inconsequential; as an indicator of the development of a sense of nationalism among noblemen known for sometimes blinkered sectionalism, it must have been heartening to Charles and his beleaguered bureaucrats.

The fall of Havana, which had anchored Spain's Caribbean defenses, and British occupation of West Florida had a twofold impact on Spain's strategists and colonial interests.[24] First, it was clear that the outer defenses of New Spain were now penetrable, and that sooner or later, English amphibious forces would be directed against New Spain's sole remaining major Caribbean port, Veracruz. Second, the year-long British occupation of Havana transformed it into a model entrepôt—almost 100 English and British North American ships brought in thousands of African slaves, North American corn, wheat, cod, beef, horses, mules, and European luxuries, and there was a surge in customs revenues. This suggested that if the English did take Veracruz, they would most likely transform it, too, into a flourishing showpiece and not pursue further territorial conquests in New Spain.[25]

The fates of Cuba and New Spain were linked in a natural order of priority. The first set of problems concerned the port of Havana and the island of Cuba, where Spanish imperial authority had to be restored. Between March and May 1763, anticipating an English withdrawal, Esquilache and his collaborators chose, from among Aranda's subordinates in the Portuguese campaign, Ricla as Cuba's captain-general and O'Reilly as army inspector, with orders to court-martial Prado y Portocarrero and other officers involved in the loss of the city, to inspect its fortifications, and to assemble an appropriate garrison. In the fall of 1763, Madrid shifted its primary focus to the defensive needs and resources of the Veracruz coast and to New Spain in general. By spring 1764, at Esquilache's request, Aranda drafted instructions for Juan de Villalba, captain-general of Andalusia, who was dispatched to New Spain with troops and junior officers, including Antonio Ramón Ricardos, to train regular Spanish and local militia units.

In sum, the disasters of the war against the British as France's ally and the search for competent officers led to the selection of men from Aranda's staff. In the Consejo de Guerra in Madrid, senior officers like Aranda and Revillagigedo now sat in judgment on Juan de Prado y Portocarrero. In Cuba, Puerto Rico, and New Spain, promising officers like Agustín Crame, Manuel Craywinckel, and Alejandro O'Reilly would go far beyond the call of duty to prepare surveys of the current situation and economic potential of the colonies.

The Trauma of Havana, 1762–1765

As we have seen, Charles III and key state servants gave priority to reviewing the metropolitan situation, finance, interest groups, and bureaucratic personnel. The necessity of a comparable colonial overhaul was not overlooked, merely postponed. But not for long. France's disasters in the Seven Years' War galvanized Madrid into a dramatic reaffirmation of the two countries' mutual defense interests in America in the shape of the Third Family Pact.[26] Then England's occupation of Havana heightened interest in reexamining Spain's transatlantic trading system. In a few years, the primacy of colonial factors in Spain's metropolitan policy would be clarified, although, as usual among imperialist powers, then and now, much understated and underpublicized.

Preoccupation with Spain's colonial possessions had cropped up repeatedly in the 1750s. "Spain's strength is her vast, opulent American possessions," a key figure in Madrid observed. Rumors circulated of English designs on Mexico and Peru; from Naples, Charles's confidant Tanucci wrote Prime Minister Wall in 1759 of England's and France's eagerness to gain access to the mines and raw materials of Spain's American colonies, adding,

"You can see the urgency for Spain of protecting itself effectively in America, more essential than in Europe."[27] While still at Naples, Charles had assured the friendly French ambassador, the duc d'Ossun, that once he was in control in Spain, his priority would be "the security of the Spanish Indies."[28] At the end of 1759, Revillagigedo, now residing at Madrid, warned the authorities, who respected his colonial expertise, that the English intended to weaken the French in America in order to move next against the Spanish colonies, "a richer and easier conquest."

In sum, Spanish authorities hardly needed reminding by a Madrid agent of Mexico City's merchants, Francisco Gamboa, of the "virtual hills of gold and silver" in Mexico only awaiting exploitation, while the French hoped to maintain the flow of millions of silver pesos from Mexico via Spain into France in return for French textiles, a flow that Choiseul considered vital to French industry. The loss of Mexico, he observed in 1759, "would be of first-class importance to France, for if the English took it, they would furnish it exclusively with their own manufactures, which would occasion a loss of trade . . . and in consequence ruin the greater part of our industry." If the English should expel the French from America, they would become "masters of Mexico."[29] As José de Gálvez observed before he sailed to Mexico as *visitador general,* English conquests in North America and naval superiority would give Spain "much to fear with respect to the empire of Mexico."[30]

Economic development of Havana and surrounding areas during the 1740s and 1750s heightened the interest of the metropolitan authorities in its defense. During these decades, Madrid had to allocate large peso transfers from the Mexico City treasury to Havana to shore up its fortifications and garrison. The French, for their part, hoped to assign a consul or commercial agent to Havana, "the operational center of the two countries," on the general proposition that "Europe's international system seems anchored on the strength of the great powers in America."[31] They vigorously protested the refusal of the newly appointed governor, José de Prado y Portocarrero, to allow French warships to resupply at Havana in wartime.

As for the English, with characteristic foresight, they laid plans for offensive operations against Havana, then the third largest city in the Western hemisphere. In the 1750s, Charles Knowles, who had participated in the previous war with Spain in 1739–48, visited the island to map Havana's defensive works surreptitiously. Then, in the spring of 1761, George Anson drafted plans for an amphibious attack, notwithstanding the city's garrison of 9,000 men, sixteen warships in the harbor, and a French squadron nearby. All London needed was a declaration of war, and this followed immediately on news of the signing of the Family Pact between Spain and France.[32]

The Franco-Spanish alliance of 1761 was based less upon strength than upon "fear and impotence."[33] To the French, who after 1757 had suffered heavy losses in Canada and the Caribbean, the alliance promised Spanish support in the event of an English attack on Saint-Domingue, then the most profitable sugar-producing colony in the world. In the long run, Foreign Secretary Choiseul valued the alliance as a tool to stabilize and even facilitate France's economic penetration of Spanish and Spanish American markets.

This formal pact avoided the sensitive issue of commercial relations, left to be handled in separate and supplementary conventions (to the relief of Spanish negotiators, no commercial treaty ever materialized).[34] Nonetheless, the threat of joint Hispano-French economic pressure on English commercial interests trading with Spain and its colonies led London merchants to denounce it as a "frightening pact for the destruction of your [i.e., George III's] subjects."[35] To Madrid, the Third Family Pact seemed the best way to prepare for an inevitable English thrust in the Caribbean following England's occupation of eastern Canada, attacks by corsairs upon Spanish shipping, and signs of England becoming "all-powerful in the West Indies." In September 1760, Spain's ambassador at London, the conde de Fuentes, warned Madrid to prepare for an English attack upon Spain's American colonies; indeed, the Spanish government's initial intention was to confine the pact's focus to joint defense of the colonies in America, not—as Choiseul insisted—upon English aggression anywhere. In September, English naval forces intercepted official correspondence from Spain and learned that Madrid would enter the war if no peace were arranged by May 1762. On January 2, 1762, England declared war preemptively against Spain and activated Anson's plans for amphibious operations against Havana and then, conditions permitting, against Veracruz.[36]

Havana's commander, Prado y Portocarrero, was unprepared and the city's defenses proved inadequate when the English fleet—40 warships, 135 transports, and 15,000 troops—passed through the hazardous Old Bahama Channel on Cuba's north coast to surprise the squadron of the marqués del Real Transporte, which was mostly demasted in the harbor. The attack commenced on 7 June and ended two months later in "the most momentous acquisition we [English] had till then ever made in America."[37] The quick surrender of both Havana and Manila undermined Madrid's bargaining position, and in September 1762, reports arrived of London's intention to move against Veracruz.[38]

In light of Spain's efforts to prepare Havana for attack, the volume of funds transferred from Mexico City to finance massive defense works, and confidence in effective naval defense by the combined Spanish and French fleets, it was not surprising that the loss of Havana shocked Spain's elite.[39] An exchange of recriminations between Prado y Portocarrero and Havana's planter and merchant magnates ensued immediately. A letter from Havana shortly after the "ignominious capitulation" recalled that Prado had been forewarned by a slaving ship from Jamaica as early as February of an imminent attack, but that nonetheless "the city was surrendered with little resistance." Prado and other Spanish officers, the letter continued, blamed the defeat upon the native Habaneros "to whitewash their conduct"; on the contrary, however, the best defense had actually been "made by local people despite the lack of veteran, professional leaders."[40]

Whatever the reasons—incompetence, surprise, the francophobic bias of the Spanish leadership at Havana—its loss galvanized Madrid to remedy conditions there. Prado formed part of a clique of Spanish aristocrats oriented toward English rather than French interests, which may account for the tepid cooperation between Havana's military and the French squadron off Saint-Domingue.[41] There remains, moreover, the possibility that Havana's defenses were weakened by the Spanish reluctance to arm blacks. As Miguel Antonio de la Gándara summarizes the racist logic at work here: "If blacks can resist the English, won't they also resist Spaniards?"[42]

The British were understandably satisfied: Havana was "in fact the most momentous acquisition we had til then ever made in America," an Englishman noted.[43] They netted about 13 million *pesos fuertes*, the equivalent of £3 million, half in government specie and goods. Of this, some 330,000 pesos were from Catalonia's Real Compañía del Comercio de la Habana alone. In contrast with the carefully managed annual undersupply of slaves by the Real Compañía (an annual average of 815 between 1743 and 1747), English merchants would import 3,262 African slaves in just eleven months of occupation, most from Jamaica. They halved the price per slave (from £46 to £21) on average. Large-scale imports of African slaves, English goods, and North American foodstuffs stimulated English merchants to expand the volume of advances to Cuban merchants and planters and reinforced the pattern of Cuban indebtedness to Jamaican factors and agents.[44] A quarter of the British shipping that arrived during the occupation came from England's North American colonies. The "taking of the Havanna . . . is a conquest of the greatest importance," Benjamin Franklin noted in Philadelphia in December 1762. "Hereabouts everyone is shocked by the loss of that port and the carelessness in adequately arming it," a correspondent wrote to the *Gazette de Hollande* when the defeated Spanish officers disembarked at Cadiz.[45] More than the psychological impact of the loss of Havana, which was bad enough, the Spaniards had to bear the shock of the costs of recovering the port: transfer of west Florida to the English, English control of the Honduras coast and its dyewoods, and abandonment of Spaniards' right to fish off Newfoundland.[46] No matter the costs, Spain had to recover Havana as quickly as possible and to block England's access to the Mexican market.

No sooner had the English withdrawn from Havana in 1763 than Esquilache appointed the conde de Ricla, an Aragonese nobleman, as the new captain-general there and gave him broad powers to revamp Cuba's defenses and analyze the potential for its economic development.[47] Ricla spent two years inspecting, repairing, and strengthening Havana's fortifications, assisted by Alejandro O'Reilly, Agustín Crame, and Manuel Craywinckel, officers chosen from among the new recruits upon whom Charles III's administration would so often rely.[48] His immediate subordinate, O'Reilly (born in Dublin in 1725), organized black and colored militia units that had acquitted themselves well during the English attack. O'Reilly was also a correspondent of Béliardi, France's commercial agent in Madrid, and would later serve as governor of Louisiana, captain-general of Cadiz, and inspector-general of the Spanish armed forces. Among O'Reilly's subordinates were the army engineer Agustín Crame, who in 1771 went to Veracruz to inspect its fortifications, and Manuel Craywinckel, a member of the court-martial board that tried the former captain-general of Cuba, Prado y Portocarrero. The Craywinckels, a Barcelona family of Flemish origin, had married into Catalan nobility. Manuel Craywinckel's brother José served in the colonial forces during the 1750s in both New Spain and New Granada, and another brother, Francisco, who in 1761 urged Esquilache to lift all restrictions on grain sales in Spain, speculated in 1762 about the impact of the loss of Havana to the English and later forcefully advocated modifying imperial trade regulations governing the Caribbean.[49]

The situation reports of O'Reilly and Crame indicate that they were more than just soldiers—they had a vision of the future of Spain's western Atlantic world. They saw the need for large military outlays to prevent further foreign occupations of the colonies with even more disastrous consequences than those of 1762. To achieve this goal, they saw, required colonial self-financing adequate to sustain an effective military presence without metropolitan contributions. These considerations in turn led them to review the general economic situation of Cuba and other Spanish-held islands and to come up with measures to tap their potential. O'Reilly's 1764 report stressed that operations of the privileged Real Compañía de la Habana had failed to provide the slaves, goods, and services needed by the island's producers.

Cuba remained undeveloped because of "the total lack of trade required to draw off surplus production, as well as the smuggling of goods and provisions reasonably priced." It was a classic example of the effects of narrowly focused, profit-oriented peninsular entrepreneurs being unwilling or incapable of planning development and growth and preferring to milk a monopoly. The Real Compañía had supplied goods of poor quality at grossly inflated prices, thereby stimulating smugglers of European textiles, particularly the popular light linens and calicoes (*bramantes, lencerías, zarazas*). In addition, the Compañía's unscheduled ship arrivals and departures had led to perishable staple exports being stockpiled. O'Reilly's major recommendations went to the heart of Spain's transatlantic system: dispense with expensive peninsular intermediaries, authorize Cuban planters to buy directly from foreign slave depots in the Caribbean, open Cuban ports to direct exchanges with Spanish ports, and lower Cuban customs duties.[50]

For his part, Agustín Crame reacted to factors underlying what he viewed as Cuba's stagnation. Traditionalists venerating "ancient maxims," he observed, preferred an undeveloped Cuba, on the erroneous assumption that "by not stimulating the wealth of those people, their subordination is assured." On the other hand, England's brief and effective *dominación* of Cuba had "opened their eyes," leaving Madrid with only one option. Cuba's inhabitants had learned how to "augment their wealth, they realize that they lack development as well as the freedom their trade needs." The crux of the matter, he judged, was an expanded labor force to increase sugar, tobacco, and cattle exports. Free European workers in the tropics, he was aware, avoided field labor and, in any case, insisted on high wages. Only blacks (the "materia prima") produced sugar profitably at current price levels; after deductions for purchase, maintenance, amortization, and interest they "produce three times their prime cost over their working lives"—the longevity of African slaves was no prime consideration. Therefore, the most effective Cuban investment was in slave labor, which was also the way to "wipe out smuggling." Crame therefore seconded O'Reilly in recommending that residents of Cuba receive authorization to sail directly to the nearby foreign ports of Jamaica and Saint-Domingue to purchase slaves.[51]

O'Reilly and Crame left no doubt that externally oriented agricultural development was *the* path to exploiting Cuban resources, and that large-scale imports of African slaves and fewer trade constraints would prove to be the main instruments of the island's economic development. As Crame formulated the options, between "the poor who have nothing to lose by revolting" and "the prosperous who risk all in an uprising," it was preferable to aid the latter.[52] Satisfied planters would handle the dissatisfied. The

Reglamento del Comercio Libre a las Islas de Barlovento of 1765 would be designed to rectify shortcomings magnified by the English occupation by opting for development over stagnation, at least on Spain's Caribbean islands.

The Special *Junta,* 1763–1765

Madrid's decision to issue the Reglamento del Comercio Libre a las Islas de Barlovento of 1765 must be seen in long-term perspective. The opening of carefully selected Spanish ports in the Caribbean should not be regarded as exclusively or even primarily a response to the shock of Havana's temporary loss, although that disaster had brought to the surface underlying, long-term dissatisfaction with the relationship of Spain and its colonies in the absence of a colonial compact.

By the 1760s, the Spanish Bourbons' commercial policy remained a patchwork of compromise and inadequacy. The Real Proyecto de Galeones of 1720, which revived the convoy system, was barely functioning at the outbreak of war in 1739; it was de facto abandoned thereafter for Peru and only partially revived in the 1750s by *flotas* only to New Spain and its colonial subsystem, Venezuela.[53] Formal renewal of the *flota* system in 1755 (actually a *flota* did not sail until 1757) had left intact the Canary Islanders' privilege of shipping directly to the Caribbean ports of La Guayra, Campeche, Havana, and Santo Domingo.[54] To critics in the 1750s, the revival of *flotas* to Veracruz, balanced by unconvoyed, licensed ships (*registros*) serving other colonial ports, was further indication of reluctance to initiate a policy of economic development that was national and comprehensive in scope rather than reflecting provincial or even urban interests. The mixed system of convoys and *registros* sailing from and to Cadiz failed, however, to come to terms with the pressures in Spain's peripheral provinces, especially in Catalonia, to exploit growth opportunities in the colonies, while Cadiz's oligopoly persisted as the principal barrier to national development based on fuller exploitation of those resources. The need to break Cadiz's monopoly on trade with the colonies was only too evident. Cadiz's colonial trade was in the hands of a few undercapitalized Spanish merchant houses, commonly financed by foreign trading firms; the transatlantic trading system formed centuries earlier in the age of Charles V favored reexporting foreign goods to Spain's colonies; and the system of taxing shipments to America based on volume (*palmeo*) regardless of value, which had been established in 1720, was inefficient.[55]

Cuba's powerful planters and slave-trading interests also demanded an end to Cadiz's monopoly, and in 1764–65, the British parliament debated reopening Kingston, Jamaica's principal port, to shipping from Spain's colonies, thus expanding covert commercial exchanges.[56] In late 1762, French observers predicted that English traders would concentrate on smuggling along the Veracruz coast, "a goal all the more interesting to them since it will undermine Spain's trade there, just as the English have done along the coast of Honduras, Yucatan, Guatemala, and Central America."[57] As a result, in part, of Spain's delayed participation in the Seven Years' War, France opened "free ports" at Martinique and Guadaloupe in 1763. Subsequently, in mid 1764, Madrid belatedly established a monthly mail boat connecting La Coruña in Galicia with Havana to ensure the flow of official correspondence and supply peninsular traders with current economic intelligence. In light of English expansion in the Caribbean and Cadiz's constraining role, one understands the French view that the British threat in the Caribbean could be countered only if Spain were "to free the American trade at all its ports and lower trade barriers at Cadiz." A new approach by Madrid, the French commercial agent Béliardi reported hopefully in 1763, "is currently under review by government officials, stirring much interest."[58]

Early in his role as Charles III's preeminent minister, Esquilache sought advice on how to improve the colonial trading system. For example, a group of ministers and "amigos" invited Miguel de Cervera to present his views on the system in late 1760 or early 1761, and his thoughtful, forceful presentation led to a request that he provide a brief summary of his "discourse" as quickly as possible.[59] Cervera drew upon a fund of information about Spain's economy garnered from observation and reading: although he had neither visited nor traded in the colonies, he said, he felt qualified to comment on colonial trade on the basis of considerable informal discussion and "buenos documentos." Indeed, he could not resist the challenge of examining Spain's relations with its American colonies, since, reasoning pragmatically, "Spain's interests and well-being have been so interconnected with the Indies since their conquest that stagnant trade with the latter degrades and impoverishes Spain."

Cervera discerned a pattern in the evolution of foreigners' penetration of Spain's overseas commercial system. Until 1700, Dutch, English, and French smugglers had limited their operations to brief illegal contacts along the coasts of Spain's Caribbean possessions. What gave the English practical intelligence about the preferences of Spanish colonial consumers and the size and composition of the market were the slave depots they established under the *asiento* treaty of 1713. Spain's porous Atlantic system came under further pressure in the ensuing phase of *registro suelto* shipping, adopted by

Madrid to maintain contact with its colonies during the War of the Austrian Succession, when French, Dutch, and other neutral shippers enjoyed authorized access to Spanish America. Smuggling subsequently reached unprecedented proportions not only in the Caribbean but also in the Rio de la Plata area in the south Atlantic (where the Portuguese controlled the port of Sacramento). Moreover, the English South Sea Company stationed factors and sought out collaborators in the Spanish colonies eager to supply the interior, where—Cervera put it candidly—even *"corregidores* are traders."

Northern European traders, Cervera concluded, were motivated differently from their Spanish counterparts. They exported national textiles in predominantly national shipping, paying few (and usually low) export duties, and would accept low profit margins. In addition, while they exchanged their wares for silver, they did not neglect the colonies' other valuable exportables, such as indigo and cochineal, for which they paid well. They followed a policy of selling their goods cheaply and paying good prices for what they bought, the reverse of Spanish commercial practice. In contrast to this more aggressive trading strategy, current Spanish policy was failing, Cervera judged. The few peninsular wares available were burdened with multiple taxes, the port of Cadiz imposed high duties on domestic manufactures entering its jurisdiction (Uztáriz had criticized this decades earlier), and government policy was contradictory. It discouraged both the purchase of foreign-built shipping *and* the construction of shipyards in Spain; consequently, traders in the Spanish colonies could offer only limited quantities of their goods at inflated prices. Worse, Cadiz's overseas representatives were interested mainly in being paid in silver, neglecting or deliberately underpricing colonial exports. Why, Cervera asked, should merchants in the colonies send silver pesos to Cadiz when English and other smugglers could transfer them to Amsterdam at a saving of 30 percent? Inevitably, as a result, "millions in silver, gold and other valuable products are carried away by foreigners."

To remedy the flaws in the Spanish transatlantic system, Cervera proposed what he called *libertad y protección: libertad* for Spanish merchants to export from a wide range of Spanish to colonial ports, in ships sailing either in convoy or singly as *registros sueltos,* without requiring licenses or manifests registered at the peninsular port of exit; *protección* for domestic manufacturing by removing the innumerable *tributos,* substituting a 10 percent sales tax collected *overseas* at colonial customshouses, and expanding Spanish shipping by encouraging investment in both colonial and metropolitan shipyards. To favor poorly capitalized merchant houses, Spanish policy in the short run should exclude the competition of privileged companies in colonial trade. As for the state's major obligations, they should encourage construction of a national merchant marine and provide ample supplies of mercury for silver refining. He phrased it epigrammatically: "Much mercury to produce much silver; and much cloth, so that all the silver comes to Spain."

Modification of the colonial trading system had been the subject of critical questioning for decades. The manuscripts of Melchor Macanaz, of the author of the *Nuevo sistema,* of Antonio de Ulloa, Bernardo Ward, Campomanes, and now Cervera accurately diagnosed bottlenecks in the Spanish economy, pinpointing major structural impediments to growth and development in the metropole and the overriding necessity of revitalizing the imperial transatlantic system. They understood that the basis of metropolitan economic development ("recovery") might lie overseas in the American colonies, and that the key to colonial growth was modifying the transatlantic commercial structures exploited by one peninsular port, Cadiz, an *estanco* that, along with the convoy system, fostered domestic and foreign smuggling. In sum, a real developmental policy had to provide for direct exchange between Spain and its many colonial ports. In 1764 and 1765, these ideas were common currency among Charles III's bureaucratic elite—Esquilache, Grimaldi, Campomanes, and members of the Junta de Comercio like the marqués de Los Llanos.

That high civil servants in Charles's administration were seriously questioning the wisdom of adhering to traditional trade patterns despite changing national, colonial, and international conditions should not blind us to the power and influence of those profiting by that policy, whether well-capitalized foreign merchants or petty traders at Cadiz. No doubt, by 1764, probably sooner, the Cadiz mercantile community and its network of like-minded businessmen among Mexico City and Lima merchants had learned of Esquilache's project for a *junta* specifically to review the whole colonial trading system and propose changes.[60]

After Esquilache's Special Junta was formed in July 1764, lobbyists of the Cadiz *consulado* carefully monitored its deliberations, and there is evidence that elements of its *consulta* were leaked by Esteban de Abaría, who had been asked in 1763 to evaluate "an anonymous project entitled 'Ydea general del comercio de Yndias' [A General Idea of Trade with the Indies]." Like Colonial Secretary Arriaga, Abaría, who was ex-president of the Casa de Contratación at Cadiz and had been a member of the Consejo de Indias since 1758, proved an ideal covert agent at court for Cadiz interests. His reports on the government's intentions inspired Cadiz to caution the Madrid authorities about how dubious "an innovation without mature examination" was and to request an opportunity to review any "project" in advance and offer counsel. It was a sign of changing attitudes at Madrid that this time around, Cadiz's bid to intervene was rejected.[61]

Nonetheless, a counterattack against the Special Junta's purpose was drafted and circulated anonymously. Internal evidence indicates the sponsorship of the Consulado de Cadiz. Furthermore, since representatives of the Consulado de México (Francisco Xavier de Gamboa and Francisco de la Cotera) were already in Madrid to forestall radical changes in the colonial commercial system that might affect New Spain's merchant community, one may assume the collaboration of both of these influential *consulados*. Moreover, no effort was spared to circulate copies of this unsolicited defense of what was essentially the Spanish transatlantic commercial system centered on Cadiz.[62]

In the opening paragraphs, the existence of a "project" to undermine the "strength of your commerce" was affirmed, then promptly smeared as part of a centuries-old "foreigners' goal to take over Spain's colonial trade and the profits of its mines and other products" advanced under the "siren song of freedom" and the promise of a "specious extension to all Spain's peninsular ports."[63] The threefold aim of this project was to allow foreigners "free trade" that would surely "destroy manufactories in America"; to increase non-Spanish imports in the Spanish colonies overseas; and, through the expansion of smuggling, ultimately to deprive the Spanish state of customs revenues. These, according to the anonymous counterattack, were the real objectives behind any policy endorsing *comercio libre*.[64]

Cadiz, argued the defense of the status quo, was far from an *estanco injusto*. It represented all Spain, since the port was open to "Vizcaynos, Navarros, Montañeses, Gallegos . . . todas las provinces de España." Extending the privilege of colonial trade to "all the ports of Spain" would actually lower the volume of transatlantic trade by dispersing it among ill-prepared, undeveloped ports. Would Santander, for instance, really have sufficient exports available, much less enough capital to invest? "If they don't have even flour exports, what can the Montañas, Vizcaya, and other provinces offer?" After all, it was the Consulado de Cadiz that had sponsored the improved design of colonial commerce in 1720, the Proyecto, that "model of wisdom, equity and justice." The Consulado de Cadiz had long been considered the "main support of the Realm," and as "parte esencial," it was invariably consulted on major commercial issues. Its advice was responsible for the current prosperity ("our trade has never been more Spanish)," with the result that "the millions of pesos coined in Mexico City's mint" flowed to Spain. In sum, Cadiz was committed to *flotas, palmeo,* and *toneladas* as the basis of the dutying system. It held to the "principio fundamental" that the Spanish trans-atlantic trading system had always been an "honorable contract between the king and the Consulado de Cadiz." The anonymous manuscript concluded that a major issue concerning "the commerce of Spain and America and consequently the whole monarchy" should not be settled without a formal hearing to obtain the views of the *consulados* of Cadiz and Mexico.[65]

This hyperbolic apologia for Spain's traditional transatlantic commercial system, centered on lower Andalusia's secular port monopoly (barely modified by the Proyecto of 1720 with *consulado* approval), was rigidly uncompromising and gratuitously self-congratulatory. The preoccupations of many critical Spanish *proyectistas*—a revised system of managed trade under a single government agency (proposed in Bernardo Ward's manuscript),[66] coupled with encouragement of domestic manufactures—were simply ignored. Instead, the Consulado de Cadiz emphasized the traditional advantages of a managed colonial commercial system: balancing Cadiz's exports (mostly reexports) against colonial imports ("the survival of the monarchy depends upon a balance between the two") and the critical financial role of the Cadiz *consulado* in making available to the state "gifts and personal favors"—more than 26 million pesos (an exaggeration) between 1700 and 1760.[67] Unabashedly, the *consulado* took credit for the government's decision in 1755 to restore *flotas* to New Spain, and then questioned resorting to *registros* in wartime; it praised the current colonial secretary, Julián de Arriaga, for abandoning his support for *registros sueltos* in favor of convoys once he realized that unregulated *registros* were responsible for oversupplying the colonies.[68] Even dutying cargo by bulk (*palmeo*) rather than value (which favored high-value textiles) was defended belligerently, turning a defect into a virtue, "because if cloth is properly compressed, it arrives in good condition . . . occupies far less space, and allows for more cargo."[69] Significantly, New Spain, its mines, and the *flota* system to Veracruz and the Jalapa fair were most frequently and approvingly cited.

One may conclude that this unabashed apologia for the status quo signaled a strategy to induce Madrid to request a formal *consulta* by Cadiz commercial interests in hope of stalling any policy innovations. Certainly, the backgrounds and outlooks of the members of the Special Junta—Nicolas Mollinedo y La Cuadra (marqués de los Llanos), Francisco Craywinckel, Simón de Aragorri, Pedro Goosens, and Tomás Ortiz de Landázuri—gave the Consulado de Cadiz and associated interests little ground for complacency. The higher echelons of the bureaucratic universe of eighteenth-century Spain were not peopled by faceless, interchangeable pawns. Given press censorship, the selection of leading civil servants, the rise and fall of ministers, their subordinates, and clientele, and their deliberately visible ranking in processions and ritual gatherings all graduated the status of individuals and interests, influence and power. Moreover, under a recently installed monarch whose bureaucratic appointments indicated readiness at the very least to question traditional patterns of policy, scrutiny of committee personnel and realistic assessment of their backgrounds, patrons, networks, and orientation were vital to the survival of individual and group interests.

Of the five-member Special Junta, we have little information about Pedro Goosens, except for possible identification with the then insignificant Cantabrian port of Santander.[70] The Craywinckels had substantial ties to the Catalan nobility. One Craywinckel, José, was a cavalry captain at Valladolid (New Spain) in 1750;[71] another, Manuel, was a member of the court-martial that in 1763–64 reviewed the causes of Havana's loss in 1762. Francisco Craywinckel had been a *corregidor* in the viceroyalty of Peru (Cochabamba). In 1760, when a member of the Junta de Comercio y Moneda, he had joined the *proyectista* Bernardo Ward in recommending that Esquilache abandon government intervention in the grain trade, a stance that put him at odds with the influential Cinco Gremios Mayores of Madrid, which then held the monopoly of Madrid's grain supply.[72] We should not overlook his analysis of the significance of Havana's temporary loss to the English.[73] Simón de Aragorri (later marqués de Iranda) in 1764 managed Madrid's municipal grain supplies, supervising the transport of imports from Mediterranean ports to Madrid. In 1761, he had anonymously printed "reflections" on economic policy, at one point criticizing proposals to limit exports of manufactures to the colonies to those made in Spain. Through the children of his sister's marriage to a Las Casas y La Cuadra, he became uncle-in-law of Alejandro O'Reilly, as well as uncle of Cuba's outstanding captain-general in the 1790s, the conde de Las Casas y Aragorri. A merchant banker and Madrid representative of France's Compagnie des Indes, Aragorri later helped funnel Spain's subsidies to insurgent forces in the British colonies in North America in 1780–81.[74] Aragorri's links to the extended families of Las Casas, O'Reilly, Castaños, and Gardoqui illustrate patterns of Spanish colonial and metropolitan financial and military networks in the last quarter of the eighteenth century.[75] His networks had roots in post-1765 Cuban economic development and figured large in the expansion of Cantabrian interests.[76]

Nicolás Mollinedo y la Cuadra (marqués de Los Llanos) had been an Ensenada associate along with Agustín Ordeñana and a fellow *vizcaíno*, Sebastián de la Cuadra (marqués de Villarias), and he had kept a low profile after the coup that ousted Ensenada. Los Llanos formed part of a Basque network centered in the Congregación de San Ignacio at Madrid (Sebastián de la Cuadra had once been a *prefecto*); a French report ranked him among those of "le plus grand crédit."[77] Esquilache's selection of Los Llanos for the Special Junta signaled the orientation he wanted. There is also a Los Llanos manuscript (1755) that sketches his policy outlook, as well as a brief paper by Francisco Craywinckel.

Drafted in 1755, Los Llanos's document, like most *proyectista* analyses, followed a traditional pattern, touching in turn on the general European economic situation, Spain's colonies, and national policy goals and how to realize them.[78] Europe's development, he reasoned, was an outcome of population growth, improved techniques in agriculture and stock raising, and expansion of shipping and foreign trade. He was eclectic in paradigm-hunting: he favored those elements in English, French, and Dutch economic models that put primary emphasis on colonial trade and shipping. For Spain to aspire to compete with the more advanced economies in the European marketplace was chimerical, he posited, because the dominant English and French interests would insist Spain fulfill the seventeenth-century commercial stipulations they had forced upon its representatives. Since in realistic terms "for many years Spain will not be able to develop an active trade with Europe," Spain must direct its energies, following English and French models, to its American colonies, which "as part of its empire, can import its agricultural products and increase its manufactories and navigation." And bearing in mind Spain's unequal commercial treaties, the reaction of the model nations, and other factors, he added with caution, "even here we must dissimulate and show patience."[79] The American colonies would provide the platform for metropolitan economic growth.

Obviously, policy shifts demanded dissimulation by the central government because of two linked factors: first, Cadiz was a one-port monopoly; second, its function was primarily as an entrepôt between European suppliers and colonial consumers. As for the metropolitan economy, Cadiz's role was dysfunctional, "perhaps worse, as if it were the port of another country."[80] At other peninsular ports such as those in Galicia, Asturias, Cantabria, Murcia, and Aragon, the situation was different: duty levels were higher, collections more rigidly enforced, and no nation had the right to have them modified—this last a reference to the imposed commercial treaties effective at Cadiz. As a result of Cadiz's control over colonial trade and commercial information, "even today . . . Castilians, Galicians, Murcians, or Aragonese barely know they are our colonies, even less about their trade."[81] He also traced the curious isolation of Spanish provinces from colonial contacts to "the favoritism shown by the Casa de Contratación's bureaucrats to Cadiz because of their residence there." Furthermore, Contratación personnel hamstrung efforts by merchants in the peripheral provinces to bypass Cadiz to trade directly with the American colonies. After 1733, Los Llanos reported, Catalans had "petitioned for trading rights to Santo Domingo, the Galicians to Campeche, Asturianos to Buenos Aires or Honduras, Montañeses and Basques for the same." None of these, however, had obtained "the least satisfaction, because these requests must have Cadiz's approval." Los Llanos was not exaggerating. Equally restrictive of colonial trade, merchant firms at Cadiz, his critique emphasized, concentrated on the gains of trade with Peru and New Spain, minimizing exchanges with less-developed colonies. If Madrid's colonial policy remained inflexible, Los Llanos predicted, the English (at Barbados), the Dutch (at Surinam), and the Danes (at St. Lucia) would shortly occupy Spain's Caribbean colonies.[82]

Los Llanos's recommendations reveal a clear regional or provincial bias. His manuscript of 1755 foreshadowed themes that would surface a decade later: the fact that metropolitan economic growth depended upon production of colonial staples—indigo, cochineal, cocoa, sugar, and especially precious metals; the necessity of opening ports on Spain's periphery for direct trade with colonial ports, bypassing Cadiz; and the desirability of abolishing the Casa de Contratación, whose personnel were overly influenced by Cadiz's mercantile interests. Although at one point he urged that the ministries of Estado, Hacienda, and Indias jointly elaborate a comprehensive project to lower customs rates and encourage shipping between other peninsular ports and the American colonies, he conceded that "for the moment, let Andalusia control trade with New Spain and Galicia that of Peru." In the long run, development of metropolitan manufactures depended upon exploiting colonial markets by "sharing the American trades among Spain's provinces."[83]

The wide variance between Bernardo Ward's concept of national planning and the fundamentally fragmented emphases of Los Llanos underscores the persistence of regionalist mentalities in these approaches to metropolitan growth. Equally obvious is Los Llanos's dedication to forming a regional economic pole on the Cantabrian coast in northern Spain to counter that of Andalusia. In fact, in the course of mentioning Galicia's potential domination of the Peruvian economy, he specified exports of Galician linens, lace, and thread.[84] From his colonial years, Los Llanos was well aware of the primacy of foreign linens in Spain's trade with New Spain and especially Peru.[85] Possibly his Galician focus reflects demographic pressures in Spain's northern provinces over the second half of the eighteenth century and the aspiration of Cantabrian mercantile interests to penetrate colonial markets hitherto accessible only to those operating through the Cadiz oligopoly.

We know that Asturias and Galicia through their legal representatives (*diputados* or *apoderados*) also petitioned the Special Junta in late 1764 and early 1765, employing arguments basically similar to those of Los Llanos.[86] Their provinces, the representatives argued, were better positioned than other regions of Spain to trade with the American colonies. They could expand shipbuilding facilities to carry linens, brandy, metalware, and other Spanish goods, which, they understood, could not compete in European markets in quality or price; however, Cadiz blocked the expansion of trade to the colonies by other peninsular ports. The solution advanced by *diputados* from Asturias and Galicia was unambiguous: "Our merchants and merchant marine will revive only by opening our colonial ports to the shipping of those two provinces."[87] The petition was signed by the provinces' representatives, the marqués de Bosque Florido and Domingo Antonio de Argandona. In fact, however, a *fiscal* of the Consejo de Castilla, Pedro Rodríguez Campomanes, had drafted it; he would boast in 1789 that it had "initiated free trade to those Islands."[88]

Curiously, the approaches of Los Llanos (a Basque) and the representatives of the peripheral provinces of Galicia and Asturias were in a sense paralleled across the Atlantic in New Spain by another Basque, an *almacenero* of Mexico City. Apparently Manuel de Lerguinazával was at odds with the merchant oligarchs of Mexico City, whose interests overall jibed with those of Cadiz. In 1764, he too was asked by Madrid's Special Junta for policy recommendations, since a letter of 1764 refers to "el comercio libre y la navegación" under review.[89]

One must recall frequent references to economic conditions in New Spain dispersed in general reports on colonial conditions in the 1750s and 1760s to appreciate Lerguinazával's response. Whereas the *Nuevo sistema* manuscript and those of Ward, Craywinckel, and Los Llanos focused on the nexus between Spain and its colonies almost exclusively, Lerguinazával focused on the colony of New Spain as the main (and for him, fortunately isolated) terminus of Spain's colonial trade. He also favored frequent transpacific shipping between Manila and Acapulco, and stepped-up interprovincial exchanges with Lima to the south — a trade prohibited but carried on nonetheless in Guayaquil cacao and Chinese and European goods. Eager to stimulate trade with both East Asia and the viceroyalty of Peru, he at the same time envisioned Spanish intercolonial trade expanding in the Caribbean, along with greater direct contact between colonial and major peninsular ports. The economic impact of the English occupation of Havana had impressed him; in one year, he exaggerated, 750 merchant vessels had entered Havana, equal to the total of the previous twenty-five years. And, he added, although Havana had been returned to Spanish control, non-Spaniards (presumably North Americans and English) continued to be the major suppliers of Cuba's imports.[90]

In common with other analysts, Lerguinazával stressed from a Mexico City perspective that the principal hurdle to colonial economic growth was Cadiz's *estanco*. Here he singled out cargo carriers who tyrannized over merchants and shippers at both Cadiz and Havana, notably during the previous conflict with England (1739–48).[91] Furthermore, he railed against devices employed by Cadiz's merchants and shippers. Under the Proyecto of 1720 (which Cadiz had warmly supported), merchants in the colonies had to place their orders solely with those registered (*matrículado*) with the Consulado de Cadiz, who could thereby charge excessive commissions and shipping fees. "After all, are those in America to be treated like Turks?" So he had to recommend "freedom of trade and navigation."[92] He did not go as far as his contemporary Juan Joseph del Ribero (self-styled "del Comercio de Indias"), who urged Madrid in a more radical vein to fashion a brand-new "model for the Indies completely different from the old one" and to shift customs collection from peninsular to selected colonial ports, "throats or passageways for imported goods subject to the same duties as at Cadiz." This, Ribero claimed, was the only tactic that could inhibit European smugglers, who "like birds of prey, have fattened on large profits from their clandestine trade."[93]

3. The First Reglamento del Comercio Libre (1765)

After innumerable conferences, calculations, and tables, we have agreed and propose that the government should pursue this general plan for the development and prosperity of our trade and navigation to America.
      "Consulta original" (1765)

Free trade from all of Spain to America is a chimera.
      G.-T.-F. Raynal, *Histoire philosophique* (1783)

In the first quarter of 1765, Madrid seemed committed to reviewing its policies toward the overseas empire. The views of Esquilache's Special Junta, its "Consulta original" of 14 February 1765, and the carefully formulated instructions that followed a month later to José de Gálvez, the *visitador general* dispatched to New Spain, should all be seen in the context of the challenge of responding to the English occupations of Havana and Manila; pressure from Cantabria and from Basques in New Spain; and the opposition of anxious Cadiz and colonial merchants, whose advice Madrid avoided.

The *consulta* had its origins seven months earlier, in July 1764, when Prime Minister Grimaldi had asked Los Llanos to handpick four members to serve on a *junta,* to be chaired by him, to "review ways to address the backwardness of Spain's commerce with its colonies and foreign nations." Los Llanos was first directed to draft an initial report (*pre-informe*), which has not been located. This was followed by a formal order for an in-depth *consulta*.[1] The charge was treated soberly. At preliminary meetings, the *junta* resolved first to isolate the "más esenciales puntos," and, one presumes, to rank them; in mid September, Grimaldi advised the members that he had reviewed their agenda with Charles III, who had warmly approved it. Much encouraged, the *junta* assigned high priority to those factors and policies of most immediate effect.[2]

The Special Junta presumably realized that decades of memoranda, both solicited and unsolicited, but rarely published, had preceded its *consulta,* and that it behooved *it* to come up with feasible recommendations. There is no denying that the "Consulta original," prepared in only five months, is an impressive model of the genre: an *extracto,* or précis, of the main report; elaboration of eight factors of backwardness (*atraso*); and analysis of seven areas where change was both imperative and possible, all buttressed by thirteen appendices, some statistical and others exemplifying proposed recommendations.

Presumably, the Special Junta's members intended no open confrontation with Cadiz's commercial interests. Instead, they focused on the systemic flaws in Spain's transatlantic trade that accounted for the country's inability to profit like France and Britain from the human and natural resources of its overseas possessions: the convoy system, the need to purchase ship licenses from Madrid, and the *tonelada* and *palmeo* (cubic) measurement fees introduced in the Proyecto of 1720.[3]

In the introduction to the "Consulta original," one is struck by the way in which structures and needs shape both the approach to a national problem and proposed solutions. The growth of domestic trade ("the foundation of a state's well-being in the development of *its* agriculture and crafts, the real way to abundance, independence, and population growth") would bear fruit, but gradually. As for foreign trade, the issue was that the export trade of Spain's European competitors was so much more developed "por su economía, perfección y poder" that Spanish competition required prior improvement of the economy's basic sectors, agriculture, craft industry and, of course, shipping. Such time-consuming formation of infrastructure, however, might be bypassed. If national policy demanded quick results, policy emphasis might have to shift from metropole to colonies, to "the trade and navigation with our colonies . . . so that [the] vast continent's rich mines, goods, and materials may stimulate our merchants, employ our workers, expand our shipping, and over the long run absorb the output of our agriculture and crafts." The reference to "ricas minas" must reflect data available to the *junta.* Between 1755 and 1761, the proportion of precious metals to total imports from the colonies on private account unloaded at Cadiz topped 78 percent.[4] In addition, the greater part (85 percent) of the duties collected at Cadiz was generated not by exports (and reexports) but by colonial products.[5]

In brief, the most effective locus of metropolitan economic growth would have to be overseas in Spain's American colonies, rather than at home. Los Llanos's *junta* was, by indirection, challenging the order of priorities in the eighteenth-century growth paradigm, which hitherto had given primacy to domestic development.

Primacy to colonial over domestic growth had two added advantages. Overseas, there were none of the entangling constraints of century-old international treaties to block policy innovation ("we don't have to enter into conflict with the regulations of another treaty"), and, second, there were no national psychological factors of inferiority, such as "the unwarranted preoccupation of foreign critics in intimidating and confusing us by attributing to idleness or national character" Spain's curious inability to exploit fully its American possessions in an effective colonial compact. As the *juntero* Craywinckel had argued in 1762 apropos of the lessons of Havana's occupation, a national growth policy for Spain might alter what many interpreted as traits of national character.

The developmental program of Europe's economic models was thus stood on its head in the *junta*'s perspective, since it made Spain's colonial economy the initial rather than the ultimate focus of policy-makers. Fixation on the colonial world also led the *junta* pragmatically to assign priority to fiscal rather than other factors, a viewpoint clarified by the *junta*'s judgment that Spain's distant "dominions divided and separated" were naturally weak, needing an external force to bind them. In turn, this meant defense forces and their financing; it would require a major tax base to have colonies underwrite expenditures on imperial economic growth and unity, transatlantic trade, and shipping. Putting this into effect, concluded the *junta*, would stimulate backward sectors of the colonial economy, precisely those areas that the metropole had consistently neglected, despite the examples of Europe's other overseas empires since the middle of the seventeenth century.

In light of post-1740 *proyectista* analyses, Bernardo Ward's and Miguel de Gándara's, for example, there is little novel in the *junta*'s compendium of the shortcomings in Spain's economic policy for the American colonies: the trade monopoly of Cadiz and the Andalusian hinterland; the *flota* and *galeon* system centered there;[6] customs duties that disadvantaged domestic products; neglect of colonial staples, demand for which was growing in Europe; inability to suppress colonial production of *aguardiente,* wines, and coarse-to-medium grade textiles that competed with Spanish and European products; and inability to gain direct access to West Africa's slave ports. Last, there was the legendary vulnerability of the imperial trading system to bribery, customs fraud, and "large-scale smuggling between foreign colonies and our American possessions." The unprecedented growth in Caribbean smugglers' operations after 1748 had to be contained.

Two statistical tables buttressed these points. As a result of the pattern of controlled shipping and multiple taxation, the *junta* calculated that a barrel of Spanish wine valued at 6.7 pesos FOB in Cadiz paid a total of 12 pesos in insurance and freight charges to Veracruz and finally sold in Mexico City for 48.5 pesos—7 percent more than a barrel of colonial *aguardiente de caña,* or *chinguirito* (45 pesos).[7] "As a result consumption is lowered, and the colonies expand vineyards . . . and production of various liquors." Everywhere in the colonies, it was agreed, locally produced wine, *aguardiente,* and *mistela* undersold wine and brandy from the Iberian Peninsula. Unless legislation outlawing colonial production of such items were effectively applied, even the remaining market for exports to New Spain would evaporate. The full financial loss to Spain's transatlantic system between 1747 and 1761 was underscored in a statistical presentation, which revealed that of an estimated annual output of colonial mines and agriculture worth 35.6 million pesos, only 19.4 million pesos, or just over half, reached Spain, while a minimum of 12 million leaked to other European countries through foreign

TABLE 3.1

Average Annual Product of Spain's American Colonies, 1747–1761
(pesos)

	Precious Metals		Staples	Total
	Coin	Smuggled	Staples	Total
New Spain	12,324,643	800,000	3,000,000	16,124,643
Guatemala	250,000	–	1,600,000	1,850,000
New Granada	1,500,000	3,000,000	1,000,000	5,500,000
Peru	7,200,000	4,000,000	1,000,000	12,200,000
Total	21,274,643	7,800,000	6,600,000	35,674,643

Source: Adapted from AHN, Estado, 2314/1, n. 13.

TABLE 3.2

Spain: Average Annual Value of Imports from America on Private Account, 1757–61
(pesos)

	Precious Metals	Staples	Total
New Spain	8,970,128	3,260,314	12,230,442
Guatemala	200,000	460,512	660,512
Lima/Chile	3,684,275	196,395	3,880,670
Cartagena[a]	1,328,106	160,032	1,488,138
Buenos Ayres	1,057,190	114,214	1,171,404
Total	15,239,699	4,191,467	19,431,166
(New Spain)	(58.8%)	(77.8%)	(63%)

Source: AHN, Estado, 2314/1, n. 10.
[a]Includes Portobelo.

TABLE 3.3
Estimated Value of Goods Smuggled from Spain's Colonies, 1747–61
(pesos)

Total	35,674,643
Retained in Colonies	4,000,000
To Cadiz (registered)	19,431,166
Total Presumed Smuggled	12,243,477
From New Spain	1,000,000
From South America	11,000,000

Source: AHN, Estado, 2314/1, nn. 2, 13.

TABLE 3.4
Distribution of Exports, New Spain and Guatemala, 1747–61
(*pesos fuertes*)

To Spain (private account)	12,890,954
To Spain (royal account)	2,000,000
Subsidies (Caribbean colonies)	1,500,000
Subsidies (Philippines)	1,000,000
Unaccounted for	583,689
Total	17,974,643

Source: AHN, Estado, 2314/1, n. 13.

colonies in the Americas (Tables 3.1–3.3). (The French agent Béliardi attributed this to "the ease in America for forwarding the product of sales in English shipping to Europe.")[8]

New Spain's output was valued at 16.1 million pesos (45 percent of the total), which provided 10.2 percent of all precious metals smuggled. Of the annual combined production of New Spain and Guatemala, valued at 17.9 million pesos, Spain received 14.8 million (83 percent), while 1.5 million went to the Caribbean colonies and another 1 million to the Philippines (Table 3.4). This was the measure of Cadiz's port monopoly and Spain's managed trade in the Atlantic that the *junta* pilloried: "We limit this trade to one port, to a certain number of vessels, decisions made not by merchants but by the ministry at Madrid; we subject it to endless formalities, squeeze it with *tonelada* duties, and without separating domestic from reexported products, we proceed to levy on both disproportionately high export taxes." This was an exercise in eighteenth-century "political arithmetic" and a recognition of real rather than virtual reality.

From this careful evaluation of the minimum gains of Spanish colonialism flowed the *junta*'s policy recommendations in three categories. Since trade monopoly exercised by Cadiz merchants and Andalusian growers formed the bedrock of Spain's "decadence," the first category of proposed change called for extending "colonial trade to all the provinces" so that all Spain might share in colonial trade. The peripheral provinces could be served by their ports, which in turn would be assigned specified colonial zones—a variant, in fact, of the earlier policy of granting incentives to privileged companies in specified colonial dominions.[9] Inclusion of Bilbao and San Sebastián is noteworthy, since they were not mentioned as serving their provinces of Vizcaya and Guipúzcoa, the *provincias exemptas* whose special customs status (outside Castilian jurisdiction) had long ago led Madrid to isolate them from direct contact with the American empire. Bilbao and San Sebastián would now operate under regulations similar to those of the Compañía Guipuzcoana (headquartered at San Sebastián) for purposes of customs collection. The aim of linking peninsular provinces to colonial development was matched by the desire to maintain existing privileged companies to which the government had already assigned other colonial areas. Hence the colonial areas serviced by the respective Compañías de Caracas, de la Habana, and Barcelona (for Santo Domingo) were left intact since, the *junta* felt, those companies warranted "particular consideración," especially the Caracas company, now considered "in a very prosperous condition." The *junta* cautioned, however, that the companies were not to participate in "comercio general."

A second category of recommendations was a logical extension of revamping Cadiz's position as sole metropolitan port for Spain's trade with its colonies. The *junta* would terminate the convoy system and register vessels and specific licenses issued by the colonial office at Madrid, along with the complex of formal ship inspections and, of course, *toneladas* and *palmeo* duties of the Proyecto of 1720. For its part, the Colonial Office would absorb functions hitherto exercised by its influential subordinate, the Casa de Contratación, a move to eliminate Andalusian influence over ship sailings.[10] The *junta* took into account that given uneven colonial resource endowments and their development, along with their differential level of demand and variety of production, the richest and densely populated areas would attract more imports than others. The *junteros* proposed therefore to channel individual *registros* only to less developed colonies like Santo Domingo, Trinidad, Cumaná, Guayana, and the Orinoco Valley, and to eliminate duties levied on Spanish items exported there. Only in its third category of recommendations did the *junta* grapple with "the main advantage a state should consider in its colonial commerce"—the singular importance of colonial markets and resources to Spain's economy. Agricultural exportables ("staples, liquids, and dry goods") would be dutied at 5 percent—

except for duty-free flour, an incentive to north Castilian wheat and flour producers, and domestic manufactures. Duties on non-Spanish manufactures reexported at Cadiz, it was well known, generated significant revenues.

The wealth of reliable detail produced by researchers for the *junta* illustrates the importance of Europe's textiles in Spain's transatlantic trades. Predictably, a 600-ton vessel for Veracruz might hold on average 200 *toneladas* in Spanish staples, liquids, and dry goods, and double that tonnage in non-Spanish textiles (*ropas*).[11] Yet the value of textiles (18.1 million *reales de plata*) was more than ten times that of the rest of the cargo (1.7 million). Among textiles, linens (59 percent, mainly French) and silks (32 percent) predominated by value.[12] In addition, Cadiz exporters exploited the differing consumption patterns of Peru and New Spain. Fine linens (and some baize) were directed to Peruvian consumers, lesser qualities to those of New Spain. A *tonelada* of *ropas* shipped to Peru paid 225 *pesos fuertes* in duties, to Veracruz almost 66 percent less. Since linens and woolens sent to Peru had correspondingly higher unit values, "in every shipment expensive items predominate," adding up to virtually double or more than "the cargo value destined for New Spain."[13] Yet to be clarified is the higher purchasing power of elite consumers in the extended viceroyalty of Peru.

Under the *junta*'s proposed duties, non-Spanish manufactures would continue to pay customary import duties, and when reexported to the colonies, another 6 percent. Since the current effective duty on reexported European goods—linens, woolens, and cottons—averaged only 3.3 percent, the new rates represented an 82 percent increment, compensated for by expected lower maritime freight rates.[14] Thus inducements to smugglers might evaporate. Along with the proposed export rate structure, the *junta* insisted that Cadiz's low level of import duties on European goods, a vestige of Spain's seventeenth-century commercial concessions to England, Holland, and France, be compensated by higher duties on their reexport to the colonies.

The *junteros*' two final recommendations unambiguously addressed the needs of the Caribbean islands and nearby New Spain. Doubtless recalling English policy during the occupation of Havana in 1762, the *junta* recommended that Spanish merchants enjoy tax exemptions on trade goods when sailing directly to Africa to buy slaves for Spain's Caribbean possessions, thereby circumventing Jamaican slave dealers, who "keep selling them to us as a pretext for introducing their goods and extracting our riches."[15] Next, apropos of colonial production of precious metals and the fact that one of the *junta*'s appendices indicated that New Spain accounted for roughly

45 percent of all colonial precious metals output between 1757 and 1761, the *junta* urged a lower price for mercury while augmenting New Spain's supplies.[16]

Statistical materials and recommendations probably point to the colonial exposure and influence of the fifth member of the *junta*, Tomás Ortiz de Landázuri. Landázuri had gone out to New Spain along with the viceroy's secretary, Francisco Fernández de Molinillo, and when Molinillo was recalled to Madrid as *oficial mayor* (head secretary) in the Consejo de Indias, Landázuri also returned.[17] Appropriately, he had made a point of surveying New Spain's main mining centers, establishing contacts with mine owners and their merchant suppliers (*aviadores*). His grasp of the overriding importance of the colony's mining sector was clear: "The largest part of the trade of our America, and that moves world commerce, consists of gold and silver, mainly the latter."[18] His standing among New Spain's commercial magnates was high; the Consulado de México considered him an "excellent protector" of its interests.[19] In 1764, one year prior to the report of the Special Junta, he had drafted a comprehensive survey, "Noticia de los minerales . . . del reyno de la Nueva España" in which mercury supply and pricing were covered extensively.[20] Probably Landázuri prepared appendix 12 of the *junta*'s report, a succinct, hands-on survey of the mercury problem at New Spain's mining centers, recommending that the mercury price be reduced from 84 to 50 pesos per hundredweight (quintal)—close to its cost to the state monopoly—in order to lower the cost of processing a higher volume of the colony's low-grade silver ores.[21] Initial losses in earnings on mercury sales at a lower price might, he calculated, be more than compensated by existing taxes (seigniorage, tithes) on higher silver production. Annual revenue from mercury sales (at 84 pesos per quintal) was 700,000 pesos, he estimated, while at his lowered rate, it might more than double to 1.5 million.

Further indirect confirmation of Landázuri's contribution to the *junta*'s report is a remark concerning silver smugglers' collaborators among the colonial population, "convents and clergymen's homes [which] are often warehouses for smuggled goods, and refuge for smugglers." On the basis of internal evidence and observations on relations with native peoples in northern Mexico,[22] Landázuri's contribution to the work of the *junta* cannot be minimized; in January 1765 (probably in recognition of his participation), he was appointed *contador general* of the Consejo de Indias.[23]

During the eight months after the *junta* submitted its *consulta*, little movement on the colonial trade system was apparent, except for a contract awarded in June to a consortium of Spaniards at Puerto Santa María (on the Bay of Cadiz) to deliver African slaves to Puerto Rico and other Spanish possessions in the Caribbean. Madrid assigned 1,000 slaves to Cuba—the lessons of England's seizure of Havana followed by the situation reports of O'Reilly and Crame had not been lost. Four months later came the first product of the *junta*'s activity, the Reglamento del Comercio Libre a las Islas de Barlovento, Spain's first major revision of its transatlantic trading system in the eighteenth century.[24]

Its preamble consists of Charles III's *determinación,* pointedly lacking the countersignature of the prime minister (Grimaldi) or colonial secretary (Arriaga). It was directed for execution to Esquilache's Hacienda ministry rather than the Colonial Office according to the accompanying *instrucción* "signed by my Royal Hand"—evidence of Charles III's full backing of the Reglamento and confidence in Esquilache. The link between the monarch and the cutting edge of change in his regime, Esquilache, was patent. The preamble displays traces of the preoccupation of Alejandro O'Reilly and *junta* members with Cuba and other Spanish Caribbean islands, their shortages of imports from Spain, and the disturbing, growing inflow of smuggled goods.

The fundamentals of the Reglamento were clear: abolition of *palmeo* and *tonelada* duties inserted in the Proyecto of 1720, simplification of shipping formalities, authorization of selected peninsular and Caribbean ports for mutual trade—all designed to open the ports of the "principales provincias de España" to profitable operations—but restricted explicitly to Spain's Caribbean colonies. Of thirty-five colonial ports recommended by the *junta* for inclusion in the Reglamento, twenty-six (74 percent) were omitted.[25] Exports of Spanish products would be duted at 6 percent, foreign re-exports at 7. Ships could now sail unescorted from authorized peninsular ports only to designated Caribbean ports. However, new formalities were introduced: customs personnel at peninsular ports now had to prepare lists recording cargo, Caribbean destination, and the monetary security (*fianza*) guaranteeing arrival at the designated overseas port.[26] Merchants in Spain's Caribbean ports would continue to export the products of their respective islands to the metropole, but were enjoined not to reexport their Spanish or European imports to other colonial ports. Intercolonial exchanges remained restricted.

The Reglamento de Barlovento as Incrementalism

The "Consulta original" was the end product of years of reviewing Spain's transatlantic system, of recommendations by—among others—the *proyectista* Ward, and of the Special Junta's exhaustive analysis. Yet the statutory outcome of the Consulta, the Reglamento de Barlovento, introduced only incremental modifications to an otherwise enduring trade pattern. The busy Basque ports of Bilbao and San Sebastián were omitted, as was overt criticism of Cadiz's *estanco*. The *junta*'s explicit recommendation to exploit the colonies for the benefit of metropolitan economic development was muted to a call to "make the most of" the colonies—hardly a declaration of a well-defined developmental policy under belated mercantilism. Granted, the fleet system was abandoned, at least for the Spanish Caribbean, but there remained the 6 percent export duty on Spanish products, where the *junta* had recommended none. Neither shippers nor agents were authorized to traffic from island to island seeking markets for their cargoes, nor could island residents reexport imports from Spain to other Spanish possessions. In sum, the government had limited change essentially to meeting Cuba's needs, the sole area recently occupied and opened by the English, by ensuring a supply of African slave labor, subsistence goods, and manufactures, and somewhat more shipping for its staple exports.

The balance of the elaborate structure of managed colonial trade was left intact, testimony of reluctance to disturb Cadiz's lucrative exchanges with Veracruz or the Guipuzcoan company's monopoly of "Caracas" trade. First, Cadiz's advantage in lower import duties compared to those of other peninsular ports was not balanced by higher export duties on shipments to the colonies; hence that port could (and would) continue to account for the bulk of Spain's reexports to the colonies. Second, the sole colonial marketplace where Cadiz oligopolists might at last encounter serious competition from other peninsular ports (essentially Barcelona) was really Cuba. On the other hand, the Guipuzcoan (Caracas) company retained its commercial preserve in Venezuela, while Cadiz still monopolized access to the most productive of all the Spanish possessions, New Spain and its Caribbean port at Veracruz. Third, there is no mention of a reduced mercury price for that colony's mine owners, which they would have communicated to Landázuri. Indeed, the fact that New Spain's secular structure of managed trade with Cadiz was left intact is all the more significant in light of the rumor current when the Special Junta was formed in 1764 that it would surely recommend what to many seemed inevitable, "la libertad de comercio al reyno de México." Perhaps the rumor indicated how onlookers had interpreted the selection of *junta* members Mollinedo and Craywinckel?[27] Rumor aside, Veracruz would still be supplied only by *flotas* from Cadiz. At Veracruz, the only innovation was the inauguration of mail packet boats to and from Havana.

Certainly, cautious *junteros* had reasonable grounds for excluding New Spain from the Reglamento de Barlovento. New Spain now produced nearly half the precious metals mined in Spanish America, as Raynal's *Histoire philosophique* soon revealed.[28] It covered its own very substantial administrative and defense outlays, dispatched annual subsidies to Spanish colonies in the Caribbean (especially Cuba) and the Philippines, yet still managed to export a surplus of millions of pesos to the metropole every year. New Spain was the linchpin of Spain's presence in Meso-America and the Caribbean. The Reglamento's clear omission of New Spain testified to Madrid's ongoing fear that *comercio libre,* once extended to the "most profitable of our Indies," would serve only to "enriquecer al extrangero y a fomentar América."[29]

Minimal as were the modifications legislated by the Reglamento, the underlying proposition in the introductory section of the Special Junta's *consulta* should not be overlooked. Raising the volume of cargo, the number of ships, and customs receipts of colonial trade might provide feedback to the economy of the metropole—the overriding priority of imperial developmentalists. Here is foreshadowed Madrid's major imperial policy reorientation in the aftermath of the *motín* against Esquilache. As Raynal would phrase it with characteristic insight, "Far from subordinating colonies to metropole, somehow the metropole was subordinated to the colonies."[30] Whatever the reasons—New Spain's overall economic importance, ingenious lobbying by Cadiz merchants' agents backed by those of the Consulado de México, perhaps even the intervention of Landázuri—no reference to New Spain appeared in the Reglamento of 1765. Yet one month after the *junta*'s report was submitted, a special investigator, the *visitador general* José de Gálvez, left Cadiz for New Spain. Pure coincidence?

The immediate response to the Reglamento's publication was mixed. For instance, one bureaucrat exaggerated that the province of Valencia would now "trade within or without, or navigate to and trade with, the Indies." In France, Raynal, ever the realist, would soon observe that "free trade from Spain to America is a chimera," echoing perhaps the opinion of France's commercial agent at Madrid that Spain's Caribbean commerce continued "to stagnate as before."[31] Perhaps the contemporaneous English historian William Robertson (incidentally, a Campomanes correspondent) voiced how English commercial interests interpreted the Reglamento when he exaggerated that "this ample privilege . . . at once broke through all the fences which the jealous policy of Spain had been labouring for two centuries and a half to throw round its commercial intercourse with the New World."[32] Or perhaps English interests deliberately exaggerated the extent of Barlovento's innovation, since its minimal changes encouraged continued smuggling operations in Caribbean waters at which they excelled?

Nevertheless, the Spanish Bourbon program of renovation pushed wholeheartedly by Esquilache, by the Special Junta's *consulta,* and the ensuing Reglamento, along with the Hacienda's ongoing probe into Cadiz's customs practices and the financial operations of its *consulado,* had exposed Esquilache to powerful, anxious antagonistic interests at Madrid, Cadiz, elsewhere in the Peninsula, and overseas at Mexico City and Lima. Worse, those integrated aristocratic, clerical, and merchant elites had reason to fear further changes that he might spearhead.

Can we trace the moderate end product of the Special Junta's deliberations to the dominant influence of interest groups in Spain's transatlantic trading system? While there is reason to accept a relatively large degree of bureaucratic or state autonomy, one must recognize the presence of integrated interest groups reluctant to adjust to new conditions in the Atlantic world. Most influential were Cadiz's exporters (both national and foreign), other corporate bodies dependent upon luxury imports, like Madrid's Cinco Gremios Mayores, and cautious Hacienda functionaries wary of any precipitous falloff in customs revenues (Cadiz still supplied the largest percentage of contributions to Spain's *rentas generales*). It was probably treasury functionaries a French observer had in mind in saying that "although the ministry was convinced of the advantages of the [new] system, it lacked power to implement it."[33] Equally influential were merchants in the colonial distribution hubs at Mexico City and Lima, and those in the colonies dependent upon smuggling activities. Nor should we overlook the fact that Mexico City's *almaceneros* knew of English and North American penetration of Havana's commercial system during the occupation of that strategic port and had weighed the consequences for the Spanish colonial trading system.

Nonetheless, given the data in the statistical tables of the "Consulta original," it is surprising that the 1765 statute turned out to be mildly reformist. Or is it? In 1622, Edward Misselden's *Free Trade* had argued for eliminating only selected monopolistic restrictions, a proposal opposed by London's powerful and well-established merchants dealing in staples.[34] Some may argue that Spain's 1765 statute reflects a planned timetable, with an implicit ultimate goal; others may claim the Reglamento was merely a reaction to the Caribbean crisis situation.

4. Privilege and Power in Bourbon Spain: The Fall of Esquilache (1766)

In carefully planned affairs, we must rely upon presumption and conjecture, otherwise a conspiracy may never be uncovered when the instigators of a certain status cannot publicly lead the unfortunate masses in such disorders.

Pedro Rodríguez Campomanes,
Dictamen fiscal de expulsión de los Jesuitas de España (1766–69)

Without clear goals, powerful vested interests, consolidating over centuries, have the power to thwart any possible reform.
José Muñoz Pérez, "La publicación del Reglamento de Comercio Libre de Indias de 1778"

Since the eighteenth century, mainly as a result of English and French experience, political systems in western Europe and the western portion of the North Atlantic have provided relatively open channels of communication between rulers and ruled, between government and people, elites and masses. The frittering away of systems of censorship, the expansion of literacy, and the complexity of interest in economic growth and/or development have inspired formal institutions providing representation to groups, classes, and interests. The most notable such institution has been the elected parliament or congress based upon political parties and a degree of freedom of the press. Acts of political terrorism in the form of guerrilla operations or urban riots as a political expression in the late twentieth century represent a breakdown in the functioning of open forms of accepted interest expression.

In the prerepresentative polities of the eighteenth century, and particularly in an old regime typified by so-called "absolutism," such as the Spanish *monarquía,* there were to be sure institutional channels through which the demands of interest groups could reach high courts and *consejos,* such as the Consejos de Castilla and Indias, and ultimately the chief executive and arbiter, the "crown." At times, however, and especially in the case of the lower classes during economic crisis, protest took the form of violent crowd action, the riot, or *motín,* as a legitimate (sometimes awesome) form of direct appeal to the crown, as the chief source of justice.

Less frequently and generally during acute political crises, powerful interests, obstructed or rejected in formal channels of redress, resorted to the *ultima ratio,* the coercive force of the managed pseudo-riot. Adroitly mobilized around a perceived injustice, such as an inflationary spiral, acute food shortage, or an affront to customary practice, the crowd was manipulated to direct violence against a prominent figure of the regime, adroitly incriminated for real or invented abuse of delegated state (or royal) authority. In this ritualized coercive presentation of "popular" demands for respect for the "moral economy," the crowd was the prime actor, and it bestowed upon a symbol of social cohesion and legitimacy, the cleric, the role of spokesman-mediator. In this context, a rioting mob marked the limits of state authority through a political object lesson, or *escarmiento,* directed at the ultimate source of secular power, the monarch of the *monarquía.*

Such an event was the urban riot, or *motín,* that occurred at Madrid in March 1766, resulting in the ouster of the minister chosen by Charles III to oversee substantive change in the metropole's economy and society, as well as in its American empire—the marqués de Esquilache. There would be a remarkable sequel: in March 1808, a similar episode at Aranjuez, a royal residence near Madrid, ended the reign of Charles IV, fired resistance to French intervention, and ultimately resulted in Spanish America's independence from Spain. The Madrid riots of 1766 illustrate the imperatives and constraints that characterized Bourbon renovation between 1759 and 1808; the crisis of 1808 marked the substantive failure of those reforms.

Here we seek to clarify the significance of the *motín de Esquilache*—an anti-Esquilache movement—as ritual mobilization of elites under stress. In analyzing the mechanics of the event and focusing on individuals and groups linked to it, we seek to illuminate cause and consequence. There is an underlying hypothesis—the primary, conspiratorial role of integrated elites composed of formal political, social, and economic groups, along with the indispensable informal ones that play roles essential to the maintenance and function of the whole society. What follows is a sketch of antecedents, an abbreviated account of the sequence of rioting, followed by analysis based on direct as well as circumstantial evidence incriminating individuals and groups, both formal and informal. Finally, we advance conclusions about the immediate and especially the long-term consequences of an episode that momentarily revealed the fragility of an "absolutist" polity.

Motín as Mass Mobilization

The *escarmiento* of the marqués de Esquilache had antecedents in Bourbon Spain. More than one leading minister of Philip V and Ferdinand VI had been forced from office by conspiracy and force. Perhaps the most relevant case was the abrupt arrest at midnight and then exile in 1754 of the marqués de la Ensenada, which aborted an earlier Bourbon attempt at reform. Esquilache's ouster, however, was more traumatic and far-reaching: he was far more closely identified with his king's aspirations and personal commitment to change, and he had in fact initiated penetrating changes in Spain's economy and polity. We must recall that Charles had insisted on bringing Esquilache to Madrid and assigning him difficult issues, fiscal and financial reorganization and economic development in metropole and colonies. The confidence of Charles and Esquilache, grounded in their Neapolitan experience and their understanding of conditions in Spain, was matched initially by the expectation of change shared by many Spaniards. Rarely in Spain's history had a monarch come to the throne under such auspicious circumstances.

Although much of Esquilache's wide-ranging program was still in the pipeline in early 1766 (some of it in fact bogged down in procedural delays), he proceeded with confidence, born partly of prior success against what appeared to be similar obstacles at Naples, partly of assurance that ample provision had been made for the economic and political security of the capital city, Madrid. All European capital cities of the time faced problems of policing rural-to-urban migration of the unemployed, the unemployable, the underemployed, or drifters (later called lumpen), who were capable of violent reaction to enforcement of public order. Esquilache's strong-arm tactics—outlawing hand arms and prohibiting certain articles and styles of dress—proved especially irritating and were readily interpreted as violating custom.

The *motín* that erupted on Palm Sunday (23 March) 1766 was the culmination of metropolitan and colonial pressures. It flared at the center of the Spanish imperial system, Madrid; its immediate objective was the ouster of Esquilache, spearhead of the reforms that followed the arrival of Charles III in 1759. In terms of achievement, it was extraordinarily successful; within twenty-four hours, the crowd forced Charles to dismiss Esquilache. The details, some still moot, are not as significant as the long shadow cast over the remaining decades of Charles's era. Records of the *motín* confirm that the episode was planned to take advantage of the conjuncture of inflated food prices, growing resentment of Esquilache's extensive program, heightened by the religious intensity of Holy Week, the holiday influx into the capital for the religious pageantry of masses and processions, and the customary return of the royal household from the Pardo palace outside Madrid just before Easter.

The precipitant—posting of dress regulations on 10 March—was carefully planned, timed to maximize crowd mobilization and manipulation. Under the pretext of "renewing earlier measures" prohibiting long cloaks and wide-brimmed hats commonly worn to conceal stolen or smuggled goods, the edict of 10 March in fact incorporated selected clauses of prior dispositions to produce a far more comprehensive (and to many, offensive) prohibition. Contradictory and ambiguous phrases imposed a blanket prohibition on wearing long cloaks and slouch hats in the capital. The edict was crafted, issued, and enforced mainly by that section of the Consejo de Castilla responsible for Madrid's public order, the Sala de Alcaldes de Casa y Corte. It did so despite the political volatility of measures seeming to violate moral polity. More critical, it was promulgated despite warnings of disaster by a *fiscal* of the Consejo de Castilla, Pedro Rodríguez Campomanes. He and others foresaw that the edict might galvanize into action a group that had recently posted the "Constitution and Ordinances" of a "new corps to defend monarch and fatherland"—a patriotic (or superpatriotic) society. During the fortnight before Holy Week, the covert opposition orchestrated a crescendo of confusion, mixed with confrontation between crowd and police, people and order, culminating in mass mobilization on Palm Sunday, 21 March.

Moving out from the traditional urban center of Easter ceremonial, Madrid's Plaza Mayor, a mob inflamed by anti-Esquilache sloganeering sacked his residence and surged on to the new Palacio Real, incorporating en route as its spokesman a prominent aristocrat, the cooperative duque de Medinaceli. An appalled Charles III refused to step outside the palace to face the crowd, instead sending a captain of the Life Guards, the duque de Arcos, popular (like Medinaceli) for "largesse and bravura," to report on the causes of popular discontent and anti-Esquilache shouting. Learning that the principal demand was Esquilache's ouster, Charles sent Arcos back to quiet the mob. It withdrew from the palace area, meanwhile entering jails to liberate those who had been imprisoned for dress violations, destroying recently installed street lighting, and carrying out "controlled depredation." The few troops garrisoned in the capital, mainly Life Guards, were kept in their barracks.

However, the next day rioters became violent, returned to the Real Palacio and, failing again to force Charles's appearance, turned on the Walloon regiment of Life Guards. Charles conferred with the Consejo de Castilla on the next steps; its members recommended concessions to crowd pressure—essentially Esquilache's formal dismissal and a mass pardon. When Charles asked for an alternative policy, the *consejo* advised lowering food prices, abolition of the Junta de Abastos managing Madrid's grain supply, and punishment of [the police] for "excesses and injustice." Appropriately, the *alcaldes de casa y corte* then posted an edict incorporating these items, but it was quickly ripped down when rioting intensified. At this juncture, the Franciscan cleric "Padre Cuenca," wearing the traditional Lenten symbol of a crown of thorns and bearing a crucifix, who had been preaching from a balcony of the Casa de la Panadería in the Plaza Mayor, was asked by the crowd to deliver reiterated demands for the removal and exile of the marqués de Esquilache to Charles.

Under such pressure, Charles consulted his immediate entourage, the duque de Arcos, the condes de Gazola, Priego, Revillagigedo, and Oñate, and the marqués de Sarriá—all military except for Oñate. In language more diplomatic than that of the Consejo de Castilla, this group recommended the same concessions already proposed by the *consejo* and, of course, a general pardon. Perhaps fearful that the mob might set fire to the recently completed Real Palacio, Charles caved in, agreeing to replace Esquilache at the finance ministry with Miguel de Múzquiz (as the mutineers demanded), abolish the Junta de Abastos, transfer its responsibilities to Madrid's town council (*ayuntamiento*) and the Cinco Gremios Mayores, and issue a general pardon. When the Madrid crowds dispersed on 24 March, the rioting seemed over.

Charles was far from reassured, however, and during the night of 24–25 March, he fled secretly with his family to the Aranjuez palace on the Tagus, thirty miles southeast of the capital. Confrontation between crowd and crown now revived at Madrid. Rumor spread that Charles had called troop reinforcements to Madrid, and others noted that Esquilache remained war minister. Madrid's crowds, again mobilized in the morning of 25 March, now converged on the residence of the governor of Spain's most important juridical-administrative body, the Consejo de Castilla, Diego de Rojas y Contreras, bishop of Cartagena. He urged the *consejo* to support the crowd's indictment of the Italian minister ("a hideous monster") and to petition Charles to return to Madrid. The indictment was comprehensive: blame for Spain's participation in France's recent conflict with England and consequently the temporary loss of Havana, for bureaucratic reorganization that displaced loyal public functionaries, for Madrid's high food prices, unnecessary taxes, mindless urban improvements, and maladministration of justice. In a remarkably pointed act of disrespect, a fugitive convict, Diego de Avendaño, was picked to deliver the indictment of Esquilache and his policies to Charles III at Aranjuez and to return with his response. Then the mob occupied the Madrid army barracks and took possession of recent arms shipments from Vizcaya. Meanwhile, Charles received a second petition supporting the indictment, now signed by Bishop Rojas y Contreras, accompanied by details of damage that Esquilache had caused Charles and the state. Reduced to the condition of a dependent and without funds, arms, or navy, the petition asserted, Charles had had to sell titles of nobility ("public honors"), while Esquilache's propensity for self-enrichment drove him to meddle in the affairs of the colonies, "with the idea of losing them" and to incite rebellion there.

The last act of the *motín* occurred on 26 March, when the convict Avendaño rejoined the crowd gathered at the Casa de la Panadería on the Plaza Mayor in Madrid. In strange solemnity, witnessed by Bishop Rojas y Contreras, flanked by members of the Consejo de Castilla, with the *consejo*'s clerk to one side and Avendaño to the other, Charles III's formal agreement (really a capitulation) to the crowd's demands was read, along with his request for an end to the *motín*.

The main objective of the *motín* having been achieved, the confrontation terminated. Esquilache left for Italy and later became Spain's ambassador to Venice, never mentioning the incident in further correspondence with Charles; Múzquiz (later conde de Gausa) became finance minister, Gregorio de Muniaín replaced Esquilache at the war ministry. The crown had, however, been the main victim of what had very nearly amounted to a *golpe de estado* (coup d'état), and it was time to restore both the image and the reality of state authority. Accordingly, Rojas y Contreras lost his governorship and was remanded to his bishopric; Aranda, an aristocrat and military officer, replaced him at the apex of the Consejo de Castilla.

Although Madrid was quiet by the end of March, mob activity spreading to the provinces made evident the underlying social malaise created by rising food prices and the ease of mobilizing the masses against constituted authority. Spontaneous or no, the menace of further rioting in the capital *and* provinces led Charles's advisers to send José Moñino, former *alcalde de casa y corte* and now (with Campomanes) a *fiscal* of the Consejo de Castilla, to investigate the provincial disorders.

More significant, perhaps, than the provincial unrest continuing into early April was a studiously phrased, long gestated, and oddly well distributed letter by the bishop of Cuenca, Isidro de Carvajal y Lancaster. It echoed most of the indictment of Esquilache presented by the freed convict Avendaño to Charles at Aranjuez, with additional criticism of state policy toward the ecclesiastical establishment. Delivered to Charles's confessor for transmission to the king, the bishop's letter pronounced Spain "hopelessly adrift" as a result of state policy, and the church "stripped of its properties, its ministers scorned, its community disregarded." It pointed to failings in colonial policy, alleging that Havana's loss signified God's wrath at the persecution of His church, as well as the "deterioration" of the Spanish possessions in America (possibly referring to recent rioting at Quito, Ecuador, in 1765). The content and date (13 April) of the letter suggest that it was prompted by the unprecedented removal as governor of the Consejo de Castilla of Bishop Rojas y Contreras, a fellow *colegial* of Salamanca's influential *colegios mayores,* and his replacement by Aranda.

If the bishop of Cuenca and his backers had aimed to revive the confrontation of late March, it was clear that Madrid's political ambient was markedly different in mid April. With Esquilache gone and Aranda in control of the armed forces and the Consejo de Castilla, the minister of Justice and Religious Affairs, Manuel de Roda, insisted that Bishop Carvajal y Lancaster substantiate his complaints. These were quickly refuted by *fiscal* Campomanes in a skillful legal opinion (*alegación fiscal*), and the bishop had to recant formally and abjectly before a session of the Consejo de Castilla held in Aranda's residence. Like the bishop of Cartagena, the bishop of Cuenca was ordered back to his bishopric. At the very least, the clerical faction had been quietly, if not entirely effectively, chastised for participating in the *motín* of 1766.

More than the symbolic rebuke of two aged, aristocratic, politically and socially prominent church hierarchs was required to resolve the political crisis precipitated by the Madrid *motín* and shore up the authority of Charles, his government, the *monarquía.* Aranda used his broad powers to ensure public order in the capital and, more to the point, began to probe the origins of the *motín* and pinpoint the mob's leadership. To this end, a special *junta* (*consejo extraordinario*) was set up at Aranjuez to get to the bottom of the *motín,* indict the leaders, and reaffirm the crown's authority.

However, the covert forces that had at minimum tolerated (if not fanned) the politically motivated March riots were already organizing to block any startling revelations. Aranda perceived immediately that the Consejo de Castilla would hamper rigorous investigation, which accounts for his insistence on the removal of Rojas y Contreras and his own appointment as the *consejo*'s governor. Meanwhile, Alonso Pérez Delgado, the *corregidor* of Madrid (formerly one of Ensenada's collaborators), joined with Esquilache's replacement at the Hacienda, Múzquiz, to exonerate Madrid city dignitaries and courtiers of any complicity in the March events—in reality, to pardon them publicly. One month after the *motín,* it was still politically dangerous to pursue the investigation in certain directions, although the authority and prestige of the monarchy badly needed public indictment and punishment of those responsible.

A tacit compromise quickly evolved. Investigation by the Special Junta continued, but with the virtually explicit purpose of incriminating the Society of Jesus as the sole party responsible. Evidence accumulated during the rest of 1766 at the direction of the *consejo*'s *fiscal,* Campomanes, became the justification for the dramatic expulsion of the Jesuits from Spain and its colonies one year after the Madrid riots. Carefully publicized in Europe, their efficient removal formally ended the episode, perhaps the most important political event in eighteenth-century Spain.

The Anatomy of the Near *Golpe*

Contemporary testimony and subsequent analysis leave little doubt that the riots of 1766 had, in fact, been foretold and were the product of a conspiracy.[1] Attribution of complicity, however, appeared difficult, even dangerous to establish at the time.[2] And while few historians have accepted the official incrimination of the Jesuits or the justification of their expulsion from Spain and its colonies, the curious disappearance of the records of the investigation ordered immediately after the riots and the fragmentary and often biased surviving accounts provide poor footing on the basis of which to proceed further. Indeed, the high priority given the restoration of the authority and image of royal power, as well as the need to reconcile the regime with groups whose acts of commission and omission pointed to complicity in the movement, obscure the record of the crisis.

Apparently at the instigation of Finance Minister Múzquiz, Madrid's *corregidor,* Pérez Delgado, early on elicited statements of self-exoneration and loyalty from the court nobility, the Cinco Gremios Mayores, and other influential organizations in the capital. Every effort was made to expunge allusions to the riots from the public record. The *Gaceta de Madrid,* for example, reported the rioting at the palace on Palm Sunday as routine religious observances by the royal family; and the hurried midnight flight of Charles and his family was recorded as an uneventful trip to the royal residence at Aranjuez.[3] The unprecedented replacement of the bishop of Cartagena at the head of the Consejo de Castilla by Aranda, a military officer and *grande,* omitted reference to the unceremonious dispatch of Rojas y Contreras back to his Cartagena diocese, although his dismissal was softened by a letter testifying to Charles's confidence in his enduring loyalty.

Attempts to minimize the magnitude and significance of the Madrid insurrection were the state's reaction to its very success, which, it was now recognized, had been at unexpectedly high cost to the fundamental institutional relationships of the monarchy's power structure. Had Charles yielded early on Palm Sunday to the crowd's insistence that he dismiss Esquilache, damage to the image of royal authority, though considerable, would have been reparable. The rioting indeed could have passed as a subsistence riot (as some historians still categorize it). But Charles's resistance and flight from his capital, the ensuing escalation of mob violence, open intervention of the Consejo de Castilla on the insurrectionists' behalf, and the use of a jailbird to deliver to Aranjuez what was clearly an ultimatum and to bring back what was clearly the king's surrender, opened a chasm between *consejo* and crown that deeply consternated the diplomatic corps and both supporters and opponents of Charles's reforms.

To no one was the isolation of the monarch and the urgency of restoring the image and reality of royal authority more apparent than to Pedro Rodríguez Campomanes, a committed regalist. One of two *fiscales* of the *consejo* (the other being Moñino), he had closely monitored the oncoming crisis, and now he desperately tried to restore a patina of cohesion and power that enlightened bureaucrats considered essential to implementing the reforms to which Charles had committed himself and his supporters.[4] Commissioned to investigate the riots following the appointment of the conde de Aranda as president of the Consejo de Castilla, Campomanes cooperated with members of the *consejo*, the aristocracy, and Charles's ministers to formulate a strategy—some have called it another conspiracy—that promised to provide a brilliant solution to the crisis: incrimination of the Jesuit order and its dramatic banishment from Spanish territory, a project long entertained by Spanish Bourbon regalists, as well as sectors of the secular church, rival orders, and agrarian and commercial interests in both metropole and colonies.

The government's efforts to restrain and shape investigation of what was certainly a case of sedition in 1766 reflects the magnitude of the object lesson (*escarmiento*) that had been applied to Charles III as monarch and patron of reform. It reveals the difficulty and danger of identifying decision-makers who manipulated the crowds to terrorize the crown into dismissing reformist bureaucrats, an extreme form of lèse-majesté. One basic ingredient of such managed violence was generating illegitimacy within the sanctum of legitimacy. On grounds of necessity (no other means to accomplish this was available) and of self-protection, leaders of Esquilache's opposition covered their tracks by manipulating the legal process in a manner that would predictably culminate in an apparently spontaneous, anonymous movement, which in fact proved to be irresistible coercion.

Under Spain's old regime, no tactic was better fitted for the purpose than to induce a high-profile government figure to approve a provision patently unjust and to some, violent, one that infringed a popular custom, style, or the "moral economy"—here, access to low-cost subsistence for an urban population. In an ambience prepared by satire, rumor, and unfounded charges, confrontation between mob and majesty would be touched off by routine execution of orders issued by the targeted minister with royal approval.[5] Success, however, hung upon choice of appropriate conjuncture—of time and place, of initiators, actors, and abettors.[6] Here one must look beyond details of mass mobilization as well as rituals of formal society and polity to examine the informal groups and institutions where common interests and bonds became shared thought, and shared thought fathered common action.

The Genesis of the *Motín:* The Edict of 10 March

Insufficient scrutiny has been accorded the legal discrepancies and deliberate obscurity about the formulation, timing, and enforcement of the edict of 10 March 1766 on dress that precipitated the March riots, which was issued and enforced by the Sala de Alcaldes de Casa y Corte, the subsection of the Consejo de Castilla responsible for the security of the capital.

The edict's immediate antecedent was a general order of 11 January 1766, signed by Esquilache, mandating military dress—short coat and tricorne hat—for the armed forces and employees of government bureaus, including the Treasury and "other offices."[7] Over the next weeks, the general order went through a curious metamorphosis. It was passed on to the Consejo de Castilla in late February, accompanied by a "decree of 24 February," which is oddly missing from the record, that made it a Madrid ordinance—the substance of the edict of 10 March. The new municipal ordinance far exceeded the general order of 11 January. Claiming merely to "renew prior dispositions," it omitted to specify that it applied only to state employees. Instead, it incorporated the language of a 1745 edict issued under Ensenada (and apparently reconfirmed in 1760) that prohibited "anyone no matter status, quality, privileges, or distinction" from wearing a slouch hat or ankle-length cloak in specified public places and contexts, such as theaters, promenades, and processions in Madrid and environs.[8] While the edict of 10 March covered all Madrid residents, it did distinguish in explicitly class-conscious fashion between the public affected ("every civilian of any class") from those excluded, "common laborers and the rest of the people prohibited from [wearing] military uniforms, although they may wear either a three-cornered hat or a cloth cap [of the kind] worn by the poorest people and beggars."[9]

Called upon to opine about the scope of the edict already posted, Fiscal Campomanes made a peculiarly ambivalent and disturbing response. First, he noted that legislative acts required careful review by the Consejo de Castilla *before* promulgation to avoid confusion and violence in enforcement, and consequently revision in the course of execution. In his *dictamen* of mid March, Campomanes cautioned that there was risk of mass reaction if enforcement proceeded without sensitivity to what was both possible and necessary. Most important—the second point—he found that the March edict was very imprecise and might ignite social violence: "It is extremely hard to define civilians of any class or distinction, since everyone claims this title, and it is the virtue of the republic that everyone claims distinction." But to sort out "those in this first class, can disturb the whole kingdom, as shown in the court during the initial application of this regulation, when people were seized indiscriminately." Campomanes considered prohibition of long cloaks unnecessary and dangerous, even prejudicial to the national interest by justifying expenditures on new dress styles and fabrics and thereby reinforcing dependence on textile imports. In any event, large-scale dress modification would require time and method.[10] He recommended that enforcement of the edict be delayed to educate the public on the issue; in which case, enforcement could follow with only moderate penalties. However, disregarding this and other caveats, eight *alcaldes de casa y corte* signed the edict, which was posted with unaccustomed fanfare on 10 March. *Alguaciles* of the *sala* enforced it loosely at first, then with rigor—even shearing infractors' cloaks publicly.[11] But once resistance organized by privileged cadres materialized and the military were brought in to control what was now an explosive situation, the show was on. Thereafter the *sala* assumed the role of victim, mere spectator of events that followed.[12]

Some aspects raise doubts about the intentions of the *sala*, which, since Ensenada's edict of 1745, had had exclusive jurisdiction over public dress in the capital.[13] First, there is the studied ambiguity of the edict of 10 March; then its promulgation without the customary prior review by the key *consejo* bureaucrats, the *fiscales*; then posting it in the face of Campomanes's warning and the *consejo*'s own experience with pitfalls in regulating public dress; and, last, the exaggerated ritual in announcing it. Presumably, the elaborate bureaucratic procedures for preparation, printing, and proclamation of such measures—obviously the consequence of bitter experience— might have precluded conspiratorial abuse of the legislative power by a small group within both the *consejo* and its *sala*.[14] It is a fact, however, that failure to follow procedures was the rule rather than exception in Bourbon Spain (a habit inherited from Hapsburg times), and the edict of 10 March was indeed issued disregarding bureaucratic formalities. It is relevant, moreover, to note that one year after the *motín,* the *consejo* made a point of reiterating that "no law, rule or new measure can be either trusted or enforced unless duly notified or published as pragmatic, cédula, provision, order, edict, announcement, or proclamation by law or high magistrates."[15]

All this raises the question: what exactly was the Sala de Alcaldes de Casa y Corte, apparently a major precipitant of the political crisis of 1766, and who ran it?

The Sala de Alcaldes de Casa y Corte

Integral to, yet a separate section of, the Consejo de Castilla, the Sala de Alcaldes de Casa y Corte exercised extraordinary power in the capital of the Spanish empire.[16] It had multiple functions: as court of high justice in criminal cases, its judgments were beyond appeal; only in civil cases could its decisions be appealed to the *consejo* itself. In its police function, the *sala* was responsible for public security in Madrid and at the court; its bailiffs and the agents of the *corregidor* of Madrid watched over public order and joined the royal *mayordomo* in guarding the royal household. It also had more mundane jurisdictions: it enforced guild ordinances against unlicensed tradesmen and monitored the capital's food supply, posting and enforcing prices of basic commodities. Particularly important was its intelligence-gathering responsibility. By comprehensive overhaul of the *sala* in late 1759, Esquilache—in one of his first initiatives—established a rigid procedure requiring that daily reports from *alcaldes* of the capital's wards on all matters of their responsibility be transmitted to the *sala*'s governor, then to the governor of the *consejo,* and finally to the king, except when the king was absent.

In 1759, the *sala* consisted of twelve *alcaldes,* headed by a governor (necessarily a member of the Consejo de Castilla) appointed by the governor of the *consejo.* The two governors worked in tandem, and evidently the responsibility of the *sala*'s governor was considerable. "The trust that the king places in the governors of the *sala* is great and very special," noted the chief clerk (*escribano de cámara*) of the *consejo* in 1764, "since on their activity, vigilance and care depend the security of the realm."[17]

The position of *alcalde de casa y corte* was prestigious: *alcaldes* were usually recruited from provincial tribunals and could advance to influential posts in the *consejos*—Castilla, Indias, Hacienda, and Guerra; for those somewhat less qualified (of "lesser vocation"), there were the *consejos* of the Inquisition and Military Orders. The *sala* was also a proving ground for career bureaucrats, many of whom had spent years at the *colegios mayores* of Salamanca or Valladolid awaiting an appointment and owed their advancement to *colegial* networks. Three of its personnel were key figures in the unfolding of the *motín:* the governor of the *sala,* Francisco de la Mata Linares y Calderón; its *fiscal,* Francisco José de Velasco; and an *alcalde semanero,* Roque de Galdames.

Born at Valladolid, where his father was dean of the *chancillería,* Francisco de la Mata Linares y Calderón came from an extended *montañés* family holding *señoríos* and prominent local offices around the Cantabrian port of San Vicente de la Barquera; the family was connected to the civil and military bureaucracy.[18] Already a member of the Order of Santiago, he graduated from Salamanca's Colegio Viejo de San Bartolomé in 1725. Over the next twelve years, he resided in the *colegio*'s hostel (*hospedaría*). He was elected rector in 1729 and awarded a chair in 1737, but he served in neither of these posts. Instead, upon his father's death in 1729, he returned to Valladolid, where he was appointed to the Audiencia of Sevilla and then, immediately afterward, to Valladolid's *chancillería.* There, he married into the extended family of the *chancillería*'s dean, José Vázquez Dávila y Arce, another well-connected *montañés* social network like his own. A decade later, Mata Linares moved up to Madrid's *sala* and then to the Consejo de Castilla, first as a *fiscal* (1754), then as full member (1758), and finally as governor of *the sala,* where he remained until 1767.[19]

As *alcalde* (1749–54) and *fiscal* (1754–58), Mata Linares had had experience in handling two major urban issues: a subsistence crisis (1753–54) and the issue of ankle-length cloaks as disguise. In 1757, the *consejo*'s governor, Bishop Diego Rojas y Contreras, reported Fernando VI's irritation over the long cloaks worn by lower-class *madrileños* in the capital's fashionable Paseo del Prado. Forthwith, the *sala* dictated new rules restricting the wearing of such cloaks by people of low status ("porters, pedestrians") to a small section of the Paseo. In 1766, as the *sala*'s governor, Mata Linares was responsible for rigorous enforcement of the dress code redrafted under Rojas y Contreras.[20]

Concurrent with governorship of the *sala*, Mata Linares accumulated other influential posts. As *juez conservador* of the Número de Receptores (100 members formed a pool of investigators for virtually all Madrid's *consejos,* tribunals, and major bureaus), he sat at the center of an extraordinarily sensitive net of intelligence gathering and influence.[21] He was also tax judge (*juez privativo de arbítrios*) and a *regidor* (by inheritance) of the Madrid and Valladolid town councils.[22]

Mata Linares's political leverage was matched by social webs of career and marriage. Through his wife's family (Vázquez Dávila y Arce) and the marriages of his brother and sister, he was further related to the *colegios mayores* of Salamanca and to the bureaucratic elites of metropole and colonies.[23] His sons were either *colegiales* or military officers; his eldest daughter married a Cagigal de la Vega y Montserrat, son of the former captain-general of Cuba and former viceroy of New Spain.[24] Was it pure coincidence that Francisco de la Mata Linares later played a central role in the opposition of Salamanca's *colegios mayores* to reform in the 1770s?[25]

Filling the next most important rank in the *sala* in March 1766 was its *fiscal,* Fernando José de Velasco y Fernández de Isla, *colegial,* former rector of the Colegio Mayor del Arzobispo of Salamanca, and a member of another *montañés* family network in the Spanish civil, religious, and military bureaucracies. His first cousin Luis Vicente de Velasco y Isla was a hero of the resistance in 1762 to the English occupation of Havana, where he died in action. Velasco joined with Mata Linares and another *colegial,* José de Rojas y Contreras, to publish a compilation of the merits, services, and careers of graduates of the Viejo Colegio de San Bartolomé and of the other five *colegios mayores* of the universities of Salamanca and Valladolid.[26] José de Rojas y Contreras left the Sala de Alcaldes for the Consejo de Indias in 1752; he was the brother of the current governor of the Consejo de Castilla (appointed in 1751), Bishop Diego de Rojas y Contreras of Cartagena. It is hardly surprising that in 1766, there was a solid core of identifiable *colegiales* among the *alcaldes de casa y corte,* nine out of fifteen.

There remain two staff members of the *sala* whose responsibility for processing legislation needs highlighting. One was the *alcalde semanero* for the week of 10 March, who selected the *alguaciles, escribanos, porteros,* and other personnel executing the *sala*'s orders that week and authenticated its *provisiones, títulos, autos,* and other regulations. His signature sufficed for the *sala*'s members to sign "without the least reservation."[27] One source identifies the *semanero* as Francisco Martínez, although possibly another *alcalde* may have served as *semanero,* in accordance with the rule that "the most recent appointees to the *salas* are made *semaneros*."[28] Finally, one other official, Roque de Galdames, a person of "special trust in serious matters," who had for some years been *oficial mayor* of the *sala*'s subordinate Escribanía de Cámara, merits attention, since as a staff member of the *sala,* he might have been decisive in drafting the edict of 10 March.[29]

The Sala de Alcaldes de Casa y Corte was, therefore, a small, tightly knit group, whose mutual association often began in the hostels of *colegios mayores* at Salamanca and Valladolid, whose personal links extended to provinces in the metropole and colonies, and who now held posts at the heart of the Spanish state. Meeting daily, their responsibilities put them frequently in contact with the Consejo de Castilla and other councils, the court nobility (in particular officers attached to the royal household), with many secular and ecclesiastical corporations of Madrid, formal and informal, and with the people of the capital. Of the *alcaldes de casa y corte,* the French hispanist Desdevises du Dézert once concluded, "No one knew Madrid better."[30]

The precise role of the Consejo de Castilla and the *sala* in processing the edict of 10 March is difficult to reconstruct. Presumably, guidelines governing internal procedures monitored the flow of legislation from draft to publication, with checkpoints en route to prevent inadvertent or (more likely) advertent insertion of unapproved material. As a matter of procedure, the governor of the *sala* would have requested a final draft, which, subject solely to the *sala*'s approval, would then be printed and posted, but where there was any doubt, the issue could be submitted by the governor of either the Consejo de Castilla or the *sala* to the *consejo's fiscales,* then to the *consejo* itself.[31] In fact, an ordinance substantially like the edict of 10 March was apparently posted weeks *before* review by the *fiscales.* What is clear is that ultimate responsibility lay with the *sala,* the *consejo,* and both governors. Any textual discrepancy between the authorized and printed versions of the edict would presumably be caught by the *alcalde semanero,* in this case, Roque Galdames, who was responsible for verifying the textual fidelity of all *consejo* legislation.

In view of the frequent consultation of both governors and the fact that the governor of the *consejo* chose the *sala*'s governor, it is no surprise that in 1766, the *consejo*'s governor was a *colegial* who had held the office for fifteen years. Diego Rojas y Contreras came from an influential extended Andalusian family holding lands, titles, and municipal office at Jaen, Antequera, Granada, and Sevilla, *señoríos* in north Spain, and an ancestral residence in Guipúzcoa. The family, like that of Mata Linares, had a long-standing stake in access by privilege to the bureaucratic hierarchy. Son of a *colegial* of San Bartolomé on the Consejo de Indias, Diego de Rojas y Contreras, after years of waiting at the Colegio Mayor de Cuenca, served at Valladolid and later as bishop of Calahorra before appointment as bishop of Cartagena and finally as governor of the Consejo de Castilla in 1751.[32] One of his four brothers, José, marqués de Albentos, had been at San Bartolomé along with Francisco de la Mata Linares y Calderón and, like him, had moved to the *chancillería* of Valladolid and then the Sala de Alcaldes de Casa y Corte before moving on to the Consejo y Cámara de Indias (1752). He had been an *oidor* at Sevilla and a *regidor* of its town council. Another brother, Bernardo, was on the Consejo de Hacienda and the Junta General de Comercio, Moneda y Minas; a third had retired from the royal navy; and the eldest, Pedro de Rojas y Contreras, marqués de Villanueva de Duero, managed the family's interests from its seat in Andalusia. A sister had married into the Moctezumas of Ronda, and two of her sons became *colegiales* at Cuenca, while a third served in the Spanish Guards at Madrid.[33] Through the marriage of another sister to a Jaen estate owner, also a *colegial* of the University of Cuenca and *consejero* of Castilla, Diego de Rojas y Contreras was tied into the landholding aristocracy and the bureaucratic elites of court and country.[34] By birthright, he was a member of Spain's integrated elites.

Which brings us to the pivotal role of Bishop Diego de Rojas y Contreras, governor of the Consejo de Castilla, in the *motín* against Esquilache. His case is intriguing, since he was the visible, key link in the bureaucratic chain between Charles III, the Consejo de Castilla, and its *sala*; the Madrid public viewed him as an unquestioned authority, second only to Charles himself. Assessments of his role are contradictory. While some have traced his behavior to weakness or incapacity and a preoccupation with keeping his position—especially after Campomanes (a *manteísta,* not a *colegial*) replaced the *colegial* Diego de Sierra y Cienfuegos as *fiscal* of the *consejo* de Castilla—others have implied that, rather than mediator, he was in fact an abettor of the March sedition.[35]

No doubt Bishop Rojas y Contreras bore a heavy responsibility for Madrid's security, and it is plausible that timing and editing, review and implementation of the dress code could not have proceeded to a blowup without his complicity or negligence. But records of his usual concern with edicts on dress make negligence unlikely. Twice before, in 1757 and 1760, he had alerted the governor of the *sala* about failure to enforce the prohibition of long cloaks that disguised the wearer.[36] Furthermore, he was aware of the explosive situation ten days before the outbreak of concerted mass action on 13 March, when Prime Minister Grimaldi—appalled by the open declaration of war on Esquilache by the cabal behind the "corps to defend monarch and fatherland"—urged Rojas to take action. "Let's do all in our power in this grave matter, so that we can never be cited for failing to punish such extreme violence," Grimaldi said after the start of the *motín*, which he clearly perceived to be no ordinary subsistence riot.[37] Rojas apparently shared Grimaldi's grasp of the gravity of the situation, since he is reported to have retorted to someone advocating forceful measures against the rioters: "You don't know the half of this; there's more than meets the eye here—the rabble is the least concern."[38] Most incriminating was the subsequent charge by Rojas's subordinate Mata Linares (probably shifting the blame), that "Rojas's henchmen . . . initiated the event," referring to the first confrontation between the *sala*'s *alguaciles* enforcing the edict of 10 March and a servant of the duque de Medinaceli's son.[39]

Rojas's complicity acquires increased credibility in a manuscript account of the "Tumult at Madrid and other places of the Realm," which reports that at the hastily called conference of Charles and the Consejo de Castilla on 24 March, the *consejeros* urged him to accept the crowd's major demands—Esquilache's removal and a mass pardon—warning that other action was useless.[40] The "Tumulto" also records the participation of the *consejo*'s governor in the final phases of the *motín:* Rojas's signature to the indictment of Esquilache and his entire program (25 March), and use of a convict to carry the indictment to the Aranjuez palace, where a coerced Charles had to capitulate to the crowd's demands in the presence of the whole Consejo de Castilla.

A visible abettor of Esquilache's dismissal and exile, Bishop Diego de Rojas y Contreras acted in multiple capacities: as a churchman representing his fellow bishops, from among whom governors of the Consejo de Castilla were chosen by tradition; as a *colegial* typifying the bureaucratic leverage of the university networks; as a lobbyist for Andalusia's landowning aristocracy; and, not least, as Spain's foremost public functionary defending the nation's most important conciliar body against encroachments by reformers within the administration.

The problem in establishing individual and collective responsibility in the behavior of *consejo* and *sala* has two facets. First, Rojas y Contreras embodied the three pillars of the old regime, aristocracy, clergy, and bureaucracy; frontal assault on these elites might shatter the already fragile authority of the *monarquía*. The second aspect stems from the opaque character of decision-making and implementation in the *motín*. The most visible actors were the crowd, whose members and manipulators were never clearly identifiable; the aristocrats of the royal household, whose privileges and functions provided immunity against criminal prosecution; the clerics, whose ostensible pacifying role was above reproach (if not suspicion); and last, the

Consejo de Castilla and its Sala de Alcaldes, which cloaked their omissions and commissions in bureaucratic ritual and multiple signatures. Aside from the number of indictables—how could so many be indicted, New Spain's former Viceroy Revillagigedo asked in advising Charles on 25 March—there was the high status of some.[41] It would be impolitic to incriminate, much less punish, Governor-Bishop Rojas y Contreras of the Consejo de Castilla for the collective recommendations of Charles's *consejeros*. This was underscored by Rojas's brother in his history of Spain's *colegios mayores,* where he took pains to point out that it was unfair to punish the head of a high tribunal for the collective decision of its members.[42]

Key to understanding the importance of the cabal of *colegiales* at the center of the movement against Esquilache are the findings of an investigation into the distribution of the bishop of Cuenca's virtual *manifiesto de agravios* justifying the anti-Esquilache elite's role. The two *fiscales* of the *consejo*, Campomanes and Moñino, were assigned to the investigation. Their preliminary work turned up seven very visible names, all former *colegiales* of San Bartolomé: José de Rojas y Contreras, a member of the Consejo de Indias; his brother, the bishop of Cartagena, then the governor of the Consejo de Castilla—both good friends of the bishop of Cuenca from their *colegial* days; two members of the Consejo de la Inquisición, Inquisidor General Quintino Bonifaz and the *consejero* Felipe Muñoz; Fernando José de Velasco (*fiscal* of the *sala*), Nicolas de Carvajal y Lancaster, the bishop of Cuenca's brother; and the duque de Frías. Such a list alone indicated that further probing might uncover others in high places among Bourbon Spain's political elite. If preliminary probing came up with these names, it stood to reason that further investigation would uncover others in high places among Spain's political class. Whatever the reason—perhaps a decision by their superiors, the *fiscales'* disorientation, or their fear of the opposition—the highly respected investigators discontinued this line of inquiry. Discouragement, however, was short-lived; it ended when a politically convenient solution in the search for presumed actors was arranged that left unindicted the pillars of the *monarquía* and restored the façade of the "absolutist" state.

Exonerating the Elite

Given the mix of explicit and circumstantial evidence linking members of the bureaucracy, aristocracy, church, guilds, *cofradías,* and *congregaciones* to the Madrid riots, the decision to charge the Jesuits alone raises questions.[43] It was based upon a covert inquiry headed by Campomanes, who submitted his findings (*dictamen*) to the Consejo de Castilla nine months later. As a result, the Jesuit Order was expelled from Spain and its colonies on grounds of conspiracy and rebellion, and its properties were confiscated. Campomanes's final report reveals much about the complex of factors—religious, economic, social, and political—involved in the crisis of March 1766.

The decision to incriminate the Jesuits cannot be divorced from the pardoning of other groups and actors granted even before the uprising had subsided. On 26 March, when Charles's capitulation to the mob was accepted by Madrid's masses in the presence of the Consejo de Castilla, members of Madrid's elite were already scrambling to exonerate themselves, the French ambassador, d'Ossun, reported to Choiseul: "Madrid's courts are reasserting authority . . . the mutineers have partly disarmed," he noted, and the Cinco Gremios Mayores were allowed to meet. This was a good idea, "first because it provided members of different bodies who had dabbled in sedition with a decent way to leave and . . . cover up their mistake. Second, every time [any of] the more sensible inhabitants of Madrid portray themselves to the king as guiltless and ask him therefore to grant mercy to the common folk, the prince will be in position to pardon [them], or at least confine punishment to a small number of individuals, without compromising his dignity and power . . . which is precisely what His Catholic Majesty would most prefer."[44] It is noteworthy that d'Ossun used the term *sédition,* far stronger than *motín,* and that he thought punishment should be limited to a small group. Well before the conde de Aranda ordered an investigation of the *motín,* Miguel de Múzquiz (Esquilache's replacement at the Hacienda ministry) proposed to the *corregidor* of Madrid (Ensenada's former collaborator Pérez Delgado) that the elite at the court seek formal reconciliation with Charles. Representatives of the grandees, nobility, church, and of Madrid's corporations would present declarations of loyalty and protest that they had had nothing to do with the *motín.* But those concerned immediately refused on grounds of infringement of both protocol and their honor.[45]

Even crisis managers who hoped that Campomanes's covert investigation would proceed in order to incriminate suspects among the elites opposed Múzquiz's proposal. Their position surfaces in two versions of the guidelines prepared for Campomanes's commission of inquiry. One version, unambiguously critical of the elite, details evidence of conspiracy suggesting the complicity of the most prominent organizations and concludes: "This persuades us that there were principal instigators and auxiliary leaders of this tumult, and [for them] to hope to exonerate [themselves] with protestations of their honor and fidelity to the king and perhaps to justify their pretensions (as they have not failed to try to do) is the greatest imaginable crime. All this obliges the king to ascertain and clarify the original causes and authors of so detestable a crime."[46]

The other version (Aranda's) ends in a significantly different fashion, diverting blame from elite bodies: "This persuades us there were actors, principals, leaders, and assistants in their tumult, although not necessarily members of the aforementioned bodies."[47] If nobility, clergy, and official corporations were to be exonerated along with the masses, a group or faction was needed for public punishment and to shore up the state's authority. Choiseul concluded in a note to d'Ossun at Madrid: "Until these three issues [the identity of the authors of the disturbances, the return of the king, and the carrying out of the capitulation] are clarified, Spain will suffer from an administrative malaise that undermines the internal authority of the monarchy and Spain's role in Europe."[48]

At what point did Madrid's bureaucratic hierarchy decide to exonerate the most visible of the *motín*'s agents and, instead, turn on a group with low visibility, the Society of Jesus? One conjecture focuses on Aranda. In the week after the *motín,* with the Consejo de Castilla busy elaborating a response to it in cooperation with loyal grandees like the conde de Fuentes and the duque de Alba, policy was still unclear. On 1 April, Aranda arrived in Madrid to find the government already in full control and the security of the capital entrusted to Alejandro O'Reilly, under the orders of the duque de Arcos.[49] Madrid's *corregidor,* Alonso Pérez Delgado, immediately assured him that the leaders of the outbreak promised no further violence.[50] Confronting the stonewalling of the Madrid authorities, Aranda could only conclude what had long been evident: Esquilache's ouster had been a carefully staged operation by a group including the Consejo de Castilla and other influential members of the elite at Madrid.

His decision followed quickly. A realist, Aranda chose to defuse the crisis by postponing the ritual exoneration of the aristocracy and corporate bodies of the capital while, as he intimated to Múzquiz early in May, conferring with high bureaucrats at Madrid and policy-makers at Aranjuez to pin blame for the *motín* on the Jesuits.[51]

The Jesuits had, of course, anticipated this possibility.[52] They were aware of the anti-Jesuit animus of Campomanes (now an influential *fiscal* of the Consejo de Castilla), of his former patron, the duque de Alba (on the Consejo de Estado), and of the minister of Gracia y Justicia, Manuel de Roda, formerly an Alba attorney and, like him and Campomanes, anti-Jesuit. Meanwhile, at Naples, Tanucci, another Jesuitophobe, who had predicted a movement against Esquilache, advised Madrid to strike at the Jesuits through their economic power in Spain and the colonies and avoid retaliating against the elite and clergy involved in the *motín*.[53]

So secretive was Campomanes's investigation that Choiseul, still anxious about the stability of the government in Spain, wrote d'Ossun on 20 May that he had as yet heard nothing about "the authors of the unrest," which he took as indicating that Madrid had yet to uncover the real or supposed organizers of the *motín*. Perhaps to answer widespread concern, Campomanes had to issue a statement (4 June) affirming that "this case is the most important ever assigned Your Majesty's ministers," and that the stability of the government required the "thorough investigation" of those responsible. Material then available showed that "the body politic was healthy." But signs of continued unrest and the need to avoid public controversy, he found, forced his investigation's transfer to a special committee (*consejo extraordinario*) of members of the Consejo de Castilla.

On 8 June, Aranda selected a committee of three to meet in his town house, Luís del Valle Salazar (who had replaced Mata Linares as governor of the Sala de Alcaldes), Pedro Ric, and Miguel María de la Nava.[54] The next day Ambassador d'Ossun, monitoring state business carefully, assured Choiseul that at the insistence of the nobility, municipal authorities, and Cinco Gremios Mayores, the Consejo de Castilla had repudiated Charles's formal capitulation to the crowd and ritually reassured the king of their loyalty.[55] Three months later, at the end of August, d'Ossun informed Choiseul, secret evidence had produced "startling proofs against the Society in question," and in September, Campomanes's special committee had a notion of the "instigation that [the] awesome movement fomented, organized, and stimulated in the guise of religion." It virtually named "a Religious Body in every branch of this vast complicated affair" that was still active and dangerous, but insisted that the rest of the clergy was "sano." At this advanced stage of the investigative commission's work, Campomanes recommended that an expanded *consejo extraordinario* review the findings, draw up an indictment, and sentence the criminals. To this *consejo*, sworn to secrecy, Campomanes turned over the result of his investigation, his *dictamen fiscal* of 31 December 1766.

Campomanes's *Dictamen* and the Society of Jesus

Campomanes's *dictamen fiscal* (finally published two centuries later) was based upon a voluminous body of materials, some divulged in 1768 to provide legal backing for the Jesuits' expulsion. It consists of 746 paragraphs, divided into chapters, offering a general critique of the order as an institution rather than its complicity in the *motín*—for here Campomanes's evidence is tenuous. While the document bears Campomanes's hallmarks, its lack of cogency—perhaps the effect of pressure to draft it hastily—and convincing reasons for the expulsion (Charles needed no elaboration of the reasons) may account for the decision to withhold the whole document from the public.[56] The importance of Campomanes's *dictamen* lies in the light it sheds on the 1766 insurrection, and on his own role at this critical juncture in eighteenth-century Spain, rather than in its broad indictment of Jesuit doctrine and the order's politicization and self-enrichment.

Probing for the ends and means of the *motín,* at the outset, Campomanes identified Charles III as the target and by extension his confessor and cabinet ministers—indeed the nation, state, and monarchy (paras. 18–22). To substantiate this conclusion, Campomanes divided the event into two distinct episodes, the preliminary phase of 23–24 March, and a second phase in which Madrid's mobs, no longer impelled by an ostensible cause (initial demands had been met and public order reestablished), virtually took over the city and arsenal and attacked Charles himself, demanding his return to the capital (paras. 5–14, 48–50, 59). Campomanes was alluding to the preliminary phase when he wrote in the *dictamen* that "everyone was resigned to it, believing the coup unavoidable, no matter human intervention, even calling it necessary and worthy." Obviously, he meant the phase of escalation when he emphasized that "no one recognized nor feared its evil" (para. 89). Those behind the criminal goals of the second phase directed at Charles were now also made responsible for the initial phase. Observing the use of palm fronds taken from Madrid balconies on 25 March to symbolize continued mobilization and religious legitimacy, Campomanes argued that there had to be a covert religious body involved, since nonreligious parties would not have dared do such a thing. He felt compelled to conclude that "the sole weapon to stir people was unwarranted resort to religion."

Only a tightly organized, influential, and well-connected group could have planned the insurrection's first stage and have accounted for the mob's furor in its second (paras. 46–48). This group he early identified as the Society of Jesus (and specifically its Colegio Imperial de San Isidro), whose wealth, power, and connections alone were able to orchestrate such a conspiracy, and whose "unbridled ambition" and "immoral" doctrines provided the motivation (para. 197). No evidence incriminating other groups existed, Campomanes asserted: moreover, had not the court nobility and guilds, supported by the "respectable" residents of the capital, explicitly condemned the role of the Madrid populace (paras. 7, 111)? The Jesuits' efforts to incriminate grandees and guilds, clergy, and especially *colegiales* were further proof of Jesuit complicity. Who could really believe, Campomanes asked rhetorically, that "these distinguished communities, which have given the country such enlightened men, would hearken to ideas so inappropriate to their loyalty . . . ?" (paras. 138, 241, 742). In view of these observations, Campomanes perhaps recognized the circumstantial fragility of his brief against the Jesuits in his final appeal to the bishops who would be responsible for sentencing. "How many classes would have seen their loyalty questioned if the sources of previous disturbances were not uncovered?" (para. 623).

The inconsistencies and circularity of reasoning in Campomanes's indictment are explicable by the need to invoke vague "vast connections" manipulated by the Jesuits to achieve their "criminal" ends (para. 592). The *dictamen* is noteworthy for repeated references to "contact and correspondence" and "intimacy" of people of all stations with the Jesuits, who enlisted as accomplices individuals who in this way could pursue their legitimate interests or those of the church as a whole (para. 734). In this sense, referring to the bishop of Cuenca's letter handed to Charles's confessor, Campomanes accused the Jesuits of exploiting the naïveté (*simplicidad*) of a "certain" bishop to persuade him that persecution of the Jesuits was really persecution of the church in general; the bishop had insinuated that an attack upon the immunities of the Jesuits was an assault upon those of the church itself (paras. 80–83, 189–90, 615, 737). On the contrary, argued the *fiscal,* the Jesuits were really the worst enemies of bishops ("true" ministers of the church), as well as of other orders, as was shown by the litigation sustained by the order against them both in America and in the metropole (paras. 616, 672). Campomanes's case clearly involved two contentions: first, the evident participation of powerful interest groups in the *motín;* second, the assertion that in doing so, these groups had merely been the instruments of the Jesuits. The former could then be exonerated, the latter condemned.

That Campomanes intended to weave together Jesuits and interest groups is suggested by a contemporaneous document tracing the connections of prominent Madrid bureaucrats, churchmen, and aristocrats to the Jesuits. Notable on this list are four individuals who figured prominently in the events of March 1766: Francisco de la Mata Linares (a member of a Jesuit tertiary order), Bishops Diego de Rojas y Contreras and Isidro de Carvajal y Lancaster, and the duque de Medinaceli. Probably, Campomanes meant these among others when intimating that there were Jesuit accomplices in high places. However, since he could not implicate them explicitly in his *dictamen* (with the exception of the bishop of Cuenca) on circumstantial evidence, he had to fall back on saying: "In carefully planned affairs, we must rely upon presumption and conjecture, otherwise a conspiracy may never be uncovered when the instigators of a certain status cannot publicly lead the unfortunate masses in such disorders" (para. 217). The critical question remains: Why were his "presumptions and conjectures" directed against a cabal in the Jesuit Colegio Imperial de San Isidro rather than a cabal of *colegiales* in the Consejo de Castilla and its Sala de Alcaldes? One might add: Why did a meticulous legalist of Campmanes's stature base his case on flimsy evidence and vague, unsubstantiated "presumptions and conjectures?"

Campomanes's circumstantial and contradictory *dictamen* should not, however, be dismissed out of hand. Despite failure to turn up convincing evidence of linkage between the "visible heads" (*cabezas visibles*) of the movement and the Jesuits, and despite his extravagant declaration that Jesuits had been behind every popular riot in recent Spanish history, but that no "bishop, gentleman, magistrate, cleric, or lady who breathes obedience, respect, and submission to throne and government" had ever been involved in such movements, the fact remains that many of the figures involved in the *motín* against Esquilache *were* reputedly connected to the Jesuits (paras. 138, 241). And as we have seen, these very individuals were also members of other interest groups more directly and immediately threatened by Esquilache's policies than were the Jesuits. On another level, Campomanes's separation of the Jesuits from others probably involved in the *motín* highlights the unintended consequences of state-sponsored reform. Notwithstanding that the groups comprising the constellation of interests attacked by Esquilache's reforms were guilty of participating in the *motín,* the Spanish Bourbon state could not afford to alienate them. An acceptable scapegoat was needed to restore power and legitimacy to the *monarquía,* and the Jesuits were an obvious choice.

Lacking concrete evidence of Jesuit responsibility for the *motín,* Campomanes fell back upon the general and popular critique of the Society of Jesus, and particularly of its status and function in the Spanish empire. He recapitulated themes of contemporary anti-Jesuit literature: Jesuits had warped the minds of royal and other elites, influenced decision-makers through Jesuit-controlled religious and educational institutions and the confessional, and undercut the autonomy of the state by creating their own state within the state. This led him to revive his long-held critique of the origins of Jesuit wealth in the American colonies and Jesuit transfers of money to Europe.

At the core of the *fiscal's* argument were the extent and illegality of Jesuit income generated in the colonies, as well as its application to criminal and even sacrilegious ends in pursuit of a program of "world domination" (paras. 225–64, 279, 292, 309–20). In the American colonies, Jesuits had perverted their proselytizing mission by enslaving Indian peoples on the empire's frontiers in order to establish profitable independent entities (paras. 309–54). The order's unwarranted tax exemptions, smuggling, and profit transfers, Campomanes continued, threatened the state (para. 353). To protect its privileged enclaves, it blocked the entry of competitive traders, regular and secular clergy, and state functionaries into its missionary zones and questioned the jurisdiction of bishops and officials collecting taxes (paras. 236, 309–59).

Campomanes contrasted Jesuit infiltration of America with colonization strategies in the Leyes de Indias, which provided that frontier areas, once proselytized, be transferred to the secular clergy and the civil authority of bishops and *alcaldes mayores,* permitting the presence of petty tradesmen. In this fashion, indigenous peoples could be drawn into Spanish colonial society via a variety of mechanisms: the courts, tribute and tax collection, propagation of Catholicism, and, of course, commercial exchanges. This, he underscored, put no drain on state finances, unlike the Jesuit Order, which was subsidized by crown contributions. Jesuit criticism of extortion by *alcaldes mayores* in the Philippines, Campomanes dismissed as libel, further proof of the order's readiness to undermine the state through its representatives abroad (paras. 369–71). In any event, if Jesuits complained about the missionary tactics of other orders, then punishing the Jesuits would be an edifying example.

Through questionably obtained financial gains, in Campomanes's analysis, the Society of Jesus had spread its influence at key points in Spain and its colonies. He offered the example of the Jesuit confessor of Fernando VI, Francisco de Rábago, who had "intervened even in matters of the Indies and Navy, as seen in the notorious case of Juan de Isla about naval construction and the lawsuit over the Jesuits' tithing" (paras. 146–47). Then he cited the Jesuit campaign of 1765 at the University of Salamanca denouncing the doctrines of Augustine and Thomas Aquinas, promotion of "fashionable" cults such as Nuestra Señora de la Luz (in the *montañas* of Burgos), and the creation of congregations of the Sagrado Corazón de Jesús in churches and schools without the approval of the state as stipulated by law (179, 181–82, 417, 593). More insidious, by operating through these congregations, the order shaped the thinking of influential individuals, especially women (paras. 181–82).

Campomanes's critique came down heavily on the Jesuits' colonial operations. They had, he claimed, competed unfairly in agriculture, industry, and commerce, not to mention political rivalry with the state in the governance of subjects of the crown. In advancing these charges, Campomanes extended the campaign against the order that had gained momentum after the ouster in the 1750s of Ensenada, his collaborators, and Fernando VI's confessor, Francisco de Rábago. With the expulsion of the Jesuits from Portugal (1759) and then France (1764), as well as the accession of Charles III, whose anti-Jesuit sentiments were manifest in royal authorization to reprint the works of Bishop Juan de Palafox y Mendoza, who had criticized the Jesuits' mistreatment of native peoples in Mexico in the mid–seventeenth century, and in the king's choice of a Franciscan friar as his confessor, the Jesuit question assumed an importance not to be overlooked in examining the crisis of 1766.

A consensus among Spain's elite to expel the Jesuit order and confiscate its property was easily achieved. The benefits were attractive: quick restoration of the image of royal and imperial authority and confiscation and transfer of Jesuit wealth and income—religious buildings, educational institutions, rural and urban real estate holdings, and tithes and tribute income—to other privileged sectors of society, including bishops, secular and regular clergy, wealthy merchants, and mine and estate owners. As for the enlightened bureaucrats surrounding Charles III, however soft the evidence against Jesuit complicity in the *motín,* most were prepared to accept Campomanes's rationale that expulsion was justified for reasons of state and for advancing the Spanish Bourbon paradigm of progress.

Opportune, justifiable, and persuasive both within and outside Spain, the attack on the Jesuits absolved those whose complicity in the *motín* was prompted by opposition to Esquilache's reform program. Esquilache's fall was a victory for privileged sectors threatened by his reforms.[57] The *motín* signaled the limits of change; to go further might imperil social and political cohesion. Both in Spain and the colonies, reforms aimed at economic growth were legitimate, but structural changes were dangerous.

Expropriation of Jesuit holdings in the colonies was symptomatic of a long-standing, implicit proclivity to solve metropolitan crises by "going to America." But it was precisely the growing contradiction between metropolitan Spain's underdevelopment and colonial growth that was the underlying cause of crises at home. This disequilibrium, which constantly surfaced in the reform models of Spanish Bourbon *proyectistas,* was, it must be recalled, the central preoccupation of Esquilache, whose policies were aimed at reordering and expanding Spain's own economy as much as the economies of its colonies. Failure after 1766 to push structural reform in the Iberian Peninsula itself and concentration instead upon increasing income from America were the most notable consequences of the crisis of 1766. Esquilache's ouster was, in this sense, the major determining event of the eighteenth century in Spain and its empire, the Spanish historian Danvila y Collado concluded, and it brought about "a profound change in the policy of Charles III."[58]

The Colonial Background of the *Motín*

The Jesuits' privileges and economic role in the colonies were not the only colonial issues in the insurgency of 1766. There was a wide gamut of underlying dissatisfaction with the way Esquilache had approached colonial affairs, patent in the popular literature during the *motín*. Allusions to the "deterioration and imminent loss of America" surfaced in charges that colonial fortifications were undermanned and ill-supplied, that Spain's navy lacked ships, and that colonial peoples were rebelling. Worse, pamphlet literature proclaimed, the state had lacked both money and credit under Esquilache; colonial funds had been wasted on Havana's ransom and on unnecessary grain imports. Moreover, Esquilache had sent his son to supervise customs collection at Spain's busiest port, Cadiz, where customs evasion was a well-cultivated art by Spaniards and resident foreigners alike. Unfounded rumors circulated that Andalusia's export trade was declining, that communication between Spain and the colonies was expensive and difficult because Madrid had imposed high new rates for mail to the colonies and had shifted the postal center from Cadiz to the inconveniently located naval base at La Coruña. Clearly, these charges criticized what the Esquilache regime considered achievements: strengthening colonial fortifications, undertaking judicial reforms, curbing illegal silver transfers, putting mail service to the colonies on a scheduled and profitable basis, and expanding trade. In the legal discourse of the time, these were arguments that both deliberately concealed the truth (*subrepción*) and falsified the facts (*obrepción*).

From the outset, American issues loomed large in Esquilache's agenda. Between 1759, when Charles wrote d'Ossun that Spain might have lost its American colonies if his brother had lived two years longer, and 1765, when major decisions on Spain's transatlantic trading system were made, Madrid was preoccupied with its colonies. Concomitant with measures to strengthen colonial defenses came moves to reorganize metropolitan and colonial finance, reorder Hacienda archives, and review "almost forgotten accounts." Long-unresolved issues came up for review in weekly ministerial sessions, where two countercurrents became evident. Since Colonial Secretary Arriaga was known to resist innovations, Esquilache had to plan reform "in secret." Between 1760 and 1763, a series of financial measures sought to correct the most obvious abuses—in particular, of course, smuggling, undervaluation of goods, and the mishandling of accounts managed by the Consulado de Cadiz.

Colonial reforms were interrupted by the war but were given high priority after 1763. While the court-martial of the officers responsible for the Havana fiasco proceeded under the presidency of Aranda, and Esquilache's finance ministry investigated the management of colonial revenues at Cadiz, Esquilache presided over the rejuvenated Junta de Comercio in 1764, when it contemplated structural changes in the colonial trade system. To improve communication with the colonies, responsibility for mail service was transferred from the Cadiz *consulado* to the navy at La Coruña. Cadiz, the *junta* discovered, had misused its mail privileges to cover clandestine commercial operations and control distribution of commercial information. Above all, the *junta* emphasized the extent of the smuggling pandemic in the Spanish transatlantic system at Cadiz and overseas. It will be recalled that between July 1764 and February 1765, the Special Junta had reviewed the defects of that system in detail, leading to the Reglamento del Comercio Libre a las Islas de Barlovento. Opening the Caribbean to Spanish exporters/reexporters was more than a cosmetic "reform of abuses," usually ineffective; it signaled a shift toward structural reform.

Although limited, Barlovento had a lasting impact, not only on the port of Cadiz, whose monopoly it weakened somewhat, but on peripheral Spain and Cuba, whose development it promoted. By excluding New Spain, Andalusia's largest colonial market and the world's greatest producer of silver, Barlovento's authors showed caution as well as consideration for powerful interests at the two termini of the transatlantic system, Cadiz and Mexico City. Cadiz merchants, however, were not blind to so notable a departure from the norms catalogued in the Leyes de Indias. The entry of merchants and their goods from other Spanish ports into the Gulf of Mexico, and particularly into Havana, promised to open New Spain to competing merchandise, breaching the traditional transatlantic conduit for goods and silver between Cadiz and Veracruz. Barlovento, threatening enough to Cadiz commercial interests, could be seen as the onset of further innovations, evidenced by the dispatch of a *visitador-general* (inspector-general) to New Spain in the same year. Cadiz and Mexico City were not reassured by the successive choices of a *visitador,* first Francisco Carrasco (who refused), then Francisco Armona (who died en route to Veracruz), and finally a recent appointee to the Sala de Alcaldes de Casa y Corte, José de Gálvez, who debarked at Veracruz in July 1765 for what turned out to be an extended investigation of six years.

The anxiety of the Consulado de Cadiz was not unfounded. During the first six months of his mission to New Spain, Gálvez stepped up his investigation of trade malpractices at Veracruz. Symptomatic of the laxity uncovered was the case of the *Nuestra Señora de la Luz*, a vessel owned by Francisco Montes, a well-connected Cadiz merchant who had formerly been resident *diputado del comercio de España* at Jalapa and was later a *tesorero general* in Madrid. At Cadiz, Montes had requested permission to shift cargo space reserved by the Proyecto of 1720 for Sevilla's exporters (*cosecheros*) of agricultural products from the *Esperidon* to his own vessel (he had received the space allocation from the convoy commander). Delayed by the alleged tardiness of *cosecheros* in filling their allotted cargo space on the *flota,* Montes's *Nuestra Señora de la Luz* departed Cadiz well after the convoy had left; and on arrival at Veracruz, it had to moor at a distance from the convoy. Montes's ship thereupon caught fire, and of its cargo, only 3,500 barrels of brandy were recovered, but quickly dispatched from the port of Veracruz into the interior of the colony without customs inspection — all before Gálvez began his inquiry there. Such concatenations of events were hardly atypical of the *flota* system.[59]

Gálvez immediately modified the rules governing unloading of ships, requiring customs inspectors to open all cargo containers for examination and to insist upon payment of sales taxes (*alcabalas*) on all items that left the port for the interior, rather than (as had hitherto been the practice) following sale at the Jalapa fair. He ruffled Cadiz shippers further by failing to side with the "comercio de España" in negotiating the terms of exchange at Jalapa. Equally unacceptable to Andalusian wine and brandy *cosecheros* was Gálvez's recommendation that Madrid accept reality and legalize the sale of *chinguirito* distilled in the colony.

The new regulations for unloading cargo at Veracruz, prior payment of sales taxes there, and preservation of what the *comercio de México* considered the *flotistas'* privileged status at Jalapa ranked high on the list of Consulado de Cadiz complaints pending at Madrid in 1765 and 1766. Under the old regime, the commercial petit bourgeoisie in both Spain and the colonies could most effectively defend its interests indirectly, acting through "retainers, agents and allies rather than directly through its own members."[60] More than likely, however, Francisco Montes, who had returned to Spain from Jalapa in 1759, helped oversee *consulado* business at Madrid before becoming its *prior* and later agent in confronting another *consulado* concern: efforts by Esquilache's Hacienda to liquidate the public debt, whose interest was secured on duties levied on imports from the colonies.

Perhaps Montes's influence at Madrid was closely related to his lobbying skill in behalf of holders of outstanding claims on state funds, known as "old creditors" (*prestamistas antiguos*), who had formed a protective association in the capital in the early 1760s. These claims had been mismanaged by the Sevilla *diputación* of the Consulado de Cadiz, and Esquilache's directives to authenticate and liquidate them had inevitably opened a Pandora's box of unverifiable claims and favoritism in the distribution of interest payments. There were immediate protests from long-term beneficiaries who did not want to liquidate their principal, much less stop receiving interest payments. The association of rentier groups centered in Sevilla, with claimants dispersed throughout Andalusia and elsewhere in Spain, sent a large delegation to the capital to protest the decision of Esquilache's Finance Ministry to oblige claimants to go to Madrid's Tesorería General rather than withdraw from government funds jointly managed by a Sevillan clique and the treasurer of the Cadiz *consulado*. Although initially willing to accept liquidation of the old debts, *consulado* officials soon perceived they could ill afford to lose the power of patronage through disbursement of payments. It emerged, however, that it was impossible to liquidate the creditors' claims. After literally decades (in some cases) of inflation without complex monetary adjustments to reflect current value, the state could neither immediately suspend interest payments to religious and secular entail holders nor tap *consulado* funds (dependent upon colonial imports) for repayment. As a result, many of the old claims remained outstanding until well into the nineteenth century.[61]

Whatever the role of Montes and representatives of *prestamistas antiguos,* Cadiz worked all its channels of access to power, formal and informal, to defend its interests in the years just preceding 1766. Undoubtedly, it was frustration in lobbying ministers, *consejeros,* and crown that accounts for the urgent note in the *consulado*'s correspondence with its agent and patrons in the capital. The removal of an invaluable patron there, the conde de Valdeparaíso, when Esquilache took over the Hacienda, was only the beginning of the Cadiz *consulado*'s sense of losing leverage.

This is not to claim a consensus within Esquilache's administration, where there were respected and influential opponents. Colonial Secretary Julián de Arriaga, appointed after the coup unseating Ensenada in 1754, was an ever-reliable supporter of Cadiz's commercial interests, as revealed by his unsuccessful "obstinate resistance" to the passage of the Reglamento del Comercio Libre a las Islas de Barlovento of 1765. He remained "extraordinarily incensed" at both Grimaldi and Esquilache, whom he accused of undermining his ministry's management of colonial finance. The Cadiz *consulado* was relieved when Arriaga returned to his post after a temporary illness, and expected him to tolerate practices at Veracruz that Gálvez attacked, such as the collection of *alcabalas* only at Jalapa. Arriaga's inability to block Gálvez's recommendations is evident in a judiciously framed letter from the *consulado* to its Madrid agent in March 1766, saying, "Although it is not proper to investigate the secrecy of the ministry, we have reason to believe that a concealed obstacle prevents the justification of Arriaga." Open to speculation is the chance that Arriaga, bypassed in his official capacity by passage of the Reglamento of 1765, tightened his ties to relatives by marriage, to the Rojas y Contreras extended family, which was well positioned in Madrid and critical of Charles III's policies and personnel. Certainly, Arriaga, who retained his post for another decade, shared with the Cadiz *consulado* relief over Esquilache's ouster and the appointment to the Finance Ministry of Miguel Múzquiz y Goyeneche, related to the Navarrese Goyeneche banking family.

Furthermore, the Cadiz commercial establishment had other conservative allies in high places at Madrid. The president of the Consejo de Indias, Juan Pizarro de Aragón y Rubín de Célis (marqués de San Juan de Piedras Albas), a Navarrese stand-patter on commercial policy like Arriaga, was another of Charles's aging bureaucratic holdovers in the aftermath of the dismissal and then the death of the conde de Valdeparaíso. José Ignacio de Goyeneche, Múzquiz's cousin, who shared his extended family's multiple interests in trade and public finance, was first secretary under Piedras Albas at the Consejo de Indias, and the Cadiz *consulado* petitioned him frequently and confidently, even after 1764, when Goyeneche became secretary of the Consejo de Castilla.

On the Consejo de Indias were others—many of them graduates of the *colegios mayores*—whom Cadiz would contact to protect its interests. José Esteban de Abaría, former head of the Casa de Contratación at Cadiz, had cooperated with the merchant guild; he too had connections at Madrid. In 1765, he was prefect of the Congregación de San Ignacio, an influential philanthropic and political action association for advancing Basque interests, whose membership included Marcos Jimeno, an *hacedor* of Salamanca's *colegios mayores*, whose clients the *consulado* cultivated; José de Rojas y Contreras, another defender of the *colegios mayores* and brother of the governor of the Consejo de Castilla; Manuel Pablo de Salcedo, *colegial* of the Colegio Viejo de San Bartolomé, who had intervened to preserve Cadiz's mail contract in 1764; Ventura Santelices y Ventura, another San Bartolomé *colegial* and a member of the Casa de Contratación; and Domingo de Trespalacios y Escandón, ex-*oidor* of the Audiencia de Mexico.

In view of what seemed the receding power of the Consejo de Indias and the marginalization of Arriaga in the early 1760s, the Consulado de Cadiz tried many channels in the labyrinth of power to reach the apex of the bureaucracy, those in Charles III's inner circle, through the mediation of friendly aristocrats and others with leverage at court. Its memorials represented a final recourse that ritually reiterated past financial "services" to the state by the mercantile community of lower Andalusia and repeated expressions of gratitude from the crown. By 1764, the *consulado* was disturbed by rumors of the special *junta* selected by Esquilache to revise the structure of trade with the American colonies. Particularly upsetting was Madrid's intention to bypass conciliar bodies where *consulado* influence was strong (e.g., the Casa de Contratación).

The *consulado*'s lobbying at Madrid at this time was expensive, since early in 1766, its officials petitioned Colonial Secretary Arriaga, successfully it appears, to free up 12,000 pesos accumulated in the *consulado*'s account for secret expenses (*gastos secretos*). Moreover, the annual allotment of 5,000 pesos fell far short of the *consulado*'s lobbying expenditures. If one tracks the quantities of fine chocolate (from Soconusco) and tobacco (from Cuba) that the *consulado* dispensed annually to friends in high places, as well as other less visible and perhaps more effective gifts of silver pesos (to Arriaga, for one), it is clear that the merchant guild had ample means of making friends and influencing people.[62]

Understandably, the correspondence of Cadiz maintained discreet silence on the March events in Madrid 1766. The *consulado*'s Madrid agent was asked to forward all "communicable" news, but recorded communication (it must have come by word of mouth) was suspended between 25 March and 8 April. Then José de Larrarte, the Madrid agent, was advised to refrain from pushing the *consulado*'s claims aggressively for the time being. "Our desires," the *consulado* directed, "although just, must be pursued at a carefully calculated opportunity, because any decision, favorable or unfavorable, depends upon the proper timing."

The ramifications of colonial interests in the crisis of 1766 cannot be measured solely by the role of the Cadiz merchant guild and its patrons spread among the Madrid bureaucracy and court aristocracy. As the *consulado* often claimed when responding to charges that it enjoyed commercial and shipping monopolies, the Cadiz business community was not a power unto itself, but represented the interests of the whole country. Those interests, it claimed, depended upon the good faith and secrecy that the *consulado*, as the point of contact between Spain and the colonies, had always shown in defending the interests confided to it. Essentially, the claim was accurate. Examination of ship registers shows a steady inflow of private funds from the colonies, some large but most small, to Spaniards in all walks of life: to grandees receiving thousands of pesos annually, to pensioned civil servants and widows collecting hundreds of pesos, religious institutions of all kinds accepting large and small amounts, and, of course, to many individual legatees of peninsular merchants, clerics, and bureaucrats deceased in the American colonies, whose beneficiaries collected sums that bordered on mere pittances. In light of the large silver balances transferred from colonial to peninsular treasuries, it is not surprising that many public works programs in the early years of Charles III's reign were financed with colonial transfers, often funds appropriated from Amerindian communities as "donations" and used for metropolitan construction projects, such as completion of Madrid's Palacio Real.

The bishop of Cuenca's complaint about the "deterioration and imminent loss of America" meant many things to many people, but they were all sure to unite in one general cause: getting rid of a minister whose reformist policies threatened to alter the distribution of the benefits of empire. However, it is unlikely that unambiguous evidence, a "smoking gun," will ever surface to reveal Cadiz's direct involvement in the coup that ousted Esquilache in 1766.

Privilege, the *Motín,* and the Limits of Monarchical Authority

In probing for origins and mechanics of opposition to the marqués de Esquilache as a prominent agent of change in Spain in the early 1760s, we have tried to identify the interpenetrating interests of groups and individuals, metropolitan as well as colonial, and their interlinkage in the hierarchical society of privilege that characterized Spain's old regime. Those interests had proliferated over time as an integral part of the exercise of privilege, and it was therefore privilege that unified the opponents of the Italian minister: privileged access to bureaucratic posts, privileged ownership of agricultural resources and control of commercial exchanges, privileged rights in the bureaucratic and economic benefits of empire, and privileged status in the protection of the law.

Such privilege was not, however, enjoyed only by the elite. It incorporated individuals and groups at all levels and served as a means of survival among the poorest, as a way of rising among the "middling" strata, and an armature of wealth and status at the apex of Spanish society. In the absence of an alternative economic dynamic, the quest for and exercise of privilege became the principle that gave the semblance of vitality to this society. With the support of associated institutions of patronage and clientelism, of kinship and family, of regional networks and religious organizations, privilege could be relied upon in a crisis of the body politic to provide the men to defend society's formal structures.

The coup of March 1766 suggests a wide consensus among privileged groups behind the decision to abort Esquilache's reform policy. The *colegiales* in the Consejo de Castilla and its Sala de Alcaldes who precipitated the *motín* were reinforced by Andalusian magnates in furnishing actors, intermediaries, and advisers in the crisis. Informal and formal webs tied these groups to the secular and regular clergy, whose participation was clarified by the activity of the bishops of Cuenca and Cartagena, the Cinco Gremios Mayores, and—less visible—the Consulado de Cadiz.

Second and equally important, Charles's unpredictable flight from Madrid forced the Consejo de Castilla openly to side with the insurrection. The escalated violence implicit in the new confrontation, symbolized by using a convict to read the royal capitulation to the crowd and by arming Madrid's lumpen, dramatized the chasm yawning between *consejo* and the crown. This violation of the accepted and acceptable ritual of the political *motín* transcended the issue of Esquilache's ouster. Equally unpredictable was the overriding imperative to restore both the image and the reality of royal authority and to reconcile the *consejo* and the crown at least publicly. The decision to appoint the conde de Aranda first as military governor of Madrid and then as president of the Consejo de Castilla was now accepted by most bureaucrats and welcomed by most aristocrats. Far from acceptable to the religious establishment and *colegiales,* however, was the loss of their traditional posts at the apex of state service, now in the hands of a military officer of doubtful devotion to church hierarchs and to the *colegial* networks long known as the "great bishop makers" ("los máximos hacedores de obispos").

Aranda's selection proved felicitous in restabilizing the Bourbon state. Recognizing the need for consensus in restoring the semblance of royal authority, he rapidly engineered what was probably the most efficient political operation of the Bourbon state: the incrimination and then swift expulsion of the Jesuits from Spain and its colonies on grounds of lèse-majesté—high crimes against the state—and primary responsibility for the *motín de Esquilache.* This dramatic act went far to restore the Spanish state's international image of stability; above all, it enlisted the support of an influential part of the ecclesiastical establishment, notably the episcopate and other religious orders that had long been rivals of the Jesuits, as well as peninsular and colonial merchant communities blocked from markets in Jesuit enclaves in the colonies. Overseas, colonial officials were shaken by the removal of Esquilache and, above all, by what he represented. This is clear in

Captain-General Bucareli's letter from Havana to Prime Minister Grimaldi at the end of 1766: "This was the year of a strange chain of tragedies; everywhere one finds obstacles to the execution of the best-thought-out projects, and it is necessary that we steadfastly await the end of evil, followed by happiness."[63]

Aranda's successful crisis-management notwithstanding, the success of the coup showed the limits of monarchical power. The lessons so dramatically—and dangerously—learned would not be forgotten either by Charles III, his successive prime ministers, Grimaldi and Floridablanca, or, later, Charles's son and his ministers, Godoy, in particular. If the paradigm of Bourbon reform in Spain remained substantially unchanged, its bureaucratic instruments and tactics turned more pragmatic and in the end proved less effective in solving the fundamental problems of Spain's economy and society. Predictably, the new orientation imposed upon the Consejo de Castilla under Aranda's presidency (1766–73) faded as the *letrado* hierarchy (the *golillas*) reasserted control and then shunted Aranda himself off to the embassy at Paris. Two years later, in a political confrontation reminiscent of 1766, Moñino replaced Grimaldi. The two *letrados* who formed part of the group to investigate the *escarmiento* of Charles III and Esquilache, Moñino and Campomanes, the former as prime minister and the latter as *decano* of the Consejo de Castilla and for a time its governor, would later preside over the Catholic enlightenment that followed the "ministerial despotism" of Esquilache and Aranda in the remaining decades of Charles III's era.

Henceforth, reform in metropolitan Spain would be pursued, not by executive fiat imposing structural reform, but through exhortation, study and more study, *consulta* and *dictamen* and compromise.

Part Two

The Colonial
Option

5. *Flotas* to New Spain:
The Last Phase, 1757–1778

[An *encomendero*'s] sense of vanity swells when [he is] called a *flotista* . . .

Juan Antonio de los Heros Fernández (1790)

Duties, more duties, duties on entry at Cadiz. Duties on departing and duties on reentry at
Cadiz, plus aggravation and details. Duties have ruined trade.

Plaint preserved in the Archivo Histórico Nacional, Madrid

By now it is evident that, unlike other eighteenth-century imperial trading
systems, the Spanish transatlantic system of managed trade operated until
the last quarter of the century out of a single metropolitan port, Cadiz,
where merchants had acquired "an exclusive trading right each exercises
with his own capital."[1] Their *derecho exclusivo* consisted of the privilege of
intermediaries (shippers, agents, factors) earning commissions "because the
bulk of their exports belong to foreigners."[2] Conspicuously absent were
the high-volume exchanges of domestic manufactures for colonial primary
products that characterized English and French imperial trading patterns of
the time.

This trading pattern assured the survival and in most cases the profitability of the trading communities of Cadiz and Mexico City. Organized and
enforced by the state through the Consejo de Indias, with the collaboration
of the Casa de Contratación at Cadiz, it facilitated collection of duties payable in specie, a welcome source of liquidity to the Hacienda. The system
also assured the salaries of the bureaucracy of the Casa de Contratación, customshouse personnel and coast guardsmen, and the wages of dockyard
workers and longshoremen. Like the state, the civil service employees lived
off customs duties, inspection and other fees, and surcharges associated with
a long-standing and involuted transatlantic trading system (which is not

to claim that it was static). The point is, all accepted and exploited a commercial and fiscal system of mutual benefit rooted in the silver mines of America. The interests of Spanish merchants and their foreign financiers/collaborators, public and private personnel, and state and private bodies converged; en masse, they had lobbied hard for resurrecting the *flota* system to New Spain and its Jalapa *feria* in the 1750s as they had for *flotas* and *galeones* in the Proyecto of 1720.

Managed Trade at Cadiz

Perhaps nothing better epitomized the Spanish system of managed colonial trade than an obsessive reliance upon a formal shell of techniques of control over shipping, crews, and goods and upon duty collection and associated fees in preparation of a vessel joining a *flota* to New Spain in the two decades after 1757. Preoccupation with step-by-step surveillance and repeated double-checking imply that evasion outweighed compliance.[3]

Dispatching a 200- to 400-ton vessel and cargo to Veracruz began with the purchase of a license from the Consejo de Indias (and often a bribe) at Madrid, with departure from the Bay of Cadiz following only months or, in some cases, years later.[4] The cost of the license—on average, 40–50,000 pesos per registered ship of 300 tons—was usually in part defrayed by surreptitious substitution of a far larger vessel. "For the licence runs only to 300 tuns at most, [but] the vessel fitted out is seldom less than 600," the Reverend Edward Clarke, an English observer, noted in the early 1760s.[5]

At this point, the shipper (*cargador*) would turn to a foreign resident for capital, goods, or both. A foreign resident with goods to sell looked for a reliable Spanish intermediary to move them to the colonies for sale. He located a *cargador* to whom to consign the merchandise (who would register and ship the goods in *his* own name); then the *cargador* chose a Spanish *comisionado* or *encomendero* to accompany the shipment, sell it, and return the proceeds in pesos or staples. Contracts between foreigner and Spaniards were unregistered and stated the true ownership of the goods entrusted and the earnings expected.[6]

Once a shipper had lined up a shipowner, or *patrón,* he furnished the shipmaster (*maestro*) with a listing (*nota*) of initialed bales, boxes, and bundles of merchandise and an estimate of their volume or weight.[7] Along with this list, the shipmaster submitted a petition (*poliza*) to the *contador principal* of the Casa de Contratación for approval (*despacho*) of the voyage to one designated colonial port, with the cargo noted in a presumably accurate manifest (*hoja de registro*). This enumerated the Spanish proprietor(s) of cargo and three alternate consignees in America, as well as the number of initialed bales, boxes, and bundles consigned. In the case of cargo bought with funds remitted from Mexico City, the manifest required a separate sworn declaration of the name of the overseas merchant. With *poliza* and *hoja de registro*, a *cargador* would proceed first to the Contaduría de Reglamento for an official estimate of the duties specified in the Proyecto of 1720 and then to the Depositaria de Indias to deposit a sum equivalent to tonnage duties.

However, before a vessel outbound to the colonies could be loaded, there were other formalities. There was the requirement of gauging a vessel's hold (*arqueo*),[8] as well as its seaworthiness, and, if necessary, completion of repairs "often mandated by willful, capricious government agents"— procedures that raised transport costs and involved delays.[9] Defenders of requirements specified by the Casa de Contratación justified these practices by observing that Spanish shipping outbound could not be compared to French and English vessels sailing to the West Indies with a cargo worth from 4,000 to 6,000 pesos; a ship to Veracruz under the managed trade system, they noted, might often carry between 1 and 1.5 million pesos' worth of goods, no exaggerated comparison. The French, who put many of their ships into the Spanish transatlantic system (foreign-built ships paid an extra tax, or *estrangería*), concurred that "high cargo value and damages, for which the carriers are responsible, oblige shipowners to take precautions far beyond those of other countries in similar cases."[10] From the Arsenal (Carraca) across the bay of Cadiz came its chief officer, accompanied by shipwrights to measure the hold and check the condition of the hull, canvas, masts, and spars.[11] On completion of this inspection (often after months of repairs) and of crew quarters and stores, the vessel received certification as seaworthy and was ready for loading.[12]

Loading, too, could be protracted. The vessel was warped to the mole for accurate assessment of duties by volume and weight as cargo was stowed. Then the president of the Casa de Contratación would order final inspection by the Arsenal's chief officer of the vessel's overall seaworthiness, possible overloading, and the condition of its armament; at the same time, he checked the crew list for unregistered seamen and stowaways (*polizones*). Spanish crews were neither small nor cheap, usually consisting of captain, mate, chaplain, surgeon, clerk, pilot, and seamen—"all paid very well."[13] At last, the vessel could clear for America, its bales, boxes, and bundles of cargo checked against the manifest, duties assessed (payment usually postponed until arrival at the colonial port of destination), and a customs seal (*sello*) on large boxes and packages. This, of course, failed to curb the ingenuity of shippers in loading substantially more goods than the official manifests indicated.[14]

The safety record of repeatedly inspected vessels in Spain's transatlantic system has yet to be compared to that of their French and English competitors. Beyond doubt, there was pressure to cut the high cost of transatlantic navigation to both shipowners and shippers. *Cargadores* confronted numerous hurdles: for "every inspection leads to a report and agents at the Contratación to push matters; this gives an idea of the expense, wasted time and many intermediaries in fitting out a vessel."[15] According to a French source, shipowners calculated that on average repairs inflated costs per ship by 25,000 pesos over those in other European ports—"an enormous difference due to the abuse at Cadiz's dockyards. . . . Repairs at the Trocadero permit the blacksmiths, carpenters, caulkers, and dockyard and warehouse owners to collude in gouging those requiring their services."[16] To be sure, no regulatory system ever receives full compliance, and shippers and shipowners alike made allowance for private deals in the form of gifts/bribes to avoid "arbitrary inspections, hurdles and chicanery by low-level customs employees."[17]

French firms (in 1753, there were 108 registered at Cadiz, 44 percent of the 244 foreign commercial houses), whose merchandise and shipping were highly visible, participated in this cat-and-mouse game at the port.[18] The pseudo-mercantilism of the Spanish state—seeking to control foreigners' involvement (usually illegal) in what Spanish authorities fostered as a national monopoly and now at last envisioned as capable of contributing to national development—seemed hypocritical to French interests. By the same token, the arbitrary tactics of petty Spanish customs officers at Cadiz in making unannounced inspections (*visitas*) of foreign and domestic shipping were a form of shakedown.[19] Spaniards, however, operating within their maze of shipping formalities and multiple duties, were convinced that following what they considered the less regulated or managed systems of France and England would bring only "confusion and disorder, like fitting Pigmy's clothing on a Giant." The graphic comparison was not hyperbolic. Such was the resilience of the system and the political influence of the Cadiz commercial community that even in the 1790s, shipping there was notoriously still "the most expensive in the world."[20]

Finally, one must add the multiple charges levied upon goods entering and then reexported to the colonies, "levies and further levies on agriculture and industry." In large measure, additional duties accounted for the inflated cost of goods ultimately discharged by *flotas* and by individual *registros* at the port of Veracruz. Merchandise entering Cadiz paid the duties of a skewed tariff schedule that privileged imports over domestic products in colonial trade; and there were also commission and insurance fees, the lifeblood of the Spanish merchant community, plus freight charges, and the not negligible wages of longshoremen organized in their *palanquinado*. Charges on goods exported through Cadiz raised prices on average by a minimum of 40 percent; and this did not include costs accruing between discharge at Veracruz and the point of final sale in the interior of New Spain.[21]

Managed Trade: Veracruz

Unloading and then moving cargo through customs at the port of Veracruz was hardly less cumbersome than the process at Cadiz. Like Cadiz's formalities, those of Veracruz inflated costs and provided an incentive for smuggling and collusion between businessmen and bureaucrats. "Although our ministers may be [like] Argos, [and] their sight lynxlike, still they cannot prevent smuggling," said a Veracruz customs official.[22]

Once moored, a shipmaster or his supercargo went ashore for permission to commence unloading. Then he saw to the construction of a temporary shelter (*barraca*) or shed within the city walls near the gate of a bureau of the local colonial treasury, the Contaduría; cargo remained stored in the shed until it had been inspected by customs officers and duties assessed and paid. The *barraca* was patrolled by watchmen (sometimes by crewmen), "who merited confidence." *Lanchas* and *botes* served as lighters to put cargo ashore as quickly as possible so that *flota* merchantmen or individual *registros* could anchor well offshore; sudden storms accompanied by high winds (the notorious Veracruz *nortes*) often snapped ships' cables, letting them drift ashore. As cargo was hauled from the hold, a watchman of the customs service tallied bales, boxes, and bundles lowered into lighters. This tally was later matched against the ship's manifest. Put ashore on Veracruz's mole, cargo was now deposited in the prepared *barraca*.[23]

In theory, cargo would now move smoothly through the Contaduría, where duties were assessed, including those levied at Cadiz but collected at Veracruz in silver. Such efficiency remained the ideal; in practice, unloading cargo by lighter from thirteen to sixteen *flota* vessels, putting it ashore at the mole, and moving it to storage sheds invariably overloaded the port's handling capacity, without considering the Veracruz customs setup. In 1776, it required five or six days just to moor and secure *flota* shipping, and another eight to unload cargo.[24] In fact off-loaded goods might remain for days, weeks, or sometimes longer in the "guarded" shed awaiting the assessment of colonial customs duties, arrangement of payment, and the arrival of consignees or their representatives. This accounts for the two months allocated for moving cargo from ship to shore, through customs, and then by mule-back inland to Jalapa before the *feria de la flota*.

With cargo in open sheds over long periods came opportunities to filch items or substitute contents before customs inspection. At night, it was possible to replace high quality merchandise with cheap items, to "remove some items and insert others."[25] There was no problem finding collaborators. One pattern of bribery occurred during the unloading of cargo; every workday, as a token of appreciation for "importing what was not duly registered," ship captains and local consignees provided snacks (*refrescos* of cakes, wine, and brandy) to longshoremen and customs personnel while cargo was being unloaded.[26] Invariably, smuggling opportunities increased when, faced with the inevitable backup of cargo and inadequate storage space, Contaduría officials permitted storage in private warehouses (*almacenes*), presumably guarded.[27]

As the major port on New Spain's Caribbean coast, Veracruz was the "throat of this vast realm," accessible both to its population centers and the principal mining zones of the central plateau and the north.[28] Yet after more than two centuries of trading with Spain, Veracruz's cargo handling procedures and facilities were inefficient and obviously porous to local and foreign smugglers. It comes as no surprise that its customs procedures were equally inadequate, equally open to collusion. "Trade to the Indies," the experienced naval commander Antonio de Ulloa mordantly commented at Veracruz in 1778, "is not for the disinterested."[29]

Part of the problem, certainly before the careful inspection in 1766–67 by José de Gálvez, the *visitador general* appointed under Esquilache, was organization and work patterns in the Veracruz customs, which Gálvez inspected twice in the months after his arrival.[30] The Contaduría was managed by a "confidential clerk," who scheduled neither fixed days nor hours for processing shipments, whether inbound or outbound. Record-keeping was appropriately informal, consisting of rough notes (*borradores de caja*).[31] This suggests an extraordinary range of discretion and arbitrariness on the part of customs personnel from the administrator-general down to the cargo inspectors, whose salaries were based on a percentage of the duties collected, in principle, an incentive for careful inspection.[32] However, in return for a gratuity, an inspector would undervalue goods or simply fail to inspect cargo. Merchants constantly invoked a regulation that once a bale or box had received a customs stamp, its contents were inviolate—beyond further questioning. Cadiz's *cargadores* commonly failed deliberately to list items on their invoices; when called to account at the Veracruz customs, their agents (*encomenderos* or *factores*) would insist that the bale or box had been properly processed by the Contratacíon at Cadiz.[33] One can imagine the problems encountered by a responsible, overworked customs inspector who insisted upon checking every bale or box against the invoice, not to speak of opening bales to verify the quality and quantity of goods packed.[34]

Hence Cadiz merchants' widespread practice of consistently undervaluing their shipments. Despite the elaborate surface structure of surveillance at Veracruz, its customshouse was as porous, perhaps even more so, than that at Cadiz.[35] As the influential *fiscales* of the Consejo de Castilla, Moñino and Campomanes, recognized on analyzing *Visitador-General* Gálvez's reports on Veracruz customs practice, officials there had reduced the "legal constraints to mere formulas, of minimal gain to the Treasury." There had been solid grounds, then, to instruct Gálvez on his departure for New Spain in 1765 to investigate the Veracruz customshouse "as his highest priority."[36]

Madrid's attempts to contain smuggling and maximize tax collection, particularly sales taxes (*alcabalas*), did not end at Veracruz. Cargo processed at the Veracruz customs received a customs seal (waybill, or *marchamo*) stamped on bales of textiles as proof of legal entry. Next, *arrieros* in charge of teams of pack mules departed from Veracruz with a register (*guía*) of bales, bundles, and packages in their care, including their names, that of the shipper (*cargador* or *flotista*), and that of the consignee, with his address. On passing through *alcabala* checkpoints, the *guía* was matched against cargo; at the checkpoint of the consignee, the *arriero* received a *tornaguía* (indicating that the shipment had arrived at destination and duties paid), which ultimately he returned or had someone return to the point of origin.[37] Years later, Valentín Foronda, when Spain's consul at Philadelphia, compared the simplicity of U.S. regulatory mechanisms with what he knew of Spanish metropolitan and colonial customs and tax practices. "The United States has no obstacles to its domestic trade. The carriers of goods are not bothered with stop for examination, I want to put my hand on your purse, pay so much for entering, for leaving, do you have the proper waybills?"[38]

The policy of monitoring trade flows in Spain's transatlantic pipeline had a primarily fiscal goal—moving more goods through checkpoints to enhance customs revenues and associated charges and minimize smuggling. Discretionary record-keeping renders eighteenth-century commercial statistics suspect. This conceded, data covering the final two decades of the Spanish convoy system, Cadiz to Veracruz, from the *flota* of 1757 to the last in 1776, provide a basis for deriving plausible trends. This is not to overlook that trade movements between the metropole and its American colonies occurred outside the *flota* system, usually in the form of mercury vessels (*azogues*) and individual *registros*.

Convoyed by two or three warships, from nine to fifteen merchant ships left Cadiz for Veracruz roughly every three or four years between 1757 and 1778. Cargo tonnage (*toneladas*) varied between a low of 5,588 (1768) to a high of 8,492 (1760) tons, ending with 8,176 in 1778. Mean *flota* tonnage was 7,320, more than double that of 1735 (3,000); after the trough of 1768, the trend is upward. José Real Díaz estimated that the cargoes of six inbound convoys varied in value between a low of 7.6 million and a high of 22.9 million *pesos fuertes*; in value per *tonelada,* they varied between 898 (1760) and 3,807 (1772) *pesos fuertes* (Tables 5.1 and 5.2). In slightly different terms, the average value per *tonelada* of four *flotas* (1765–78) was two-thirds higher than those of the previous *flotas* of 1757–60.

A striking percentage of outbound shipments consisted of foreign textiles, on average 84 percent.[39] As for the relative proportion of Spanish to non-Spanish cargo, one estimate put Spanish products at 12.6 percent, below English (15.2) and far behind French products (36.6).[40] The percentage of imports ordered by Mexico City merchants from Cadiz *corresponsales* ranged between 11 and 20 percent.[41] Meanwhile, Cadiz interests were growing: between 1757 and 1776, the number of their agents (*cargadores* and *factores*) more than doubled. Aboard the first of the renewed *flotas* (1757), there were listed 99 *cargadores* and 13 *factores* (agents), while the last convoy in 1776 surprisingly contained between 250 and 300 *cargadores/factores* registered with the Cadiz *consulado* and trading at Jalapa.[42] Not only was New Spain drawing peninsular representatives, it was also responsible for 56 percent of the silver exported (352.3 million *pesos fuertes*) from all of Spain's American

TABLE 5.1

Shipping, Toneladas, *and Return Values:* Flotas *to New Spain, 1757–78*
(*pesos fuertes*)

Year	Ships[a]	Toneladas	Value: Real Díaz	Value: Morineau
1757	13	7,669	15,160,205	16,289,504
1760	17	8,492	7,624,862	8,620,677
1765	13	8,013	14,323,701	16,222,364
1768	11 (8?)	5,558	14,087,947	16,010,083
1772	14	6,010	22,881,617	22,329,355
1778	17 (15?)	8,176	11,830,366	19,509,875
Mean		7,320		

Sources: Adapted from Real Díaz, *Ferias de Jalapa,* 126 nos. 1–2; Morineau, *Incroyables gazettes,* 399–415.

[a]Includes escort vessels.

TABLE 5.2
Return per Tonelada
 (*pesos fuertes*)

	Real Díaz	Morineau
1757	1,976.8	2,124.0
1760	897.8	1,015.1
1765	1,787.5	2,024.5
1768	2,521.1	2,865.0
1772	3,807.2	3,715.3
1778	1,446.9	2,386.2

Sources: Adapted from Real Díaz, *Ferias de Jalapa* 126 nos. 1–2; Morineau, *Incroyables gazettes,* 399–415.

colonies to the mother country between 1756 and 1778. No wonder the riches of New Spain mesmerized the Peninsula.[43]

Beyond question, New Spain's mines, financed mainly by resident merchant capitalists, and its demographic patterns and high level of import demand made it Spain's most coveted overseas possession, a fact lost upon neither Cadiz merchants, enterprising young peninsular emigrants, nor the merchant community of Mexico City. The drawing power of New Spain for Cadiz's *cargadores* and *factores* (and foreign merchant bankers financing them) emerged vividly in an inquiry ordered by Madrid and executed by the Contratación at Cadiz, then headed by the former commandant of the 1757 flota, Joaquin Villena, now marqués del Real Tesoro. Madrid wanted to know how many duly licensed *cargadores/factores* had sailed to the American colonies in the decade 1757–67 and returned within the required time period. Of 536 whose destinations were ascertained, 50 percent (265) had chosen New Spain, by far the largest number to go to any colony—despite constant friction between *flotistas* of the *comercio de España* and the *comercio de México* (merchants based in Mexico City, also called "vecinos de México," or simply "americanos," by their Iberian counterparts) at the designated exchange center, Jalapa's *feria de la flota.*[44]

The *Comercio de España* Versus the *Comercio de México:* The Jalapa Fair Destabilized

Although Madrid had mandated a *feria de la flota* at Jalapa in 1728, the colonial authorities at Mexico City were left to hammer out specific local procedures. Presumably, the situation at the colonial capital was too fraught with conflict for Madrid to formulate new regulations for the Jalapa exchanges. Then, in 1729, Viceroy Casafuerte formulated new procedures ending the halcyon period of "libertad recíproca"—the Consulado de México's overly roseate retrospective view of the time when the *cargadores* and *flotistas* of the *comercio de España* had accompanied their goods to the colonial capital for sale, and when Mexico City's *almaceneros* had been able to remit funds to Cadiz to buy goods to be shipped to Veracruz on the following convoy.[45]

Casafuerte's ground rules for "uprooting the vices and regrettable results of merchants' activities" were few, simple, and privileged well-capitalized merchants. First, all imports brought in convoy would be transferred up-country from the port of Veracruz to Jalapa for sale within the assigned stay of *flota* vessels in the Veracruz harbor, approximately seven months. For Cadiz shippers and their foreign investors/partners, this translated into the traditional pattern of one round-trip every three years and might lower the cost of borrowed capital and expenditures on ship and crew maintenance while in port. Second, the *feria* would end on the departure of the *flota's* merchant vessels for Cadiz via Havana. At this point, all imports sold by the *comercio de España,* as well as those ordered and shipped from Cadiz by Mexico City's *almaceneros,* could at last be dispatched to Mexico City or other cities and towns of New Spain. In the third place, *flotistas* holding unsold merchandise (*rezagos*) would have to sell to prospective buyers at Jalapa alone; neither *cargadores* nor *factores* would now be permitted to abandon Jalapa to arrange sales in person at the capital or elsewhere in New Spain.[46]

Over the next half-century, despite friction between the two sectors of the commercial duopoly operated by the *comercio de España* and the *comercio de México,* Casafuerte's basic ground rules were maintained, altered occasionally to meet abnormal conditions. Continuity of practice is evident in Viceroy Bucareli's instructions for handling the convoy of 1772, in cargo value and tonnage one of the largest of the eighteenth century. The first section of Bucareli's directives dealt with the unloading of merchandise at Veracruz, its transfer solely to Jalapa in full compliance with *guías, marchamos,* and numbered packages properly identified, and the provision of food and lodging at reasonable prices at Jalapa, so that "Merchants avoid unwarranted extorsion in freight charges and rents." Profit-gouging by Jalapa residents at *feria* times was notorious. Bucareli allotted two months for freighting *flotistas'* goods to Jalapa, where the merchant *diputación* from Cadiz would meet its Mexico City counterpart to settle problems at the forthcoming fair; there, *flotistas* hoped to separate New Spain's buyers from their silver. Members of the Mexico City *diputación* delegated by the *consulado* would reside at Jalapa for the duration of the *feria* to join in arbitrating issues involving *flotistas* and New Spain's businessmen.[47] Both *diputa-*

ciones were enjoined to avoid covert business deals ("tratados, conferencias o negociaciones") that might distort their presumably transparent trading. Market forces were considered paramount, "since each individual enjoys without constraint the use of his goods and interest." Duopoly did not exclude the concept of some competition.

Into a second category fell directives affecting the duration of the *feria* and its internal operations. Following two months of preparation, the fair would last six months and allow for another two months to settle accounts and prepare return cargo (mainly but not exclusively silver). According to this timetable, ten months after arrival at Veracruz, the *flota*'s merchant vessels would depart for Cadiz. Bucareli's viceregal *bando* emphasized the original, underlying concept of two spheres of commercial operation, with Jalapa as sole locus of exchange and the mutual boundary: under no circumstance could *flotistas* abandon Jalapa for Mexico City or other points of the colony to sell goods or collect debts. Here the intervention of the colonial state was explicit and direct. To facilitate on-time departure of returning *flotas* carrying silver pesos, which were the heart of the convoy system, Bucareli mandated that all New Spain's treasuries forward "las platas" to the capital "so that merchants and others may avoid delay in shipping funds in the interest of increasing [the] silver carried by *conductas:* this is an appropriate way to facilitate the *feria* and hasten the return of the *flota*."[48]

Regulations shape the ideal, to which reality usually fails to conform. Obviously, there were many independent variables in the *feria* system at Jalapa. For example, how much capital would Mexico City's *almaceneros* forward to Cadiz to cover their independent purchases? Would *almaceneros* continue to reject the high initial asking prices invariably set by *flotistas* once the Jalapa *feria* opened? For their part, would *cargadores-flotistas* be ready to lower prices to dispose of imports as the date approached for a *flota*'s scheduled departure for Havana and Cadiz? The efforts of the Spanish state to revive a late medieval institution, the fair, in a colonial context at Jalapa, in order to guarantee the "remission of funds to Spain in the shortest possible time," attempted to create a delicate balance between state *dirigisme* and individual economic rights in the marketplace.[49]

Two developments soon destabilized the system thought up in Madrid and elaborated by Viceroy Casafuerte in 1729. First, over the course of three convoys (1728, 1732, and 1735), capital flows from Mexico City to buy goods at Cadiz—what Cadiz shippers complained about were "large remissions of funds and orders by the Americans"—were understood as threatening their role in the fair system. Without consulting Mexico City's merchants, those of Cadiz, supported by Lima's *consulado,* lobbied to have the Spanish government prohibit such capital flows from the colonies, a ruling Mexico City's *almaceneros* managed to have rescinded in 1738.[50] A second development occurred during the War of the Austrian Succession (1739–48): in the absence of convoys, individual *registros* of neutral vessels met New Spain's import needs. Their shipments were transported to Jalapa, where they remained on sale for one month only, a travesty of *feria* practice.[51] Thereafter, unsold imports (*rezagos*) could be moved by the *cargadores* and *factores* of the *comercio de España* to Mexico City. Once in the capital, they profited from wartime import shortages to inflate prices and speculate among themselves in both imports and locally produced goods—activities specifically outlawed by Casafuerte's regulations.[52] Implementation of Madrid's concept of distinct commercial compartments at the Jalapa fair seemed inoperable.

In 1749, at the request of Cadiz, probably in reaction to the volume of merchant capital received from Mexico City to order goods, Madrid reinstated controls.[53] Remittances were permitted provided that orders were placed with merchants registered with the Cadiz *consulado* and that purchases were consigned to Jalapa using registered *cargadores*.[54] By law, then, Mexico City's *almaceneros* could now place orders at Cadiz, their imports competing with the merchandise offered at Jalapa by *cargadores* from Cadiz. In practice, however, their shipments were still encumbered by informal webs of interest and power linking the Consulado de Cadiz, the Casa de Contratación, and the wider community of Cadiz shipowners, shippers and ship captains, *cargadores, encomenderos,* and *factores.* Mexico City's *almaceneros* complained that it was hard to get cargoes loaded at Cadiz, since "by virtue of an obscure dispatch, Cadiz's merchants have suppressed the special dispatch that the Consulado de México obtained."[55]

Convoy resumption in 1757 to supply New Spain's import needs and capture millions of silver pesos did not occur under optimal conditions. Both entrepôts, Cadiz and Mexico City, preferred to share a regulated duopoly in *flota* and *feria* over the less manageable *registros* between 1739 and 1757. Jointly they petitioned Madrid to delay the *flota*'s departure until 1757 in order to dispose of an accumulation of unsold goods (including some smuggled), the *rezagos,* before the predictable postwar influx of lower-priced imports. Mexico City's warehousemen introduced another factor, the inadequate supply of money available to cover cash purchases of a predictably large volume of imports on the next *flota.*[56] There remained, finally, the *comercio de México*'s distrust of *flotistas* from Cadiz. Fearing *flotistas*' attempts to exit Jalapa for Mexico City and other commercial centers in the interior of the colony, *almaceneros* insisted that *flotistas* remain restricted to the *feria* area until they had disposed of all their imports—a basic element of Casafuerte's rules, they insisted, that no viceroy should countermand.

On the 1757 *flota* to Veracruz, the first since the late 1730s, cargo value and volume were impressive, as were the subsequent earnings of Cadiz merchants and creditors.[57] If anything, friction between Cadiz *flotistas* and Mexico City *almaceneros* was heightened by the viceroy's one-sided decision: after the *flota*'s arrival at Veracruz, he permitted the goods of *flotistas,* if sold, to be shipped out of Jalapa immediately, while retaining imports ordered by Mexico City merchants from Cadiz until the end of the *feria.* When they insisted upon equal treatment for their merchandise, the viceroy rejected their petition. At stake was the real cost advantage of ordering goods from Cadiz on their own account. By remitting funds there to cover imports carried by *flotas,* Mexico City *almaceneros* saved a minimum of 7 percent on a variety of middlemen's fees; in consequence those who could preferred to buy from fellow *almaceneros* rather than from *flotistas.*[58]

Once again international conflict, this time Spain's alliance with France in the Seven Years' War, moved the colonial authorities in New Spain to depart from the ground rules governing the Jalapa fair. In 1761, Viceroy Cruillas terminated the *feria* (with most of the cargo unsold), although the *flota* itself had to remain at Veracruz.[59] Later, fearing an English assault upon Veracruz and the chance that it might penetrate inland as far as Jalapa, Cruillas broke another *feria* regulation: he ruled that the *flotistas* and their unsold goods go to Mexico City.[60] But once in the large marketplace of the colony's capital, members of the *comercio de España* broke out of the constraints of the *feria* to speculate among themselves, trading goods brought out on the *flota* of 1760 back and forth and bidding up the prices both of imports and of local products. To be sure, high flyers went bankrupt when the war ended sooner than predicted and the speculative bubble collapsed, underscoring the hazards of an alternative to the rules of the convoy-and-fair system.[61] When the Consulado de México petitioned Madrid to postpone the *flota* scheduled for 1765, the proposal was rejected by Esquilache's administration, desperate for income collectible on *flota* operations.

The postwar *flotas* of 1765 and 1769 heightened the contest at Jalapa between the commercial interests of Cadiz and Mexico City. Although sales remained strong, *flotistas* were nonetheless left with unsold items when the *feria* ended. These they sold in small lots to small-scale provincial retailers ("comercio de tierra adentro"), who were now opting to travel down to Jalapa to buy directly from *flotistas* at prices below those charged by Mexico City's *almaceneros.* This reduced the volume of *rezagos* but created other problems. To increase sales, *flotistas* had extended credit to undercapitalized, illiquid (and not well known) provincial retailers; when the time came for the *flotas'* return, they had to petition local colonial authorities for permission to leave Jalapa to collect personally from their inland debtors. Quite simply, the problem was the "delayed payment spread over three or four years to liquidate purchases" at the Jalapa fair.[62]

Almaceneros countered that retailers from provincial centers were diverting payments to Jalapa's *flotistas* instead of first satisfying their Mexico City merchant creditors.[63] Moreover *almaceneros* still fretted over *feria* rules requiring them to store goods they had ordered and had shipped at Jalapa until the end of the fair, leaving *flotista* competitors free to sell their imports first. In effect, Mexico City merchants found their capital, often sizeable sums borrowed from the colony's religious bodies, tied up in prior remittances to Cadiz to cover direct purchases, shipping costs, and, once the goods arrived at Jalapa, storage for up to a year or more, depending upon how long the *flota* stayed. A credit crunch affected both the *comercio de España* and the *comercio de Mexico.* The point is that Mexico City's *almaceneros,* rather than the provincial merchants, were key to the success or failure of Jalapa's *temporada de flotas,* where customarily they bought in large lots, either singly or, often, in consortia with fellow *almaceneros.* After all, they alone could mobilize a large volume of local capital to cover their purchases. Although both "comercios" engaged in price-fixing, it is also true that Mexico City warehousemen holding highly desirable *pesos fuertes* deliberately postponed closing their deals until the last days of the *flota,* when desperate *cargadores* and *factores* had to slash prices to minimize *rezagos,* collect specie, and sail for Cadiz. Mexico City's oligopsonists knew that although the Spanish state had established *ferias* to privilege *flotistas* from the metropole, it could not coerce them to buy what *flotistas* had brought at the prices they tried to impose on merchants in the colony.

By delaying purchases, they often forced postponement of a *flota's* return and, among other effects, raised the *flotistas'* operating expenses, since food, rent, and related expenditures invariably skyrocketed at Jalapa during the fair. In part, the strategy accounted for unsold goods *flotistas* had to dispose of after the *flota* departed. As a consequence, in 1772, Jalapa retained over a million pesos' worth of *rezagos,* including merchandise unloaded from the earlier flota of 1765; meanwhile, colonial administrators had to expand the period of the fair, undermining the original principle that sailing schedules alone determine the length of a *flota's* stay, the *temporada.*[64] Unpredictable shifts in consumer preferences also resulted in *rezagos.* New Spain's wholesale and retail traders in the capital and provincial centers had to select items from *flotistas'* assortments according to what they thought colonial consumers might find fashionable. There was never a guarantee, a "regla fija," that all *flota* merchandise would sell equally well. A combination of factors—changing consumer tastes and a growing volume of shipments from Cadiz exporters—were eroding many of the advantages of managed trade. Moreover, the fact that certain imports enjoyed a justified reputation for durability and utility was no longer an assurance that new items would not displace them, especially given new smuggled goods. Consumer vagaries and aggressive merchandisers were already at the core of commercial speculation.

What produced a major break with *flota* ground rules was Madrid's decision in 1772 to authorize the transfer from Jalapa of all items sold before the end of the *temporada de la feria*. This promised to reduce inventories at Jalapa; and it led both the Cadiz and Mexico City merchant communities to petition the metropolitan authorities for further state intervention "to control and set the volume of *flotas* to avoid misuse and disorder so characteristic until the present"—in short, to lower the volume of exports to New Spain.[65] Madrid's new strategy for handling the overhang of imports at the conclusion of the Jalapa fair was aggressively implemented by Miguel de Goyeneche, who disembarked from the *flota* of 1772 as *factor* of Madrid's Compañía General de Comercio, formed with capital from Madrid's Cinco Gremios Mayores, to supervise the sale of silks and hats produced in manufactories established and subsidized by the Spanish state.

Goyeneche's litigation at Mexico City illuminates the link between state economic policy and empire in America. In 1757, when *flotas* to New Spain were resumed, the Spanish government realized that the woolen mills it had planned, financed, constructed, and now operated at Guadalajara, San Fernando, and Brihuega were markedly underperforming.[66] These enterprises exemplified early vertical integration, from dyestuff cultivation to marketing finished products, but their output was uncompetitive in terms of price and, in many instances, in quality and style.[67] Furthermore, the government also operated silk and hat mills at Madrid and Valencia, employing up to 3,000 workers and as many as 250 looms in the late 1760s. State officials then turned to the private sector, to the Cinco Gremios Mayores, a wealthy corporate body grouping Madrid's principal artisanal and commercial guilds, upon which the Spanish government relied for tax-farming and financing the public debt. The Cinco Gremios could mobilize members' capital as well as funds deposited by both individual investors and religious and lay corporations.

Confronting mounting costs and inventory backups, Madrid officials urged the Cinco Gremios to take over management and related costs of the state-owned and -operated mills. Significantly, government officials by-passed the Cadiz merchant community, doubtless because the ministry rec-ognized that the trade center was dominated by foreigners far more inter-ested in reexporting their national products than Spain's. Or did Madrid put its faith in the few economic nationalists among the members of the Cinco Gremios?

Madrid's solution for the large inventory of state-produced woolens was typical of a colonial power: it chose to continue to dump metropolitan prod-ucts in presumably unsophisticated, captive colonial markets. The contract of 1757 between the state and the Compañía General de Comercio stipulated that every convoyed merchant vessel would carry a minimum of 250 bolts (*piezas*) of woolens from state-owned mills, and that every convoy include one vessel (of 400–500 tons burden) of the Compañía General laden with such woolens made price-competitive by exemption from export duties, maritime freight charges, and colonial sales taxes. Article 24 specified the details and the bureaucratic vision of the colonial economy, "since the col-onies were major consumers of Spanish manufactures, and the woolen mer-chants' Gremio complained of sales problems of merchandise shipped on government account—despite many duty and fee exemptions." To further stimulate overseas sales, the state exempted from "sales taxes woolens shipped from Spain, to facilitate consumption."[68]

In 1772, the Compañía General shipped a large consignment of silks and hats from state manufactories on the *flota,* but by then colonial demand for them had fallen off. Because this convoy also carried English calicoes (mis-labeled as Catalan) and French linens valued in millions of pesos, shipping 2 million pesos of Spanish-made woolens, hats, and silks on it was inop-portune.[69] At Jalapa's *temporada,* sales stayed sluggish month after month, and Goyeneche, who oversaw the Cinco Gremio's shipments, soon learned that ever since 1757, the "least preferred" products (as he put it), those of Spain's state-owned mills, had not sold well in New Spain. Reluctant to abandon his shipment unsold and return to Spain, Goyeneche insisted that Viceroy Bucareli free his goods from the required "retention in the small town of Jalapa" and permit him to accompany them to the capital to ar-range sales exempted from the sales tax.[70] To buttress his case, he produced an order from Madrid authorizing him to "move into New Spain's interior provinces and reside wherever convenient as long as necessary."[71] It is plau-sible that Goyeneche was simultaneously pursuing a kind of class action in behalf of the *flotistas* and their goods, and that Madrid officials for their part were testing Mexico City *almaceneros* to see how changes might be made to privilege peninsular interests in the *temporada de la feria.*[72]

Goyeneche based his petition on a Madrid *cédula* issued virtually to coincide with the departure from Cadiz of the 1772 *flota* for Veracruz, designed, at least on the face of it, to limit how long a convoy's imports had to remain at Jalapa. It was a meliorist measure typical of Spain's old regime. Viceroy Bucareli incorporated the new rules in his edict (*bando*) of August 1772 covering the arrival at Veracruz of the 1772 convoy, but elaborated them in a fashion perhaps never intended by Madrid. In his interpretation, once both deputations concurred that 80 percent of the *feria*'s imports by value had been sold, he could authorize "shipment from Jalapa into the interior of merchandise sold by *flotistas* from Spain, as well as those [items] ordered by residents of this kingdom directly from Cadiz and brought by a *flota*." Inventories, which would have to list every major unsold item, its price, quality, and ownership, would remain at Jalapa until all items were sold; the duration of the *feria*—regardless of the *flota*'s departure for Spain—was fixed at twelve months; and only then could *flotistas* market their unsold goods through agents in the capital or provinces. Last, once the twelve-month period had passed, all sales would be subject to sales and other taxes at Jalapa.[73] It was a carrot-and-stick approach to lowering the ongoing friction between the *comercio de España* and the *comercio de México*.

Madrid's intentions were clear: on the one hand, to pressure Mexico City's wholesalers to buy from *flotistas* at Jalapa by encouraging them to remove their purchases before the expiration of the *feria;* on the other, to induce *flotistas* to sell to the colony's *vecinos* before sales and other taxes became effective there. Goyeneche, and behind him the *comercio de España,* wanted a more flexible interpretation of Madrid's *cedula:* to allow a viceroy to authorize *flotistas* to leave the fair grounds with their unsold merchandise in order to deal directly with buyers in the capital or towns of the interior. Ultimately, Bucareli accepted an accommodation offered by Mexico City's Audiencia: unsold imports brought by *flotistas* could under no circumstance be moved from Jalapa, a prohibition covering those ordered by Mexico City *almaceneros* too. Still, Madrid and Bucareli had yielded concessions: both *flotistas* and *almaceneros* were free to dispatch their sold items from Jalapa at some agreed-upon point prior to the termination of the twelve-month *feria*. Moreover, after drawn-out litigation, Goyeneche received permission to accompany his unsold imports for sale at Mexico City. And since Bucareli's decision, based upon the Audiencia's recommendation, might establish a troublesome precedent for future *ferias,* he forwarded the case to Madrid for ultimate resolution—the classic formula for shaping metropolitan directives to colonial reality.[74]

The Last Phase: Ulloa's *Flota*

The veteran naval officer Antonio de Ulloa, who commanded the last *flota* to Veracruz in 1776, limited himself to describing Veracruz and Jalapa, avoiding any comment on Spain's *flota*-and-*feria* system, which seemed by the mid 1770s to have weathered the pressures on it. While there was conflict, there also was accommodation. Besides, those who might have sought the system's total overhaul or even elimination—perhaps among undercapitalized merchants at Cadiz and in the interior of New Spain, or small-scale Catalan wine and brandy merchant-exporters—did not seem persuasive.[75]

Born at Sevilla in 1716, the son of a bureaucrat and economist, Ulloa was no stranger to Spain's American colonies.[76] In 1730, at the age of fourteen, he had shipped on a convoy to Portobelo, and in 1734, as a member of the first class of naval cadets trained at Sevilla's naval academy, he was posted to Peru, along with his fellow naval officer Jorge Juan. Formally, they were to participate in a scientific expedition led by Charles-Marie de La Condamine;[77] in fact, Madrid dispatched them to report on the political and economic situation of the extended viceroyalty of Peru, where they were to remain until 1746. An aseptic version of their survey of that vast viceroyalty appeared with government approval in 1748.[78] Ulloa's subsequent "Discurso y reflexiones políticas sobre el estado presente de los reynos del Peru," a remarkable and uncomfortably detailed critique of colonial administration and economy in the viceroyalty, drafted at the request of Ensenada, was designed for the government's internal use only, since in his own words, "this reserved material" should not be published, lest it recall (and give credence to) Bartolomé de Las Casas's denunciations in the sixteenth century, "which have so discredited us."[79]

For decades, Ulloa's "Discurso" circulated in manuscript among personnel in the Consejo de Indias and other Madrid bureaus. Competent, reliable, and ever discreet, Ulloa later served in colonial administration, first as director of Peru's corruption-ridden Huancavelica mercury mine, where he failed to stop collusion between colonial bureaucrats and mining contractors, later as governor of Louisiana.[80] During his residence in Peru, he inevitably became aware of widespread illegal commercial practices; at Lima, he became a "grand ami" of Marc Cabanes, the agent of an influential French Huguenot firm at Cadiz, Cayla, Solier, Cabanes, Jugla et Cie. Abbé Raynal learned much about Peru's trade from Jacques Jugla at Cadiz; and we know that Ulloa's Peruvian wife placed family funds with this French merchant house for investment in colonial trading operations.[81] At the age of sixty, when he brought out the 1776 convoy, Ulloa was a cosmopolitan, observant career naval officer. Like Campomanes, he was leery of attacking "abuses, as well as the people . . . responsible for them [which] are linked together."[82] As a reformer, however discreet, Ulloa had been burnt too often.

Ulloa's 1776 convoy was the second largest in volume since convoys to Veracruz had resumed in 1757, and possibly the most valuable ever—estimates range from 19.6 to from 28 to 32, or even 40, million pesos.[83] Regardless of complaints about the unsold merchandise of previous *flotas*, Asian imports via Acapulco, and goods smuggled from Caribbean islands, Cadiz merchants still shipped large amounts of non-Spanish merchandise to New Spain in response to its rising mining production, increasing monetization, and demographic growth. So eager were Cadiz's *cargadores* to participate in Ulloa's convoy that they managed to get Madrid's approval to add more merchant vessels to his *flota*.[84] Cadiz's optimism, or simply blind faith, contrasts with that of the *almaceneros* of Mexico City, who had appealed to Madrid in 1776 to authorize only one convoy every three years, with a maximum of 4,000 tons of dry goods, reserving 10 percent of the cargo by value for merchandise ordered by them.

Curiously, Ulloa's letters from Veracruz to Viceroy Bucareli do not resonate with the tension between the two oligopolistic *comercios*. His aim was pragmatic. "What I would like to do is carry away a lot of silver," he said bluntly.[85] Cadiz's *consulado* and Spain's elite could scarcely have disagreed with that aspiration.

Actually, the candor of Ulloa's letters from Veracruz to Bucareli at Mexico City reflected bonds of background and career experience. Both were Andalusian: Bucareli's family ranked among the largest estate owners in that province, and some of its members invested in Cadiz's colonial trades. Both had colonial experience: Ulloa in the viceroyalty of Peru, then in Louisiana, Bucareli as captain-general of Cuba (1765–71), then viceroy of New Spain as of 1771. Both owed key career appointments to Spanish figures notable for their dedication to *renovación:* Ulloa to Ensenada, Bucareli to Esquilache, whom he respected and admired. (In a letter to the banished Esquilache from Havana in 1768, Bucareli concluded: "Consider me your true and grateful Friend, wherever and whenever . . ."）[86]

Ulloa was committed to the success of the *feria* system, which he never questioned. Like most Spanish colonial officials, he held a dim view of the physical and mental capacity of the colonial peoples of Spanish America, whether Amerindian, African, or Creole, and was convinced that they had a natural propensity for malpractice. His colonialist attitude emerges in comments about Veracruz, where he spent most of the extended period of eighteen months during which the *flota* remained in port.[87] The climate of the Caribbean, especially the brilliant sun (and heat) of the Veracruz coast, weakened both flora and fauna, he felt, producing animals and humans lacking "the strength to match their vitality." For example, in New Spain, he found six draft animals doing the work of what in Spain would require only two oxen. Similarly, the inhabitants of the colony lacked the endurance to sustain "regular concentration on mental activity," whether by day or night. If forced to great mental concentration, an individual's health suffered. This applied to both resident Europeans and Creoles; at home, he was sure, Europeans were capable of "double or triple the mental activity" of those in the colonial world.[88]

The residents of Veracruz—Ulloa found its population surprisingly small—were divided into whites, including both Creoles and resident Spaniards, blacks, and other people of *color.* Some white families had respectable fortunes, and Ulloa speculated as to how they had achieved them. They generally began as shopkeepers (*pulperos*) dealing in local items, he found, then branched out to handle both colonial goods and some imports until, with luck and diligence, they became respected merchants marked by wealth and credit—a pattern, he recalled from colonial experience in Peru, that is "the same in most colonial ports." Nonetheless, Veracruz's few wealthy families, he conceded, lived unostentatiously: only six or eight had their own carriages; the rest used public vehicles to visit outlying areas.[89]

Overall, Ulloa found Veracruz unappealing. One might have expected a port known worldwide for the "treasures" it exported to be "beautiful, large, wealthy, and populous," but rather it gave the impression of being one of those "impoverished cities lacking a large, profitable trade." Its location, surrounded by sand hills, was unfavorable, Ulloa admitted, and it lacked gardens or kitchen plots. Its buildings were dark-stained, unimposing, and totally devoid of "sumptuousness" and "grandeur." The few large ones were designed less for permanent residence than as temporary quarters for ship captains, *cargadores,* and *factores,* and as warehouses for their goods.

Recent street paving, Ulloa commented with faint praise, might reduce the incidence of yellow fever, which normally coincided with the fall season, when Europeans disembarked from convoys. However, he could not find a reliable chart of the port itself "all the more deplorable since so many *flota* commanders have come here and regulations prescribe the preparation of one, [but] no one has bothered to do so."[90] In sum, although "the substantial commerce at that city provides large profits," its people did not match up to its wealth.[91]

Certain colonial institutions did inspire praise, however, and he singled out two in particular for their public utility. The Franciscan church and monastery had long assumed responsibility for providing last rites and burial for the crews of convoys and *registros;* in return, crewmen offered contributions, which were assessed at meetings chaired by the convoy commander, with the participation of the Sevilla seamen's association, the *universidad de mareantes.* Royal naval personnel maintained their small hospital in a rented residence. Both institutions served Veracruz's transient rather than permanent residents.

Ulloa was surprised to find Veracruz hardly an emporium in the European mode, despite the enormous wealth in goods and silver flowing through it. It was merely a funnel, he said, "a point of transit where everything passes." "This city is world-renowned for the treasures it has exported to Spain, but they are not matched by what Veracruz's capacity, wealth, and people should be."[92] Its activity oscillated with the arrival, stay, and departure of convoys. There were no manufacturing establishments. For the proprietors of large residences, rental income was important, since they leased their buildings to ship captains, *cargadores,* and *flotistas,* as well as to those arriving from the interior of the colony to make their purchases. By no measure was Veracruz a self-sufficient enclave ("it produces nothing"), for subsistence needs linked it to the surrounding countryside. Water as well as food came by muleback and cart from Antigua Veracruz, Alvarado, and Tlacotalpan, and from truck farms more than a league away. The local beef, like the cattle it came from, lacked "sustancia" and flavor, but there was a plentiful supply of game, delivered daily, and considerable consumption of local alcoholic beverages like aguardiente. And there were daily boatloads of maize, eggs, yucca, bananas, and pork unloaded at Veracruz in exchange for imported olives, olive oil, brandy, and small lots of European textiles.

The roads leading from Veracruz to Jalapa and beyond were poor, especially in the period from March to November. Then winds from the south and southwest brought torrential rains, roads became impassable, and the ground, according to Ulloa, "exhaled vapors," to which he ascribed fevers and other ailments. In summer, clouds of mosquitoes forced residents to seek protection under netting even during daylight hours. Dry weather came with the onset of winds from the north, Veracruz's notorious *nortes,* which often reached gale force ("nowhere else are they as steady and violent") and were dangerous to vessels moored in the port. But they also helped dry out the city and countryside.[93]

These observations prefaced brief remarks about commerce at Veracruz. Ulloa was impressed by the bustle and confusion when the *flota* was in port, first the unloading of goods "at the height of summer under extremely hot sunlight and sudden squalls," and much later, the phase of embarking colonial silver and valuable primary products, trekked in by streams of mule trains transporting "los tercios de plata," along with indigo and cochineal, for Cadiz. Over poor roads and worse bridges, imported goods were carried to "the finest fair in the world" at Jalapa, locus of the exchange of European imports for the colony's silver, gold, indigo, cochineal, vanilla, hides, and sarsaparilla. Jalapa's climate, Ulloa found, made it an ideal site, removed from the miasmas and epidemics of Veracruz. Its buildings, like those of Veracruz, were undistinguished, but ample for storing *flota* imports.[94] In contrast to the monotonous sand hills of Veracruz, Jalapa had forests, open fields, and a backdrop of the mountains of New Spain's eastern cordillera, dominated by the peak of Orizaba. Its population, too, differed from that of Veracruz, including white Spaniards and Creoles, a few wealthy families among them, and many mestizos and Amerindians, but few blacks or mulattoes. The muleteers (*arrieros*) responsible for the flow of goods from central Mexico through the fair town to Veracruz were Amerindians.

In the fall of 1777, Ulloa began preparation for his *flota*'s return to Cadiz via Havana. Earlier that year, he had reported that sales at Jalapa were sluggish, but he remained optimistic; "Let's see if they pick up next month as *flotistas* hope . . . they bemoan the buyers who want to settle their accounts only when the next *flota* is due, which makes them reluctant to sell."[95] Mexico City's *almaceneros* continued to postpone closing deals with anxious *flotistas,* and in September, Viceroy Bucareli decided to intervene by ordering Ulloa's *flota* to postpone its departure. This "most appropriate ruling," the relieved *flotistas* wrote to their representative in Mexico City, Domingo de Lardizábal, "has removed a worry from our commerce . . . and we trust that when the time to sail arrives, many buyers will come down [to Veracruz] bringing cash and credit to cover at least most of our stock of fine goods." Ultimately, New Spain's numerous *mercaderes viandantes,* petty traveling tradesmen who peddled small, artfully selected lots of imported as well as local products to low- and middle-income consumers in hundreds of New Spain's rural hamlets, proved to be "this *feria*'s best resource."[96] Ulloa too greeted the viceroy's decision to delay his *flota*'s sailing date for three months, from October to January 1778, with relief; Bucareli had "raised the spirits of both trades, which were so depressed and dispirited."[97]

Meanwhile, the British government's efforts to suppress the American Revolution, and the presumption that sooner or later, France and Spain would openly support it, made Madrid anxious about a surprise attack by English naval forces upon Ulloa's returning *flota* and its extraordinarily valuable silver cargo. Prime Minister Grimaldi worried about going to war without prior warning to Spanish shipping in colonial ports. "We are awaiting the *flota*'s return . . . we risk enormous losses in the opening months of hostilities," he noted, and he recommended dispatching warning notices to America.[98] The authorities in Madrid foresaw the repercussions of the English defeat at Saratoga, for in mid November 1777, Grimaldi gloated to Bucareli, "according to all reports, the English have had their heads bashed; it's considered a decisive action."[99] In addition, Colonial Secretary Gálvez wrote Ulloa that Charles III "hopes you will sail as soon as possible," and by December, Ulloa resolved to depart Veracruz on 15 January, estimating that he would arrive at Havana three weeks later and at Cadiz in early April. Meanwhile, by circulating sailing notices to New Spain's major provincial centers, Ulloa ensured that the flow of silver and other outbound cargo down to the Caribbean coast at Veracruz would accelerate in order to complete loading the returning convoy vessels on schedule. He fretted, however, over the "ridiculously insignificant amount of money registered at the last minute . . . we can't estimate precisely the volume of treasure to be carried by the *flota*."[100] Ulloa knew precisely what Cadiz and Madrid wanted.

Ulloa's spirits fluctuated with the rate of silver flowing into Veracruz for export. In early January, he was complaining about the delays in loading silver, which he blamed upon the "sluggishness and apathy of the supercargoes in charge of registering silver to be loaded," yet only days later he exulted that in one 12-hour loading period, all the chests available, filled with 5.5 million silver pesos, had been put aboard two warships, a sum subsequently raised to 8 million pesos.[101]

Once he had arrived at Havana with his convoy intact, Ulloa delayed departure for Cadiz, fearing a surprise by English naval forces. Ever cautious, he decided to change his route to Cadiz "to proceed safely," and without warning he proceeded to take the *flota* across the Atlantic by the southern (and longer) route via the Canaries, where he arrived "short of water, food and daily rations."[102] Between Tenerife in the Canaries and Cadiz, he encountered small Spanish vessels that had been on station for two months to warn him of the approach of any English naval squadrons, and by mid July, his convoy had anchored in Cadiz's harbor. Now he wrote Bucareli regretting that he had not delayed his departure from Veracruz to take aboard even more silver. "In any event," he could write with satisfaction, "the *flota* has been the largest and most important ever to have returned." Ulloa had convoyed into Cadiz probably most of the 30.6 million pesos exported from Veracruz in 1778—5.8 million on government account alone—and could justifiably claim that "a luckier *flota* has never arrived at Cadiz, nor [one] as long at sea, nor [one] as rich, nor [one] so anticipated."[103]

A grateful Spanish state, soon to join France in open support of the

American Revolution against England, welcomed the skilled convoy commander. In mid August, six months after his *flota* had cleared Veracruz homeward bound, Ulloa wrote from Spain to Bucareli that "the people at court have overwhelmed me with congratulations, and the ministers with attention," to which he added with justification, "this is the fruit of my labors and sleepless nights; I am satisfied."[104] A naval career begun as a young officer aboard a *galeón* in convoy to the moribund Portobelo fair of 1730–32 had now closed with command of a *flota* to what still seemed Jalapa's flourishing *temporada de la feria* and its return to Cadiz intact.

There was, however, a downside, detectable in Ulloa's deliberately opaque expression of disappointment that high officials in the Floridablanca ministry had failed to debrief him about the overall situation of the colony of New Spain, a marked contrast with his return after years in the viceroyalty of Peru and discussions with Ensenada. "There have been no immediate debriefings," he commented to Bucareli from San Ildefonso in August 1778, "as were once customary; in these circumstances, I remain silent, for it's better not to say what is not asked."[105] Ulloa was oddly oblivious—at least in his otherwise candid correspondence with Viceroy Bucareli—to the fact that in February, just before his return to the Peninsula, Madrid had extended the pattern of *comercio libre,* originally limited to the Caribbean area in 1765, to Buenos Aires and the ports of Peru and Chile. It is hard to believe that Ulloa had not learned from *flotistas* at Jalapa in October 1777, months before he left Veracruz, of the "dread affecting everyone's spirits, that they are considering free trade for the Americas, which dismays both trades."[106]

6. The Second Reglamento del Comercio Libre (1778)

The Atlantic economy to which the young Ulloa was first exposed in the 1730s had changed dramatically by the 1770s when the mature Ulloa brought his extraordinarily valuable convoy safely into the Bay of Cadiz. Both shores of the Atlantic were now in a phase of rapid expansion. Europe's exports of manufactures were matched by a corresponding rise in raw materials and precious metals exports from Spain's New World colonies, expanding the base of unequal exchange between Europe and its colonial periphery, which in the nineteenth century would emerge as the international division of labor. In the eighteenth century, this "colonial pact" was hardly questioned, because it seemed naturally and mutually beneficial. As a result, the requirements of the English and French colonial economies in the Caribbean (the "West Indies") in the 1760s induced London to formulate its Freeport system to attract merchants from nearby Spanish possessions, and Paris to open its colonies to trade with all French ports, as well as with England's North American colonies.[1]

In the Spanish sector of the Atlantic system in the last third of the century, the potential for overall growth through diversification by adding the agricultural and ranching export economies of Cuba, Venezuela, and the

Rio de la Plata to the mining complexes of New Spain and Peru was probably greater than in the Spanish metropole itself—ultimately justifying Madrid's decision to choose the colonial option. In the silver-mining centers of New Spain and Upper Peru, output was rising and population recovery was evident, as was increased agricultural production for internal consumption and intercolonial trade (encouraged by Madrid after the early 1770s). To Spanish analysts, growth in Cuba's trade and Catalonia's exports to that colony after about 1765 (and even earlier) pointed to what an extensive reform in the Spanish transatlantic trading system might generate. Accompanying colonial economic growth came the diffusion of monetization—the process of incorporating Indian and mestizo consumers and producers into the European market economy by drawing upon their liking for Spanish wine and brandy, European linens, woolens, silks, cottons, laces, and hardware—including, it was hoped, Spanish textiles, when available. Symptomatic of the appearance of these new colonial consumers was the move to eliminate the *reparto de mercancías,* a form of forced commercialization of colonial peoples that had long been an aspect of the economies of New Spain and Peru.

In effect, by the 1770s, the Spanish transatlantic economy was outgrowing the constraints of the convoy system, which had been refurbished a little in 1720 (with the addition of the Jalapa fair), then suspended in 1739, and revived only for New Spain in 1757. When Madrid introduced new taxes—*toneladas* and *palmeo*—on colonial trade in 1720 and systematized the accumulation of duties ("Santelmo, extrangería, visitas, reconocimiento de carenas, habilitaciones, licencias para navegar") to some extent, the objective was fiscal, not developmental. Fifty years later, fiscal needs remained paramount, but the intention of Madrid policy-makers in the 1770s was to broaden the tax base by a developmentalist strategy, first applied to the metropole and then, once Esquilache's *renovación* had been stalled, redirected primarily to the colonial world. Colonial trade became the engine of peninsular growth for many governmental and private sector analysts.[2]

The Spanish state was reacting to a variety of pressures to adjust its secular patterns of trade between Peninsula and colonies. Agricultural and commercial interests developing in peripheral Spain were now impatient to break into the colonial trading enclave so long the monopoly of Andalusian interests, first at Sevilla and then, in the eighteenth century, at Cadiz. They were irked too by the few surviving privileged trading companies, notably the Havana and Guipuzcoan companies. In Galicia, Asturias, the *montañas* of Burgos, the Basque provinces, and Catalonia—provinces characterized by marked population growth, proliferating medium and small landholdings, by primary education for males, and by a pervasive peasant mentality of work, saving, and community and family responsibility—people wanted direct commercial contact with the more prosperous American colonies, to which many were called by relatives, and whence flowed back financial support to individuals and communities. Catalan producers of wine and brandy, along with merchants and shipowners, were among the first in peripheral Spain to take advantage of opportunities emerging in Cuba's sugar sector, many even before the advent of *comercio libre* of 1765.[3] To be sure, Cadiz continued to attract the lion's share of a growing pool of domestic savings in private and ecclesiastical hands, as well as French capital managed by resident French merchant houses. Nonetheless, there remained savings that merchants in Santander and La Coruña, Barcelona, Alicante, Málaga, and Cartagena also hoped to tap for their colonial commercial enterprises.

The Debate over Managed Trade to New Spain

Such regional pressures upon commercial structures long dominated by the enclave of Cadiz interests reinforced the state's policy of raising the volume of colonial revenue while broadening peninsular participation in colonial exchanges. They account for Esquilache's decision in 1765 to send José de Gálvez as *visitador general* (inspector-general) to New Spain to carry out a broad inquiry into the shortcomings of its fiscal management.

Gálvez had been broadly sensitive to colonial problems long prior to being selected as *visitador*, and his service in New Spain gave him a hands-on grasp of its economy. It also confirmed the key role of Mexico City's commercial establishment, which he was aware of even before sailing from Cadiz. When he was subsequently appointed colonial secretary in 1775 after the death of Julián de Arriaga, Gálvez took office prepared to address a broad spectrum of colonial issues in trade, mining, and administration. Moreover, he was no isolated figure. His outlook and policies mirrored regional demands for development in metropolitan Spain, as well as the views expressed in manuscripts and publications by bureaucrats and businessmen: civil servants like Pedro Rodríguez Campomanes, Tomás Ortiz de Landázuri, and Fernando Magallón; prominent commercial entrepreneurs like Juan Antonio de los Heros; and—not least—the French-born banker Francisco Cabarrús. Meanwhile, the new prime minister, José Moñino (later conde de Floridablanca), tolerated a climate of intellectual thaw, or *apertura,* in which associations of local notables, such as Madrid's Royal Economic Society and those of Cantabria and Guipúzcoa, figured prominently. Typically, the state subsidized the mildly critical publications of Campomanes, Floridablanca's close collaborator and a leading member of the Consejo de Castilla—notably, his landmark *Memorial ajustado* on agrarian reform and his revision of Bernardo Ward's *Proyecto económico* manuscript (1762). And although those of a profoundly critical spirit, like León de Arroyal in the 1780s, would scarcely have found it a heady time, it was nonetheless an era far more tolerant of "responsible" proposals for cautiously calibrated adjustments to domestic and international pressures than the controlled ambience preceding the accession of Charles III in 1759 had been.

Equally influential in forcing policy changes upon Madrid was the renewed emphasis given to the colonial dimension by Gálvez's appointment. He left Veracruz for Spain in late 1771, before the arrival of the 1772 convoy and the sustained legal maneuvering of the Cinco Gremios Mayores' agent, Miguel de Goyeneche, to counter the merchants of the Consulado de México, who had sharpened the decades-old conflict between Cadiz's *flotistas* and Mexico City's *almaceneros*. The issue was not new to Gálvez, who in the late 1750s had drafted an unsolicited and career-enhancing think piece rehearsing the major issues requiring state intervention in New Spain. In his "Discurso y reflexiones," he gave extended coverage to trade ("the heart of the issue on which Spain's prosperity depends") and—presumably on the basis of contacts with French merchants at Cadiz—to what he termed the "opposition of the merchants of Cadiz and the colonies."[4] Subsequent residence in New Spain had sensitized him to the techniques Mexico City merchants applied to Cadiz's *cargadores* and *encomenderos* during the protracted Jalapa fair bargaining in order to purchase on terms they could dictate, and neither did Galvez minimize the prominent investment role of Mexico's *almaceneros* in financing silver-mining operations. Furthermore, confining the sale of *flota*-borne imports to Jalapa enhanced the leverage of Mexico City's large-scale merchants over the many medium- and small-scale provincial distributors of imports. The *oposición*, Galvez recognized, required resourceful handling, since the metropole relied heavily upon New Spain's silver production, just as it depended upon the multiple roles of the trading communities at Cadiz and Mexico City.

Like other Madrid bureaucrats, Gálvez had to balance peninsular and colonial interests, Cadiz and Mexico City. He was ambivalent: although he wrote from Mexico City in 1766 that Madrid had to "to block the schemes of Mexico's *almazeneros* and other merchants for damaging the interests of *flotistas*" and that all the convoys to Veracruz (that of 1729 excepted) had been commercial failures, he could be equally critical of the Cadiz trading community for forcing the resumption of *flotas* in 1757 by corralling the "support of others registered for the *carrera de Indias*." No one, he insisted, could "without dismay see our colonial traders dammed up at Cadiz, the Peninsula's most expensive port."[5]

The volume and value of *flotas* to New Spain signaled that the colony's import capacity continued to outstrip Cadiz's managed supply mechanisms, thereby providing an incentive for smuggling along New Spain's Gulf coast north and south of Veracruz and reducing the metropole's potential income from colonial customs duties and sales taxes. Both convoys and Jalapa fair had outlived their purpose, it seemed, and to critics like Gálvez, traditional colonial trade controls had turned counterproductive. The limits to trade growth were two clusters of oligopoly: Cadiz, dominated by Spanish and foreign (largely French) merchants and their shippers and dependents, and Mexico City, where a coterie of Spanish-born *almaceneros* controlled the circulation of goods and financed the colony's mine owners. Oligopoly, by limiting shipping between Spain and its colonies, whether in convoys or *registros sueltos,* inhibited competitive shipping, kept ocean freight rates artificially high, discouraged handling high-volume but low-value agricultural products of both the metropole and the colonies, and—an eyesore to Spanish proto-nationalists—nourished a well-financed foreign commercial enclave at Cadiz. On this point, Gálvez's sentiments were clear. He wrote Prime Minister Grimaldi from Mexico City that foreigners (he had to mean the French) were the real proprietors of a large percentage of the merchandise sent to the colonies from Cadiz, "leaving in our country only insignificant commissions as well as losses incurred by forced sales that shipowners must make to push sales." And he continued: "There are so many who survive by lending their names to cover foreigners and by working for them just to earn their daily bread."[6] Moreover, Gálvez, former legal counselor of the French embassy at Madrid and lawyer for French firms at Cadiz, was no francophobe.

The encouraging response of the Cuban economy captured the attention of, and heartened, Madrid policy-makers and businessmen once that island (along with Santo Domingo and Puerto Rico) had been opened to direct trade with nine metropolitan ports by *comercio libre* in 1765. Havana promised to fulfill overseas the predictions of those who believed that a less managed, more open imperial trading system might activate Spain's peripheral provinces and colonies; they were also encouraged by Catalans who grasped opportunities to export wine, brandy, and manufactures—even prefabricated coffins—to Havana, which reciprocated with sugar.[7] Long a proponent of fewer imperial trade barriers, Campomanes found Catalonia exemplifying "the progress that an active colonial trade promises to Spain," and his multivolume *Apéndice a la educación popular,* circulated with a government subsidy in 1775–77, expressly included data on Cuba's external trade.[8] So rapidly had Havana's trade expanded that its customshouse could not handle the upsurge. With considerable hyperbole, some marveled at Havana's "brilliant splendor" after 1765, when the flow of imports turned the port into a "general storehouse of goods and provisions" at surprisingly moderate prices compared to the monopoly pricing of the Companía de la Habana.[9] With an extension of *comercio libre* to the rest of the American empire looming in mid 1778, the banker Francisco Cabarrús reminded Madrid's influential Royal Economic Society how direct trade with Havana had transformed Catalonia into "an industrious province" by providing a colonial outlet for its "factories and agriculture."[10] He minced no words about the threat to Cadiz, where "they are removing the fetters of monopoly." Years later, Mexico City's *fiscal* Lorenzo Hernández de Alba, among other observers of the colonial scene, would recall his astonishment when serving at Havana at the "evident improvement in the [Caribbean] islands, their population, agriculture, and exports."[11]

Despite optimistic assessments of the likely results of the 1765 statute, Catalan merchants trading directly with Havana and other Spanish windward islands noted shortcomings. In practice, they discovered that textile goods—woolens, linens, silks—shipped aboard a *flota* from Cadiz to Veracruz paid an effective exit duty of only 2.12 percent; yet similar items shipped from Barcelona to Havana were dutied at 6 percent, or 7 percent, if of non-Spanish origin. Moreover, on entry at Havana, Barcelona's exports were burdened with aggregate duties of 27 percent; on the other hand, when Cuba's staples reached Barcelona, they paid only 11 percent. These disparities, Barcelona merchants argued, supported by Intendant Joseph Castaños, were an incentive to smugglers. Pleading protection for their infant industries, they petitioned for a 5 percent duty on reexports of foreign items.[12] It is entirely plausible, of course, that Catalan exporters exaggerated the inequities of duty schedules at Barcelona and colonial ports to reinforce their plea for tariff protection.

Predictably, discordant views also came from the Cadiz community, arguing that Catalan products were cheaper at Havana because Catalan shipping under *comercio libre* regulations paid no *tonelada* fee, that few financial backers in Spain would venture their capital in the Cuban trade from Barcelona under existing conditions, and that Havana's prosperity under *comercio libre* would be short-lived. Cabarrús would later extol the effects of 1765 upon the Cuban economy, but the Cadiz *consulado* insisted that the proverbially penny-pinching Catalans profited from shipping between Barcelona and Havana solely because they hired small crews, provided "miserable" rations, and adhered to an "extraordinaria economía" that no other Spanish province would apply. It remained convinced that Spain's trade with other American colonies necessitated larger ships and crews, along with officers recruited elsewhere in the Peninsula.[13]

Meanwhile, other critics traced the upsurge in Cuba's external trade to one factor alone, smuggling reexports to New Spain. One source estimated that 50 percent of the 8 million pesos' worth of goods annually imported by New Spain from the metropole were, in fact, Havana reexports.[14] Testily, others dismissed Cadiz's dissent as an expression of "the barely concealed, personal interest of some who are unenlightened, and the maxim of leaving matters just as they are, as our ancestors sang." But few dared openly contest the lobbying tactics of the "Guild of Shippers to the colonies, established at Cadiz, which considered that trade as its patrimony" until the state finally spelled out its position in March and October of 1778.[15]

In fact, ways of reducing the Cadiz monopoly of colonial trade were contemplated repeatedly in the 1760s and 1770s. In 1771, Tomás Ortiz de Landázuri was assigned to draft a report on how to minimize friction among traders at the Jalapa fair. Probably Madrid turned to him because he had spent sixteen years as a colonial bureaucrat in New Spain and had been *contador general* in the colonial office since 1764. It will be recalled that in that year, he had recommended suspending the convoy system to New Spain and all export duties on domestic products, and opening many peninsular and colonial ports to direct commercial contact in a report that had been utilized by the Special Junta that recommended *comercio libre* in 1765.[16] Landázuri's 1771 report reaffirmed his earlier recommendation to terminate the revived convoy system to New Spain, and he offered to draft a fuller report on request.[17]

About the same time, Mexico City's *consulado,* irked by the tie-up of its imports at Jalapa and alleging a rising volume of competitive smuggled merchandise, petitioned Madrid to cap the growing volume of imports carried by *flotas* to Veracruz. But when Madrid sought trade specifics on New Spain's consumption and preference patterns, characteristically, Mexico City failed to respond. Madrid's initiative suggests that changes once contemplated under Esquilache were still under consideration in the subsequent administrations of Aranda and his successor, Grimaldi. Finally, with the appointment of Floridablanca as prime minister and Gálvez as colonial secretary, along with government sponsorship of Campomanes's *Apéndice a la educación popular,* "filled with suggestions and convincing arguments" in favor of a liberalized imperial trade policy, the climate for further adjustments in the imperial trading system improved.[18] Furthermore, in 1776–77,

Madrid's civil servants could hardly overlook the revolution under way in England's North American colonies, where colonials were rejecting London's commercial and fiscal policies. Not to mention that Spain's colonial officials had already diagnosed "Anglo-America's" westward expansion as a threat to New Spain.

Circulating in bureaucratic circles were two views of New Spain's role in the colonial trading system. Many had long believed that extending participation in colonial trade to other peninsular ports might generate metropolitan feedback, stimulating agriculture and creating an industrial base; enlarged access to New Spain's population, silver production, and agricultural exportables could implement this objective markedly. Others, however, were less sanguine about the effects of extending *comercio libre* to Spain's most populous and productive colony. Despite friction between the *comercio de España* and the *comercio de México* at Jalapa, the two oligopolistic blocs preferred managed trade (*comercio arreglado*). More to the point, neither set of Atlantic interests wanted to abandon the system of *flotas* and *ferias*. Mexico City's *almaceneros,* it is worth recalling, wanted the right to transmit funds to Cadiz to buy directly from suppliers there, and they objected to Cadiz's insistence that their purchases be consigned solely to *encomenderos* registered with the Cadiz *consulado* who accompanied (or used agents to accompany) their consignments across the Atlantic. Still, Mexico City's merchant elite never insisted upon building or purchasing its own oceangoing shipping. In this sense, Cadiz and Mexico had forged an economic interdependence despite complaints that the Spanish state privileged one oligopoly over the other.

There was also another, more sophisticated and, in the long run, more convincing case for preserving the *flota* system to Veracruz—or, to put it differently, for isolating New Spain from the forces reshaping Spain's Atlantic economy. An anonymous report to Gálvez shortly after he was appointed colonial secretary argued that "commercial growth is useless if it fails to improve a nation's balance of trade with other nations and may even be prejudicial if they obtain the most advantage from such a development." This was especially relevant in the case of New Spain, which was primarily an exporter of silver, on both government and private account. Silver had a fairly stable international value, and the colony's production was obviously rising. New Spain's consumers—at least those in the monetized sector—displayed a growing import capacity, which was satisfied by what everyone recognized were mainly non-Spanish reexports. Since Spanish *cargadores* at Cadiz remained short of capital and continued to finance their trading activities by borrowing from foreign residents, it was realistic to assume that

Mexico City's *almaceneros* could and would augment their direct purchasing at Cadiz. Moreover, if convoys were replaced by unscheduled but frequent *registros sueltos,* the anonymous report reasoned, Atlantic maritime freight rates would tend to fall, along with the final prices of goods entering New Spain. This might translate into higher volume but lower profit margins per unit for Cadiz exporters. However, while, over time, developing metropolitan manufactures might supply New Spain's elastic import appetite, in the immediate as well as foreseeable future, the availability of goods manufactured in Spain would remain problematic.

From this anonymous analysis flowed disheartening conclusions: inclusion of New Spain in an expanded process of *comercio libre* would result in more imports of non-Spanish origin, rising trade deficits, massive transfers abroad of colonial silver—not to mention an upsurge of colonial smuggling. Extending *comercio libre* to New Spain, a mining colony par excellence, was "in no way appropriate," because it would not "furnish the same advantages as [in the case of] predominantly agricultural colonies." This realistic analysis soon bore fruit.[19]

Comparable reservations about including New Spain in modifying the imperial trading system also surfaced in a report drafted in December 1776 by Contador General Tomás Ortiz de Landázuri of the Consejo de Indias.[20] Evidently, while supporting the broad concept of commercial innovation, Landázuri believed nonetheless in preserving the convoy system to New Spain.[21] Certainly, his relations with the Mexico City and Cadiz business communities were solid: at Mexico City, he came to know prominent merchants such as Ambrosio Meave and Juan José Martínez de Aguirre, and in Madrid, he maintained contact with the agent of the Cadiz *consulado,* Joseph de Larrarte.[22]

In 1771, when Cadiz and Mexico City businessmen complained to Madrid about the large volume of merchandise carried by convoys to New Spain and factionalism between the two competing oligopolies that seemed ineradicable, Landázuri had recommended extending the 1765 *comercio libre* statute to the colonies in South America and to New Spain, promising to elaborate his recommendation on request.[23] But once an official request materialized in 1773, he delayed three years before submitting a plan that his superior Floridablanca, along with Múzquiz and Gálvez, one may assume, intended to use as a position paper for their grand design of "broad-scale regulation of trade."

He may now have come under heavy pressure to preserve their managed trade system in toto for Cadiz and Mexico City commercial interests.[24] Hence, to minimize the predictable opposition from the "influence and maneuvers of such a trade body as the consulado de Cadiz" and the "inconvenience and hindrance that would ensue by granting it a formal hearing," the planning group avoided soliciting viewpoints from "any body or group of merchants."[25] Predictably, rumors of the *junta*'s deliberations circulated unofficially, and by September 1777, letters were arriving at Mexico City with the "bad news that Madrid is reviewing the matter of free trade for America," along with heartening assurance of opposition to its extension to New Spain. The Cadiz community through its Madrid agents had learned of the contents of position papers, including Landázuri's, that had been circulating for months among members of the Consejo de Indias.[26]

In his report (*informe*) of 1776, Landázuri recalled that over the preceding two hundred years, the Spanish state had tolerated European interests establishing control over "the main substantial activity," its colonial trade.[27] And although Madrid had reaped fiscal advantages from that trade, non-Spaniards, who were "sharper and more attentive to their real interests," had improved their manufactures, shipping, and exports during the eighteenth century "in proportion to the demand we facilitate." At this point, Landázuri's realistic analysis—surely a product of his years in New Spain—disaggregated the transatlantic trading system, whose internal logic was consistent with chronic, purposeful undersupply of shipping and goods, high operational costs, reexports rather than national exports, one privileged port, and necessarily high profit rates. The problem was that this system conflicted with the state's current obligation to spread development to many areas of the metropole, discouraged producers of high-volume but low-value agricultural exportables in both Spain and its colonies, and—most destabilizing to colony/metropole commercial relations—induced some entrepreneurs in the colonies to invest in local manufacture of woolens, silks, and cottons, which had achieved "considerable perfection." In the long run, he prophesied, "by drawing upon domestic inputs, they will not easily be kept dependent." Economic autonomy and colonialism were antithetical. Furthermore, the state policy of micromanaging the supply of exports to its colonies encouraged smuggling and the distribution of such goods to colonial consumers at prices "one-half below ours." Landázuri had not wasted his years of colonial service in New Spain.

In general, his recommendations reiterated his position in earlier *informes* of 1764 and 1771 on colonial commercial structures. Some of the most constraining features he would eliminate: Cadiz's hegemony over colonial trade, Madrid's licensing of shipping, time-consuming and expensive inspection of ships and crews, and, above all, abolition of the major provisions of the Proyecto of 1720, *tonelada* fees and dutying by cubic capacity (*palmeo*).[28] He would open all major peninsular and colonial ports to intra-imperial trade, although he conspicuously omitted Veracruz, as well as those Venezuelan ports under the jurisdiction of the Compañía Guipuzcoana. However, sailing papers would be available on demand at the port of departure, where ship captains would deposit copies of manifests and indicate their colonial port of destination. Last, since he had no confidence in the cooperation of Contratación bureaucrats, whose collusion with *cargadores* was legendary, he would shift supervision of shipping and merchandise to Gálvez's Colonial Office and its agents in colonial ports.

Behind these recommendations lay Landázuri's developmental strategy for exploiting the American colonies' rich untapped resources for the metropole's benefit. In his mildly incrementalist approach, only Spanish-built shipping could participate, manned by crews that were at least two-thirds Spanish; authorized vessels would proceed directly only to one specified colonial port, whence they were obliged to return to their metropolitan port of departure. Long exposed to colonial praxis, Landázuri could hardly overlook widespread smuggling in colonial ports and the consequent drainage of state revenue. Utilizing official data for the period 1757 to 1761, he estimated that fully one-third of the annual combined exports of New Spain, Peru, and Central America (about 12 of 35 million pesos, mainly in precious metals) leaked away to foreign ports, 4 million was retained for circulation in the colonies, leaving only 19 million pesos for the metropole.[29] To narrow the gap between the prices of legal and smuggled imports, he proposed to scale down tariff rates to favor national products over European imports and to make the tariff schedules of all peninsular ports uniform—a distortion that had helped sustain Cadiz as Spain's principal port in the eighteenth century.

Colonialist to the core, Landázuri insisted that the American colonies remain subordinate to metropolitan interests. Just as he would terminate competitive colonial textile manufactures, so he would discourage the exploitation of colonial mercury mines, as he put it candidly, "to keep those possessions dependent and encourage trade and navigation by transporting that commodity."[30] It is hardly surprising that Esquilache's administration had brought to Madrid a colonial officer of Landázuri's experience and decidedly metropolitan outlook to occupy a post of major fiscal responsibility in the Consejo de Indias.

Landázuri's *informe* of 1776 was consistent with his hope of improving colonial fiscal practices, mining, and trade. Assignment to the Zacatecas area had attuned him to its mining interests and to the fundamental role of the Spanish merchant community of New Spain not only in commerce but in mining investment. His colonial career points to identification with Mexico City's influential *almaceneros,* an identification maintained following his return to the Peninsula. At Madrid, he supported the opposition of Mexico City's *almaceneros* to Gálvez's proposal to privatize *alcabala* administration, his tactics in remodeling accounting procedures in the colonial treasury, and to Gálvez's intention to legalize the reexport of European imports from Veracruz to Yucatan and Campeche (instead, Landázuri urged prior consultation with the *consulados* of Mexico City and Cadiz).[31] And to protect the interests of Andalusian and Catalan brandy exporters, Landázuri also opposed Gálvez's plan to legalize the sale of New Spain's *chinguirito.*[32]

There were, however, inconsistencies. Landázuri remained intolerant of fiscal sloppiness in the Consejo de Indias, which he found invariably compliant with the interests of Cadiz and Mexico City businessmen. From 1765 onward, he tried to shift responsibility for auditing colonial treasury accounts from the Consejo de Indias to the more autonomous Contaduría de Indias, a shift finally approved in 1774.[33] Ever dedicated, in the mold of Esquilache and Campomanes, to making Spain's colonialism efficient and profitable to state and society, Landázuri appreciated the economic weight of New Spain—its mine owners, merchants, and growing body of consumers—in the Spanish imperial system. Consequently, in late 1776, this veteran of service in New Spain's fiscal bureaucracy would not jettison the convoy system serving that colony, a position inconsistent with one expressed in 1771.[34]

In December 1776, only months before his death, Landázuri virtually confessed to the contradictions in his position on *comercio libre* when he wrote that "while I have tried to show how prejudicial to trade the convoy system is in peacetime," other considerations still made it imperative to maintain the convoy system centered on Cadiz "while our commerce develops in the Peninsula." The metropolitan economy simply needed more time for development before terminating the *flota* system centered on Cadiz. Not only did Landázuri magnify the role of Cadiz, he exaggerated that of Andalusia's hinterland as the major exporter of wine, brandy, olives, and other products to the American colonies, clearly overlooking Catalonia's remarkable response to Cuban demand before and after 1765. This was distorting reality to make his point: it would take years, he argued, for Spanish as well as European suppliers to establish warehousing and other facilities comparable to those at Cadiz, "currently the general warehouse for all the merchants embarking for the Indies," at other peninsular ports. Only at Cadiz and nearby Puerto Santa María, San Lúcar, and Xerez, he felt, had merchants and growers acquired the expertise to operate profitably in colonial trading, know-how still lacking elsewhere in the Peninsula. Significantly, this appeared at the end of his thirty-second recommendation: until other peninsular ports developed personnel and resources to trade with New Spain "in a way similar to what is proposed for other possessions, *flotas* to New Spain and *ferias* at Xalapa or Orizaba can continue." Meanwhile, assignment of shipping to New Spain should be handled exclusively (*privativamente*) by the colonial office, a recommendation Gálvez accepted. Over the thirty-six months during which Landázuri had delayed submitting his *informe,* pressures from Cadiz and Mexico City must have been irresistible.

The *Dictamen* of the Consejo de Indias

Landázuri's *informe* was part of the renaissance of interest during the 1760s and 1770s in improving Spain's imperial trade circuits. To recapitulate: in 1771, he had offered to draft an extended analysis of what could be done in response to complaints about the volume of goods on *flotas* to New Spain, but he received no request to do so until 1773, when Madrid resolved to tackle this issue "from the bottom up."[35] It took Landázuri three years to meet this charge with a scarcely radical but influential position paper. Those three years were critical for the emergence at Madrid of fresh bureaucratic leadership convinced that priority in imperial development should go to those colonies capable of contributing most to metropolitan growth.

Pragmatism now dictated turning around Esquilache's emphasis on the priority of change in Spain itself. As we have seen, when Floridablanca replaced Prime Minister Grimaldi in 1776, he installed José de Gálvez as colonial secretary. It was both logical and appropriate to have Landázuri, a veteran of the colonial service with a flair for economic issues and an intimate knowledge of the key colony of New Spain, draft a position paper on imperial trade for review by the Consejo de Indias. In the Spanish bureaucratic tradition, Gálvez could not formally call on any one Cadiz merchant— for example, the conde de Villamar (Lorenzo Beyens y Huwin), his confidential correspondent at Cadiz—for an official position paper. Besides, this policy review had to be executed "in the strictest confidence and secrecy."[36] There was, moreover, the strong presumption that input from the Cadiz *consulado* or the Casa de Contratación would be deliberately delayed in order to postpone a decision on what was now an urgent matter.

The choice of Landázuri was deliberate. Gálvez, Floridablanca, and the cooperative finance minister, Múzquiz, must have picked him because of his colonial experience; connections, efficiency, and dedication as *contador general* of the Consejo de Indias; and respect earned even among *consejeros de*

Indias who might be critical of Landázuri's ideas, like Pedro de Rada, who nonetheless valued Landázuri's "knowledge, sound judgment, outstanding intelligence and other factors of clarity and common sense." Probably, they had learned that Landázuri had backed away from his earlier position on eliminating *flotas* and *ferias,* while still remaining critical of major defects in the transatlantic trading system: inadequate economic development of the metropole and its effect upon smuggling, a pseudomercantilist program affording little effective protectionism, high shipping costs, and the dominant role of foreign colonies at Cadiz.[37]

Nonetheless, even Landázuri's toned-down recommendations failed to win over traditionalists of the Consejo de Indias. Two of three conservative *consejeros,* José Pablo de Agüero and Rafael Antúnez y Acevedo, had long been exposed to the influence of Cadiz *flotistas,* having served in the Casa de Contratación at Cadiz until promotion to the Consejo de Indias at Madrid (Antúnez's father had also been on the Contratación's staff at Cadiz). The third, Pedro de Rada, had spent his bureaucratic career in the Colonial Office, rising to *oficial mayor* (1765–72), apparently interrupted by a brief tour of duty in the viceregal secretariat of New Spain (1766–69); in 1776, he became a *consejero de Indias.*[38] The three *consejeros* were appointed (1773–76) under the aging, stand-pat colonial secretary, Julián de Arriaga, Gálvez's predecessor. There is no reason to doubt that Cadiz had been pressuring *consejo* members, perhaps subsidizing some.

The viewpoints of the conservative *consejeros* emphasized three issues: opposition to "libertad absoluta" in colonial trade, the advantages of the much-criticized convoys and individually licensed shipping, and the utility of concentrating colonial trade at Cadiz.[39] Agüero, ex-*oidor* of the Audiencia of Santo Domingo,[40] recalled that in the sixteenth century, the participation of many peninsular ports in colonial trade had promoted "deception and harm" to customs collections; he insinuated that under the *comercio libre* of 1765, growth in Cuba's customs revenues was mainly the effect of illegal reexports from Havana to Veracruz. For his part, Antúnez was convinced that the English policy of permitting major metropolitan ports to engage in colonial trade was far less effective than the French strategy of merely lowering duties and surcharges. He referred favorably to the manuscript later attributed to Campillo and circulating among *consejeros de Indias* (he called the "Nuevo sistema" a "tratado") that recommended opening a number of peninsular ports to colonial exchanges. However, Antúnez insisted that vessels *return* to one peninsular port, Cadiz, which alone should be authorized to handle reexports of foreign goods (the major items in Cadiz's exports) to the American colonies.

All three believed that the current convoy system to New Spain, supplemented by licensed individual shipping to the Caribbean and South American colonies, was a more efficient mechanism than commonly held. They insisted that under the system of *comercio convenido* or *arreglado* (terms, incidentally, also used by the Cadiz *consulado*), merchants and shippers at Cadiz could assemble, process, and ship in two months what at other ports required two years. This managed system would continue, they believed, to balance supply and demand, leaving ample time to distribute goods to colonial mining and other centers in the interior of New Spain and collect payments in order to settle accounts in the metropole in hard currency. In their opinion, "unregulated" shipping from Spain would oversupply the colonies, drain away hard money, and expand the volume of sales on credit, always costly and often risky. They also defended the *palmeo* system of duty collection: its mix of high- and low-value goods raised the average value on which duties were collected and was more efficient in generating revenue than one based on itemized but grossly undervalued and falsely sworn to bills of lading.

What Rada, Agüero, and Antúnez were justifying was the dominant role of Cadiz in colonial trade. In their view, far from being an enclave of oligopolists, the Cadiz merchant community was a "cuerpo respetable" mobilizing capital and credit, whose warehousing facilities provided access to a wide assortment of merchandise, and that maximized its commercial techniques—in a limited sense, tenable points. Moreover, Cadiz was hardly an exclusive corporation; people from all Spain's provinces could register with its *consulado,* and their earnings, Rada, Agüero, and Antúnez took pains to point out, ultimately flowed into the other provinces of Spain. Not surprisingly, this precisely echoed the argument made by the Cadiz *consulado* when claiming responsibility (and gratitude) for the "mule teams carrying silver and gold dispatched regularly from this city to help those in the provinces of Spain, so they may share without trouble in the earnings of relatives and friends established in this and colonial ports, benefits otherwise not available if divided into many ports."[41] Rada, Agüero, and Antúnez did not deny the importance of foreign merchant houses at Cadiz, whose capital, credits, and merchandise were indispensable to the transatlantic system linking metropole to colonies. However, the current growing presence of Spanish merchants and their expanding capital base—Rada exaggerated that they could now finance a *flota* of 30 to 40 million pesos—offset foreigners' financial power. As for peninsular ports that Landázuri would open to colonial trade, the *consejeros* predicted that very few would be able to attract the capital to finance the shipment of as little as 100 tons of goods, and even then would need twelve months to accumulate this. There were other risks in spreading colonial trade throughout Spain, since most peninsular ports lacked "practical understanding, economy, and means of completing profitable" overseas commercial operations and would therefore have to tolerate the entry and dominant role of foreign firms. Finally, the three *consejeros* noted with satisfaction that Cadiz had shown over decades that it alone could mobilize financial resources that the state could rely upon to cover unexpected deficits. If Cadiz's financial capacity were weakened, they asked rhetorically, could other Spanish commercial centers replace it?

The major features, as well as the tone, of the arguments advanced by Agüero, Rada, and Antúnez—*consejeros* perhaps too long attuned to the commercial establishment controlling Spain's colonial trade—prepared the ground for their recommendations: minor simplification of shipping controls, tariff reductions, and preservation of the underpinning of the Spanish transatlantic system, convoys to Veracruz coupled to tonnage ceilings. In this sense, their disagreement with Landázuri was not as sharp as expected. Yet only one of the three *consejeros* explicitly stated his position on the principal issue. "We propose," opined one of the Cadiz establishment's strongest supporters in the Consejo de Indias, Rafael Antúnez y Acevedo, "under the new Proyecto that *flotas* continue with limited volume and that *registros sueltos* be authorized for all areas"—in short, the status quo.

Such support for the established commercial order must have surprised neither Floridablanca nor his colonial secretary, Gálvez, both of whom could recall the obstacles encountered earlier in advancing the Barlovento changes under Esquilache's ill-fated administration. The impression is that they followed bureaucratic strategies, pursuing their objective by blending the Bourbon administrative innovation of ministries with the Austrian inheritance of conciliar bodies, here the Consejo de Indias; they knew the Consejo's stand-pat majority. Their strategy included more than consultation with conservative-minded Consejo members, however; it required a well-argued, plausible dissonance within the Consejo, and this they obtained from Fernando Magallón, recently appointed *consejero,* probably at Gálvez's initiative.

Magallón brought a far more cosmopolitan background than that of his tradition-minded fellow *consejeros* to the central issue posed by Landázuri's *informe*—whether to adopt "total freedom for all the provinces and people of the Peninsula," thereby changing the way colonial trade had been maintained "solely from the Port of Cadiz."[42] During the 1760s, Magallón had served as secretary at the Paris embassy under the Aragonese conde de Fuentes, who was succeeded in 1774 by another Aragonese nobleman and fellow *militar,* the conde de Aranda. In that year, Magallón returned to Madrid as a *consejero de Indias.* Like another former embassy secretary, Bernardo de Iriarte (in London during the late 1750s), Magallón had cultivated a European perspective on his country and its problems. In his Paris years, he found the conduct of colonial trade—essentially the diffusion of capitalistic market structures—by Europe's imperialist powers his constant preoccupation when France and Spain confronted English commercial and naval expansion threatening their overseas possessions. The connection between metropolitan trade policy and colonial instability was obvious; Magallón insisted that now was the strategic moment to examine that relationship, given the "trouble of the English nation with its colonies." Did he mean that being temporarily distracted by tension in North America, Britain was incapable of vigorous reaction to Spain's attempts to curb smuggling in its colonies, or that its difficulties in North America underscored Spain's need to lower tensions between metropole and colonies over imperial commercial policy?

The gravity of the issues addressed by Landázuri and his fellow *consejeros* did not escape Magallón, "because the rise or decline of our American trades depend upon these decisions"—clearly no hyperbole. A modest man, he confessed to a sense of inadequacy in resolving the issues; a perfectionist, he would like, he remarked, to "fully understand trade with the Indies and that of Cadiz: to be informed in detail of the current status of crafts and manufactures in Spain." For the metropole's rudimentary industrial structures were a key component of his analysis, and he was convinced that a backward metropole incapable of producing manufactures at competitive prices could never cope with "what is most destructive to our trade" overseas in the colonies—smuggling. At the time of his writing, along with Landázuri, he did not doubt that the Spanish metropole was in no "condition to supply the needs of our colonies."

The metropole's export shortcomings brought Magallón to two revealing observations. The first, reminiscent of Gálvez's earlier warning in his "Discurso y reflexiones," drafted before taking up his assignment in New Spain, was that a rigorously enforced mercantilist strategy might invite English retaliation against Spain's colonies as had occurred in 1740 and again in 1762. Second, Magallón, who as embassy secretary had grasped the importance of international silver transfers from Cadiz to Paris (now a function of the Real Giro) in settling Spain's perennial deficits on current account, considered the outflow of colonial silver to Spain's European trading partners to be sound "political arithmetic." It might deflate those partners' aggressive tendencies and, moreover, represented sound monetary policy for dampening price inflation. In earlier times, he perceived accurately, "while the money supply doubled and tripled, so [too] the price of what was bought and sold doubled and tripled." In the eighteenth century, however, the "prodigious" silver shipments "de nuestras minas" had raised the import capacity of metropole and colonies with minimal inflationary consequences, since "silver has flowed quickly from our to foreign hands." This was tantamount to transforming chronic national economic insufficiency into an international boon.

In Paris, seeking to clarify the relationship between Spanish policy, colonialism, and the rampant smuggling in both metropole and colonies, Magallón had read, reflected on, and discussed a major interest of his, the historical experience of the more advanced English, Dutch, and French economies. Europe's political elites, he felt, had long studied "the main sector of political economy"—trade—and he concluded that his model European economies had encouraged agriculture, manufacture, and transport infrastructure between hinterland and ports *before* achieving success in exploiting their overseas colonies—in Magallón's time still an intriguing hypothesis. Their expanding output depressed relative prices and discouraged smuggling; hence, a strong domestic economy was indispensable for profitable colonial trade relations.

Magallón had apparently grasped how Spain's underdevelopment had been a significant factor in the economic growth of competing European economies, judging by the way English, Dutch, and French interests had capitalized on Spain's incapacity to supply its American possessions by encouraging smuggling. They had also learned from initial colonial failures that privileged companies, in general, and designated metropolitan ports for overseas trading—en bloc misguided economic intervention by the state—hindered the growth of colonial trade. Louis XIV's pragmatic minister Colbert, Magallón believed, had radically turned around French colonial policy by opening France's Caribbean colonies to all French shippers and "from that moment, the look of things changed." In extending colonial trade to companies and individual entrepreneurs alike, cutting shipping formalities to a minimum and authorizing multiple rather than selected metropolitan ports to engage in colonial operations, England, France, and Holland fostered a climate of "ease and freedom" in which colonial commerce flourished. Magallón believed a revised Spanish commercial strategy might achieve comparable success in the Caribbean despite aggressive European competition. He found France's annual Caribbean trade of 20 million *pesos fuertes* and England's of 14 million impressive, for example, not to speak of the hundreds of ships and thousands of seamen involved. This was, to say the least, his implicit criticism of Spain's reliance and fixation upon mining rather than colonial export agriculture.

Magallón reserved his sharpest criticism for Cadiz's hegemony over colonial trade, which was perhaps what Gálvez and his collaborators needed to strengthen their case. Not only was that port's monopoly a brake upon trade, it was dominated by resident foreigners, who furnished both exports and financing, while Spaniards functioned merely as *factores* and *encomenderos,* accounting at most for 10–12 percent of all exports by volume to colonial ports.[43] Was it not curious, Magallón asked caustically, that knowledgeable Spanish merchants denounced monopoly positions exploited by "privileged bodies and companies"—an allusion to Cadiz merchants always bemoaning colonial competition from the Havana, Catalan, and Guipúzcoan privileged companies—when in fact the Cadiz merchant community "is nothing but a commercial firm with a monopoly privilege, trafficking by itself in a few known lands, whose profits are assured . . . ?" Should Cadiz, he asked rhetorically, continue to enjoy a monopoly, "when it could share it with the nation's other provinces and ports to the state's advantage?"

Savvy in the protective tactics of the Spanish bureaucracy, Magallón knew that the best weapon in undermining an established policy supported by influential pressure groups was to cite former distinguished, outspoken, but state-tolerated critics (the tactic recently adopted by Campomanes in his *Apéndice a la educación popular* of 1775–77). So Magallón quoted José de Carvajal y Lancaster, president of the Consejo de Indias and former prime minister, an earlier eighteenth-century critic of the Cadiz mercantile community's stranglehold on colonial trade, who had asserted in his "Testamento Político" that he did not know what entailment (*derecho de primogenitura*) conferred upon Cadiz its monopoly. The Cadiz merchants, Carbajal had insisted, well before Adam Smith, were in fact a "bad, formless company" that met the definition of a privileged company, namely, "a pool of many individual capitals in a business in which they alone participate . . . ; such is the Commerce of Cadiz, where only those duly registered do business with the Indies, only their capital is used, only their elected consuls manage it."[44]

Magallón's incisive remarks about the one-port monopoly and Landázuri's analysis ultimately formed the basis of the recommendations of the Consejo de Indias. Its *dictamen* held the Cadiz interest-group responsible for Spain's poor economic performance and lack of a sizeable merchant marine, as well as for the disproportionately large participation of foreign interests in the exploitation of the "inmensas riquezas" of the colonies. The *consejo* adopted the position of Landázuri and Magallón on the broad issue of "libertad del comercio," electing to suppress *palmeo* and *toneladas* and extend the *comercio libre* of 1765 to Central and South America, but—here hewing closely to Landázuri's cautious approach—preserving *flotas* between Cadiz and New Spain until conditions warranted a change. These recommendations the *consejo* linked to the necessity for the government to develop the infrastructure of overseas trade—manufactures, artisan crafts, agriculture, and population—"incesantemente"; otherwise, "the general provisions applicable to an Indies trade will serve for little."[45] With the support of the informed opinions of Landázuri and Magallón, Floridablanca's administration had now managed to garner restrained support for incremental change in Spain's transatlantic trading system, albeit at the price of leaving intact its eighteenth-century core, Cadiz-to-Veracruz *flotas*—a position incidentally also backed by Floridablanca's ever-cautious colleague on the Consejo de Castilla, Campomanes.[46] We have no reason to believe Gálvez hoped to include New Spain at this juncture. After all, he had *his* connections with Mexico City's *almaceneros*.

What *is* puzzling is Madrid's apparent inability or unwillingness to move quickly after hearing from the Consejo de Indias. In this connection, it is worth recalling that Landázuri had delayed his report (1773–76), and that Floridablanca's ministry had delayed its review, apparently preferring to make commercial changes piecemeal. Did delay stem from fear of Cadiz commercial interests operating through their influential Madrid networks? By its own admission, the *consejo* had refrained from consulting the Cadiz *consulado* in order to avoid that body's well-honed delaying technics—the "influence and deals of groups like the merchants and *consulado* of Cadiz; the inconvenience, accusations, and obstacles to follow by granting them a formal hearing in a matter setting the general interest against their personal, private interest."[47]

The Second Reglamento, 1778

In February 1778, professing to detect a slowdown of smuggling following the withdrawal of Portuguese forces from the Rio de la Plata, the Floridablanca ministry extended the regulations of the 1765 statute of *comercio libre* to the Buenos Aires area and the Pacific ports of Chile and Peru.[48] The February decree, countersigned by Colonial Secretary Gálvez, specified that nine peninsular ports now qualified for colonial exchanges (two more were added in March 1779). Thirteen years after these commercial modifications were legislated in 1765 for Spain's Caribbean possessions and their *amplificación* in February 1778 to most of South America (but still excluding New Spain and Venezuela), the climate in the metropole, in the opinion of its political class, could now tolerate limited public debate about "the commonweal" and even some confrontation with the "few hundreds involved in Cadiz's monopoly" who still deluded themselves that Spain was "the most powerful, strong, and wealthy nation, and that by avoiding change in long-established commercial regulations, it will always be the master of the world."[49] In the following month (March), these remarks were read to Madrid's Royal Economic Society, reminding the audience that before February, one had not publicly discussed trade issues, lest it appear that the society was meddling in "the government's secret affairs." The February decree had, it seemed, changed all that.

Looking backward two decades in 1778, Charles III's ministers could agree that since 1759, their regime had introduced limited modifications in those long-standing colonial commercial structures barely refurbished in 1720. In 1739, war with England had ended convoys (*galeones*) to Cartagena and Porto Belo on the north coast of South America, and subsequent legalization of *registros sueltos* in wartime proved effective in maintaining Spain's transatlantic communications, a practice begun even earlier when Madrid began to license individual shipping for the Buenos Aires area. Under Charles, the Barlovento decree of 1765 opened Cuba and other Spanish Caribbean possessions to trade with several peninsular ports, and in February 1778, it was extended to Spanish South America; to many, this represented in retrospect "the initial phase of a prosperous system" and badly needed "national development."[50] Still excluded, however, were Santa Fe (Colombia), Venezuela, Guatemala, and, of course, New Spain. For Prime Minister Floridablanca, then newly raised to that office, and Colonial Secretary Gálvez, eager to leave his mark in the one area of the empire where change was possible and the gains potentially great, the colonies in and around the Caribbean, a deliberately publicized incremental change was in order. In the months after February 1778, and peaking in September, Gálvez and his collaborators formulated a further *amplificación* of 1765, now to include Santa Fe and Guatemala. This would be the showpiece offered as a *reglamento completo* incorporating colonial modifications legislated since 1765, plus two new tariff schedules covering the export-import trade with the colonies.[51]

So spectacular a policy change necessitated covert preparation for maximum effect on both national and international publics and to dampen the reaction of Cadiz interests, "those 20 to 25 wealthy individuals who, although lacking the offices or warehouses common among merchants in Europe and the colonies, employ 200 Spaniards."[52] Gálvez learned, of course, that the Cadiz *consulado* had protested that the February 1778 decree hardly improved on the earlier Barlovento statute (1765), which, it argued, had produced poor results since "hardly any well-capitalized or creditworthy people are in our colonial trade, only those whose debts and misfortunes have led them to it, despite creating a false appearance of what they really are."[53] In addition, other sources warned Gálvez of a countermove by Cadiz interests "able to oppress and restrain our nation as in the past."[54] Gálvez therefore took pains to admonish his brother Matías, then supervising the printing of the new Reglamento, that he "take care to print it with all possible secrecy," while a similar observation came from another Gálvez (and earlier with Esquilache) collaborator, Director General de Rentas Rosendo Saenz de Parayuelo—"let's keep it secret."[55]

At the same time, Gálvez was backed by disaffected and exasperated regional interests critical of Cadiz's dominance of colonial trade. "Does it benefit the state," questioned one such critic from Burgos, "that a small group disregard this whole kingdom to deprive it of participation in this trade?"[56] Gálvez's principal correspondent at Cadiz, Lorenzo Beyens y Huwin, conde de Villamar, a wealthy Cadiz-born merchant with twenty-five years' experience in colonial trade and currently *síndico* of the Cadiz town council, kept him abreast confidentially of the attitudes and lobbying activity of the Cadiz mercantile community. Villamar, descendant of a Flemish family, possessor of a capital of 250,000 pesos and part owner of a frigate, was no partisan of Cadiz's monopoly; in June 1778, he wrote in support of the February decree and urged Gálvez to extend it to cover New Spain.[57] For supporting such innovation, he was considered at Cadiz a kind of class traitor, "enemigo de [su] Patria."[58]

Working under such conflictive pressures, Gálvez, his brother, and other collaborators oversaw the printing of more than 9,000 copies of the Reglamento y aranceles reales para el Comercio Libre de España a Indias de 12 de Octubre de 1778, which the government disseminated widely. Distribution was carefully planned: copies went to five *consejos* in Madrid, to *consulados* in Spain and the colonies, to church hierarchs, to the directors of privileged companies and other corporate bodies in colonial trade (the Guipúzcoan company, Cinco Gremios Mayores of Madrid, and Seminario de San Telmo of Sevilla), and, in an uncommonly gracious gesture, to distinguished, memorable political figures like Esquilache (now Spain's ambassador to Venice) and former Prime Minister Grimaldi. Prime Minister Floridablanca, aware of the possibilities of shaping elite perceptions and through them "opinión pública," also circularized the recently created royal economic societies, urging them to contribute to the *reformación* that the Reglamento symbolized.[59] Esquilache, who had been responsible for initiating *reformación* under

Charles III and had countersigned the Barlovento statute of 1765, responded that "such a great regulation will enhance commerce and the Treasury," which must have gratified Gálvez; Grimaldi wrote from Rome that these were "appropriate measures to develop national industry and trade"; and the *regente* of Mexico City's *Audiencia,* Francisco Romá y Rosell, a political economist in his own right, praised the Reglamento as a "chef d'oeuvre de la Política económica en este ramo."[60]

The government distributed its new Reglamento widely to convince the skeptical of the Spanish state's commitment to innovation via *reformación* rather than *novedad,* just as for similar reasons, it had recently distributed thousands of copies of Campomanes's *Discurso sobre la industria popular* (1774) to parishes throughout Spain.[61] In a real sense, the Reglamento of 1778 was emblematic of the regime that authorized it. To be sure, the terms of Spanish public discourse had changed markedly between the refurbishing of the old colonial commercial order (the Proyecto of 1720) and the effort to modify elements of that system by the *comercio libre* of 1778. Yet one cannot assign twenty-first-century understandings of *libre* and *libertad* to eighteenth-century usage in the Hispanic world. Oligopolists of Cadiz had no fears of *libertad.* By liberty, they understood freedom to operate behind the protection of a managed, controlled colonial trading system without state-imposed formalities hindering their small-scale operations; they welcomed the multiple formalities buttressing *their* economic enclave against outsiders. In this context, Cadiz viewed competition from well-capitalized, regionally based privileged companies chartered by the state—Madrid's Cinco Gremios Mayores, San Sebastián's Compañía Guipuzcoana, or Barcelona's Real Compañía de Comercio, for example—as constraining merchants' liberty. The convoy system on the other hand, Cadiz's economic traditionalists insisted, formed the bedrock of what they liked to call *comercio arreglado,* with its connotations of order and rationality rooted in peninsular and colonial reality. The high personnel of the Spanish state, it must be underscored, had no intention of undermining one of the primary aspects of its domestic and colonial economies, transatlantic trade. If one interprets *comercio libre* as trade relieved or freed of certain outgrown encumbrances, one approximates the meaning of *libre* to Madrid authorities.

There is a further sense in which the Reglamento of October 1778 expressed the state's purpose. The economic core of the imperial system, although fundamentally dependent for survival upon the nature and magnitude of colonial responses, would remain the metropole, its economy, its interests, and its imperial hegemony, expressed in the balance of the law's title, "comercio libre de España a Indias." To the ingenuous, the title of the

Reglamento promised much; to the skeptic, it offered a variation on a long-practiced commercial system that the underdeveloped metropole, a variety of the European old regime, needed to survive as an Atlantic power. As the Cadiz *consulado* would confess decades later with uncommon candor apropos of the Reglamento of 1778: "We should view it only as an effort to loosen the restrictions and prohibitions of the old system."[62] This, however, was the candor of hindsight in 1810. At bottom, the Reglamento must be seen as the tardy, incremental response of a late medieval regime to inescapable external pressures.

The initial attempt formally to chip away at Spain's secular transatlantic system did have innovative elements. Barlovento in 1765, propelled by Esquilache's administration, turned out to be an encouraging experiment, which the Reglamento of October 1778 amplified and extended to Colombia (Santa Fe), Yucatan, and Guatemala. Now in 1778, thirteen rather than nine ports in the metropole and the Canaries were certified as *habilitados* for one-on-one contact with twenty-four colonial ports in the Caribbean, Central America, and South America. Still conspicuously omitted were Venezuelan ports, which remained the preserve of the Compañía Guipuzcoana, and—most important—Veracruz, the major Atlantic gateway to New Spain. The Spanish state's extreme sensitivity to Veracruz is evident in the fact that its exclusion from the October 1778 Reglamento surfaced when dealing with the elimination of the complex formalities embedded in the 1720 Proyecto. Nowhere was it explicit that *flotas* would continue between Cadiz and Veracruz; article 6 contained merely the cryptic phrase, "withholding my decision to issue a corresponding [regulation]."

The articles on shipping displayed a distinctly nationalist and mercantilist cast, calling for Spanish-built ships (a condition undermined by a two-year grace period for purchasing and nationalizing foreign-built vessels), Spanish ownership, Spanish officers, and a crew that was at least two-thirds Spanish. No authorization of shipping owned and operated by residents of the colonies appears for trade between colonial ports and Spain, an impression reinforced by a provision obliging *consulados* (presumably those in the metropole) to develop "navegación a mis dominios de América."[63] Only in shipping between colonial ports (with cargo restricted to products of colonial origin) were colonials (*vasallos americanos*) mentioned specifically, a notable departure from article 10 of the Barlovento rules of 1765 permitting natives of the Caribbean islands to carry only *their* products to peninsular ports.

Much was made of eliminating the cost-inflating, time-consuming, and essentially restrictive requirements integral to the traditional convoy system—Madrid's control of ship licensing, Cadiz's maddeningly painstaking gauging inspections, *palmeo, toneladas, San Telmo, extrangería, visitas, reconocimientos de carenas, habilitaciones*—that Barlovento had already dispensed with. The emphasis was justified: by switching the basis of export duties from bulk rate (*palmeo*) to ad valorem, Madrid hoped to raise duties on exports to the colonies by an estimated 80 percent.[64] However, government oversight of shipping, crews, and passengers resurfaced in less overt fashion: manifests listing domestic and foreign cargo separately, and the volume, value, and duties levied had to go to Madrid for approval; sailing permits then went back to port authorities (*jueces de arribadas*) for delivery to shipmasters; and still stipulated was the inspection (*revista acostumbrada*) of officers, crews, and those accompanying their cargo, as well as passengers, who still needed licenses from the Consejo de Indias at Madrid.[65] Moreover, Madrid recognized the informal power of government employees to manipulate office for personal gain. Customs and treasury personnel were enjoined neither to request nor accept "duty, tip, nor emolument" from shipowners, captains, shippers, *factores,* or *encomenderos* in expediting shipping and cargo. Tight controls were now applied to *cargadores* in peninsular ports: they could accompany cargo only when valued at more than 53,000 reales, they had to be "Spanish" (there was no mention of "American"), and if married, they had to post bond and return within three to four years.[66] Neither before nor after 1778 did Spain's transatlantic system offer an open door to emigrants from the metropole.

A markedly nationalist note absent from Barlovento's regulations of 1765 surfaced in the Reglamento's articles on cargo, designed to favor national over foreign products in colonial trade. The apparent intention was to manipulate tariff schedules both for fiscal ends—the perennial priority behind state intervention in external trade—and economic development of the metropole. There was also an effort to screen out smuggled goods, that other constant preoccupation of the metropolitan authorities.[67] Domestic and foreign merchandise were therefore to be packed separately ("never to be combined") and listed separately on manifests, which were to state both the value of the merchandise and the duties payable on leaving Spain, as well as the sole authorized colonial port of destination, where local authorities would be able to check the accuracy of the manifests against the cargo unloaded.[68]

Obviously, *comercio libre* retained many features of "managed trade." Export duties were calibrated to channel goods into hitherto neglected colonial zones, since Gálvez and his collaborators understood that colonial ports where silver exports bulked large invariably attracted the most shipping. To encourage the development of neglected colonial ports, export duties to these were lowered to 1.5 percent on domestic products and to 4 percent on foreign ones; export duties to more frequented colonial ports, such as Havana, Callao, and Rio de la Plata, were somewhat higher, 3 and 7 percent respectively. And although exit duties on colonial trade were uniform in all authorized peninsular ports, the basic valuations (*aforos*) on items entering colonial ports varied from 8 to 20 percent higher than in peninsular ports, depending upon distance from the metropole and the level of commercial activity. Colonial import duties were, of course, uniform; thus imported merchandise exiting colonial ports for the interior paid duties of 6 percent on national products and 14 percent on foreign.

The ambivalence of state intervention in manipulating colonial demand for metropolitan products was revealed in the handling of what Madrid's planners viewed as vanguard manufactures, hardware and woolen, cotton, linen, and silk textiles. Government personnel allowed such domestically produced items to exit peninsular ports and enter colonial ports duty-free. Since the transformation of imported textiles originating in England, France, Silesia, and Italy into "Spanish" products had become a national industry, the government insisted that all textile exports to the colonies prove Spanish provenance, including certification by local officials, indication of locale of production on all bolts of cloth, and factory seals. Furthermore, no imports of ready-made clothing such as shirts, dresses, and dressing gowns could now be reexported to colonial markets.[69] Yet article 31 negated such pseudoprotectionist provisions, leaving a loophole for the "concealed reexport" of imports provided that local entrepreneurs had modified items "such that appearance, use or destination are changed after entry."[70] Here was implicit recognition that domestic production facilities were simply incapable of matching the import needs of even "a tiny corner of the Indies," and that Mexico City's *almaceneros* were somehow managing to order direct from foreign suppliers.[71]

Finally, continuing the traditional pattern of the Spanish transatlantic system, all colonial products would have to be exported solely to the metropole. (There was nothing comparable to the "enumerated" items, the selected colonial products that under the English Acts of Navigation could be exported only to the metropole.) Madrid lifted all import duties on colonial staples entering the metropole—on sugar, coffee, dyestuffs such as cochineal and indigo, and raw wool—demand for which was rising in western Europe. To reduce illegal outflows of precious metals, the duty on colonial silver entering peninsular ports was cut from 10 to 5.5 percent; of this, 4 percent went directly to the Treasury; 1 percent to organizations like the

Colegio Seminario de San Telmo (the Spanish naval academy, hitherto subsidized by the *tonelada* duty) and to finance construction of the major highway between Madrid and Cadiz ("of major interest to the Commerce of Cadiz"); and 0.5 percent to the Consulado de Cadiz to liquidate outstanding government debt incurred in the seventeenth and early eighteenth centuries. Montesquieu was not far off the mark on the inverse relation between Spain's colonies and their metropole when he commented that "the Indies and Spain represent two powers under one master; the Indies, however, are chief, Spain the accessory."[72] There was one further aspect of colonial exports, precious metals, upon which state and economy in the metropole depended. As we have seen, a major drawback of the convoy system had been long delays in remitting the product of colonial sales predominantly in silver. Now, providing no royal naval vessel was available, merchant shipping could bring back the product of colonial sales in silver plus other funds up to 1,000 pesos per ship/ton.

Although *comercio libre* of 1765 and 1778 shared developmental concerns, they were not indicated in similar fashion. In 1765, Esquilache had clearly spelled out the state's intention to increase the trade of Cuba and other Caribbean possessions in order to stimulate "Spain's major provinces." In the Reglamento of 1778, countersigned by Gálvez, there was only a brief introductory reference to reestablishing the metropole's former "vigor" in agriculture, industry, and population. On the other hand, Gálvez's statute reiterated the state's commitment to revitalizing the metropolitan economy. To this end, Madrid proclaimed its intention to found *consulados*—those eminently traditional corporative bodies—in peninsular ports newly authorized for colonial exchanges, which, joined by the recently formed regional economic societies, might foster agricultural, manufacturing, and shipping enterprises for the colonial trade.

In all of its fifty-five articles, the new Reglamento went little further than that of 1765, except for extending the zone of *comercio libre* and the formulation of a comprehensive colonial tariff schedule. In effect, Gálvez countersigned what had been tested in the Caribbean (and adjusted to the special situation of New Orleans in recently acquired Louisiana). Barlovento's earlier success, one must recall, had been a measure of the capacity of Cuban and Catalan agriculturists to expand production and exchange between Havana and Barcelona. Yet Barlovento had not proven that the metropolitan economy could respond, at least immediately, to colonial demand by creating manufacturing capacity in textiles and hardware, which in theory lay at the heart of Spain's developmental strategy to curb smuggling and customs fraud. Second, the Reglamento of 1778 still isolated the richest colony, New

Spain, which was still subordinated to the hegemony of one metropolitan port and its commercial community. Madrid was determined to avoid in New Spain what Antonio Valdés would later term the "inevitable . . . abuso de una libertad absoluta."[73]

Of course, there was underlying resignation to the fact that sooner or later, Madrid would have to open New Spain to *comercio libre.*[74] On balance, however, despite Madrid's deliberate effort to isolate the commercial interests of Cadiz and Mexico City from consultation in the course of drafting the Reglamento, their unique commercial role was respected and survived intact. Gálvez's and Floridablanca's commercial *reformación* seems, in fact, only an *amplificación* of Esquilache's initiative of 1765. Last, critics' long-held objective of reducing Cadiz's primary role in imperial trade, based upon its pool of shipping, a large foreign community making available capital, credit, and goods, and a core of experienced merchants au courant with the changing composition of colonial demand, was abandoned to the operation of market forces. In this light, one wonders what the intent of a subsequent warning to officials in colonial ports to treat all peninsular merchants with "politeness and respect, avoiding extortion or delay" was.[75] To avoid discrimination against ships and cargo from metropolitan ports other than Cadiz?

New Spain Isolated

Nothing better exemplifies the gradualist and often ambiguous approach of the Spanish state to changing conditions in the Atlantic over the eighteenth century than the handling of the centerpiece of its transatlantic commercial system, New Spain.

The Reglamento of 1778 left that colony in limbo. In a kind of addendum to article 6 that eliminated the long-criticized formalities and duties of the 1720 Proyecto, Madrid expressed its intention to formulate a similar *reglamento* for New Spain at an unspecified future moment; meanwhile, ships laden with mercury (*registros de azogues*), an indispensable input for New Spain's silver refineries, were also licensed to carry Spanish products according to the new colonial tariff schedule. Nowhere mentioned were *flota, feria,* or Spanish port or ports of origin. To sum up: the Reglamento of 1778 was no striking break with the Spanish state's incrementalist policy; it conformed to long-existing "distributional coalitions."[76]

Why, then, such caution in handling what the Consulado de Cadiz would later categorize as only an effort to "loosen" the restrictions and prohibitions of the old system two decades into the reign of Charles III?[77] The question goes to the heart of the decision-making process in a unique type of old regime, one by definition lacking overt organs of frequently renewed elective representation for economic interests and social classes. In no small measure, the moderation (not to say, conservatism) of the eighteenth-century Spanish state testified to the flexibility of its bureaucratic elites in compromising their conception of state needs with the more narrowly focused goals of powerful vested interests. Also it must be kept in mind that the Consejo de Indias did not speak with a united voice. Only Magallón's vote explicitly broadened *comercio libre* to include New Spain; three *consejeros* claimed they needed more information, and another three failed to clarify their positions. There were, after all, lines of communication to high-level bureaucrats through the Casa de Contratación at Cadiz and the lobbyists at Madrid in the pay of the *consulados* of Cadiz and Mexico City. Given the impasse in the Consejo de Indias, the decision to proceed with policy changes necessarily fell to those high civil servants directly responsible for the trade initiative, to Floridablanca and Gálvez.[78] Both realized the necessity of proceeding cautiously.

Floridablanca, only recently appointed prime minister, had to omit New Spain until, as he expressed it ambiguously, "we can see the effects" of *comercio libre*.[79] Understandably, many among Madrid's high-level public servants recognized the influence of "our singularly unique commercial center for the deposit of funds"—Cadiz—as well as that community's "horror" at any "inovación." In addition, there was anxiety that a persistent shortage of competitively priced imports would aggravate smuggling in the Caribbean and, as Floridablanca wrote Múzquiz, lead to "craft shops and other branches of industry" in the colonies and to "independence from their metropole, which we must skilfully guard against."[80]

Gálvez was no radical reformer. Years earlier, he had opted for a middle position between the *flota* system and unrestricted peninsular shipping to supply New Spain; around 1760, he had floated the proposition to send *registros sueltos* to Veracruz and the sale of their cargoes at annual Jalapa fairs—hardly radical departures.[81] But during his *visitación* to New Spain, he had perceived the importance of mercantile groups at Cadiz and Mexico City in colonial and metropolitan finance. For example, both corporate bodies helped finance Gálvez's operations in northern Mexico, and Mexico City's *almaceneros* remained a principal source of loan funds in the colonies.[82] Moreover, was it coincidental that in August 1778, anonymous merchants offered the Spanish government 9 million pesos at 4 percent interest, repayable over twenty years, and that the following December, the Mexico City *consulado* shipped 24,000 pesos to two prominent Cadiz merchants,

Francisco Fernández de Rábago and a consul of the Cadiz *consulado,* Gerónimo Maza Alvarado? For lobbying purposes? Subsequently, Gálvez arranged a "gift" of 175,000 pesos to the royal heirs, Charles and María Luísa, from merchants in the Consulado de México and mine owners in the Tribunal de Minería.[83] This is convincing, albeit circumstantial, evidence of Gálvez's willingness to decouple the Cadiz–Mexico City trade link from the Reglamento, at least temporarily.

Contemporaries provided a variety of explanations, complementary rather than contradictory, for excluding New Spain. Grimaldi justified it on several grounds: Ulloa's *flota* had left the colony loaded with imports, smuggling was controllable, and, most important, time was needed before metropolitan agricultural production could adequately supply the colony.[84] A decade later, Galvez's successor as colonial secretary, Antonio Valdés, expressed fear that New Spain's combination of silver exports and consumer demand would lead to "concurrencia excesiva" among Spanish merchants, and consequently to oversupply and falling prices. Better to continue the *flota* system to Veracruz, he suggested, "managed, however, to avoid the inconvenience of the *flotas* method." In other words, enforce a maximum tonnage per convoy.[85] Antúnez y Acevedo who, as *consejero de Indias* had recommended maintaining convoys and a tonnage maximum, later asserted that he had no explanation for excluding New Spain, perhaps because he chose to overlook very effective lobbying by Cadiz and Mexico City.[86] While influential interests evidently opposed *comercio libre,* it is equally evident that Madrid feared that the inclusion of New Spain at that conjuncture might lead to a shortfall in customs revenue, at least in the short term.[87] In sum, fear of serious repercussions on state finances was real, if exaggerated. As a confidant of Charles III, the conde de Férnan Núñez, encouraged Gálvez, "May God grant you good health to continue your work, to render Spain prosperous as is absolutely necessary—otherwise the patient is hopeless."[88] Was Férnan Núñez thinking of the unreconstructed opposition of the major metropolitan mercantile interest, which remained inalterably convinced that Madrid's gradualist policy of expanding areas under *comercio libre* would undermine *its* transatlantic system?

Despite friction between the merchant groups of Cadiz and Mexico City over the ground rules of Jalapa fairs, neither ever proposed to eliminate the source, the periodic convoy system, whose cargo volume was rising in the 1760s and 1770s. Between 1772 and 1776, in fact, both *consulados* petitioned Madrid to set a maximum of *flota* volume: initially, Cadiz proposed 4,500 tons (based on assumed annual import requirements of 1,500), while Mexico City favored a higher level of 6,000.[89] However, in 1777–78, this issue faded away when both commercial centers were preoccupied with government study groups exploring ways of extending *comercio libre* to all colonial ports, including Veracruz. In March 1777, Mexico City's merchants pressured the viceregal administration unsuccessfully to authorize a deputation to Madrid; later that year (in July), Cadiz similarly petitioned Gálvez to grant its representatives a hearing on the proposal for *comercio libre,* also without success.[90]

Incensed by inability to present its case, and perhaps disoriented by Gálvez's strategy of unannounced printing and wide distribution of the decree (making recall by the government an embarrassment, and consequently virtually impossible), the Cadiz *consulado* reacted vigorously to the "grande novedad" itself, the first of the two 1778 decrees on *comercio libre* forwarded by Gálvez via the official channel of the Casa de Contratación for delivery to the *consulado.* Unanimously, a general assembly of the *consulado* voted to have a small committee petition for suspension of enforcement of the 2 February decree, issued, it complained, "without a hearing and to the prejudice of our rights."[91] The *consulado*'s argument was two-pronged. First, it rejected Madrid's gradual elimination of the convoy system in favor of unregulated shipping, *registros sueltos.* Its tunnel vision went back two centuries, to that moment in 1529 when colonial trade had been opened to the metropolitan ports of La Coruña, Bayonne, Avilés, Landa, Bilbao, San Sebastián, Cartagena, and Málaga, along with Sevilla, then suppressed because *registros sueltos* were returning from the colonies with "much gold and silver that, smuggled out and unregistered, they carried away to foreign kingdoms"—an accurate interpretation. To tolerate a return to such "libertad"—although it confessed that liberty in general was the "alma del comercio"—was now inconceivable, since the smuggling of precious metals could not be contained at Cadiz, despite the dense system of surveillance in place there.

A second line of argument constituted a fall-back position. The Cadiz *consulado* wanted the new decree delayed in order to gain time to recoup 10 million pesos' worth of merchandise sold on credit at Buenos Aires, Lima, and Valparaíso, ports now opened to *comercio libre.* To strengthen its case, the petition recalled the "disorder" in colonial trading during war with England in 1740–48, when the government had to suspend *flotas,* and merchants could not cope with unregulated arrivals of imports at Veracruz. It also cited the situation of Ulloa's *flota* at Veracruz, where mere rumors of *comercio libre* had discouraged New Spain's would-be distributors, who, the petition averred, had left half the *flota*'s cargo unsold at Jalapa.[92] A general slowdown of commercial activity had ensued in New Spain, delaying the repatriation of sales income.

Since the *consulado* had been denied a preliminary hearing, it now chose to exploit this opportunity to list what it considered the shortcomings of the preceding Barlovento decree of 1765, enlarged on the smuggling opportunities encouraged between Havana and Veracruz (calculated at 3 million pesos annually), and then lauded the national role of the port of Cadiz, whose colonial trade drew, it remarked proudly, "Bizcaínos, Gallegos, Montañeses, Navarros, as well as those of other provinces of Spain." Concentration of colonial trade since the sixteenth century, first at Sevilla and then at Cadiz, "theoretically opened it to the whole kingdom." As proof, the Cadiz merchants pointed to caravans (*conductas*) of silver and gold sent on from Cadiz to assist residents in other provinces quietly to enjoy the earnings of their relatives' and friends' commercial enterprise in the American colonies. Finally, the *consulado* again requested a formal hearing, adding that commercial statistics generated by the recently promulgated *comercio libre* decree specifically excluded 20 million pesos still expected at Cadiz from sales returns on merchandise exported before 1776 to New Spain and South America.

The length and vehemence of the Cadiz *consulado*'s representation suggest a hope of rolling back or at worst delaying enforcement of the first of the 1778 decrees. Cadiz merchants didn't "know how to rid themselves of what minimizes profits," even at the expense of the national interest, Miguel de Vallejo, administrator-general of the Cadiz customs, one of Gálvez's nationalist correspondents in the Cadiz bureaucracy, commented, and he advised the colonial secretary to act firmly to ward off any "attempt to keep the old trade structure."[93] There is no reason to believe the overblown acquiescence of an assembly of Cadiz businessmen when formally advised of the second (October) decree on *comercio libre*. The president of the Casa de Contratación wrote Gálvez that the merchants had unanimously applauded "so artfully elaborated a work," whose benefits "the blindest self-interest cannot neglect."[94] Nor could Gaditanos warmly have greeted a subsequent order countersigned by Gálvez requiring colonial customs officials to pay special attention to merchandise dispatched at Cadiz and to compare carefully ships' manifests (*registros*) with shippers' invoices (*facturas*) to prevent entry of unlisted items.[95]

Not until late March 1779 did Gálvez reveal how Madrid intended to supply New Spain. The promised special *reglamento* for that colony did not materialize; instead, the government allocated eleven ships to the port of Veracruz for that year, assigning six to Cadiz alone, which were authorized to carry both mercury and national products.[96] Abandonment of a convoy to Veracruz showed the Spanish government's fear of England's naval forces in the Atlantic once Spain joined France in supporting the American Revolution. "How depressed would our nation be if a rich convoy from New Spain were intercepted at sea?"[97] One need only recall Antonio de Ulloa's extraordinarily elaborate precautions in taking his convoy back to Cadiz via the long southern route to the Canaries. Practically speaking, in Gálvez's order of March 1779, the trading interests of Cadiz and Mexico City achieved what they had supported in the early 1770s, a cap on exports to New Spain.

Attempted Rollback: The Montes-Landaburu Initiative

Three years later, in the summer of 1782, the Cadiz *consulado* demonstrated through connections to the state bureaucracy how unreconstructed its opposition remained to recent modifications in the imperial trading system, and how effective its lobbying might be. At this conjuncture, Spain's participation in the conflict with England on the side of the North American insurrectionaries, and that colonial war's repercussions upon silver remittances and state finance, provided another opportunity for Cadiz and associated interests to attempt a rollback of the commercial legislation of 1778.

Repeated international conflict invariably destabilized the fragile fiscal systems of eighteenth-century European states, whose revenues came from unsystematic taxes on foreign trade and mass domestic consumption. When coupled to inadequate budgetary oversight and discretionary allocations, preconstitutional European state systems in crisis usually fell back upon financial legerdemain and the confidence of small investors, mainly through merchant-banking houses using their own and depositors' liquid assets. Conflict with England invariably threatened the financial stability of the Spanish imperial state, always dependent on income from its colonies across the Atlantic.

The instability returned in 1779, and over the ensuing three years, 1779–82, average state expenditures climbed 37 percent over the preceding four-year period, and defense outlays just under 28 percent, although defense as percentage of total outlays remained constant (in the 60 percent range).[98] Madrid searched for fresh revenue sources to meet defense obligations and compensate for temporary suspension of colonial revenue, conservatively estimated at 20 percent of Spain's total annual state income. In fact, adding customs receipts (*rentas generales*) from the colonial trade at Cadiz and at other peninsular ports raises that percentage appreciably. Fresh financial infusions were critical, since the state's internal security forces were far from omnipotent (as the *motín* de Esquilache had memorably shown), and Madrid refrained from drastically increasing the tax burden on a generally impoverished, heavily taxed peasantry. It was a time, then, for inventive finance, financial innovation, much speculation, and super-profits for national and international investors. The financial and commercial problems arising from the war in 1779–83, and the solutions adopted, foreshadowed those of the critical 1797–1807 period.

Once war against England had begun in 1779, Floridablanca's administration first turned to what had become the state's principal financial resource in the private sector in the eighteenth century, Madrid's Cinco Gremios Mayores, for 70 million reales (about 4.6 million *pesos fuertes*) in monthly installments of 10 million.[99] In mid 1780, when the Cinco Gremios backed out of the contract after two installments, Francisco Cabarrús—a young, ambitious twenty-eight-year-old French immigrant who was rapidly making a career in Madrid banking circles[100]—proposed the device of *vales reales,* treasury notes in 600-peso denominations bearing 4 percent annual interest and redeemable at par over twenty years; apparently, Cabarrús had learned of the paper money issued by the U.S. Continental Congress. *Vales* were negotiable, the 1780 issue made clear, for payment of customs duties and general financial obligations, an attraction to the commercial communities of peripheral Spain. What ensured the success of the contract of Cabarrús & Aguirre with Finance Minister Múzquiz—it would market 9 million pesos of *vales* over the second half of 1780—were their multiple contacts with well-capitalized French bankers at Madrid, and with French merchants and merchant bankers established at Cadiz, where for decades they had both financed and supplied *registros sueltos* as well as *flotas.* Of the top ten Cadiz commercial firms purchasing 3.8 million pesos of *vales,* four—Laserre, Magon y Lefer, Cayla, Solier y Cabanes, and Lecouteulx—were French.[101] (In 1771, the Cadiz *consulado* estimated the annual incomes of two French houses, Magon y Lefer—30,000 pesos—and Cayla, Solier Hermanos, Cabanes y Companía—40,000—as by far the largest incomes of any firm there.)[102]

The high visibility of French merchants and financiers behind the contract negotiations of Cabarrús & Aguirre with Múzquiz in the fall of 1780 increased over the eighteen months between December 1780 and April 1782, as financing an emptying treasury in wartime became a dominant preoccupation. As a consequence of at least two other government contracts thought up and executed by Cabarrús & Aguirre and its successor, Cabarrús & Lalanne, both involving French capital, French firms in colonial trade at Cadiz seemed likely to acquire political leverage that might undermine the oligopolistic strategies of the Cadiz *consulado* and related interest groups.

Both financial operations proposed by Cabarrús entailed direct access by French shipping to Veracruz or Havana—invariably off-limits to non-Spanish vessels, except under special conditions—in order to return with government silver mined in New Spain and minted at Mexico City. In August 1781, Madrid's Hacienda reserves fell to 2 million reales (100,000 pesos), while 3.5 million in outlays were needed on short notice. At the end of the month, Cabarrús & Lalanne contracted with Múzquiz to deliver a million pesos (less Cabarrús's commission of 7.6 percent) to the Spanish authorities at Cadiz; once again Cabarrús's arrangements involved prominent French firms at Cadiz, Magon y Lefer, Lecoulteux, and Laserre. In recompense, a French warship sailed to Havana in late September to take aboard a million pesos for delivery to the French treasury.[103]

Far more threatening to nationalist-minded Cadiz merchants and sympathizers like Francisco Montes, a *tesorero general* in the finance ministry, was an earlier and more ambitious proposal by Cabarrús in December 1780. For decades French merchant houses at Cadiz had hankered after the chance to participate openly in convoys to New Spain, shedding the mutually tolerated subterfuges necessitated by the restrictive Spanish commercial code. Taking advantage of the deepening financial crisis, Cabarrús's package offered the Spanish treasury millions of pesos and French merchants at Cadiz direct trade with New Spain.

Cabarrús's leverage was an offer to deposit 100 million reales (5 million *pesos*) in the Madrid treasury in exchange for permitting a French ship to pick up five million *pesos* of government silver at Veracruz. No commission was charged; instead, Cabarrús asked that two or three French merchant vessels be authorized to carry 1,000 tons of duty-free goods (which Cabarrús valued at 60 million reales, or three million *pesos fuertes*) to Veracruz; in addition, private sales proceeds in silver and exports of colonial cochineal and indigo would also pass duty-free at Veracruz and Cadiz. Not surprisingly, Colonial Secretary Gálvez found Cabarrus's terms unacceptable on several counts: in the first place, the real value of the merchandise to be sent to New Spain, high-priced linens and silks, would not be 60 million reales but more realistically 100 million in prices current at Cadiz. When sold in New Spain, these goods would probably bring double that amount—as much as 200 million reales, or 10 million pesos. In all, estimating the real value of such imports at Veracruz, returns in silver and colonial dyestuffs, as well as the duty-free status of outbound and inbound cargo, Gálvez concluded that

Cabarrús and his associates stood to earn 47 million reales—an extraordinary commission. Based on Cabarrús's investment of 100 million reales loaned to the government plus 60 million in merchandise forwarded to Veracruz, Cabarrús stood to make just under 36 percent on his investment.[104]

Over the next eleven months, Cabarrús saw his proposal cut back. In exchange for one million pesos (and 3 percent commission) deposited in government treasuries at Madrid and the port cities of Sevilla, Cadiz, and Cartagena, French ships (without cargo) were licensed for Havana, there to load one million silver pesos. On this modified contract, Cabarrús and his backers probably garnered a net profit of 25 percent.[105] The contract was signed in November 1781 by the Spanish government, which was scrambling for funds to support its naval and military operations and unwilling to adopt the old regime's traditional economy measures—suspension of salary and pension payments, coupled with privatization of some tax collection. Madrid was in a crisis of unprecedented proportions, whose solution was access to government silver held at Veracruz, Havana, and other colonial ports until peacetime, a point hammered home by Cabarrús's contracts. Once again a colonial resource, now mainly Mexican silver, remained more fundamental than ever to Spain's financial solvency.

There remained another major financial resource linked to colonial trade that the ministerial core consisting of Floridablanca, Múzquiz, Campomanes, and Gálvez had yet to tap once more, the Spanish merchant community at Cadiz. To be sure, Cabarrús had readily located buyers of *vales* and lenders to the government among well-capitalized, internationally recognized French merchant establishments there. The government's delay in tapping potential Spanish investors at Cadiz is understandable; as a tactical matter, Madrid had consulted neither the Cadiz nor the Mexico City *consulado* on the sensitive issue of amplifying Barlovento (1778). Apparently, reluctance to approach Cadiz's merchants evaporated when, in the first eight months of 1782, the Hacienda was inundated with appeals for funds from Spain's naval arsenals and the ground forces besieging the English naval base at Gibraltar. Doubtless Finance Secretary Múzquiz consulted with Floridablanca and Gálvez before approaching Cadiz indirectly through a *tesorero general,* Francisco Montes. In August, through an old friend, Matías de Landaburu—who was prominent in the Cadiz merchant community, in contact with the Mexico City business community (notably with the *almacenero* Francisco Ignacio de Yraeta), and, like himself, a former prior of the *consulado*—Montes offered the Cadiz merchant community an unexpected opportunity to have Madrid abandon its *comercio libre* policy. On inspection,

Montes's scheme presented at Cadiz by Landaburu was no more far-fetched than some of Cabarrús's extravagant proposals.

Montes and Landaburu typify the migration in the eighteenth century of young men from northern Spain (Montes from the *montañas* of Burgos, Landaburu from Guipúzcoa) to Cadiz and on to the colonial commercial world, especially New Spain. At Cadiz, Montes had initially clerked in a commercial house and then, probably financed discreetly by French firms like Béhic (who used him as *prestanombre* early in his trading career in New Spain), spent the next ten years (1749–59) as a *diputado del comercio de España* at Jalapa. Back at Cadiz in the 1760s, he made the acquaintance of three other successful merchants, from towns in the *montañas,* Polaciones, and the Liévana respectively—Ignacio de la Torre, Gerónimo Maza Alvarado, and the Cadiz *consulado*'s secretary, José Fernández de Cosío. For his dedicated work at Madrid facilitating payments to *prestamistas antiguos* who had lent funds decades ago to the central government via the Cadiz *consulado,* correspondents addressed him as "compañero y amigo" and often commended his "efficiency and goodwill." The officers of the Cadiz *consulado* lauded him for his "influence and good offices that have earned our confidence," his readiness to defend "the interests of this body and every member." Conversely, a critic later lampooned him as "Francisco de Cerros" or "Cerote," portraying him as a mere "paymaster of damages by hunters" whose business skill consisted of "trading in turnips and eggs." By the late 1760s, the French considered him an ingrate, because although early in his career in New Spain, he had relied upon their financial backing, he later championed what they considered excessively xenophobic legislation. As *tesorero general* along with the marqués de Zambrano, Montes reacted negatively to Cabarrús's financial legerdemain.[106] For his part, Cabarrús distrusted him, at one point insisting that Montes have no part in reviewing his proposals for trade with New Spain.

At Cadiz, Montes had formed business relations and a durable friendship with another migrant from northern Spain, the Biscayan Matías de Landaburu (from Durango). During the 1750s, Landaburu enjoyed the confidence of the Mexico City *consulado,* which gave him power of attorney to press its campaign to legalize direct buying at Cadiz by Mexico City merchants; he also corresponded with prominent Basque merchants established in Mexico City, *almaceneros* like Manuel de Aldaco, Matías de Urrutia, and Francisco Ignacio de Yraeta. After serving as priors of the *consulado,* Montes and Landaburu enjoyed high status in the Cadiz merchant community: Montes became an early member of the Order of Charles III, and Landaburu purchased an estate from the conde de Aranda, along with the title of vizconde de Biote y Bayo. In 1782, Landaburu contributed 20,000 pesos to an interest-free loan offered to Madrid by the *comercio de España* at Jalapa, repayable after the war with England, when silver would finally arrive at Cadiz.[107]

Montes's financial initiative with Cadiz began when Finance Minister Múzquiz showed him a letter from the Ministry of the Marine warning that the Cartagena naval base would shortly run out of funds. Similar petitions followed. The commandant of the El Ferrol base "laconically and energetically" noted his department's delayed payments, urging immediate remittance of 2 to 3 million reales. *Tesorero* Montes, exasperated by the pile of complaints touched off by the "lack of funds at every treasury office," complained to Múzquiz that "although we ship the treasuries every cent received at Cadiz and Sevilla and cover the most important needs, everyone criticizes the Tesorería Mayor, the army's finance division, and the Depositaria de Indias, as if they could match funds to demands."[108] Three days later, Múzquiz told Montes that he had spoken to the king of Montes's dismay at the financial situation, and that Charles had concluded that somehow Montes was capable of meeting the immediate financial needs of the forces besieging Gibraltar "because of merchants' high opinion of him, especially at Cadiz." Múzquiz directed Montes to seek out potential buyers of a million *pesos fuertes* in *vales* at no or very low interest among "firms that trust him" at Cadiz.[109]

Presumably, Charles simply concurred with the decision of Múzquiz, Floridablanca, and Gálvez to use Montes to pry the kind of substantial financial commitment proffered by the French commercial community at Cadiz from *consulado* members. What Madrid had recently denied the Cadiz community—the opportunity formally to air its opposition to enlarging the imperial trading system through *comercio libre*—it was now belatedly prepared to offer through Montes.

Montes advised Finance Minister Múzquiz that he could not readily raise a million *pesos fuertes* at Cadiz because of *comercio libre*'s negative effects. He contrasted the current wartime situation at Cadiz with conditions during another war, in 1740–48, when Cadiz businessmen had invested heavily in shipping goods to the American colonies, disregarding the eventuality of a postwar inundation of imports there by unregulated shipping from the metropole. At that juncture, Madrid expected to profit from *tonelada* fees and customs duties (sometimes as high as 250,000 pesos per *registro*). However, *comercio libre,* Montes claimed, had clouded merchants' perspectives.

On rumors of impending *comercio libre* circulating in 1777, those of Mexico City's *almaceneros* who had foreseen that New Spain would be incorporated into the system sooner or later, but had nonetheless "considered buying goods brought by Ulloa's *flota,* now desisted on learning of the certainty of *comercio libre*" and reduced their purchases. At Cadiz, sales and prices fell, and inventories climbed.[110]

When hostilities commenced with England in 1779, a few ships chanced the Atlantic crossing, many of which were taken as prizes; realistic merchants had little expectation of recouping losses with profitable postwar sales. Since *comercio libre* had promised a large volume of exports to the colonies, but low unit profits, peninsular exporters confined themselves to purchasing small lots, "just enough for daily expenses." Nowadays, Montes claimed, a Cadiz merchant would not venture to ship as much as formerly, which, he noted, explained why customs receipts at Cadiz had fallen. Furthermore, many proprietors of respected firms had abandoned colonial trade for their country estates "to avoid losing under *comercio libre* what they had earned under managed trade," while firms whose proprietors had died found heirs either wasting their inheritances, incompetent at business, or moving on to other careers. Cabarrús—whom Montes disparaged—had managed to market over 6.1 million pesos of *vales* mainly because he could relate to selected French firms at Cadiz, even sharing his banker's commission with them.[111] Yet although he had promised redemption with interest to others (presumably Spanish investors at Cadiz), his proposal was not specific about the time of repayment, which dissuaded many potential investors. Last, Montes confessed, the current high interest rate of 13 percent at Cadiz "makes it difficult to carry out the king's orders."[112] Montes's pessimistic outlook was not exaggerated; Landaburu wrote from Cadiz that the port was flooded with *vales,* which soaked up all available silver specie; even merchants reputed to control fortunes of 500–700,000 pesos reported that they had had to sell their *vale* holdings to meet household expenditures.[113]

To Cadiz colleagues on whom he could depend "in all commercial matters there," Montes now proposed a different assessment. Along with copies of his royal commission and personal correspondence with Finance Minister Múzquiz, he expressed the conviction that once they had invested their *pesos fuertes* earned on colonial sales in *vales,* "I am quite sure of the recognition and good impression this service will make upon His Majesty, with respect to our merchants in general or individually." Was this based on a prior off-the-record understanding between Múzquiz and Montes? More explicitly, Montes advanced the questionable belief that if the Cadiz community responded favorably to the *vales* proposition, it might "open the door to the return of the old managed system, because the king will listen to us."[114]

A week later, Landaburu managed to persuade Manxón, the president of the Casa de Contratación, and *consulado* officials to call a general assembly (*junta general*) of the *consulado* membership. There, Landaburu read to an enthusiastic audience Montes's exposition to Múzquiz of the depressive effects of *comercio libre* of 1778, coupled with the government's proposal to sell *vales* for silver pesos. He concluded, to quote from reports of the assembly, with Montes's prediction that "[i]f we merchants give the king a million pesos, he expected and even believed certain that His Majesty would reestablish managed trade, abolishing what had been harmful to his Treasury and subjects."[115] This was no minor commitment.[116]

The *junta* proceedings were immediately reported to Gálvez by his informal agent and correspondent, Villamar (one of Cadiz's wealthiest merchants and a veteran *consulado* member), who expressed relief that he had not been present. Otherwise he would been obligated to clarify at no small personal risk what he courteously termed Landaburu's delusion, "since I would create many enemies by defending freedom of trade." Revealing of the ambience at Cadiz was Villamar's request that Gálvez conceal the source of his information.[117]

In fact, Gálvez did not need Villamar's report (3 September) of how Montes, Landaburu, and Manxón had misinterpreted Múzquiz's order by calling for a general assembly of the Cadiz *consulado* as if so authorized by Madrid, rather than by privately trolling for potential Cadiz investors in *vales*. For, two days earlier, on 1 September, Gálvez had apparently concluded from anonymous sources that Montes's quid pro quo to the Cadiz merchant community for the purchase of a million pesos in *vales* would obligate Madrid to rescind the recently promulgated *comercio libre* decrees. Had Múzquiz deliberately rephrased the royal order to give Montes latitude in its interpretation, or had Montes decided on his own to manipulate his commission to help the Cadiz *consulado* roll back the decrees?

Gálvez adopted a charitable pose toward Múzquiz. Putting the best face on a disagreeable situation, he wrote him that Montes's letters to Landaburu had distorted Múzquiz's instructions and were, as he put it, "phrased in such a way as to stir up merchants addicted by habit to the old custom of colonial trade and"—obviously incorporating Villamar's position—"disturbing those who have experienced the advantages of the modern one." Galvez could hardly overlook the colonial trade and merchant banking interests of the Goyeneches(the maternal side of Múzquiz's family), and he may also have assumed that Múzquiz was more interested in a quick fix for state deficits than in defending *comercio libre*. His handling of Montes's initiative was another matter. On 1 September, Gálvez informed Múzquiz of a forceful royal order, presumably drafted by Gálvez, and subsequently "fully confirmed" by Charles III, requiring Manxón as president of the Contratación to lose no time in retrieving from the Cadiz *consulado* and from Landaburu all relevant papers and letters "so that there is no record of the documents discussed" at the general assembly convened "contrary to the intention of the king" and Múzquiz. And to preserve the fiction of the king's infallibility as the executive of the "absolutist" state, an incensed Gálvez had Charles III insist that "neither vestige nor memory remain of a manifest violation of the sovereign will."[118]

Notwithstanding Gálvez's efforts to eradicate evidence of sharp ministerial friction over perhaps *the* major issue of colonial trade policy and the purposeful misinterpretation of Charles III's intent by contending cabinet officers, bureaucrats in the Colonial Office long remembered Montes's intervention and drew their own conclusions. Thirty years later, Francisco Viaña, who had entered the Colonial Office in 1782, where he made his career, recalled the affair in contrasting an "enlightened" minister (Gálvez) with a committed pro-business type (Montes). Múzquiz, Viaña judged, had simply forgotten that commercial policy should be made by public servants, not merchants.[119]

This is not to say that business interests did not continue to press public servants (with whom they continued to maintain contact) like Montes at the Hacienda or Antúnez y Acevedo at the Consejo de Indias to preserve policies and structures they considered necessary. Montes's continuation as a *tesorero general*, despite Gálvez's reaction to his performance at Cadiz, was a measure of the influence of merchants at Cadiz and Mexico City and the dependence of the Spanish Bourbon state upon them. Commercial and financial fine-tuning of the form of *comercio libre* of 1778, the Banco de San Carlos, and the emission of *vales* could not erode the faith of many public functionaries and men of business in the efficacy of traditional sources of state finance and continuity in colonial trade policy. A propos of the resistance to *comercio libre* of merchants in the Spanish commercial system, Valentín Foronda, an observer of the Spanish transatlantic trading system with an internationalist's perspective, once commented that "such is the influence of custom and ignorance upon weak minds, many who listened to Cadiz's monopolists bewailing their loss of exclusive trade came to believe all commerce ruined simply because of this handful of merchants."[120]

Supporters of traditional structures never lost sight of the link between the liquid assets and capacity of a prosperous Cadiz to respond to financial emergencies of the Spanish state. After all, the Cadiz *consulado,* joined by Madrid's Cinco Gremios Mayores, had repeatedly helped finance the state during the eighteenth century, at least until the late 1770s. By that time, however, prominent civil servants were reluctant to continue to rely upon these corporations, since their assistance obligated reciprocity, that is, reaffirmation or even extension of privilege. To many in state service, the repeated challenges of the century necessitated flexibility, which the affirmation of privilege inhibited. Montes managed to escape prosecution for his role in 1782, perhaps because he was an important intermediary between the central government at Madrid and the funds of the Cadiz community. As long as the metropole derived invaluable income and liquidity from the American colonies, Cadiz would retain its influence in commercial policy.

Montes's activity after differing with Gálvez illustrates the survival of old ways of thinking both in the Madrid bureaucracy and in the Cadiz community he represented unofficially but loyally. Responding in 1784 to a request from Múzquiz for suggestions on how to cover continued state deficits, he could still argue for the role of Cadiz as Madrid's paramount financial resource, providing the state restored earlier trade structures, the Proyecto of 1720 and *tonelada* and *palmeo* duties. Under the old Proyecto, he claimed inaccurately, merchants had never complained. The presumed decline of the metropole's major commercial emporium only began after 1778, when the regulations of 1720 were discarded, the Proyecto's special duties were voided, and other peninsular ports were authorized to engage in colonial trade. The result was, he argued, vessels departing from peninsular ports for the colonies laden with non-Spanish goods financed by non-Spanish merchant houses, their profits not retained but exported—all because neither the newly authorized ports in the metropole nor their provincial hinterlands offered exportables: "They lack goods and manufactures." The flip side of this coin was an upsurge in smuggling. Now, with Spanish authorization, ships from the United States could introduce goods smuggled in flour barrels at Havana, just as ships under contract to Cabarrús & Lalanne carried smuggled merchandise rather than ballast to Havana.

There was little new in Montes's argument or details. What is surprising is the repetition. In 1784, almost two decades after the initial hesitant step of Barlovento had slightly opened the Spanish transatlantic commercial system, and six years after the amplifications of 1778, Montes—and through him, the chorus of Cadiz merchants—still tendered old remedies for dangerously changing conditions. Commerce had always been an ever-flowing "wellspring of riches," Montes philosophized to Múzquiz in 1784, always "the best resource in any urgency." Implicit was his experience as a former merchant in the trade to New Spain, which confirmed that the cooperation of Cadiz interests depended on the state's readiness to compromise its vaguely defined and imperfectly executed developmental policy. In other words, if Cadiz was then in no condition to lend to the state, there still remained a solution: return to the pre-1778 transatlantic commercial structures of managed trade. "Let trade with the Indies return to its former prosperous state, reestablish the regulations of 1720 or others like them," Montes urged Múzquiz. "Terminate immoderate freedom, and I promise to find the means of support for the state without prejudice to the Treasury, with benefit to the trade of America and of these kingdoms."[121]

This mentality, and the aggregated business interests of Cadiz, Mexico City, and Lima sustaining it, go a long way toward explaining the maddeningly halting pace at which Spain persistently made basic changes in colonial affairs. It accounts for the omission of New Spain from *comercio libre* in October 1778, and why another decade had to pass before that colony was finally included.

7. The Aftermath in Spain

In evaluating the repercussions of the comprehensive October 1778 statute on colonial trade, one must take into account the broad policy considerations of the Spanish state for the metropolitan and colonial economies. Probably because of the virtual stalemate in the metropole in the aftermath of the fall of Esquilache in 1766, economic initiatives shifted to Spain's colonies in America, where, Madrid concluded, policy could be more successfully implemented, because resistance would be less effective. In 1778, the Spanish state's major preoccupation was to augment its income from its extended American empire, especially from New Spain and Peru, through duties on exported goods, its most reliable source of financial liquidity, given Spain's agrarian economy. A second priority was the development of agricultural exportables, especially wine and brandy from Andalusia and Catalonia; in the colonies, there was emphasis on exports of sugar, tobacco, hides, cochineal, and indigo, which metropolitan intermediaries redirected to European consumers and manufacturers.

There was, finally, a third priority integral to the Bourbon paradigm that *proyectistas* had been contemplating over the first half of the century: creation of a broad base in manufactures permitting (belatedly, to be sure) the metropole to match the achievement of competing European colonial powers, a colonial pact whereby national manufactures were exchanged for prized colonial staples. Although perhaps not considered realizable in the short term, behind the fiscal priority was a protectionist factor favoring an import-substitution model that privileged what was still small-scale manufacturing of woolens, linens, silks, and cottons. Bernardo Ward's *Proyecto económico,* originally written in 1762, had broached this, and his editor, Campomanes, had supported the concept in his *Industria popular* (1774), expounding on cottage industry that might avoid grouping potentially dangerous proletarians in large workshops. These interlocked objectives required more shipping capacity and a stimulus to lower maritime freight and insurance rates, which under the convoy system had discouraged shipments of high-volume agricultural staples with low unit value. Taken together, these measures might reduce the widespread smuggling of European manufactured goods (which was cheaper by far than reexporting them through Spain's transatlantic trade system), a perennial problem in the Peninsula, and one now increasingly encountered in the Caribbean. Smuggling—the parallel economy in both metropole and colonies—translated into serious leakage of New Spain's minted and unminted silver to non-Spanish suppliers and an irreplaceable loss of government revenue.

Silver minted at Mexico City figured large in official and unofficial calculations. Analyzing the gap between silver minted in New Spain and the metropole's receipts over a twelve-year period, 1767–78, Madrid's Royal Economic Society found a difference of 45 percent. Over the following wartime period, 1779–83, the gap virtually doubled, reaching 81 percent.[1] Even after making allowance for silver retained in New Spain's internal economy, its customary subsidies to colonial governments in the Philippines and Cuba, and for silver withdrawn from Havana under contract by Cabarrús & Aguirre during the war, the gap was disturbing as a measure of the extent of smuggled imports and silver exports, on both counts a revenue loss. "[R]est assured . . . it is no exaggerated estimate that over six years, foreigners have supplied three-quarters of New Spain's imports," the Royal Economic Society's report hammered home. A more conservative estimate lowered this to 50 percent.[2]

Internal contradictions plagued attempts to curb smuggling in colonial markets. While the 1778 Reglamento removed the Proyecto's *toneladas* and *palmeo* fees, among others, it increased the base prices of selected exports to colonial ports from 5 to 20 percent.[3] In addition, the tariff of 1782, although effectively liberating Spain from the unequal commercial treaties of the seventeenth century, raised import duties between 14 and 25 percent on items constituting two-thirds of exports to the colonies, such as woolens, silks, thread, mercury, and hardware.[4] Moreover, colonial import prices were inflated further by equating the colonial *peso fuerte* with the metropole's *peso sencillo,* cutting colonial purchasing power by 25 percent.[5] Thus, despite the government's intention to provide the colonies with imports at price levels reasonably competitive with English, French, and Dutch goods circulating in the Caribbean, its financial priorities in fact promoted smuggling.[6] Clandestine colonial specie exports were encouraged by minting fees and export duties at colonial ports, on arrival in Spain, and on reexport to European suppliers. And there was a further anomaly. The home government, despite its publicized *comercio libre* of 1778, continued to allow Colonial Secretary Gálvez to set the number of ships and allocate tonnage (but not value) in supplying its most important American colony on the basis of unreliable commercial reporting.[7]

These factors gradually surfaced after the war years, when maritime traffic between metropole and colonies resumed. The cycle of expansion and contraction in Spain's colonial trade between 1783 and 1787, the result of Cadiz's speculative exuberance, led Gálvez's immediate successor as colonial secretary, Antonio Valdés y Bazán, to solicit opinions in 1787 from interested parties in metropole and colonies before implementing further modifications in the Spanish transatlantic commercial system of shared and still managed monopoly.

Dazzling Appearances, Detestable Bad Faith

At Cadiz, the impact of the 1778 Reglamento was contradictory. Notwithstanding the commercial crisis and a shakeout of overextended firms through bankruptcies, other data indicate a remarkable expansion of colonial trade and silver inflows, which the port continued to dominate.

To well-established domestic and foreign businessmen in the colonial trade, the 1778 statute threatened Cadiz's commercial domination by weakening the main constituent of its bargaining power with the Spanish state, financial leverage. With the development of capitalist institutions, state finance in Spain was shifting to new sources, to *vales reales,* the Banco Nacional de San Carlos, Amsterdam bankers, and Mexico City's wealthy merchants, and away from domestic lenders such as the state-managed Real Giro, the Cadiz *consulado,* and Madrid's Cinco Gremios Mayores.[8] Furthermore, Cadiz's hegemony over the lucrative trade with New Spain, long protected by the rules governing the Jalapa *feria* system and its distribution of economic "space" between the *comercio de España* and the *comercio de México* now seemed obsolete when *almaceneros* of New Spain's capital city shipped funds to Cadiz and even directly to European suppliers in England,

France, and Italy in order to cover their orders.[9] So many Gaditanos thought; whether it occurred on the massive scale claimed has yet to be confirmed. Anxiety can be more motivating than reality.

If the stepped-up flow of merchants' capital from colony to metropole was more imagined than tangible, this could not be said of the rash of bankruptcies registered (and publicized) at Cadiz after about 1786 and considered a direct consequence of the October 1778 Reglamento. The roots of this phenomenon were evident: a surge of exports and reexports to the colonies, especially New Spain, in 1784 and 1785, where supply (it was claimed) outstripped demand; the persistence of traditional trading practices, along with expectations nurtured by the convoy system; and that basic ingredient of entrepreneurial skill, the spirit of speculation.

At war's end in 1783, Cadiz shipowners and shippers hurriedly dispatched ships and goods to supply consumers in the colonies and to tap the backup of precious metals there. Colonial Secretary Gálvez proceeded to assign ships and cargo capacity (*toneladas*) to peninsular ports now eligible to trade directly with New Spain; cargo value was, of course, unlimited. He had an extraordinary degree of discretion, since, as Campomanes recognized, shipowners "must apply to Madrid for a license, while the ministry sets the number."[10] Exercising this discretion "without calculating demand and without data on stock," Gálvez exposed himself to the risk of "losing objectivity, privileging a port of individuals." Between 1784 and 1787, he assigned Veracruz an unusually high average of 10,000 tons annually. Andalusia remained the favored Spanish province: in 1784, Gálvez allocated 42 percent to Cadiz and a further 27 percent to Sevilla and Málaga.[11] New Spain received shipments far above its expectations and capacity to absorb. Reexports to Veracruz of goods with high unit value produced a rise in customs revenues and satisfaction to traders on the Cadiz-Mexico City axis. As a result, 96.5 percent of New Spain's precious metals exports to Spain in 1783–87 went to Cadiz.[12]

Inflows of precious metals from colonial ports in 1784 promised to fulfill the expectations of Madrid bureaucrats and dispel the anxiety of Cadiz merchants. Dubious Gaditanos warned, however, that the promising volume of sales recorded in New Spain was abnormal and simply reflected the pent-up demand of the war years. But when millions of pesos flooded into Cadiz in 1784 and again in 1785, most Cadiz merchants responded with a conditioned reflex. "No one accustomed to a method changes under different circumstances until experience shows the new way." They settled outstanding accounts with foreign suppliers, diverted higher than usual earnings to personal expenditure, bought real estate in and around Cadiz, began to invest in recently issued treasury bills (*vales*), and plowed funds into more exports to Veracruz and other colonial ports, such as Havana and Cartagena.[13] Joining in this export boom were Catalan and Andalusian shippers of wine, brandy, and other agricultural products, profiting at last from reductions in overseas freight and insurance costs.[14]

The downside of the postwar overexpansion, a crisis whose repercussions affected domestic and foreign merchants along with the merchant bankers of Cadiz, made its appearance in 1786. Not only had New Spain imported an unusually high tonnage of European goods, but its merchants had meanwhile been speculating in smuggled merchandise introduced by the English from Jamaica, the French from Saint-Domingue, and by traders from New Orleans, all advantaged by the differential between the current prices of legal imports from Spain and those of smuggled items at colonial ports, an appreciable margin of between 30 to 35 percent.[15] After absorbing a high volume of goods over two years, inventories were backing up in New Spain in 1786, and a number of Cadiz firms faced a liquidity crisis when forced to settle accounts with creditors from whom they had borrowed at higher than usual interest rates.

The investment climate at Cadiz, Madrid, and elsewhere in the Peninsula had been changing rapidly in the early 1780s as both domestic and foreign investors discovered new opportunities in the purchase of *vales* and shares in the Banco de San Carlos, and in the financing of a major construction enterprise, the Canal de Aragín—all, relatively speaking, gilt-edged investments. But by 1786, merchants and shipowners seeking fresh capital for promising colonial ventures encountered rising interest costs, which many tolerated in the hope of continuing inflated returns on colonial speculation. For many at Cadiz, illiquidity was also the product of real estate speculation and an excessively high level of personal expenditure on housing, servants, carriages, and entertainment, rather than investment in manufacture or agricultural enterprise. These factors, to be sure, were important but accessory to a predictable downturn of sales by 1785 in Cadiz's major overseas marketplace, New Spain.[16] The bulge in the number of Cadiz bankruptcies was undermining the port's credit standing and commercial operations.[17]

In late 1784, one year after the war's end, the rate of Cadiz bankruptcies began to climb, signs of business failures multiplied in the number of sealed-off offices and warehouses and business records sequestered.[18] The main bankrupt firms "very early evidenced disquieting signs; few at Cadiz remained calm; then rumor undermined credit; but what sustained firms were their interconnections; they scraped together funds among associates to try to improve their luck, using more or less reliable calculations," noted an investigator appointed by the Cadiz *consulado,* which feared that the cumulative impact of business failures would bring the transatlantic trade into disrepute.

Confidence, the bedrock of the *cuerpo comerciante,* was at stake and as the most influential corporate body representing the commercial interests of Spain's busiest port, the Cadiz *consulado* was in an ambiguous position.[19] It was under pressure to block the "scandal of multiple bankruptcies" and its ripple effects. On the other hand, the *consulado* held that its charter limited its role, and that it was merely there to "witness, authorize, and enforce" agreements worked out by creditors, even when they were recognizably neither well thought out nor equitable to all parties.[20] Under the discretion granted to creditors' agreements and the presumed neutrality of the *consulado,* settlements were often discriminatory, the product of "secret arrangements and assurances obtained in advance by the biggest, well-connected firms." The deliberately confusing tactics of wily bankrupts left the general public caught between those who had proceeded in good faith and those who had prejudiced "la causa publica."[21] To dissatisfied creditors, the *consulado*'s neutrality disguised favoritism to some bankrupts and their creditors, improper conduct so frequent that it had "become a customary tactic of well-known utility."[22]

A five-part typology of bankruptcies was formulated by the *consulado*-appointed investigator Juan de Mora y Morales (a lawyer) after research into the "real time of origin, frequency, and circumstances behind the chain of bankrupts." Three varieties of bankruptcy were most common. First came bankruptcies predictable when the prospect of profitable commercial undertakings opened by the October 1778 Reglamento drew in undercapitalized but highly motivated newcomers intent on fulfilling their financial obligations promptly in order to "buy confidence." Straining to meet all creditors' demands sooner rather than later, "adjudications are hurried, the chronology of contracts broken," then "honor disappears," followed shortly afterward by "the bankruptcy evident from the beginning."[23]

A more "criminal" variety was bankruptcy caused by "ostentatious traffic in bills of exchange . . . luxury" and in flamboyant displays of wealth, which could "confuse the keenest eye." Ever pressed for liquidity, such merchant houses sold merchandise bought on credit below cost, paid the most demanding creditors first, and accepted bills of exchange drawn on them without hope of funds to honor them. Finally, overwhelmed by accumulating "obfuscation, confusion, and disorder," they closed their doors, leaving records so disorganized that "the sheer irritation of reading [them] saps the need to examine [them]."[24]

A third type, involving shipowners (*navieros* or *expedicionistas*), was a result of the increase in shipping to the colonies produced by the 1778 Reglamento. Such maritime enterprise commenced on a narrow base, usually ownership (real or simulated) of a merchant vessel, in some cases bearing a license from the Colonial Office giving access to Veracruz. *Navieros* fantasized about overseas speculation, pushed up costs by borrowing at the high rates of sea loans (*a riesgo de mar*) to cover the cost of a ship license, buy or fit out a vessel, and meet other incidental outlays. Often their ships failed to sail on schedule or, once in a colonial port, failed to fulfill their contracts within the stipulated time, sometimes even assuming more debt. Forced liquidation of the bankrupts' assets usually fell far short of the outstanding debts, "causing losses to many" and discrediting responsible shipowners.[25]

Business failures at Cadiz in the 1780s cut across the commercial community and affected not only French firms like Béhic & Gomez, Meray & la Case, Ribeaupierre, and Medard y Cia. but Spanish houses such as those of Matheo Bernal and Mariano Bernabé de Frías. Bernal was typical of those Spaniards who went to the colonies as the factors or agents of Cadiz merchant houses, husbanded their savings, and then returned to Cadiz to establish their own firms, in Bernal's case with a surprisingly large capital base of almost 700,000 pesos—or so he claimed, although this does not square with large purchases on credit for reexports to the colonies. After three decades trading in New Spain and Peru, Bernal opened his own business in 1778, dealing with Irish firms such as Tierry & Cia., Guillermo Thompson & Cia., and O'Connor y MacNamara Hijos & Cia. Bernal later blamed arrangements contracted with these firms for his downfall. He bought on credit, repaid on time (he said), and used Pedro del Puerto Vicario, Vicario, and Saenz de Santa María as his consignees at Veracruz.[26]

After the peace settlement of 1783, eleven Irish commercial houses approached Bernal and, according to his deposition, produced letters from correspondents overseas at Veracruz urging fresh shipments of woolens and mercury, further confirmed by a fellow Cadiz trader, Ignacio Rodríguez de Lorenzana, who assured Bernal that "America needed those goods." Such personal market information formed the sole basis of business decision-making in the absence at Cadiz of government-sponsored or private-sector trade periodicals. Markets, after all, are driven by information, and also by intangibles—speculation about how others will react to new commercial intelligence and by crowd psychology. The Irish firms sweetened their proposition with verbal assurances that they would not pressure Bernal to sell merchandise below cost even if conditions at Veracruz so warranted. Their contract stipulated one year for repayment, that Bernal consign shipments to firms in New Spain designated by them, so that Bernal could not take independent action without their approval. Here Bernal seems to have been a *cargador* fronting for non-Spanish merchant houses.

It is hard to believe that Bernal failed to realize that in accepting such conditions, "he had no more participation in the matter than lending his name for two reasons, first, to ship to America what foreigners could not under their own names, and second to be responsible for the predictable losses."[27] By his own admission, Bernal had acted squarely in the tradition of *prestanombres* when he "bought" 183,000 pesos worth of textiles and mercury on credit from his "partners."

What soured this transaction, Bernal complained, was the inferior quality of the goods he obtained on credit during the postwar colonial trade boom of 1785 from his Irish suppliers, Felipe Magnamara (*sic*) and Domingo Thomas Terry, which were overpriced (*recargados*) by 25 to 35 percent according to Bernal's Veracruz correspondents, who advised that they could not dispose of his shipments "because of poor quality and overpricing."[28] From Veracruz, Pedro del Puerto Vicario wrote that he would have to match textiles received against invoices, warning Bernal to ship no more linens "whose local prices would not cover even prime costs in Spain," nor calico prints (*indianas*), nor *angaripolas,* since Catalans were selling them far cheaper. Suspend shipments, Puerto Vicario admonished Bernal, until Veracruz conditions improved, since other ships were unloading the same types of goods and "[t]he Americas are oversupplied." Meanwhile, a whole shipload went unsold, and mercury fetched only 15 percent over prime cost at Cadiz. As for a second shipment, "I don't know what the devil got into you to buy those English Camillones or so many second-rate serges and duroys with no hope of sales," an exasperated Puerto Vicario wrote. "[T]here will be enough goods hereabouts to supply your grandchildren."[29] Bernal reacted by ordering his Veracruz consignees to suspend sales until marketing conditions improved, a decision angering Bernal's Cadiz creditors and sponsors, who demanded his immediate liquidation (*cesión de bienes*). Bernal's accounts reveal that he had yet to receive full returns on 293,556 pesos' worth of merchandise exported to the colonies, the bulk (66 percent) to New Spain and Guatemala.[30] Bernal's is a classic case study of a straw man (*prestanombre*) who failed his backers.

Mariano Bernabé de Frías offers another example of an overextended shipowner overtaken by rapidly changing colonial market conditions in the immediate postwar years. His bankruptcy conforms closely to the flamboyant type sketched by the *consulado*'s investigator. Like Bernal, Frías was no newcomer to the colonial trade; he claimed that his grandparents had been traders, and that since about 1760, he had engaged in "steady trading with the Americas" as a *cargador* and *factor* aboard his own ships, operating on earnings from freight, efficient shipping techniques, commercial contracts, and "intelligent, practiced, and diligent" management. In the early 1780s, he prospered enough to buy and renovate two residences at Cadiz, which absorbed a whopping 402,000 pesos, and spent another 16,000 pesos annually on wages and household and other expenses. Meanwhile, he managed to purchase three large foreign-built vessels (each of about 500 tons burden) for 170,000 pesos, then had them overhauled for another 60,000. He leased them to the Spanish government for the siege of Gibraltar, receiving in return from the Colonial Office a license (really a *privilegio*) to send two *registros* loaded with goods to Veracruz. In 1783, he borrowed *a dos riesgos* (sea loans covering outbound and inbound voyages) from at least three prominent Cadiz commercial houses (Lopedeti, Noble, and Pons), and from other French, Irish, and Italian firms, at the then prevailing high interest rates, in order to buy over half a million pesos' worth of merchandise "best adapted to the consumers" of New Spain, which he shipped to Veracruz, where he set up his son as agent.[31] Then, as "proprietor of the laden ships," he awaited the profits of the enterprise, "which promised prosperity to his legitimate conjectures."

Like Bernal, Frías could not adapt to competitive post-1778 conditions of supply and pricing at Veracruz. Sales proved unexpectedly slow, the shipping business stagnated, and Frías's son failed to remit funds to satisfy his father's creditors, who refused to renegotiate terms of repayment. As Frías described his predicament, "suddenly after he had spent funds, his speculations were cut short, [with] his ships at anchor, [and he was] overcome with debt." In April 1786, he declared bankruptcy to the Cadiz *consulado,* his creditors, and his merchant colleagues, among whom he counted Spaniards (Caraza y Santa María), French (Verduc, Jolif y Sere), Irish (Rian), Italians (Greppi y Marliani), and English (Duff, the British consul), as well as agents of Madrid's Cinco Gremios Mayores.[32] However favorable his character references, the Consejo de Indias ultimately got to the heart of his and similar cases. Frías's failure occurred, it determined, because he had undertaken more than either his capital base or market conditions warranted, bought three unnecessarily large vessels, and borrowed at high interest rates to make them seaworthy. "Customarily, many ship goods purchased on credit." It concluded dryly: "This is what happened to Frías."[33]

Bankruptcy proceedings like Frías's were all too common at Cadiz in the late 1780s, but his became notorious when outraged creditors rejected the *consulado*'s decision in his favor, appealing first to the local Juzgado de Alzadas and then to Madrid's Consejo de Indias. Perhaps his creditors were encouraged by changes in Madrid's high bureaucracy when ministers more critical of the Cadiz *consulado*'s policies and political influence like Pedro Lerena at Hacienda and Antonio Valdés at the Colonial Office took control. Frías's creditors—Pons, Bulle, Vega—charged *consulado* officials with failure to adhere to its customary bankruptcy proceedings, "rules they have religiously observed until now." Where once the *consulado* had proceeded fairly and promptly, the creditors argued, now it badly mishandled such cases.[34] They faulted its lenient attitude toward Frías: it had called on short notice for what turned out to be a poorly attended assembly (*junta*) of creditors, where Frías, without taking oath, had offered no documentation ("without referring to his ledgers") to support his case. The creditors then refused to discuss his proposed settlement: a limited number of creditors would be paid off, some to 70 percent of their exposure, others to 50 percent over a five-year period, leaving Frias high and dry in uncontested control of his assets "and with ample resources to continue with prejudice to all his creditors." *Consulado* officers then hastily accepted his proposal without requiring the assent of all creditors. But on appeal to the Juzgado de Alzadas of the Casa de Contratación at Cadiz, the creditors were vindicated. Both the *junta* called by the *consulado* and its settlement were judged illegal, Frías was ordered jailed, his assets, records, and other relevant papers were impounded, and a second creditors' *junta* was called to review the "documents proving credits and persons involved."[35]

Nonetheless, the *consulado* balked at executing the Juzgado de Alzadas's resolution, claiming it required the Consejo de Indias's approval. When this materialized, the *consulado* still resisted action against Frías. "All one can say is the *junta* has met again without drawing up a list of the real debtors." As for Frías, he stayed out of jail and neither presented a sworn statement of assets and credits nor demanded that creditors substantiate their claims. In fact, two years after Frías had declared bankruptcy, the dissatisfied insisted that many creditors were still unnamed, "on the contrary, they suspect they are fake or fraudulent" and believed that others had been secretly paid off "to induce them to accept the agreement."[36] If the *consulado* had ever enjoyed a reputation for evenhandedness in its commercial court, now it stood publicly accused of gross negligence in handling the illegal actions of a prominent Gaditano shipper and *consulado* member with manifest partiality. At stake, as the *consulado*'s own investigator noted, was confidence in the *consulado* as representative of the Cadiz commercial community, confidence "it has always inspired among everyone in the principal ports, centers, and factories of Europe and America."[37] Boom times were unmaking obedience to customary norms of business behavior.

The Parallel Economy at Cadiz

Equally damaging to the image of the *consulado* and the commercial community it served was a four-year-long inquiry (1785–89) ordered by Lerena's Hacienda ministry into Cadiz's notorious smuggling complex—really a parallel economy—linking customs officers to Spanish and foreign businessmen and giving the port the reputation of handling in one day "more smuggled goods than all the authorized ports in the Peninsula over a whole year."[38] Given the peso value of Cadiz's trade, this was hardly hyperbole. Not that smuggling was a novelty at Cadiz, at other peninsular ports, and in the colonies. It was an everyday, common, unavoidable, necessary (to some even legitimate) way of doing business, and for many a means of economic survival. However, the operations of this parallel economy undermined the fiscal aims of Charles III's policy planners. Before and after coming to Madrid, Charles's government continually received reports of smuggling at Cadiz and in the American colonies. Officials could hardly have been startled by Miguel de Cervera's observation that while Cadiz was filled with "innumerable customs watchmen, inspection boats making rounds, yet millions of illegal pesos are introduced."[39] Accordingly, Esquilache, Charles's first Hacienda secretary, had assigned high priority to investigating Cadiz's operations, with meager results by the time of his ouster.[40] Madrid was well aware that English merchants considered "the bullion trade . . . the most valuable commerce in the world," and that their share in that trade came from the sale of English products reexported to the Spanish colonies and from smuggling in the Caribbean.[41] (Miguel de Cervera calculated in 1765 that, by importing directly from Jamaica rather than from Cadiz, merchants in the Spanish colonies saved 20–40 percent.)[42] With good reason, the large surplus in Spain's colonial trade account was in the main transferred through Cadiz to European suppliers, justifying the complaint that "foreigners are making off with silver . . . directly from America's mines to London, Paris, or Amsterdam."[43]

As tariff barriers to imports of European textile products—woolens, cottons, linens, silks, and yarns—were raised in the October 1778 Reglamento and the 1782 schedules "to favor our manufactories," the flow of unlisted and mislabeled reexports through the Cadiz customs rose proportionately.[44] The oversupply of imports in the colonies was not the result of the October 1778 legislation, Thomas Southwell insisted in 1788, but of "smuggling and illicit exchanges." Southwell, an Irish-born officer in the Spanish navy and mathematics tutor of one of Charles's sons, meant by illicit trading what was becoming almost standard practice at Cadiz and other peninsular ports trading with the colonies, the purposeful mislabeling of European re-exports as "Spanish."[45] Collusion among Spanish and foreign merchants with Cadiz customs officers had always been common, but it burgeoned in the late 1780s, when statistical data generated by the October 1778 Reglamento pointed to huge revenue losses to the Spanish state because of the way customs personnel dutied foreign and colonial trade. One such calculation in 1787 indicated that Madrid should have collected five times more from external trade than its actual receipts (14.8 million reales).[46]

Importing European products excluded by customs regulations from reexport to the colonies to Cadiz and slipping undervalued imports past customs officers were time-tested practices of the Cadiz commercial community. Before the era of Charles III, a ritualized compromise had existed for two centuries under which, for example, a *flota* that was excessively freighted with both prohibited and undervalued cargo would have its merchants assessed a fine (*indulto*) on returning to Cadiz. Sometime after 1739, the government tried to break the established pattern, which underscored its pseudo-mercantilism, by investigating the *administradores, vistas,* and *guardas* of the Cadiz customs bureaucracy. With the arrival of Charles III, Spanish policy moved to implement a developmental policy—an early import-substitution approach—which entailed reducing competition from imports then reexported to the American colonies. However, as Esquilache's abortive efforts had shown, mutually profitable collusion between officers and merchants outwitted and outlasted inspection teams and reformulations of oversight. By the late 1770s and early 1780s, however, parameters had changed. Colonial demand for quality imports rose concurrently with the disposable income of upper-class colonial consumers and even of more modest income groups. A propensity for luxury is not solely characteristic of the wealthy.

In the second place, conjoined protectionist and fiscal objectives crafted to exploit the colonial world inflated tariff levels in Spain and the colonies along with sales taxes, not to mention the fees of Cadiz brokers and commission agents, which made the colonies' legitimate imports far more expensive than goods deliberately undervalued at Cadiz or smuggled from Caribbean islands. Depending on the elements included, estimates of customs duties, maritime freight, insurance, commissions, and sales taxes imposed on goods imported into New Spain from Cadiz vary from a low of 16 to a high of 70 percent of base prices at Cadiz.[47] The rationale for a proto-import substitution policy in the reign of Charles III was the expectation of success within a tolerable, short-to-medium time frame. That policy was reduced to a fiscal device when domestic coupled to colonial demand outdistanced the low-quality, overpriced, and limited supply of metropolitan output. In the late 1770s, techniques for undermining customs regulations and personnel were widespread, well honed, and virtually ineradicable at Cadiz. Their survival is a measure of the incapacity of the preconstitutional (whether "late feudal," "absolutist," "enlightened despotic," or "mercantilist") state to enforce its directives upon a small, conniving, resourceful commercial bourgeoisie and its foreign collaborators.[48]

A variety of evasive stratagems of long elaboration and official toleration had compromised the effectiveness of the Spanish state at its principal commercial entrepôt. Incoming vessels from Europe's Atlantic ports introduced merchandise that was often consigned to anonymous bearers (*al portador*), who thereby avoided prosecution for customs evasion; or cargo was not marked clearly for entry, whether into the Peninsula or "in transit" for reexport to the colonies.[49] Ship captains might register only a fraction of total cargo at customs, retaining the balance aboard for months instead of unloading within eight days as required by Cadiz port regulations. Only gradually would cargo be off-loaded, put ashore, and inserted secretly into the metropolitan market, or loaded aboard vessels bound for the colonies—in any event, without passing through customs. Merchantmen moored in Cadiz's harbor served in effect as long-term floating warehouses—to quote a weary Hacienda minister, as a "free port, maintaining storage from which to land [goods] or load [them] aboard shipping outbound for America to avoid import duties."[50] Equally traditional evasion took the form of gross undervaluation of items listed on ships' manifests (*registros*) deposited with the Cadiz customs.

Somewhat more novel tactics came with improvement in cargo packaging. Densely packed bales were put through customs for dutying and shipment to colonial ports. Accepting the claim that the bales could not be opened and repacked quickly, customs officers failed to inspect their contents, accepting the number and value of bales listed on manifests.[51] (In colonial ports, those claiming the cargo then used the approval of Cadiz customs to rebut accusations of mislabeling, undercounting, or undervaluing.) In a celebrated case involving a determined Lima customs inspector who discovered that a shipment of silk thread and stockings had been mislabeled as Spanish products, the Cadiz *consulado* insisted that once the Cadiz customs service had so classified it, the contents could not be questioned.[52] Frequently, high-value items would be concealed in barrels containing relatively cheaper agricultural products; Havana shippers often concealed precious metals in sugar boxes.

Far more vexing were techniques designed to circumvent the state's infant-industry policy. In the 1770s and 1780s, merchants and foreign manufacturers colluded to smuggle prohibited textiles (e.g., cotton prints, silk stockings, and yarns) in two ways. Imported prints, French and Genoese silk stockings, and Flemish yarns were either stamped in their country of origin with counterfeit seals of Spanish manufacturers, or foreign entrepreneurs set up manufactories at Cadiz and Valencia for which they managed to import finished goods only to stamp them with local seals for reexport to colonial consumers as "national" products.[53] There were at Cadiz, it was reported, "producers whose main function is to label, as national products, embroidered silk stockings from Nîmes, then ship them to Spanish America."[54] In this fashion, the specific injunctions contained in the protectionist articles of the October 1778 Reglamento requiring customs to demand proof of domestic manufacture (articles 27–29) were systematically ignored. Inevitably, in the late 1780s, the supply of foreign textiles like woolens was so large in colonial markets that "we can't dispose of the large back-up at the Guadalajara, Segovia, and other factories."[55] Serious as was the situation at Cadiz, it was only symptomatic of all southern Spain, where large, well-armed bands transported a variety of smuggled items—tobacco, muslins, cottons, kerchiefs, gauzes, and shawls—from Portugal's frontier towns and from Gibraltar and Málaga. Prohibition or no prohibition, "muslins" had become fashionable in Spain and a kind of popular challenge to an inoperable state policy.[56]

Typically, a merchant of Valencia, who surely knew of the pseudo-ateliers counterfeiting imported silks as national products, shifted the blame for the impressive scale of smuggling operations onto the state bureaucracy, a myriad army of "clerks, inspectors, accountants, guards." Why, he asked, should public servants trouble to block illegal shipments? "If they confiscate items, only more work and perhaps vexing arguments [result]; if they don't confiscate, it's collusion. If the guards look away, they get what they want by calling fine linens *sheeting*. If the center of bales holds prohibited items, they [nonetheless] treat them as licit; so wherever they look, they find only licit goods and none other as they follow their instructions."[57]

Trying to break down the symbiotic relation between ineffective government protectionism and tenacious private sector smuggling at Cadiz became a preoccupation of Floridablanca's Hacienda minister, Pedro López de Lerena, who was appointed hard on the death of Múzquiz y Goyeneche, in 1785. Lerena and Múzquiz were not cut from the same cloth. Múzquiz's connection with the Cadiz community was without friction. On the ouster of Esquilache in 1766, Múzquiz was the choice of those who had supported the *motín;* the French commercial agent welcomed his appointment, since presumably he might give priority to supporting the Franco-Spanish alliance. The maternal (Goyeneche) side of the Múzquiz family had investments in the Cinco Gremios Mayores and its colonial trade and, it will be recalled, Múzquiz initiated the attempt of Francisco Montes, former Madrid agent of the Cadiz *consulado,* to arrange a loan for the government among members of the Cadiz community in return for suspending the *comercio libre* of 1778. As treasury secretary, Múzquiz had backed the financial legerdemain of Francisco Cabarrús, behind whom stood the influential bloc of French resident merchants and bankers. Cabarrús's eloquent elegy on Múzquiz's death was hardly disinterested.[58]

Lerena came from a different mold, distanced from French mercantile and banking interests. Of more modest social origins (Townsend dismissed his father as a "miserable publican"), Lerena had served as Floridablanca's private secretary during the investigation of the bishop of Cuenca's role in Esquilache's removal, followed Olavide as intendant of Andalusia and *asistente* of Sevilla, and was Floridablanca's choice to replace Múzquiz.[59] More of an economic nationalist than Múzquiz, Lerena concerned himself with Spain's economic development, which earned him the confidence of nationalists like León de Arroyal, a small landholder and regional Hacienda official.[60] Characteristically, Múzquiz had disregarded reports of the disarray of Cadiz's customs procedures and personnel, the ineffective processing of cargo, and the consequent "confusion resulting from disorder."[61]

When Lerena took over the Treasury, he found on his desk complaints from whistle-blowers at Cadiz. From Manuel María de Heredia (an official in the important Contaduría del comercio libre de Yndias), he learned that sugar boxes containing concealed silver were moving undetected past customs (colonial sugar was duty-free), and from another source, of imports reexported to the colonies as "made in Spain and falsified with Barcelona and Valencia seals."[62] Heredia accused the commandant of Cadiz's customs guards (*resguardo*), Antonio de Gálvez (a brother of the colonial secretary), of openly tolerating if not colluding with Gaditano smuggling rings. For his part, Antonio de Gálvez had lodged his own charges against local "people of power and standing."[63] Amid unprecedented postwar euphoria, the Cadiz business community was no peaceable kingdom.

Lerena wasted no time checking cautiously into how the Cadiz customs establishment processed the rising volume of trade with the colonies and Europe, since his oversight could be a measure of the effectiveness of the state's fiscal and protectionist policies. He drew immediately from the pool of competent and prestigious *alcaldes de casa y corte* of the Consejo de Castilla to pick Francisco Pérez Mesía, invested him with the broad authority of a *visitador-general,* and provided a set of secret depositions about the official conduct of the *comandante general del Resguardo* of Cadiz, Antonio de Gálvez. Mesía's broad investigative authority, the French consul at Cadiz reported, worried Cadiz's *consulado* and especially "our merchants," who might now have to open their business files for inspection. The consul observed that everyone realized how the privacy of business records affected a merchant's sense of security, and how fear of compromised security haunted them.[64] Mesía's immediate suspension of the customs administrator Andrés Montero Hijo was a disturbing straw in the wind.

Antonio de Gálvez had wind of the oncoming investigation, and just before Mesía's appointment, he wrote Lerena that he wished to retire, confessing that smuggling was beyond his control. He had entered government service in 1768 as an inspector (*vista*) in Málaga's state tobacco monopoly and in 1775 (the year his brother became colonial secretary) was posted to Cadiz as *Resguardo* commandant. Hard work, he complained, had affected his health, he no longer had any influence, and no one followed regulations, which explained the "wretched state of this monster, clandestine trade that controls Cadiz." Lerena, he had to assume, must surely know about the situation at Cadiz, its "treacherous bay, the port where faithlessness dominates, ably assisted by those who ought to be grateful." Gálvez then took sick leave and departed for Málaga, but on learning that, in his absence, Madrid had designated a cavalry colonel, Pedro Corvalán, as his interim replacement, he hurried back. He could hardly have been reassured by the insinuations of Alejandro O'Reilly, captain-general of Andalusia, and Visitador Mesía that he leave Cadiz.[65]

Mesía lost no time establishing contact with knowledgeable informants—"all important men of affairs"—willing to testify only at night "and at regular times so they won't be noticed."[66] Via informants and personal inspection tours, Mesía concluded that despite the apparent simplicity of the tariff accompanying the October 1778 statute, it was "defective," leaving merchants without adequate guidelines for certain prohibited imports, valuations, or duty rates, which explained customs officers' errors at Cadiz and colonial ports.[67] This did not, however, excuse businessmen from bypassing regulations by covertly loading vessels ready to depart for the colonies. Indeed, one year after arriving, assisted by Juan de Indart, Mesía drafted a 77-page set of new regulations covering customs procedures at Cadiz (his *Instrucción*), which Lerena quickly authorized.

Far more intractable and in the long term incorrigible was the protective self-interest of Cadiz's customs personnel. Not that their practices differed materially from those of their English counterparts at a time when customs regulations were mostly "burdensome and complicated."[68] Until the 1780s, ties of clientelism, patronage, and friendship placed personnel in the London customs service drawn largely from "Country Fox Hunters, Bankrupt Merchants, & Officers of the Army and Navy." Salaries were inadequate, obliging appointees to accept bribes for services and creating an environment for "corrupt agreements with merchants to facilitate fraud and smuggling." It was a system based upon "Bribery and Corruption . . . much practis'd from the Collectors down to the Tidesmen and Extra men."[69]

In this light, Mesía's assessment of Cadiz customs personnel, while brutally frank, was not uncommonly so by then current standards. He found the temporary administrator-general, Blas Sánchez Ochoa, incapable of managing the "many complex sections of their administration, omitting that of *commercio libre a Indias*," and that neither subordinates nor merchants could tolerate his "confused ideas and impatience."[70] At least Ochoa's defects had the virtue of good intentions; not so those of the important *contador* Andrés Montero Hijo, who had a "pasión" for befriending merchants, whom he allowed to remove goods from customs warehouses without following required procedures.[71] Montero's performance was matched by that of a lieutenant-commander of the *Resguardo,* Francisco Ortega, who handed out "passes for unloading ships and for the free entry and exit through city gates of bales, packages, bundles, and chests without search."[72] Mesía scorned the *vistas* who demanded bribes to spend on "luxury, gambling, and loose women"; to cultivate "untrustworthy merchants," the *vistas* would downgrade goods and, for example, record 6,650 yards of cloth as 665.[73] There were customs collectors like Manuel González Miera, formerly a merchant, who continued to ship goods (presumably fraudulently) to the colonies while maintaining "links or commercial relations with those to whom he owes his good fortune." Mesía's solution: select low-level personnel from candidates trained outside Andalusia who still feared punishment and were ready to "tolerate necessity and work."[74]

In Mesía's judgment, part of the problem at Cadiz was the unit of *guardas,* which was basic to the government's customs controls there. The *Resguardo*'s small harbor craft (*falúas*) met all incoming ships and put aboard from one to three *guardas,* who accompanied them to their moorings and then transferred shipmasters to shore along with their official documents. Upon the commandant of the *Resguardo* fell responsibility for his subordinates' "purity, disinterest, and vigilance," to quote from Mesía's *Instrucción* of 1786; under no circumstance should *guardas* be permitted to moonlight as merchants.[75] Mesía was now convinced that the *Resguardo*'s commandant, Antonio de Gálvez, had set a poor example. Under "high protection at court" (his brother, the colonial secretary), Gálvez permitted goods to be deposited in customs "without orderly accounts," merchants to show only samples (*muestras*) of cargo, and the bulk of incoming goods to be delivered to consignees "without examination or duties." No wonder "untrustworthy merchants" never considered requesting "the dispatch of goods from customs, because there were more advantages in leaving samples than paying duties." "With these tactics, Antonio de Gálvez had enriched himself, bought properties in Puerto Real [across Cadiz Bay] and in Málaga, as well as ships managed under the cover name of 'Pablo Mayo.'"[76]

Mesía, a civil servant, had to be tactful in offering this thumbnail exposé of Antonio de Gálvez's performance, for in 1789, the friends of the recently deceased José de Gálvez still occupied high places at Madrid. Although he painted a damning portrait of Antonio de Gálvez—he was ineffective, sloppy, authoritarian, and self-interested—Mesía thus only obliquely charged him with open collusion with Cadiz's commercial community. His evaluation of Gálvez was drafted in late August 1789, only weeks after Mesía's recall to Madrid, and suiting the cautious style of reformers in the age of Charles III, he recommended that Gálvez be retired on an annual pension of 20,000 reales.[77] Structural defects in the system were criticized but left unreformed; problem-solving consisted of changing personnel, as the conde de Aranda once advised the young Charles IV.

Lerena's extended commission of inquiry, like the one ordered two decades earlier by his aggressive predecessor in the Hacienda ministry, Esquilache, turned out to be equally fruitless. In 1787, the fate of Mesía's investigation was predicted by a Cadiz businessman who requested anonymity and immunity from possible persecution before exposing to Lerena the underworld of tolerated smuggling. Mesía's reforms, the anonymous "Zelante Patricio" foresaw, would evaporate once hardened smugglers resumed operations "whether by merchants or Manipolistas [*sic*], or the very officials and personnel of His Majesty. The Manipolistas or, rather, the brokers of such arrangements are already proposing them and have already realized them."[78]

Mesías's inquiry and its meager results underline the dilemma of Spain's tardy developmentalists in the last half of the eighteenth century when confronting massive falsification of textiles and related imports as "national" for reexport to the colonies. "Either this kingdom will have the means to supply America" with Spanish products, an anonymous report noted, or it would have to tolerate reexports of select imports for colonial consumption.[79] The issue could not have been put more clearly: could a "late-feudal" old regime circumscribed by entrenched interest groups carry out a policy of delayed industrial development? Could a colonial market adequately undergird Spain's infant manufacturing sector?

State Policy and Regional Growth: Catalonia and Andalusia

Assessment of the impact of the Spanish state's changing colonial trade policy after 1765 upon major regional economies of the Peninsula turns up, as in the case of Cadiz, contradictory indications. Between 1765 and 1785, growth and some development appeared, but were they traceable to state policy?

Over the eighteenth century, Catalonia was perhaps the single bright spot of economic performance in the metropole. Whereas Cadiz grew but did not develop, remaining an international entrepôt funneling reexports to the American colonies, Barcelona drew upon the agricultural resources of its hinterland and, in the second half of the century, also upon manufacturing nuclei in both the city and the countryside. In this case, development of a peripheral province in the metropole, its exportables, and colonial demand were interconnected and remained so over the next century and more.

Located on the western periphery of the Mediterranean, easily accessible to imports of grains and other provisions from producers around the Mediterranean, Catalonia's economy was able to shift from subsistence crops into export-oriented vineyards. After initially exploiting northern European and colonial outlets for the sale of its wine and brandy, after 1750 Catalonia galvanized its export agriculture and capital accumulation, forming an entrepreneurial core among medium- and small-sized landowners and port merchants.[80] These, in particular the small commercial bourgeoisie of Barcelona, were positioned to move into colonial trade between 1740 and 1758 using individual sailing vessels (*registros*).[81] Catalan agents at Cadiz, who for decades had handled the province's wine and brandy, now formally registered themselves and their shipping with the Cadiz *consulado* and began exporting both European imports and Catalan products to colonial ports, forging Catalonia's "primer momento de esplendor."[82] Earnings in silver from sales to preferred colonial ports like Veracruz were applied partly to cover Catalonia's food shortages, partly to expand its vineyards. After midcentury, Catalan entrepreneurs also began to invest in textile manufacturing, first in traditional woolens and linens, later in cotton prints, producing Catalonia's well-known *indianas*.[83] Colonial exposure over six decades of the eighteenth century prepared Catalan businessmen for two paths of involvement in colonial trade. One, the more traditional form, was a privileged stockholding company, the Real Compañía de Barcelona, chartered by the Madrid government in 1756 to benefit from tax concessions in trading with designated Caribbean colonies, Puerto Rico, Santo Domingo, Margarita, and later Cumaná in Venezuela. The other—far more attractive to cautious, hard-headed, profit-oriented investors—led Catalan merchants, shipbuilders, and shipowners organized in extended family-sized firms to probe the opportunities opened by the first and second *comercio libre* statutes. A few commercial firms trading with the colonies then eased slowly into cotton and paper manufacture, turning Catalonia into Francisco Mariano Nipho's rather exaggerated "little England."[84]

As a state-sponsored privileged company whose Catalan exports had duty-free status (but not a trade monopoly) when directed into its assigned colonial marketing "space," the Compañía de Barcelona replicated Cadiz's colonial commercial structures on a minor scale at a point when state policy was aiming to create a climate of competition for colonial markets among the metropole's ports and the peripheral provinces they served.[85] In this economic climate, the Compañía barely managed to place fewer than half of its 4,000 shares, most sold before 1765; always capital-short, it abandoned the sale of equity after 1771 for loan capital.[86] Just three months before the October 1778 statute was promulgated, its inefficient management had to suspend the dividend promised months earlier, and the following January, it halted payments to its creditors. By the early 1780s, the Compañía was, to all effects, moribund.[87] Aside from low returns to its stockholders, the Compañía did provide a vehicle for colonial sales of Catalan alcoholic beverages and flour (although some French flour imports were also included). Very few Catalan cotton goods were shipped to the colonies, and the Compañía's other textile exports (e.g., coarse linens and yarn) were probably purchased through Cadiz's foreign merchant houses.[88] Catalan printed linens, and to a lesser degree woolens (but virtually no cottons), constituted an insignificant 9 percent of the Compañía's total exports, and according to some reports, shipments of so-called Catalan linens were, in fact, imported cloth marked in Catalan mills with Barcelona seals and stamps.

To be sure, the tariff of the October 1778 Reglamento legitimated this practice and even encouraged it, leading recent analysts to conclude that the tariff's protectionism favored the products of cottage rather than factory industry.[89] In this context, state industrial policy pursued the strategy outlined by Campomanes in his *Industria popular* (1774) for stimulating small- rather than large-scale manufacture, thereby sidestepping the perceived social hazards of the factory system.[90] In no way did the Barcelona Compañía serve Catalonia's infant textile industry, "either because of the industry's inadequacies or the Compañía itself, which was naturally more preoccupied in protecting the capital invested than in stimulating national industry."[91]

Evidence indicates that Barcelona's Real Compañía, while a logical outgrowth of earlier Catalan involvement in colonial trade through Cadiz, came on the scene when its time had already passed. Directors and shareholders held out for the traditional security of monopoly when state policy through *comercio libre* was prodding Spanish merchants toward cost reduction and export volume, toward competition within the space of the Spanish transatlantic enclave.[92] The Compañía's assigned colonial territory—western, cocoa-growing Venezuela—remained an economic backwater on the periphery of the dynamic colonial economies of New Spain and Cuba, from which the company's charter specifically excluded it. The directors tried but failed in 1783 to have Madrid assign it 1,500 *toneladas* of annual exports to Venezuela *and* Veracruz over a ten-year period, both markets covered by other dispositions of the Colonial Office.[93] And when the Compañía attempted to exchange its fiscal privileges for participation in trade to colonial areas opened to other peninsular ports by the October 1778 statute, it could not compete with Catalonia's small-scale, extended family networks based on limited capital invested in a spectrum of enterprises—shipbuilding, textile printing, and, of course, colonial trade.[94]

These family firms rejected the stock offerings of the Compañía de Barcelona, investing instead in their own enterprises. Challenged by the commercial possibilities created by state policy in 1765 and broadened further in 1778, Catalan entrepreneurs preferred the potentially high earnings (and risks) of competition over those offered by Barcelona's privileged company. They competed by building small, efficient ships that reduced crews and turnabout time, by trimming transatlantic freight costs, and by adopting a penny-pinching frugality (for which they were often caricatured) that contrasted markedly with the exuberant business practices and lifestyles of Cadiz merchants.[95] Meanwhile, Catalonia's infant textile industry, deficient in technology and overall expertise, could hardly match demand in the colonies for high-quality goods; in fact, in the late 1780s, perhaps two-thirds of Catalan shipping returning from colonial ports brought back unsaleable items, principally Catalan textiles.[96] As the Catalan economy responded to *comercio libre* after 1778, efforts were concentrated in the agricultural rather than the manufacturing sector. Returns on Catalan agricultural exports remained higher than those from local manufacture.[97]

The two paths of Catalonia's strategy, one in the traditional monopoly mode, the other more competitive, proved complementary. Both channels exploited conditions created by *comercio libre* to push the region's agricultural rather than industrial exports. But even before 1765, one must recall, Catalan businessmen were beginning to branch out into Spain's transatlantic commercial system, positioning themselves to expand sales overseas in the colonies after 1778 and to double Barcelona's precious metals imports between 1784 and 1787.[98] Although Catalonia's colonial participation grew, in the mid 1780s, it still only had a minimal average share of Spain's total exports to the colonies (4.34 percent).[99] Nor should we exaggerate the competitive mentality of those Catalan businessmen who did not buy into the Barcelona monopoly company. Colonialists to the core, they, too, hoped to throttle competition overseas from producers of brandy and textiles in New Spain, the better to develop their own regional economy.

The other region of the peninsular economy affected by changing state policy for colonial trade after 1765 was lower Andalusia. Since the sixteenth century, its two principal port cities, first Sevilla and later Cadiz, had hosted Spanish and foreign merchant groups engaged in maximizing opportunities for managed trade with the colonial world. The convoy system of limited shipping and spaced departures favored low-volume, high-value cargo; after the last quarter of the sixteenth century, Andalusia's agricultural products were both minimized or rejected outright by shipowners and shippers in favor of reexports of high-quality northern European textiles, following the maxim offered by Eugenio Larruga in 1787, "A trader earns more handling foreign rather than national goods."[100] In marked contrast with Catalonia, Andalusia had an extraordinarily skewed system of land tenure, in which large landed estates concentrated in a handful of aristocratic families—Osuna, Alva, Medina Celi, and Medina Sidonia—dominated the countryside, along with a small agrarian bourgeoisie. Farming was carried on by leasing and subleasing arrangements with market-oriented entrepreneurs, employing a large reserve of seasonally employed, low-paid day laborers; Andalusia lacked a significant group of medium and small owner-operated farms.[101] Of course, property concentration was present elsewhere in the Peninsula but not on the Andalusian scale. León de Arroyal probably had in mind Andalusia's miserable rural day laborers—then as now Andalusia was Spain's internal "third world"—when he reminded Hacienda Secretary Lerena that despite widespread demand for agrarian reform, "nineteen years have been wasted on diagnoses, and one may conclude the prescription will come after the patient dies."[102] There have been many Cassandras in Spain's economic history.

Until mid-century, as elsewhere in the Peninsula, Andalusian grain output rose, not because of the introduction of new technology, but because of territorial expansion, the classic way, favored by the "open" resources of the province.[103] Then, as in Catalonia, the profit possibilities of export agriculture began to multiply, and proprietors, producers (generally renters and subrenters), and merchant intermediaries experimented with bringing estate lands under intensive cultivation. In hilly zones of the province, they shifted from grain to cattle, while on the plains, they replaced wheat with vineyards and olive and orange groves. Export earnings covered a growing volume of wheat imports from North Africa, supplemented by shipments from Naples, Sicily, and Sardinia.[104] Andalusian growers and shippers were now supplying an expanding colonial demand for wine and brandy, as well as raisins, olives, and almonds, a trade made profitable as a consequence of the competitive shipping that lowered transport costs following the *comercio libre* of 1765 and 1778.[105] Competition for cargo as the Spanish merchant marine expanded lowered maritime freight rates by roughly 75 percent, while insurance rates fell by half. Where once shippers had rejected agricultural products, now they found such cargo desirable. For their part, Cadiz exporters plowed earnings from colonial sales into purchasing more Andalusian agricultural exportables.[106] Clearly, agricultural specialization and commercialization in Catalonia and Andalusia were largely, if not wholly, regional responses to colonial import possibilities developing during the early decades of the eighteenth century and accelerated by *comercio libre*.

The internal conditions of growth in the two regions were, however, profoundly dissimilar, with long-term consequences. Whereas the pattern of rural property ownership in Catalonia produced export earnings flowing to small and medium growers and a multiplicity of export merchants, in Andalusia, income remained concentrated and *jornaleros*' wages depressed. Unlike Catalonia's, Andalusia's rural demand could not even partially support an infant textile industry, and Cadiz exporters, dependent upon imported textiles and foreign credits, would not invest in less profitable, far more speculative local manufacturing. They preferred "monopoly over re-exports of foreign goods" to "dependence upon local industry."[107] Moreover, as Antonio García Baquero has perceptively noted, foreign merchants at Cadiz continued to exercise "control sustancial" over Cadiz's colonial trade.[108] Catalan manufacturers and Andalusian and Catalan growers and exporters concurred in demanding that Madrid direct colonial governments to suppress New Spain's output of competitive products, whether alcoholic beverages like Mexico's *chinguirito* or textiles.

On balance, by the mid 1780s, at least in Catalonia and Andalusia, the Spanish state seemed to be achieving some of the objectives of the incremental, hesitant, eminently pragmatic colonial commercial policy that was materializing under the administration of Charles III. Levels of agricultural exports rose, along with customs revenue from colonial trade flows. A physiocratic emphasis upon improving agricultural output promised rewards to Andalusian *cortijo* owners, while leaving intact the structures of land tenure and associated *derechos señoriales*. In both regions, there were responses to colonial demand, in Adam Smith's sense, a "vent for surplus." An ambivalent, at times backward-looking, protectionism failed, however, to generate manufactures to underpin Spain's exchanges with its American colonies and perhaps curb the burgeoning parallel economy there. *Comercio libre* in the 1780s showed few signs of either overcoming Spain's secular industrial retardation or reducing smuggling, especially in the crucial Caribbean.

Comercio libre and Spanish Manufacturing

Contradictory indicators and interpretations of the impact of government policy and *comercio libre* on Cadiz and the provinces of Andalusia and Catalonia also surface in evaluating the performance of Spanish manufacturing in the second half of the century. The epigraphs to this chapter encapsulate the contradictions. Floridablanca's introduction to the census of 1787, where he purposely underscored population growth, expressed the government's effort to present a modern face to counter criticism of Spain's backwardness by European publicists and intellectuals in general. Earl Hamilton's optimistic assessment of "remarkable progress" has received little substantiation by researchers in recent decades, not to mention the pessimism of Spanish observers of the time.[109] The metropole's disappointing protoindustrial performance is all the more perplexing in that *proyectistas* in the first half of the century had tried to formulate an economic policy of balanced growth, clarifying the connections between agriculture, population, and the formation of a manufacturing base. Moreover, under Charles III's administrators, protectionism brought controls on imports of linen and cotton prints, and later on all cottons and some woolens. In fact, in 1779, the Junta de Comercio, the state economic planning agency, floated a project for an industrial bank, the Gran Banco de Manufacturas, which apparently went no further than the projects of Múzquiz at Hacienda or Gálvez at Indias.[110]

How then is one to account for poor industrial performance almost seven decades after state policy had initially clarified national development goals, and after Charles III's aggressive, wide-ranging finance minister Esquilache had launched an inquiry into the situation of Spain's state-subsidized manufactories, notably the woolen mills of Brihuega, San Fernando, and a showpiece at Guadalajara ("the largest manufacturing establishment"), directing the commissioners to review the utility of government subsidies and concessions granted and pinpoint those enterprises that were notable failures.[111]

Perhaps a major (but not the only) obstacle to the growth of manufacturing, according to recent Spanish historiography, was persistent, insufficient domestic demand—a chronic bottleneck in a traditional economy where food production, demography, and prices intersected. Adjusted estimates of Spain's population yield an increase of one-third between 1712–13 (8.15 million) and 1787 (11.0 million), which works out to an annual rate of 0.4 percent.[112] As long as grain production increased in the first half of the century, prices remained fairly stable. But as the limits of traditional agricultural techniques were reached after about 1750 and population continued to grow, real rural incomes failed to keep pace with grain prices. The result was consumer resistance to the purchase of domestic woolens and linens that were costlier (and, to many, less stylish) than imports from France, England, or Germany, for which there had long been a Spanish and colonial market.[113] Not to mention the customary preference of consumers in underdeveloped economies for imported over domestic products.[114] It was the stagnant domestic market for the products of state-subsidized mills that induced state officials and factory managers early on to consider dumping inventories in colonial markets, "since our Indies are the greatest consumers and principal destination of our manufactures."[115] The disappointing level of metropolitan demand, joined to growing perceptions of demand overseas, was transforming the colonies into the main prop of a metropolitan industrialization effort.

In the case of peninsular woolens, it was not just the quality of Spanish woolens that biased consumers in favor of imports, whether legal or smuggled. There were other factors—inadequate lines of credit to large-scale buyers, transport costs, and national, provincial, and local taxes, along with the resistance of an agrarian society to the installation of manufacturing enterprise and female employment. In short, by the late 1770s, and probably sooner, state-sponsored textile enterprises still needed fresh capital infusions, while management was pressured to dispose of inventories in colonial markets. This is at best a gross simplification of the development of underdevelopment in eighteenth-century Spain, but it approximates the current explanation of the Spanish phenomenon of the eighteenth century.

Take the case of the woolen manufactory at Guadalajara, set up at state initiative early in the reign of Philip V "to benefit the commerce and interests of the Spanish crown."[116] Its operations, along with those of San Fernando and Brihuega, had acquired multiple objectives, at least from the viewpoint of Madrid in the 1750s, when an official statement equated them with the "well-being" of the nation and its people in metropole and colonies, a stimulus to trade ("a major principle"), reduction of specie outflows to cover trade deficits and, last, with disciplining a workforce of peasants for employment in manufacturing. "If many are employed in decent work that prevents idleness and pays for food and clothing, it makes them industrious." As if these ambitious goals were not enough, by mid-century, the state aimed to make Guadalajara operations vertically integrated, including "equipment for buildings and shops, raw materials, labor force, cultivating dyestuffs and trees, and many other operations."[117] It was a petition for further state investment that induced Esquilache to order an investigation of the management and operations of Guadalajara and similar establishments in 1761.

Despite repeated state subsidies, Guadalajara's enterprise could not measure up to state objectives. It was plagued by unpredictable deliveries of basic inputs; by work schedules disrupted by shutdowns for shipments of inputs; by holidays and variations in the duration of the work day, which together made for fluctuating wages and poor living standards for workers.[118] It was also plagued by poor sales as a result of the colors, types, and pricing of its woolens in highly competitive domestic markets also supplied with English and French goods.[119] The sustained backup of company inventory had led Goyeneche, the agent of the Cinco Gremios Mayores (under contract to dispose of the products of the state enterprises), to obtain from New Spain's viceroy special tax concessions for woolens shipped on the 1772 *flota* to Veracruz, where Spanish woolens including ratteens, druggets, and *bachillas* enjoyed some popularity despite competitively priced English and French woolens.[120] The inventory buildup led the manager of the Guadalajara operation to petition Madrid in 1788 to suspend reexports of non-Spanish woolens to the colonies, pointing out that he had tried but failed to make a dent in 14 million reales' worth of warehoused woolens, despite granting prospective buyers a year for payment in full. Nor could he afford to be optimistic about colonial sales. Response had been discouraging, he confessed, and "we can't expect to reduce our stocks in this way, while no one trading to America has ordered shipments despite many notices from us."[121] Meanwhile, in Mexico City, the experienced *almacenero* Francisco Ignacio de Yraeta remained convinced that the problem was that Spanish woolens were aimed at high-income consumers, when in practical terms "a trade that does not deal with the poor is neither large nor profitable."[122] Here was the dilemma of Spanish manufacture: at home, there was little demand for the line of products aimed at discriminating consumers, while a mass market in the colonies required low-priced goods able to compete in quality with non-Spanish imports.

Following Madrid's temporary suspension of woolen reexports to the colonies in 1788, colonial sales performance received careful analysis.[123] Two factors were found accountable for poor sales. First, the incapacity of the Guadalajara mill to produce a sufficient volume of blue-dyed woolens to complement other colors in the same shipment; second, colonial consumers preferred "cloth of many qualities and widths that our shops do not turn out like interseasonal woolens, lightweight and adapted to the climate and tastes of those consumers." Here the explanation was what an anonymous specialist termed the Guadalajara plant's "abandono," coupled to production guidelines and guild labor restrictions that shackled "freedom to operate and discourage[d] capacity to imitate, invest, and vary operations and products."[124] The rigidities of Spain's traditional economy were certainly in part responsible for Guadalajara's inflexibility, uncompetitiveness, and ultimate failure. Perhaps equally responsible was the colonialist mentality, which assumed that consumers overseas would accept Spanish products simply because they came from the metropole.

By the late 1780s, after almost a decade of *comercio libre,* state officials still oscillated between providing full protection for woolens produced in manufactories supported by decades of state subsidies, and abandonment of that policy. Madrid's Junta de Estado in June 1788 first adopted a hard-headed stance when the Guadalajara management petitioned for higher tariffs on imported woolens. If existing levels of protection were inadequate, the *junta* replied, "don't expect this tactic to provide any advantages."[125] Yet pressure for protection shortly led to a compromise later in September. The government decreed that since colonial markets were flush with non-Spanish woolens blocking sizeable sales at the Guadalajara and Segovia mills, as well as at other state-supported enterprises, further woolen reexports were temporarily suspended.[126] The next year, Madrid softened this position, permitting up to one-third the value (but not volume) of all woolen exports to the colonies to consist of foreign imports.[127]

Comercio libre had not proven to be the hoped-for panacea for the structural problems of delayed industrialization and colonial undersupply, and smuggling in the colonies was becoming uncontrollable. Moreover, adopting the model of France's royal factories had produced disappointing results. Guadalajara's big woolen goods factory, which focused on items attractive to high-income consumers in Spain and its colonies, exemplified state intervention where neither private venture capital nor independent entrepreneurial talent could readily be mobilized. The state's commitment was long-term, and its capital investment was large, but although this and other state-sponsored manufactories survived more than fifty years, their products remained uncompetitive.

Other attempts at proto-industrialization in eighteenth-century Spain were dependent less upon large-scale commitment by Madrid (necessary, if not sufficient) and rather more upon cooperation between individual initiative and local secular and religious authorities in what was still a profoundly peasant, Catholic—in a word, traditional—society. Perhaps the case of Joseph Diez's textile operation at Soria, a town on the Duero in north-central Spain, in the 1770s—a tale of self-interest, a conception of the public good, and a web of local resistance that ultimately resulted in failure—clarifies the factors behind Spain's meager industrial progress in the eighteenth century better than that of the Guadalajara factory. Diez, an entrepreneur of peasant origin, mixed advancement of his own and his family's status with creating opportunities for an underemployed peasant labor force, mobilizing the support of the distant central authorities at Madrid, local representatives of the state (here, the *corregidor*), and Soria's *ayuntamiento* and bishop. There is no reason to question Diez's confessed pride in his "personality opposed to inactivity," which he combined with his concept of the public good to "encourage industry, reduce begging, make the people proper, hardworking, and useful to the state," as he phrased his objectives in 1778, goals generally subscribed to by members of the bureaucratic intelligentsia committed to changing traditional societies in the eighteenth century.[128] Trained in woolen manufacture, Diez was in his sixties when his name came to the attention of Campomanes, the *fiscal* of the Consejo de Castilla, who had just published his *Discurso sobre el fomento de la industria popular* (1774) with a government subsidy, and whose goals matched Diez's own. Campomanes's objectives may be understood as fitting an early industrial policy to agrarian structures and mentalities: cottage industry could soak up spreading rural unemployment by drawing upon women and children as spinners at home, it required low initial capital investment, used local inputs, and supplied local markets. Moreover, protecting cottage industry rather than large-scale factories had an added advantage made explicit in an early manuscript of José de Gálvez: it might lower the antagonism of English and French textile interests heavily involved in Spain's colonial markets and thereby their diplomatic pressure. Invited to Madrid by Campomanes, Diez was assured that the state would look favorably upon his project for a textile mill at Soria.

A spinning and weaving mill, Diez knew by experience, needed capital investment beyond his means, and he settled on what he believed to be more manageable, a linen and cotton printing establishment. He contracted two specialists in linen and cotton production from Barcelona, and print-block and printing technicians from Madrid. Their contracts stipulated that they teach their skills to Diez's workforce, a form of on-the-job training. By late 1775, he had erected spinning, weaving, and printing sheds on a bank of the Duero outside Soria, cleared a large field for drying cloth, and hired forty employees, including many women and adolescents, who walked from town to the works. The adolescents received instruction in the use of the spinning wheel to produce yarns—the preindustrial textile bottleneck—for Diez's weaving operations.

At this point, difficulties began. Diez's mill was located in the interior of Spain, in a peasant economy where the commonalty of rural poverty generated resentment of the self-made capitalist, and where ecclesiastical interests and influence were manipulable and pervasive. First came personal attacks from "many who knew me when I was less well off and now envied my improved status," charging him with unconscionable greed that profited from the "sweat of the poor." Since we have only Diez's account, prepared for his main government contact, Campomanes, it is impossible to evaluate the validity of the criticism. Then public outcry was directed at the critical area of his enterprise, the yarn shed. His hand spinners were said to be grossly underpaid, the school for spinning was called a refuge for "fallen women," who were mocked by daily macho verbal assaults and catcalls directed at women trudging from town to workplace. As a result, female employees began to quit. In January 1776, only months after Diez's enterprise began integrated operations, a mysterious fire completely destroyed the plant, consuming raw materials, yarn stocks, spinning wheels, looms, and printing blocks. It was hardly an auspicious beginning.

To rebuild, Diez turned for assistance again to his influential sponsor, the Consejo de Castilla, which awarded him temporary use of the confiscated buildings of a former Jesuit school. Formal notice of the award failed to come, however, because "malice had the skill to conceal it, so that news of the grant never reached me." Meanwhile, a local ecclesiastical body, consisting of the Canónigos de San Pedro, petitioned for the same ex-Jesuit buildings to serve as their collegiate church; this returned the case to the Consejo de Castilla. Backing Diez were, apparently, the Soria town council, the *corregidor,* a local notable (the conde de Gómera), and the bishop; somehow none of the supporting representations came to the Consejo's attention, since "they managed to misdirect them." On a hunch, Diez went to Madrid; there the *consejo*'s governor and *fiscal,* Campomanes, had Diez's petition placed ahead of that of the canons of San Pedro. As proof of his mill's capacity, Diez submitted samples of his prints (*platillas, trúes, cotones, indianas, fernandinas, bombases*), along with an assortment of printed goods exhibited to an audience of the *consejo,* guild representatives (probably from Madrid's Cinco Gremios Mayores), and others. The *consejo* resolved to grant him full control of the contested buildings.

Along the lines laid out in Campomanes's *Discurso sobre . . . industria popular,* Diez planned to employ local women and children in the spinning shed. The school for training skilled yarn spinners was basic to the whole operation; at first, he had intended to operate 100 looms, but yarn shortages limited him to 20. Diez viewed the school as "one of the most appropriate ways to promote the textile industry," to employ women, and to "keep them from licentiousness contrary to the modesty of the sex." The purpose was commendable, but its execution backfired. Women were hard to attract from the town of Soria, where, he noted bluntly, welfare had its charms ("alms make them lazy and idle"). He drew up a budget to build and maintain the school, offering to pay the master spinner and to purchase spinning wheels, raw materials, and, of course, the yarn produced. In return, he expected the local authorities to furnish workers with three meals daily as a public service. To this end, he recommended tapping local religious funds nominally at the discretion of the bishop for purposes of charity, or, alternatively, diverting the proceeds of a tax on wine collected by Soria's *ayuntamiento*; he called upon Soria's recently established Real Sociedad de Amigos del País to administer them. He also circularized a budget estimate to interested parties. Diez was, however, insensitive to the fact that his implicit criticism of the traditional expenditure of church and *ayuntamiento* funds on supporting the poor of the Soria community rather than on what he considered his more socially useful enterprise might destabilize local society.

The response was mixed. The bishop offered some help, a local notable joined in, and soon twenty female spinners were being supported. Soria's *ayuntamiento* volunteered to send offal from the slaughterhouse at prices charged other charitable institutions, which stirred up local butchers' dissent. The eight *jurados de la Quadrilla* petitioned the *corregidor* to force the *ayuntamiento* to withdraw its offer, and attacked Diez and his spinning school in such violent terms that the *corregidor* had the *jurados* jailed, then released them at the intercession of "perhaps the very author" of the petition, "presumably the source of the outrage." This ambiguous discourse suggests why Diez feared generating further antagonism. The blowup was followed by "a whole range of greater and lesser idiocies" perpetrated against the cloth-drying terraces along the Duero, which spoiled between 200–300 pieces extended there; and then Diez had to move his fulling operation when a grain mill owner suddenly so demanded. As if this were not enough, there was friction with Diez's technicians: the print-master, joined by a block maker, refused to instruct Diez's apprentices, thereby breaking their contracts. Diez retaliated by contracting by mail for another printer and print-block maker from Paris, all expenses paid (they took three months to arrive). But the newly hired printer proved incompetent, was discharged, and proceeded to bring suit against Diez. As a result, textile printing was suspended for months.

Undaunted by these problems, Diez remained an eighteenth-century projector. He resolved to ask the Consejo de Castilla for financial assistance in moving the equipment and personnel of a muslin factory at Metz (France) to Soria. The Metz director went to Madrid, where he and Diez worked out a deal, which was submitted to the Hacienda for review and action; in November 1778, the decision was apparently still pending.[129]

Self-made, possibly paranoiac, and surely sexagenarian, Diez now confessed to his patron on the Consejo de Castilla, Campomanes, that he viewed himself as "isolated, not merely abandoned by everyone, rather persecuted by many, because I struggle against the current prevailing in this country where the poor"—here he returned to his repeated complaint—"need no more energy to maintain their existence than to go about begging." In a traditional society of custom, hierarchy, and patronage, to get ahead necessitated, he well understood, the "high, effective and powerful protection" that Campomanes could provide. He then resubmitted a petition for further concessions by the state to support his Soria operations: tax-free status for products of his mill both on entry into Madrid, at royal residences, in the province of Navarra, and on export to the "countries of America and adjacent islands." And given the "importancia" of his services to the Spanish state, the anti-traditionalist Diez petitioned for the status of "nobleza perpetua" for himself and his family.

Compared with the findings of general analyses of Spanish textile manufacturing between 1750 and 1790, roughly the age of Charles III, the cases reviewed confirm disappointing results. One must recall that in Spain, as in its American colonies, the bulk of woolen and other textiles came from local *obrajes,* workshops turning out coarse products for local consumption. High-quality textiles like Valencia's silks and the woolens of Guadalajara and Segovia found a market niche among Spain's high-income consumers, landlords, churchmen, bureaucrats, and the professional and commercial bourgeoisie. But these were hardly competitive in the wider domestic and colonial markets, because production and distribution costs, and consequently the final prices, were too high, and in type and quality, the textiles themselves were often out of vogue.

In the case of Barcelona's cotton weaving and printing mills, progress was evident. But Catalan *indianas* survived mainly because *comercio libre* broadened colonial outlets for them; and one must take into account that Catalan print shops at this time chiefly used imported cloth. Significantly, the most "active" smugglers were textile manufacturers who used their workshops to stamp their seals on imported print cloth.[130] According to the *comercio libre* rules of 1778, each bolt of cloth exported to the colonies required the manufacturer's mark, place of production, quality, and quantity—all to prevent the magical transformation of foreign into "national" products. This requirement was extended in 1779 to all fabrics, whether sold to domestic or colonial consumers, but given the incentives, it barely dented smuggling.

It is hardly surprising that criticism in the last decade of Charles III's reign focused upon the disappointingly low volume of Spanish textile production, its failure to adapt to domestic and colonial fashions, and smuggling. In a widely read (and lamentably short-lived) Spanish periodical that circulated among Spain's political class and social and economic elite, *Espíritu de los mejores diarios literarios que se publican en Europa,* an article in 1788 commented on the close nexus between metropolitan productive capacity and colonial consumers, concluding that "since we cannot meet our own needs, we can hardly expect to supply those of our vast dominions overseas."[131] With this judgment, the Cadiz *consulado* complacently agreed. The products of Spain's factories were in no "condition to compete with foreign ones. These have expanded and profited by shipping them to America benefiting from the same exemptions as Spaniards."[132] Other observers, like Manuel García Herreros, a Spanish *almacenero* established in Mexico City, reported that he found few buyers for Spanish textiles, since his colonial consumers did not wear "heavy clothing"; in addition, Spanish-made textiles were less marketable because of "carelessness in finishing and packaging."[133]

One of the most devastating, because well informed, critiques of the Floridablanca ministry's "hallucination"—its mirage of industrial progress and of manufactures exportable to the colonies—came from a prominent, respected merchant at Cadiz in 1788. Writing to the recently appointed, activist colonial secretary Antonio Valdés, who had just replaced the deceased José de Gálvez, Tomás Izquierdo marveled at the government's capacity for self-delusion in interpreting as "good fortune and affluence" what he as a pragmatic merchant considered "more properly misfortune and backwardness." Openly skeptical of Floridablanca's hyperinflated *feliz revolución* in colonial trade, the exasperated Izquierdo pointed to misleading data forwarded to Madrid on the value of so-called Spanish products recently exported to the colonies. "The ministry observes that many ships are sent to America. From customs, it hears of extraordinary shipments of goods made in Spain. It reviews its legislation and regulations to conclude there is substance and wealth." But all this was nothing but "a fable, our own noise, and mere show for the whole world."[134]

The Official Story: Floridablanca's Euphoria

In October 1788, only weeks before the death of Charles III, Floridablanca drafted a *memorial* (really an apologia) covering his eleven years as prime minister, which, like the *instrucciones* left by New Spain's outgoing viceroys, sought to justify his ministry's performance and indirectly to rebut critics.[135] In one sense, it was an insider's response to the infighting among Madrid's irrepressible political class, many exasperated by Spain's lack of enlightenment in the age of enlightenment. It was published in the first volume of the eagerly read *Semanario erudito de Valladares,* another expression of short-lived *glasnost* in the twilight of the era of Charles III.

By late 1788, the prime minister had in hand "completas notícias," statistics on exports to the colonies compiled by the Hacienda, some already published in the official *Gazeta de Madrid.*[136] When compared with 1783, the data showed striking increases not only in total exports by value but, more controversial, in the share of so-called "national" products, which had risen by a factor of 5 between 1783 and 1785.[137] These data legitimated the prime minister's reference to "esta feliz revolución" in the metropole's exports to the colonies, a clear reference to the October 1778 statute issued early in his administration.[138]

Floridablanca buttressed his euphoria with comments on the results of economic policy since 1777, and in particular on the broad spectrum of state support for industrial development: importation of skilled labor and machinery to produce "every type of woolen and cotton cloth," and higher tariffs on foreign manufactures (an affirmation of sovereignty), thereby unilaterally withdrawing the trade concessions yielded by the Spanish state under the Austrian dynasty in the late seventeenth-century phase of "former weakness." There was praise for the Hacienda's secretary, Lerena, for facing down the "defenses and obstructions" of those opposed to the government's program of "reforma de abusos."[139] Now, for the first time, a Spanish prime minister publicly criticized the merchant community of Cadiz, ever antagonistic to the elements that made for the "fortunate revolution." Satisfied with their "one-port monopoly," Gaditano merchants, he claimed, "were enslaving poor Indians" (*this* was strong public criticism from a leading Spanish statesman), inhibited the growth of the metropole's industrial and agricultural enterprises, and, by steering "everything via the narrow bottleneck of Cadiz," continued to earn superprofits.[140]

On the other hand, Floridablanca barely mentioned the state's incapacity to control the sizeable underground economy in both metropole and colonies. So he exaggerated the effectiveness of Mesía's inquiry into smuggling at Cadiz, terming his effort an "arrangement," while putting the best face on an unmanageable phenomenon.[141] To blunt criticism, he turned to hyperbole rather than the desperate candor of Antonio de Gálvez on the subject of the "monstruo" of smuggling at the Cadiz entrepôt. This conformed, of course, with Floridablanca's strategy for moving Europe's political elites and critical intelligentsia to view Spain and its American empire through his rose-colored lens.

Behind the prime minister's public euphoria, one detects the tactic of minimizing Cadiz's commercial crisis of 1787–88, visible in the rash of bankruptcies there, in order to highlight the overall success of delayed Spanish *dirigisme.* Supported by data collected by the Hacienda on the growth in exports (reexports?) to the colonies, Floridablanca could dismiss complaints from Cadiz's *consulado* and merchant community that "the Indies are full of unsold stocks of merchandise," and that an alarming number of its respected merchant houses were going bankrupt. This had happened before, Floridablanca argued with reason and, besides, France and England were also experiencing the same postwar phenomena. He did not attempt to relate depressed prices in the metropole and "abundancia" in the colonies to the postwar boom and short-term recession; in optimistic market-oriented fashion, he predicted that low prices and ample supply would soon invigorate "the desire, tasks, and practice of buying and consuming there." Here was public, official avowal that colonial consumers could be the engine that pulled along the metropolitan economy.

The real problem, Floridablanca emphasized, was not the business cycle but the propensity of *arriviste* Cadiz merchants for the "monster of display and disorder," for squandering income and capital to imitate their betters, "as if they enjoyed the steady income of great señores." Here, he felt, bankruptcy was the unavoidable corrective for spendthrift merchants whose patrimony was insecure and invariably subject to "risky contingencies." Wealth, he insisted, should be the reward of frugality rather than "disipación."[142] Himself, like Campomanes, the product of more frugal times, and since the

1750s associated with the world of landholding aristocrats at the court of Madrid, Floridablanca could neither tolerate nor wanted to understand the psychological effects of the postwar boom in colonial trade upon Cadiz businessmen who had dissipated their monopoly profits of 100 to 200 percent as if they were merchant nobility. Like figures peopling Goya's work of the early 1790s, Cadiz's new-rich merchants, Floridablanca seemed to say, were somehow bewitched by the twin "monstruos" of consumerism and contraband. Was he simply echoing the sentiments of the physiocratically inclined landed classes about "buying cheap and selling dear," rather than engaging in truly productive activity?

Fitting together contemporaneous analyses of the commercial situation at Cadiz in the late 1780s with recent studies, it appears that Floridablanca's optimistic conspectus had some factual substantiation. He was inaccurate in blaming the crisis primarily on merchants' high personal expenditures, and he underestimated smugglers' tenacity, yet he was politically correct in uncritically accepting statistics on the export sector in the postwar years and about the inevitability of recovery and expansion of colonial trade. Three sets of figures, while not in agreement on details, confirm an export peak in 1785, followed by a decline at varying rates. Significantly, what must have been data released by a government agency indicate a peak far above the maximum estimated in John Fisher's 1985 analysis. In any event, the export surge was unprecedented, even compared to a prewar base year, 1776.[143] From data supplied by the Cadiz *consulado,* the value of average annual exports to the colonies in 1784–86 of 36.4 million pesos (of 15 reales), rose by 50 percent over that of the two prewar years 1776–78, or 24.3 million.[144] Metropolitan receipts of precious metals (mainly silver) representing colonial sales earnings and the transfer of funds from colonial treasuries peaked earlier in an "avalanche" of silver in 1784, followed by a decline in 1787 of 41.3 percent; precious metals receipts from Veracruz dropped more, by 58.2 percent. Overall, Michel Morineau calls the five-year period 1781–85 "the most brilliant in the whole history of the Spanish Atlantic." Nevertheless, despite a falloff in exports from the metropole after 1785 and in imports of colonial precious metals after 1784, both categories remained reassuringly above prewar levels.[145]

No doubt, the downside of the business cycle followed the boom in exports to Spain's major colonial market, New Spain, whose wine and brandy imports were far out of line with normal consumption levels.[146] Cadiz and Barcelona exporters had responded enthusiastically to early reports of high sales and profits in 1784 by doubling export levels the following year; by the end of 1785, their colonial sales were sticky, and merchants in the colonies became anxious about the fresh supplies of wine, brandy, and textiles expected at Veracruz and Campeche.[147] The fading postwar export boom had the greatest effect on Cadiz, which handled roughly 80 percent of peninsular shipments, but Barcelona shippers were also affected.[148] At Cadiz, the economic downturn toppled Spanish firms like that of Frías, along with foreign firms financing them, French merchant houses from Languedoc, Brittany, and Paris. Apparently, not only the Breton group, including Verduc, Jolif, and Sere y Cia., but also firms from Languedoc, such as Jaureguiberri and Laborde, were severely affected.[149] Floridablanca was accurate in observing that foreign firms were as much affected as peninsular ones. Meanwhile, at Barcelona an excess of exports to the colonies had comparable effects: wine and brandy prices tumbled in late 1785 on pessimistic sales reports from correspondents in New Spain, while sales of Catalan textile exports also suffered. Not surprisingly, between 1786 and 1788, Barcelona had a 32 percent bankruptcy rate.[150]

To label these phenomena typical of a crisis of late commercial capitalism in an Atlantic empire of the eighteenth century misses the point. Unlike the contemporaneous English and French economies, which exploited the colonial pact by which colonial raw materials (staples) were exchanged for metropolitan manufactures, Spain's late-developing economy remained basically agrarian, with minimal capacity for production and export of domestic manufactures. This was a long-standing structural defect, rooted in what Floridablanca called its "debilidad anterior," a euphemism for stagnation under the previous dynasty of "los Austrias." Since the sixteenth century, the Spanish metropole had imported European manufactures for reexport to the colonies through lower Andalusia. The eighteenth-century heir to Sevilla's port monopoly in the Spanish transatlantic system, Cadiz, persisted as the commercial center of peninsular, international, and colonial interests. As the residence of well-capitalized and internationally linked foreign merchant enclaves, Cadiz could draw upon their capital and had larger inventories and shipping facilities greater than those of other peninsular ports recently authorized for colonial trade, Málaga, Barcelona, and Santander, first in 1765, then in 1778. The unbroken primacy of Cadiz for the foreign interests involved in Spain's colonial trade was recorded, appropriately, by a French commentator, who observed: "Despite the laws of February and October 1778 that allowed Spain's other ports to share the privileges long reserved for Cadiz, our shipments have almost always followed this route and continued to do so before the revolution."[151] In the recently *habilitado* ports, merchants maintained traditional structures, practices, and attitudes in Spain's system of colonial trade in order to explore opportunities opened up by *comercio libre:* they reexported non-Spanish manufactures to the colonies in order to obtain more silver from Veracruz, Havana, Lima, and Buenos Aires. In Catalonia, when industrial development slowed in the late 1780s, investors shifted smoothly from industry to trade.[152]

The crisis of the late 1780s at Cadiz should be viewed in the long perspective of the era of Charles III. In the aftermath of the coup against Esquilache, state policy was directed increasingly toward exploiting the colonies — consumers, silver, and a few staples of relatively recent demand in Europe, such as raw hides and dyes. Increasing what the colonies imported and exported, paid in taxes, and remitted in silver to a penurious metropole received higher priority in state policy than development, which may explain the euphoria expressed in Floridablanca's memorial of 1788 apropos of the fiscal tangibilities of the *feliz revolución*. Development through diversification into manufactures was soft-pedaled; recent Spanish scholarship emphasizes that the tariff structures in the October 1778 statute, as well as that of 1782, were formulated to satisfy fiscal needs rather than long-term effective protectionism. In addition, *comercio libre,* backed by Colonial Secretary Gálvez, by the successive treasury secretaries Múzquiz and Lerena, and by Prime Minister Floridablanca, promised a painless, inexpensive route to growth without social disorder. There would be no dangerous proletarian classes.

The other achievement of which Floridablanca made much, the Banco de San Carlos, was not given developmental objectives. It was fashioned to mobilize capital for state ends, to handle Spain's growing international payments for a commission, and to manage the state's new interest-bearing treasury bills, the *vales*. Even the modest savings of Amerindian communities in the distant American colonies were forcibly invested in shares of the Banco, diverting them from local colonial projects. Growth without development meant more reexports to the colonies, but insignificantly greater exports of national manufactures, mounting trade deficits with western European suppliers, and massive smuggling. The Spanish state under Charles III's ministers, some of them enlightened, proved incapable of harnessing colonial resources to update or modernize the metropolitan economy. In 1788, however, many officials in the central government at Madrid were convinced that the policy for colonial trade applied minimally in 1765 and hesitantly in 1778 would show its full benefits only when extended to Spain's principal American possession, New Spain, without prejudicing control over its most important export commodity, silver from the world's richest mines.

8. A Colonial Response to *Comercio Libre:* New Spain

Mexico flourished as never before when Cadiz's controls . . . loosened somewhat: in the decade from 1778 to 1788, customs revenues doubled and the empire flourished.

El Sol (Mexico City), 1823

This trade has been very inappropriately called free; it has never been, [since] shipowners must petition the court for licenses . . . and the ministry sets their number. What data or information are available? This explains the excessively large shipments.

Manuscript in the Biblioteca del Real Palacio, Madrid

On reviewing data for those sectors of the economy of New Spain closely watched by bureaucrats and businessmen in the metropole seeking to gauge the impact of the *comercio libre* of 1778, there were grounds for their guarded optimism by 1787.

Colony watchers in the metropole paid attention to at least two statistical series, the output of the Mexico City mint, which theoretically coined all bullion produced in the colony, and transfers of silver from Veracruz to Spain, directly or via Cuba. The reasons were obvious: these data both helped Madrid better manage current and future outlays on bureaucracy, defense, and infrastructure and aided businessmen in settling accounts with creditors at Cadiz and in western Europe. Under the fleet system, news of the safe arrival of inbound convoys from Veracruz invariably electrified the public and private sectors. Comparing the two most recent five-year periods of peace in the late 1780s, observers found that the coining of silver had increased by over 12 percent between 1773–77 and 1783–87, accelerating a trend that had begun in the second quarter of the eighteenth century (although it slackened briefly in the 1760s).[1] And if they turned to data on precious metals shipped from Veracruz to Spain and its Caribbean possessions in the same five-year periods, they discovered an extraordinary surge of 98 percent.[2] The statute of 1778—omitting the special circumstances of the war years, 1779–82—seemed only to have accelerated the upward trend in the economy of Spain's principal American colony.

Other economic indicators were also followed, notably data on metropolitan exports to colonial ports. It was state policy to use 1778 as the base year (although 1776 has recently been suggested as more representative). In any case, the average annual value of exports to the colonies in 1783–87, in constant official prices, topped the benchmark year (1778) by a factor of more than five.[3] To be sure, other sources indicate a more conservative but still impressive rise of 50 percent. Spain's Treasury had done well out of *comercio libre,* the French diplomat Jean-François Bourgoing noted, with metropolitan customs receipts rising from 6.8 million reales in 1778 to over 55 million a decade later.[4] Concomitantly, government receipts in New Spain in 1778–90 rose to almost double those in 1765–77.[5] Given such comforting indicators of economic expansion in New Spain in the 1780s, we may ask, were transatlantic silver transfers and rising state revenues responses to recent modifications in colonial trade policy or reflections of longer-term trends?

A Pillar of the Spanish Monarchy

Over the eighteenth century, roughly six of New Spain's mining districts put that colony far ahead of Peru as the mining core of the Spanish empire in America. New Spain's principal mining areas were concentrated north of Mexico City in a zone stretching from Guanajuato to Zacatecas, and from Guadalajara eastward to San Luís Potosí. Three districts—Guanajuato, Zacatecas, and Catorce—produced about 50 percent of total eighteenth-century output. Overall, silver production in New Spain rose at an annual rate of 1.4 percent; but Richard Garner has computed that in the period 1772–83, minting rose at almost double that rate (2.65 percent) and silver exports at the phenomenal annual rate of 9.6 percent. *Comercio libre* coincided with extraordinary growth in silver production and coinage; in concrete terms, between the ouster of Esquilache in 1766 and 1783, annual coinage by the Mexico City mint soared from 11.2 million pesos to 23.1.[6]

To note that New Spain's mining and trade expansion coincided underscores the long-term connections among silver, the colony's overall economy, its Spanish metropole, and the Atlantic system. Silver mining was *the* measure of New Spain's significance to its metropole; New Spain had no other major export to link it to the Atlantic or, for that matter, the Pacific world. Sugar production in New Spain increased during the eighteenth century, and there was sustained internal demand for it, but transport costs over poor roads to Veracruz made Mexican sugar uncompetitive in European markets with sugar from the Caribbean and Brazil. Silver was the cutting edge of capitalism in New Spain as in Peru, a function shared with Brazil's gold and diamond mines, as well as its sugar plantations and those of the Caribbean.

Silver drew Spaniards, Creoles, Amerindians, Africans, mestizos, and mulattos alike north beyond New Spain's densely populated central zones as mine owners and mine workers, merchants, shopkeepers and pack peddlers, artisans, bureaucrats, and priests. In turn, the mines stimulated production of maize and beans, horses, mules and oxen, hides, timber, and salt. Around mining towns, as Angel Palerm has reminded us, "an important agro-ranching complex was organized with amazing speed; large haciendas typical of the Bajío, ranches and haciendas typical of the Altos de Jalisco." In this fashion, the peripheral and lightly inhabited mine-based north of New Spain was transformed into an "espacio organizado."[7]

Over time, mining performed an integrative rather than a purely enclave function by breaking down regional compartmentalization and absorbing products from distant regions of the colony, thereby continuing the monetization of the colony's economy through payment in specie. Silver expanded the volume of credit and money in circulation, fueled commercial expansion, and contributed to price rises as population rose and agricultural bottlenecks appeared. It monetized transactions once limited mainly to barter.[8] In more graphic terms, commercial capitalism began and developed along a spinal column that commenced at Veracruz, passed via Jalapa and Orizaba to Puebla and Mexico City, then moved northward via Querétaro and San Luís Potosí, Guanajuato, and Guadalajara to Zacatecas and Durango. This is not to minimize the role of agriculture and ranching in the colonial economy, but rather to highlight silver mining as its main source of liquidity—*pesos fuertes*. In the eighteenth century, silver production was the mainspring of the colony's growth and prosperity, enriching mine owners and their financial backers in the merchant community, expanding employment directly and indirectly, widening the market for food and services, and providing specie for the local money supply, credit, and "most of what is needed and supplied from outside."[9]

Furthermore, there was the international dimension of silver mining. While New Spain's output enriched mine owners and their backers among the colony's merchant class, it also subsidized the colonial state and its Spanish metropole. The greater the production and coinage of silver, the larger the volume removed from local circulation and exported by the colonial state and merchants to the metropole, and through it to western Europe and East Asia. Without silver, the monetization and commercialization of the colonial and Atlantic economy would have proceeded far more slowly, the metropole would have gained little by colonialism, and without a profitable export, strong links to Europe and Asia would not have materialized.[10] In this sense, silver functioned as the "organizing principle of the colonial economy," as observers reiterated then and still do.[11] Humboldt put it crisply in the early nineteenth century when he commented that in the colony of New Spain, silver was the "regulator of public prosperity" and that New Spain's pesos were the "raw materials that fuel the operations of most European mints."[12] Mining was not just one sector of a multisectoral colonial economy, it was *the* "main engine of the . . . economy" that the Spanish state—primitive as it was—fostered for centuries, even more so in the second half of the eighteenth century. As the knowledgeable secretary of Veracruz's *consulado* phrased it in 1803, in New Spain, silver mining was "one of the tallest, most robust and solid columns supporting the Spanish monarchy."[13]

The Spanish state also played an influential, even dominant, role in creating and maintaining conditions favorable to sustained growth of the whole mining sector. By cutting the tax burden on silver production from 20 to 10 percent, standardizing the weight and fineness of coinage, providing for the security of mining sites and highways, supplying the mercury (often on long-term credits) required for ore amalgamation, and taking control of the Mexico City mint when the private sector compromised its integrity, the Spanish state monitored, and ministered to, colonial mining interests. New Spain provides an early model of "an administrated, regulated economy, not a market economy," Angel Palerm observes.[14] Between 1750 and 1760, when coinage leveled off with the recession in Zacatecas's output (prior to the spectacular surge of Guanajuato's "Quebradilla" and "Valenciana" mines), and after the last of the Mexico City *bancos de plata,* which had specialized in financing mines, disappeared in 1770, Madrid was, if anything, even more sensitive to the need to stimulate the supply of mercury and investment capital to the mines. That sensitivity surfaced early in the era of Charles III among bureaucrats influential in shaping state economic policy for the colonies, like José de Gálvez, Tomás Ortiz de Landázuri, and Pedro Rodríguez Campomanes, as well as among lobbyists for Mexico City's merchant magnates such as Francisco Xavier Gamboa.

Gálvez had long been interested in America ("the part of the world whose discovery and advances have been the first cause of Europe's political system"), and in his "Discurso y reflexiones de un vasallo sobre la decadencia de nuestras Indias," a manuscript mémoire probably drafted between 1759 and 1762, well before he was commissioned to investigate and report on New Spain, he reviewed the influence of Spain's European competitors on trade, government, and mining in Spain's American empire.[15] Gálvez was convinced that change there was unavoidable. The English and French envied Spain as "possessor of the rich ores of gold and silver that drive the world's commerce" and schemed continually to "share in our riches." Officials born and educated in the colonies should be posted far from their birthplaces, Gálvez stressed, since "such is the spirit of faction and partnership that even fictive parenthood generates powerful alliances."[16] (That he overlooked similar factors operating in the metropolitan bureaucracy is another matter.) In fact, the "Discurso" demonstrated distrust of colonial elites and awareness of polarization between Spaniards and Creoles in the colonies, on the one hand, and Spaniards in the metropole, on the other.

In a brief section on mining, Gálvez reviewed the supply and pricing of mercury, which regulated the "principal riqueza" of the American colonies. Silver production in New Spain, he concluded, had recently risen proportionate to the availability of mercury and to its improved distribution. He added that New Spain's mine owners still paid 82 pesos per hundredweight of mercury, which in fact cost the state only 20 pesos CIF delivered to Mexico City. The implication was evident: a cheap, ample supply of mercury could produce more silver.[17] José Antonio Fabry and others had earlier pointed to the benefits that could be expected from reducing the price of mercury. Gálvez's preoccupation with the mercury issue reveals how sensitive Madrid's political class had become to the economic role of the state.[18]

Gálvez based his analysis on second-hand information, which was not the case of the report drafted at Madrid by Tomás Ortiz de Landázuri, *contador general* in the Consejo de Indias.[19] Unlike Gálvez, Landázuri focused solely on New Spain's mining districts, covering each administrative unit—Nueva Galicia, Nueva Vizcaya, Nueva España—in detail. Landázuri's "Noticias" collated many data on the mines of Zacatecas, Fresnillo, Sombrerete, Bolaños, and Veta Grande in the jurisdiction of the Audiencia of Guadalajara, as well as on those of Guanajuato, shortly to become the world's most spectacularly productive mining district.

What emerges from the report is Landázuri's appreciation of the wealth in the colony's mines, the roller-coaster fortunes of mine owners, the constant friction among mine developers, between mine owners and their financial backers (*aviadores* such as the Aldaco and Valdivielso merchant bankers, who in Landázuri's time still operated *bancos de plata*), and the extraordinary success of mine owners like José de Sardaneta and merchant financiers like

Francisco Sánchez de Tagle, Domingo de la Canal Lanburu, "and other well-known [firms]" in Mexico City. Landázuri repeatedly refers to the mine owners' merchant backers, such as *aviadores* in Chihuahua ("where there reside powerful merchants and agents of many firms of Mexico City") and San Luís Potosí ("wealthy merchants who do business with the mining complexes at Guadalcázar, Charcas, and Mateguala"). Guanajuato gave grounds for optimism: the "Mellado" and "Rayas" mines were "so marvelously engineered, in the rest of the world there are no equals, since their nature, rich ores, and their owners' drive and attention have led to shafts and stonework admired by all the experts who have studied them carefully."[20]

Landázuri marveled that since 1698, the two mines had produced over 150 million pesos, and that despite unfavorable terrain, Guanajuato's mines had created a city of "churches, magnificent buildings, and homes" for a population he estimated at 80,000. With an annual output worth 3 million pesos and the "tremendous backing of those in Mexico City," Guanajuato's future was assured, providing there were adequate supplies of mercury. Landázuri also recommended that mines taken over by the state in bankruptcy proceedings resulting from mine owners' defaults on mercury purchases be made available to those prepared to work them. But henceforth, he warned, the state should not accept mines as collateral for mercury bought on credit.[21]

Mining Inputs: A General Supply Company and Mercury Pricing

Predictably, Gálvez and Landázuri, as Peninsula-born colonialists, put metropolitan above colonial interests. A markedly different perspective was provided by Francisco Xavier Gamboa, a Creole from Zacatecas who had made his career in the colonial capital and went to Madrid in 1755, accompanied by a Spanish-born merchant, Francisco de la Cotera, to lobby in behalf of the Consulado de México for restoration of the *flota* system to Veracruz and institutionalization of relations between merchants and mine owners.[22] More specifically, Mexico City's mercantile magnates intended to preserve the oligopoly of their *bancos de plata* over New Spain's mine owners.[23]

Gamboa's involvement, as a lawyer linked both to mining interests and to the capital's *almaceneros,* in litigation between mine owners and their merchant backers, led him to grasp the fundamental interdependence of mercantile and mining interests. As he put it in his *Comentarios a las ordenanzas de minas* (1761), "the prosperity of commerce depends upon the extent to which the mines are worked"—a valid perspective for understanding the evolution of New Spain's economy.[24] After five years' residence at Madrid, he was a seasoned, amply financed lobbyist at the Spanish court for Mexico City's influential commercial establishment, as well as being a good friend of Manuel de Aldaco, a wealthy Basque merchant in Mexico City, who had married into the Fagoaga family of silver bankers.[25] Gamboa justified his clients' role and increased the impact of his *Comentarios* by quoting the peninsular cleric and intellectual Benito Jerónimo Feyjóo, widely respected as an example of Catholic enlightenment, and one of Charles III's favorite authors. "The gold of the Indies keeps us poor; and worse than this, it enriches our enemies," Feyjóo observed. "In return for our maltreatment of the Indians, we Spaniards are now the Indians of the rest of Europe. It is for foreigners that we dig our mines, for them that we bring our treasure to Cadiz" (and although Gamboa buried this comment in a footnote, he quoted it there in full).[26]

Gamboa's *Comentarios* praised the financial policies of Esquilache as secretary of the Hacienda and of Charles III, "a king . . . who in a reign of a few months, has not only surpassed the hopes but has even outrun the wishes of his subjects . . . remitting royal claims and crown debts to an enormous extent, [and] paying off numberless hereditary debts"—which was accurate.[27] Ostensibly, the *Comentarios* were a manual on silver-mining technology in New Spain, but Gamboa's hidden agenda (on instructions from the Mexico City *consulado*) was to enhance the image of Mexico City's merchant magnates and promote the continued insulation of their economic space from the *flotistas* of the *comercio de España* at Jalapa, both during and after *ferias. Almaceneros* at the colonial capital sent him to lobby Madrid to resume convoys and fairs, an objective that might block *flotistas* from selling their imports directly in Mexico City, in provincial capitals, and even in the major mining centers of Guanajuato and Zacatecas, where they had managed to penetrate during the years of *registros sueltos,* 1748–55.

When Gamboa's *Comentarios* were published at Madrid in 1761, the *flota* issue had already been resolved in favor of Mexico City's *almaceneros.* There remained, however, two interrelated issues of the Gamboa-Cotera hidden agenda: financing mining exploration and operations, and ensuring a dominant role for Mexico City merchants in silver production. He lost no time in reminding readers of New Spain's mining wealth. To begin with, he portrayed New Spain as a "Theatro de las minas."[28] "The prosperity of commerce depends upon the extent to which the mines are worked, and these again depend, in turn, on commerce for supplies and support," he said. "By reciprocally assisting each other, therefore, the greatest possible advantage will be produced to both, especially in a country so rich in ores."[29] Mexico

City's mint, he accurately reported, was producing 13–14 million pesos annually, much of it shipped to the metropole on returning *flotas*. With proper organization, regulations (*ordenanzas*), and state protection, New Spain's silver mines could become inexhaustible sources of wealth for the metropole—an approach welcome to Madrid's Hacienda, then scrambling to finance Spain's naval defenses. Gamboa dangled before his Spanish readership the mirage of "literally mountains of these precious metals and of other minerals in New Spain," which introduced his real agenda, fusing mine finance and provisioning into one chartered company, to be managed by the Mexico City *consulado*.[30]

A general supply company fitted the eighteenth-century Spanish practice of chartering privileged companies, some with and others without state shareholder participation. In fact, however, Gamboa's merchant sponsors had been on weak ground since the 1760s, an effect of the strong backlash against state-chartered monopolies, considered exploitative of consumers and unprofitable to shareholders and the state. But to Gamboa, the resources of the Consulado de México guaranteed responsible oversight, because "the commercial body, as represented by its head, the consular tribunal of Mexico, and no other, is competent to give effect to such an enterprise . . . from the impartiality and good faith with which it discharges its duties, and the great confidence [of] the proprietors, whether merchants or of other classes."[31]

By extolling the *consulado,* Gamboa was implicitly separating well-capitalized Mexico City *almaceneros* from smaller commercial houses speculating with capital-short mine operators. Gamboa's projected general mine supply company could stimulate silver production, at least in theory, by lowering the cost of credit and inputs to mine owners below the levels offered by medium-sized provincial merchant *aviadores* competing with Mexico City's amply funded *bancos de plata.* In fact, he minimized those petty *aviadores,* who, "filled with distrust, nonetheless furnish the necessary advances. . . . If new works are required, they withhold advances, because they see no silver; as for mine owners who have provided them with large earnings and profits, they usually abandon them when they're in trouble." And while many petty *aviadores* had lost millions, not so with New Spain's *cuerpo de comercio,* which found its status improved by the earnings of mining investments.[32]

By depicting small-scale *aviadores'* operations in an unfavorable light to Madrid's policy-makers, Gamboa aimed to preserve the oligopsony of silver controlled by Mexico City's merchant magnates, a few still operating *bancos de plata,* despite recent heavy losses. *Almaceneros* feared that, in the collapse of silver banks, *flotistas* from Cadiz might compete to finance large mining enterprises.[33] His proposed general supply company would both underwrite and provision the colony's mines. To ensure that the proposed company commanded adequate capital resources, Gamboa insinuated that the *alcabala* tax farm, which Madrid had recently removed from management by the Mexico City *consulado,* should revert to its private administration. Subtly, Gamboa was packaging a number of issues close to the interests of the colonial capital's commercial elite. Profits from a renewed *alcabala* farm, he promised, would be recycled into the company's capital fund, while the financial solidity of the *consulado* would guarantee a broad spectrum of investors in the colony—"whether lay or clerical, convents, communities, merchants or agriculturists, in short, all persons of property throughout the kingdom."[34] Gamboa's proposal for mobilizing capital for speculation in mining enterprises played upon the financial reliability of the Mexico City *consulado* to restore confidence in silver mining; otherwise, he felt, "the ecclesiastical communities will take very good care, in future, not to trust a miner with a single dollar . . . they are content to purchase houses. . . . And they have lost immense sums in trade, and also through the miners supplied by the merchants."[35]

Fitting the pieces of Gamboa's lobbying strategy into a pattern suggests that Mexico City's merchants and allied mining interests proposed to solidify and legitimate their dominant position in the colony's mining, finance, and trade. Resumption of the system of *flotas* and *ferias* promised to keep intact control of their trading space in the Spanish transatlantic commercial system; reprivatizing administration of the *alcabala* farm would revive their edge over competing merchants operating in the interior of the colony. At bottom, oligopolistic financing and provisioning of the mines by Mexico City's magnates could preserve their hegemony over the leading and most lucrative sector of the colony's economy, at the expense of competitive Gaditano interests, the *comercio de España*. Campomanes immediately grasped both the scope and effects of this ambitious strategy when a copy of Gamboa's *Comentarios* came to his attention in 1761.

Criticism of Cadiz's port monopoly, it will be recalled, was one facet of Campomanes's dislike of Spain's experiment in replicating Dutch, English, and French models of privileged overseas trading companies. Not that he was against development; he was, rather, a late mercantilist in the sense that he opposed concentration of economic power *inside* the perimeter of Spain's colonial trading system, whether in the metropole or the colonies.

Campomanes was obviously primed to flush out Gamboa's agenda. He welcomed his technical exposition and emphases upon formulating ordinances regulating colonial mining, "the wellspring of the greatest riches of America." Silver mining's integrative function in the international economy he recognized as "the zeal encouraging the workmen of Europe and Asia," which in turn regulated exchanges among "the four quarters of the world." For Campomanes's colonialist mentality, it was also the root of the "luxury and laziness of the Americans."[36] Gamboa's proposed general supply company designed to reinforce the mercantile interest at the core of the economy of New Spain was, however, unacceptable. After all, Gamboa himself noted that a similar proposal had been tabled in 1745 on the advice of two well-connected merchant bankers in Mexico City, the Creole Francisco Manuel Sánchez de Tagle and the Spaniard Manuel de Aldaco. Conveniently, Campomanes overlooked that both were heavily involved in a *banco de plata*.

Aside from the generally unsatisfactory performance of Spain's privileged companies, Campomanes distrusted the financial power of another company whose monopoly of capital and credit might set off a "remarkable revolution in Spain's political and commercial system." In addition, he perceived another drawback: the solidity and potential profitability of a *consulado*-backed general supply company might attract wealthy investors among New Spain's ecclesiastical corporations, which would remit even more earnings to Rome — an oblique allusion to Campomanes's bête noire, unmonitored Jesuit capital transfers to Europe from the colonies. Uppermost in his view was the real possibility that such a general supply company run by the Mexico City *consulado* might become the Spanish empire's most formidable corporate body, able to manipulate its monopoly over silver to dominate, first, "the merchants from the Peninsula," and then "the metropole itself." Through control over silver production, merchants in the Consulado de México would overwhelm the *comercio de España*, since "with the funds in its banks, it would dominate our merchants from Europe."[37] This was Montesquieu's view of the inverse relationship of Spain's American colonies to their metropole. Distrust of concentrated economic power at Cadiz and among merchant groups in the colonies — colonial interests dominating the metropole — remained a determining source of Campomanes's unwavering support for *comercio libre*. For him, the epoch of privileged trading companies was over, and he believed that colonial silver production could best be increased by regulatory guidelines, adequate capital, and credit, and especially by keeping the prices of basic inputs like mercury low.

Mercury was a particularly troublesome issue in the seventeenth century, when the supply and price at Mexico City had oscillated erratically.[38] Around 1700, Madrid had scrambled to obtain supplies of mercury in Europe, Asia, and Peru, and the price in New Spain had risen at one point to 120 pesos per hundredweight, then fell to 82, where it remained until the 1760s.[39] State control remained profitable, although management was inefficient, perhaps purposefully so. A quintal of mercury cost the state 13 pesos delivered at Sevilla; transshipped to Mexico City, its cost rose to 30 pesos, but even including freight charges from the colonial capital to mine sites, the final price of 82 pesos to purchasers, whether mine owners or merchants (*aviadores*) servicing them, still left substantial profits.[40] Merchants who bought mercury from the state sold it to small mine owners at monopoly prices, and the distribution network was permeable: the bureaucrats who controlled distribution, like the administrator-general and *oidor* of the Audiencia de México, Joseph Fernández de Veytia, abused their positions for gross self-enrichment, and the Amerindians who handled the leaking mercury-filled goatskins peddled it on the black market.[41]

At his death, Veytia's will stipulated that half his estate (it topped the extraordinary sum of 800,000 pesos) be returned to the state "in the most proper and covert manner possible."[42] The perks of an *oidor* of the Mexico City Audiencia raised the lifestyle of a Peninsula-born *letrado* to heights undreamed of in the metropole. Moreover, by maintaining a high final price, the state-generated income then cycled into other operations, such as the purchase of Cuban leaf tobacco for processing and sale in Europe.[43] As for broadening mercury exploration in the colonies to stabilize amalgamation operations in the mines in wartime, when shipments were usually curtailed or suspended, experienced officials like Landázuri reminded Madrid policy-makers of an imperative of colonialism: "Mining of mercury in the Indies is inopportune, for we must keep those dominions dependent in order to foster our navy and navigation through its transport."[44]

Maintaining artificially inflated mercury prices over the first half of the eighteenth century should not be construed as a sign of state immobilism with respect to New Spain's mining problems. A Zacatecas *junta* meeting between 1716 and 1720 urged halving the state's tax from subsoil rights, the 20 percent (*quinto*) levied on mining production, to encourage mine operators, a recommendation implemented in 1723.[45] In the 1720s, too, alerted by reports of debased coins cut by the Mexico City mint, which was then leased to private contractors, Madrid authorized an investigation into the Casa de Moneda's operations, leading ultimately to deprivatization of the *fundición, ensaye,* and *marca* by the public sector.[46] Predictably, state revenues rose, although the tax was now reduced to a tenth, the *diezmo.* In the 1730s and 1740s, it will be recalled, proposals surfaced in New Spain and Peru for setting up privileged mine supply companies; the government rejected these, accepting the advice of merchants and others who "managed slightly more than two million [pesos]"—hardly disinterested advisors.[47] These were obstacles to state intervention by powerful colonial interests, among them New Spain's *aviadores,* mostly emigrants from Spain.

Beginning in the late 1760s, a number of factors—technology, state initiative, and the sheer persistence and luck of mine owners—touched off a remarkable surge in silver production, and consequently government income, launching New Spain's greatest silver age. Not the least factor was, first, the use of blasting powder in underground operations.[48] Next came the serendipity factor, the unexpected economies of scale through skillful restoration and expansion of Guanajuato's "Valenciana" mine complex, which after 1778 consumed 90,000 pounds of powder annually, seventy times as much as Zacatecas in 1738, making "Valenciana" the world's most profitable mine of the period.[49] In the third place, one should not minimize two recommendations by Gálvez as high commissioner to New Spain and again on his return to Spain, when he became colonial secretary: first, to reduce the price of mercury, and second, to respond to the need of New Spain's mine owners to have their own tribunal, or corporate body, an organization comparable to the merchants' *consulado,* to solve the problem of mine finance and to put to rest repeated proposals for a general mine supply monopoly. Both became state policy.

Gálvez's final report, or *informe general,* detailing his activity as high commissioner to New Spain (1765–71) was a far cry from his "Discurso" around 1759, which covered mining only summarily and tangentially. His *informe* should be viewed in context: the disproportionate space devoted to mining reflected the secret instructions drafted under Esquilache's supervision directing him to survey mine owners' capital and credit, mercury supply, and all else "that could increase the harvest of precious metals."[50] Accordingly, the *informe* respected the mining sector as the Spanish empire's "main nerve" and Mexico City's mint as the "crown's most important property."[51] There is an oddly ambivalent attitude toward mine owners. Gálvez made much of consorting with prominent mine owners such as Borda and Romero de Terreros ("restorer of this profession"), along with the silver banker Aldaco.[52] At the same time, he sympathized with medium and small mine owners, who were "wretchedly impoverished," perennially starved of capital to pay for drainage and other expensive works, and exploited by their *aviadores* and other businessmen, who underpriced ore entrusted to them for refining and provided mercury "a precios excesivos." In the past, he noted approvingly, increases in silver output had followed increases in mercury supplies to small mine owners.[53]

In general, Gálvez absorbed the mine owners' opinion that they were tyrannized over by their multiracial workforce of "Indians, mulattoes, and other castes" crowding New Spain's mining sites, where they formed a mass of "idlers, loafers, and delinquents" whose "ignorance, disorder, and thefts" were responsible for "outrageous rioting and repeated rebellion," financial loss, and mine owners' discouragement. With a colonialist mind-set, Gálvez probably expected to find the urban proletariat and lumpen proletariat of New Spain's mining camps docile, subservient, and respectful of private property and the imperial state's representatives, despite the horrendous conditions of their workplaces.[54] Silver mines, Gamboa had reported, with no exaggeration (and presumably Gálvez knew them firsthand), were "like dark, damp, suffocating caverns emitting noisome vapors; life-threatening risks in ascending and descending, not to mention cave-ins; the mine workers are naked and lacerated carrying heavy bars and ores; sickness and rotting widespread; foundries and mercury operations are poisonous; humidity, fire and the vapors make sicknesses incurable. It's a hell." It was hardly surprising, then, that mine workers stole silver and mercury at the smelters "openly, in sight of the foremen," or that "the workers and ore bearers drink, gamble and spend what they earn." These were "men without greed, who live day to day. They dress in expensive clothing and the next day descend into the mine where in their finery they wield wedge and pick." And he summed up, "if these are the servants, can you imagine what the masters are like?"[55] Gálvez and Gamboa, it seems, had little respect for mine workers as a group.

No doubt Gálvez had been unsettled by local response to his surgically efficient execution of Aranda's directives for the expulsion of the Jesuits, an unnerving "uprising of the plebeians and riffraff of the mines" of Guanajuato, although he was convinced that his ruthless repression there had improved silver production. For this reason, he rejected pleas from Guanajuato's mine owners and refiners to eliminate the head tax (*tributo*) paid annually by mine workers (Gálvez's *canalla*) on the grounds that they would lose "respeto y obediencia" to the authority of the colonial state.[56] Bureaucratic efficiency, enlightenment, and a sense of humanity are not necessarily linked.

Of three major interventions by Gálvez and hence by the Spanish state in New Spain's mining sector, two were quickly implemented without opposition. Less than two years after arriving in the colony, Gálvez ordered a 25 percent reduction in the mercury price to 62 pesos per hundredweight and placed blasting powder manufacture and sale under state administration, with a further price reduction. Nine years later, in 1776, the state lowered the price of mercury by another 25 percent, to 41 pesos, half the level of 1766.[57] As a result, mercury consumption climbed steadily; a comparison of the consumption level of 1762–66 with 1778–82 shows an increase of 66 percent.[58] Gálvez's pricing policy was quickly accepted by the Mexico City merchant establishment. The *consulado* praised the state's new policy, pointed to the processing of neglected low-grade ores, a corresponding rise in silver output and coinage, and the way this rippled through the colony's economy, "with consequent increase in consumption of imports" distributed by the local commercial establishment.[59] Silver production remained the most dynamic factor underlying fluctuations in New Spain's external trade.

Characteristically, the Spanish metropole shifted the financing of mercury imports to colonial consumers. As demand rose and breakdowns in metropolitan production (at Almadén) recurred, Madrid turned to Austrian suppliers for delivery of 12,000 quintals annually, then ordered New Spain's officials, as well as those of other colonies that imported mercury, to advance funds to Madrid to cover future shipments.[60] As usual, the colonies had to finance their own growth.

Odd, but nonetheless true, Gálvez found the mining industry dispirited, its "mineros de profesión" lacking respectable status, enduring "perjudicial descrédito." Litigation among mine owners was both misunderstood and mishandled by "ordinary judges and their subalterns." Only too conscious of the wealth, influence, and status of the members of Mexico City's *consulado*, Gálvez concluded that New Spain's mining community needed a separate set of ordinances establishing a privileged body, "just like the commercial *consulados*," and dedicated to solving the major problems of working capital and civil litigation.[61] However, Gálvez's third intervention, creating the Tribunal de Minería, did not materialize overnight.

The Tribunal de Minería

The immediate origins of what became New Spain's mining tribunal were the industry's capital shortages as well as cost-reduction imperatives. These, it may be argued, were aspects of the boom-and-bust cycle—perennial problems of any large-scale enterprise. Yet this apparently static perspective on New Spain's major economic sector obscures factors making the last seventy-five years of colonial rule in New Spain both novel and crisis-prone, such as the surge in output that began with the extraordinary development of Guanajuato's "Valenciana" and Zacatecas's "Veta Grande" mines, both requiring large-scale investment in infrastructure—including timbering, drainage, and whims. In this sense, New Spain's silver-mining sector in Gálvez's time was entering a new phase, the apogee of more than two centuries of activity. Another factor was the more general, nebulous, but nonetheless real pressure of private and public peninsular interests to offer the metropole and the growing numbers of emigrants from the *montañas de Santander* and the Basque regions greater opportunity in wealth-producing sectors of Spain's colonial possessions, notably (but not exclusively) in New Spain. In this connection, at least four interest groups were not hard to define: Creole mine owners and their Mexico City *almacenero* backers, local silver refiners hoping to circumvent Mexico City's commercial oligopolists, Cadiz *flotistas* pressing to enter mining as *rescatadores,* and recent immigrants from Spain's Cantabrian provinces.

It was Gálvez's successive roles as *visitador general* to New Spain, *consejero* of the Consejo de Indias, and then colonial secretary that led him to respond to private and public interest peninsular groups vitally involved in the economy of New Spain. Six years there had sensitized him to mine owners' problems. When he returned to Madrid, soon to become colonial secretary and seeming arbiter of colonial policy and its implementation, he kept in contact through former staff members in Mexico, including Joaquin Velázquez de León, a Creole who had served under him on his northern expedition. He could also rely on civil servants with substantial colonial service who occupied key positions in Madrid's high bureaucracy, among them Landázuri; Francisco Machado, who had also served under Gálvez in New Spain and later became a viceregal secretary before being recalled to Madrid; and Antonio Porlier, ex-*oidor* of the Audiencias of Charcas and Lima.[62] Gálvez's problem was not whether but how the state might intervene in the colonial mining sector in order to provide capital equitably, a judicial system attuned to mine owners' rather than *almaceneros'* issues, and technical assistance, all the while circumventing the *almaceneros* of the Mexico City *consulado* and the Creole *oidores* of the Audiencia, notably Francisco Xavier Gamboa. In other words, how to block Gamboa's proposed general supply company, likely to be dominated by the (largely peninsular) commercial oligarchs of the colonial capital; and to provide a degree of autonomy to mining districts precisely when a new wave of bonanza-seekers from Spain's northern provinces were penetrating those districts.

Gálvez probably drafted the royal *cédula* (warrant) of November 1773 directing Viceroy Bucareli to choose a committee drawn from the key colonial bureaucracies, principal mining districts, and the Mexico City merchant community to review mercury pricing and distribution and frame new regulations for the industry.[63] Bucareli circulated the warrant in February 1774 and, surprisingly, within just nine days, received back a comprehensive analysis (*representación*) prepared by two mining experts, the Creole Joaquín Velázquez de León and the Spaniard Juan Lucas Lassaga, and seconded by deputies from the mining districts of Bolaños and Sultepec.[64] To no one's surprise, their report, which was immediately published, underscored the industry's capital needs and the lack of updated mining regulations or a mining court along the lines of the merchants' *consulado.* More significant were their recommendations. After considering and then discarding Gamboa's proposal for a *consulado*-controlled company to provide working capital, they proposed that a percentage of the state's coinage fee be set aside to cover interest payments on a mining investment fund (*banco de avío*) of 2 million pesos administered by the Tribunal de Minería. Once the latter body was established, its chief officers—administrator-general, director-general, and three deputies-general—would be chosen by delegates elected by regional mining groups, the *diputaciones territoriales.*[65]

Basically, the recommendations of Velázquez de León and Lassaga (Bucareli made them his key aides) covered funding of the investment bank (1776) and the responsibilities of the tribunal's administrator-general and director-general (Lassaga and Velázquez de León, appointed in 1777). After years of intermittent review by Gálvez, assisted by Machado and Porlier, a set of ordinances was finally issued in 1782. Gálvez and his associates had rejected the opposition of the dean of the Mexico City Audiencia (the Spaniard Domingo Valcárcel), Mexico City's *almaceneros,* and their supporter on the Audiencia (Francisco Gamboa) to an independent mine owners' tribunal.[66] The Audiencia's *oidores* were incensed among other things by the independent judicial authority vested in the Tribunal de Minería; it meant *oidores* would lose the supplemental income they had previously earned in handling mine owners' litigation.

On balance, it had taken almost four decades for the mining community and the colonial and metropolitan bureaucracies to create an institution modeled on Mexico City's merchant guild to meet mine owners' long perceived needs. It had also taken Gálvez a decade to establish the tribunal, an investment fund, and a judicial body that promised to minimize the influence of Mexico City's merchant oligarchs and friends among the *oidores* of the Audiencia, while enhancing the influence of the mine owners' *diputaciones territoriales.* Indisputable evidence that Gálvez had a clear vision of the structure of the tribunal and its regulations is confirmed by the drafting of the November 1772 *cédula,* the immediate involvement of Velázquez de León and Lassaga, Bucareli's reliance upon them as key *junta* members, and Gálvez's elaboration of the ordinances with Porlier and Machado. Tribunal and ordinances bore the birthmarks of planned parenthood, not accidental paternity. Later, mine owners would reward Gálvez handsomely for his paternity with an annual pension of 4,000 pesos.[67]

Over the initial three years of its formal operation (1783–86) the Tribunal de Minería seemed to meet the objectives of Gálvez, Machado, Velázquez de León, Lassaga, and the *deputaciones territoriales,* to judge by the allocation of loans from its investment bank (the *avío* funds) and election of Guanajuato's *deputación* in 1783. Although a major role of the tribunal was supposedly impartial allocation of investment funds, Gálvez's handpicked officials, Velázquez de León and Lassaga, processed applications with virtually no supervision. Evidence is overwhelming that both authorized loans without careful review of a mine's physical condition and the owner's experience and competence—an indication of "laxness and complacency in financial matters," not to say gross mismanagement.[68] In 1784, rumors critical of the chief officers' competence circulated, probably inspired by discontented Guanajuato mine owners, but no action came until the deaths of Velázquez de León and Lassaga, within a month of each other, in February–March 1786. Then at the end of May came a warrant countersigned by Gálvez ordering a review of the management and investment policy of the capital fund and appointment of two external observers "agreeable to the merchants and aviadores" of Mexico City whenever the tribunal's officers processed "economic matters." This led to audits by the tribunal itself and by an auditor, Pedro María de Monterde, sent by Mexico City's treasury accounting office, to the formation of a reorganizing *junta,* and ultimately to the revamping of the tribunal itself. Where once only mine owners had been entitled to participate, deputies drawn from Mexico City's "merchants and mine financiers"—a significant departure—were now to "sit with the tribunal in *acuerdo.*"[69]

Monterde's exhaustive audit permits a comparison of the major objective set for the tribunal, its capital fund, or *banco de avío,* to finance mining enterprise, with performance over a decade of activity, 1777–87. First, the tribunal's income side. Over the decade, receipts totaled more than 3 million pesos, including one million borrowed but immediately "donated" to the metropolitan government; there was no borrowing specifically to form a capital fund, and financial assistance to mine owners began only seven years after the tribunal's formation. On the disbursement side, 51.7 percent of all expenditure went to non-mine-related activities, including 1.3 million pesos to the metropolitan government, another 150,000 to the princes of Asturias (the future Charles IV and María Luísa), 33,000 to Gálvez's pension, another 20,000 to Velázquez de León for services rendered in establishing the tribunal, and even 30,000 pesos to the recently created Academia de San Carlos, Mexico City's art school.[70]

Meanwhile, less than half of all disbursements (40.16 percent) was allocated by Velázquez de León and Lassaga to mine owners, plus another 1.28 percent to fruitless efforts to locate and exploit mercury resources in the colony when demand shot up and Almadén shipments faltered. More revealing was the pattern of distribution within the mining community: more than half such allocations (55.27 percent) went to five of twenty-one recipients located in the Pachuca/Real del Monte mining district; far less went to Guanajuato, which received a mere 3.31 percent. Perhaps more significant, the borrowers—with the exception of a Creole mining magnate of Guanajuato, José Mariano de Sardaneta y Legazpi, second marqués de San Juan de Rayas—were newcomers to mining. Some had only minimal mining experience; others had only tenuous title to their properties. Yet others lacked both experience and sound title. As a group, the borrowers probably drew on their connections to influential colonial and metropolitan officials; networking seems to have been the principal factor behind their loans. The tribunal's financial resources, Walter Howe concluded, were "grossly mismanaged."[71]

There is a strong presumption that favoritism rather than realistic assessment of the potential return to a mining enterprise shaped decision-making in allocating loans. In mid 1784, for instance, Francisco Rojas y Rocha received 25,765 pesos for operations at Real del Monte; three years later, he was still indebted for 93 percent of the loan's principal. This performance could have been predicted. On-site inspection of the enterprise when the loan request was under review had turned up warning indicators: the mine shaft required immediate enlargement, mine walls were solid rock, and there were no levels, ore samples showed poor quality, and, most important, Rojas y Rocha although lacking any mining experience had purchased the property for 200,000 pesos. He was an obvious risk, as Deputy-General Julián del Hierro pointed out in substantiating his reservations.[72]

The case of Rojas y Rocha, in which family and marriage networks played influential roles in career advancement, was not unique in the colonial world. Details reveal the countless minor labyrinths of power webbing together colonial and metropolitan, "old" and "new" worlds. Rojas's father was peninsular, his mother was a *criolla*, and he was one of fifteen siblings. In Spain, Rojas had married a León y Pizarro, whose brother's Andalusian wife, Rojas's *concuñada*, was a tireless "mover" at Madrid in the early 1770s—her wire-pulling activities in behalf of husband and family earned her the sobriquet of "La Pizarro." One suspects that her socializing at Madrid put her in contact with the rising Andalusian bureaucrat José de Gálvez, leading to her husband's appointment to Quito, and to an *alcaldía mayor* in the prospering cochineal-raising area of southern New Spain (Teposcolula/Yanhuitlán) for Rojas. Hence his gratitude to Gálvez and his family and an epic poem dedicated to Matías de Gálvez.[73]

In view of the 40 percent of total tribunal outlays over a decade allocated to mining operations and the disproportionate share to the Pachuca/Real del Monte district, the *avío* fund could not have been a major factor in the mining upsurge of the late 1770s and 1780s. Contemporaries concluded accurately that "at this time one cannot count on this resource." A major objective of the mining guild—easing the financial problems of mine owners and lessening their dependence on Mexico City's *comerciantes y aviadores*—was not met.[74] There is reason to believe the capital outlays to the Pachua/Real del Monte group of mines were misspent. These observations aside, there remain Madrid's irresistible demands for a huge, "prompt and cheerful" forced loan of a million pesos for a long war, along with a 300,000-peso "gift" to Spain for a shipyard and docks at Cuazacualco, and perhaps another 100,000 pesos to cover peace negotiations with Morocco, described as of "benefit to all the subjects of these kingdoms and the Indies." Typically, the million-peso wartime loan was omitted from the Tribunal de Minería's ledgers by viceregal accounting legerdemain.[75]

Gálvez and his associates, it will be remembered, had come up with the idea of the Tribunal de Minería primarily to offer New Spain's financially strapped mine owners an alternative to Mexico City's merchant bankers. It is in the light of the less than acceptable performance of its officers during the tribunal's first decade that the pattern of appointment to tribunal office by Colonial Secretary Gálvez just before his death must be seen. While Gálvez was still minister in 1786, elections to fill vacancies were suspended and a protégé of his, the Basque mining engineer Fausto de Elhuyar, was appointed director-general, and two of the three deputies-general, Antonio Basoco and Antonio Barroso, widely respected representatives of the Basque and Montañés communities in the "cuerpo de comerciantes y aviadores" of the colonial capital, were handpicked from among the Mexico City merchant oligarchy.[76] Furthermore, the *junta de arreglo* selected by Mexico's viceroy in 1787 to oversee the tribunal's operations contained eleven members, of whom six were the most prominent Mexico City *almaceneros* (Basoco, Barroso, Echarri, Yermo, Goya, and Dongo).[77]

There was yet another facet to Gálvez's policy for stimulating the entry of new mine owners by reducing the traditional financial dependence upon Mexico City's merchants: his intention to limit the judicial preeminence of

Mexico City's Audiencia by granting the *diputaciones territoriales* and the tribunal wider authority in settling litigation over mine boundaries, claims to abandoned mine shafts, and mercury allocations.[78] Moreover, if Mexico City's jurisdiction were curbed, the entry of newcomers into mining districts hitherto dominated by a few well-capitalized consortia would allow them ultimately to shape local policy in mercury allocations and in settling property boundary disputes brought to regional mining courts. In fact, the tribunal's ordinances shifted litigation from civil courts to the *diputaciones territoriales,* and in 1785, Gálvez directed that appeals be carried to local officials, *corregidores* and *alcaldes,* a clear sign of intent to limit the influence of Mexico City's courts over mine owners' factional disputes.[79]

Factional issues and their effect on New Spain's principal mining district at the time, Guanajuato, are a case in point. Guanajuato's first *diputación* to the tribunal was elected (and manipulated) by a *junta* of seven electors, chosen by the district's qualified mine owners. Between 1779 and 1783, when the tribunal began formal operations, the well-established Creole mine owners Antonio Obregón, his partner (*socio*) Pedro Luciano de Otero, and Vicente Manuel de Sardaneta y Legazpi, and their Basque associates, controlled the district's electors. As a result of their influence, the tribunal authorized the million-peso "donation" to Spain during the war with England, despite protests from the merchant community, while the Creole proprietors of the "Valenciana" and "Rayas" mines (Otero, Obregón, and Sardaneta) received a disproportionately high percentage of the scarce mercury available in wartime (1781). Meanwhile, under the first *junta de electores,* dominated by established Creole mine owners, the Spanish *montañés* merchants Francisco Septién y Arce, Manuel García de Quintana, and José Hernández Chico, to whose interests Galvez seemed to respond, moved into silver refining.[80] They manipulated the selection of new Guanajuato electors in 1783 (all seven were *peninsulares,* four of them *montañeses*) to win local control and thereby, they hoped, elect *peninsulares* rather than *criollos* to the *diputación territorial.*

The outgoing Creole deputies reacted by presenting a list of those who might replace them as *diputados,* while the insurgent *montañés* group insisted that only the new electors were entitled to "nominate those they considered most appropriate." In effect, the outgoing deputies were imitating the electoral strategy of the Consulado de México whereby former and outgoing officials (*priores, consules*) rigged elections by presenting prearranged slates of candidates for office to the electors of the *montañés* and *vizcaíno* factions.[81] So bitter was this factional dispute that Viceroy Mayorga passed the issue on to Madrid, really to Gálvez, who must have shaped the decision that "the electors [of the *diputación*] from Guanaxuato must be able to nominate deputies freely, not the old practice of nominations by outgoing officeholders."[82] Apparently, Gálvez sided with the *montañés* newcomers to Guanajuato's community of mine owners.[83] The Creole mine owner Antonio Obregón thereupon proposed to Gálvez that future selection of *diputación* members be removed from the mining districts and shifted to the authorities in Mexico City, either the chief tribunal officials or the viceroy. Predictably, Gálvez ignored this hardly disinterested proposal.[84]

These were manifestations of deepening factionalism that would plague the mining community over following decades and become acute in the critical months of mid 1808. More to the point, formation under state auspices of a corporate body in theory protecting the interests of all mine owners became a guarantee of security to the wider merchant community seeking to invest its growing earnings in what was again becoming a booming industry of "startling prosperity" in the post-1770 decades. Mining paid wages, bought supplies from haciendas and estancias, from workshops (*obrajes*) and independent artisans, from local shopkeepers and Mexico City's large warehousemen. Mining monetized the colonial economy, pulling along agriculture and commerce.

Assuming the accuracy of observers then and now of the symbiotic relationship between silver mining, coinage (the motor of the colonial and, for that matter, of the metropolitan economy), and other sectors, the resurgence of silver production in the 1770s had stimulated agriculture and commerce before the impact of 1778 was manifested. Data on coinage and its export from Veracruz substantiate the upward trend of the 1770s. The recovery in silver mining—the result of bonanzas, capital, and state policy—laid the groundwork for what to contemporaries seemed New Spain's broad-based economic expansion from the 1780s onward. Through Madrid's intervention in reducing the cost of mercury, iron, and steel imports, in tax exemptions or reductions, and in the mining tribunal and *comercio libre* of 1778, the Spanish state augmented the multiplier effects of New Spain's mining sector. Fausto de Elhuyar, who was not given to hyperbole, perceptively noted mining's multiple effects, including the "increase in mine workers, in materials needed, and in feeding people and animals," adding that "since most of their provisions and equipment come from outside their area, those—even in those far distant zones—gain from mining prosperity."[85]

Agriculture: Growth without Development

Surging silver production and coinage, striking phenomena to eighteenth-century observers in both Spain and New Spain, were matched by population growth and transformation of the colony's other major economic sector, agriculture. With the exception of Great Britain, everywhere in the North Atlantic world of the time an increase in agricultural products can be traced, not to marked productivity growth per acre, but to planting different crops, expanding the area under cultivation, and, above all, applying more labor.[86] To contemporaries, population growth ("more hands") translated visibly into more production and ultimately a more expanding economy, society, and polity; hence the emphasis that political economists in the government placed upon census and tax records of one sort or another. At one point, even the volume of New Spain's mail became a crude measure of demographic growth, despite its obvious shortcomings.[87] The prosperity of "any kingdom is generally regulated by population, and therefore everyone hopes it will grow in order to draw its favorable consequences," Eusebio Ventura Beleña, an *oidor* of Mexico City's Audiencia, observed.[88]

Extrapolating from data for the period 1743–1810, New Spain's population rose at an average annual rate between 1.5 and 1.9 percent, although that of the colonial capital—Mexico City was the largest urban center in the Western Hemisphere—grew far less.[89] Probably overall demographic growth was greater, taking into account undercounting in the 1790 census, when "many people avoided the census, besides the fact many common folk have no fixed residence and live in the streets."[90] Although scattered data indicate regional variations in growth rates, a general pattern is discernible.

Between 1650 and 1750, the rate of demographic recovery from the holocaust of epidemic disease and cultural disorganization in the sixteenth century was high. In Michoacán between 1697 and 1720, the annual increase reached 2.14 percent; in the Bajío's San Luís de la Paz and Guadalajara, it was slightly lower.[91] Around 1750, growth rates began to slacken as a result of recurrent epidemics in 1761–62 and again in 1785–86, land shortages, and the consequent immiseration of Indian communities and lower rural living standards. While fertility remained around 5 percent annually, mortality rates were often far higher; in San Luís de la Paz, the growth rate fell 92 percent.[92]

Not that population stagnated, for in the large Michoacán bishopric between 1745 and 1785, it more than doubled, from 315,000 to 675,000. But in general, "the great upward surge of the eighteenth century lost momentum at its close," as demographic studies at the regional level indicate.[93] Evidently, the colony's population was growing (if more slowly) in the last half of the century, while rural migrants flowed to Mexico City, the provincial capitals of Puebla, Valladolid, and Guadalajara, and to mining centers at Guanajuato, Pachuca, Zacatecas, and San Luís Potosí. No doubt the colony's increasing urban population raised the demand for regional products from both near and distant sources, for food, clothing, and draft animals, and for European and Asian imports through Veracruz and Acapulco.[94] Agricultural expansion in the last half of the eighteenth century rewarded hacienda and estancia proprietors large and small alike with higher prices, propelled by the demands of a growing colonial population. The pattern of mid-century stagnation in mining followed by rising output seems in general to have been duplicated in agriculture, but without, to be sure, the spectacular performance of mining centers like Guanajuato. In any event, the parallel suggests some reciprocal, even symbiotic relationship between the two major sectors of the colonial economy. In the case of agriculture, however, demand seems periodically to have outstripped supply, forcing food prices upward.[95]

Maize and beans, wheat and sugar satisfied mainly local and intraregional consumption, with some interregional traffic in wheat, sugar, and probably rum (*chinguirito*) that could bear shipping costs. A number of factors help explain what has been termed with exaggeration "startling increments" in agriculture, which contemporaries measured by tithe receipts.[96] Mining expansion absorbed more workers and their families, food and clothing, and "tallow, hides, mules and horses, and grain."[97] Mine owners and merchants invested in land and cattle, in irrigation works for crops like sugar and wheat, and, when price levels warranted, in maize. There developed a large-scale interregional flow of products from northern New Spain to the center following the mines' lifeline, the Camino Real, sending sheep and wool to the workshops (*obrajes*) of Querétaro and Mexico City, as well as cattle on the hoof.[98] Maize was the basic staple for humans and for hundreds of thousands of mules, burros, horses, and pigs. But high freight costs by mule and cart over poor roads, as well as limited storage capacity, placed ceilings on agricultural production; on average, haciendas, lay and ecclesiastical, could store a maximum of about two years' production.[99] To be sure, some products could bear transport costs, accounting for exports of high-value cochineal and indigo and attempts to sustain shipments of wheat and flour from Puebla to Cuba, and of sugar from Cuernavaca, Izúcar, and Orizaba to Spain. Nonetheless, flour and sugar exports could not long be sustained, since they could compete neither with U.S. flour shipped from Baltimore to Havana nor with Cuban sugar at Cadiz, Málaga, or Barcelona.[100] Such exports aside, the Consulado de México diagnosed the problem accurately when it stated that New Spain's agriculture "requires greater stimulus than other areas, since we lack good transport facilities."[101]

These were among the main conclusions of a survey of New Spain's agriculture that Madrid requested from Mexico City's *consulado* in order to assess the impact of adjustments in its commercial policy after 1778.[102] Juan Antonio de Yermo y Larrazával, who provided detailed crop-by-crop coverage, was a peninsular immigrant from Güenes in Vizcaya's *encartaciones* who entered Mexico City's commercial world sometime in the late 1750s and prospered between the 1760s and 1780s, becoming a wealthy *almacenero,* consul of the *consulado* (1785–86), and a member of the mining tribunal's *junta de arreglo,* along with his fellow *almaceneros* Basoco and Dongo.[103] (His daughter María Josefa married her first cousin, Gabriel Joaquín de Yermo y la Bárcena, the son of Juan Antonio's brother.) The *consulado* turned to Juan Antonio de Yermo because like other merchant oligarchs, he owned and operated as part of his multiple operations two large sugar plantations in the Cuernavaca valley, which his nephew and son-in-law Gabriel Joaquín later acquired as part of his wife's dowry.

Yermo's survey was filtered through a successful, aggressive merchant's perception of the gap between the potential of colonial commercial agriculture and the constraints limiting its realization: lack of capital for medium and small farmers, shortage of storage facilities, high freight costs, biases in state policy, and last, but not least, insubordinate rural workers. Yermo reviewed maize, wheat, beans, pulque, tobacco, cochineal, cotton, and sugar, crop by crop, with acute observations about ranching. Not unexpectedly, he reserved the most extended treatment for the crop he knew best, sugarcane.

New Spain's cane plantations in the bishoprics of Mexico, Puebla, and Valladolid (Michoacán) benefited, he believed, from better soil, water, firewood, and weather than in Cuba. Yet the industry remained underdeveloped.[104] Demand in the colony's urban centers was strong and growing in response to increased consumption, by all social classes, of cocoa from Guayaquil, cheaper than and fast displacing Venezuelan imports. (Yermo could not resist reporting that "Caracas" exporters had tried to limit New Spain's imports of Guayaquil's competitively priced cocoa). Local cane production, he predicted, could be doubled from the current level of around 800,000 *arrobas* to become a prized export on a massive scale, provided that Madrid legalized processing New Spain's molasses into *chinguirito.* This legal constraint, from which Cuban rum producers were exempted, discouraged planter/merchants like Yermo from experimenting with lower production costs to compete with Cuban cane products at Cadiz, other peninsular ports, and in European markets. Citing an issue of the official *Gaceta de Madrid* of 1784, he foresaw a growing export trade in New Spain's sugar, even to distant Baltic and Russian ports. In the current situation, however, Yermo reported that New Spain's unsold molasses was simply dumped or diverted to production of unrefined brown sugar (*panocha*) for purely local consumption. As a result, he added, "our sugars end up too expensive for transport, unlike those of the Windward Islands; our expansion is a response only to New Spain's consumption."

Yermo blamed Cuban planters, their Cadiz brokers, and "Españoles de Barcelona," who were able to reexport Cuban rums because they had pressured Madrid to hamstring competition from New Spain, for the plight of Mexico's cane growers. Why, he asked rhetorically, did Catalans systematically downgrade New Spain's *chinguirito* as "of low quality and sickening, while they applaud that of Cuba, which they sell profitably in Europe?" Since a barrel of good Andalusian white wine sold for 40 pesos in New Spain, while Catalan brandy went for only 5 pesos, "such praiseworthy brands must consist of the dregs and other matter of the mother wine and"—he slyly added—"even other unknown substances." On the contrary, such was the high quality of New Spain's rum that it was widely used in hospitals and pharmacies, where it was held to be "better than what comes from Spain." And resorting to the concept of comparative advantage in a market-based economy, Yermo recommended that Catalan brandy producers switch to other products if they could not match New Spain's competition. In this case, he pointed out, Spanish shipowners would at last be able to count on return cargoes of up to 700,000 *arrobas* of New Spain's sugar. Like other *vizcaínos* in the last half of the eighteenth century, Yermo had migrated to New Spain from the Basque country without establishing strong ties to the Cadiz commercial community, and with an inbred regionalist bias against Catalans.

For that matter, like Mexico City's business community and most of New Spain's elite, Yermo held racist views of the indigenous people who made up most of the colonial labor force. As a landowner, he also had a vested interest in preserving his workers' dependency, subordination to his paternalism, clientelism, and low wages. To block provisions in the proposed intendancy system designed to limit lending to native peoples by estate owners, merchants, and local officials to a maximum of five pesos per year, he looked to a *representación* drafted in late 1785 by a group of concerned citizens of Mexico City calling itself the *Junta de Ciudadanos*, which expanded on two principal constraints upon agricultural growth from the employers' viewpoint: field workers' "insubordination" and the colony's badly maintained road system.

Junta members feared the impact of government curbs on the borrowing capacity of the colony's native peoples, partly because sales in a monetizing economy might fall, but mainly because without sizeable advances and consequent growth in consumer debt, "they can find no Indians willing to work for an advance of only five pesos." Otherwise, only hunger would then drive Amerindians into the rural labor reserve.[105] As for their purchases of cloth or clothing (textiles, as we have seen, were Spain's main reexport to New Spain), Yermo was convinced that "in general that's what least interests them, for they are satisfied with a poor *fresada,* shabby hat, worthless pants, and jackets of goatskin or sheepskin."[106] In the perverse logic of colonialists, the visible effects of poverty and degradation under colonialism, the rags of the poor, became cause rather than effect. Even Indians who participated in the marketplace with their livestock and truck crops were, the *junta* believed, now withdrawing, because "they no longer can count on someone for advances." Pragmatic market- and profit-oriented colonialists believed that innate, congenital characteristics explained the reluctance of indigenous peoples to expose themselves to market mechanisms imposed by colonialism. Thus the cardinal cause of the colony's agricultural stagnation (Yermo's term was *decadencia*) was the imperial state's intention to limit exploitation of native peoples by imposing curbs on lending or consumer indebtedness. The elite's understanding of native modes of resistance was presumably persuasive with Madrid officials, also predisposed to a racist view of subaltern peoples.

Complementing the resistance of badly needed Amerindian laborers to enter the marketplace, and a further factor of agricultural "decadence" in the *junta*'s view, was their *poca subordinación.* While *junta* members confirmed the devastating effects of frosts and ice storms upon crops in mid 1785, nonetheless plantings were not saved in time, because Amerindians would not work for advances of less than 5 pesos, compelling *hacendados* to compete for "insolent" field hands who insisted upon their customary work practices. (The *junta*'s case becomes plausible if one changes "insolence" to "resistance" to the work regimen imposed by estate owners). Workers, the *junta* complained, insisted upon resting one or two hours "following general custom here, at eight or half-past eight in the morning, the same at midday. Not a minute less, since they have not eaten since seven o'clock the night before. They leave for work without breakfast. Can you keep working until midday without eating?" In addition, "they insist on a midday rest, not one hour (the custom) but two hours according to the regulation. They want to return to their pueblo for a rest period, which allows some to get drunk, and others to get cool to the idea of returning to work, which they abandon." Rural workers had been politicized by overly solicitous government labor provisions, by "gentle measures designed to provide the good treatment we must give them." Now they believed they could no longer be punished and, if punished, reacted "insolently and impudently." If threatened, they called it mistreatment, protesting even the "slightest well-deserved push" and then litigating.

The resistance of rural labor was not yet generalized throughout the colony, the *junta* noted with relief; rather, it was still confined mainly to Mexico City and nearby provinces, precisely those most affected by market-oriented agriculture and labor relations in transition from clientelism to a mixture of paternalism and wage labor. The *junta*'s members welcomed agricultural development to supply the colony's internal demand and exports to Europe, but they were disturbed by adversarial relations with their workers. Of course, they distanced themselves from the paternalism of the past, "a kind of slavery," under which, they admitted, Amerindian field hands had often been exploited with "the most unrestrained greed" and could not preserve their "livertad." In reality, the *junta* hankered after a utopia far from Mexico City—unspoiled by migration, commercialization, urban density, rootlessness, and poverty, one located somewhere on "haciendas in the interior" near Querétaro to the north or Oaxaca to the south, where workers dressed decently, "suffer no food shortages and live far from the misery of Indians in nearby provinces," where well-intentioned estate owners "whose sole interest is the benefit of the Indians, provide needed clothing at cost, or at moderate profit," paid workers' church dues (*obvenciones*) and head taxes (*tributo*), and supplied weekly rations of maize and meat.

Not that the colony's agriculture stagnated, we now know; rather, it was a striking case of growth without development, a colonial economy whose entrepreneurs emphasized cheap labor over technological improvement and, moreover, aside from precious metals, had few exports. Agricultural expansion therefore had to be lateral, inasmuch as both private landowners and, in some areas, Amerindian communities brought under cultivation unoccupied or unused land in a process compared recently to a kind of "internal colonization."[107]

In the valley of Mexico, an uninterrupted expansion of maize and pulque estates occurred at the expense of land held by Amerindian communities, turning the closing decades of the eighteenth century into a golden age for the valley's approximately 160 large and medium hacienda owners, both secular and ecclesiastical. "The large hacienda," Enrique Florescano has observed, "now dominates the city."[108] There were other changes too: an increase in storage capacity on large estates, more use of irrigated fields in areas like Michoacán. As food prices rose, farms displaced pasture, wheat displaced maize, and pulque plantations expanded in the valley of Mexico and nearby Puebla to supply Mexico City's profitable *pulquerías,* owned by *hacendados* and merchants. Eric Van Young has argued persuasively that the phenomenon of rising food prices in the closing decades of the eighteenth century requires explanation, which he locates in agricultural expansion and higher capital investment pushing the final product to the margin; in short, production costs rose. As population and consequently demand grew, while productivity lagged, prices inexorably crept upward, at times dramatically. But while estate agriculture prospered, lagging real wages and inflation immiserated farm workers and their families, a rural proletariat in formation. The prosperity of estate owners in most cases was a measure of their skill in manipulating the labor reserves created by the increase of landless indigenous people.[109]

Expansion of silver production and coinage that increased the volume of specie leaking into the colony's economy, the growth of urban population and a rural proletariat, and the diffusion of wage labor in agriculture (however poorly remunerated) suggest the circular fashion in which mining, commercialization of agriculture and artisanal activity, and growing import capacity combined to erode barriers to the internal trade of New Spain and to the monetization of its economy. More efficient collection of the state's head tax (*tributo*) from native peoples and *castas* (blacks, mulattoes, and mestizos) alike was designed to impel the lower classes to participate in the marketplace to obtain the necessary specie.[110] The process was not entirely unplanned. In the same fashion, the state's efforts to limit lending to indigenous peoples to no more than a few pesos probably induced native producers to cultivate their plots more intensively and to bring more products to market. Finally, monetization was reflected in rising textile imports after 1763, shipped mainly by Spain's suppliers in western Europe.

Transport Bottlenecks: *Caminos* and *Arrieros*

Both Mexico City's Junta de Ciudadanos (1785) and Yermo's situation report (1788) pointed to the colony's inadequate road system and high transport costs as additional bottlenecks responsible for the "decadence" of agriculture and slow commercialization of the rural economy. The primitive and poorly maintained road system had long been an issue; while the colonial state saw to the maintenance of military garrisons along the mining route to the north, the Camino Real, it allocated little from the colonial treasury to construction or maintenance of other roads, which were abandoned to provincial and municipal authorities.[111] The main arteries between Mexico City and Veracruz on the Caribbean and between the capital and the Pacific coast port of Acapulco carried precious metals exports to Europe and Asia, and low-volume, high-value luxury imports; for such items, shipment by muleback long sufficed, and the state's contribution to maintenance was minimal. "The roads of this area," Intendant Manuel de Flon once wrote candidly to Viceroy Revillagigedo, "remain the way things are when neither cared for nor repaired. Consequently, in the rainy season, they are terrible, and in the dry season force unavoidable detours."[112]

One suspects, however, that by the last third of the eighteenth century, pressures from an expanding interregional economy, monetization, and consumerism induced merchants in the capital to explore the possibilities of the domestic market and external trade more intensively. Road conditions, the organization and functioning of mule drivers (*arrieros*), their subordinate *chinchorreros* and *mozos,* and their strings of mules (*recuas*), along with higher taxes and tighter fiscal surveillance of freight in transit, came under review from the 1770s onward. The underfinanced infrastructure was no longer adequate for transporting silver from the mines to the Mexico City mint, and then on to the east and west coast ports, and for interregional flows of goods, once confined mainly to exchanges between large-scale producers and large-scale consumers.[113] An expanding colonial economy was transforming the once tolerated high-cost transport system into a major bottleneck. "Exports are expensive," officers of the Consulado de México complained and explained in 1788, "because of high freight rates."

Uppermost was the sheer physical deterioration of heavily trafficked roads. Depicting the difficulties small traders had to endure (and perhaps revealing an unconscious recognition of nascent Mexican nationalism), the *consulado* cited the example of the preconquest Amerindian traders described in Torquemada's *Monarquía indiana* two centuries earlier. Torquemada's native informants had told him that when young Aztec traders were about to begin their first trading expedition, a retired, experienced merchant would customarily try to toughen them psychologically for what they would encounter on the road—"hunger, thirst and weariness . . . stale bread, wet tamales . . . water both muddy and bad-tasting"—conditions still encountered in the 1770s by those "trafficking in the interior provinces."[114] In the 1790s, the heavily used Mexico City–Veracruz road was still regarded as impassable in the rainy season, causing shipping delays "because it is impossible to travel through mud and swamps," until dry weather, when one encountered "loose stones and broken terrain and no chance to take alternate paths." An exasperated secretary of the Veracruz *consulado* lamented in 1803 that despite the favorable impact of external trade on the colonial government's income, "New Spain has no bridge, inn, canal, or other resource," and another early nineteenth-century critic commented that in over three centuries, Spain had not built a cart road from Mexico City to the colony's principal ports.[115]

Shipping by mule team (*arriería*) was done by professionals.[116] The *recua* of an *arriero-patrón* might consist of several teams (*atajos*) of anywhere from 10 to 40 mules each; a 40-mule enterprise was adequate for local operations, but only a large number of *recuas* with adequate equipment (harnesses, bridles, and leather coverlets, or *puangoches*) could operate profitably on the long Camino Real.[117] The largest, most elaborate, and most heavily capitalized *recuas* were owned by firms of silver shippers, the *conductores de plata*, who possessed hundreds of mules, usually raised on their own ranches, and employed scores of muleteers. One such *conductor*, Diego Fernández Peredo, had 28,000 pesos invested in "recuas propias," eight *atajos*, or 360 mules, plus 110 saddle mules and their equipment. Amerindians and "other lower classes" predominated among *arrieros*, many from the *feria* site at Jalapa; *arriería* was a monopoly of those born in the colony.[118] Given the distances covered, limited mail service (until 1792, only one weekly mail was dispatched on "all the highways" of the colony) and the customarily high value of cargo, *arrieros* were prized and respected for honesty and reliability. It was common for a Mexico City *almacenero* to entrust to an *arriero-patrón* dozens of boxes filled with hundreds of thousands of silver pesos for delivery at Veracruz or Acapulco. *Arrieros* would leave receipts for items entrusted to them, which they often signed with a cross "because illiterate," since "most of those in the *arrieros'* profession are quite uneducated."[119]

Arrieros canvassed merchant houses for freight to be dropped off along distant routes, "at the same time carrying freight to other places, towns, and haciendas along the roads they transit," ran one careful description in 1767, "until they reach the last stop. When an *arriero* arrives at Mexico [City], he can handle ten loads for Chiguagua if he has extra mules." So he would seek freight to be delivered en route there. To cover costs, an *arriero* hired others, his so-called *ahijados;* and now as *arriero-padrino*, he would "take responsibility from merchant houses for cargo destined for many places, handing some of the shipments to subordinates; they travel together until they must separate. Arriving at a hacienda, for example, they unload chests of spurs, stirrups, shoes, tools, and other goods, then continue dropping off two to four *tercios* of goods from Castille. This is the pattern followed by all in the trade."[120]

Mexico City's centrally located Plaza de Santo Domingo and its imposing late-eighteenth-century Aduana (customshouse) was the capital's distribution and transportation center. Mules, horses, and wagons mingled outside and inside the large building, through which moved goods imported from Veracruz and Acapulco, as well as exports. The clatter of *atajos* of mules was heard all day as shod hooves struck cobblestones, producing "the peculiar sound of a never-ending storm," mixed with the high-pitched whistles of *arrieros* summoning their animals.[121] In the patios of the customshouse, there was a daily crush of "people, mules, and horses," *arrieros* hurrying to clear goods and paperwork, occasionally slipping away for refreshment, leaving their mules or horses and cargo unattended in the patios, and on their return discovering something missing, or their places occupied—a source of quarrels and "hindrance, confusion, and inconvenience."[122] At the Veracruz customs, the confusion was of a different order. Exhausted after long days on the road, *arrieros* usually went directly to the Aduana, unloaded cargo in the patios, and then turned their mules out to pasture. They would put off reporting to the consignee that cargo had been deposited to the next day, which meant an extra fee charged to the Veracruz consignee for cargo left at customs.[123]

Processing the waybills (*guías* and *tornaguías*) prescribed by the colonial treasury office to ensure payment of *alcabalas* in each excise zone, and to reduce the entry of smuggled or prohibited goods into regular distribution channels, also fell to the *arrieros*.[124] On the hide wrapping, or *puangoche*, of each *tercio* loaded on muleback, the customshouse stamped a royal seal (*marchamo*) to indicate that it had been properly dutied; by law, *arrieros* needed a detailed waybill for goods consigned to each excise zone (*alcabalatorio*). On arrival, *arrieros* presented *guías* to the appropriate local authority, whether the *administrador de alcabala* or, in his absence, the local judge, or even the curate, who, after checking the *guía* against the merchandise presented, signed a receipt (*tornaguía*), which had to be returned to the issuing office within a fixed period, the *arriero* otherwise incurring a fine.[125] In 1767, however, as *visitador general*, Gálvez modified the procedure, shifting responsibility for returning *tornaguías* from the harried *arrieros* to the merchant shippers. So complicated had fiscal surveillance by the colonial state become through "customs regulations covering waybills, reply to sender by the responsible *arriero*, showing separate invoices and the rest," one suspects that apparently inflexible formalities masked a flexible indifference, a wheeling and dealing among shippers, tax collectors, and *arrieros*. Actually, freight carriers—*arrieros, traginantes,* and *carreteros*—were considered prime suspects when it came to *alcabala* evasion and precious metals' smuggling to and through the port of Veracruz.[126] The burden of such paperwork had Mexico City *consulado* officers longing for an easing of restrictions such as that reported to have been accorded Madrid's grain trade in 1766 to stimulate supply. New Spain, they decided, also needed deregulation of a sort ("la libertad del tráfico") in order to "maximize mining operations" and accelerate the flow of merchandise in which public and private sectors were interested. Trade goods, after all, "attract and finance the work of the mines."[127]

Gálvez's Compromise: New Spain's Import Allocations

To accelerate the flow of goods and precious metals between colonies and metropole and fulfill the Spanish Bourbon state's fiscal goals constituted core elements of its policy of controlled deregulation of the Spanish transatlantic trading system initiated in 1765 and amplified thirteen years later. With respect to the colony of New Spain, where Mexico City's *almaceneros* wielded economic power and political influence greater than that of their Cadiz counterparts, that policy was fortunately implemented with piecemeal, at times noticeably hesitant, incrementalism. High profile figures of Madrid's political class—Prime Minister Floridablanca, Colonial Secretary Gálvez, Hacienda Secretary Múzquiz, and Campomanes, the *fiscal* and later *gobernador* of the Consejo de Castilla—wherever possible avoided confrontation with Mexico City's commercial magnates, whose financial resources were essential to colonial and metropolitan treasuries. The gradualism of these high-level bureaucrats, by contrast with Esquilache's brief assault on the inefficiencies in Spain's managed transatlantic trade, laid the groundwork for the consensus that decades later would bind together the elites of Spain's transatlantic empire in counterrevolution in Mexico City, Cadiz, Barcelona, and Madrid.

From the viewpoint of those monitoring the repercussions of *comercio libre* of 1778, a reassuring index in the last decade of the thirty-year era of Charles III was the volume of exports to the colonies and especially to its wealthiest colony in America, New Spain. This justified Floridablanca's reference to a "feliz revolución" produced by *his* colonial trade policy. Between 1783 and 1785, it was reassuring to follow three indicators of a growing economy: the rising value of exports from Cadiz, as well other metropolitan seaports, recently authorized to trade with the American colonies; a barometer of New Spain's trade, *alcabala* receipts in the principal fiscal districts of Puebla, Mexico, and Valladolid; and, most encouraging, specie outflows from Veracruz to Havana and on to peninsular ports on public and private account. To contemporaries, silver mining undergirded the rising tide of the colony's prosperity, while its import capacity was substantially raised by the 33 percent upward revaluation of Mexico's silver *peso fuerte,* from 15 to 20 *reales de vellon* in the metropole's currency (*peso sencillo*).[128]

Compelling considerations in 1778 had shaped Gálvez's strategy of limiting access of peninsular ports to New Spain's single major Caribbean/ Atlantic port, while opening Spain's South American harbors to peninsular shipping. One was the probability that Veracruz would draw the interest of most exporters in metropolitan ports authorized in 1778 for colonial trade; the sheer unprecedented volume of New Spain's silver specie exports from the early 1770s onward was an irresistible magnet and drew a disproportionate share of the metropole's colonial traffic. Another was the colonial secretary's confidence that the state could fine-tune commercial policy to minimize the negative effects upon the interests of *almaceneros* dominant in the Mexico City merchant guild. Wealthy Peninsula-born merchants in the colonial capital had financed Gálvez's expedition to northern Mexico, and they still chafed at Madrid's rejection of their bid to renew the *alcabala* tax farm, and the loss of economic leverage that rejection inflicted. Also, Gálvez knew, in the third place, that they were preoccupied with possible extension of *comercio libre* to their colony.

In essence, the Mexico City commercial establishment formed a Peninsula-oriented, close-knit interest group on which Madrid depended for finance and loyalty. For a variety of reasons, Floridablanca's ministry and the Consejos de Castilla and Indias felt impelled to accord special treatment to New Spain's merchant magnates. Such factors explain the omission of New Spain from the 1778 Reglamento and Gálvez's decision in March 1779 personally to allocate among peninsular ports shipping and cargo space to the port of Veracruz. No longer would that port receive *flotas* from Cadiz; instead, the colonial secretary would monitor the amount of shipping and cargo from peninsular ports destined for Veracruz.

Years earlier, one must recall, Mexico City's *consulado* had urged the government to put a ceiling on *flota* cargo to the colony, and in 1779, Gálvez clearly intended to restrict both shipping (*registros*) and space (*toneladas*).[129] Under his policy for New Spain, total annual tonnage remained high, frequent sailings to New Spain promised to lower ocean freight rates, and the costly, cumbersome fees and inspections of the 1720 Proyecto were largely eliminated. Now Barcelona's exporters would participate directly in trade with New Spain (its privileged company faded away in the 1780s), and that perennial source of friction between Mexico City and the *comercio de España*—the Jalapa fair syndrome—disappeared too. Gálvez's solicitude for Mexico City warehousemen brought rewards. During Spain's participation in the North American insurrection against Britain, Francisco Cabarrús recouped his loan to the Spanish government with interest, with drafts on government silver shipped by New Spain's treasury to Havana. At the same time, Mexico City's *consulado* cooperated by drumming up a one-million-peso "donativo" for Madrid among private investors and amply endowed religious corporations. The colonial capital's capitalists were then flush with silver pesos. Part of the high level of silver transfers on private account from Veracruz to the metropole in the immediate postwar years represented a peso buildup from profit-taking during the war in 1779–82. In the immediate prewar years, the extraordinary volume and value of Ulloa's *flota* (1776–77), rumors that the imminent 1778 Reglamento might discriminate against certain foreign goods (i.e., hosiery and yarns), and the threat of interrupted maritime communications had induced Mexico City's *almaceneros* to stockpile quantities of European imports. Then at the war's end, specie retained by Mexico City mercantile firms poured out to the metropole, in turn funding large-scale imports by New Spain's merchants between 1783 and 1785. The economic expansion of the 1770s followed by wartime profiteering created a platform for postwar speculation and expansion during the 1780s.

Madrid's authorization of silver transfers through Havana from its Mexico City treasury to subsidize the North American insurgents postponed full implementation of the 1778 statute until 1784. In wartime, unscheduled ship arrivals at Veracruz were few. With peace, Madrid put into effect the decision taken in March 1779 to set the number of ships to Veracruz annually, distributed among metropolitan ports (the *puertos habilitados*) authorized for colonial trade, as well as the total cargo tonnage—another form of managed trade. Evidently, this was Gálvez's compromise package with the Mexico City merchant oligarchs: the *flota* system would end, but New Spain's trade exchanges with the metropole would not be decontrolled.

In 1779, for example, the Colonial Office licensed a total of eleven vessels (*registros*) for Veracruz, allocating six to Cadiz, including mercury ships (*azogues*), but only one each to Málaga, Alicante, Barcelona, Santander, and La Coruña.[130] Thereafter the annual number varied; for example, between 1785 and 1787, Barcelona's allocation oscillated from seven to thirteen *registros*.[131] Normally overlooked is that the 1778 Reglamento at no point authorized merchants *in the colonies* to charter their own shipping to freight colonial exports eastbound across the Atlantic to Spain. The conclusion: Madrid still supported Cadiz's oligopolists by blocking merchants in New Spain and other American colonies from direct communication with peninsular ports in their own ships.[132] Moreover, Gálvez's Colonial Office restricted licenses to merchant shippers registered with local *consulados,* and, judging by complaints, privileged Cadiz, Sevilla, and Málaga over other ports, even favoring commercial houses like Uztáriz y San Ginés, Francisco Sierra, and Alvarez y Frías.[133] This closely monitored ship-licensing program simply extended the favoritism and clientelism of the *flota* era. According to one accurate critic, shipowners had to "petition for licenses to the court, and the ministry sets their number"; another pointed to the bureaucratic tangle of "steps, formalities, and petitions to manage to obtain a *registro* license."[134] Unscheduled *registro* arrivals at postwar Veracruz ("one after the other") were initial indicators of readjustments in colonial managed trade policy resulting from the 1778 statute and termination of the Jalapa fairs. In the short run, the substitution of frequent unscheduled *registros* for spaced-out *flotas* cheapened maritime freight rates and offered peninsular shipowners the inducement of return cargoes from Veracruz such as flour to Havana and more cochineal and hides to Spain.[135]

Only months after the assignment of annual *registro* licenses, Gálvez's Colonial Office felt compelled to pacify anxious Mexico City *almaceneros*—still wedded to the "regulated" *flota* system despite underlying tension over economic space between the *comercio de México* and the *comercio de España*—with a large tonnage maximum to the port of Veracruz. Actually, Gálvez conceded to the Mexico City *consulado* what its membership had petitioned for during the *flota* system, an agreed-upon import quota to "avoid the misuse and confusion that in general has been the pattern until now."[136] However, to judge by the volume assigned in 1784–87, the ministry's target figure was far higher over this three-year period than that of previous large *flotas*. Assignment of an impressive volume was foreshadowed in late 1779 when Madrid ordered the viceregal staff in Mexico City to draw up annual accounts of silver and gold minted and agricultural, ranching, and artisanal production entering the market, along with the staff's estimate of import demand—all to firm up an empirical basis for setting both shipping and volume ceilings.[137] The policy received clarification in 1784, when the initial maximum was fixed at the high volume of 9,600 tons, 79 percent assigned to three Andalusian ports and Barcelona; predictably, the largest single allocation (4,000 tons) went to Cadiz.[138]

Such was the theory of matching supply to crude estimates of demand; the reality was another matter. In practice, Gálvez's office established annual tonnage limits, to cite one review, "without data or calculation, solely from private reports in the secret correspondence of the viceroy with [Gálvez]."[139] Viceregal data forwarded may have been optimistically inflated (or, worse, uncritically accepted); or was the Colonial Office mesmerized by the mirage of silver in the west, while undervaluing other factors responsible for aggregate colonial demand? Or perhaps fine-tuning a distant overseas economy was an art requiring more sophisticated instruments? As a result, Gálvez's tactics ran the risk of "going wrong by privileging a port or individual."[140]

Unfortunately, Gálvez failed to reckon with the combined impact of high morbidity and mortality rates on aggregate import demand in New Spain, following poor harvests, widespread famine, and high subsistence prices in 1783–86. As a result, imports of Catalan brandy and wine in 1786 were far above New Spain's normal consumption levels.[141] When Cadiz and Malaga merchants urged Gálvez to lower his 1787 tonnage ceiling to half that of 1786, he complied with 6,000 tons, of which only one-third was utilized by peninsular shippers, down to 20 percent of the previous two years' average and less than any in the era of *flotas.* Was Gálvez maintaining unrealistically high levels of exports to Veracruz because, like Floridablanca, he aimed to advertise the success of the 1778 Reglamento? These decisions produced the unsettling oversupply of imports in New Spain in 1787 and 1788, and Mexico City's troubled *almaceneros* soon proposed a maximum even lower, 1,500 tons. Paradoxically, merchants in Spain's transatlantic trade had, it appeared, lost the vexing friction of *feria* chaffering between Cadiz's *flotistas* and Mexico City's *almaceneros,* only to confront the uncertainties of controlled deregulation: oversupply, growing competition, and a rash of bankruptcies — the downside of "unmanaged" trade.

The Rise of Veracruz

Modification of the external dynamics of trade between metropole and colony induced by the 1778 Reglamento had lasting internal repercussions upon the structures and relations of New Spain's mercantile groups in the following decades. Along with the fifty-year-old Jalapa fair, the implicit boundary separating peninsular merchants from those in New Spain disappeared. Under the *feria* system, most of the colony's exportable specie had been held by Mexico City *acaudalados,* who spent months of ritual bargaining with *encomenderos-factores* from Spain (the *monopolistas*), each side seeking to get the most for its silver or merchandise. Obviously, the Jalapa marketplace had excluded most of the small players, provincial traders, and merchants whom Mexico City's *almaceneros* supplied with goods and credit. In the 1780s, however, the latter were no longer able simply to pass on to the smaller traders, and ultimately to their customers, the cost of spending interminable months at the Jalapa fair, commission fees of 5 percent, and the 6 percent *alcabala* on all merchandise entering the Mexico City customs zone. Provincial merchants now had the option of exchanging their silver for European imports themselves in Veracruz, where they could choose what they wanted in a few days and avoid transaction costs in the capital.[142] By 1785, the declining role of Jalapa led one of its residents to lament nostalgically that "neither the powerful merchants of Mexico [City] nor the rich men of Guanajuato nor of other opulent cities in the kingdom have come . . . , as they used to, to Jalapa to employ their wealth in the purchase of our goods."[143]

Jalapa's changed situation testified to the colony's apparent prosperity, its mining boom, the spreading commercialization of agriculture and ranching, and the more widespread use of wage labor—overall, the monetization of native producers and consumers. By the 1780s, the burgeoning number of small- to medium-sized merchants in provinces and capital alike was a widely recognized phenomenon.[144] *Pulperías, tiendas, tiendas mestizas,* and *viñaterías* increasingly supplied the urban and rural poor with imported wine and brandy, cloth and clothing, and hardware and spices, along with locally produced cotton and woolen cloth, sugar, cheese, and seeds, paid for in small change: "tlacos, cuartillos, medio reales."[145] Recently arrived *montañeses* from the upper valleys of the Deva, Nansa, Pas, and Cadagua rivers and other overpopulated microregions of Spain's Cantabrian mountains set out hopefully to trade with Amerindians in the *alcaldías mayores* and *corregimientos,* hitherto virtually captive consumers exploited through the *reparto de mercancías* by local officials financed and supplied by Mexico City merchants. Decontrol of New Spain's external trade and introduction by Madrid of the intendancy system, the newcomers believed, would create a kind of internal *comercio libre* that would allow them to penetrate these monopolies.

The 1778 Reglamento also altered relations between the merchants of Mexico City and those of Cadiz. No longer were there legal mechanisms to constrain Mexico City *almaceneros* from ordering directly from Cadiz suppliers, although for at least five decades, the former had tried to circumvent the Jalapa fair mechanism by remitting funds to cover their purchases at Cadiz. Now legal restraints on direct relations with Cadiz commission agents collapsed, inspiring them to complain that New Spain's wealthy merchants had extended their "trading activities on their own or others' account with the metropole," that they enjoyed the "advantage of buying directly from European nations their products, which we carry off," and—what must surely have been painful to confess—"now Americans trade with Spaniards the way formerly Spain traded with America." *Comercio libre*, many in the metropole were now convinced, would inescapably shift control over the metropole's transatlantic trade to the colonies.[146] Here was further peninsular recognition of Spain's long-term dependence on American silver, foreshadowing the pivotal hegemonic role of merchant communities in colonial capitals in the preservation of Spanish rule in America.

When the preceding comments were made in 1787, it was still moot whether Mexico City *almaceneros* had in reality become that hegemonic. A more balanced analysis of the situation came from a Veracruz perspective two decades later. José María Quirós, secretary of the *consulado* in that port, concluded in his 1808 summary that the 1778 changes had benefited colonial consumers in several ways: above all, they had weakened the dominance of roughly 100 "influential merchants" of Mexico City over the colony's distribution system, preventing these "men of wealth" from automatically engrossing whole shipments of imports, comprising "those items most scarce and most sought," and overcharging small traders of the capital and the provinces, as well as colonial consumers of all classes. Moreover, the changes had also curbed the "unbridled greed" of Cadiz's "monopolistas," who tried to fix prices arbitrarily for textiles and other wares their agents sold at Veracruz or Jalapa.[147] But in asserting that *comercio libre* had reduced smuggling from Jamaica, Quirós was either naïve, misled, or blind to reality.

Jalapa's eclipse was more than compensated for by the growth of Veracruz, where year-round ship arrivals now became the rule, and merchants from central and southern New Spain came down to replenish stocks. Veracruz was transformed, at least to a recent immigrant and local booster, from a "gloomy, ugly" little port filled with ramshackle construction into a resplendent, renovated city, whose "elegant and growing" population soon quadrupled.[148] Visitors from Mexico City and the provinces found information about merchandise and trade readily available, whereas under the Jalapa fair system this had always been hard to come by. Under recently instituted *alcabala* regulations, importers now presented customs officers with their waybills, which listed the quality and current prices of their goods, and this information rapidly got about.[149] With envy, exaggeration, and some truth, the capital's merchant magnates lamented that "*comercio libre* has transformed Veracruz into New Spain's most vigorous commercial city" and that "merchants from the interior" had abandoned Mexico City, hitherto the "warehouse for goods brought from Europe."[150]

Observing the seaport's quickening activity and the stream of *tenderos* and *arrieros* from the interior in the aftermath of the 1778 Reglamento, Veracruz's leading merchants, mainly *montañeses,* resolved to probe Madrid's limited promise, contained in a closing article of the Reglamento, to charter *consulados* in Spanish ports now authorized for colonial trade. They were in effect prodding the imperial state to include what had been specifically neglected by Gálvez: new merchant guilds in the colonies. Yet no new *consulado* materialized either at Veracruz or elsewhere in the colonies under Charles III, because, one suspects, Gálvez—mindful of the well-oiled lobbying of the long established *consulados* of Mexico City and Lima—sat on such pretensions. Veracruz's hopes would be realized thirteen years later, early in the reign of Charles IV, under Gálvez's replacement, Antonio Valdés y Bazán.

Prosperity and Decapitalization

Perhaps nowhere were the effects of *comercio libre* of 1778 more subtle yet pervasive than upon the linked factors of mining and money supply, monetization and commercialization, fiscal policy and capital export. To meet changing conditions, Mexico City's *almaceneros* made adjustments in order to preserve their hegemony over the colony's economy and the *pesos fuertes* coined by the Mexico City mint, internationally prized in the Atlantic and Asian economies.

The passing of the Jalapa fair system posed an immediate liquidity problem. No longer could *almaceneros* in the capital buy imports in whole lots paying in hard currency spread over perhaps twelve to eighteen months, or even two years, that is, until the next *flota* sailed for Cadiz. The new conditions of Spain's Atlantic commerce now facilitated repeated purchasing, but placed a premium on fairly rapid payment in specie. The Mexico City *consulado* itself described the new and conflicting pressures for liquidity and specie export in vivid, hardly disinterested prose. "Formerly, silver shipments left each year, or after eighteen months, even after two years. During these months, money circulated among trading parties. Now, no sooner is silver mined than it goes directly to the firms freighting silver to Veracruz because it may be loaded aboard a vessel of any size. No longer is there any point in large, long-term transactions."[151] Earlier, in 1785 or 1786, the Colonial Office had facilitated the turnaround time of ships at Veracruz, first by modifying article 47 of the 1778 Reglamento to authorize captains to return to Spain *before* all cargo was sold provided their vessels carried back in specie the value of "duties charged on entering the customs office." Madrid wanted customs duties levied at Cadiz and collectible at Veracruz forwarded to the metropole as soon as possible. In the second instance, vessels of a minimum of 400 tons burden could load an extra 1,000 pesos of cargo per ton.[152] While this benefited Cadiz exporters by shortening the term of their borrowings and hence lowering interest costs, they found that many of the small and medium merchants who now traveled down from the interior to purchase directly from their *encomenderos* at Veracruz were more often than not poor credit risks. Such doubtful receivables were a factor in Cadiz bankruptcy proceedings in the late 1780s. These problems aside, the 1780s were boom times in New Spain: increased silver production and coinage, monetization of the rural economy, and flows of colonial and imported goods throughout the interior contributed to rising sales volume.[153] Using unadjusted *alcabala* receipts as a good proxy of sales volume, by conservative estimate, volume rose more than 100 percent over two seven-year periods (1770–77 and 1780–87).[154]

At this conjuncture of swelling internal demand and supply drawn from both locally produced and imported goods, the budgetary expenditures of the Spanish imperial state put pressure on colonial monetary stocks in the form of capital export—a "withdrawal of money" (*saca de dinero*)—on public (royal) account. Esquilache's strategy of scrutinizing the Spanish Bourbon state's financial structures and long-term commitments, revenue sources, and (most important) revenue leakages, then scrupulously enforcing existing tax legislation, was more successfully and probably more ruthlessly applied to the colonial than to the metropolitan economy. From the 1760s onward, colonial fiscal policy turned out to be surprisingly effective, vindicating the bureaucratic consensus at Madrid on initiating change in colonial structures after the impasse in metropolitan initiatives evident in the overthrow of Esquilache and his policy. Annual receipts of New Spain's Real Hacienda virtually doubled between 1770 and 1789; over two seven-year periods, 1770–77 and 1780–87, the colony's aggregate revenues in current pesos climbed 57 percent (from an annual average of 11.5 to 18.0 million *pesos fuertes*) as major components in *alcabala, tributo,* tobacco, and seignorage taxes rose.[155]

Fiscal data on both the colony's revenues and specie exports from Veracruz to Cadiz reinforced Madrid's long-standing policy of transferring any surplus in New Spain's treasury to Spain and paying for better defense of Havana, threatened by British naval bases in the Caribbean. At the same time Madrid also drew upon colonial income to finance outlays on the metropole's armed forces and other budgetary items. Moreover, customs receipts, especially those at Cadiz, on goods imported from European suppliers destined for reexport to New Spain and other colonies contributed significantly to Spain's general revenues (*rentas generales*). Government expenditures to which colonial income had been, was, and could be applied drove the economic policies of Esquilache and his successors, Gálvez's *visitación* to New Spain, and the hesitant deregulation of the imperial trade system. In the latter half of the eighteenth century, as English naval forces repeatedly threatened Spain's economic lifeline in the western Atlantic and the Pacific, income from the colonies became increasingly indispensable for the preservation of a vast overseas empire.

These imperial and metropolitan budgetary pressures explain the bureaucratic fixation on annual coinage at Mexico City's mint, on New Spain's revenues, and on the extraordinary volume of capital transfers on public account from New Spain to both Spain and Cuba after about 1766. To contemporaries, coinage formed the basic index of the colony's economic expansion and its overseas trade: between *flota* and post-*flota* years, between 1770–77 and 1780–87, average annual coinage rose by 13 percent (from 16.8 million to 19 million *pesos fuertes*).[156] Reflecting this monetary stimulus, moreover, the colony's tax receipts in these periods rose even faster, by 57 percent.

Ultimately, the success of Madrid's fiscal policy in New Spain lay in its capacity to transfer colonial surplus to the most needy points. And here a breakdown of government specie outflows between those from Veracruz to peninsular ports and those to the "Islas" (largely Cuba), based upon data prepared for the viceregal secretariat of the second conde de Revillagigedo, is instructive. Comparing two thirteen-year intervals, 1766–78 and 1779–91, total specie outflow from Veracruz on public and private account rose 44.4 percent—an "astronomic increase."[157] Specie shipments on government account alone destined for Cadiz and other peninsular ports climbed by 96.8 percent, while transfers to the Caribbean ("America") jumped upward 117.4 percent. Note, however, that the largest sums exported, those on private account, over the whole period, 1766–91, constituted 58 percent of total specie exports.[158] No doubt transfers to the "Islas" included specie sent to Havana to cover Spain's outlays on subsidies for French naval and military intervention in behalf of the North American insurgents fighting for independence. By indirection, data on *pesos fuertes* shipped to France from Saint-Domingue in 1783–89 can serve as a proxy for the magnitude of Spain's transfers of silver from Veracruz.[159]

More than ever, defense of the Spanish Caribbean rested on the fiscal ruthlessness of the metropolitan government in the mining colony of New Spain. Still, massive diversion of colonial Mexico's government surplus to Havana did not escape criticism by Spain's political class. In an unsolicited letter to Pedro Llerena, the secretary of the Hacienda, León de Arroyal, an Aragonese provincial treasury official, physiocrat, radical poet, and polemicist, referred caustically to "the movement of funds from Havana via Philadelphia and Paris" during Spain's war with England between 1779 and 1783.[160] Equally critical was the inquisitive, hard-driving, and opinionated Viceroy Revillagigedo. After poring over colonial treasury accounts listing specie exports from Veracruz during the quarter-century ending in 1791, he reached the obvious conclusion that for every *peso fuerte* transferred to Spain, 2.6 had gone to Cuba, Louisiana, and Santo Domingo. "New Spain's net revenues are enjoyed more by the islands or, through them, foreigners than by Spain itself."[161]

Revillagigedo was not far off the mark in emphasizing the magnitude of New Spain's silver peso transfers from Veracruz to Havana and other Caribbean possessions rather than to the metropole. Oddly enough, however, he overlooked (or chose not to recognize) what *comercio libre* had seemingly enhanced, the growing volume of specie transfers on government account. Reviewing the phenomenon at three points, 1766–69, 1770–79, and 1780–89, it becomes evident that average annual exports of colonial government funds accounted for 25.6, 32.7, and 37.5 percent respectively of total Veracruz specie exports. Furthermore, the sheer volume of such transfers leaped 246 percent, from an annual average of 2.5 to 8.7 million pesos. Another facet of the phenomenon was the startling success of metropolitan policies directly impinging upon the liquidity position of Mexico City's *almaceneros*. Over the same three intervals between 1766 and 1789, as coinage, colonial trade, and state revenues rose, the colonial treasury's capital exports rose faster, from 22 to 23 and finally to 46.8 percent of coinage by the Mexico City mint. Hence the justification of the complaints of the Mexico City commercial establishment about the *saca de dinero*—decapitalization—the transfer of colonial resources that has recently drawn scholars' attention.[162] And the data do not cover the omissions between what was ostensibly shipped from Veracruz to the metropole and what in fact was recorded on arrival.

To meet the challenge of Madrid's incremental tampering with the framework of Spain's transatlantic trade system, Mexico City's *almaceneros* devised a variety of stratagems. The economic hegemony that Mexico City's commercial elite had enjoyed since the end of the sixteenth century was not to be relinquished without resistance. Perhaps it is exaggerated to claim that the merchant oligarchs of the largest city in America believed themselves beleaguered by Madrid; on the other hand, many *were* convinced that recent changes would in the aggregate undermine their position.

There had been, first, the *consulado*'s failure in the 1750s to renew the lease of the *alcabala* farm: its last tender was, state officials at first suspected and later learned, far below the farm's effective yield, raising justified suspicion of stewardship by the private sector.[163] Absorption of the administration of the excise tax was part of the metropole's intent to maximize revenue sources the better to form a firewall to English commercial interests probing for access to Spain's silver-producing colonies. Then there were the subtle changes introduced by the Reglamento of 1778 that promised gradually to phase out controls over the timing and volume of imports, both hallmarks of the *flota* system centered on the Jalapa fairs. Third, by transforming Veracruz into the principal point of exchange with shippers from Spain, the Reglamento of 1778 threatened to undermine key elements of Mexico City's hegemony, the jurisdictional and economic control of the capital's *almaceneros,* which inspired Veracruz's mainly *montañés* merchants to petition Madrid for a separate merchant guild. Last, the entry of Cantabrian immigrants, notably *montañeses,* into New Spain's commercial circuits long dominated by *vizcaínos,* heightened competition for supplying the colony's mining centers. Coupled to the disappearance of the last *bancos de plata* controlled by Mexico City's Basque mercantile magnates, the surge of *montañés* immigrants posed a challenge to Basque *almaceneros'* access to specie and liquidity, hence to their control over the colonial economy's money supply, investment, and trade.

The response by Mexico City's merchants took many forms. Major mercantile establishments diversified. They reduced the proportion of imports handled, purchased more of the locally produced agricultural and artisanal items, ranging from cloth and clothing, cotton and wool, and cochineal and indigo to wheat, sugar, and pulque. Competition for prized exportables led to the observation that "everything has a fresh look, cotton, wool, indigo, cochineal, and hides now sell at more than double their former levels." They expanded investment in rural and urban real estate, in maize and sugarcane haciendas, in cattle-raising and urban properties.[164] And as the mining boom of Guanajuato, Zacatecas, and Catorce showed no sign of slackening, more merchant capital—encouraged by state intervention in behalf of the mining tribunal—was also shifted into mining, and it was noted that investors "are no longer ashamed to invest in these enterprises so important to the state." Mining prosperity and state intervention helped dissipate some of the inveterate "distrust and even contempt" in which mining ventures had once been held.[165]

Expanding horizons in trade and mining matched with impressive capital exports on public and private account worsened the liquidity problem of New Spain's merchant community. In response, merchants multiplied the use of bills of exchange (*libranzas*) to ease the specie shortage while preserving the centrality of the capital's *almaceneros* in colonial finance. To enlarge their capital pool, they increased their acceptance of local deposits (*depósitos irregulares*) at 5 percent interest and for their own part borrowed heavily from religious bodies—convents and monasteries, hospitals, chaplaincies, and other pious institutions—offering the security of real estate.[166]

Finally, to these survival strategies, Mexico City's merchants added a traditional reflex in an effort to reregulate trade with their metropole. Here the

Consulado de México had a basis for complaint—the temporary oversupply of imports partly caused by the lowered internal demand resulting from widespread famine in 1784–86 and the consequent contraction of expenditure. In part, too, oversupply at Veracruz and subsequent bankruptcies among Cadiz merchants uncovered the shortcomings of Gálvez's strategy based on the licensing of ships sailing to New Spain and his estimates of the colony's import needs. His estimates of New Spain's import requirements reflected at best unreliable data supplied from New Spain, the hope of supplying enough imports to reduce the rising tide of smuggled goods, pressure from Cadiz interests, and more probably, Gálvez's own reluctance to ruffle his merchant supporters at Cadiz and Mexico City. Now the *consulado* chose to petition for a reduction in shipping entering Veracruz.

In late 1787, Madrid furnished the Consulado de México with an opening when it requested the guild to prepare recommendations covering a range of issues, including those of "benefit to our commerce," namely, the volume of imports for the following year. In response, *almaceneros* presented two major recommendations, one concerning liquidity, the other the volume of imports. They hoped, first, to confine the export of specie aboard "silver" ships (*registros de plata*) to one prearranged period every year, "prohibiting monetary exports until that vessel's complement is met." The second proposed that shipping from Spain enter Veracruz, again, within a short designated period of fifteen to twenty days annually, and that non-Spanish products be assigned a quota every two or three years. This was a thinly disguised resurrection of managed trade under the old *flota* system.[167]

Madrid's request was hardly routine. Rather, it was one of the opening moves by Gálvez's replacement as colonial secretary, Antonio Valdés y Bazán, apparently responding to complaints about an oversupply of imports at Veracruz and its repercussions rippling through the merchant communities of both Cadiz and Mexico City. It was an initial gambit of a ministerial group emerging in the twilight of the era of Charles III, preparing to deregulate the Spanish transatlantic system further. The effects of the limited deregulation of New Spain's external trade since 1778 had been encouraging, they reasoned. The colony's resources in mines and consumers, its mine owners and merchants, required careful handling, since its revenues, now rising steeply, could be channeled to the metropole's continued advantage. In the closing decades of the century, Spain's dependence upon New Spain was both apparent and growing.

9. Incorporating New Spain into *Comercio Libre* (1789)

The issue of our commerce with America [is] the most important of those that may now lay the foundation of the Spanish empire and the strength of its navy and merchant marine.
Pedro Rodríguez Campomanes, governor of the Consejo de Castilla, to Colonial Secretary Antonio Valdés y Bazán (1788)

Our American subjects must be content to cultivate and process the fruits of the soil, and in exchange receive our fruits and manufactures.
Consulado de Barcelona, "Informe sobre el comercio de América" (1788)

As Spain's dependence upon New Spain's *pesos fuertes* deepened in the 1780s, the commercial and financial interests of Cadiz and Mexico City monopolizing that colony's external trade necessitated sensitive handling by state authorities. By 1787, four years after a long war in the Atlantic and an extraordinary short-term postwar trade boom, Madrid's earlier decision in 1778 to shield New Spain's commercial interests from a full program of Spanish-style *comercio libre* needed reexamination, particularly when merchants in peninsular ports were convinced that they were suffering a commercial depression with wide repercussions in New Spain. In October 1788, first a mémoire by Prime Minister Floridablanca to the aging Charles III—effectively, an accounting of his ministry's policies—and then a widely circulated anonymous political lampoon, involving characters transparently identifiable as Charles III, Floridablanca, Gálvez, and Treasurer-General Francisco Montes, signaled to Spain's political class how Madrid intended to manage the commercial crisis in New Spain: the full incorporation of the silver-producing colony of New Spain into the imperial system of *comercio libre*.

Floridablanca's apologia for eleven years as prime minister, which expatiated on his administration's major policy initiatives, expressed marked satisfaction with two in particular, the Banco de San Carlos and *comercio libre*. The Reglamento of 1778, claimed the memorial, had "tripled" colonial trade, "doubled" the empire's customs revenues, and created a "fortunate revolution in the trade of Spain to its colonies." Three paragraphs on *comercio libre* show that Floridablanca used data from sources both within and outside the bureaucracy that buttressed that policy.[1] To the perceptive among the political class, the memorial foretold Floridablanca's intent to extend *comercio libre* to New Spain—which recently deceased Colonial Secretary Gálvez had scrupulously kept separate in 1778—despite the opposition of the influential Cadiz and Mexico City merchant establishments.

Within a week, Floridablanca's memorial was followed by an anonymous "Letter from an Egg Merchant of Fuencarral [Cadiz] to a Lawyer [Floridablanca] on the Egg Trade," in which a well-informed satirist pilloried the Cadiz commercial community for resisting imperial trade adjustments, lampooned the Consulado de Cadiz's former lobbyist in Madrid's bureaucratic networks, Treasurer-General Francisco Montes (satirized as "Cerote who is artful"), and criticized the late Gálvez (a "trouble-making clerk") for ineffective implementation of *comercio libre,* because "his head was not screwed on right" (an insider's allusion to rumors of Gálvez's mental illness during his commission of inquiry in northern New Spain, which Mexico City's *almaceneros* had helped finance).[2]

Floridablanca's apologia and the satire reveal how important the inclusion of Spain's wealthiest American colony under *comercio libre* had now become, an issue impressed upon Gálvez's successor, Antonio Valdés, appointed in July 1787. Valdés, then forty-three, came from a well-connected Asturian family that for at least two generations on the paternal side had been in state service. His grandfather had been an army officer, his father *intendente-corregidor* of Burgos. At thirteen, in 1757, Valdés joined the navy, and in 1762, he participated in the defense of Havana against the English. Twenty years later, he was navy minister and an activist who urged Floridablanca to revitalize the Junta de Estado in order to put a stop to interministerial bickering; on Gálvez's death, Floridablanca appointed him interim secretary of the Guerra and Hacienda de Indias ministry. Immediately, he circularized colonial officers for reports on local conditions, ordered fiscal data from the colonies and pressed the Casa de Contratación at Cadiz for more commercial data. Small wonder that the "Carta de un Huevero" praised him as a man who was "most honorable, judicious, [who] wants the best, and tries to understand by listening to all parties."[3]

Gálvez died on 17 June 1787, and just three weeks later, the government declared that it would henceforth fix the volume of exports to New Spain "according to the state of the economy of New Spain, its exports and imports" and how they were to be distributed among peninsular ports, at the beginning of each year.[4] In a confidential letter to Valdés on 20 July 1787, Tomás Izquierdo, a prominent Cadiz merchant with commercial contacts to New Spain who was critical of Cadiz's *consulado,* singled out two factors responsible for the "decline" of trade with New Spain: the excessively high volume of Cadiz's reexports to the American colonies, deliberately mislabeled "national" products, and the reluctance of local businessmen to conform to regulations prohibiting direct participation of foreign resident merchants in colonial trade. "All Europe trades with America and sends whatever is wanted," Izquierdo observed.[5] Three months later, a busy Valdés turned to Izquierdo for more details, about the time he received an incisive analysis of the commercial crisis in New Spain from the Consejo de Indias.

Within the Consejo de Indias (of which Francisco Moñino, Floridablanca's brother, was the recently appointed president), a group that included veterans of colonial service in New Spain had competently sized up the economic situation at Cadiz, at other peninsular ports, and in New Spain.[6] According to the group's analysis, the current commercial crisis could hardly be blamed upon the 1778 Reglamento as the "ignorant herd charmed by the song of former monopolists" was insisting. "Ignorant herd" and "former monopolists" were code words for Cadiz's commercial establishment. Besides, *comercio libre* was not "free" if one considered the new duty schedule of the 1778 Reglamento, the level of protectionism provided in the tariff of 1782, and New Spain's *alcabala* tax increases. To a considerable degree, the overlay of customs duties and excise taxes was really responsible, the Consejo de Indias group believed, for the volume of competitively priced European (non-Spanish) products reexported from New Orleans and smuggled into New Spain through Tampico and Veracruz. The sheer volume of such goods slipping into the colony might alone, the *consejeros* implied, account for the current slowdown in New Spain's sales.

The Consejo de Indias group also introduced another aspect of the commercial crisis, the inflexibility of Gaditano merchants resisting pressures to revamp traditional business practices tolerated under pre-1778 monopoly trade conditions. The Consejo itself then approved what must have been Valdés's intention to test the "sentiments and viewpoints" of peninsular and colonial *consulados* about this "very thorny matter": it resolved to seek many opinions.[7] Two weeks later, on 19 October, Valdés countersigned an order announcing the state's intent to circularize a questionnaire seeking information about economic conditions in New Spain, a notable departure from the unpublicized, in-house bureaucratic practice employed in the imperial trade modifications of 1765 and 1778.

The ostensible goal of Valdés's seven-point questionnaire was a quantitative and qualitative data base to calculate New Spain's annual import capacity and distribute export tonnage to participating peninsular ports, as Gálvez had interpreted the 1778 Reglamento's article 6. Annual tonnage quotas, the colonial ministry apparently implied, might produce "regulated" trade between the Peninsula and Veracruz, avoiding the "abuse of complete freedom" in the form of "excessive competition" once the *flota* system and other constraints of pre-1778 vintage were abandoned. Meanwhile the Colonial Office's data on shipping and trade and colonial production and price levels still remained markedly inadequate and highly unreliable.[8]

By indirection Valdés's questionnaire criticized Gálvez's tonnage assignments for New Spain as arbitrary, designed primarily and unrealistically to placate the business communities of Cadiz and Mexico City. It skirted what peninsular businessmen interpreted as a commercial crisis in New Spain and its metropolitan repercussions, except to claim that colony's annual import quota had to be set quickly and accurately lest New Spain suffer the "foolishness of a few merchants" lacking "sound principles" and the ability to speculate prudently—remarks no doubt mirroring critiques crossing Valdés's desk. The Colonial Office emphasized that the immediate goal was an appropriate level of exports to New Spain in 1788. From the spectrum of data that the questionnaire sought—the impact of "liberty" on New Spain's external trade; the volume of the metropole's exports of manufactures and staples to the colonies in America; the composition of such exports, distinguishing between "national" and "foreign"; and, most important, New Spain's annual consumption of Spain's principal exports, namely, brandy and wine—one may suspect that Valdés's real design at the outset was to establish a convincing rationale for incorporating the colony of New Spain as a full participant in *comercio libre* and for pushing Cadiz to reduce its dependence upon the "assured exorbitant profits," once virtually guaranteed by the pre-1778 trading system, undergirding Cadiz's notorious "ostentation and pomp." This is a plausible interpretation of a point in the introduction to Valdés's questionnaire: "it would appear that we should let commerce seek its own level." The marketplace would correct the distortions of oligopoly.

Behind Floridablanca's mémoire, the "Egg Merchant" lampoon, and ultimately Valdés's questionnaire was the troublesome oversupply of imports in Spain's principal colonial market, New Spain. Measured by its repercussions upon peninsular ports and their provincial hinterlands, and upon the metropole's recently inaugurated central bank (the Banco de San Carlos), responsible for private and public specie transfers abroad and for issuing the government's new treasury bills (*vales*), New Spain's trade recession seemed the epicenter of a systemic crisis requiring state intervention. This was all the more imperative since the level of New Spain's economic activity determined how that colonial government's revenue surplus was partly diverted to Havana, other Caribbean outposts of empire, and the Philippines, partly to public finance in the metropole.

Many factors, some predictable and others not, contributed to the recession in New Spain's economy in the late 1780s. Overall, there was a decline in demand for imports, but preordered supplies continued to arrive at Veracruz. And, more troublesome, there was the expansion of smuggling along New Spain's Gulf coast north and south of Veracruz from New Orleans, Havana, Jamaica, and (probably through Havana) Saint-Domingue.

It was not that clandestine imports from foreign sources in the Caribbean were a novelty, but rather that both the volume and value of smuggled goods were rising in proportion to population in New Spain. Spain's colonial commercial policy was a blend of half-hearted protectionism and heavy-handed fiscalism. The Reglamento of 1778 had imposed new duties to replace those dropped; then came the protectionism of the general tariff of 1782, not to mention New Spain's excise tax structure. This fiscal system, compounded by high transaction costs, pushed the final prices of legally imported goods in the colony of New Spain well above those of smuggled items, providing an irresistible attraction to all engaged in illegal trafficking—foreign suppliers, local colonial officials, and businessmen and their clients. Not all policy-makers, however, were oblivious to the contradictions between development and public finance: "It is in vain that an activist minister decides on measures for national development, setting high duties on imports of foreign goods and on exports of national raw materials," "Ugartiria" observed. This might satisfy metropolitan developmental interests, but when it choked off customs income, "Where are we to find the funds to cover the state's expenditures?"9

More to the point, New Spain's recession had spread across the Atlantic to its metropole, where one of the first sectors affected was export agriculture, especially the growers and shippers of Andalusian and Catalan wine and brandy attracted by the colonial opportunities created by the commercial adjustments of 1765 and 1778. Furthermore, contraction of Spain's imports of European products for reexport to New Spain and other American colonies led to a drop in customs collections, which figured prominently in the Spanish state's general revenues and its capacity to reduce the overhang of wartime deficits and now to borrow from Amsterdam bankers. In brief, New Spain's commercial crisis affected the liquidity of the Spanish state at a critical juncture and was a principal factor pressing Colonial Secretary Valdés to seek "reports from *consulados* in all ports authorized to trade with the Indies and Mexico."[10]

The Response to Valdés's Questionnaire: I. Cadiz, Barcelona, and Sevilla

For six months, the Cadiz commercial establishment stalled its response to Valdés's eight-point questionnaire of late October 1787. In preparation, it reprinted and circulated copies of the questionnaire for members' comments; after replies trickled in, a sixteen-member committee, or *junta*, of *consulado* officers and special invitees met repeatedly to cobble together a representative response. Some *junta* members were veterans of trade with European suppliers or colonial merchants; a few were also estate owners and manufacturers. A collective portrait of the signers of the final *consulado* document indicates that of eleven listed in the *matrícula* of the *consulado*, eight had been in business at Cadiz for at least twenty years and ten under the pre-1778 *flota* regime.[11] Anxious about the impact of their long delay in replying to Valdés, *consulado* officials urged their Madrid agent to monitor official reaction when delivering their response and, if necessary, to explain that the *junta* had to sift many opinions in order to "choose the view worthy of the members' approval."[12]

The leitmotiv of many traditionalists in the Cadiz business community was, predictably, pessimism about the impact of the 1778 Reglamento upon the metropolitan economy. Growth in colonial trade had occurred but was "disordered," responsible for its "ruin" and "backwardness." From the perspective of old-line businessmen, fresh openings in trade after 1778 had drawn a "crowd" of inexperienced exporters who had heedlessly overspeculated, with disastrous consequences. Unlike the veterans of colonial trade at Cadiz, newcomers "make their fortunes early in their meteoric career, only to vanish and appear unhappily before the courts." Oversupplied colonial markets had forced cutbacks in prices and sales, compelling "shippers, factors, and agents" in the metropole to accept long-term repayment schedules. Currently, the *consulado* document calculated, "America" was indebted for "muchos millones a Europa."[13]

The impact of the 1778 statute upon metropolitan manufacturing had been negligible, the Cadiz businessmen's *junta* reported. Production was still inadequate, and in any event, the products still remained uncompetitive with European imports in quality and price. No one at Cadiz could calculate even approximately the value of peninsular manufactures exported to the colonies, partly—the *junta* confessed publicly, and probably for the first time—because a high proportion were in fact disguised reexports. Overly trusting, inexperienced Cadiz exporters mistakenly shipped goods Spain's "semi-fabricantes" had artfully disguised in order to slip them through customs as national. "The trusting merchant in an authorized port who buys Spanish goods so labeled is likely to be compromised at state bureaus," it was noted, and not only in peninsular but in colonial ports as well. Despite official reports covering the period between 1784 and 1786—boom years in colonial trade—realistic estimates of exports put domestic sources as supplying at most 20 percent of all manufactures shipped from Spain to the colonies. The *junta* felt that official data were misleading, since they showed the proportion of domestic to foreign exports to be roughly equal.[14]

These were the narrowly focused responses of the Cadiz merchants to Valdés's questionnaire. By way of recommendation, they would suspend reexports for one year or perhaps more, a facile concession to economic nationalists in the upper levels of the state bureaucracy. But on the most sensitive point of Valdés's questionnaire—his request for a reasoned calculation of peninsular export tonnage to meet the demands of New Spain's consumers—the otherwise knowledgeable Cadiz *junta* could propose no caps for domestic manufactures or agricultural products, alleging the absence of reliable data, since "vagueness and confusion . . . complicated knowledge" of conditions at Veracruz and Mexico City.[15] The *junta* offered only the remote hope that at some future date, Madrid would somehow match the output of New Spain's coinage (the customary yardstick of its import capacity) to the supply of exports from the metropole, setting a "fixed indication of tonnage" annually. Consistent with this stance, it refused to support the government's intention to assign the main producing areas in Andalusia and Catalonia quotas for brandy and wine exportable to New Spain. Presumably this kind of "desorden" was tolerable.

State intervention of another order was, however, recommended. Heedless of the possible reaction of New Spain's cane growers and distillers, Gaditano exporters urged the government to suspend sales of New Spain's *aguardiente de caña,* or *chinguirito*. And in an obvious attempt to minimize competition from small-scale entrepreneurs eager to exploit New World economic opportunities, the Cadiz group further proposed that only shippers and shipowners registered with peninsular *consulados* be allowed to participate in colonial trade, and that vessels under 250 tons—Catalan shipping was generally below this size—be excluded from imperial transatlantic trade. Cadiz did not welcome Catalan competition in its colonial trade.

In answering the last of the eight points formulated in Valdés's questionnaire, inviting broad rather than specific views on improving the performance of the metropolitan economy, the Cadiz *consulado*'s leading businessmen revealed the depth of their animus to growing competition from mercantile interests in New Spain. Implicit was a nagging fear of losing privileges long enjoyed by peninsular merchants overseas in the colonial trading system. Now the Cadiz mercantile establishment demanded a level playing field, asserting that the 1778 Reglamento was consolidating a dominant role for merchants operating in New Spain. It hoped to revive the prohibition of 1745 preventing that colony's merchants from transferring funds first to Spain and thence to Europe's Atlantic ports in order to place orders directly with producers and exporters, bypassing commission agents at Cadiz.[16] Recently, complained the Cadiz *junta,* fully half of New Spain's imports had consisted of merchandise ordered direct by Mexico City *almaceneros.* It proposed that once reexports of European goods resumed, an annual average of 2,000 tons be channeled exclusively through Cadiz, which it suggested should "be designated the sole authorized port for the export of foreign merchandise and products to America." It followed, then, that Jalapa be redesignated the sole locale for initial exchanges between merchants from the Peninsula and the colony, and that the *comercio de España* be permitted to extend temporary residence in the colony for its representatives (*factores, encomenderos*) to five years from the current maximum of three.

Examined en bloc, these proposals lead to the obvious conclusion that driven by a pessimistic prognosis of the impact of change in the Spanish transatlantic commercial system, Cadiz's commercial oligarchs aimed unsubtly at a modified restoration of the *flota* regime. They hankered after large oceangoing vessels operated by registered shipowners and shippers, a pattern of "regulated" or "managed" exchange at Jalapa of Spanish and European goods for New Spain's silver, and the suppression of colonial *chinguirito*, which competed effectively with Spanish brandy.

Cadiz's reservations about *comercio libre* were shared, with minor yet sometimes striking divergences, by businessmen at Barcelona, the center of Spain's most dynamic regional economy at that time and already the peninsula's second largest exporter to the American colonies. Unlike Cadiz, which was virtually an island entrepôt and lacked important productive facilities, Barcelona was simultaneously an urban industrial center, an exit point for provincial agricultural and manufactured output, and an international port. In replying to Valdés, Barcelona's *consulado*—self-styled the "body representing the opinion of the province"—confessed, like that of Cadiz, to a lack of reliable data for assessing the overall impact of *comercio libre*. It pointed out there was no annual balance of trade equivalent to those published by the British and Dutch governments with "exactness and care"; even local Barcelona customs officers had failed to furnish promised statistical series on external trade promptly.[17]

Left to its own resources, Barcelona's *consulado* formed a small working group of *redactores,* who canvassed merchants with "casas de comercio en América" and shipowners (*patrones*) recently returned from the colonies, while sifting through "bad news" in correspondence from representatives overseas and the "the politico-commercial reflections and calculations" of those with the "curiosity to evaluate the progress and lags of national prosperity." Where the Barcelona group's response to Valdés's questionnaire parted company with Cadiz's is in very candid emphasis on hard-headed recognition of the volume of non-Spanish products in the metropole's exports to the American colonies. Since Spain's colonial trade, as the Barcelona group well understood, formed "the main and virtually only one we have," it urged metropolitan analysts to avoid self-deception with overly optimistic reports of incoming shipping from the colonies "bearing cargoes of millions of *pesos fuertes* and valuable staples." In fact, two-thirds by value of the metropole's exports to the colonies were really reexports ("goods purchased from foreigners"), Spain was running a perennial trade deficit with its colonies, and these issues demanded solutions.[18] To hammer home the danger of self-deception, Barcelona's merchants dissected published government data showing a remarkable trade reversal between 1785 (when so-called reexports surpassed exports of Spanish manufactures by 92 million reales) and 1786 (when "national" goods exported apparently exceeded reexports by 23 million reales). They argued that in 1785, Europe's exporters had funneled goods improperly labeled as Spanish to colonial ports via Cadiz. The following year, however, they modified their strategy, avoiding peninsular ports and instead shipping their products directly overseas for illegal introduction into Spanish-American ports. There, "in addition to the immense profits usually earned on their clandestine operations," they could count upon "just the export of *pesos fuertes* whose intrinsic value is superior to that of many other nations."[19]

Catalonia, they reported in self-congratulatory fashion, had responded energetically to colonial opportunities by rapid growth in the immediate postwar years, the most favorable epoch for "agriculture, crafts, factories, navigation and trade in this *principado*."[20] Vineyards had expanded and employment had virtually doubled in "workshops of prints, woolens, crepes, belts, and burlap." Catalan producers and exporters were understandably sensitive to competition overseas in wine, brandy, and textiles, whether from colonial producers or from smugglers. European printed cottons (*indianas*) and linens smuggled into New Spain and other colonies had caused almost a 50 percent falloff in Catalan textile exports, from a high of 862,000 *piezas* in 1784–85 to less than 430,000 in 1786. The problem, Barcelona's *consulado* felt, was preventing smuggling, complicated by the dumping of underpriced goods in Spain itself.

On the critical issue of setting an annual export tonnage to New Spain, Barcelona's mercantile elite was ambivalent and cautious. In principle, its merchants supported full decontrol, all the more since there were few reliable data on economic conditions in the Peninsula, or, for that matter, in New Spain; they recognized that the issue was overshadowed by the interplay of "large interests, which raise the power and energy of passions." However, pressed to reply to Valdés's questionnaire, the Barcelona group suggested a ceiling of 6,000 tons of reexports ("géneros extrangeros"), three times higher than what Cadiz's *consulado* had proposed, leaving the volume of domestic exports unlimited.[21] Unlike the Cadiz practice of favoring large-capacity vessels, Barcelona would limit ships to those under 300 tons, keeping Catalan vessels under 200, for the practical reason "that this is the average capacity of most of its ships."[22]

Given Catalonia's expanded production and export of wine, brandy, and printed textiles, Barcelona's *consulado* intended to improve the competitive position of these export items in the potentially large marketplace of New Spain and other Spanish colonies. The state, ran the thinking of Barcelona's merchants, should ease or remove multiple duties on domestic products shipped to the colonies "to give them preferential treatment." Similarly, metropolitan duties on silver imports earned by colonial sales should be lowered drastically or eliminated. Drawing upon account books made available to the *junta* (omitted, however, from the published version of the Barcelona *informe*), a Barcelona exporter's silver earnings from one cask (*pipa*) of brandy (*prueba de aceyte*) shipped to Veracruz paid a total of 183.3 percent of the cost FOB Barcelona in accumulated duties, excise taxes, and the peninsular tax on imported silver. A cask of red wine paid 95.5 percent at Veracruz, and 135.4 percent if forwarded to Mexico City. (Receipts remitted in the form of hides, sugar, or cocoa paid even higher rates.) Such fiscal burdens were "exorbitant" and "prejudicial" compared to those France and England imposed on trade with their colonies. Exports from France to its colonies paid no duty, it was claimed, and colonial sugar and raw cotton imports were taxed a mere 3 percent on entry into France.[23] "How many advantages does a foreign merchant have over a Spaniard," the *junta* asked rhetorically, "and what are the benefits and superiority that smuggled goods acquire over national goods by [reason of] the difference in duties . . . ?"

However, no sooner had mercantile interests raised the issue of tax abatement than Hacienda officials, who contemplated "with horror the slightest drop in their receipts," invariably invoked the "insuperable obstáculo"—revenue losses to the state.[24] Usually, this sufficed to silence critics, since the Spanish public lacked information about the country's balance of trade and the Treasury's income and expenditures. In short, Spanish fiscal policy encouraged French and English smuggling in America and clarified why the Catalan merchant community felt that Spain, "conqueror of America, mistress of its vast, rich possessions, [and] distributor of virtually all the precious metals circulating in Europe, instead of improving its wealth, population, and power, has left those increments to the trading nations, undermined from within and by the industrial war waged by them against her."[25]

What emerges from the Barcelona group's wide-ranging *informe* is a profound undercurrent of economic regionalism, rather than nationalism, combined with commitment to maximizing Spain's imperialist hegemony over its American colonies. Paralleling the Cadiz community's assessment of the expanding financial and commercial power of merchants resident in the colonies, Barcelona's merchants remained wary of the agricultural and manufacturing potential of New Spain. The interests of Catalonia, Spain, and its American colonies had to be harmonized by mutual sacrifice in order to confront the "preponderancia" of colonial interests. The social basis of Catalan economic discourse was clear: "The well-being of society demands from every individual, community, or province certain sacrifices, without which the harmony and happiness of all cannot exist." Hence the state's responsibility to limit the "libertad de sus dependientes" in the general interest of imperial hegemony.[26]

Here "harmony" was the codeword for colonialism, for the need to eliminate the textile workshops of Mexico City, Querétaro, and Puebla in New Spain, which sold their products as far south as Peru. If Madrid failed to halt the expansion of New Spain's agriculture and manufacturing, "which can supply the metropole, the basis of their mutual union and happiness will begin to erode."[27] Effective "unión y felicidad" necessitated elimination of colonial brandy and manufactures, leaving colonials to "be satisfied with the cultivation and profits of the soil, exchanging them for the fruits and the products of our industry." This was the colonial compact envisioned by Barcelona's entrepreneurs, which later would be justified as the international division of labor and comparative advantage.

In 1789, with the Spanish press enjoying a brief relaxation of censorship on the eve of the French Revolution, Barcelona's "Informe sobre el comercio de América" was published at Madrid in the *Espíritu de los mejores diarios literarios*, edited by Cristóval Cladera. It was also carefully read in the colonies. In 1802, in his annual mémoire for local merchants, Vicente Basadre, the Peninsula-born secretary of Veracruz's *consulado,* later noted that "regrettably" there were Spaniards with an "impolitic preoccupation" who believed that the colonies should produce neither manufactures nor primary commodities if to do so were prejudicial to metropolitan producers.[28]

Ministerial "despotism" in the era of Charles III could not suppress regional rivalries in Spain's transatlantic trading system, and Sevilla's *consulado,* another merchant guild responding to Valdés, brought its distinctively regional (and rival) interests to its view of colonial trade under *comercio libre*. Unlike Cadiz (purely an entrepôt port) or Barcelona (an outlet for both agricultural and manufactured goods), the interests of Sevilla's agricultural hinterland suffused its *informe* with markedly physiocratic priorities, foreshadowing Andalusia's free trade position vis-à-vis Catalan developmentalism in the nineteenth century. Agriculture, Sevilla's exporters affirmed, remained the "first pillar of the state, which needs much stimulus."[29] Sevilla's recently resurrected *consulado* found that since 1765, modifications in colonial trade regulations had, in fact, privileged manufacture and shipping; competition among proprietors of vessels under 250 tons had lowered maritime freight rates and brought to Spain primary materials from the colonies previously neglected because of exorbitant freight rates. The self-interested business practices of Cadiz's shipping oligopolists over the eighteenth century remained a sore point, since Sevilla's primary exports—wine, brandy, almonds, and dried fruit—were often rejected by Cadiz shippers, who preferred to reexport imported textiles, which could absorb high freight rates.[30]

It followed that Sevilla's merchants bore little sympathy for Cadiz's bankrupts of the mid 1780s, who to their mind had been justly punished for overspeculation. In sum, Sevilla's merchant community found no fault with the principles behind a government strategy designed to metamorphose Spain's colonial trade from a one-port monopoly into a broad oligopoly of metropolitan ports. Saying that "liberty" was the essence of a sound colonial trade policy, Sevilla's *informe* rejected ceilings on exports, reexports, or on tonnage of goods apportioned among authorized peninsular ports and saw no reason why any peninsular port should be blocked from participation in colonial trade.[31]

There were, however, two reservations about implementing *comercio libre* that Sevilla's *informe* underscored. Convinced of the overall utility of "libertad absoluta" in colonial trade, the report detected one serious drawback: the continued commercial hegemony of Cadiz. Without further intervention by Madrid, virtually everything shipped to New Spain or to other American colonies would inevitably continue to exit from that port alone. Had not Gaditano merchants "boasted" that in 1785—a peak year for peninsular exports—their port still managed to handle at least 80 percent of shipments to the colonies, reaching 87 percent the following year?[32] Sevilla's *informe* conceded that Cadiz enjoyed well-recognized facilities in shipping, credit, and insurance, along with warehouses that foreign resident merchants kept well stocked. With ill-concealed exasperation, however, it added, "That's why the whole wealth of this nation is piled within the walls of the tiny precinct of Cadiz." When Cadiz recommended that Valdés allow its port to handle most of the reexports to the colonies, it simply intended to "reduce commerce to its former monopoly."[33] Sevilla advanced its own radical agenda: simply prohibit Cadiz from reexporting foreign goods to the colonies. Notwithstanding their liking for "liberty," however, Sevilla's exporters did not fail to impress upon Madrid how prejudicial to Andalusia's winegrowers the manufacture of New Spain's *chinguirito* was, and they urged that the sale of it be banned and violators vigorously punished.[34]

Smuggling was *comercio libre*'s second shortcoming, the main cause of oversupply and depressed prices at Veracruz and Mexico City. The "radical cure," the way to "double" the metropole's exports to its American colonies and reach the "strongly desired level of remittances and consumption" was the elimination of smuggling. This, according to Sevilla's *informe,* was entirely the fault of state policy, both at home and in the colonies, through the unfortunate combination of high tariffs in the 1782 schedules with multiple *alcabalas* collected in New Spain, "burdensome in its rates as well as levied both on national and imported goods."[35] And just as the government's fiscal system drove up the price of a barrel of Andalusian wine sold at Mexico City by at least 19 percent and resulted in lower consumption, so cumulative levies—*almojarifazgo, alcabalas,* and local colonial taxes—made reexports from metropolitan ports uncompetitive with similar items shipped directly from English ports to Jamaica and then routed clandestinely into New Spain. To make their case more convincing, the Sevilla merchants reinforced their point by citing a London textile exporter who could sell a roll of coarse, durable woolen cloth (*sempiterna*) to a merchant from New Spain for 13 *pesos fuertes* at a Jamaican port, undercutting the same item reexported from Sevilla or Cadiz by at least 18 percent, not to mention the fact that the smuggled silver that the English merchant would accept as payment in

Jamaica avoided both colonial taxes and duties of 10.5 percent payable at Cadiz.[36] Sevilla's *informe* argued that smuggling was ineradicable as long as Madrid maintained a tax pyramid that diverted "most of the commerce of New Spain" to English competitors.[37]

The Response to Valdés's Questionnaire: II. New Spain

By contrast, the reply of the Consulado de México to Valdés's questionnaire, although warily critical of the 1778 commercial changes, displayed little sense of friction between metropolitan and colonial interests.[38] Criticism of the *comercio de España*—unlike the *consulado*'s attitude before 1778— was strikingly subdued, mildly touching upon the unnecessarily speculative practices of some "Europeos" in New Spain, or needling them for failing to furnish products designed for surprisingly volatile colonial tastes.

Oddly enough, Mexico's *consulado* (whose members were overwhelmingly Spaniards) seemed unfazed by an issue to which Catalan and other metropolitan exporters were highly sensitive: expansion of colonial manufacturing capacity. It even ventured to recommend "prudent rules to help the industry of the people of this kingdom."[39] Perhaps this was an effort somehow to adapt the colonial economy to the proto-industrial strategy sketched in Campomanes's widely circulated *Discurso sobre el fomento de la industria popular* (1774), designed to reduce widespread rural unemployment and underemployment through dispersed, small-scale cottage industry. The rationale for this was explicit enough: artisanal employment would provide wages to those enduring "a wretched, shameful existence" including women ("a sex truly scorned") to spend on "consuming the manufactures of the nations of Europe," for which New Spain's consumers had a "strong preference."[40] Still, more than charitable paternalism or the hope of supporting the imperial economy may have motivated interest in artisans' purchasing power or spending preferences. Mexico City's *almaceneros,* members of their extended families, and their business associates invested in the textile workshops (*obrajes*) of Querétaro, Mexico City, and Puebla, financed Amerindian weavers of popular cotton cloth (*manta*) in Oaxaca in southern New Spain, and sold these textiles at a profit to low-income consumers.[41] Were they, in fact, targeting a growing local demand for low- and medium-priced goods neglected by metropolitan exporters?

As businessmen of the hub city controlling the distribution of imported and domestic merchandise everywhere in New Spain, Mexico City's Spanish merchant oligarchs obviously appreciated the pivotal role of "our trade." To impress Madrid's Colonial Office, they played upon the "valuable treasure" they remitted annually to the metropole, which, they pointed out, resulted from their large-scale mining (and risk-bearing) investment, although frequently "losing millions of pesos in this very risky business, to the point of bankruptcy, even the most affluent firms." Before getting down to the main features of New Spain's trading system, they emphasized in introductory comments how their operations differed from those of their metropolitan counterparts at Cadiz and Barcelona, the reasons for their recommendations to Valdés, and how the needs of the *mercader americano* (that is, merchants in New Spain) might be harmonized with those of the *mercader europeo*.

The Mexico City merchants knew that Cadiz exporters had little working capital and relied on credit and loans (usually both) from resident foreign merchants. "Convenience for the European merchant consists not only in selling profitably but also in selling quickly," they noted, adding inaccurately (or was it purposely misleadingly?) that metropolitan merchants were under pressure to advance domestic manufacturers capital for materials and wages. Implicit was the Consulado de México's recognition that the cost of capital borrowed at Cadiz cut into profits when silver receipts from colonial sales were delayed; to the *mercader europeo* (read Cadiz exporter), it was always imperative to receive "returns as timely as possible."[42] At best, this was a reminder that Cadiz exporters in the main were straw men for European merchant houses at Cadiz.

The business world of the *mercader americano,* argued the Consulado's *junta,* had other perspectives. The capital's *almaceneros* distributed imports and domestic merchandise over a network of poor roads, and to maintain sales and prices, they needed predictable supplies, shielded from the uncertainties of new products, and months to recover the value of sales on long-term repayment schedules. "Unregulated" arrival of imports after 1778 had upset established business practice, leading the *mercader americano* to cut back on purchasing and to shift investment from trade into urban and rural properties, returns on which, although low, were reliable. "This is what we have found recently, proven by the repeated arrival of *registros.*" Here the Mexico City *junta* pinpointed a weakness in Spain's transatlantic trading system: by curbing import buying, *almaceneros* lowered earnings in specie that *cargadores* from the metropole were obliged to remit overseas quickly to satisfy creditors at Cadiz and other peninsular ports. Furthermore, when *cargadores* failed to find well-financed "cash-paying buyers of their wares," they turned to other, less capitalized, less creditworthy buyers in the provinces, who asked for long-term repayment schedules and then often defaulted, ultimately dumping their merchandise, "to the prejudice of all the other merchants." This scenario was no doubt overdrawn, although basically accurate.

These introductory remarks, a preamble so to speak, contained guarded criticism of *comercio libre* as applied conditionally to the colony of New Spain under Gálvez. This cautious approach resurfaced in the Consulado de México's observations apropos of two major innovations of 1778: unscheduled arrival of imports and repeated silver transfers from New Spain to the Peninsula on both public and private account. Imports, the Mexico City group advised Valdés apropos of some "arrangement of maritime trade," ought to arrive annually within one twenty-day interval; silver exports could be scheduled for a year later, also within a brief time frame, to allow "money, prior to export to Spain, to circulate two or three times within this colony to help the provincial sectors that generate it."[43] This was a logical tactic to minimize the local effects of constant decapitalization by the private and public sectors remitting money to the Peninsula. Spaced specie exports would halt the "constant extraction of money, since no sooner is it coined at the mint, than it disappears," causing capital shortages for the all-important mining industry.

As for Valdés's basic request for an informed estimate of an annual maximum (*toneladas*) of the colony's imports, the Mexico City *junta* sidestepped a calculation based on population, agricultural production, tithes, or even *alcabala* receipts. Characteristically, it fell back upon the experience of *flota* times and proposed an implausible 1,500-*tonelada* ceiling per annum on non-Spanish products, abandoning to Cadiz *cargadores* "complete freedom to ship what they considered appropriate" in national products.[44] It required little imagination to realize that Mexico City's merchants, like their Cadiz counterparts, hoped to revert to the status quo ante 1778; still, it was a far less blatant call than that of the Cadiz *junta* for a return to the *flota* regime.

In reacting to Valdés's questionnaire, the eight-member special *junta* formed by Mexico City's *consulado*—like the *consulados* at Cadiz and Barcelona—exploited the chance to push their own agenda rather than the Colonial Office's.[45] This is clear from the common theme of more than half the final *informe*'s 184 paragraphs, what the *almaceneros* termed the "imposition of duties," which in their view had undermined the colony's commercial sector, that "highly useful machine to the state." The principal factor behind the condition in New Spain that Madrid ought to ameliorate, namely "decadence in every sector," was, according to the Mexico City merchants' *junta*, fiscal pressure by the state in the form of assorted import duties, the *almojarifazgo* and repeated sales taxes (*alcabala, alcabala de reventa*).

The *junta*'s extended and sometimes confusing retrospective of the evolution of colonial sales taxes in the colony since the last quarter of the sixteenth century had as its raison d'être to prove that the fiscal policy of the Spanish state was responsible for the colony's exorbitant retail prices, limited consumption of what they chose to import, and for what they determined was the "decadencia" (that is, decline) of Mexico City as the colony's distribution center.[46]

The historical overview opened with the initial 2 percent *alcabala* imposed in 1575, which, the *junta* claimed, had been set low because the state intended that the "comercio de America" apply surplus income to finance mining operations, already the "crux of happiness."[47] By 1635, Spain's entanglement in international conflict had tripled the rate to 6 percent, where it remained for more than a century. Another era of international conflict, in 1744–57, saw the tax rise to 8 percent, after which it fell to 6 again, until war in 1779–83 drove it back up to 8. As the *junta* noted, under the pre-1778 flota system, the *alcabala* was collected only once; after 1778, however, *alcabalas* were required in each zone (*alcabalatorio*) through which merchandise moved, thereby raising the final price of non-Spanish imports by at least 44 percent, and national goods by 36 percent, above principal cost.[48] Recent *alcabala* changes were probably an initiative of the newly appointed Colonial Secretary José de Gálvez, drawing upon observations in the colony as *visitador general* in the late 1760s. Even more irksome were his measures to ensure *alcabala* collections and hamper smugglers by imposing waybills (*guías*) and customs stamps (*marchamos*) as evidence of customs payment.[49]

Buttressed by these fiscal details drawn from the *consulado*'s archives (it had farmed the excise tax for decades until 1754), the *junta* now advised Valdés on how to lighten fiscal pressures, of course pursuing its own agenda. These included eliminating *guías* and *marchamos;* permitting unsold merchandise to pass untaxed through successive *alcabalatorios* until the point of final sale; and, perhaps most important to the Mexico City merchants, reprivatizing *alcabala* collection, while maintaining collection by the state in the key commercial hubs of Veracruz and Mexico City.[50] (Realistically, Mexico City's mercantile elite entertained little hope of recapturing the capital's *alcabala* farm.) As tax collector, the private sector would be less arbitrary in tax assessments, the *junta* declared, than the notoriously undersalaried state personnel, whose zeal was overstimulated by their mandated percentage of gross *alcabala* collections. Left for last, "since it especially benefited Mexico City's commerce," was the *almaceneros'* proposal to lower the *alcabala* in their zone to 4 percent, leaving the rest of the colony to continue at a 6 percent rate. With this 2 percent advantage, Mexico City aimed to draw back provincial buyers, who after 1778 went to Jalapa and Veracruz to purchase directly from peninsular *cargadores,* avoiding what had in effect become an added tax burden at the capital.[51]

On a major issue raised by Valdés—how to expand colonial demand for Spanish manufactures and spirits—the Consulado de México's report was notably reticent. Metropolitan manufacturers could expand colonial sales, it was suggested, by reproducing "samples and models" forwarded from the colony in recent years to produce goods "to suit the Americans' customs and taste." There was no mention of an annual quota of brandy and wine for the metropole's major producing areas, on the plausible grounds that reliable data were unavailable. In this fashion, the Mexico City merchant elite skirted the keen regional rivalry between Catalonia and Andalusia.[52]

Final consideration went to mining, which was crucial to colonial trade, manufacture, agriculture, and "everything else that benefits both kingdoms and the treasury." Here the merchants' focus appears more technical than substantive, aloof to expression of concern about the recently formed mining tribunal or its financial operations. Instead, the capital's warehousemen would modify legislation by granting permanent ownership of mercury sites to those who discovered them, in order to compensate for well-known production problems in peninsular mines at Almadén. They also proposed to remove the *alcabala* from major mining inputs—wrought iron, steel, animals, tallow, hides, and canvas.[53]

The reply of Mexico City's *consulado* to Valdés is at bottom a regionalist document, permeated with observations regarding local colonial concerns, but never wider imperial interests, such as those voiced by peninsular *consulados.* A digest of the *informe* prepared for the *consulado*'s agent (*apoderado*) at Madrid, Santiago Saenz (who was paid the princely annual sum of 12,000 pesos), reveals that the first seven of its twenty-five points lobbied for reductions in multiple sales taxes, duties, and unrealistic maxima on annual silver remittances to Europe; for a cap on the volume of foreign goods; and for the stimulation of Spanish exports, that is, national, products.[54] In this sense, Mexico City's *almaceneros* followed their expressed intention to underscore that their situation differed from that of the *mercader europeo.* They made no effort to situate the problems of Spain's wealthiest overseas possession in an imperial context, for example, to reduce dependence upon Europe's suppliers of Spain's large volume of reexports. Their narrow approach was not novel: an earlier report, apparently drafted in the late 1760s during Gálvez's commission of inquiry, had been similarly focused.[55]

The backward-looking mentality of Mexico City's business elite, inflexible in its fixation on the earlier *flota* regime, surfaces in the introductory sentences in which *consulado* officers acknowledged receipt of Valdés's questionnaire. In a baroque clientelist paragraph, the *consulado,* whose external trade was second only to that of Cadiz in the metropole, gushed about its "inexpressible joy" and "humble gratitude" for the "imponderable mercy with which our August Monarch stimulates and revitalizes his fortunate subjects," while deprecating its own "limited intelligence" in handling matters "of such great importance," not to mention its sense of "confusion and reverent fear." The *informe*'s core is comparably baroque, speaking of "the incomparable mercy of our Catholic king," addressed with "the greatest veneration." It drew comfort from the conviction that "neither the Lord nor the King demand from the *consulado* anything other than that it provide the means to excuse its shortcomings if its efforts fail to overcome them."[56]

Beyond doubt, the *consulado* took its responsibility for drafting a response seriously. Eager that their views receive full consideration, one month after dispatching the *informe* to Valdés, *consulado* officers also sent their Madrid agent a 25-point digest of their principal findings so that he might proceed to "promote the aforementioned issues, which have the highest importance." However, references to smuggling from New Orleans, Havana, and Kingston through Veracruz and Tampico, a complaint recurrent in the *informes* of the peninsular *consulados,* were significantly absent, except for a comment on "presumed frauds committed fraudulently."[57] Better to let sleeping dogs lie?

The Response to Valdés's Questionnaire: III. Madrid

Such were the perceptions of the effects of the 1778 Reglamento by those on the Peninsula's periphery at Cadiz, Barcelona, and Sevilla, and on the periphery of empire at Mexico City. The responses to Valdés's circular had much in common, albeit with some notable exceptions. All were reluctant to quantify annual tonnage allocations, the bedrock of Gálvez's special (and highly personal) handling of New Spain's mercantile elites. Their excuse, unavailability of reliable commercial data, is implausible. True, the Spanish government had yet to publish an annual trade balance; equally true on the other hand, knowledgeable Cadiz merchants worked pragmatically with their own estimates of New Spain's import capacity, which they concealed from competitors, just as Cadiz long balked at sharing its data on colonial trade with Madrid's ministries. Significantly, only Cadiz and Mexico City, the main beneficiaries of the *flota* system, implicitly suggested reversion to the pre-1778 system.[58] Another point in common was the tendency to lay the blame for smuggling, not on inadequate metropolitan production, lack of goods in certain categories, or the overt complicity of customs officials and contrabandists, but rather on the colonial tariff system.

The peninsular *consulados* agreed in explicitly opposing colonial production of items competitive with those of the metropole; colonies, peninsular merchant guilds argued, should confine their economic activity to silver mining and producing noncompetitive export staples like sugars, dyestuffs, raw cotton, and untanned hides, a position advanced by the Barcelona and Sevilla *juntas.* All in all, interest in national industrial development received at best sporadic support. How else interpret the general critique of protectionist schedules in the 1782 tariff? One explanation: merchants in the metropole were convinced that Madrid's real, thinly disguised goal was to increase tax revenues.

Did assessment of the 1778 commercial adjustment made at Madrid, which although the capital of Spain's imperial system had no direct involvement in colonial trade, differ from that of the ports on the periphery and overseas in the colonies? In the first place, the constellation of interest groups at Madrid differed from those elsewhere in the empire. To name only the most obvious, there were the Cinco Gremios Mayores and the recently formed Real Compañía de Filipinas (into which the Guipuzcoan Company had been folded), both controlling large capital resources, which if put to work at Cadiz, for example, might overwhelm the perennially undercapitalized, small-scale Spanish merchant houses there. For decades, Cadiz merchants had aggressively opposed colonial operations by the Cinco Gremios Mayores, and in the 1780s, they complained of the Compañía de Filipinas's efforts to introduce Asian products directly into New Spain at Acapulco. Second, another corporate creation of the 1780s, the state's Banco de San Carlos, monitored transfers of silver from commercial centers like Cadiz and Madrid to European creditors supplying merchandise for reexport to the colonies. Also at Madrid were high-level bureaucrats with a long-term policy interest in the empire's transatlantic trade system like Campomanes (now *gobernador* of the Consejo de Castilla) and his correspondent Tomás Southwell, a foreign-born naval officer. These, along with members of Madrid's influential Real Sociedad Económica, tended to support the state's commercial strategy gradually unfolding under Prime Minister Floridablanca, seconded by Colonial Secretary Gálvez. They kept urging the government to look beyond special interest groups and the complaints of a handful of "imprudent or incompetent" bankrupts in order to pursue a national vision of "general harmony, the integrity of the great machine of state."[59] Such exhortations from the Compañía de Filipinas to Colonial Secretary Valdés were, one suspects, not entirely disinterested.

The report of Madrid's prestigious Real Sociedad Económica, whose members included figures prominent in government, finance, and commerce, was drafted by Francisco Xavier Uriortua y Villanueva. Apparently, it was unsolicited by Valdés or Floridablanca. Uriortua, the brother of Juan Manuel Uriortua, the prior of Sevilla's revived *consulado* and a prominent landowner, expressed no reservations about the advantages of the 1778 statute over the former "inhuman commercial system."[60] Under that system of trade contrary to the "happiness of mankind," Spain's American colonies "have been supporting us since the reign of Philip III." In the grim vein argued decades earlier by Melchor Macanaz in unpublished manuscripts, Uriortua found that that system had deformed the colonial economy by diverting investment from potentially productive land ("in some areas the best in the world") into "painful, harsh labor in the mines," whose output had fueled vast smuggling networks in the Caribbean ever since the early years of the eighteenth century. Between 1764, when Madrid had authorized regular mail packet boats between La Coruña and the colonies, and 1778, Uriortua felt, a great transformation had begun, despite opposition from those dedicated to preserving "las antiguas maximas."

As spokesman for the Real Sociedad Económica, Uriortua judged that either "malice" or "ignorance" had led certain unnamed interests to find contradictions, inescapable whenever "new paths" threatened an established order by "the very reforms intended," and to attempt to reconcentrate in one port all exports of foreign merchandise to the colonies. In 1778, Madrid had ended Cadiz's monopoly but had not provided the "libertad" that might expand Spain's imperial trade.

Uriortua insisted that the larger volume of maritime freight at lower rates made possible by the 1778 statute might have improved sales in New Spain and other American colonies had not unpredictable developments intervened. Perhaps the foremost obstacle to successful implementation of the state's commercial policy was the uncontainable surge in smuggling from non-Spanish Caribbean ports into Cuba, Puerto Rico, and particularly New Spain. Once again, Madrid's fiscal policy (or was misguided protectionism his real target?) came under fire as the prime stimulant to smuggling.[61] Uriortua underscored metropolitan duties on reexports under the 1778 Reglamento, to which Madrid had subsequently added the higher rates of the 1782 tariff schedule, inducing what he termed "very fatal consequences for the trade of America." Smugglers undersold legal imports in the colonies by at least 20 to 25 percent, while still pocketing large profit margins; the sheer volume of smuggled goods, he insisted, made accurate determination of colonial consumption of imports impossible. "The high volume of smuggling other trading nations carry on with New Spain will undermine even the best-thought-out operations."[62] Furthermore, Uriortua noted, reopening Spanish New Orleans in 1784 for direct trade with France's Atlantic ports only complicated control of smuggling. Such were the contradictions in the course of modifying the "old establishment."

The second and unpredictable obstacle was monetary, whose effects, Uriortua judged, provided further incentive for smuggling between New Spain and European ports in the Caribbean. Spain's peso devaluation (Uriortua's "monetary changes") had induced a rise in foreign exchange rates, reflected in higher prices paid by metropolitan merchants for reexports to the colonies, which were passed along to colonial consumers. In turn, price changes negatively affected the metropole's customs receipts, which figured so prominently in Hacienda's *rentas generales.* In New Spain itself, those paying in uncoined silver often avoided the tax bite of Mexico City's mint and applied the savings to the purchase of more illegal imports. In fact, circumventing mint fees had become one of the "strongest attractions of clandestine commerce; as long as they remain, it cannot be extinguished."

Uriortua's solution was drastic. He proposed to reduce all duties on foreign merchandise reexported to New Spain to a flat 6 percent, complemented by removing licensing and other shipping formalities, in order to sustain the "level between the goods we send and those that other countries have in their trading ports." He shied away from further criticism of monetary policy, alleging failure to receive information that he was convinced government bureaus had compiled. Indeed, one of his closing recommendations was government-sponsored publication of an "exact, reliable, and useful" trade journal providing businessmen with commercial intelligence. This later materialized in the extraordinary *Correo mercantil de España y sus Indias.*[63]

Perhaps interconnections of the elite membership of Madrid's Real Sociedad Económica to government and business, along with the frequent presence of high-level bureaucrats at its sessions, account for the national rather than provincial or peripheral perspective that Uriortua's report projected. Crony capitalism has its advantages. The Real Sociedad, we know, made a point of pressing its views at the highest levels of state.[64] This may explain Uriortua's frank reference to Spain's unending deficits on current account with the European producers of goods reexported to its colonies, which made the metropole perpetually dependent upon New Spain's silver. Without specie from that colony, Spain could never hope to finance its colonial trade, and, he had to add regretfully, "support itself."

Probably the Real Sociedad's report was drafted and submitted after mid May 1788, when most replies sought by Valdés's Colonial Office had already been received. Until August, almost one year after Valdés's circular was distributed to *consulados* at home and overseas, the great debate over New Spain's ambiguous status in the Spanish transatlantic system remained unpublicized. But rumors about it circulated, of course, in business circles at Cadiz and other metropolitan commercial centers. "They are working out the structure for commerce," a letter from Cadiz reported accurately in January 1788, for example. "They seek the opinion of the kingdom's *consulados,* on the basis, however, of keeping the prejudicial authorization of specific ports."[65]

Only in August did the political class, the "public," begin to learn officially of the commercial controversy in the pages of the recently founded and widely read *Espíritu de los mejores diarios literarios.* First the editor published the initial installment of a succinct, provocative defense of the one-port monopoly at Cadiz by "F.X.B.," which he followed with Uriortua's unsolicited report (in seven successive issues), then a second installment from "F.X.B." The latter was probably Francisco Xavier Bustamante (y Fondevila), who had family ties to the merchant communities of Cadiz, Santander, and Mexico City, as well as to the upper levels of Madrid's bureaucracy. Only a year earlier, in November 1787, Bustamante had read, perhaps even helped draft, the quickly prepared response of Santander's *consulado* to Valdés's circular.[66] It was indicative of the fluid political climate in the last decade of Charles III's reign that position papers of an important government review process, customarily restricted to internal bureaucratic eyes, were now spread before the metropole's political elite. The priority given Cadiz's defensive stance suggests that the censored press hoped to avoid the complaint that the government had sidelined that port's interests as inconsequential. It is equally plausible that Bustamante's defense of Cadiz was used by the editor of the *Espíritu* to justify publication of Uriortua's far longer and critical *informe.*

Bustamante focused upon binary elements in Spain's colonial trade, which, he assumed, had been in equilibrium prior to the modifications made in 1778. Interpreting the mentality of Gaditano and Mexico City merchants, he treated the number of effective consumers in the colony as a fixed quantity and the other element, silver, as an independent variable. There was a factual basis for the concept of equilibrium: New Spain's silver output over the eighteenth century tended to rise, while demographic recovery after the awesome losses to epidemic disease in the sixteenth century was slow and per capita income growth negligible, despite gradual commercialization. Thus, the periodicity of the *flota* regime corresponded to a perceived reality: in his view (unorthodox for the time), the *feria* system centered on Jalapa had, in fact, adjusted the "regulated," or managed, supply of imports, not to the quantity of silver held by peninsular merchants resident in Mexico City, but to a limited number of consumers. Bustamante's argument was not all that far-fetched. This was the prized equilibrium of "comercio arreglado" (Gaditanos and their spokesmen avoided the word *monopoly,* their critics' weapon). For Bustamante, a stand-in for tradition-minded merchants on both shores of the Atlantic, with a honed incapacity to confront change in the international economy of the eighteenth century, it was simply a matter of locating a "means of fitting shipments to consumers in the colonies, rather than to their silver exports."[67]

As long as a handful of *casas fuertes* at Cadiz continued to dominate colonial trade restricted to that port, Bustamante claimed, the *flota* system had remained functional and efficient. However, the changes mandated by the 1778 Reglamento, by increasing the number of peninsular ports in colonial trade (his *ampliación de puertos*) had destabilized well-capitalized firms by facilitating the entry of *aventureros.* Disregarding the size of effective demand, newcomers of the exuberant 1780s had shipped to the colonies all the goods they could finance, just as, Bustamante noted, manufacturers and exporters in France, England, and Germany offered "an unlimited supply of goods" to match the "unlimited quantity of money" of the colonies rather than the number of estimated consumers. Here one detects the rationale of the Cadiz traders who declared bankruptcy in the 1780s. Hence, the "liberty" provided by the state in its *ampliación de puertos* had brought disorder (*desorden*).[68] Bustamente's incapacity for change became clear in his recommendation that Madrid return to the halcyon era of trade equilibrium by adjusting exports (in point of fact, reexports) to the "consumption levels of preceding years" and by restricting shipping to "one port where they will make appropriate calculations."[69]

What the anonymous "F.X.B." failed to factor into his analysis was that adjusting exports to effective colonial demand was no longer uncomplicated if the supply of desirable European goods expanded but the manufacturing capacity of the Spanish metropole remained totally inadequate. Spaniards involved in the colonial trade were still mere "agents for the rest of Europe, because the goods they should be delivering, we deliver, which benefits us, since we buy them for 3 and sell overseas for 6." Logically, Bustamante observed maliciously, Madrid's recent innovation of "liberty" might ultimately legitimate the flow of Europe's manufactures "from production centers to America," since "this is a commerce all the nations of Europe should be carrying on with America."[70] The reasoning was impeccable: the issue confronting the Cadiz commercial establishment in the changing circumstances of the Atlantic economy was how to rationalize an "unfree" colonial trade.

Here Bustamante reverted to the logic of the imperialism of merchant capital in its late eighteenth-century phase. For his merchant's mentality, as for that of Cadiz, Barcelona, Sevilla, and Madrid, justification was rooted in the fact of conquest. Colonial consumers, he insisted, were "our feudal vassals," and hence Europe's manufacturers and exporters had to use Spain as intermediary for funneling their products into Spain's colonies in America.[71] Spain's trade monopoly (*estanco*) inhibiting the "natural" flow of trade between European producers and Spain's colonial consumers required "reglas" to maintain imperial hegemony. No matter that, under the 1778 statute, exports of colonial staples had increased; this only proved that commercial modifications tilted the balance to favor "los Americanos." Asked Bustamante rhetorically: "What is our benefit in enriching Americans?" More important to the metropole were the benefits of colonialism. The Spanish system was operable provided colonial consumers "have only what they need." And since by right of conquest, Spain enjoyed a monopoly over its colonial trade, "we extract very large profits, since we are the commercial agents for one part of the world." In fact, he had to add, "we must do so." Economic liberty was incompatible with Spain's imperial rule: colonial trade "is not nor can be free"; it had to have "reglas."[72]

Beyond doubt, "F.X.B." (or Bustamante) accurately encapsulated the attitude and mentality of a majority of Spain's metropolitan and colonial commercial elites. *Consulados* at Cadiz, Barcelona, Sevilla, and Mexico City favored the existing Atlantic trading system, albeit with some divergences. The sole body fully supportive of ending the anomalous status of New Spain was Madrid's Real Sociedad Económica, which, to be sure, was neither a commercial body nor had been formally asked for its views. All of which raises the question, who were those behind decision-makers in Spain's Bourbon state—the Consejo de Indias, the Junta Suprema de Estado, Prime Minister Floridablanca, the new colonial secretary, or the "Ministerio en general"—who resisted the pressures of the commercial groups entrenched in the imperial system?

Comercibrilistas: Campomanes, "Ugartiria," and "Pretensa Libertad"

Supporters of the ministry's initiative shared two characteristics. In the first place, they had a healthy respect for the political and financial power exercised through "machinations at court" by the commercial interests of Cadiz and elsewhere in the empire, and they worried lest the *consulados' informes* might dominate government policy without serious contestation from other sources.[73] Merchants and merchant organizations were the interests "that higher government authorities customarily consult in commercial matters like the one before us," such as the Cadiz merchants, who "are the least knowledgeable about trade, and the reason is," as one critic put it, "that [since] they have focused exclusively on colonial trade, they have scorned busying themselves with commerce's many sectors."[74] Second, to development-oriented civil servants, the Spanish merchants at Cadiz were, on the whole, hardly producers of real wealth, but rather what a later generation would call a comprador bourgeoisie: "Those who buy, transport, and sell are just agents, mere traffickers [*traficantes*]." Instinctively, Spanish merchants contested developmentalists in the state bureaucracy who aimed to raise production and widen distribution; as harvesters of the market, these traders were interested in limited volume and correspondingly high profits. "They have a great interest," as the same critic noted, "in being few, transporting little, buying cheap and selling dear what they carry from Europe."[75] Tenacious defenders of their imperiled interests, they were psychologically incapable of taking a national view of "el bien público."[76]

Examined dispassionately, New Spain's commercial crisis and the associated wave of business failures at Cadiz had resulted from uncontrolled speculation, from "lack of facts and the misconduct of some merchants who can't grasp what a merchant needs to know to proceed knowledgeably."[77] There had always been bankrupts at Cadiz, only now Gaditanos could conveniently blame the phenomenon on Madrid's efforts to adjust commercial policy to the changing reality of the Atlantic world. The role of government supporters, in the view of the Compañía de Filipinas, was to remain impassive in the face of "the collapse of a few imprudent, hapless individuals, counterbalanced by the discretion of those who learn from their erroneous example."[78] This—bankruptcy—was an outcome of the operation of the impersonal law of competition and the market, the Compañía seemed to say. Not to be overlooked among the causes of bankruptcy were the lavish spending propensities of Cadiz merchants, exemplified by the "dining rooms of many merchants, comparable to those of ministers of state, such as are not evident even in many of the grandest homes at Madrid." Cadiz's newly enriched commercial bourgeoisie appeared to lack appropriate reverence for those of higher status; they merited, it seemed, a kind of divine justice.[79]

A second shared characteristic of the government's supporters were certain recommendations. They agreed that too many pre-1778 trade and navigational constraints survived, and that the external trade of New Spain "has not been as free as some claim: it has been carried out with licences issued by the colonial secretary, and therefore merchants cannot abuse a freedom they have not had [in the past] nor have today."[80] In addition, there were the flagrant shortcomings of metropolitan merchants in those peninsular ports recently authorized for colonial trade—their crass "ignorance of the geography of the Indies, or the current structure, condition, and traffic with them, along with their passive exchanges with other Europeans for so many years."[81] So the government's supporters wished to remove the requirement that exporters and shipowners register with *consulados,* just as they proposed to open more peninsular ports to the colonial trade: "Those authorized ports: don't they represent precisely the exclusion of all others?" They rejected ceilings on the volume or value of exports to New Spain—one of Valdés's principal issues—and, what was critical, quotas for reexports. It was illogical, they also seemed to say, to block reexports, "since Spain does not yet produce them [i.e., equivalent items], nor will for years to come."[82] Official propaganda in Madrid's *Gaceta* of 18 April 1786 aside, most exports to the colonies originated in "foreign manufactories, and no one thought they [i.e., Spanish national products] might constitute even one-tenth."[83]

This said, those behind Valdés's initiative among high civil servants advocated no radical transformation of colonial trade policy; rather, their agenda concerned only fine-tuning *comercio libre* already in place. This meliorist approach, with its historical perspective, insight, and unavoidable contradictions is best exemplified by the unsolicited comments of Floridablanca's long-time colleague and fellow functionary in the Spanish state apparatus, Campomanes.

In early August 1788, after the *consulados'* responses to Valdés had been digested, and while Floridablanca, Valdés, and the Consejo de Indias were crafting a solution for New Spain in the transatlantic trading system, Campomanes, now governor of the Consejo de Castilla, who had been interested in Spain's colonial trade for decades, drafted unsolicited reflections (he termed them "Apuntaciones," or "Notes") on "our commerce with the Indies, in its most decadent state ever."[84] (By decadence, Campomanes, like other eighteenth-century writers, meant no more than the aggregate of factors limiting growth.) The importance of Spain's colonial trade to the national economy should not, he felt, be underestimated, since "this subject, so important to the nation, is extremely difficult to restructure with half-measures." Commerce, he allowed, remained the "principal factor in national wealth" and—here spoke the fiscally attentive bureaucrat—"in the growth of the Treasury."[85] As he observed in a covering note to Valdés, colonial trade remained key to improving the economy of the *imperio español* and its merchant marine and naval forces. It was, he recognized, a complex matter, which required historical perspective, along with analysis of how other European economies had managed to strip Spain of the "gran parte" of its colonial exchanges, "relying upon no secret device other than bringing cheaper what they sell to our vassals overseas and accepting in exchange the many staples that we cannot distribute."

He confessed that several considerations motivated his unsolicited "Apuntaciones," which he forwarded to Valdés and, along with a private note (*adición particular*), to Floridablanca. He noted that he had kept abreast of Spain's colonial trade for decades and had serious reservations about the narrow range of issues raised by Valdés's questionnaire, which—incorrectly, he believed—assumed that trade with the colonies was *libre* by 1788, when in fact it was not. "Just read carefully the regulation of what is called *comercio libre,* and even the least informed will quickly recognize that those regulations reveal the very defects and counterprinciples that afflicted the commerce of Cadiz."[86] After examining Barcelona's recent *informe* to Valdés and discussions with those sharing his trade preoccupations, he found himself questioning the advantages of seeking the opinion of the *consulados*, whose views were invariably informed solely by their own narrow interests. "Overseas, for a long time, the same monopolies and constraints have been adopted (the questionnaire omits them), and they are maintained by the Consulados of Mexico and Lima with the same tenacity as the Consulado de Cadiz, out of similar interests." Ever sensitive to powerful lobbies, internal as well as external, Campomanes warned in his private addendum to Floridablanca that implementing any decision detrimental to the Mexico City merchant establishment, or for that matter to English interests expanding in the Pacific, would require "maximum discretion and shrewdness."[87]

Campomanes was a rationalist in the Catholic context of the Spanish enlightenment—analytical while limiting remedial action to avoid antagonizing influential interests. He recognized inefficiencies in the peninsular and colonial economies, and, as a physiocrat, he felt compelled to try to improve upon Spain's old regime. He was comfortable under the old order. A talented legal mind, he had risen through the layers of Spanish bureaucracy at Madrid by virtue of merit and a finely honed capacity for suiting ideology to praxis, to Spain's social structure and political processes, ecclesiastical establishment, and landowners and merchants—that is, to the institutions, interest groups, and mentalities of the old regime. This sense of balance (or compromise?) surfaced and resurfaced in his rhetoric, for example, when he explained why trade issues stirred up such conflicting opinions. Conflict of interest occurred, he affirmed, "either because we are really moved to push our opinions excluding anyone else's, or because interests blind us, or because some yield easily to novelty while others tenaciously cling to the old."[88]

Probably motivating Campomanes's observations was a real possibility that once again the mercantile establishments of Cadiz, Barcelona, and Mexico City might persuade Valdés and Floridablanca to abandon trade adjustments already mandated, even to return to the status quo ante 1778. In his historical perspective, he found a rationale for Spain's colonial trade monopoly centered in Andalusia since the sixteenth century—"as if the merchants of Seville and Cadiz were interested in depriving the other ports of the Peninsula of this traffic, and abandoning it to enemies or foreigners."[89] The trade monopoly of the two ports had led to the neglect, not to say virtual abandonment, of many Caribbean islands where English and other European interests had penetrated in the late seventeenth century. In the eighteenth century, however, conditions were changing far more rapidly. Campomanes observed colonial demographic growth and a consequent upsurge in import demand, matched by development of new colonial export staples; he prognosticated that English commercial interests, battered by the recent success of the American Revolution, would seek to compensate for their losses in North America by expanding illegal commercial contacts with Spain's remaining Caribbean colonies and especially with the Pacific coast ports of Central and South America. The English, he speculated, might choose to operate even from faraway India to establish another Jamaica somewhere in the Pacific as a base for clandestine trade networks.

This brought him finally to what he judged to be the fundamental flaw in the Spanish trading system: the increasingly unstoppable clandestine exchanges between Spain's colonies and British and other northern European possessions in the Caribbean, while Madrid persisted in restricting the colonial trade to a few ports. "Is it possible to reconcile that monopoly with adequate supplying of our West Indies and the export of their products?" he asked.[90]

In analyzing British commercial expansion in the Caribbean, Campomanes seemed to offer a paradigm for peninsular merchants. Here, no doubt, he mirrored the admiration for English institutions of Asturian intellectuals in the eighteenth century that suffused the economic thought of Jovellanos, Canga Argüelles, and others. The English, he recalled accurately as an autodidact historian, had exploited the slave supply contract that the Spanish government had had to concede them in the first half of the century to set up supply posts or factories to provision slave depots in agreed-upon Spanish colonial ports. In practice, the English trading enclaves had provided hands-on training for English commercial agents in the categories of merchandise Spain's colonial consumers preferred, in the terms and methods of repayment, and in the export staples available—all the "information we have never had," he said bitterly—and perhaps most valuable, one-on-one commercial contacts.[91]

No sooner had the Spanish government failed to renew the *asiento* in 1738 than English exporters transformed Jamaican harbors into entrepôts with well-supplied warehouses—an "orderly, steady system" grounded in "true principles of a reciprocal and lasting commerce." Campomanes chastised peninsular merchants in the colonial trade for ignoring an inescapable reality and labeling as "clandestine a commercial system carried on before our eyes, and as smuggling a traffic that, because of our neglect, is indispensable to avoid the depopulation of those regions." Moreover, England, as a colonial power in North America, had set enviable standards by supplying domestic manufactures in return for its colonies' agricultural staples, which were preferable to the "artificial products of industry." Campomanes could not restrain his deep physiocratic convictions. Such reciprocity between metropole and colonies also had a political facet: it had nourished a "government and republic" in England later transformed into "a European nation ranked among the most cultured"—no small accolade from a Spanish imperialist of Campomanes's stature and convictions.[92]

By contrast with the aggressive, innovative flexibility characteristic of England's colonial trade policy that Campomanes explicitly admired, by 1778, the Spanish state's inflexible policy of confining most colonial exchanges to one lower Andalusian port, where direct involvement of foreign resident merchants was formally prohibited, had induced in the metropole "a political lethargy, lacking a mercantile spirit when confronting the extraordinary wealth that [the American] continent offers."[93] In Campomanes's judgment, the 1778 legislation on Spain's transatlantic system had failed to activate peninsular mercantile communities. The attitude of metropolitan *consulados* formed in the aftermath of 1778 mimicked that of Cadiz, he said; "they do not fully support commerce and display all the monopoly tactics of Cadiz, with similar exclusionary provisions spread systematically and contagiously throughout the Peninsula." Since foreign residents were still deprived of the right to participate directly in Spain's colonial trade on their own account, Campomanes could not but regard *comercio libre* as a "pretended freedom."[94] Whereas England, France, and Holland made no distinction between the colonial operations of nationals and resident foreigners, Spain had naturalized Irish Catholic émigrés, while "clearly excluding them from trading with the Indies." It had even excluded Spaniards not registered with peninsular *consulados* from the colonial trade. Lower Andalusia's obstinate support for such exclusionary practices marginalized foreigners and their sons "born and raised in this kingdom" (*genízaros*), stripping them of rights conferred by "nature upon all born in Spain." At a time when both colonial population and import capacity were rising, the pool of merchants in Spain remained small, because ultimately foreigners emigrated with their earnings and their children, abandoned trade for investment in landed properties, or sent their sons abroad for education. All this was a net loss to Spain.[95]

In his note to Floridablanca accompanying the "Apuntaciones," Campomanes put Valdés's questionnaire on New Spain in the wider context of "the great issue of how to correct our colonial trade." It was a complicated matter, he conceded, "hard to grasp unless its many loose ends are brought together."[96] Valdés's major preoccupation, the management of New Spain's trade, he treated as a minor issue, the theme of only one of ten observations. Possibly, he disproportionately magnified what many *comercilibristas* feared, that the lobbying networks of the Cadiz mercantile establishment at Madrid might bring about a dramatic policy reversal, restoration of Cadiz's former port monopoly over the transatlantic trade. Or perhaps, as governor of the Consejo de Castilla, he had little opportunity to pursue what was now at best an absorbing avocation, colonial trade issues in historical perspective, much less to master the complexity of New Spain's mining economy, commercialization of agriculture, and urbanization. While admitting that New Spain's trade was "the most important of that continent," he went no further than to echo the complaints of Cadiz merchants and their *factores-encomenderos* trading with that colony under the former *flota* regime about the overpowering financial resources of Mexico City merchants. "In that land, they constitute a body exclusively of merchants" able to order merchandise from European suppliers, and in that capacity, they constrained large towns like Zacatecas, Guanajuato, Querétaro, and Valladolid to purchase "secondhand what they can and ought to acquire firsthand."[97] Campomanes appears to defend the abandoned Jalapa fair, where in theory provincial merchants could purchase directly from Cadiz's agents.

Campomanes's inability to grasp the nature of New Spain's economic situation in the 1780s underlies the banality of his recommendations for Madrid's colonial trade policy. Perhaps that banality reflected his haste in drafting the "Apuntaciones," although he confessed to Valdés "for many years I've tried to keep informed about what I boiled down in this paper."[98] He recommended authorization of additional colonial ports to trade with the metropole; uncontested participation of naturalized merchants in the colonial trade to make unnecessary their recourse to Spanish straw men (*prestanombres*); and, last, maintenance of permanent, well-stocked warehouses (really, English-style *factorías*) at major colonial entry points such as Veracruz for distribution of goods to merchants from New Spain's provincial centers. From these colonial ports, peninsular factors and agents would be able to maintain a flow of correspondence with metropolitan ports, forwarding customarily scarce information on prices, supplies, and consumer tastes. And he would have Madrid grant rebates on reexports in order to dissuade any clandestine trade.[99]

His final category of recommendations, possible ceilings on shipping and cargo volume, magnify his shortcomings. Campomanes was an archetypical high-level public functionary of an old state bureaucracy and a physiocrat reverential of Spain's imperial old regime. Throughout a long career, he was invariably predisposed to turn from incisive analysis to meliorist palliatives, leaving aside his vigorous recommendations for decontrolling Madrid's grain prices and justification of the ruthless expulsion of the Jesuits from Spain and its colonies decades earlier.

But now in his unsolicited "Apuntaciones," when at last he addressed Valdés's principal preoccupation, Campomanes simply separated New Spain from other colonies on pragmatic rather than conceptual grounds. With only one major port for its large Atlantic exchanges, New Spain's external trade was, he held, still manageable. In effect, Campomanes sided with Mexico City's *almaceneros:* he would retain that colony's ambiguous status under *comercio libre.* Unlike other informed observers, he claimed that it was easy to discern the trend of export data over the previous two decades and arrive at a credible estimate of New Spain's current annual capacity for absorbing imported textiles (*ropas*) and its exports of specie and raw materials. "New Spain," he concluded, "is the only place in the Indies where it is appropriate, for the moment, to fix the number of *registros.*"[100] Intelligence and capacity for study and hard work, joined to unquestionable dedication to Spain's old regime and its principal interest groups, gave Campomanes a survival kit as a reliable state servant. He was an admirable high-level servant of the state (*covachuelo*).

In essence, his was a position staked out by the *consulados* of Barcelona, Cadiz, Santander, and Mexico City, organizations Campomanes had long criticized for their inability to adjust practice to change. Now in cautious recommendations for dealing with merchants in New Spain's external trade, he once again revealed his tendency to yield to the enduring pillars of the Spanish imperial state, whether aristocratic landlords, high churchmen, or—as in this instance—merchant oligarchs. Decades of devotion to Spain's *monarquía* had rendered Campomanes incapable of innovative thinking in the closing years of his career. One cannot minimize his reluctance openly to challenge Mexico City's wealthy Spanish merchant oligarchs, who, he accurately foretold, would seek to "maintain the monopoly they enjoy at any cost, at the expense of the commerce of all Spain."[101] In the addendum to his "Apuntaciones" sent to Floridablanca, he characteristically warned him to avoid overt confrontation with "Mexico" and, instead, resort to "slow, gradual means to allow the whole country to profit peacefully."[102]

Campomanes drafted his moderate recommendations in mid 1788. In March 1789, a letter signed "Ugartiria" on Spain's colonial trade, published in the *Espíritu de los mejores diarios,* revealed how far official toleration of public debate of large commercial questions had advanced.[103] "Ugartiria" avoided irritating inveterate traditionalists among metropolitan merchants and their bureaucratic connections, but his proposal for a closed imperial system contained radical elements whose publication the regime would scarcely have tolerated less than a decade earlier. Small wonder that the author resorted to a pseudonym.

His core argument was simplicity itself. The policies based upon "our enlightenment," on the one hand, and state fiscal pressure, on the other, had failed to bring about metropolitan economic development, while most of the coined silver of New Spain (he estimated 24 million pesos minted annually in the early 1780s) and of Peru and New Granada (8 million) continued to trickle abroad to other European economies through legal and clandestine channels.[104] American silver, he observed, anticipating subsequent diagnoses of the trajectory of Spain's economy, was *the* source of its "decadence." The "extraordinary expansion of Spain's monetary stock as a result of American silver, especially during the reign of Philip II, and continued thereafter, ruined our national industry, rendering it unable to compete in price with imports."[105]

"Ugartiria's" solution for a stagnant economy was an imperial trading system minus internal barriers, open to all citizens of Spain and its colonies, unrestricted as to type of economic enterprise. "In my view," he wrote, "everyone must sow, cultivate, harvest, process, and sell freely, without the least constraints, whatever, whenever, and wherever he wishes in Spain and our American colonies: this freedom, the soul of industry and agriculture and procreator of population, is the foundation of public happiness, without which no state can achieve real prosperity."[106] He welcomed investment in "all the workshops possible in our American colonies." His system, he added, reflected the principle of equity, of "rights and prerogatives" shared by all members of the "polity of this monarchy."[107] "Ugartiria" was boldly advocating the adoption of a national and imperial *política comercial* for the Spanish empire.

To traditionalists obsessed with the "fantasma político" that wealthy, populous, economically developed possessions would inevitably seek independence and sovereignty on the model of England's North American colonies (predicted in Raynal's recently published *Histoire des établissements européens*), "Ugartiria" had a reasoned response: England had brought on the rebellion itself by denying the colonists "rights and prerogatives" as English citizens (which suggests that "Ugartiria" had absorbed the pamphlet literature of the North American colonies' revolutionaries). He was confident that Spain's American possessions would remain in "unity with the metropole" as long as the Spanish imperial state guaranteed them "prosperity, liberty, and security."

The publication of "Ugartiria's" letters in a censored periodical alerted the *Espíritu*'s readership to the fact that the Floridablanca administration was committed to change in a key area of concern to the Spanish state. In *consulado* reports, unsolicited opinions of both corporate bodies and concerned individuals, and "Ugartiria's" two explicit essays, there is an underlying preoccupation with the overriding importance of the special relationship of Spain's American colonies to its economy. It was, we now recognize, a relationship unique to Spain and Portugal in the development of the Atlantic economy: a metropole's marked dependence upon its colonies, rather than the reverse.

Properly decoded, this is virtually made explicit in "Ugartiria's" first letter, where he calculated government income from metropolitan and colonial sources. By shifting some income categories from metropolitan to colonial sources—crediting to colonial revenue a minimal estimate of 50 percent of *rentas generales* contributed by customs, as well as duties on colonial silver reexported from Spain, for example—colonial revenue as a percentage of total imperial revenue reaches virtually 65 percent.[108]

"Ugartiria's" essays appeared in the *Espíritu de los mejores diarios literarios* immediately after Madrid had resolved the status of New Spain under *comercio libre,* although the second letter on expanding colonial trade was dated 10 February 1789, two weeks *before* the order affecting New Spain. *Espíritu*'s editor, Cladera, had deliberately held up publication of "Ugartiria's" second letter.

Finale: The "Teatro de los Sueños"

In airing conflicting views of Spain's economic situation and policy options in a new periodical, Madrid's weekly *Espíritu de los mejores diarios,* Floridablanca's administration signaled that it would proceed cautiously and firmly, preparing selected interest networks for imminent policy changes. By late January 1789, only weeks after Charles III's death and the accession of his son, rumor mills were at work among Madrid's political class in "gossip, stores, the Puerta del Sol, cafes and salons" where people shared stories generated by "overheated imagination," by bureaucrats consumed with "envy and perversity," and by the optimism of the "Teatro de los Sueños" (theater of dreams). At one nobleman's townhouse, guests arriving for dessert, coffee, and conversation—basic ingredients of the *tertulia*—gossiped about impending changes in the bureaucracy and particularly in the most sensitive ministry (Hacienda), predicting that "they will shortly announce the system henceforth to be followed concerning trade with our Colonies in America."[109] In fact, the gossipmongers were on to something: the Floridablanca administration could no longer postpone what it had gingerly broached eighteen months earlier when Antonio Valdés replaced the recently deceased José de Gálvez at the Colonial Office.

One week after "Ugartiria" cited current gossip in the pages of the *Espíritu,* the Consejo de Indias circulated a digest of *consulado* responses to the critical items of Valdés's questionnaire. In a *dictamen,* it summarized contradictory assessments of the supply of the most valuable items exported to the colony of New Spain, non-Spanish merchandise; while Mexico City and Veracruz reported that their inventories were about right, metropolitan *consulados* harped on New Spain's unsold inventories and depressed prices. Proposals for annual tonnage ceilings for foreign merchandise ranged from a low of 800 (Barcelona), to 1,500 (Mexico City) to a high of 2,000 (Cadiz and Málaga). All had concurred, the *consejo* noted, that Cadiz remained by far the main entrepôt for exports and reexports to the colonies.[110] As for national products, since colonial demand was unpredictable, exports should be left to merchants' "news and calculations." In the long run, competition would expand overseas demand by lowering prices.[111]

Within two weeks, Floridablanca presented his *dictamen* to the Junta Suprema de Estado, the interministerial group he had revived. As regards national exports to New Spain, the marketplace and consumer preferences would establish an equilibrium between vendors and buyers, he observed; "supply increases consumption, and once the consumer becomes accustomed to using those items, he seeks, buys, and thereby helps growth in commerce." However, for 1789, he would set reexports at a maximum of 33 percent of a vessel's cargo outbound for the American colonies. Probably recalling reports sent by the exasperated *visitador* Mesía on the devious tactics of Cadiz's customs agents, he warned that this would oblige them to use "much caution not to confuse national with foreign goods in following regulations that prevent falsification."[112]

In two meetings over the next three days, 16–19 February, the Junta Suprema de Estado reviewed the opinions submitted by Floridablanca and other ministers in detail, then drafted its own view, which contained the substance of the final resolution of the status of New Spain in Spain's transatlantic commercial system. No limits were placed on the volume of national products exported to the colony or the tonnage of ships in colonial trade, and the registration requirement for shipowners and merchants was dropped. To encourage exports of national manufactures and semi-manufactures (but not agricultural products), these would now benefit from a 10 percent across-the-board reduction in export duties in the Peninsula, plus another 10 percent in colonial import duties.

Most critical was the decision with respect to reexported non-Spanish goods, hitherto Cadiz's virtual monopoly. While accepting Floridablanca's recommendation that reexports be permitted to constitute up to one-third of all cargo, the Junta Suprema now mandated perceptively that the basis of calculation be value rather than volume in order to dissuade exporters from investing more in the permissible one-third of volume than in "the other two thirds, to the detriment of national commerce." If customs officials questioned the national origin of exports "to prevent the often practiced ruse of utilizing foreign manufactures labeled national in colonial trade," a subsequent special meeting of the Junta Suprema directed that the opinion of trade experts be solicited and, if any doubts remained, that the goods in question be dutied as foreign. On 19 February, the Junta Suprema authorized Secretario de Guerra y Hacienda de Indias Antonio Valdés to oversee "como costumbre" publication and distribution of an *orden* based upon its determinations.[113]

The final product of the Junta Suprema's deliberations, the order of 28 February 1789, whose title declared "free for trade with New Spain and Caracas all agricultural products and manufactures of national origin" was an amalgam of bravado and rejection of the aspirations of Cadiz's commercial establishment. Bravado showed up in the explanatory preface: Madrid stated as fact what still was moot, that the "libertad del Comercio a Indias" had led to expansion of domestic manufactures, the merchant marine, and exports of colonial staples, lowering prices to the benefit of colonial consumers and "comercio en general." Bankruptcies had been inaccurately ascribed to *comercio libre,* when speculators' "imprudence or ignorance" was really what was responsible. Buried among these observations was the root impulse for changing New Spain's anomalous status: it had proven impossible for Gálvez's Colonial Office to adjust that colony's import quotas to local demand, "since unforeseeable factors determine variations in consumption"—oblique abandonment of Gálvez's coddling of Mexico City's *almaceneros.* Closely adhering to Floridablanca's view of the conditions for New Spain's incorporation into *comercio libre,* the order of 28 February rejected Cadiz's request for mandatory registration, reexport ceilings, and a monopoly of reexports. In conformance with Floridablanca's recommendation as modified by the Junta Suprema, non-Spanish exports could be up to 33 percent by value of a ship's cargo.

By comparison with the 129-page printed version of the 1778 Reglamento, the two-page 1789 order incorporating New Spain into the system of *comercio libre*—to be sure, not quite fully, since there remained limits on the proportion of foreign to national goods shipped from the Peninsula— seems laconic.[114] Excluded in 1765 and again in 1778, New Spain was now tersely, even surreptitiously, included. It was almost anticlimactic. Of course, in issuing the *real orden* of 28 February covering New Spain, Madrid had more than this goal in mind. It chose the same day to break with tradition and open the African slave trade to the colonies to Spanish and, for two years only (it was later extended indefinitely), foreign slave-runners as well, largely at the insistence of Cuban planter and commercial interests, whose representative at Madrid then was the lobbyist Arango y Parreño. Madrid thus tied the development of the Cuban economy in the nineteenth century inextricably to sugar and slavery. It was hardly coincidence that the *Espíritu de los mejores diarios literarios* printed both measures in its issue of 16 March 1789, along with "Ugartiria's" essay on colonial commerce.

Incorporating New Spain into the system of *comercio libre* closed a cycle of intermittent, hesitant efforts begun almost seventy years earlier to adjust the traditional Spanish transatlantic commercial regime to changes in the Atlantic economy. The cycle's last phase (1778–89) was designed to isolate Spain's wealthiest colony by limiting the volume of its imports, allocated and distributed by Colonial Secretary Gálvez in collaboration with colonial officials and members of Cadiz's and Mexico City's merchant elites. Gálvez's death and a lingering trade recession in New Spain together served to justify a wide-ranging reappraisal of that colony's position in the colonial commercial order.

At this point, one may speculate as to why Gálvez and other highly visible public officials at Madrid like Tomás Ortiz de Landázuri, and Francisco Viana (*contador general* and *consejero* respectively of the Consejo de Indias), both veterans of New Spain's colonial service, had omitted that colony from *comercio libre* in 1778. Perhaps they had hoped to give Mexico City's *almaceneros* and Cadiz's *cargadores* time to adapt to now inescapable change. Perhaps they had hoped to preserve New Spain's ambiguous position as long

as possible. Perhaps Gálvez, manipulating an implicit patron-client relationship, banked upon future claims on the financial resources of Mexico
City's business elite, as in fact he did in behalf of the state during the war
with England, and of the Bourbon heirs-apparent, Charles and María Luísa.
All were further indices of the dependence of Spain's state and economy
upon control of New Spain's economy. Speculation aside, Gálvez's secretive, ad hoc, and discretionary tactics for fixing New Spain's import levels
annually after 1779 had failed to avert the unsettling trade recession of 1786–
87 in New Spain and its backlash in Spain itself. State intervention now
became imperative in view of the metropolitan public and private sectors'
need to capture as much as possible of the colony's trade and revenues.

Noteworthy in the last phase of *comercio libre* was the innovative style of
the process. Consultation with those directly involved, the *consulados* in
metropole and colonies, had been rare in Spanish policy-making over the
eighteenth century and was a measure of the high priority given New Spain.
In circularizing mercantile bodies, state bureaucrats sought consensus rather
than to exercise what critics already labeled "ministerial despotism." To be
sure, circumstances required such collaboration. If one goal of *comercio libre*
was to elicit merchants' satisfaction, it followed that their participation
raised customs revenues, which in turn boosted the overall growth rate of
Spain's *rentas generales* by 6.3 percent annually between 1775 and 1792. An
analysis of the estimated customs revenues of 1787, for example, reveals
that 58.5 percent were obtained from peninsular duties on colonial trade.[115]
Contacts between a handful of policy-makers in the upper levels of Spain's
state bureaucracy and elements of the business and financial world of the
Peninsula were beginning to forge a national rather than regional outlook,
heightening the priority of public over private interests. In general, however, bureaucrats and businessmen recruited from the ranks of the Peninsula's mid-level gentry still shared an interest in preserving Spain's underdeveloped economy, traditional society, and—need one add—an empire in
America whose full potential they were only beginning to tap.

10. The French Connection: Spanish Trade Policy and France

The canal from the Indies passing through Spain, the one bringing cash in silver to France, is the one we must cultivate.
Masson de Plissay

Freeing our commerce and Your Majesty's authority over ports and customs duties from the pressures exerted by England's power in previous treaties and times. Secret agreements and adjustments with France concerned these issues.
José Moñino, conde de Floridablanca, to Charles III (1788)

At the end of the War of the Austrian Succession (1740–48), French merchants and shippers could expand only inside Spain's transatlantic trading system, now centered on Cadiz, not Sevilla. They exploited trade concessions by the Spanish Hapsburg governments in the last half of the seventeenth century that effectively lowered duties on imports of French linens and other selected items.[1] As for the concessions themselves, "France considered these privileges the foundation of its trade in Spain, indispensable to its continuation."[2] At mid-century, large-scale French commercial penetration of markets overseas in Peru and New Spain was facilitated by an influx of wartime profits earned by French firms at Cadiz, which they invested in overseas speculation when the Spanish transatlantic system assured high earnings during and immediately following the war. Until the Revolution, the French remained the largest foreign merchant enclave at Cadiz, conspicuous and ever sensitive to infringement of their treaty rights. Omitting a sudden peak of 154 firms in 1771, on average there were, over the decades 1724 to 1778, about 60 principal French commercial houses, described as "maisons très opulentes."[3]

Charles III came to Madrid when it was already evident that the English were winning the Seven Years' War and might move aggressively against

Spanish possessions in and around the Caribbean. For France as well as Spain, which Charles judged isolated in western Europe, his accession provided the opportunity at last to renew a dynastic alliance of mutual convenience, the "Family Pact" between the two Bourbon monarchies, a "collaboration of maritime forces to resist common enemies."[4] In light of the Franco-Spanish diplomatic and defense collaboration symbolized in the pact, Madrid's planners expected French private and public sectors to tolerate Spain's tardy efforts at protectionism, which they hoped might render their country effective in the joint containment of English commercial and naval expansionism in the Caribbean.

Sifting French consular and commercial reporting at mid-century, one discerns the main factors behind French involvement in Spain's empire in America. A prime consideration was the significant percentage of French textile production shipped to Cadiz for reexport; consequently, sales of linens, woolens, and silks at Cadiz for colonial markets directly impinged upon employment levels and earnings in France's textile centers. French industry also absorbed appreciable quantities of Spain's primary exports—wool, soda ash, raw silk—along with Mexican and Guatemalan cochineal and indigo dyes. From the French viewpoint, Spain had every reason to import French manufactures for reexport to its American colonies, since it was understood that perhaps only 10 percent of cargoes destined for the colonies consisted of Spanish-made goods; the balance could (and, to some, should) be drawn from the production of Spain's ally, France. There was, moreover, more than just the export factor of concern to French interests: sales to Spain's colonies generated a counterflow of silver into the private banking system centered on Paris and Lyons.

In probing Spain's economic relations with France in the age of Charles III, certain problems become prominent. Could Spain's centuries-old imperial system based upon precious metals remain dependent upon colonial silver while belatedly fostering a manufacturing sector in the metropole—this, in the last phase of highly competitive commercial capitalism? Could an arrangement under the Hispano-French alliance satisfactorily harmonize French and Spanish policy objectives, balance French economic interests with Spanish developmentalism, and integrate two economies in different stages of commercial capitalism, one relatively advanced, the other underdeveloped? Perhaps answers may emerge from a detailed examination of three interrelated issues vital to the French economy: illegal transfer of American silver overland to France, the stagnation of France's traditional exports of woolens and linens to the Spanish colonies, and the French reaction to Spanish developmentalist efforts. These factors played a part in the crisis France experienced in 1789, as well as in the crisis in Spain two decades later.

Silver Flows from Spain to France

Like other European merchants at Cadiz, French businessmen received the bulk of their sales earnings in colonial silver, and only to a lesser degree in gold. Exports of linens, woolens, and silks and the counterflow of pesos were major facets of the complex international economy of the eighteenth century dominated by Anglo-French competition for economic hegemony in the Atlantic. French firms loaded silver aboard vessels of the Compagnie des Indes that stopped at Cadiz en route to the Far East; more silver, after payment of an export tax, went by sea or overland to France; and a large and still unquantified percentage was smuggled overland to Lisbon, or to Madrid, and thence to the French border cities of Bayonne and Montlouis.[5] At the end of the 1780s, the Spanish authorities' effort to control silver outflows led to a crackdown on massive smuggling into France. Clearly, the incentive to smuggle silver was the possibility of avoiding the export tax levied on remittances; those to France were considerable, and by this time, the center for settlement of Spain's international accounts was Paris, where the Banco de San Carlos established a major branch.[6] A descendent of the prominent Lecouteulx merchant banking house of Paris, Rouen, and Cadiz once recalled that French speculators in smuggled pesos during the old regime had pressured their government to protect their access to colonial silver transfers.[7]

Furthermore, there was an added stimulus to silver outflows from Spain to France. Between 1725 and 1785, European governments devalued silver, modifying their gold : silver ratio. In 1772, in response to rising silver production in New Spain, and in an effort to reduce imports, Spain adjusted its gold : silver ratio to 1 : 16, parity with the Portuguese ratio, but higher than that of England (1 : 15⅛) or France (1 : 15½). So French speculators shipped gold to Spain in exchange for silver, which was then shipped to France and sold to "monnoyes [i.e., monnayeurs] ou au commerce français avec un bénéfice de 1½ ou 2 pour cent suivant le cours."[8] Production of Mexican, Peruvian, and other New World mines was critical to French trade growth throughout the eighteenth century, inasmuch as France did not develop the banking and credit instruments pioneered by Holland and England.[9] This motivated an experienced Spanish merchant with decades of colonial residence to note in 1775 that France was the European state "where that circulating medium [silver] is most abundant." It explains why later in the century, Boislecomte rather boastfully asserted that "half the gold and silver from America's mines crosses the peninsula to flow into France."[10]

The pattern of precious metals transfers is clear. Colonial pesos—New Spain's gold and silver coins were especially prized—were reshipped from Cadiz to Lisbon or to Madrid and thence via Soria and Logroño to Bilbao or San Sebastián and on to Bayonne. Later, once Catalonia established large-scale contact with the American colonies, silver was reexported from Barcelona to Marseilles or Montlouis and thence to Toulouse, Perpignan, and Narbonne. From Marseilles ("the repository and channel carrying an immense quantity of pesos and silver and gold bars to Lyons") precious metals moved up the Rhône valley via Nîmes to Lyons and beyond to Switzerland.[11] France's trade with North Africa also needed New Spain's silver pesos, so insisted Berber merchants; and pesos also flowed from France to trading partners in the Near and Far East.[12] Contemporaries estimated that a high proportion of the American silver entering France remained to cover goods sent to the Spanish colonies and to Spain; the balance went to London, Amsterdam, Hamburg, Geneva, and Genoa—all suppliers of manufactures reexported from Barcelona and Cadiz to Veracruz, Cartagena, Montevideo, and Callao.[13]

For their financial intermediation, a small group of Paris merchant bankers netted commission fees on the volume of silver handled. Hence their involvement in well-organized silver convoys entering Bayonne, a free port after 1784; from there the "barrils de finance" (silver pesos) were carted to Paris and Lyons. An estimated two-thirds of the pesos imported paid for French manufactures, grains, and cattle. French seasonal workers in Aragon also returned home with their wages in silver. By the 1780s, Bayonne had become the main center for Franco-Spanish overland trade flows. Into Bayonne from Spain came raw wool and silk, along with pesos both legally and (mostly) illegally exported from Spain, while from Bayonne into Spain went French goods, substantiating the view that "at Bayonne, trade consists entirely of smuggled goods."

Bayonne's principal source of precious metals, however, was colonial silver and gold entering from Santander, Bilbao, San Sebastián, and upper Navarre. It was hardly pure coincidence that merchant bankers like Francisco Cabarrús, who initiated his career at Madrid, and two of the first directors (Lafitte and Basterrèche) of the Banque de France established under Napoleon, came from southwestern France, or that one of Napoleon's financial advisers was a Lecoutelx de Canteleu whose family had for generations maintained a merchant house at Cadiz.[14] Defending the role of the Banco de San Carlos in French finance before the Revolution, Mirabeau acknowledged that Spain was the source of the "enormous quantity of pesos feeding the money supply that enriches France."[15]

Expansion of Spain's trade with its American colonies after 1778, coupled with international exchange speculation, enhanced Bayonne's position in the 1780s as an entrepôt for the flow of New Spain's silver into France and thence to western Europe. Broadly speaking, Spain's transatlantic trade stimulated silver smuggling at Cadiz, and the operations of international smuggling rings speculating in short-term fluctuations in silver prices on exchanges at London, Paris, Amsterdam, Marseilles, and Genoa. It led to Spanish countermeasures, the founding of the Banco de San Carlos authorized to monitor silver transfers, and, after 1786, a crackdown on silver smuggling. Smugglers, however, were able to bore from within the bank itself.[16]

Details of international smuggling operations linking the Spanish and French economies via silver shipments materialized in the 1780s when the French government, reviewing its customs income, noted the unprecedented silver inflows at Bayonne and Bordeaux. Although the fiscal objective was inadequately implemented, customs reports vividly clarified cross-border movements. For example, customs officials at Montlouis reported in 1785 that French bankers were accepting silver pesos from Barcelona on bills of exchange sent to Madrid and other Spanish cities. "Not a week passes but that Roussillon gets between 50 and 60,000 pesos (each valued at 5 livres, 6 sous, 2 deniers). These pesos, whose export Spain severely prohibits, buy French manufactures, silks, woolens of Languedoc, hats, and other finery. Just between Montlouis and Perpignan, 30 to 40 million livres are shipped." This commerce, the official added admiringly, "is carried on with remarkable fidelity and faith; the convoys are guarded only by their muleteers."[17] Smugglers, of course, easily arranged the collaboration of Spanish customs officers and agents.[18] From Narbonne came comparable reports of precious metals exiting Spain "freely without registry or weighing," permitting merchants to garner commissions of 1.5 to 2 percent.

Given the Spanish government's sensitivity to unlicensed precious metals exports, the French (like the English) government diplomatically did not insist upon accurate customs reporting or publicize data available. French inspectors at a major entrepôt like Bayonne did not demand that businessmen dealing in pesos make full customs declarations, since "there's no purpose in insisting on detailed declaration of an item merchants are interested in keeping secret." Notwithstanding, derived estimates of peso shipments were made. Customs employees simply counted the *voitures de terre* or *charrettes* entering France proper from the Bayonne free zone, each freighted with fifteen boxes of 15,000 *livres tournois*. Despite rough calculations at frontiers and the deliberate omission of considerable Bordeaux and Nantes peso receipts from the French West Indies, it was commonly understood that "[*piastres*] are an important item in our Balance of Trade."[19] One simply avoided advertising it. By the eve of the Revolution, silver and gold inflows from Spain in specie or bars were a critical factor in French domestic and foreign trade, and markedly so in commercial exchanges between the more developed French and the less developed Spanish metropolitan and colonial economies. These flows were also the result of Spanish bankers' making France "their financial intermediary in payments to different areas of Europe."[20]

The critical role played in the French economy by Spain's colonial specie flows immediately preceding the Revolution, and long before the financial crises of the Directory in 1797–99 and the Empire in 1805–6, is confirmed by the available data. Enquiry into legal and illegal peso flows into France in 1784–89 showed the importance of Bayonne, Montlouis, and Labourde as entry points, and Bayonne, Pau, Toulouse, and Perpignan, where precious metals reexported from Spain were coined or recoined, accounted for 59 percent of the total output of French mints, which peaked in the mid 1780s, reflecting the fact that Spanish treasury officials began to crack down on unlicensed outflows after 1785. French businessmen complained about the "baleful stagnation in the credit of our principal commercial centers"; the Banco de San Carlos, it was said, "absorbs all."[21]

Major counteroperations by Spanish treasury officials to interrupt smuggling of Mexican and Peruvian pesos from Cadiz by sea or overland occurred in 1785–87. To be sure, smuggling was not new, but it expanded noticeably around 1757, about the time of the resumption of the long-suspended *flotas* to Veracruz and the return inflow of Mexican silver in coin and bars. Aware of such activity, the Madrid government issued fresh regulations covering foreign warships "visiting" Cadiz.[22] Not until the 1780s, however, were measures taken to curb the flow of specie through Spain's "provinces exemptes" (Vizcaya, Guipúzcoa, and Alava) and Navarre in payment for shipments of goods, grains, and cattle from France.

Apparently disturbed by rumors of massive silver smuggling following the end of hostilities in 1782 and perhaps by the intensive customs investigation at Cadiz in 1785, Madrid treasury officials in 1786 began to check the connections to Lisbon of a foreign firm at Sevilla, Keyser & Butler, and at Cadiz, the operations of long-established French firms known to provide Mexican pesos to Asia-bound vessels of the Compagnie des Indes——Jugla, Solier & Cie. and Magon, Lefer Frères & Cie.—as well as a third firm, Pierre

Lenormand & Cie.[23] It was common knowledge that two prestigious Paris firms, Lecouteulx and Magon, received silver through connections at Cadiz.[24] Only the business papers of Keyser & Butler produced incriminating evidence that the Lisbon firm of Dhormand, often agent for Lecouteulx, mailed requests for silver in the form of bills of exchange drawn on Keyser & Butler at Sevilla and at Cadiz on Diego Duff and Jugla, Solier.[25] Simultaneously, Spanish investigators picked up the trail of silver from Cadiz to Madrid and on to Logroño, San Sebastián, and Bayonne, organized by firms in which the well-known charter director of the Banco de San Carlos, Francisco Cabarrús, was implicated. After 1786, Cabarrús limited his overt participation in the flow of silver that linked firms at Cadiz, Madrid, Bayonne, Bordeaux, and Paris, as well as in a well-organized overland transport network operating from headquarters at Cervera (Navarre); no doubt the operations involved payoffs to Madrid officials as well. But not until 1790, the onset of the Revolution and the accession of Charles IV did Finance Minister Lerena order that Cabarrús be arrested and his papers seized. This is at best a simplification of the still poorly investigated case of the smugglers' ring nicknamed "The Mint." It shows another dimension of the link between New Spain's silver mines, the peninsular entrepôt, and the French economy at the end of the eighteenth century.[26]

The Crisis in French Textile Manufacturing

In the late 1780s, coincident with the Spanish government's efforts to curb silver-running into France and the consequent sharp drop in the output of Bayonne's mint, textile manufacturing, a major sector of the French economy, was affected by international competition for overseas consumers in Spain's principal colonies, where sales of manufactured goods generated silver specie. The export performance of French linens, woolens, and silks, while already disappointing since the late 1760s, turned critical when English and German (Silesian) products began to cut into French sales of textiles at Cadiz destined for major consumer centers in Spanish America. France's exports to "Spain"—most were reexported to the colonies—were further affected by the Spanish state's limited efforts to develop its own high-quality textiles, emulating the French model of economic development.

First, an overview of French textile exports through Spain to its American colonies is in order.[27] Between 1660 and 1700, French linens and woolens predominated in exports both to Spain and its colonies. Initially, linens constituted the major export item from the Breton and Norman hinterland, followed by Rouen's woolens. There was a degree of international reciprocity, for Spanish merino wools were far superior to local French supply and indispensable for producing the high-quality woolens on which the French industry concentrated in order to match the similar goods of England, Holland, and Flanders. A second phase came after the Peace of Utrecht, when French producers relied upon French merchant houses with established outposts at Cadiz, such as Magon & Le Fer of Saint-Malo and Lecouteulx of Rouen. They freighted *flota* and galleon convoys, as well as unescorted licensed ships (*registros*) to expand shipments of high-quality textiles to Mexico City and Lima. In periods of Anglo-Spanish conflict between 1739 and 1762, French producers and exporters prospered in the temporary absence of English and other European competition.

In peacetime, however, English medium-priced woolens and German (chiefly Leipzig) linens competed successfully with higher-priced French products. Until the 1760s, the linens of Brittany and Normandy, the fine woolens of Amiens, Reims, Sedan, and Abbeville, and silks from Nîmes and Lyons still found their largest foreign outlet in the Spanish empire, mainly in its colonies. At least two-thirds of sales to "Spain" were in fact reexported to the colonies and paid for in bullion and readily negotiable pesos (*piastres*) from the Mexico City and Lima mints. One indicator of French textile exports' importance is the high percentage of *ropa,* or cloth (which included ready-made clothing), in the four *flotas* to Veracruz between 1757 and 1769, a percentage fluctuating between 80 and 86 percent of the total cargo by value. At mid-century, woolens and linens constituted "the principal article in foreign trade with Spain." Exports of French cottons were minor, but the late growth of the trade in slaves from West Africa to the French Caribbean islands by way of Nantes induced what became the cotton-printing industry there.[28] As the abbé Béliardi, France's commercial agent at Madrid, reported in 1762, French linens and silks continued to dominate sales at Cadiz, while the English enjoyed clear superiority in woolens. But he underscored the expansion of Silesian linen sales at Cadiz, as well as the skill of English exporters in smuggling woolens such as *bayetas, serges,* and *perpetuanas* directly to the Spanish colonies from Caribbean islands.[29]

In the third phase, between 1770 and 1789, French textile exports to Cadiz failed to grow as rapidly as English and South German ones. In part this may have been because the number of colonial consumers of luxury goods grew slowly, providing at best a narrow base for production requiring economies of scale.[30] However, French silk producers continued to boast of their high-quality fabrics, whose production, they immodestly claimed, had been lifted to the "highest level of perfection," rendering France "the mother of luxury and style for all Europe" and providing an "incalculable commercial advantage."[31] In contrast, English woolen manufacturers continued to concentrate on their lower-priced products, broadening the base of demand and relying upon domestic supplies of high-quality raw wool. Simultaneously, Silesian linen manufacturers tinkered with quality to turn out cheap "counterfeit" French-type linens; between 1740 and 1780 Silesian linens jumped from 25 to 66 percent of Cadiz's reexports of linens to the colonies.

Successive Spanish finance ministers, beginning with Esquilache and continuing with Múzquiz and Lerena, chipped away at the special tariff rates conceded under pressure to English, French, and Dutch textiles in the middle of the seventeenth century. However, French textiles, once dutied at between 5 and 10 percent, were equalized in the eighteenth century with others at a general level of 15–20 percent, undermining the competitive position of French imports. Hence, in 1769–84, Lyons suffered a 16 percent loss of silk weavers, whose numbers fell to 9,200 from 11,000, and a corresponding drop of 28 percent in the value of output, from 46 to 33 million *livres tournois*.[32] There was some truth in Adam Smith's observation that Rouen and Bordeaux aside, "there is little trade or industry in any of the parliament towns of France," substantiated by the lament of France's commercial agent at Madrid in the 1770s that in woolens, "France has lost a prodigious amount" of what it had formerly sold to Spain and its colonies. To be sure, French manufacturers also confronted a serious technical problem: the *sempiternes* of Montpelier and Nîmes, the *bayettes* of the Cevennes and Beauvaisis, and the *serges* of Châlons, Ambois, and Tours lacked the highly desirable softness of English woolens.[33]

The Spanish government soon complemented its equalization of import duties with tariff modifications, setting quotas on reexports to the colonies. The *comercio libre* of 1778, it will be recalled, limited foreign reexports to 33 percent of cargo by value. Spanish economic development policy fixed upon selected luxury products as the focus of proto-industrialization, which weighed heavily upon French products, because "luxury items constitute a large part of French commerce."[34] Brittany, Languedoc, and the Rhône valley soon felt the repercussions, leading to a report to Necker that analyzed the surge in Spain's imports of Silesian and Swiss linens and silks, along with English fabrics, and concluded pessimistically: "If France does not give this serious attention, her manufactures will decline, or at the least lose their outlet in Spain, hitherto France's largest foreign market."[35] Perhaps this was a prediction of, rather than actual loss of, colonial sales, just as reports exaggerated the emigration of skilled French artisans to Spain and Portugal in search of employment. France's foreign trade data for 1715 and 1787 in current *livres tournois* (which do not reflect at least 100 percent inflation) indicate that France's textile imports rose tenfold, while its textile exports increased by only a factor of three. Overall, French industrial output in the late 1780s stagnated.[36]

Against this background, we can examine the performance of the major sectors of French textile manufacturing, woolens and linens, and their export through Cadiz to Spanish colonial markets.

Several factors conditioned the evolution of the French woolen industry in the eighteenth century: the supply, quality, and price of imported raw wool and access to Spanish and especially Spanish American consumers. Until the last third of the seventeenth century, production of French woolens was directed mainly to the domestic market; it was Colbert who reoriented manufacturers to the production of woolens competitive with those of England and Holland. This necessitated select raw wools (not then produced in France) at reasonable prices, since the raw material constituted about 65 percent of the cost of the finished product.[37] Colbert, who hoped to see French manufactures compete with those of Holland, which "exclusively" used Spanish wool, insisted upon merino wool imports from Segovia and León in Spain. The principal raw wool merchants and their warehouses supplying French manufacturers of *draps, serges, cadis,* and *roses* at Carcassonne, Elboeuf, Louviers, Abbeville, Amiens, Aumale, and Sedan were located in southwestern France, close to the Spanish border, at Bayonne, Oléron, Toulouse, and Montauban.[38] Dependence upon Spanish wools, indispensable for upscaling French woolens, continued throughout the eighteenth century. In 1789, raw wool imports still represented 40 percent of total French raw wool consumption, and as late as 1806, a Franco-Spanish consortium of bankers—Martínez de Hervás, the Recamiers, Charles Geyler, Louis Jordan, and Alexandre Barillon—financed imports of Spanish wools in a profitable operation.[39]

As a result of state intervention by Colbert and other bureaucrats who envisioned potential sales overseas in the Spanish colonies, French manufacturers, exporters, and merchant intermediaries resident at Cadiz in the first half of the eighteenth century shifted from woolen goods (*cadis, cordeillets, brevettes, droguets*) to finer fabrics such as *bayettes, sempiternes, perpetuanes,* and *anacostes* —"stuffs of new manufacture."[40] At Abbeville and Reims, producers imitated the English "cloths called *redingots,*" or what the French termed "hunter's cloth"; at Cadiz, French importers marketed the medium and finer fabrics against English competition, which had the advantage of cheaper raw materials and more attractive finish. Elboeuf's finer products sold well at Cadiz in the 1730s, but it was difficult to compete in the medium quality range aimed at low-income consumers, since French producers could not "price their woolens as low as the English." French import houses at Cadiz continued to hope that France might produce woolens to fill the gap between the grades of Elboeuf and Monfors.[41]

What allowed the French to hold on to market share at Cadiz at this time were, first, tariff privileges dating back to the *convenio de Eminente* of the late seventeenth century given to English, Dutch, and French importers at Sevilla, later at Cadiz, and, second, those periods of Anglo-Spanish conflict when Spain could prohibit English imports. During the War of the Austrian Succession, for example, French firms at Cadiz forwarded to French producers "samples of *bayettes* and other English and Dutch woolens of considerable consumption in Spain and the Indies, to have them produce the same quality, to fold and package them the way the English and Dutch do, in order to sell them to Spain and the Indies at the same price." This late-comer's strategy brought annual French woolen exports to Spain and its colonies up to 5–6 million *livres tournois* annually. Almost fifty years later, François Sahuc, a wealthy and influential French entrepreneur at Cadiz, continued to prod French manufacturers to imitate popular lines of English woolens. "Application and care," ran the praise of France's ambassador at Madrid in 1774, "account for the increase in sales at Cadiz and the Indies of Abbeville woolens made by Van Robais." Sahuc claimed credit for persuading Rouen manufacturers to produce a *serge imprimé* sold at Cadiz as *séraphine*.[42]

Sales of French woolens in Spain and its colonies peaked in the 1750s and 1760s. Around 1750, approximately 25 percent (later rising to 36 percent in the 1760s) of the woolen output of the Rouen *généralité*, a major producer of fine goods, was exported via Cadiz to Spanish America; the drop in Elboeuf's output in 1752–53, like its subsequent rise in 1763–67, reflected fluctuating Spanish domestic and colonial demand.[43] However, once English woolens reappeared at prices generally 20 percent below those of France at the end of the Seven Years' War in 1763, they affected production of the *sempiternes* of Montpelier and Nîmes, *bayettes* of the Cévennes and Beauvaisis, and *serges* of Châlons, Ambois, and Tours.[44] In the 1760s, English producers' access to quality wools at relatively lower prices, along with technical efficiencies, pressed Elboeuf's manufacturers to cut corners in order to remain price competitive—with predictable effects.

These were pinpointed in 1768 by Béhic fils, son of a merchant family established over more than six decades at Sevilla and later Cadiz, "entrepôt of the vast trade with Spanish America." Commenting on the quality slippage of Elboeuf's products over the previous six to eight years, he complained "that branch once considerable is now insignificant because of the poor quality of its woolens." In his view, "manufacturers introduced the pernicious method of dyeing woolens by the piece, not the wool." Consequently, "the woolens are poorly dyed; and the rejects that cannot be sold in France, in colors not suited to Spain, are nonetheless redyed and shipped." Worse, on the long sea voyage from Cadiz to Veracruz and other colonial ports, those "redyed woolens are stained because the first color inhibits the proper imprint of the second; they are unsaleable."

Wary Spanish merchants and shippers now examined French goods "with the most scrupulous care" and—since complaints transmitted to French manufacturers had no effect—"their consumption is virtually nil." Béhic fils could only conclude there was "collusion between French inspectors and manufacturers."[45] A decade later, French commercial agents at Madrid reported that French woolen exports to Spain had fallen off "prodigiously," virtually no ordinary French woolens were selling at Cadiz, and even sales of the better qualities were slipping. Moreover, English woolens of quality, superior in "finished appearance" and cheaper, supplied 50 percent of total sales to Spain and its colonies; for example, merchants in New Spain reported in 1788 that "the heavy clothing ordinary women use are English *bays* [i.e., baize] and *sempiternes*." Concurrently, Elboeuf's chamber of commerce confessed that its members could no longer compete effectively in foreign markets against the cheaper grades of English woolens.[46]

French exports to Cadiz and elsewhere in Spain enjoyed a brief wartime reprieve in 1779–83, but sales stagnated or even declined when peace brought a large flow of English woolens targeted at average and low-income consumers. For French manufacturers, exporters and resident merchants at Cadiz, survival in Spain's colonial markets depended upon exports of superfine woolens requiring imported Spanish wools. And even this market niche for luxury goods became precarious as Spain's policy of implementing economic nationalism gradually stripped French and other imports of tariff privileges enjoyed at Cadiz since the late seventeenth century. One French estimate of tariff increases on quality woolens between 1765 and 1787 was 35 percent, and as a result, the best French superfine blue cloth sold one-third higher than the English.[47]

A variety of data point to the crisis of France's traditional woolen manufacture in the closing decades of the century. Production of woolens shows a long-term tendency to decline after 1764, peaking abruptly in 1785 at the highest level of the century, then falling precipitously. The output of the Rouen area, which included Elboeuf, Louviers, and Darnetal, where France's finest woolens were produced for domestic and foreign sales, rose irregularly to a peak in 1787, only to fall below the 1750 level in 1788 and

1789; production probably bottomed out under the Directory and Consulate.[48] Other sources point to a decline in the number of looms devoted to woolens.[49] Caen shifted in the 1760s from short cloths (*petites draperies*) to silks, and Darnetal and Bolbec to cottons, and between 1785 and 1789, Abbeville and Amiens lost 39 percent of their looms. No wonder Abbeville bitterly denounced the Anglo-French commercial treaty of 1786.[50]

The trajectory of France's other major export industry, linen, followed the pattern of woolens. In the first half of the century, there was growth in exports to "Spain" and in the last half an apparent contraction of sales. A striking departure from the pattern, however, was the extraordinary importance of the Spanish colonial market to producers in and around Rouen.

During the eighteenth century, as earlier, linen was widely used by middle and upper income groups in western Europe and America for undergarments, sheeting, tablecloths, curtains, dresses, shirtings, trousers, and even to make varieties of lace.[51] Already in the last decades of the sixteenth century, Breton and Norman linen from Elboeuf and Laval, and Vitry and Pontivy, were a principal item in France's trade with Spain and in its favorable merchandise balance with the Peninsula. "All West France seemed enlivened by the weaver's profession" when Simón Ruíz started out as an importer of Brittany's *toiles* in sixteenth-century Spain. Linen manufacturing continued to be a widespread cottage industry in Brittany and Normandy, whose products became household words—*bretañas, ruanas,* and *pontivíes*—in what French commercial agents called the "vast Spanish outlet." Sizeable shipments of these linens were already reaching Cadiz by 1691, earning average returns of 40 to 50 percent for French intermediaries there.[52] Such was colonial demand at this time that even Chinese exporters shipped linens via Manila across the Pacific to Acapulco, accurately imitating swatches of French and other European linens sent by Mexico City's wholesale merchants.[53] As a result of French cultural and economic influence during and after Louis XIV, French *toiles* enjoyed the advantage of low import duties, perhaps as low as one-third the rate of the competition, at Cadiz under the *convenio de Eminente*. Hence, until well into the eighteenth century, French linen manufacturers could rely upon a high volume of re-exports from Cadiz to Veracruz and other ports in the Spanish empire in America and upon their returns in *piastres*.[54]

Indeed, in certain categories, such as common *toiles,* duck (*coutil*), and especially the fine *blancards* of Elboeuf (often labeled *ruanes* because they were shipped from Rouen), exports marked for "Spain" were remarkably high in volume. For over half a century, between 75 to 94 percent of all Rouen's linen and duck exports to Europe, and fully 94 percent of the finest linens (*blancards*), went to the Iberian Peninsula.[55] This was the era when the leading linen merchants of Brittany and Normandy set up their own *maisons de commerce* at Cadiz, a practice Postlethwayt found "extremely advantageous," because the returns were "generally made in cash"—silver. At Cadiz, French merchant houses found "ways and means to make up their assortments for the Spanish West Indies" in their "Bretagnes and . . . Rouens."[56]

Yet even before the Seven Years' War, and certainly immediately afterward, signs multiplied of strong competition in *bretagnes* and *rouens* from English producers and exporters, and, more significant, from Silesian newcomers.[57] The war, in addition, cost France a number of European markets, magnifying those in Spain and its colonies in the postwar years. In the 1760s, France's assiduous commercial agents Puyabry, at Cadiz, and Béliardi, at Madrid, warned Breton and Norman manufacturers and shippers that their relatively high prices generated a preference in Spanish America for Silesian imitations (*contrefaits*), and that future sales would be gravely affected "if shipping for America were to leave from other Spanish ports where French linens don't enjoy the duty reduction provided only at Cadiz." Evidently, Rouen's *blancard* shipments to "Spain" fell off markedly after the peak postwar years (1763–64) perhaps, as was the case of woolens treated earlier, because Elboeuf's manufacturers lowered the quality of their products to maintain competitive pricing. The French resident merchant Béhic fils reported in 1769 that Spanish exporters at Cadiz were inspecting *blancard* shipments bale by bale and "even bolt by bolt" or were shifting to "Rouens de Silésie et de Hollande." On a recent *flota* to Veracruz, Béhic himself failed to load a single bale of *rouens de France*.[58]

Businessmen are notorious for exaggerating current or future losses, and Béhic fils, it would appear, was no exception. Although they fell off in the 1770s, Rouen's exports of ordinary linen and duck to Cadiz for reexport to the American colonies were still respectable in the years 1770–76. In the late 1770s, French agents could cite the volume of ordinary French linens exported to Spain that helped balance French imports of Spanish soda ash, raw silk, wool, and dyestuffs.[59] Yet this did not belie the danger signs. In 1777, as a stimulant to Catalonia's infant industry, Madrid prohibited further imports of printed linens, which only aroused French agents' suspicions of favoritism, since they reported that 60 percent of printed linens aboard the next *flota* to Veracruz were English rather than Catalan.[60] Moreover, while Rouen's linen exports to "Spain" were falling in the 1770s, Silesian imitations were taking a larger percentage of expanding colonial demand. Whereas Silesian imports furnished about 25 percent of Spanish colonial demand in 1740, according to French estimates, they topped 66 percent four decades later. France's competitive position in linens deteriorated further when Madrid implemented its policy of economic nationalism in the late 1770s by erasing the *convenio de Eminente* and raising duties on all linen imports to 15 percent ad valorem. This virtually tripled import duties on French linen.[61]

This action by the Spanish authorities was followed by new duties on reexports to the colonies stipulated in the *Reglamento del comercio libre* of 1778. Thus a combination of heightened international competition and belated Spanish protectionism produced repercussions in areas such as those supplying Rouen's exporters. Sharply affected among others were Breton and Norman production centers at Saint-Georges-du Vieure, Combourg, Fougères, Morlaix, and Laval. In the early 1780s, Necker learned that among French textile exports linens had declined the most. The "États de Bretagne" fired off complaints about Spain's revised tariff regulations of 1782 to Paris, while other disaffected French groups blamed Spain's finance minister for the "destruction" of French sales to "Spain." Lerena had abolished the *convenio de Eminente,* "such a terrible blow; he raises duties, he is the source of the blows suffered by trade and nation, he shows the most animosity and bad faith."[62] The complainants overlooked a remarkable phenomenon of the early Industrial Revolution: the abrupt and massive shift by consumers from linen to relatively cheaper, but equivalent, cotton fabrics. For a variety of factors, even before the French Revolution, French linen and woolen manufactures were beset by growing structural problems and shifting consumer preferences.[63]

Stagnation is the leitmotiv in the response of French manufacturers and merchants to concessions to English textile manufacturers in the much-debated Anglo-French commercial treaty of 1786. To judge from evidence offered by a member of the Lecouteulx extended family and published in both Rouen and Paris under *Observations de la chambre du commerce de Normandie sur le traité de commerce* (1786), the French textile industry was barely holding its own against English and Silesian competitors and had already lost its leading position in Spain's reexports to its colonies. On the eve of the Revolution, the *Observations* was the portrait, not so much of a triumphant bourgeoisie about to exert its hegemony, as of a segment of the French bourgeoisie that felt betrayed by a government insensitive to its manufacturers and merchants, who were determined for their part to maintain and even expand their position in transatlantic trade, despite possible diplomatic and military repercussions.

As part of the background research for the treaty, its principal architect, the civil servant Dupont de Nemours, almost certainly consulted France's former commercial chargé d'affaires at Madrid (1772–84), Edouard Boyetet, whose diplomatic career, first at St. Petersburg and later in Spain, had made him aware of England's industrial and commercial growth. Boyetet had reservations about making concessions to English products in the French market, and he may have supplied Lecouteulx with data on England's market share in Spain's transatlantic trade. Furthermore, Spanish government officials, who had long balked at commercial treaties with England and France, followed the debate over the treaty closely. For what English manufacturers and exporters obtained from France might foreshadow English demands upon a far less commercially and industrially developed Spain.

Lecouteulx's *Observations* carefully reviewed the condition of Elboeuf's woolen industry along with that of other French manufacturing centers. Elboeuf, he found, lacked a reasonably priced domestic supply of raw wool for the cheaper grades of its woolens. More disturbing to producers at Louviers, Abbeville, and Sedan were the fine woolens of Wiltshire and Gloucestershire, which contained a high proportion of imported Spanish wools. The output of short cloths such as *serges, flanelles, satins, camelots,* and *étamines* from 40–50,000 looms in and around London seriously affected French manufacturers at Darnetal, Aumale, Beauvais, Amiens, Lille, Rheims, and Le Mans. Only when Madrid briefly suspended trade with England during wartime in 1779–82 had Spanish exporters at Cadiz ordered more French goods than usual—orders immediately canceled at the war's end, when English exports were offered at 20 percent below French quotations.[64]

This long-term decline in overseas sales of woolens was matched in linens, that other long-established Breton and Norman textile specialty. Although Lecouteulx omitted references to tampering with quality by woolen manufacturers, he was explicit about Norman linen producers' decision to match Silesian imitations by cutting quality "in order to lower prices." This might be effective in the short run, but in the long run, France would lose linen sales overseas, too, as a result.

The *Observations* underscore English technological breakthroughs in areas where France had experimented least, in cotton spinning, dyeing, and printing. English cottons were, Lecouteulx insisted, "better finished, the result of more even spinning, in short, prettier than ours"; moreover, they were cheap, and soon, he predicted, English manufacturers would reproduce East Indian muslins. In starting up the industry, the English government had provided protection, and now the Manchester countryside poured out ginghams, for which its manufacturers had created an "immense" demand. Meanwhile, the livelihood of an estimated 15,000 French weavers was at stake.

Overall, Rouen's analysis of the situation of the French textile industry in the late 1780s was a worrisome compound of fact and fear. Indisputably, England was technologically ahead in woolens, and far ahead in cottons— "she has developed manufactures to perfection"—threatening French manufacturers, workers, and merchants by invading the French and, most dangerous, the Spanish colonial market. For so brief a pamphlet, the frequent references to Spain and its colonies are revealing: for example, a recent *flota* from Cadiz freighted with over 30,000 bolts of English cotton cloth; English short cloths displacing French products in Spain and Spanish America; Norman linen weavers who, by lowering quality, risked losing "both reputation and sales in the Spanish Indies." These fears were mirrored in the assertion that French workmen, "discouraged, without work or bread," might emigrate to employment in Spain where, the pamphlet claimed, the state was developing an industrial base to supply domestic and colonial demand and to block foreign goods. Only months before the meeting of France's Estates-General in 1789, Rouen's merchants and manufacturers believed, rightly or wrongly, that their government overtaxed merchants, scorned them, along with "any citizen without public office," and consistently failed to seek the opinions of "merchants on all issues related to commerce." No matter that French textile interests knew that Dupont de Nemours, Gérard de Rayneval, and other policy-makers put their faith in the capacity of French entrepreneurs "swiftly to regain superiority in this important industrial sector, the manufacture of cotton goods." They were convinced that French industrial backwardness was the result of too much rather than too little *dirigisme.* Protectionism, responded Dupont de Nemours to Rouen's chamber of commerce apropos of publication of the *Observations,* had stifled innovation and provided incentive to smuggling; it was shameful that "we do not deign to awaken industry and only know how to invoke prohibitions."[65]

More to the point, disaffected French manufacturers and merchants would no longer tolerate a Bourbon regime that seemingly failed to pressure the Spanish Bourbon state to privilege France's trade with Spain's overseas possessions. "Our rights and privileges have been discarded," complained a French merchant at Valencia to Foreign Minister Vergennes in 1787, "and here we live like captives in Barbary, no nation is less respected than ours, and the reason is, the excess of goodwill and indulgence you have shown them."[66]

Comercio Libre and the French Dilemma

French manufacturers and exporters in the 1780s had to accept the fact that the ambience of business at Cadiz had been changing since the halcyon interwar decade of *registros sueltos,* 1745–56. For the cause of their declining position at Cadiz, they turned outward to the Spanish bureaucracy and commercial legislation, and to what they convinced themselves was their own government's diplomatic passivity, its repeated unwillingness to pressure the authorities at Madrid and Cadiz in their defense. The contrasting approaches of the state and the private sector, of French bureaucrats and businessmen, to the defense of French interests in the Spanish empire were fundamentally differences over the meaning of the Family Pact. The French business sector viewed the alliance as confirmation of its commercial rights at Cadiz, but French bureaucrats and some of their Spanish counterparts saw no incompatibility between strengthening the Spanish economy and joint defense against English trade and naval expansionism. For years, success of the Franco-Spanish alliance depended upon two unpredictable factors: could Spanish protectionist policy form a viable industrial base in the short run; second, if not, would Spanish economic policy accept French products to fill the widening gap between colonial demand and peninsular output?

French sensitivity after 1759 to the repercussions of Spanish economic nationalism under Charles III's ministers is understandable, since French businessmen had a large stake to protect. Blocked from direct participation in Spain's colonial trade by statute, French resident merchants employed a variety of mechanisms tolerated (and often shared) by Spanish authorities: direct legal sales to Spaniards registered with the Cadiz *consulado* for the colonial trade and the illegal dispatch of goods under the names of Spaniards collaborating as straw men (*prestanombres*).[67]

There was a third mechanism widely used after 1745, when French speculators invested wartime profits in Cadiz's highly profitable colonial trade, an "international mobilization of often large credit." Capital came from investors at Saint-Malo, Laval, Paris, Lyons, Orléans, Bayonne, Carcassonne, and Perpignan for speculation at Cadiz by prominent firms such as Lecouteulx, Lenormand et Cie., and Jolif, Magon, Lefer et Cie.[68] These lent to Spanish exporters on the security of ships and cargo in the form of sea loans (*à la grosse*), which promised attractive returns varying from 30 to 40 percent or higher; repayment was contingent, however, only on successful completion of the venture, hence the high rate of return.[69] Although repayment often included colonial dyes required for the textile industry, along with other staples, the French and their Spanish collaborators were mainly interested in bullion and specie earnings. In the decade after 1745, French merchants forwarded cargoes on *registros sueltos,* but they preferred the more controlled system of escorted convoys, the *flotas.* Consequently, they backed Spaniards at Cadiz and Mexico City who argued in the mid 1750s for the resumption of *flotas* to New Spain and speculated heavily on successive *flotas* to Veracruz.[70]

At mid-century, French merchants and consuls at Cadiz and commercial agents at Madrid had a solid grasp of demand in the Spanish colonies, the potential there for diversification from silver into other exports, and the state of the Spanish metropolitan economy, which visibly lagged behind England and France in manufacturing. Through observation, analysis of commercial data obtained from Cadiz customs personnel, and discussions with members of the leading French Huguenot firm at Cadiz, Cayla, Solier, Cabanes et Jugla, the abbé Raynal demonstrated the quality of French commercial intelligence around mid-century.[71] Like other French observers, he noted the American colonies' high propensity to import, which development of new colonial exportables and liberalization of commercial policy might increase significantly.

There was, however, a downside to this optimistic economic scenario. Colonial exports and population growth would, French observers forecast, far outstrip Spain's manufacturing capacity, certainly for the foreseeable future. In 1759, however, French commercial interests still felt well positioned to supply that demand. The *convenio de Eminente* privileged French linens over those of Silesian and Swiss competitors, and French merchants and shipping were still protected against searches in the absence of the French consul at Cadiz. Litigation involving French citizens was still settled in Spanish military rather than civil or commercial courts, and French business papers disclosing partners, assets, working capital, profits, and inventories, as well as the firms' journals and correspondence, were safe from government inspection. Already shielded by the Utrecht treaties that had confirmed the privileges of extraterritoriality conferred upon subjects of England, Holland, and France in the seventeenth century, French businessmen felt even more protected by the Family Pact of 1761. "Protected by the treaties, these nations have continued to do business in Spain and to supply most of their requirements."[72]

Realistically, were there grounds for complacency? Although French observers invested the alliance with the "spirit" of improving Franco-Spanish trade in Europe, the family alliance made no reference to equal participation in Spain's colonial trade, despite tacit recognition that "the French invest large sums there in operations under the name of Spaniards." In addition, Spanish bureaucrats left no doubt that ultimately they would try to modify the terms of the pact, to "break with and abolish burdensome treaties," on the grounds that they were bottlenecks for Spanish trade and manufacture.[73] Since the outset of Charles III's reign (and even earlier), Spaniards and Frenchmen had had divergent economic goals, and the result was a dialogue of the deaf on trade policy.

An unexpected finding confirmed Madrid's pursuit of a policy of economic nationalism: Spanish straw men at Cadiz were emancipating themselves from dependence on French merchants and competing with their former creditors.[74] The locus of influence of Cadiz merchants remained the Cadiz *consulado,* linked through the Casa de Contratación and its president (who was also the governor of Cadiz) to the Consejo de Indias in Madrid. Spanish entrepreneurs in both trade and agriculture now supported a policy of economic development. The core problem for French export interests was that the Spaniards wanted a total rather than shared monopoly of the colonial trading system.

Between 1765 and 1778, Madrid put into effect nationalist measures that were seen by the French as threatening, although they remained optimistic about retaining a stake in Spain's colonial trade and continued to invest in goods and credits on *flotas* to Veracruz. A statute of 1769, for example, aimed to eliminate indirect channels of foreign investment in the colonial trade by requiring customs officials in colonial ports to sequester any cargo found registered or consigned by foreign merchants at Cadiz on arrival; those considered non-national traders included Spanish-born sons (*genízaros*) of foreign fathers and Spanish mothers, whom many Spanish merchants considered natural straw men for foreign competitors.[75] The statute's intent was evident: to disrupt indirect involvement of the French in the *flota* system to New Spain and force foreigners instead to depend upon Spanish intermediaries. Fortunately for the French, their commercial agents detected a split in the Spanish ministry over this issue; Prime Minister Grimaldi and Colonial Secretary Arriaga opposed the measure, while Múzquiz, Esquilache's successor as secretary of the Hacienda, supported it. When the French protested, the measure was not enforced.[76]

More vexing was an order of 1767 pushed by Cadiz merchants to oblige all merchant houses at Cadiz to register their firms' charters with a notary and provide a copy to the Cadiz *consulado.* Insisting on transparency in capital, assets and liabilities, partners and associates, procurement patterns, earnings, and profits would reveal vital commercial data and business strategies to Spanish competitors.[77] Following strong representation from the French consul at Cadiz, this measure was also suspended, but, like the statute of 1769, not cancelled. It was revived in 1775 on Charles III's recommendation, but again suspended. Compromise was achieved under the new colonial secretary, Gálvez, who softened the impact of the registry by making it applicable only to newly established foreign firms.[78]

France's success in forestalling such nationalistic measures and optimism about the fate of its stake in Spanish colonial markets reflected a harsh reality: Spain's imperative need to support the Family Pact, on the one hand, and its inability to build a diversified economy to match growing colonial consumer demand, on the other. Over decades, a variety of stimuli had failed to produce goods marketable in Spain and the American colonies that were competitive in quality and price. Nonetheless, with the appointment of Floridablanca as prime minister and, in 1776, of Gálvez as his colonial secretary, a developmentalist strategy was pursued, mainly in the economic sector that had shown the most growth potential, the colonial trade concentrated at Cadiz.

When Floridablanca's ministry proceeded with the Reglamento of 1778, French commercial agents assumed that "liberalization" of the Spanish colonial trading system might open up unparalleled opportunities for expanded exchanges ("this navigation will triple shortly") between the metropole and the American colonies, and for increased silver flows to Europe.[79] In the spirit of the Family Pact, France's diplomatic representatives stationed in Spain reasoned that French producers and exporters of traditional manufactures might expect to provide a growing share of Spain's expanding colonial demand. Their logic dictated a Spanish colonial trade policy blending measured nationalism with the commercial collaboration of the French ally. But logic and raison d'état are not usually synonymous.

Instead, Spanish policy between 1778 and 1782 seemed to fall most heavily upon French interests at Cadiz and elsewhere in Spain, as if designed to undermine them, at a time when France (later joined by Spain) was financially and militarily supporting the American Revolution. In Spain's Reglamento of 1778, the French found that former customs procedures were dropped; now goods were dutied by value rather than volume, which translated into higher effective rates on high-quality goods. There was a flat 15 percent import duty, another 7 percent on reexports to the colonies, and a further 7 percent on entering colonial ports; the statute also included a long list of prohibited goods, many of French provenance. More radical, the time-honored specific arrangements of the *convenio de Eminente* were unilaterally eliminated. No longer were French linen exports to the Spanish colonies ("the largest segment of our exports to Spain") privileged over those of Silesia and other European competitors; and this was confirmed in the general tariff revision of 1782 (the 1778 statute affected only Spain's colonial trade; the tariff reform of 1782 made customs practices uniform at all peninsular ports).[80]

The thrust of Floridablanca's colonial trade policy changes in 1778 and

1782 was unequivocal: Madrid aimed to remove tariff exemptions, augment income from customs, set up protectionist barriers, and—a key objective—lessen incentives for the worrisome increase in smuggled goods moving from English Caribbean ports into Spanish commercial centers at Havana, Veracruz, Cartagena, and La Guayra. Hoping against hope, France's Madrid agent Boyetet found positive elements in Gálvez's role, since his "main goal was suppression of smuggling and forcing all nations to participate in this commerce via the channel of Spain." With this goal, French officials and businessmen had no quarrel, even trusting that the 1778 Reglamento might open "the largest outlets for all the foreign manufactories positioned to supply Spain."[81]

Edouard Boyetet's Guarded Optimism

For a balanced assessment of the short- and long-term implications of Floridablanca's colonial trade policy for French manufacturers and exporters, we have two analyses by Edouard Boyetet, well regarded for "long experience in trade affairs" as commercial agent at Madrid from 1772 to 1784.[82] In December 1778, he drafted a brief report, followed in September 1779 by a far more comprehensive one for Foreign Secretary Vergennes.[83] Both reports gave high priority to commercial issues, and to this end he had established "close relations with several Spanish ministers" including a key cabinet officer (and former lawyer for the French embassy), Colonial Secretary Gálvez.[84] A "feel" for Spain and even a degree of empathy, as well as contact with key Madrid officials and a grasp of their attitudes, bureaucratic structures, and decision-making patterns, rendered Boyetet an effective, perceptive defender of French economic interests and the diplomatic axis linking French business to Spain's colonial economy.[85]

Only weeks after publication of the 1778 Reglamento, Boyetet drafted a preliminary evaluation of what he soon termed with some hyperbole Spain's "nouvelle révolution." Like some of his predecessors at the Madrid embassy, he believed that trade liberalization might open a market of eleven million colonial consumers—"a vast outlet for every agricultural and industrial product of Europe"—adding that this had not escaped Colonial Secretary Gálvez; rather, it shaped his policy. Spanish nationalists with whom he was in contact, he confided, fantasized about Spain's imminent economic self-sufficiency, convinced that they might "shatter and shake loose from any and all understandings with friends and foes." Boyetet foresaw pitfalls in Spain's go-it-alone economic policy, however. If Spanish manufacturers failed to produce goods acceptable to colonial consumers, the latter might opt for the "power of any other country." Furthermore, whatever the outcome of the bitter struggle then going on between England and the North American insurgents, he predicted that a "formidable et très redoubtable" England would soon scheme to "invade the trade" of the Spanish colonies.[86] To assist in protecting its American possessions, Spain could count on only one ally, France; however, Spain's policy of excluding non-Spanish participation in its colonial commerce was hardly "the way to invite participation, rather it strips Spain of the advantages that render our union useful." Here, in a nutshell, was the dilemma: how to preserve France's overseas markets while not antagonizing Spanish nationalists. French merchants readily interpreted this attempt at balance as privileging the interests of *haute finance* over those of manufacturing.

Nine months later, Boyetet fleshed out these and other issues in an extended synthesis of his previous reports for Vergennes with disturbed and confused complaints filed by French firms at Cadiz about the Spanish government's intervention in their affairs.[87] Boyetet's second report combined realism and utopianism, trying to reconcile what Vergennes probably found irreconcilable: economic cooperation between two economies in unequal phases of development.

Boyetet was empathetic toward nationalist Spanish officials who considered the commercial treaties of the seventeenth century a "very humiliating yoke." His Spanish contacts were committed to achieving "the independence enjoyed by other nations who reject such treaties." Over eight decades of Bourbon administration, the Spanish economy had evolved, he concluded, from a "total state of demise," obliged to import many of its necessities, to a condition in which it was possible to reduce such external dependence. Economic nationalism might have been pursued more vigorously had there been no obstructive tactics by Cadiz merchants ("ever inimical to any changes"), and had Spanish authorities not feared English retaliation. Now that the English were embroiled in a colonial war, he felt, Madrid's officials were awaiting the moment when such retaliation would be minimal in order to accelerate their policy. Pursued without due nuance, however, Spanish economic nationalism might backfire; isolating foreigners from direct or indirect participation in colonial trade at Cadiz, for example, could disadvantage French interests at a time when Spain was collaborating with France to support the insurgents in North America. Still, in Boyetet's prism, the xenophobic policy was neither ostensibly nor necessarily francophobic, although he granted that many Spaniards would relish anti-French policies.

Rather than viewing Spain's mercantilist policies as the brainchild of a small interministerial group, Boyetet discerned a new phenomenon, a "widespread ferment" in support of mercantilist policies, with two negative consequences for French exporters. First, such policies might include outright prohibition of specific imports being reexported to the colonies, such as "printed cloth, ribbons, [and] all sorts of knitted woolens," with the aim, he thought, of protecting nascent Catalan manufacturing. Second, foreign businessmen in Spain confronted "antipathy and jealousy," which tended to focus on the many "more active and hardworking" French nationals who dealt in luxury goods in Spanish ports, making them especially visible ("plus frapants" [*sic*]). Boyetet, who covered Gálvez's operations attentively, recognized the colonial secretary's commitment to a "system of freedom that should make Spain wealthy and powerful." Gálvez's commitment to the 1778 Reglamento was designed, Boyetet judged, to afford at least a 30 percent level of protection for domestic manufactures exported to the colonies and to minimize the dominant presence of foreign merchants in Spain's colonial trade.

On the surface, Boyetet tolerated Spanish economic nationalism, conceding that in the late mercantilist spirit of the time, "each nation seeks to make the most of its position and advantages and achieve self-sufficiency." Yet, toleration aside, as a French civil servant, he could not bear to have the products of Spain's closest ally, France, more disadvantaged by Spain's developmental policy than those of their mutual antagonist, England. Not only did the recent Reglamento raise duties on linens, France's principal export to Cadiz for reexport, it specifically excluded other French exports, such as half-beaver hats (a specialty of Paris, Lyons, and Marseilles) and, in particular, Nîmes' silk stockings, worth at least two million *livres tournois* annually and expressly designed for Peruvian consumers. On the other hand, most medium- and low-priced English woolens (*draps, bayètes, serges*), which Boyetet claimed clothed "more than half the common women in Spain and its Indies," could better support the high duties now levied on principal cost rather than volume.

Overall, Boyetet's assessment of the impact of Spain's economic growth policy on French exports was tempered with optimism. He had no illusions about economic development under Charles III's ministers. Spain's industrial achievements, he judged, "have fallen far short of what they might have been, because finding no resources in a nation that was poor, uninformed, and inactive, instead of seeking remedies, they have only thought of exclusive privileges, chartered companies, and manufactories on royal account"— all exemplifying failed state intervention. The Spanish government recognized its shortcomings but "left matters alone without further attention." So, despite reworked tariff rates and a few outright prohibitions, government-subsidized Valencian silks and Guadalajara woolens were (and would continue to be) uncompetitive in terms of quality with the silks of Lyons and Nîmes or the woolens of Elboeuf, Abbeville, and Sedan. At Valencia, he pointed out, Madrid had intervened by importing skilled French workers, along with Vaucanson and Piedmontese looms. But poor plant management, overregulation, and disgruntled immigrant workers produced silks lacking the "perfection of Lyons textiles."

In the second place, behind the 1778 Reglamento, he detected grounds of optimism for beleaguered French interests. To reduce smuggling by English merchants from Caribbean ports, Gálvez and his fellow civil servants would be willing to tolerate a low level of non-Spanish exports to the colonies. They might even be satisfied if peninsular producers supplied just one-third of aggregate domestic and colonial demand, allowing French merchandise to fill the gap that Spain could not, "given the extensive outlets in the Indies." A final source of Boyetet's optimism was what he judged the major structural weakness in Spanish economic development: the fact that Spanish traders at Cadiz still relied upon the "fonds considérables" of foreigners (mainly French) and their long-term credits—practices tolerated of necessity by the Spanish state. As Boyetet commented dryly, "Were it possible to prevent the French from offering Spaniards long-term credit, they would very soon find how far they are from carrying on this commerce without their help."

These observations undergirded Boyetet's conclusion that Franco-Hispanic economic relations would remain complementary rather than confrontational. Both nations had to compromise certain national interests to abort a dangerous "guerre intestine." Effective collaboration, Boyetet insisted, depended upon containing Finance Minister Múzquiz, who showed no interest in implementing the economic articles of the Family Pact, and the short-sighted individuals among "the juntas, corporative organizations, and all those advice-givers" who lacked "vision." Compromise required free trade between Spain and France in virtually all products (he conceded that French policy had systematically blocked importation of many Spanish products), and on Spain's part, total suspension of commercial contacts with England.[88] Spain, Boyetet recommended, should no longer serve as the "immense market" for English industrial goods and the "greatest source" of England's wealth. His policy recommendations, he concluded, were dictated by "reason and reciprocity." Decades later, similar reasoning and notions of reciprocity would blossom into Hauterive's federative system and Bonaparte's Berlin decree severing Spain's and the European continent's trade with England.

Pessimism and Realism

Boyetet's alloyed optimism was rooted in faith that somehow Hispano-French military and naval cooperation beginning in 1779 during the war against England might soften Spain's mercantilist policies, and that Madrid might extend the military alliance into the commercial cooperation foreshadowed in the Family Pact. Boyetet's optimism proved transitory, however, and was soon counterbalanced by his own and others' pessimism. Sometime between 1780 and 1783, a reasoned French analysis appeared that was colored by profound disillusionment, even despair over the direction and ultimate effects of Spain's delayed policy of economic development.[89]

That policy prompted an anonymous nationalist French agent to predict, unlike Boyetet, the imminent "total collapse" of French commercial activity at Cadiz and elsewhere in the Iberian Peninsula, a prediction grounded neither in exaggerated suspicion nor fear, but in "unquestionable facts that cannot be interpreted otherwise." He found petty officials at Madrid and Cadiz engaged in "every kind of underhanded activity" directed against French merchandise, shipping, and the special military courts where cases involving French citizens were tried. He complained about the list of prohibited trade goods, excessively high duties on others, inflated official values on which duties were computed, and the confrontational attitude and "injustice . . . vexation . . . and meanness" of petty customs and revenue officers at Cadiz to French residents. Although Spanish customs officers were insisting that the new import duties did not surpass 15 percent, given unjustifiably inflated base prices, the effective import rates now averaged over 25 percent. Inexorably, French merchants and goods in Spain's colonial trade were losing the privileged treatment guaranteed by treaty. The agent reported that Hacienda Secretary Múzquiz had told the administrator of Cadiz's customs that "the French could not ask for more privileges than the Spaniards." Since the French "cannot survive without privileges," their withdrawal would force the French either to abandon Spain or become Spanish nationals. Most would choose to remain, opined the agent, and here notions of French ethnic superiority erupted. Inevitably, the children of Frenchmen accepting Spanish nationality would fall victim of the "widespread inertia of that nation" and represent a loss to France, since "we must never expect from them or the Spaniards either interest or vigor" in marketing French agricultural and industrial products.

Particularly disturbing were the disappointing results of what had promised to tighten the bonds uniting France and Spain, the Franco-Hispanic Bourbon Family Pact. Now, at a moment of special "union intime" in wartime, Spanish officials had chosen instead to pressure French interests, to "strip the French of all advantages granted by treaties and this pact." Shipping between France and Cadiz and other peninsular ports no longer enjoyed preferential treatment, and French grain ships could no longer participate in Spain's coastal traffic. French linens had been stripped of the benefits of Eminente's *convenio,* a gratuitous action since it was well known that Spain had virtually no linen industry to protect. And by way of a final example of harassment, there was the imminent loss of legal protection for French nationals against unwarranted governmental prosecution by carrying their cases to Spain's military courts, for generations the "baze [*sic*] de l'existence du commerce de la France." There, French interests had been shielded from the "excesses of tax collectors" and unauthorized search without the presence of the French consul.[90]

Boyetet's view in 1779 implied but did not fully develop the contradiction between the public rigor of Spain's developmental legislation and its implementation by Madrid, along with the informal verbal concessions offered by Spanish officials on French products that compensated for the shortcomings of Spanish manufactures in colonial commerce. Boyetet's optimism blurred his perceptions. Was he convinced that more than Spanish legislation was at issue, and that some of the blame fell upon French manufacturers who preferred special treatment to efficiency and competitiveness? On the other hand, citing Prime Minister Floridablanca on the need to confine colonial trade only to Spanish and French hands, the anonymous critical report made explicit the dilemma that Boyetet sensed, and that was turning acute in the decade before the French Revolution, asking: "Is Spain in a condition to be self-sufficient and to dispense with foreign aid?" And most important, "Have the interests of its people and finances become incompatible with agreements made with France about commerce? Do they foretell their total destruction?"

Taken together, Madrid's unexpected activism in colonial commercial policy in the decade after 1778 represented the high point of delayed developmentalism under Charles III's ministers, especially under Prime Minister Floridablanca. Success seemed assured by several developments: an upsurge in colonial trade after 1783 and the remission to Cadiz and other peninsular ports of earnings retained in the colonies during the war;[91] a rise in reexports to the colonies as Spanish and non-Spanish merchants alike sensed a sustained demand fueled by colonial economic growth;[92] legislation transferring litigation involving French nationals from military to civil and commercial courts; closer watch over foreign shipping in the harbor of Cadiz, where smuggling was endemic; and outright exclusion of non-Spanish woolens from the colonial trade in 1788.[93] Mercantilism applied to colonial commerce seemed to some Spanish optimists to have produced tangible results. Now a kind of euphoria flourished in certain Spanish government circles, buoyed by a mix of protectionist measures formulated to secure effective domination of the colonial trade for Spanish manufacturers and merchants and revenues and profits in the form of colonial silver.

There was also a more down-to-earth perception of the situation in the 1780s. The perspective of French businessmen at Cadiz was based upon two facets of colonial trade: the composition of exports to the colonies and the corruptibility of Cadiz customs inspectors. No matter the statistics published by Madrid, a high percentage of exports to the colonies were in fact not "national" but reexported goods, many of French provenance. French merchants hoped their merchandise would continue to excel Spanish workshops' small output of woolens, linens, and silks. Despite subsidies from the Spanish state, French merchants remained convinced that the volume and quality of Spanish textiles would not, and in the immediate future certainly could not, cover the shortfall between colonial demand and metropolitan output.

Second, long experience at Cadiz had taught French businessmen how to circumvent Spanish economic nationalism by co-opting customs officials at Cadiz. Over decades of trading there, French merchant firms had established channels bypassing trade regulations. The major channel involved exporting colonial coin and bullion. The magnet of profit was irresistible, and the risks of detection were low. "Smuggling money always yields 6 percent profit." Although silver was registered at Spanish ports of entry, it moved risk-free through illicit channels up to the French border. In the late 1780s, perhaps 50 to 60 million *livres tournois* moved from Spain into France.[94] For their part, shippers at colonial ports like Veracruz collaborated by submitting inaccurate manifests, reducing the value or totally omitting any record of silver cargo. And much colonial silver simply escaped registry at the Cadiz customs.[95] Often silver was transshipped at sea when vessels from Veracruz and other colonial ports rendezvoused with French ships off the Spanish coast; sometimes it was transshipped inside the Bay of Cadiz just before a merchant vessel cleared for France, or put aboard French warships conveniently calling at Cadiz.[96]

Recognizing the sensitivity of Spanish authorities to evasion of colonial silver, English and French official trade statistics simply omitted details of the movement of precious metals. At Cadiz, to be sure, the Spanish authorities remained suspicious of the source of silver pesos and ingots that certain large, well-established French merchant firms delivered to outbound vessels of the French East India Company, and of French warships suspiciously delaying departure. Repeatedly, French and other European vessels were impounded with cargoes of illicit silver, and shipwrecks near Cadiz often turned up equally illicit cargoes of precious metals.[97]

Both the upward revision of export duties in the Reglamento of 1778 and prohibitions and duties imposed on imports of European manufactures in the tariff of 1782 brought an upsurge of smuggling in the mid 1780s. Measures to enforce the prohibited list or collect duties in full were ineffective given the collusion of business and bureaucracy. Shipmasters and French consignees at Cadiz, with the cooperation of customs agents who customarily boarded incoming vessels, arranged for secret off-loading of prohibited silks and woolens and falsified bills of lading. A French representative at Cadiz was candid: French merchants "conspire with ship captains who carefully avoid mentioning prohibited goods when presenting cargo manifests. Consignees, colluding with captains and even the customs guards who board ships on their arrival here, find ways to remove various prohibited items, and to steal the shipping bill from the customs agents." Shipmasters' collaboration was profitable: they received double the going freight costs of the concealed cargo.[98]

Other strategies facilitated the introduction of legal goods but evaded full duties. Since bills of lading generally lacked full data on bales when consigned to an anonymous "bearer" who claimed them on arrival, shippers undervalued them by 50 to 75 percent; to block action against a defrauding consignee, manifests omitted his name ("he is merely designated as the bearer of the shipping bill").[99] Sometimes this tactic failed: customs agents stopped and searched a shipmaster on entering Cadiz and discovered in his possession an order to deliver to the " bearer" five trunks of prohibited silk stockings omitted from his manifest.[100] In handling silk stockings from Nîmes, there was another technique. The smuggled hosiery was delivered to silk "manufacturers" at Cadiz, who then affixed their seals on it as a "national" product that could legally be exported to the colonies. As a result, Peru's upper-class women "will make much of this ridiculous, old-fashioned stocking [from Nîmes]."[101] (Europeans selling in colonial markets did not have to admire their customers' tastes.) For French merchant houses at Cadiz, it was always possible, moreover, "through close relations with customs people" to avoid duties by paying customs inspectors small sums per bale or box. Taking advantage of this arrangement in 1786, the French simply increased the contents of each bale or box.

Of course, French and other foreign firms at Cadiz accepted the risks and advantages of operating in the parallel economy of "énorme contreband," taking advantage of "greed and pillaging of the king's duties at the hands of customs employees." Efforts by Madrid to suppress corrupt practices proved fruitless; smuggling, it was reported in 1786, "is carried on with a bravado unheard of even among Spaniards, and by channels so protected that under a show of rigor, the king of Spain does not collect even half the duties owed."[102] The extent of collusion between the customs bureaucracy and Spanish and foreign businessmen at Cadiz ("this . . . treacherous bay, the port where infidelity dominates, where no one fears God or king"), induced Finance Minister Lerena in 1785 to order Mesía's three-year-long investigation of the customs, with special attention to "foreign goods sold in America as Spanish under the spurious trademarks of Barcelona and Valencia."[103]

Guided by this pragmatic appraisal, many French commercial agents and consular officers continued optimistically during the 1780s to envision a role for French products in reexports to the Spanish colonies in America and especially to New Spain's expanding market. They appraised Spain's colonial trade policy as fundamentally pseudomercantilism, in form developmentalist and nationalist, in practice a strategy encouraging corruption by businessmen and bureaucrats.[104]

Spanish statesmen committed to the economic development of their country—first Esquilache, Grimaldi, and Múzquiz, then Floridablanca, Campomanes, Gálvez, and Lerena—had to walk a tightrope between espousing Spanish state and private interests and mollifying French diplomats and interests.[105] To be successful, the policy of maintaining a national monopoly over colonial trade demanded ambiguity, which inevitably begat misunderstanding. France's commercial agent Béliardi once alluded to such ambiguity when commenting that while Finance Secretary Múzquiz believed that the prosperity of France and Spain depended on their unity, as a "prudent" bureaucrat, he could not "compromise himself under these circumstances."[106] Floridablanca was probably sincere when he postulated an ideal Hispano-French relationship in which both would be able to "concentrate all those commercial advantages their position made possible." More realistically, both Múzquiz and Floridablanca wanted interdependent collaboration to achieve a more self-sufficient Spain; equally realistic, the French banked on Spain's permanent dependence upon France.[107]

French diplomatic reporting from Madrid indicates that the complaints of French businessmen about the nationalistic policies and harassing tactics of the Spanish bureaucracy and businessmen, especially but not exclusively at Cadiz, were faithfully transmitted to Paris. Whether in fact the French authorities remonstrated forcefully with their Spanish counterparts remains moot. The French government in the 1780s could hardly risk pressuring

Madrid forcefully lest Spanish authorities weaken the Bourbon alliance by opting for closer ties with England.[108] More significant, Paris could not afford to antagonize Madrid and thereby imperil massive imports from northern Spain into France of colonial silver critical to the French money supply and the private banks then making Paris a major European financial center. Their political weight was evident; witness the comment of Jean-François Bourgoing in 1795, who had spent eight years in the French embassy at Madrid: "No longer do we have those financial groups whose greedy calculations and shortsightedness hampered the former government."[109] French merchant bankers along with the "large commercial firms established in Spain" had drawn "every bit of interest our former government could conserve in its commercial relations with Spain." Given the profitability of smuggling silver at Cadiz and elsewhere in Spain, as well as French investors in the Banco de San Carlos and other Spanish enterprises, French government officials cooperated with Paris bankers who, fearful of losing the "privileges and franchises, reserved for their firms, which were sometimes criticized, kept a culpable silence."[110]

There was, however, a downside to this informal policy. A respectable body of petty French tradesmen (*voyageurs, pacotilleurs, portes-balles*) were convinced that their government left them "abandoned and defenseless."[111] Justified or not, these were the perceptions of French merchants in Spain like Jacob Lenurb, who wrote to Vergennes in 1787 that "we need a clear-headed, solid consul-general at Madrid who knows how to defend our rights," and who would forward their complaints to Paris. France's diplomatic representatives, he complained, had been too willing to cooperate with Madrid. Then, denouncing a recent decision by the Spanish government to raise import duties on French woolens, he concluded his jeremiad with "All this makes clear their intention to crush the commerce of your subjects and, if Your Highness does not defend it, it will disappear forever!"[112] There was a conspiracy to deliver the wealth of France to foreign countries and its "natural enemies," Nantes's chamber of commerce charged.[113]

The French old regime seems to have operated on the premise that fear of English economic and naval aggression would keep Spain within France's orbit and preserve France's stake in "a part of the riches of all the nations of Europe, those of Spain, Mexico, and Peru."[114] And although they understood why Spanish nationalists in public and private sectors wanted a proto-industrial policy, France's leaders invariably reckoned on its ultimate failure.[115] In any event, French agents predicted privately that Spain's industrial development would lag, and that "the needs of Spain and its industry will continue for a long time to keep it tributary to foreign industry."[116] Here was the opportunity for French manufacturers and export merchants, since demand for French woolens and linens was, as J.-A.-C. Chaptal later observed, "stronger in Spain and its overseas possessions than in France itself." There remained the ultimate weapon, too: in response to seemingly inflexible Spanish protectionist policy, the French government might "par degrés" limit cooperation in preserving Spain's possessions in America.[117]

While French manufacturers, exporters, and merchants at Cadiz chafed over the immediate impact of Spain's nationalist legislation, France's high public officials had to confine themselves to formal remonstrances via diplomatic channels. When the Spanish government mounted a strong protectionist campaign after 1782 that affected French products, French diplomats believed they detected the real target: "There is no reason to doubt," commented the marquis de Castries, "that Spain's ministers envisage England as the primary threat to the commerce and industry of this nation, and France as a secondary one."[118] Hence Boyetet at Madrid recommended joint Franco-Spanish economic cooperation to counter England's challenge in the 1780s. Spaniards' self-interest, he felt, would lead to the recognition that French interests could be satisfied as long as the Spanish government "assures us of that share of goods and labor that the production of its nascent industry will not satisfy."[119]

What French agents at Cadiz and Madrid overlooked in the 1780s was the chasm yawning between France's high finance bourgeoisie and dissatisfied commercial and industrial bourgeois.[120] The two social groups had divergent aims in participating in Spain's transatlantic system. No wonder that the French commercial community at Cadiz, along with manufacturers and exporters at home, would complain in the 1790s that the old regime had failed to support them, that "for a long time our ambassadors have abandoned us to pursue their own interests at the Spanish Court," that French trade with Spain had "absolutely collapsed," and that the fate of "ruined families weighed on the events of our revolution."[121]

French commercial agents and bureaucrats, like their Spanish counterparts, failed (or did not want) to realize that by the last third of the eighteenth century, both the Spanish and French versions of the mercantilist growth paradigm were becoming inoperable. Spain remained hostage to a bullionist policy, while the French vision of the international economy remained mercantilist. From mid-century onward, French commercial representatives continued to think in terms of a constant, rather than an expanding, world market, and imagined that France along with the less-developed economies of the southern tier of western Europe—Spain, Portugal, and Italy—might form an economic bloc to limit commercial relations with

England. They pressed this view repeatedly on Spanish bureaucrats, who remained unconvinced. What few wished to recognize, at least as revealed in the French correspondence examined here, was that England's industrial development would generate products whose price and quality would permit them to penetrate any and all protectionist barriers, and that the greater Spain's intervention to enforce late protectionist legislation, the greater the metastasis of smuggling. With the old order coming to an end, and the new already in sight, many in Spain and France refused to believe what was happening; for traditionalists, the past was the preferred guide to the future.

There were, finally, unintended consequences of Spain's late economic nationalism. It contributed to the crisis of the old regime in France by alienating manufacturers in traditional industrial sectors and associated export merchants from the Bourbon state, which seemed to subordinate their interests to those of high finance. For them, foreign trade was the most dynamic factor of France's economy in the eighteenth century.[122] Once freed from the decorum of the Bourbon Family Pact and strengthened politically (if not economically) by their Revolution, the French would attempt to reestablish their lost dominance in Spain's colonial trade.

11. Euphoria and Pessimism

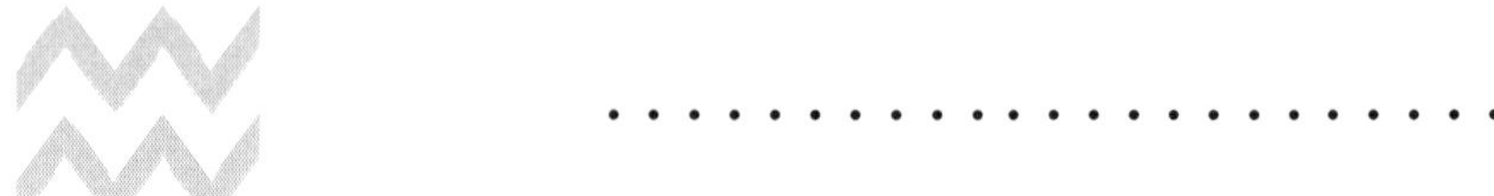

Do you think any cultivated nation does not know of our current situation. . . . ?
Julián Marías, *La España posible en tiempos de Carlos III*

. . . the fables that denigrated our past and that by virtue of monotonous repetition created an inferiority complex among Spaniards.
Felipe Ruiz Martín, *Las finanzas de la monarquía española en tiempos de Felipe IV*

The closing years of Charles III's long reign were a time of stocktaking, drawing up a balance sheet of what Spain's political class and leading policymakers had managed to achieve. Charles's life (1716–88) spanned most of the first century of the Spanish Bourbon dynasty, which many hoped would bestir both the metropole and its American colonies from the stagnation of the later reigns of the Spanish Hapsburgs. For many in the state apparatus, among them Campillo and Ensenada under Philip V and Fernando VI, and Esquilache and Floridablanca under Charles III, it was imperative to find a way to dispel the psychology of national inferiority with respect to Spain's government, economy, Roman Catholic establishment, and society as a whole, expressed by seventeenth-century *arbitristas* and later *proyectistas*. Matching the patent progress of England, Holland, and France by revitalizing peninsular and colonial institutions was one way, and it was hoped that Spanish Bourbon achievements might ultimately earn the recognition, even the respect, of the "model" European states.

After 1777, under Floridablanca, long-desired developments began to materialize: limitation of Cadiz's monopolization of the Spanish transatlantic trading system; large-scale investment in major public works projects in the Peninsula, including canals in Aragon and Castilla's Tierra de Campos; the establishment of a national bank and the issuing of treasury notes to shore up government finances and bring under control the troublesome reexport of American silver from Spain to the rest of Europe; and the revival of the Suprema Junta de Estado to coordinate decentralized, overlapping ministries and conciliar bodies, where "every minister considers himself absolute master over his department."[1] In international affairs, Spain helped France support the successful struggle of the colonists of British North America to form an independent republic. At last, it seemed, Spain had begun to share characteristics of "enlightened" and "absolutist" Europe.

On the other hand, some Spaniards remained troubled by the way the thought-control arm of the Catholic church, the Inquisition, was allowed to humble admired figures like the *asistente de Sevilla,* Peruvian-born Pablo de Olavide, and by the predictable reaction in France and elsewhere in Europe to the handling of this enlightened and cosmopolitan figure.[2]

An even greater shock to official complacency about progress under Charles III was the appearance in the widely read *Encyclopédie méthodique* published in Paris by Panckouck of a remarkably well-informed and surprisingly sympathetic article on the Spanish empire by the French critic Nicolas Masson de Morvilliers.[3] To be sure, Voltaire, Montesquieu, and Raynal had been critical of Spain's role in Europe's evolution, but neither as explicitly nor as forcefully as Masson. His article was really about the burden of Spain's Hapsburg legacy and the failure of Spaniards to make the most of the resources of the metropole and, worse, of the American colonies. Indeed, Masson, like his predecessors, hammered home that Spain's European trading partners were garnering most of the benefits of Spanish colonialism by supplying goods from their workshops and siphoning off most of the silver remitted to Spain. As Masson phrased it: "Truly it is a blessing for Europe that Mexico, Peru, and Chile are possessions of a sluggish nation." France, England, and Holland prospered by trade with Spain's colonies via peninsular ports, while Spain itself stagnated. What after all, Masson questioned at one point, did Spain really represent in Europe? Masson recommended that Spain be shocked out of its "lethargie politique." For Spain had "gradually suffered a decline from which it will arise with difficulty."[4]

Under Floridablanca, Madrid had to orchestrate a response to European critics by carefully selected optimists about Spain's trajectory under the Bourbons. True, Floridablanca's administration had issued the Reglamento del comercio libre covering the South American possessions in 1778, and the third and final Reglamento incorporating New Spain into the imperial *comercio libre* trading system in 1789. In 1779, it had authorized publication of Bernardo Ward's *Proyecto económico,* and in 1789, its partial incorporation into the *Nuevo sistema de gobierno económico para la América* attributed to

José del Cosío y Campillo, whose recommendations for Spanish America—some partially realized, others soon to be—promised to put the regime in a favorable light. Finally, Floridablanca had also undertaken the colonial reorganization that came with the intendancy system, first in the viceroyalty of Peru (1784), then in New Spain (1786). Madrid's orchestrated response took many forms: subsidies to collaborating intellectuals like Juan Pablo Forner and Antonio de Cabanilles;[5] publication in the official *Gaceta de Madrid* of statistical data marking growth in colonial trade (and the unprecedently high percentage of "Spanish" products exported there) resulting from *comercio libre* covering the Caribbean and South American possessions.[6] And since population growth was taken as one reliable indicator of national prosperity promoted by judicious state policy, Floridablanca's administration ordered a census in 1787, by which he intended to disprove critics abroad who claimed that Spain was impoverished partly because it was depopulated.[7]

Optimists

Appropriately, the centerpiece of the orchestrated response was Floridablanca's "Memorial presentado al rey Carlos III y repetido a Carlos IV," an extended apologia for his eleven-year tenure (1777–88) and an expression to Charles III and the nation at large of his grand design for restoring "this great monarchy, raising it to the power and splendor in happier times."[8] The "Memorial" covered the spectrum of his administration's activities, ranging from foreign relations, church-state affairs, and the readiness of the armed forces (he boasted that in 1781–83, the country's naval forces were the largest "Spain had ever seen") to the condition of the metropolitan and colonial economies.[9] The government had pushed ahead with *comercio libre* (in Campomanes's opinion, "the most important gift . . . to the nation"), by founding the Banco Nacional de San Carlos ("grande obra"), and the issue of treasury notes (*vales*) as a wartime financial measure.[10] Floridablanca also applauded his collaborators, Múzquiz at the Hacienda, Gálvez at the Colonial Office, and the merchant banker Francisco Cabarrús ("this active, skillful merchant").[11] In late 1788, many initiatives were still in process, still hotly debated both within and outside the administration. These were not serendipitous, Floridablanca assured readers, but the product of "well-pondered, systematic, and sustained" planning to overcome Spain's "debilidad anterior" (code for the Hapsburg legacy).[12] Overseas, in the South American colonies, he had secured Portugal's support against "internal convulsions" (an allusion to Jesuit-inspired resistance in South America to the treaty of 1750); in the Rio de la Plata, Spanish troops had destroyed smugglers' bases, while in the Caribbean they had removed the threat of foreigners (read: the English) scheming to "destroy and disable the great kingdom of New Spain, the most valuable of our Indies."[13] The American colonies' silver and export staples, he was confident, would expand trade under *comercio libre,* leading to the "advance of our industry" and growth in domestic and foreign trade, enabling Spanish producers to overcome the "advantages of foreign products over ours"—goals advanced by *proyectistas.*[14] The Floridablanca ministry's imperial design was clearly delineated, but its execution was still moot.

In light of the emphasis on colonial trade in Floridablanca's "Memorial," it seems hardly coincidental that two articles on *comercio libre* were published in the *Memorias* of Madrid's prestigious Sociedad Económica (they had, in fact, been presented to the society's members nine years earlier), and that others appeared in the September, October, and November issues of the recently inaugurated *Espíritu de los mejores diarios literarios.* The subject of colonial issues after the *motín* against Esquilache is prominently discussed in Floridablanca's "Memorial."[15] Floridablanca, whom Charles once appraised accurately as "solid regalist, prudent . . . but steady,"[16] boasted that his administration had effectively terminated foreigners' hold over Spanish trade policy created by tariff concessions negotiated by "those who farmed the customs in former times," pressed ahead with *comercio libre* in the face of opposition orchestrated by the "narrow throat" of Cadiz interests, and— most important and still premature—removed the causes of "our former weakness . . . the real source of our ills."[17]

As if to prove that state and church could at last tolerate public circulation of criticism and opinion by a minority of "enlightened people" dispersed among a mass of "melancólicos" and "ignorantes," in mid 1787, two periodicals began to appear in Madrid. Their editors took advantage of a cautious relaxation of state censorship: in 1785, a decree had laid out the ground rules governing surveillance and authorization of periodicals, and three years later the Consejo de Castilla published regulations to orient censors, editors, and translators about what could and could not be published. Freedom of the press was very narrowly defined.[18] Together the periodicals were indicators of a "sound albeit unfounded optimism" by a minority (including Charles III, one of their readers) disposed to air past errors and learn from the experience of neighboring modernizing societies. The *Semanario erudito,* edited by Antonio Valladares, reverted to Campomanes's stratagem in the multivolume *Apéndice a la educación popular* (1775), obliquely criticizing the present by publishing manuscripts critical of the later Hapsburg and early Bourbon periods of Spain's past. Valladares hoped thereby to demonstrate that Spaniards might debate national shortcomings in order to "restore the nation to its proper condition." Meanwhile, he took on those "weak souls who not only hope to conceal defects but will also consider criminal publicizing them."[19] In the context of Spanish Bourbon press censorship, this was a remarkable development.

Among other things, the *Semanario erudito* reviewed the debatable policies of Philip IV's *valido* conde-duque de Olivares; printed uncomplimentary material on the Jesuits by Bishop Palafox (who had served in New Spain and was a favorite author of Charles III) and Andrés Marcos Burriel; extolled the seventeenth-century economic nationalism of France's Sully, Richelieu, and Colbert, and of Spain's *arbitrista* Manuel de Lira; and resurrected some of the less vitriolic manuscripts of Melchor Macanaz, whose overt regalism had resulted in his being censured by the Inquisition and obliged to take refuge in France.

Next, in the summer of 1787, Cristóbal Cladera was allowed to publish his *Espíritu de los mejores diarios literarios que se publican en Europa*. In its 42-month life, the *Espíritu* culled materials from seventy-six foreign (mainly French) periodicals for at least 870 subscribers, and many more readers. It graduated quickly from short, human interest trivia to lengthy thought-provoking pieces. Cladera printed a fictive debate between Columbus and Las Casas on the handling of America's native peoples (a sensitive topic); a refutation of Cornelius de Pauw's theory of the natural inferiority of American flora and fauna; Raynal's discussion of America's utility (or the reverse thereof) to Europe; and articles on the inhumanity of the slave trade and slavery (another charged theme), *comercio libre,* the radical views of Valentín de Foronda on Spain's political economy, and Benjamin Franklin, John Adams, and the American independence movement. His periodical was a "medium for presenting different ideas to the public," who could then judge for themselves, Cladera said.[20] Together with *El Censor,* the two periodicals represented a kind of *appertura* that some of a new generation of Spanish intellectuals warmly welcomed. Others, of course, were irritated by the critical tone of *Espíritu* articles and proceeded to spread rumors "with evil intentions" that the government intended to close it down.[21] The hope was father to the thought.

Appropriately from Francisco Cabarrús, one of the collaborators whom Floridablanca had specifically singled out in his "Memorial," came three publications between 1786 and 1788 also lauding the achievements of Charles III's reign.[22] His observations were in Floridablanca's optimistic mode, with one notable reservation.

Like Floridablanca, Cabarrús believed that Spain's Bourbon monarchy had modified structures at home and in its American possessions that had congealed under the Hapsburgs; that, in the words of another contemporary optimist, the Bourbon regime had "regenerated" Spain from its "very sad, terrible state."[23] According to Cabarrús, Hacienda ministers from Patiño and Ensenada to Esquilache and Múzquiz had profited from the strategy and goals of French proto-nationalists of the seventeenth century. Múzquiz, Cabarrús noted, had consistently rejected the notion of national inferiority, never accepting that "in Spain nothing can flourish."[24] In greater detail than Floridablanca, he revisited features of Hapsburg colonial policy in a fashion reminiscent of Macanaz: the fixation on precious metals, inhumane treatment of native labor, trade monopoly, and monopsony in New Spain. He had no toleration of the privileging of the trinity of colonial labor policy, mining, and monopoly, which he detected behind the attitude of colonialists in Spain at the end of the eighteenth century who considered "América como esclava," its resources as "the foremost support of the state."[25] By consistent support for *comercio libre* ("this great act, Charles III's greatest"), Múzquiz had helped shake off the "lethargy in which monopoly had kept the provinces."[26] Free trade within the imperial transatlantic system and the inauguration of frequent, scheduled *avisos* between metropolitan and colonial ports ("internal communication with the remotest parts of a great empire") were changing that system. And like Floridablanca, Cabarrús unequivocally underscored his optimism and confidence in the permanence of *ilustración* in colonial trade policy: "The system that the government has now adopted is the effect of enlightenment," he said, and, he added, "this system will not change."[27]

Cabarrús was equally positive about domestic policy under Charles III. To his credit, Cabarrús courageously risked criticism when he extolled a deliberately unnamed activist-predecessor of Múzquiz at the Hacienda ministry (obviously Esquilache) as "a person tested [by Charles III] in the same position at Naples, and whose effective role justified that appointment."[28] Esquilache, he recounted, had planned to reduce grain imports (an avoidable capital drain) and promoted internal colonization schemes for agricultural development in the Sierra Morena (continued briefly by Olavide) along with completion of large-scale irrigation projects and elimination of government grain pricing. In Esquilache's successor, Múzquiz, Cabarrús discerned a confirmed protectionist, responsible for the tariff of 1782, a two-pronged instrument of national policy affording "protection for our, and a barrier to foreign, industry," while at the same time reducing state revenue losses caused by the former "complicated, excessive and, worse, arbitrary and unfair duties" perennially defended by Cadiz commercial interests.

Matching Múzquiz's colonial policy innovations were financial ones that permitted the state to mobilize domestic capital and monitor (and profit from) silver transfers abroad: the Banco Nacional, treasury notes, and careful management of the bewildering multiplicity of old (Hapsburg) and new (Bourbon) public debts.[29]

Despite his optimism, Cabarrús had few illusions about the sustained and widespread resistance to meliorist initiatives under Charles III and earlier. He bore witness to Múzquiz's struggle to overcome the "backbiting and snares of that faction too numerous by far that in every country defends abuses and fights to preserve them."[30] Perhaps this explains Cabarrús's approval of Charles III's decision in 1767, following the rioting against Esquilache's activism, to expel "una orden famosa" (the Jesuits) as well as Cabarrús's lambasting (like Floridablanca) of Cadiz's merchants as "a small group of monopolists who for two centuries divvied up among themselves the plunder of the provinces in America and Spain, defended it as their patrimony, and used every stratagem to keep it." And as for the level of criticism of *comercio libre,* the jewel in Floridablanca's oeuvre: "What a mishmash of gloomy predictions, lies and ridiculous arguments."[31] The Cadiz community was now fair game for its critics.

There had been progress, Cabarrús seemed to argue, yet he could not end his elegy of the late Charles III without confessing that manufactures in Spain had not progressed very far, certainly not to the degree necessary to match European models. Ruefully he admitted that more was involved than adapting Spanish economic policy to a changing international environment; in what was a troubling reservation, he hinted that Spain's national problem was far more serious, "because our system is fundamentally flawed."[32] He gave no details; he could hardly afford to.

There is no reason to question the sincerity of the optimists' belief in Spain's general progress under Charles; they took comfort in a certain distancing of the country from the "lethargy" associated with Hapsburg times, a loosening of state and ecclesiastical censorship, and the "reform of abuses" in colonial trade, finance, and administration. Although they had serious reservations, a dose of excessive euphoria from a spokesman like Floridablanca, the circulation of a few closely monitored new periodicals, and the optimistic observations in 1786 of a prominent financier and counsel like Cabarrús were warranted to confront pessimists at home and abroad.

Pessimists

Optimists could not overlook the doubting Thomases, those profoundly pessimistic about the condition of the machine of state and its foreign policy, unconsciously breaking with the old regime, yet without a vision of a new paradigm, or the "gloomy crowd" among Cadiz's small commercial bourgeoisie convinced that meliorism in colonial affairs would not work and that "experience" counseled a reversion to the fondly recalled pre-1765 era of managed trade.[33] The pessimists' writings remained unpublished for decades but the manuscripts were shelved in private libraries (often those of official censors), and they were read and circulated clandestinely.

Floridablanca's policy of wartime collaboration with France in support of American independence had the backing of the conde de Aranda, Charles III's choice to head the government in the immediate aftermath of the anti-Esquilache coup of 1766, and later posted to Paris as Spain's ambassador. Charles's son and heir, the príncipe de Asturias, wrote Aranda at the Paris embassy in 1781 for advice on the future management of what he described as "this disordered machine, the monarchy." Aranda (whose "integrity and patriotism" the future Charles IV admired) replied pessimistically, although clinging to faith in the promise of Spain's potential in agriculture, manufacturing, and science.[34]

Both Aranda and Charles III's heir confronted the growing, bewildering complexity of society and government at the end of the century of enlightenment. There was a crisis of authority in Spain, with ministries competing with *consejos* for jurisdiction, and a pervasive sense of lack of direction. Charles III's government under Floridablanca, Aranda confessed, had failed to "fashion a masterful machine" to match its hope of improvement. Most troublesome to Aranda was the Colonial Office (which he likened to an "Ymperio"), where the secretary (he did not name Gálvez) dominated both his ministry and the parallel Consejo de Indias (he was also its *gobernador*) and concentrated all aspects of colonial administration—defense, justice, finance, and appointment—in his own hands. These should be separated, Aranda felt, and the Colonial Office's "useless" personnel (it was a "trash bin for the scum of Spain") should be replaced.[35] And there was an even more worrisome aspect of colonial affairs: Aranda, who had many contacts with the colonial world, noted that when elite Creoles came to Spain, they got little respect and returned home alienated. Unless colonial policy changed for the better, he said, no doubt thinking of the insurrection in the British colonies in North America, "sooner or later [they] will foment revolution."[36] Whether through family interests or military personnel posted to colonial service, Aranda had an uncommon grasp of colonials' sensitivity to Spanish imperialism.

Two years later, Aranda's pessimism deepened in the wake of the 1783 peace settlement with England. He now concluded that it had been unwise to yield to France's urging to support the North American insurrectionists in a war "opposed to our own interests." The now independent North American colonies he found a source of "grief and fear," since their success would inevitably expose Spain's nearby colonies to "terribles convulsiones." A realist, Aranda queried why Spain should now trust independent North Americans not to covet that "rich country," New Spain? Driven by this prognosis, he now opted for a policy of cutting the inevitable losses he foresaw: he recommended that Spain abandon the viceroyalties of Mexico and Peru, retain one South American foothold as depot for Spanish traders, and hold on to only two Caribbean island possessions, Cuba and Puerto Rico.[37] He was prescient: in another five decades, those islands would be Spain's sole remaining colonies in the New World.

Floridablanca's fiscal and financial policies led León de Arroyal, an intellectual, poet, and Hacienda agent in a small town of Aragon, to review economic policy under the Hapsburgs. Arroyal, who had attended the university of Salamanca in the 1770s, was decidedly a loner among Spanish intellectuals, although he was later friendly with Pedro Estala and José Juan Cadalso.[38] What most interested him was the relationship under the Spanish monarchy between government, fiscal policy, and the burden on the mass of Spanish taxpayers. More specifically, he probed the boundaries between the central government (*autoridad soberana*) and individual liberty (*libertad civil*) and tracked how sovereign power (the king/state) had created gross inequities in Spain's tax system and the chasm between the privileged and the people. Although Spaniards and foreigners had long been aware of Spain's persistent poverty, he observed, "whether from fear or ignorance, no [Spaniard] has pointed it out until now." For Arroyal, the ideal state was one where "each partner contributes to the common expenses in proportion to benefits from the common fund." How to achieve this condition was "the great secret of politics."[39]

In tracking the use and misuse of the power to tax and spend under the Hapsburgs, Arroyal underscored the fiscal exemptions still enjoyed by Spain's privileged sectors under Charles III, notably those of the ecclesiastical establishment and nobility. The Hapsburgs had bequeathed to the Spanish Bourbon state a structure (*constitución*) consisting of "crude bits, disproportionate, confused, and contradictory," a government both "unsteady and accidental," whose tribunals were "arbitrary and corrupt, as uncouth as our upbringing."[40] This was the result of a pattern of patrimonial state formation through inheritance and conquest, he concluded, which left the aggregated but not unified provinces with their own legislation, while depriving Charles III's *autoridad soberana* of that "uniformidad" necessary to "felicidad pública." Since Arroyal believed that no one had diagnosed this condition correctly, he proposed to embark on a series of manuscripts, the first of which (his *Sátiras*) was an early critique of "enlightened Spanish society in its totality."[41]

Arroyal's five letters to Hacienda secretary Lerena (Múzquiz's successor) over three years (1787–90) provide a well-informed "crítica exacta" of Spain's rulers and policies from 1500 to 1700, their reliance upon consumption imposts (*alcabala, sisa, nieve, fiel medidor, sal, tabaco*), and how they impinged on the lower social strata.[42] To formulate a new public income policy (his *nuevo sistema de rentas*), he picked apart the structure of state, bureaucracy, clergy, and nobility, isolating for criticism the growth of property ownership by clergy and nobility through tax privileges, mortmain, and entailment. Floridablanca's glowing canvas of an *España ilustrada* became Arroyal's dark landscape of backward Spain, where "agriculture pleads for an agrarian law," postponed for nineteen years, "the highest authority is dispersed among a multitude of councils, juntas, and tribunals," and the "royal power is carved up."[43] (This was not very far removed from the prince of Asturias's "disordered monarchy.") Employing Necker's vivisection of France's fiscal system as a surrogate for his view of Spanish conditions, Arroyal reported "an infinity of destructive taxes" in France that financed useless employment and the uncontrolled expenditures of the vast royal household. Omnipotent sovereignty was therefore guilty of "the most harmful abuses." Arroyal therefore distanced himself from the ad hoc policies of Floridablanca, Múzquiz, and Cabarrús, which during the recent war had forced the government to rely upon high-cost borrowing backed by silver transfers from Veracruz to Havana to Philadelphia and ultimately to Paris, along with the invention of paper money—measures that, he added maliciously, "would make the economic talent of Sr. Cabarrús' sweat."[44]

Arroyal's references to the American colonies were few but trenchant. He warned that it was risky to rely upon transatlantic trade as the "great link" tying vast overseas possessions to Spain. In his view, colonialism was a weak reed, and Spaniards disregarded the lessons of their country's imperialist past in Europe at their peril. "We lost Flanders, we lost Italy," he said, and, in a vein reminiscent of Aranda's 1783 memorial, asked, "why can't we lose Mexico and Peru?" And if this happened, "what will our role be in the world?"[45] Spain had to develop its internal resources ("the Peninsula is the core of our power"), which, he insisted, exceeded those of the colonies in America and construct a more equitable tax structure that could provide annual revenues covering both ordinary and extraordinary contingencies. From a more equitable distribution of the tax burden, there would come a fresh initiative. To forge the indispensable bond tying people and sovereign, to weaken omnipotent sovereignty, and inspire "trust and common interests," the state should tolerate "freedom to think, write, speak."[46] On the eve of the French Revolution, some of Spain's *ilustrado* elite were inching toward political liberalism.[47]

There remain tantalizing ambiguities—inevitable in a society of official press censorship—in Arroyal's play on *constitución* and *revolución*. We are never sure whether he envisioned a formal charter defining the state's structures and powers or referred only to the fiscal order, or, in the case of the "feliz revolución," to gradual and sustained meliorism or radical change in the existing order. How are we to interpret his recommendation for "a general renovation of our constitution," rather than halfway measures that, he said, would "be futile no matter how many efforts are made to check abuses."[48]

Floridablanca's official euphoria had highlighted colonial trade expansion through *comercio libre,* which, he was confident, would lead to "progresos de la industria." However, faith in the linkages of colonial trade was not shared by well-informed foreign observers. Surely Floridablanca knew of the comment in a current London periodical that Spain was "a mere commission agent of foreign factories" and of Raynal's curt dismissal of Spain's experiment in *comercio libre* as a chimera.[49] Moreover, there was a hard core of peninsular merchants (Cabarrús's "small number of monopolists") who were equally pessimistic about the development of domestic industry in response to colonial markets. While they could not doubt Spain's overall trade growth after 1778, and particularly after peace with England in 1783, they questioned assertions about the high percentage of Spanish-made goods in recently published colonial trade statistics. Merchants on the Cadiz-Sevilla axis and in Barcelona knew of the dishearteningly low percentage of Spanish merchandise in the transatlantic system—the official published data for 1784–87 indicated 44 to 52 percent, when in fact it was far less, just as they knew foreigners knew this too.[50] By 1788, officials at Cadiz reported that Madrid was deluding itself in believing that "an extraordinary supply of goods made in Spain" flowed to America through the Cadiz customs. It was common knowledge that at least 66 percent of linens, woolens, yarns, silks, hardware, and mercury exported to America still had to be bought from European manufacturers. "It's all a fable," one official at

Cadiz told Colonial Secretary Antonio Valdés in 1788, "we're listening to our own noise, we stand like dull-witted fools before the rest of the world."[51]

In handling the critical issue of the inadequate state of Spanish manufacturing in the era of Charles III, Andalusian and Catalan merchants engaged in mutual recrimination. Cadiz, joined by Sevilla, accused Catalan competitors of falsifying manifests by labeling as national what were really reexported imports. For their part, Catalans blamed disappointing progress in manufacturing on the national tax system and on New Spain's workshops (*obrajes*) turning out cotton prints, woolens, and hats. On two points, however, the disaffected merchants agreed. Official data were gravely misleading because of uncontrollable smuggling in both peninsular and colonial ports. From the "narrow channel" at Cadiz in 1788, Thomás Izquierdo reminded Colonial Secretary Valdés of the covert "substitution of foreign for national goods" exported at that port, and of the unenforceable regulations against trading with foreign smugglers in the colonies. The reaction of these realists suggests that the official euphoria of the 1780s had created a credibility gap, deepening both their pessimism about the regeneration or restoration of the Spanish state, society, and economy under Charles III and the national psychology of inferiority. Or was this another instance of the glass being either half empty or half full?

12. By Way of Conclusion

Monographs by their nature emphasize detail to be convincing. Hence the detail should fit into a wider context to avoid irrelevance. In a long retrospective view, eighteenth-century Spain could not recover from the effects of the drawn-out, wasting conflict with the Netherlands that ended in the middle of the seventeenth century. To consolidate support among the new and old aristocracy, Hapsburg policy had enhanced the institutions of privilege, which then effectively blocked efforts to curb them. As a result, Bourbon Spain's political class in the eighteenth century, from Patiño to Campillo, Esquilache, and Floridablanca, could at best initiate cosmetic change when more radical change was made imperative by the rapidly developing English and French economies of the time. Which is to say that Spain's policy-makers were not "reformers" but merely anxious to preserve the colonies in America from direct exploitation by English and French merchants. Their project may best be described as a form of "defensive modernization."

Empires, we all know, decay, and the earliest of the overseas empires of occidental Europe were contracting or, as some would have it, declining around 1700 or even earlier. The process should not be exaggerated: Spain would hold on to its American continental possessions for another century, and would only retreat from Cuba and Puerto Rico (and the Philippines) two centuries later. Like Portugal, Spain managed to stretch out its decline. What slowed it down was the decision of Spain's elites around 1700 to accept a Bourbon as monarch, the basis of an informal alliance with France against England that would become the formal Family Pact of 1761.

For most of the eighteenth century, the output of silver mines in New Spain and Peru was considered basic to the metropolitan economy. Of course, indirectly, silver leaked out to western Europe via English and French

Caribbean ports, to the English colonies in North America, and to Asia via the Philippines. Growth of the empire's nonmining exportables from Cuba (sugar, tobacco) and the Rio de la Plata (hides, dried beef) came mainly in the last quarter of the century. Madrid's colonial policy over the century after 1700 had to focus on isolating New Spain from the merchant community in Kingston, the major port of England's major sugar economy in its "west" Indies, Jamaica.

Madrid turned to Bourbon France because together they might hope to reduce the threat of English expansion in the Caribbean to the traffic and ports of Veracruz, Havana, and Cartagena. Barbados, Antigua, and Jamaica became imperial England's overseas engines of growth, exporting sugar and tobacco, importing merchandise and African slave laborers, and reexporting goods to Spain's possessions in the Caribbean in exchange for silver pesos. Kingston functioned as a Caribbean emporium: handling traffic with Britain, with the British colonies in North America, with Africa, and with Spain's colonies around the Caribbean. London's Freeport Act, a reaction to Madrid's decision in 1765 to permit Havana and other island ports to trade with many peninsular ports other than Cadiz, confirmed the importance of smuggling between Kingston and nearby Spanish colonial ports.

England's Caribbean complex, a portion of its American empire stretching from Newfoundland to Barbados, needed naval protection to sustain its transatlantic flow of goods, people, and silver, as well as the unity and influence of the "master class" of its plantations. It required seamen and officers, ships, shipbuilding and maintenance facilities at home, and, overseas in the Caribbean, naval stations suitable for wintering warships. In wartime, those naval units could be shifted from defense to offense, to capturing enemy shipping and blockading enemy ports. The Royal Navy was the core of military policy in the "long" century of English economic growth after 1660. For its time and place, the scope of public intervention by the English state was unique and extraordinarily successful: consider the size of inputs for ship construction in the form of wood, ironware, rope, and canvas, in repair facilities at home and abroad, in officer training, and in at one point provisioning as many as 40,000 men at sea. Ranked against such massive state intervention, the operations of England's private sector were minor. The buildup of naval power was the handmaiden of English economic development. By the time of the Seven Years' War, the great war of the eighteenth century, between 1756 and 1763, England's naval establishment could mount simultaneous operations in the western Pacific at Manila and in the Caribbean at Havana. Charles III's wife did not exaggerate when she wrote from Madrid to Tanucci at Naples after the loss of Havana that the English could now become "los dueños de México."

Madrid sought to maximize the mineral, agricultural, and financial resources of its most important New World possession, New Spain, as well as to make the most of that colony's consumers from a trading perspective. New Spain's trade with the metropole was confined to Cadiz until 1789, almost twenty-five years after Cuba, Puerto Rico, and Santo Domingo had been opened to trade with other peninsular ports. Madrid privileged silver mining with improved supplies of mercury and blasting powder at subsidized prices. Meanwhile, New Spain's corn and wheat growers were encouraged to export their flour to feed Cuba's growing slave labor force. Furthermore, an impressive proportion of the colonial government's surplus funds was earmarked for financing Havana's defenses, not to overlook the purchase of Cuban tobacco for the lucrative metropolitan tobacco monopoly, while New Spain's private sectors—mainly religious corporations and Mexico City's merchant oligarchs—were pressured to contribute "gifts" and provide loans, both interest-free and interest-bearing. Decapitalization occurred in the form of New Spain's subsidization of the defense of Spain's Caribbean possessions and transfers to Madrid on both private and public (royal) account.

What is clearly beyond question, commercial groups at Cadiz and Mexico City—the former mainly small-scale operators dependent upon resident foreign merchant capitalists for funds and goods, the latter immensely wealthy (and politically influential) merchant princes—can be pinpointed as *the* principal interest groups opposing (or, in the end, watering-down) overdue adjustments in imperial commercial policy. That neither was a vehicle of change should surprise no one. Adam Smith in the eighteenth century and Maurice Dobb in the twentieth, among others, underscored the profound conservatism of the bourgeoisie of the mercantile system when confronting imperatives of change. Exceptions to this pattern have all too often been mistaken for dynamic agents of economic change.

Did the mercantile elites of Cadiz and Mexico City constitute a bourgeoisie in the era of Charles III? Answering this entails a historical definition of the merchant, his function, and his outlook or mentality. In the long evolution of commercial capitalism, two prominent bourgeois types surface. There is the merchant of the fifteenth and sixteen centuries who bought cheap in one port to sell dear in another, invested sparingly, and pursued the highest immediate returns. Such merchants operated in a world of few cities, low population growth, minimal per capita income, and poor communications—an essentially rural economy. They were still on the margins of late medieval structures and institutions and formed part of an isolated, subaltern social group aspiring to incorporation into seignorial society, which was sometimes accommodating.

Another type of merchant bloomed in the eighteenth century when the English, French, and Dutch expanded the universe of trade to Europe's colonies in America, to the African coast, and to Southeast, South, and East Asia. Large investments amortized over long terms were commonplace: merchants, individually or in association, operated simultaneously in many geographically separate commercial worlds. Unlike earlier merchants, the eighteenth-century variety was only one segment of a larger group of "bourgeois"—financiers, manufacturers, professionals—some, but not all, critical of seignorial values, no longer marginalized, and some pressing for juridical equality—for a society of contract, not privilege.

This summary typology of the commercial bourgeoisie suggests that what determines the social type is not function—buying and selling—but the larger world of which the merchant is a part, that is, the system. And the system that shaped, regulated, and ultimately integrated the economies of New Spain and Spain and at the microlevel, Mexico City and Cadiz, with those of England and France was constructed upon silver mining. This formed an enclave economy of limited linkages in both colony and metropole, which raised silver output but restrained both economies from diversification and development. Silver functioned as a major pole of growth in the essentially agrarian, backward economies of colony and metropole, as in preceding centuries. In New Spain, merchants of various levels were drawn into mining investment or the agricultural and ranching activities ancillary to it. In Spain, the Cadiz community served as the entrepôt for incoming flows of silver and outgoing flows of reexports. At the same time, Cadiz attracted investment from abroad and the rest of the Iberian Peninsula, siphoning capital from canal and road construction projects, from agriculture, and, except in Catalonia, from manufacturing. Indeed, inflows of silver at Cadiz maintained, even expanded, a metropolitan rentier structure that involved small and large private investors—merchants, civil servants, military officers, gentry, churchmen—and the central government, anxiously awaiting its colonial revenues. Thus there was a bourgeoisie sui generis, the peculiar product of an imperial economy based upon silver.

Acceptance of silver as the pole of growth in the Spanish Atlantic system, and of Cadiz as the exchange point between New Spain and Europe, was compatible with the interests of Spanish merchants at Cadiz and Mexico City, but incompatible with the goals of Bourbon economic nationalists in the era of Charles III. Mainly bureaucrat-intellectuals, these embarked upon a developmentalist, that is to say, mercantilistic, policy designed to transform a "passive" or entrepôt bourgeoisie into an "active" bourgeoisie primarily handling national goods, and thus to fulfill the colonial pact. They failed to take into account, however, the secular attachment to bullionism that had formed an economy and bourgeoisie that was not viable in the international context of the eighteenth century, yet was incapable of transforming itself or being transformed. Hence mercantilistic legislation and continuing incapacity to develop manufactures took the form of pseudo-mercantilism, in which prohibitions and discriminatory tariffs provided merchants and bureaucrats alike with the opportunity to combine personal and public interest for profitable survival. This meant rigorous pursuit of privilege and precedent, lip service to the national weal and evasion of national priorities. These were a measure of the autonomy of this merchant elite within Spain's transatlantic system. In the closing decades of the eighteenth century, these practices exhausted the system's possibilities precisely at a time when external pressures upon the Spanish Atlantic system were growing exponentially.

So the fixation upon silver kept the mercantile bourgeoisie of Mexico City and Cadiz small in numbers, inward- and backward- rather than outward- and forward-looking, deeply religious in a Catholic counterreformation spirit. And after 1789, its members believed that the preservation of their enclave of privilege required undoing even the modest alterations achieved in Charles III's years.

One objective of Charles's reign was quietly abandoned: the hope of creating an industrial establishment in the metropole capable of providing manufactures for colonial consumers in populous colonies like New Spain. The aim of raising domestic demand in Spain by implementing reform initiatives was blunted by the reaction of the regime's privileged classes to Esquilache's program; meanwhile, overseas in New Spain, both the supply and quality of non-Spanish imports reexported from Spanish ports or smuggled from English entrepôts in the Caribbean grew uncontrollably. By Charles's last decade, Spain's economic policy for New Spain and other possessions was no longer designed to control the inflow of foreign-made goods but to reduce the threat of English and North American traders eventually penetrating the internal circuits of New Spain's trade.

This policy seemed feasible when Charles died in 1788. It was dangerously imperiled by the unintended consequences of revolution in France, which led Charles IV to abandon the protection of the French alliance when Spain joined the First Coalition and briefly invaded southwestern France. In retrospect, what followed over the next fifteen years appears inevitable.

Notes

Abbreviations and Acronyms

AAEPar	Quai d'Orsay (Paris)
AE	Affaires étrangères
AEA	*Anuario de Estudios Americanos*
AESC	*Annales: Economies, Sociétés, Civilisations*
AGI	Archivo General de Indias (Sevilla)
AGN	Archivo General de la Nación (Mexico City)
AGSim	Archivo General (Simancas)
AHDE	*Anuario de Historia del Derecho Español*
AHH	Archivo Histórico de Hacienda
AHN	Archivo Histórico Nacional (Madrid)
AHR	*American Historical Review*
ANPar	Archives Nationales (Paris)
BAE	*Biblioteca de Autores Españoles*
BLAR	*Bulletin of Latin American Research*
BMus	British Museum (London)
BNMad	Biblioteca Nacional (Madrid)
BNMex	Biblioteca Nacional (Mexico City)
BNPar	Bibliothèque Nationale (Paris)
BRAHM	Biblioteca de la Real Academia de la Historia (Madrid)
BRPal	Biblioteca del Real Palacio (Madrid)
CC	Correspondance Consulaire
CH	*Cuadernos hispanoamericanos. Los complementarios/2*
CP	Correspondance Politique
DGR	Dirección General de Rentas
EHR	*Economic History Review*
EMDL	*Espíritu de los Mejores Diarios Literarios*
HAHR	*Hispanic American Historical Review*
HMex	*Historia Mexicana*
HPE	*Hacienda Pública Española*
HSA	Hispanic Society of America (New York)

JEH	*Journal of Economic History*
JIS	*Journal of Inter-American Studies*
JLAS	*Journal of Latin American Studies*
M et D	Mémoires et Documents
MN	Museo Naval (Madrid)
NYPub	New York Public Library
PP	*Past and Present*
REP	*Revista de Estudios Políticos*
RH	*Revue Historique*
RHA	*Revista de Historia de América*
RHCF	*Revue de l'Histoire des Colonies Françaises*
RHisp	*Revue Hispanique*
RHMC	*Revue de l'Histoire Moderne et Contemporaine*
SEV	*Semanario Erudito de Valladares*

Preface

EPIGRAPH: Bernal, *Financiación*, 294.

1. From Naples to Madrid

EPIGRAPHS: Garofalo, *Monarchía borbónica a Napoli*, 17–18; María Amalia to Bernardo Tanucci, quoted in Danvila, *Reinado de Carlos III*, 2:38–39.

1. Villani, *Feudalitá, riforme, capitalismo agrario*, 61. Around 1730, out of 369,019 "hearths" only 71,961 "obbediva direttamente al rei." Schipa, *Regno di Napoli*, 2:192. The population of the kingdom of Naples reached 3.9 million by 1765.

2. Danvila, *Reinado de Carlos III*, 1:82 n. 1, 132–34; Buttà, *Borboni de Napoli*, 1:23.

3. Chorley, *Oil, Silk and Enlightenment*, 140 ff., 150–51, 177–78; Schipa, *Regno di Napoli*, 2:126–27, 170–71, 186.

4. Chorley, *Oil, Silk and Enlightenment*, 90.

5. Danvila, *Reinado de Carlos III*, 1:274–75, 288.

6. Schipa, *Regno di Napoli*, 2:195–96.

7. Ibid.

8. Ibid., 1:292 ff.

9. Acton, *Bourbons of Naples*, 32.

10. Schipa, *Regno di Napoli*, 1:58 ff.; Danvila, *Reinado de Carlos III*, 1:96, 139; Ajello et al., *Bernardo Tanucci*.

11. Rousseau, *Règne de Charles III*, 1:16–17; Ferrer del Rio, *Historia del reinado de Carlos III*, 1:244–45; Schipa, *Regno di Napoli*, 2:15–16; Danvila, *Reinado de Carlos III*, 3:299–300; AHN, Estado 2872, no. 23.

12. Ensenada had been accused of secretly urging Charles to oppose the Treaty of Madrid (1750) that partitioned disputed areas in the Rio de la Plata basin between Spain and Portugal. Spanish Jesuits violently opposed transferring certain Jesuit missions from Spanish to Portuguese sovereignty.

13. Chorley, *Oil, Silk and Enlightenment*, 24–25.

14. Schipa, *Regno di Napoli*, 2:93–97, 102, 105.

15. Chorley, *Oil, Silk and Enlightenment*, 85, 90–98.

16. Danvila, *Reinado de Carlos III,* 1:274–75, 288.

17. Schipa, *Regno di Napoli,* 1:195–200; 2:114.

18. Ibid., 2:114.

19. Villani, *Feudalitá, riforme, capitalismo agrario,* 69. Charles's ministers have been accused of operating "senza un disegno prestabilito, senza metodo, tumultuariamente." Schipa, *Regno di Napoli,* 2:101.

20. The upwardly mobile included "il mezzano di estrazione di monete, il mediatore o commissionario di esportazione, di derrate; il cambista . . . di lettere de cambio" and the "capitalista che trafficava sulla publica finanza." Schipa, *Regno di Napoli,* 2:193.

21. Ferrer del Rio, *Historia del reinado de Carlos III,* 1:207; Buttà, *Borboni de Napoli,* 1:35.

22. Danvila, *Reinado de Carlos III,* 1:372.

23. Charles's government had to cancel even a mild attempt to curb the jurisdictional privileges of the *baronaggio,* not to mention those of the Supremo Magistrato del Commerzio, Villani points out (*Feudalitá, riforme, capitalismo agrario,* "La questione feudale," 58). Charles himself was "debole, bigotto, incapace di grande idee e di altretanto grandi realizzazioni," Garofalo says (*Monarchía borbónica a Napoli,* 17–18).

24. Danvila, *Reinado de Carlos III,* 1:336.

25. Mateo Dorado, "Actividad de Carlos III," 1:299–321.

26. Danvila, *Reinado de Carlos III,* 3:383, 404–5.

27. Christelow, "French Interest in the Spanish Empire," 519–20. Note the comment of Charles III's wife (reflecting her husband's preoccupation) to Tanucci that "[con] los establecimientos hechos," the English "se pueden convertir en los dueños de Mexico." Palacio Atard, *Tercer pacto,* 95 n. 24.

28. Aguado Bleye and Alcázar Molina, *Manual de historia de España,* 3:158–59.

29. Choiseul to d'Ossun, in Christelow, "French Interest in the Spanish Empire," 520.

30. Palacio Atard, *Tercer pacto,* 279.

31. Quoted in Christelow, "Contraband Trade Between Jamaica and the Spanish Main," 313 and nn. 8–9. The mémoire writer adds: "The English . . . admit that the most considerable branch of trade which they have in America is the Contraband trade which they have with the dominions of Spain . . . it reaches at least 6 million pesos each year."

32. Voltes Bou, *Carlos III y su tiempo,* 173.

33. Bourguet, *Duc de Choiseul et l'alliance espagnole,* 21.

34. Béliardi to Berryer, Madrid, 19 Nov. 1759, BNPar, MS Fonds Français, 10767, f. 123.

35. Lafuente, *Historia general de España,* 14:144–45. For French complaints about the treatment of French naval vessels by the recently appointed governor of Cuba, Prado y Portocarrero, see Béliardi's comments in BNPar, MS Fonds Français, 10769.

36. Gálvez, "Discurso y reflexiones de un vasallo," BRPal, Ayala 2816, f. 127v.

37. Dahlgren, *Relations commerciales et maritimes entre la France et les côtes de l'océan Pacifique,* 256–57.

38. Bustos Rodríguez, *Comerciantes,* 29. Sevilla's *consulado* had set the pattern in

the previous century, providing a "loan" of 1 million *escudos* (1649) and a "servicio" of 2.2 million (1691–92)—the price of its port monopoly. Bernal, *Financiación,* 219.

39. Bustos Rodríguez, *Comerciantes,* 13, 35, 202–3, 238–40.

40. Gómez-Centurión Jiménez et al., eds., *Herencia de Borgoña,* 72–77, 169, 182.

41. Bustos Rodríguez, *Comerciantes,* 202–4, 238–40.

42. Ibid., 18; Bernal, *Financiación,* 279.

43. Louis Béhic is probably representative. Born at Bayonne, he came to Cadiz in 1720, where together with Jean Casaubon and others, he founded Casaubon, Béhic y Cia. In 1735, he married the Spanish daughter of another French immigrant, Gilles Pain. Casaubon, Béhic sold goods on credit, loaned *a riesgo de mar,* and shipped its own merchandise to the Spanish colonies.

44. García-Mauriño Mundi, *Pugna,* 87; Bernal, *Financiación,* 297.

45. García-Mauriño Mundi, *Pugna,* 87; Bernal, *Financiación,* 297.

46. García-Mauriño Mundi, *Pugna,* 65; Bustos Rodríguez, *Comerciantes,* 53–54. See also Garmendia Arruebarrena, *Tomás Ruiz de Apodaca.*

47. Bustos Rodríguez, *Comerciantes,* 300.

48. Cf. Bustos Rodríguez, *Burguesía de negocios y capitalismo en Cádiz: Los Colarte,* 73: "Obsérvese la insistencia en los nombres españoles, únicos legitímamente autorizados para penetrar en los mercados indianos."

49. Ibid., 25–30, 37–39, 48–51, 58, 67–84.

50. Ibid., 112–14, 125–26, 190. Colarte's direct descendants avoided "contacto directo . . . del mundo de los negocios; o terminan sucumbiendo ante la competencia de otras naciones mejor afianzadas en este siglo (los franceses, por ejemplo)" (ibid., 238).

51. Dornic, "Commerce des français à Cadiz," 311–12.

52. Ibid., 312.

53. Ibid., 313.

54. Bernal, *Financiación,* 277, detects the shift to finance under way by the early eighteenth century.

55. Aside from three elected officers (prior, two consuls), the personnel of the *consulado* consisted of twenty-two employees. There was also an agent or lobbyist at Madrid. Bustos Rodríguez, *Comerciantes,* 18.

56. The *consulado* dispensed "contribuciones" to the central government totaling 660,000 pesos between 1701 and 1723—an impressive sum at the time. Bustos Rodríguez, *Comerciantes,* 29.

57. García-Mauriño Mundi, *Pugna,* 62.

58. Ibid., 69–70, 76–78, 80. Coincidentally, the *consulado* offered another "servicio" of 120,000 pesos.

59. Ibid., 83, 89–90.

60. Ibid., 93, 103.

61. Bustos Rodríguez, *Comerciantes,* 31–34. In 1771, Cadiz's Junta de la Única Contribución confessed to a lack of income data because "ha sido imposible conseguir la conclusión de una empresa ardua en Cádiz" (75). At the same time, Madrid had to accept the *consulado*'s petition to "no realizar declaraciones juradas, y evitar las pretendidas averiguaciones sobre la fortuna de sus miembros" (46).

62. Bustos Rodríguez, *Pugna,* 80.

63. Hussey, *Caracas Company;* Matilla Tascón and Capella, *Cinco Gremios Mayores de Madrid;* Gárate Ojanguren, *Comercio ultramarino e ilustración.*

64. See, e.g., Christelow, "Contraband Trade Between Jamaica and the Spanish Main," 309–43, and Ramos, *Contrabando inglés en el Caribe y el Golfo de México.*

65. Mörner, *Political and Economic Activities of the Jesuits in the La Plata Region.*

66. Jenkinson, *Collection of the Treaties of Peace, Alliance and Commerce.*

67. Béliardi, Madrid, BNPar, MS Fonds Français, 10766, f. 66.

68. Béliardi, Madrid, BNPar, MS Fonds Français, 10768, f. 582.

69. See materials in ANPar, B III series, in BNPar, MS Fonds Français (Béliardi papers), and AAEPar, M et D and CP.

70. AAEPar, M et D, Amérique 33, no. 4, f. 185.

71. On Carrasco's career, especially his investigative role in the Consejo de Hacienda, see Moxó, "Medievalista en el Consejo de Hacienda," 609–50. Carrasco formed part of the "grupo alrededor de Esquilache" for whom Esquilache retained a warm friendship. Esquilache's correspondence from Venice with Carrasco is in the Real Academia de la Historia, Madrid.

72. Danvila, *Reinado de Carlos III,* 2:299–300; Ferrer del Rio, *Historia del reinado de Carlos III,* 1:244–45.

73. AAEPar, M et D, Amérique 33, no. 4, f. 185.

74. Béliardi, "Conclusions," BNPar, MS Fonds Français, 10768. Of course, selection of new appointees for high posts at home and abroad at the expense of the aristocracy ran the risk of alienating "les premiers seigneurs de la cour." Béliardi, letter, Madrid, 24 Mar. 1760, BNPar, MS Fonds Français, 10764, f. 147v.

75. J. A. de Armona to Pedro Antonio de Paul, Havana, 1 Mar. 1772, HSA, HC 427/6.

76. Cantillon, *Essai de la nature du commerce en général,* 258.

77. Kagan, *Students and Society in Early Modern Spain.*

78. Lafuente, *Historia general de España,* 14:15.

79. Vilar, "Structures de la société," 428–29; Anes Alvarez, *Antiguo régimen,* 69–75; and esp. Carrasco, "Ultima representación al Rey . . . sobre amortización. Madrid, 27 Agosto 1766," BRAHM, Mata Linares, 87. A measure of Esquilache's recognition of "zealous" reformers was the fact that Carrasco was his first choice as *visitador general* to New Spain in 1765. Carrasco declined; the third choice was Gálvez.

80. Carrasco, "Ultima representación al Rey."

81. Campomanes, "Apuntaciones," BRPal, Ayala. 2867; Mörner, *Political and Economic Activities of the Jesuits in the La Plata Region,* 40 n. 30.

82. Among its influential alumni were Julián de Arriaga (colonial secretary), the conde de Valdeparaíso (treasury secretary), and Padre Rábago (royal confessor). Raynal termed them "une société de marchands qui, sous le voile de la religion, n'étoient occupés que d'un interêt sordid" (*Histoire philosophique,* 4:148). Another organization included the Congregación de San Ignacio at Madrid, as well as the *montañeses* from the Liébana, associated with the cult of Nuestra Señora de la Luz.

83. Armona, "Catálogo," HSA, HC 427/6, f. 208.

84. Danvila, *Reinado de Carlos III,* 1:310. For Tanucci on the Jesuits, see ibid., 1:303.

2. Renovation under Esquilache

EPIGRAPHS: "Carta . . . por un caballero de Madrid a otro en Cádiz" (1766), AHN, Estado 2872, n. 35; Turgot, "Mémoire" (1779), in *Oeuvres de Mr. Turgot, Ministre d'État précédées et accompagnées de mémoires et de notes sur sa vie, son administration et ses ouvrages,* 9 vols. (Paris, 1808–11), 8:463.

1. Navarro Latorre, *Hace doscientos años,* 20.

2. Danvila, *Reinado de Carlos III,* 2:299–300.

3. AHN, Estado 3211, pt. 2; Ferrer del Rio, *Historia del reinado de Carlos III,* 1:422, 455; Moxó, "Medievalista en al Consejo de Hacienda," 610–68.

4. Béliardi, BNPar, MS Fonds Français, 10764, ff. 136v–137. Béliardi was posted by the French Foreign Ministry under Choiseul to Madrid in 1757 as commercial agent to restrain the hispanophile French ambassador d'Ossun, a good friend of Charles III. Béliardi, always close to French merchants and financiers at Madrid, envisioned a Franco-Spanish economic "union" in which Spain might fulfill its role in the colonial compact, France furnishing the manufactures Spaniards could not yet produce satisfactorily. Via detailed reports to Choiseul (Carrasco considered Béliardi the "alma de Choiseul"), especially his "Grand mémoire sur le Commerce des Indes," Béliardi shaped Choiseul's approach to Spain. Muret, "Papiers de l'Abbé Béliardi," 657–69; AHN, Estado 3211, pt. 2.

5. BNPar, MS Fonds Français, 10764, esp. ff. 226v, 283v.

6. Ibid.

7. Danvila, *Reinado de Carlos III,* 2:304.

8. BNPar, MS Fonds Français, 10764.

9. Ibid.

10. *SEV* 12 (1788): 281; BNPar, MS Fonds Français, 10764, f. 154; BNMex, Lafragua, Miscelanea 626, f. 27; Rousseau, *Règne de Charles III,* 2:21–22.

11. BNPar, MS Fonds Français, 10767, f. 183.

12. Ibid., 10768, f. 107.

13. Anes Alvarez, "Sociedad y economía," in Congreso internacional sobre Carlos III y la ilustración, *Actas,* 2:107.

14. Moñino, "Alegación fiscal," *BAE,* 59:28. A statistical survey ordered by Campomanes in 1764 revealed that 16 percent of rural property in Castile belonged to the church. Noel, "Campomanes and the Secular Clergy," 213–14 and 214 n. 5.

15. Noel, "Campomanes and the Secular Clergy," 214, 231, 233.

16. Ibid., 231; Moñino, "Alegación fiscal," *BAE,* 59:28. On the growth of ecclesiastical acquisitions of rural properties in the eighteenth century, see Francesco Carrasco to Miguel de Múzquiz (1766), "Representación," BRAHM, Mata Linares, 87.

17. Noel, "Campomanes and the Secular Clergy," 214, 233, 267.

18. BNPar, MS Fonds Français, 10764, f. 238v; Campomanes, *Memorial ajustado . . . sobre . . . los abastos de Madrid,* 1:505–506; Hamilton, *War and Prices in Spain, 1651–1800,* 158.

19. Valera Marcos, "Primer reglamento para el libre comercio," 258.

20. "Memoria sobre la política comercial de Inglaterra en America," BRAHM, 9-9-8, 2008, n. 1. English merchants made no bones of their intention to ship their goods via Spanish New Orleans to New Spain, for that city would "deliver to us the

key to the wealth of Mexico." Christelow, "Contraband Trade Between Jamaica and the Spanish Main," 315.

21. Voltes Bou, *Carlos III,* 173; Andrien, "Economic Crisis," 104–31.

22. Cf. *Ordenanzas* (1768), Tratado 3, titulo 6, art. 21, p. 147: "pues a lo que ha de aspirar cada uno por la carrera y honor de las armas, es a mantener y aumentar si puede el lustre de su familia, y si no, adquirirlo, y con sus méritos personales deja a la posterioridad memorias de sus apreciables circunstancias."

23. Béliardi to Choiseul. BNPar, MS Fonds Français, 10764, f. 297v.

24. See Kuethe, *Cuba,* ch. 2.

25. Tornero Tinajero, *Crecimiento económico.* During the English occupation, customs revenues jumped to 400,000 pesos, compared to a prewar annual average of 30,000. Christelow, "Contraband Trade Between Jamaica and the Spanish Main," 314 n. 11.

26. Palacio Atard, *Tercer pacto.*

27. BRPal., MS Ayala, 2852, f. 155v; Tanucci to Wall, in Palacio Atard, *Tercer pacto,* 29.

28. Béliardi to Berryer, Madrid, 19 Nov. 1759. BNPar, MS Fonds Français, 10764, f. 123; Rousseau, *Règne de Charles III,* 31; Bourguet, *Choiseul,* 21.

29. Christelow, "French Interest in the Spanish Empire," 520; María Amalia, letter to Tanucci, cited in Palacio Atard, *Tercer pacto,* 95 n. 4. Data prepared for the Esquilache administration covering 1747–61 underscored the importance of New Spain's mining and agricultural export production. That colony produced 43.6 percent of all precious metals from the Spanish colonies in America, and 51.4 percent of the agricultural exports. Of total Spanish colonial exports of precious metals and agricultural staples, New Spain alone accounted for 45.2 percent. AHN, Estado 2314, no. 13.

30. Gálvez, "Discurso y reflexiones de un vasallo," BRPal, Ayala, 2816, f. 1124.

31. Béliardi to Berryer, Madrid, 2 Nov. 1761. BNPar, Fonds Français, 10764, ff. 244–44v.

32. Guerra y Sánchez, ed., *Historia de la nación cubana,* 2:110–11; Thomas, *Cuba,* 1–2; Pérez de la Riva, ed., *Documentos sobre la toma de la Habana,* 18, 23; Syrett, comp., *Siege and Capture of Havana.*

33. Béliardi, BNPar, MS Fonds Français, 10766, f. 66; Palacio Atard, *Tercer pacto,* 279.

34. Esquilache resisted committing Spain to a commercial treaty with France, viewing it as "un piège" undermining Spanish tariffs. "Plan de Convention," BNPar, MS Fonds Français, 10766, f. 206.

35. Palacio Atard, *Tercer pacto,* 255–56; Pérez de la Riva, ed., *Documentos,* 265–66.

36. Palacio Atard, *Tercer pacto,* 74–75, 117, n. 26, 132; Pares, *War and Trade in the West Indies,* 583.

37. Pérez de la Riva, ed., *Documentos,* 23–24; *Guía de fuentes para la historia de Ibero-América,* 2:274; Anderson, *Historical and Chronological Deduction,* 3:33.

38. Guerra y Sánchez, ed., *Historia de la nación cubana,* 2:45.

39. Béliardi to Choiseul, Madrid, 18 Oct. 1762, BNPar, Fonds Français, 10764, f. 297v. The British capture of Havana produced shock waves in European capitals. Dickson, *Financial Revolution in England,* 9.

40. Juan Manuel Palomino, Havana, 29 Aug. 1762. BNMad, MS España 423, ff. 224–26v; "Carta escrita en la Habana . . . 1762." BRPal, MS 1855.

41. For example, the court-martial of Havana's Governor Prado y Portocarrero was criticized in 1766 by the bishop of Cuenca, who, in turn, was refuted by a *fiscal* of the Consejo de Castilla, Campomanes. See the latter's "Alegación," 63; Béliardi to Choiseul, BNPar, MS Fonds Français, 10764, f. 297.

42. Gándara, *Apuntes,* 242–43. See also Thomas, *Cuba,* 6 n. 33.

43. Pérez de la Riva, ed., *Documentos,* 30; Thomas, *Cuba,* 50, 65.

44. Moreno Fraginals estimates that the 4,000 slaves imported virtually doubled Havana's slave population. In seventeen months (Nov. 1763–Apr. 1765), another 5,037 were imported. Moreno Fraginals, *Ingenio,* 1:35–36; Tornero Tinajero, *Crecimiento económico,* 34–36.

45. Perez de la Riva, ed., *Documentos,* 32, 35 n. 98, 260.

46. Thomas, *Cuba,* 53; Moreno Fraginals, *Ingenio,* 4–5.

47. On the conditions that the Spanish military encountered, see Kuethe, *Cuba,* 25.

48. Ricla, friend and collaborator of Aranda, remained in Cuba (1763–65) and later rose to be war minister (1779–80). On Ricla, see Guerra y Sánchez, ed., *Historia de la nación cubana,* 2:50–60, and his *Manual de la historia de Cuba,* 179 ff.; Delgado, "Conde de Ricla," 51–77.

49. Cf. Craywinckel, "Papel útil y curioso de reflexiones . . . ," 111–50; Vilar, *Catalogne,* 2:393.

50. Alejandro O'Reilly, "Descripción de la isla de Cuba." BRPal, f. 331v, 333–33v. O'Reilly furnished a copy of his report to France's commercial agent Béliardi. AAEPar, B III, 9 Sept. 1765.

51. Crame, "Discurso político," ff. 237, 243v, 244v, 251.

52. Ibid., f. 237.

53. In 1750, Ensenada had said the government might eliminate the Cadiz monopoly of colonial trade. Ensenada to Andrés de Hoyo, 14 Sept. 1750, "Derecho . . . según los precios actuales, que son los mismos que se han pagado en Cádiz en el despacho de la última flota," BMus, Add. MS 13976, f. 286.

54. French agents monitored closely the Canaries' trade with America, since Tenerife was authorized to import foreign (what turned out to be largely English) merchandise. D'Hermand, Tenerife, 1 Apr. 1786, ANPar, AE. B III, n. 344.

55. A classic formulation of dissatisfaction with the existing Spanish transatlantic system appears in an anonymous letter to Colonial Secretary Julián de Arriaga. After a knowledgeable review of the system concentrated at Cadiz, the writer proposed what in fact nine years later became the Reglamento de Barlovento. "Propónese, pues, que se dé libertad para que de qualquier puerto de España se puede navegar por Españoles a los Puertos e Islas de nuestra dominación desde la Isla de la Trinidad . . . hasta el puerto de Cartagena. . . ." Anon., letter, Buen Retiro, 20 Aug. 1756, AHN, Estado 3208[1]. Arriaga was no partisan of such modifications.

56. BMus, Add. MS 33030 (Newcastle Papers), ff. 69–69v.

57. Parry and Sherlock, *Short History of the West Indies,* 129, 133; Béliardi to Choiseul, Madrid, 13 Dec. 1762. BNPar, MS Fonds Français, 10764, ff. 305–305v.

58. Béliardi to Choiseul, Madrid, 31 Jan. 1763. BNPar, MS Fonds Français, 10764, f. 312v.

59. "Discurso . . . para acreditar el orígen y decadencia del comercio de España," 26 Feb. 1761, AHN, Estado 2851, no. 112. The following paragraphs are based upon this unpaginated manuscript.

60. This is also the conclusion of Varela Marcos, "Primer reglamento," 245–46.

61. [Anon.] "Ydea general del comercio de Yndias, Tolosa de Guipúzcoa, 1 marzo 1776," NYP, MS Rich 19, reprinted in Florescano and Castillo, eds., *Controversia,* 1:23–68. By February 1764, Cadiz knew of a "proiecto cuio asumpto es persuadir . . . lo útil y conbeniente que sería la libre navegación . . . a los [puertos] de America. . . ." Consulado de Cádiz to Madrid, 17 Feb. 1764, AGI, Consulados, Correspondencia de España, bk. 80, ff. 120–20v. Predictably, Abaría, who had joined Prime Minister Wall and other ministers (Eslava, the conde de Valdeparaíso, and Francisco Fernández de Molinillo) in recommending renewal of *flotas* to Veracruz in 1755, was critical of the changes in commercial policy advanced in the "Ydea general." Real Díaz, *Ferias de Jalapa,* 95 n. 10. In late 1764, a note in the correspondence of the Cadiz *consulado* with its Madrid agent (Larrarte) refers to "Abaría . . . sobre la protección de los assumptos que este tiene pendientes; lo que no declara de su jurisdicción y integridad." Consulado de Cádiz to Larrarte, 23 Oct. 1764, AGI, Consulados, Correspondencia de España, bk. 80, f. 120v.

62. At least three versions of the counterattack exist: Anon., AGI, Estado 86 (unfoliated); "Comercio de España y América," BNMex, Colección Lafragua, Misc. v. 626; "Impugnacion del comercio libre de América favoreciendo el de Cádiz," BRAHM, Mata Linares, 6. Benito Mata Linares accompanied José de Gálvez to New Spain (Priestley, *Gálvez,* 135).

63. "Comercio de España y América," ff. 1, 6.

64. "Impugnación del comercio libre de América," ff. 210v–211.

65. Ibid., ff. 216–17, 218v.

66. Ward objected to overlapping ministries supervising commercial affairs: "Nuestro comercio está dividido en diferentes retazos . . . sin conexión, ni armonía; pues el de América va por un Ministro, el de España por otro; los recursos en materia mercantil en unos casos van al Consejo de Guerra, en otros a la Junta [de Comercio]; algunas Compañías giran baxo la dirección de la Junta, otras por la vía reservada." *Proyecto económico,* 122–23, 150.

67. "Impugnación del comercio libre de América," f. 216.

68. Cadiz's cordial references to Arriaga must be put in context. No doubt the Cadiz *consulado* knew indirectly that the Consulado de México had recently rewarded Arriaga for unspecified favors with an impressive 32,000–peso gift (omitted from its accounts "por el sigilo que devía observarse"). Consulado de México, 23 Dec. 1754 and 6 Mar. 1758, AGN, AHH, 129–31.

69. "Impugnación del comercio libre de América," ff. 218, 220.

70. Perhaps this was Pedro Francisco de Goosens, later a *tesorero general* at Madrid (1765–87)? Pieper, *Real Hacienda,* 88.

71. José Craywinckel was later *governador interino* of Sonora (d. 1763). Varela Marcos, "Primer reglamento," 249 n. 7.

72. "Papel útil y curioso de reflexiones . . . al marqués de Squilace . . . sobre el comercio de trigo. . . . ," 131–50. Not to be overlooked was his analysis of the impact of Havana's brief occupation by English forces in his "Discurso sobre la utilidad que la España pudiera sacar de su desgracia en la pérdida de la Habana." Cited by Delgado i Ribas, "Floridablanca . . . política agraria," 657.

73. Ibid., 657.

74. Hale, *Franklin in France,* 75.

75. Ferrer del Rio, *Reinado de Carlos III,* 4:248.

76. Simón de Aragorri y Olavide (a Guipuzcoan) was presumed by Francisco Craywinckel to be the anonymous author of *Reflexiones sobre el estado actual del comercio de España* (Madrid, 1761) which inspired Campomanes's extended comment. Campomanes, *Reflexiones sobre el comercio español a Indias,* 409, n. 73.

77. AAEPar, M et D, Espagne 81, ff. 202–204v. He participated in arranging the Concordat of 1753 and was a *consejero* in the *cámara* of the Consejo de Castilla. Valera Marcos, "Primer reglamento," 249 n. 6. Mollinedo was also responsible for an edition of the seventeenth-century *arbitrista* Sancho de Moncada. Vilar, *Oro y moneda,* 45 and n. 109.

78. Marqués de los Llanos, "Papel . . . haciendo presentes . . . ," BRAHM, Ayala 2872, ff. 101–11. Note that Manuel José de Ayala—his manuscript collection is in the BRPal—was then the recently appointed archivist of the Colonial Office (Despacho Universal de Indias). Manzano Manzano, ed., *Notas a la recopilacion de Indies,* x.

79. Los Llanos, "Papel," f. 104.

80. Ibid., 104–104v.

81. Ibid., f. 106.

82. Ibid., ff. 108–10.

83. Ibid., 106v–107, lllv.

84. Ibid., f. 107v.

85. To quote from the Consulta of 1765: "las Lencerías que se embían al Perú son mas finas que las que se remiten a Nueva España y entre ellas van muchas encages" ("Consulta original," AHN, Estado 2314/1, f. 32).

86. "El Reyno de Galícia y Principado de Asturias . . . suplican. . . ." (1765), AHN, Estado 3188[2].

87. Ibid., ff. 1–2[2].

88. Campomanes to Antonio Valdés, 3 Aug. 1789, AHN, Estado 3208[1]. Understandably, Charles III insisted on frequent meetings of the Consejo de Indias to review colonal matters. Colonial Secretary Arriaga resisted change. More sensitive to overseas threats, Esquilache maintained his reserve, while making his own plans. Present at these sessions was Francisco Carrasco, a *fiscal* of the all-important Consejo de Hacienda. Ferrer del Rio, *Historia del reinado de Carlos III,* 1:452.

89. Fray Andrés de Echeandía to Manuel de Lerguinazával, Mexico, 16 Oct. 1764. A Mercederian, Echeandía had been asked by Lerguinazával for his views of "los comercios [que] son los mas graves empeños de las monarquías." Trade, he judged, had become "la sustancia, fuente y manantial de todos los Reynos." He was startled by the scale of smuggling in Manila-Acapulco shipping. Lerguinazával was listed (1767) as one of 128 *mercaderes/almaceneros* in the *vizcaíno* faction of the Consulado de México. AGI, Mexico 1515, n. 123. In 1776, he joined other *almaceneros* (Rodríguez de Neyra and two Rávagos) in criticizing officers of the Consulado de México for their mismanagement of surplus *alcabala* funds. AGN, AHH, 791–8.

90. Lerguinazával, "Thesoro de España. Discurso sobre el comercio," BRPal, Ayala, 2819, ff. 30–31v, 39.

91. Cf. ibid., f. 42: "si quieran [los cargadores] hacer . . . sus remesas, paguen los fletes a su antojo, mayormente quando giran Registros Sueltos en tiempo de guerra."

92. Ibid., ff. 44–45.

93. Juan Joseph del Ribero del Comercio de Indias, "Méthodo fácil i conveniente de impedir los contrabandos . . . 1761," BRAHM, Mata Linares, 76 n. 7.

3. The First Reglamento del Comercio Libre (1765)

EPIGRAPHS: "Consulta original," AHN, Estado, 2314/1, ff. 44v–45; Raynal, *Histoire philosophique,* 6:54.

1. Varela Marcos, "El primer reglamento para el comercio libre," 245–46. Varela considers Esquilache to have been the "alma de la política de libertad" (258).

2. "Consulta de una Junta formada de orden de SM por el marqués de los Llanos, Francisco Craywinckel, Simón de Aragorri, Pedro Goosens, Tomás de Landázuri, sobre el Proyecto de comercio de América. Acompaña un extracto de ella y otros documentos," Madrid, 14 Feb. 1765, AHN, Estado, 2314. There are copies with varying titles: [New York] Cadiz. Junta de Comercio, "Estracto del Proyecto para fomentar el comercio de las Indias en el que se consignan las modificaciones que debieron introducirse en el estanco del comercio en Cádiz. . . ," HSA, HC 371/63; [Mexico] "Extracto de consulta hecha a SM sobre comercio libre y arbitrios que propone para su aumento y progresivo desarrollo," AGN, Historia, vol. 279. Since the AHN copy of the "Consulta" lacks foliation, citations for quotations are omitted in the following paragraphs.

3. In the clear prose of the "Consulta original": "Como se paga [tonelada] por el Dueño del Navío antes de salir a navegar, y recae su importe sobre el coste principal del Navío, y crecidas expensas de su avilitación, son raros los que tienen facultades proprias para sufrirle: de que resulta, que muchas licencias concedidas quedan sin efecto, por la imposivilidad de los sugetos, a quienes se dieron: con que se reduce la Navegación a un corto número de individuales ricos, que embarcan de su quenta, o de sus socios, y Amigos, sostienen el alto precio de los fletes y privan al comun de Comerciantes pobres españoles de la libertad de embiar sus Mercadurías, prefiriendo el negociar con Casas Extrangeras, para ocupar los buques de su quenta: siendo digno de reflexión, que un derecho que desconcierta y aniquila nuestro Comercio, produzca en la Real Hacienda el corto interés, que se demonstrará en su lugar." AHN, Estado, 2314/1, f. 12v.

4. *Colonial Imports on Private Account, Cadiz, 1755–61*
(*pesos fuertes*)

Precious Metals	15,239,699	(78%)
Staples	4,191,467	(22%)
Total	19,431,166	(100%)

Source: AHN, Estado, 2314/1, "Consulta Original," ff. 33–34.

5. *Revenues from Colonial Trades, Cadiz, 1755–63, Excluding 1762*
(*reales de vellon*)

Exports	28,340,416	(9%)
Palmeo, etc.	18,698,899	(6%)
Imports (precious metals, staples)	261,751,055	(85%)
Total	308,790,370	(100%)

Source: AHN, Estado, 2314/1, "Consulta Original," ff. 33–34.

6. The costly formalities of managed trade via convoys obliged "los Negociantes a hacer mayor embíos en cada buque, y por consecuencia, hacer el negocio con mayores riesgos, y sin arbitrio para economizar los fletes ni gastos de comisiones." Not to introduce the "incertidumbre del número de Navíos, que si se ha de emplear, y de los que serán preferidos en el Ministerio, precisa a los Armadores matriculados a mantener dos tercios más de buques, de los que regularmente se emplean." AHN, Estado, 2314/1, "Consulta original," ff. 9v–10.

7. AHN, Estado, 2314/1, n. 2. *Reales de plata* have been converted to pesos of 15 *reales*.

8. Béliardi, BNPar, MS Fonds Français, 10766.

9. Catalonia, for example, would channel its colonial trade via the port of Barcelona, Aragon via Tortosa, Valencia via Alicante, Murcia via Cartagena, Granada via Málaga, Andalusia via Cadiz, Sevilla or Sanlucar, Galicia via Vigo and La Coruña, Asturias via Gijón, Castille via Santander, Santoña or Laredo, and La Rioja, Navarre, and part of Aragon via Bilbao and San Sebastián.

10. The file or dossier of the "Consulta original" contains a brief, polished, unsigned recommendation to "extinguir la casa de la Contratación de Cádiz pues cesa los motivos de su establecimiento." Also recommended was termination of the charters of all privileged companies within two years. Neither recommendation was implemented in the final statute.

11. According to a *reglamento* of 21 Jan. 1735, *flotas* would depart from Cadiz with cargo divided into *frutos* (one-third) and *ropas* (two-thirds). AGI, Estado, 86.

12. *Cargo Distribution of 600-Ton Ship to Veracruz*
   (*reales de plata*)

Frutos, Caldos, Abarrotes		(200 *toneladas*)
Wine	335,500	
Paper	318,000	
Cinnamon	579,384	
(Other)	473,885	
Subtotal	1,706,769	
Ropas		(400 *toneladas*)
Linens	10,781,100	
Woolens	1,455,780	
Silks	5,809,258	
(Other)	56,962	
Subtotal	18,103,100	
Total	19,809,869	(600 *toneladas*)

Source: AHN, Estado, 2314/1, "Consulta Original," n. 6, "Cálculo de un navío de 600 toneladas para Veracruz."

13. "Cálculo de un navío de 600 toneladas para Veracruz," in AHN, Estado, 2314/1, "Consulta original," n. 6.

14. The *junta*'s claim of an effective reexport duty rate of 3.3 percent is in part substantiated by Barcelona exporters, who calculated the level of export duties on textiles loaded aboard a *flota* for New Spain in 1772 at 5.38. See also "Derecho . . . segun los precios actuales, que son los mismos que se han pagado en Cádiz en el despacho de la ultima flota," BMus, Add. MS 13976.

15. Fortune, *Merchants and Jews.*

16. *Spanish America: Precious Metals Production, 1757–61*

All Spanish Colonies	29,074,643	100.00%
New Spain	13,124,643	45.14%

Source: Adapted from AHN, Estado, 2314, app. 15, "Noticia de los productos de las Américas en plata y oro y frutos, con distinción de reynos."

17. Valera Marcos, "Primer reglamento," 262 and n. 17.

18. "Consulta original," ff. 40–40v. The state, Landázuri added, should "animar a los Mineros" because "los quintos, señoreage y monedage, hacen un Ramo muy considerable de la Real Hacienda en aquellos Dominios, y a su venida en España repiten otro aumento en los derechos de entrada y necesitandole todas las Naciones que comercian en Levante y Oriente a donde va a pasar, para sacarlo de España pagan otro indulto sobre él de los frutos o mercaderías que entregan por su valor principal."

19. Valera Marcos, "Primer reglamento," 265.

20. BRPal, MS Ayala, 2824, ff. 131–59. There is a copy in NYP, MS Rich 9.

21. At the end of the seventeenth century, a quintal of mercury was priced in New Spain at 60 *pesos fuertes,* and subsequently raised to 84 despite repeated protests by mine owners. Since mercury distribution was handled by the private sector (*por dirección de particulares*), mainly Mexico City's *almaceneros,* the distributors balked at lowering the price ("tuvieron arte para sofocar tan justificada instancia"), arguing that were the state to administer mercury supplies, the colonial treasury would not receive its mercury revenues on time. AHN, Estado, 2314, n. 12.

22. Landázuri was probably the source of the observation that "en la Nueva Vizcaya y Nuevo México se celebran dos ferias cada año, con los Gentiles . . . a las que concurren las Naciones Apache, Comanche, Caiguas, Alas [?], Pimas y Yroqueses, que hacen el convalache con nosotros, y se reduce a Pieles preciosas, y entre ellas las de Castor." AHN, Estado, 2314/1, "Consulta original," f. 27.

23. Whatever Landázuri's stand in 1765, in 1771, he proposed including New Spain in the expanding system of *comercio libre.* Hussey, *Caracas Company,* 229n. See also Valera Marcos, "Primer reglamento," 251, 253–54 n. 9.

24. Levene, ed., *Documentos para la historia argentina,* 5:197–98, no 40. Apparently colonial issues, including trade, had dominated the cabinet's agenda in the first quarter of 1765. The weekly interministerial meetings included Prime Minister Grimaldi, Colonial Secretary Arriaga, Hacienda Secretary Esquilache, and a rising *fiscal* of the Consejo de Hacienda, Francisco Carrasco. Grimaldi told Béliardi, for example, that "les affaires de l'Amérique l'avoient tellement occupé ces derniers jours." Béliardi to Choiseul, July 1765, BNPar, MS Fonds Français, 10764, f. 357; Ferrer del Rio, *Historia del reinado de Carlos III,* 1:452.

25. The thirty-five ports are listed in AHN, Estado, 2314/1, ff. 19v–20.

26. Rodríguez Labandeira, "Política económica de los Borbones," in Anes Alvarez et al., eds., *Economía española al final del antiguo régimen,* 4:173.

27. See AHN, Estado 86, "Dictamen leído . . . ," 12 May 1777.

28. Raynal, who had access to reliable data on Spain's foreign and colonial trade, published data indicating that New Spain alone absorbed virtually 46 percent of

Cadiz's total exports to America. *Histoire philosophique,* vol. 3, "Tableau des marchan-dises."

29. AHN, Estado 3188², "Observaciones" (1778).

30. Raynal, *Histoire philosophique,* 4:154.

31. Ibid., 221–22; Béliardi to Choiseul-Praslin, Madrid, 17 Feb. 1766, BNPar, MS Fonds Français, 10764, ff. 427–427v.

32. Robertson, *History of America,* 3:337.

33. AAEPar, M et D, Amérique, 33, ff. 185.

34. Edward Misselden, *Free Trade, or, The Meanes to Make Trade Florish wherein, the causes of the decay of trade in this kingdome are discouered: and the remedies also to remouve the same, are represented* (London, 1622), cited in Schumpeter, *History of Economic Analysis,* 355.

4. Privilege and Power in Bourbon Spain: The Fall of Esquilache (1766)

EPIGRAPHS: Campomanes, *Dictamen fiscal de expulsión de los Jesuitas,* para. 217; Muñoz Pérez, "Publicación del Reglamento de Comercio Libre," *AEA* 4 (1947): 620.

1. Cf. "Carta del Conde de Aranda a D. Manuel de Roda, 9 de Abril de 1766," AGSim, Gracia y Justicia, leg. 1009, ff. 47–48, cited in Navarro Latorre, *Hace doscientos años,* 26–27: "El orden que se observó en el mayor desorden; la especie de disciplina y obediencia en los repentinos movimientos para el alboroto y para la respectiva quietud cuando les convenía; las Centinelas que tenían y avisos que se daban; la ocupación de las Puertas de Madrid; el ningun temor a la Tropa ni a la Justicia; el arrojo con que se presentaron a Palacio, a los Tribunales y Magistrados . . . no es fácil comprehender que lo practicasen sin ser gobernados con instrucción, regla y disciplina." And see also d'Ossun to Choiseul, Aranjuez, 10 Apr. 1766, AEParis, CP, Espagne, 545, ff. 264–71.

2. Contemporaries clearly perceived the role of churchmen and the nobility but would not identify those responsible. See d'Ossun to Choiseul, Aranjuez, 27 Mar. 1766, AEPar, CP, Espagne, 545, ff. 227–28. "Quien las fomentó (directamente sin duda contra el marqués de Esquilache) es arriesgado adivinarlo. . . . Celebramos la quietud que gozamos," wrote a "Gentleman of Madrid to another in Cadiz" late in April 1766. AHN, Estado, 2872, n. 35.

3. *Gaceta de Madrid,* 25 Mar. 1766. See also ibid., 8 Apr. 1766: "El Martes 25 del próximo pasado por la Manaña el Rey y demás Personas Reales se trasladaron felizmente desde este Palacio al Real Sitio de Aranjuez, y alli disfrutan de perfecta salud."

4. Campomanes, "Alegación fiscal . . . Obispo de Cuenca," in *BAE,* 59:65.

5. According to Rodríguez Casado, *Política y los políticos,* 140–41, "los más de los fautores se retiran a la sombra, atizan el descontento, prenden la chispa y esperan tranquilamente el resultado."

6. Navarro Latorre, *Hace doscciento años,* has proposed the concept of initiators, actors, and abettors.

7. *Novíssima recopilación,* lib. vi, tit. viii, ley xix.

8. Ibid., lib. iii, tit. xix, ley xiii, n. 6; Martínez Salazar, *Colección,* 448–52.

9. *Novíssima recopilación,* libro iii, tit. xix, ley xiii; Danvila, *Reinado de Carlos III,* 2:309–10.

10. Campomanes, "Dictamen de los fiscales sobre prohibición de capas largas y sombreros redondos. Madrid, 4 de marzo de 1766," in Eguía Ruíz, *Jesuitas y el motín de Esquilache,* 349–59; Danvila, *Reinado de Carlos III,* 2:310–11.

11. Campomanes, *Dictamen . . . Jesuitas,* para. 7.

12. Danvila, *Reinado de Carlos III,* 2:314–15.

13. Martínez Salazar, *Colección,* 448–52; Sala de Alcaldes de Casa y Corte, Archivo, *Catálogo por materias,* 161–62, 672 (sombreros de tres picos, 1760, 1761, 1766); Danvila, *Reinado de Carlos III,* 2:81–82.

14. Martínez Salazar, *Colección,* 211–14. See also ff. 460–73, 476–77, listed in Sala de Alcaldes de Casa y Corte, Archivo, *Catálogo por materias,* 283: "Expediente formado para evacuar el informe pedido por el consejo sobre las penas que pueden imponerse a los que falseen la de SM y Señores, con el informe que se hizo (1784)."

15. *Novísima recopilación,* lib. iii, tit. ii, ley xii.

16. Sources of the vignette of the *sala* are Martínez Salazar, *Colección,* 317–485, and Desdevises du Dézert, "Chambre des juges," 1–51.

17. Martínez Salazar, *Colección,* 380–81. The dean of the *sala* replaced the absent governor in most functions. Its supporting staff included a *fiscal* and his agent, two *relatores,* a lawyer, a counsel for the poor, clerks, and about forty sheriffs, or *alguaciles.* The *sala* met daily, and its committees supervised public ceremonial, prisons, and hospitals.

18. Rojas y Contreras, *Historia del colegio viejo de San Bartolomé,* 722–28. Unless otherwise indicated, this is the source of biographical and genealogical data on the governor.

19. Luís del Valle Salazar replaced him in 1767. What lay behind his appointment as governor and then his departure is not clear. Cf. Sala de Alcaldes de Casa y Corte, Archivo, *Catálogo por materias,* "Aviso del Governador de la Sala y nota de lo practicado el día que tomó posesión el señor don Francisco de la Mata . . ." (1765), f. 142.

20. Martínez Salazar, *Colección,* 449.

21. Ibid., 730–39. The leverage of the *juez conservador* waxed in the seventeenth century in proportion to the financial gifts of the *receptores,* who then purchased and sold their office.

22. A *regiduría* in Andalusia's capital associated Mata Linares with the provincial nobility dominating Sevilla's *ayuntamiento* (the so-called *veinticuatros*), who controlled both municipal taxes and land. Sevilla's town council along with others in the metropole were targets of Esquilache's program to revise municipal financial practices based on manipulation of *proprios* and *arbitrios.* On this point, see Julián Saiz Milanés, "Orígenes y historia de los bienes de propios," in Estapé y Rodríguez, ed., *Textos olvidados;* Martínez Salazar, *Colección,* 123; and Anes Alvarez, *Crisis agrarias en la España moderna.*

23. A nephew, Fernando de la Mata Linares y Vásquez de Acuña—his brother's son—attended San Bartolomé; his sister's marriage linked Mata Linares to the Movellán family also from San Vicente de la Barquera and to its merchant members in both Cadiz and Mexico City. On his mother's side, Mata Linares was related to Francisco Calderón de la Barca y Barreda, who resided in the *hospedaría* of San Bartolomé (1765) and in the next decade joined Mata Linares in opposing reform of the *colegios mayores.* Rojas y Contreras, *Historia,* 894; Sala Balust, *Visitas y reforma de los colegios mayores de Salamanca,* 150–51, 182.

24. Benito de la Mata Linares y Vázquez followed his brother (Juan de Sahagún) in a scholarship at San Bartolomé in the 1760s, later serving in the colonial bureaucracy and finally in the Consejo de Indias. A younger brother, Francisco de Paula, was an intendant at Concepción in Chile. Like the first conde de Revillagigedo, who preceded him as Cuba's captain-general, Francisco Antonio Cagigal de la Vega profited from the slave trade and investments in the island's economy.

25. Mata Linares spoke for many *consejeros* of the Consejo de Castilla when protesting reform of the *colegios mayores* in 1771 and later helped block its implementation at Salamanca. Minister of Justice Manuel de Roda singled him out to his like-minded collaborator Bishop Beltrán of Salamanca: "El alcalde mayor de esa ciudad, que está destinado al Colegio de San Bartolomé, es protegido del señor Mata, que hace de cabeza hacedor, y es el que más se ha singularizado entre los ministros en el empeño que comuniqué a VI, y por eso fué mas severa y particular la advertencia que se le hizo en nombre de SM para que se contuviese . . . se sabe su pasión e inteligencia con este ministro." Sala Balust, *Visitas y reforma,* 57–59, 78. In 1775, Mata Linares's Madrid home was considered a "nidal de los colegiales," the source of stratagems to stem the state's reform drive. Mata's sons joined their father's campaign of resistance. Regulations on the dress of *colegiales* notwithstanding, they were reported to authorities: "Usan capas blancas ambos Matas y Calderón, del Viejo . . . y Mata, el mayor, sale al público con medias blancas y sombrero de plumaje." Roda recalled that in 1766, a *colegial* group had appealed for their use of long cloaks, "suponiendo su necesidad de venir a la corte y, quitado este disfraz común, no poder ir como los demas." They petitioned for special treatment, the wearing of distinctive dress to match the prestige of their scholarships. Ibid., 100–101.

26. Justice Minister Roda was suspicious of the circumstances of the publication of the compendium. In 1771, as the campaign to reform the *colegios* began, Roda discovered that the edition had been printed (1766–70), left unbound, and then moved to the Colegio Mayor de San Bartolomé at Salamanca; although dedicated to Charles (without permission), a copy had never been presented to the king. Roda urged careful examination of the text for its supposed distortions. Sala Balust, *Visitas y reforma,* 88–92. Velasco's co-editor, José de Rojas y Contreras, remained profoundly attached to the Colegio Viejo: its hostel had been his home for fifteen years, it had "fixado la rueda" of his fortune, and his admiration was expressed in both introduction and comments throughout the work. Rojas saw the *colegiales* as prime factors in the "sacred work of church and state" and paid tribute to the "corto número de Individuos que hayan producido tan abundantes frutos de santidad, sabiduría y prudencia," whose alleged shortcomings were the product of envy rather than the zeal of critics. In defending *colegiales,* Rojas recalled that in 1762, Charles III had promised the *colegios* that "sus quexas hallarían siempre en la Real Justificación . . . el apoyo que corresponde a la estimación que hace de los Colegios y de sus Individuos . . . pues este Real apreciabilísimo honor debiera ponerlos a cubierto de todo insulto." After March 1766, the state had a different view of the *colegios mayores.* See Rojas y Contreras, *Historia,* vol. 2, introduction.

27. Martínez Salazar, *Colección,* 211–12, 421.

28. Cf. decree in AHN, Archivo de la Sala de Alcaldes de Casa y Corte.

29. Ibid., *Catálogo por materias.*

30. Desdevises du Dézert, "Chambre des juges," 8.

31. This protocol is outlined in Martínez Salazar, *Colección*, 211–17.

32. Rojas y Contreras, *Historia*, 2:694–709; "Casa de Rojas. Rama Sexta," in García Carraffa, *Diccionario heráldico y genealógico*.

33. Pedro de Moctezuma y Salcedo (a *regidor* of Ronda) enjoyed an annual pension of 1,000 pesos drawn on the Mexico City colonial treasury as sixth great-grandson of the Aztec "emperor." Rojas y Contreras, *Historia*, 2:707–8. José de Moctezuma y Rojas became a lieutenant under one of the royal princes (Pedro), *Hermano Mayor* of the Maestranza of Ronda, a prestigious honorary militia. Such organizations proliferated in Andalusia in the eighteenth century, conferring privilege and influence on their memberships, which listed prominent estate owners and merchants of the distant colony of New Spain. The Maestranza of Ronda was one of the first paramilitary organizations to be ordered to conform to the new prohibition of cloaks and slouch hats. Archivo del Ayuntamiento de Sevilla. Colección Aguila, vol. 41, n. 65.

34. By his sister's marriage, Diego de Rojas y Contreras had as nephews Joachín de Melgarejo y Rojas (marqués de Quiroga), a royal equerry (*caballerizo*) and *mayordomo de semana* at court; Luís, *colegial* of Cuenca and on the Chancillería of Granada, and Francisco Xavier, a naval officer. Rojas y Contreras, *Historia*, 2:707–8.

35. Ferrer del Rio, *Historia del reinado de Carlos III*, 1:414–15. Danvila, *Reinado de Carlos III*, 2:337, 361–63, and Navarro Latorre, *Hace doscientos años*, 18, blame his weakness. Ferrer del Rio sees him sympathetic to the rioters (*Historia del reinado de Carlos III*, 2:31–33), as does Amador de los Rios (*Historia de la villa y corte de Madrid*, 4:245). Lafuente calls him "prudent" (*Historia de España*, 14:173), and Rousseau "equivocal" (*Règne de Charles III*, 1:189).

36. Martínez Salazar, *Colección*, 449, 453.

37. Danvila, *Reinado de Carlos III*, 2:313.

38. Ferrer del Rio, *Historia del reinado de Carlos III*, 2:45.

39. Navarro Latorre, *Hace doscientos años*, 10.

40. After the Walloon Guards came under attack, the "Tumulto" relates, Charles "hizo llamar a Palacio a todo el Consejo de Castilla, y le mandó se juntase allí mismo, y le consultase los medios que juzgase oportunos para apaciguar al Pueblo. El Consejo obedeció, congregandose en las piezas de la Secretaría del Despacho de Indias, y expuso a SM como único remedio para aplacar el tumulto la deposición y destierro del Marqués de Squilace, objeto de la ira publica. . . . No se conformó SM con este dictamen, y le mandó pensase luego en sugerir otros medios." While suggesting a lowering of food prices and withdrawal of the edict of 10 March, the *consejo* insisted that "no juzgaba se diese por satisfecha la plebe, insistiendo en . . . el propuesto antes [hecho] por el mismo Consejo." BMus, Egerton, "Tumulto de Madrid" (1766), ff. 221v–222.

41. Danvila, *Reinado de Carlos III*, 2:333.

42. Rojas y Contreras, *Historia*, vol. 2.

43. The literature on the Jesuits in the *motín*, although generally subject to polemics, provides considerable documentation and some elucidation of the issue. Among those who have insisted on the Jesuits' noninvolvement is Eguía Ruíz, *Jesuitas y el motín de Esquilache*.

44. D'Ossun to Choiseul, Aranjuez, 27 Mar. 1766, AAEPar, CP, Espagne, 545, ff. 227–38.

45. Danvila, *Reinado de Carlos III,* 2:372–77 and n.

46. AGSim, Gracia y Justicia, 1009, "Puntos que quiere el Rey para su honor y seguridad del pueblo," ff. 47–48, cited in Navarro Latorre, *Hace doscientos años,* 26–27.

47. Aranda to Múzquiz, Madrid, 8 May 1766, AGSim, Superintendencia de Hacienda, 1061.

48. Choiseul to d'Ossun, Versailles, 20 May 1766, AAE, CP, Espagne, 545.

49. Béliardi to Choiseul, Aranjuez, 28 Apr. 1766, AAE, CP, Espagne, 545, f. 531.

50. Danvila, *Reinado de Carlos III,* 2:386.

51. Danvila, *Reinado de Carlos III,* 2:322, long ago concluded on examining Aranda's report that in "la versión mas autorizada del motín de Madrid . . . no se encontrará nunca, por mucho que se rebusque, dato ni antecedente que justifique el nuevo rumbo que tomaron las investigacioanes a poco de ser nombrado [Aranda] . . . governador del Consejo de Castilla.".

52. Eguía Ruíz, *Jesuitas y el motín de Esquilache,* is convinced that the anti-Jesuit groundswell gained momentum with the ouster of Ensenada and the removal of Fernando VI's confessor, Padre Rábago.

53. Danvila, *Reinado de Carlos III,* 2:362; Ortí y Brull, *Doña María Manuela Pignatelli,* 1:90–92.

54. AGSim, Gracia y Justicia, 1009, ff. 10–12.

55. D'Ossun to Choiseul, 9 June 1766, AAEPar, CP, Espagne, 545.

56. Danvila, *Reinado de Carlos III,* 2:613. Apropos of Campomanes's hallmarks, note para. 234, where a parallel is drawn between the Jesuits and the Knights Templars, suppressed by the pope in 1312, whose history Campomanes—a historian by avocation all his life—had researched early in his career. See his *Disertaciones históricas del orden y caballería de los Templares* (Madrid, 1747).

57. Cf. Townsend, *Journey Through Spain,* 200–201: "All [Esquilache's] well digested plans for the reformation of the finance, the encouragement of manufacture, and the renovations of the empire were rendered ineffectual and banished with himself."

58. Danvila, *Reinado de Carlos III,* 2:614.

59. AGI, Consulados, Libro de correspondencia 80, ff. 132, 164–164v, 179, 189, 194, 241; Garmendia Arruebarrena, *Apodaca,* 316.

60. Baran, *Growth,* 153 n. 34.

61. *Consulado* correspondence with Madrid on the "old creditors" and related matters fills AGI, Consulado, Libro de correspondencia, 80.

62. AGI, Consulados, Libro de correspondencia, 80, ff. 273v–274, 280v; AGN, AHH, 129–31.

63. Quoted in Delgado i Ribas, "America" (1987), 139. Bucareli's admiration for Esquilache shines through in a personal communication to the latter in 1768, two years after the *motín:* "Conserva VE el conocimiento de lo seguro de mi afecto y gratitud de lo que me distinguió en el tiempo de su ministerio. Los acaecimientos después que VE dejó la corte han justificado lo mismo que dije a VE en la carta a que se sirve responderme, tanto puede el obrar vien, que no basta la malicia mas acreditada, a manchar la conducta de quien solo trataba de servir al Rey." Bucareli to Esquilache, Havana, 22 Jan. 1768, AGI, Ind. Gen., 1629.

5. *Flotas* to New Spain: The Last Phase, 1757–1778

EPIGRAPHS: Heros Fernández, *SEV* 26 (1790): 197; AHN, Estado, 2851, n. 112.

1. José María Quirós, "Memoria de instituto . . . 1819," AGI, Mexico, 2519, n. 3, quoting John Nichols.

2. Bernal, *Financiación,* 313.

3. The following synthesis of Cadiz shipping formalities is based upon García del Prado, *Compendio general,* one of the manuals "para instruir las formulas y diligencias presedentes, y subsiguientes a la profesión de cargadores, encomenderos, sobrecargos, navieros, et., estando en perpétuo y desigual convate todas las relaciones que debían referirse a un fin." José Donato de Austria, "Memoria de instituto . . . 1803," AGI, Mexico, 2996. See also "Formalidades que oy se practican [1764] para el despacho de los Navíos que van a las Indias," AHN, Estado, 2314/1, n. 6.

4. AHN, Estado 2314/1, n. 6: "no puede despachar ningun navío para la América, sin licencia de la corte. Para este fin acude al Ministro de la secretaría de Yndias, por mano del Presidente de la Contratación de Cádiz, o por los Amigos, o Agentes que tienen en Madrid." "Formalidades que oy se practican para el despacho de los navíos que van a las Indias."

5. Clarke, *Letters Concerning the Spanish Nation,* 258. Since the cost of a license was a component of ocean freight rates, it forced export merchants wherever possible to avoid peninsular staples "que son por naturaleza mas voluminosas que los efectos finos extrangeros; y del mismo modo acorta y retrae los retornos de frutos y materiales de América." Furthermore, the high cost of licenses limited their purchase to "un corto número de individuos ricos . . . sus socios y amigos" generally the foreign merchants resident at Cadiz. AHN, Estado 2314/1.

6. Bernal, *Financiación,* 355.

7. Shipper (*cargador*), shipowner (*dueño*), and shipmaster (*maestro de navío*) all had to be registered with the Consulado de Cádiz, with proof of "naturaleza de estos Reynos, de limpieza de sangre, y de no ser de los nuevamente convertidos a nuestra Santa Fe Cathólica." "Formalidades que oy se practican," AHN, Estado, 2314/1, n. 6, item 1a.

8. As late as 1826, the Mexican government gauged the tonnage of foreign shipping entering Veracruz in a similar fashion, i.e., following "Burgos measurements." Espinosa de los Monteros to H. G. Ward, Mexico City, 23 Oct. 1826, Public Record Office, Board of Trade, 6/54.

9. "Examen du nouveau règlement sur le commerce libre des Isles Espagnoles. . . ." BNPar, MS Fonds Français, 10769, f. 134v.

10. Ibid. In the last third of the century, the use of foreign-built merchant shipping purchased by Spanish shippers for the colonial trade rose. Consulado de Cádiz to Francisco Manxón, 19 June 1780, AGI, Consulados, Copiador de cartas, f. 44.

11. AHN, Estado 2314/1: "se arqueó el Navío por el capitán de las Maestranzas de la Real Armada, ante un Oydor, el Fiscal, y el Capitán de la Maestranza. Se toman las medidas en presencia de un escrivano de la Contratación, quien forma una certificación que se agrega a los Autos." Once the "certificación de las Toneladas" has been sent to Contratación, there follows "la visita, y señalamiento de obras por el Capitán de Maestranza de la Real Armada y Maestros Mayores de Carpintería y Calafatería de ella, dando . . . testimonio necesario, y que por el Consulado y Uni-

versidad de Cargadores a Indias, se informe sobre el abono del interesado, y que hecho lo vea el Fiscal." Finally, "informe el Consulado lo que se lo ofrece en virtud del Auto del Presidente."

12. The incidence of careening per vessel was high, since the Consejo de Indias often failed to issue licenses to the same petitioners on successive *flotas,* leaving their vessels moored unused for extended periods. See Boyetet, "Idée générale . . . ," BNPar, MS Fonds Français, 10769, ff. 13v–14. And see also [Anon.] "Ydea general del comercio de las Indias," Tolosa de Guipúzcoa, 1 Mar. 1776, NYP, MS Rich 19, case 1: "Muchos pretendientes para tan corto numero de licencias, se quedan sin obtenerlas, de que resulta inutilizarse en el Puerto, y quando llega el caso de que naveguen, tienen que hacerlos [navíos] nuevos."

13. [Anon.] "Ydea general del comercio de Yndias," Tolosa de Guipúzcoa, 1 Mar. 1776, NYP, MS Rich 19, ff. 4v–5.

14. When caught for overloading by colonial customs officials, the "error" was then blamed upon metropolitan customs officials. Blas Sánchez Ochando to Antonio Valdés, Cadiz, 19 Sept. 1788, AGI, Ind. Gen., 2313.

15. "Demostración del comercio exterior español . . . ," BRPal, Ayala MS 2822.

16. "Examen du nouveau règlement . . . ," BNPar, MS Fonds Français, 10769, f. 135. The average repair cost of 50,000 pesos was a minuscule percentage (3.3–5%) of the value of the cargo, often set at 1–1.5 million pesos. Apparently, delays in sailing were the major complaint.

17. "Examen du nouveau réglement . . . " BNPar, MS Fonds Français, 10769, f. 135.

18. García-Baquero, ed., *Cádiz, 1753,* 44–45, 60. More revealing, if less visible, the few French firms averaged earnings 700 percent higher than 285 Spanish wholesalers.

19. These and other practices are fully sketched in "Oficio de la Francia sobre visita de navíos," AHN, Estado, 4570[1].

20. BRPal, Ayala MS 2822; Fiscal de Indias (1790), AGI, Ind. Gen., 2318.

21. Cf. Miguel de Cervera, "Discurso" (1761), AHN, Estado, 2851, n. 112.

22. Simón Joseph Vives, Veracruz, 1766, AHN, Consejos, 21463, n. 46, f. 46v.

23. Consulado de México to *virrey,* "Representación," 6 Dec. 1773, AGN, AHH, 502–17.

24. AGI, Consulados, Libro de correspondencia, 85, ff. 183–88.

25. Consulado de México to *virrey,* "Representación," 6 Dec. 1773, AGN, AHH, 502–17, f. 126. Since the *palmeo* duty was levied by volume of "fardos, tercios, frangotes," which customs inspectors did not examine at Cadiz or Veracruz, merchants or their agents at Veracruz could easily introduce smuggled goods in crates and barrels in the open storage sheds. AHN, Estado, 2314/1.

26. "Interrogatorio de la provanza de oficiales reales de Veracruz," AHN, Consejos, 21463, pieza 2, n. 19.

27. Consulado de México to *virrey,* "Representación," 6 Dec. 1773, AGN, AHH, 502–17, ff. 126v–127.

28. Pedro Antonio de Cosío, Veracruz, 9 Apr. 1781, AGI, Mexico, 2994.

29. Antonio de Ulloa to Bucareli, Veracruz, 7 Mar. 1778, AGI, Ind. Gen., 1631.

30. Gálvez, *Informe general.*

31. Cf. AGI, Mexico 1250, paras. 360–62: "Lo que hacían los oficiales reales de

Veracruz antes de pasar el visitador [Gálvez] era tener un cagero confidencial que cobraba y pagaba todo perteneciente a Real Hacienda, sin tener días fijos, ni tiempos determinados para hacer entradas de caudales . . . desculpandose todos con la imposivilidad de cumplir las leyes a la letra, y con la práctica tolerada de aquel gobierno de Nueva España."

32. Francisco Ignacio de Yraeta, BNMex, MS 1334, f. 89v: "el método establecido de aplicarse a los administradores el 34 por ciento sobre lo que recauden para su subsistencia . . . está a la vista el que estos han de tratar solamente de engrosar sus sueldos . . . por los medios injustos de abaluar las partidas de efectos."

33. Consulado de México, 27 Aug. 1800, AGN, AHH. 635-1: "haviendo pasado las mercaderías . . . de los puertos y aduanas . . . no se pueda hacer ni haga causa de denunciación ni visita."

34. Cf. AHN, Estado 2851, n. 112, on the situation at Cadiz, where "hay muchos guardas, barcos visitadores y rondas; con todo esso, son muchos los millones de pesos que se ocultan, y es constante que . . . hay mas metedores y ocultadores."

35. In 1771, irritated by complaints of Mexico City's *almaceneros* of the excessively high official valuations of their imports, Gálvez reminded Viceroy Bucareli with a wealth of detail of "los reprehensibles medios de que por punto general se valen los Comerciantes [of Mexico City] para ocultar los géneros, su verdadera calidad y valor, y conseguir por estos y semejantes arbitrios en perjuicio de los intereses de la Real Hacienda aumentar los suyos, para que suelen creerse autorizados de la viciosa tolerancia, que ellos mismos ponderan de haberlo executado así los anteriores ultimos empleados." Gálvez to Bucareli, "Sobre licencias para embiar Diputados a Madrid," 26 Mar. 1771, AGN, Historia, 125, folder 8, f. 140v.

36. AGI, Mexico 1250, paras. 360–62; Priestley, *Gálvez*, 405–6; Fonseca and Urrutia, eds., *Historia General de Real Hacienda*, 4:614.

37. Juan Antonio de Areche, "Oficio del visitador . . . ," Cuzco, 18 Feb. 1779, BRAHM, Mata Linares, 108.

38. Valentín Foronda, "Apuntes ligeros . . ." (Philadelphia, 1804), NYPub, MS Rich.

39. *Exports, Cadiz to Veracruz, 1757–68*
   (*pesos fuertes*)

Flota	Total Value	Foreign Textiles
1757	18,054,067	15,463,925 (85.6%)
1760	24,057,510	20,696,150 (86%)
1765	16,702,581	12,984,550 (77.7%)
1768	13,097,917	11,299,275 (86.3%)
Mean percentage foreign textiles		84%

Source: AAEPar, M et D, Espagne, 207, n. 2.

40. Brown, "Anglo-Spanish Relations in America," 463n. In 1775, foreign merchants at Cadiz were judged "dueños de la mayor parte de la cargazón de una flota." Heros Fernández, "Discurso sobre el comercio," 10. In 1776, it was believed that Spanish textiles and other products of a quality saleable in the colonies "escasamente pueden cargar dos navíos" of a flota to Veracruz. BRPal, Ayala, 2862, "Disertación sobre los abusos . . ." (1776).

41. BRPal, Ayala, 2862, "Disertación sobre los abusos . . . "(1776).

42. Ibid.; Real Díaz, *Ferias de Jalapa,* 96 n. 16.

43. Morineau, *Gazettes,* 417, table 61.

44. "Razón de los sujetos que han sido habilitados por la Real Audiencia de Contratación a las Indias, para cargadores y factores, y para cargadores solamente desde . . . 1757 hasta . . . 1767 ambos inclusive," AGI, Contratación, 5532.

Cargadores/Factores, *Colonial Destinations*
(known destinations only)

Destination	No. *Factores*	%
New Spain	265	49.4
Cartagena	100	18.6
Buenos Aires	48	9.0
Mar del Sur	83	15.5
Honduras	33	6.2
Havana	7	1.3
Total	536	100.0

Source: AGI, Contratación, 5532.

45. Consulado de México, Dec. 1776, AGN, AHH 791–8.

46. Details from Casafuerte's eighteen-part proclamation of 7 Nov. 1729, in Real Díaz, *Ferias de Jalapa,* "Documentos. III," 133–44. *Oidor* Beleña was convinced that Casafuerte's rules placed medium- and small-capitalized Mexico City merchants under the domination of "los comerciantes ricos de México." Beleña, "Informe reservado . . . ," in Florescano and Castillo, eds., *Controversia,* 1:214.

47. Both *diputaciones,* ran Bucareli's directives, were to "promover y facilitar . . . la más pronta celebración de la Feria, procediendo con el mayor empeño a superar y allanar todos los reparos o embarazos que . . . puedan retardar la ultima perfección de las negociaciones y contratos entre los Individuos de ambos Comercios." Antonio Bucareli, proclamation, 18 Aug. 1772, AGN, Consulado, 113, n. 5. See also Yuste, ed., *Comerciantes mexicanos en el siglo XVIII,* 189–245.

48. Bucareli, proclamation, 18 Aug. 1772, AGN, Consulado, 113, folder 5.

49. Areche, Mexico, 15 Jan. 1774, AGN, Consulado, 113, folder 5.

50. Consulado de México, "Representación a SM," 28 Feb. 1765, AGI, Consulados, Libro de correspondencia, 80, f. 200.

51. AGI, Consulados, Libro de correspondencia, 80, f. 203, 5 Mar. 1765.

52. "Apuntes sobre comércio de Europa con Nueva España," Mexico, 31 Dec. 1792, BNMex, MS 1396. According to the unsympathetic Consulado de México, in 1753, the colonial capital contained "500 más casas y almacenes poblados por individuos del comercio de España, y en muchos se vende por menudo y vareo, quanto van a comprar los marchantes, aunque sea una bretaña o un par de medias, o quatro varas o menos de paño; y los mercaderes de México están sugetos a comprar a los de España para revender." Consulado de México to *virey,* 2 Dec, 1753, AGN, AHH, 635–5.

53. The Cadiz *consulado* claimed that such was the volume of capital forwarded to Cadiz for direct buying by merchants in the colonies that no capital would be left when the next *feria* was held. Bernal, *Financiación,* 312.

54. Once again, Madrid had yielded to Cadiz's insistence on its commercial intermediation, since "el comercio colonial no reporta a los españoles otro beneficio

que la encomienda, por pertencer a extranjeros la sustancia de las exportaciones." Bernal, *Financiación*, 313.

55. Consulado de México, Dec. 1776, AGN, AHH, 791–8, ff. 50v–51: "Para que el comerciante de Yndias logra emplear en España, necesita remitir a aquellos Reynos con mucha anticipación los caudales . . . ; padece el riesgo de ida del dinero; tolera el desconsuelo de haver de valerse de agena mano para buscar lo que necesita; . . . pagar derechos por el dinero que transporta; satisface encomienda el que la recibe en Cádiz; satisface así mismo otro encomienda al que le compra los efectos . . . y después de haver pasado por tantas demoras y desembolzas tiene el desconsuelo de que se le retengan sus efectos hasta que regresa la Flota."

56. Consulado de México, "Instruzión" (1755), AGN, AHH 635–8, ff. 1–2.

57. Puyabry to Choiseul-Praslin, "Mémoire," Cadiz, 19 Apr. 1765, AAEPar, M et D, Espagne, 32, n. 28.

58. Consulado de Cádiz, "Consulta . . . ," 2 Feb. 1765, AGI, Consulados, Libro de correspondencia, 80, f. 200.

59. Cruillas, proclamation, 3 May 1761, in AGI, Consulado, Libro de correspondencia, 80, f. 196v. This intervention permitted imports already sold by *flotistas* and Mexico City merchants to be moved from Jalapa into the interior.

60. AGI, Consulado, Libro de correspondencia, 80, f. 171v, 4 Sept. 1764; Real Despacho, 24 Apr. 1772, AGN, Consulado, 113, folder 5.

61. Real Despacho, 24 Apr. 1772; AGN, Consulado, 113, folder 5; Beleña, "Informe reservado," in Florescano and Castillo, eds., *Controversia*, vol. 1.

62. Miguel de Goyeneche to *virrey*, Mexico, 12 Dec. 1773, AGN, Consulado 113, folder 5, ff. 11v–12.

63. Cf. Consulado de México, Dec. 1776, AGN, AHH, 791–8, f. 49: "los mercaderes de Tierradentro ocurren en derechura a emplear de los flotistas, con la esperanza de lograr la comodidad de la primera venta, y sólo se acercan a México aquellos que por estar enteramente faltos de facultades, solicitan al fiado, todo lo que pretenden, y esto, con el peligro . . . de no poderlo pagar al plazo, por que encuentran la Tierradentro, tan surtida en derechura desde Xalapa, que venden tarde, mal o nunca, lo que emplearon en México."

64. Areche to Bucareli, "Respuesta fiscal," 2 Apr. 1774, AGN, Consulado 113, folder 5, f. 73.

65. Real Orden, 24 Apr. 1772, AGN, Consulado, 113, folder 5, ff. 40–40v. Here Madrid ordered both communities to furnish data on "consumo general que considere en esse Reyno con distinción de frutos y mercaderías y número de toneladas," suggesting the latitude with which Madrid authorized aggregate *flota* tonnage.

66. For details on mismanagement in these royal factories, see the comments of Heros Fernández, "Discursos sobre el comercio. . . . "

67. Miguel de Goyeneche to Bucareli, Mexico, 12 Dec. 1773, AGN, Consulado, 113–5, ff. 7, 9. The mills had such large inventories that Treasury Minister Conde de Valdeparaíso resolved to turn management over to the Cinco Gremios. Béliardi, "Réponse au mémoire . . ." (1761), BNPar, MS Fonds Français, 10768, ff. 160 ff.

68. Miguel de Goyeneche to Bucareli, Mexico, 12 Dec. 1773, AGN, Consulado 113–5, ff. 8–8v.

69. ANPar, AE, B I 792, f. 50.

70. Miguel de Goyeneche to Bucareli, Mexico, 12 Dec. 1773, AGN, Consulado, 113–5, ff. 10–10v.

71. Real Orden, 23 Dec. 1772, AGN, Consulado, 113–5, f. 42.

72. As representative of the "interesados de España" in the shipment on the 1772 *flota,* Goyeneche recognized that investors in the Compañía General could be justifiably anxious about the "falta de caudales que acaso se prometerán registrados en el primer navío de bandera para sobstener las crecidas erogaciones que hazen en el fomento de dichas fábricas." Goyeneche to Bucareli, Mexico, 14 July 1774, AGN, AHH, 113–5, f. 88v.

73. Bucareli, proclamation, 18 Aug. 1772, AGN, Consulado, 113–5. Reacting to Bucareli's insistence on the registry of all items unsold, the *comercio de España* advised him that "no hay comerciante alguno que deje de establecer por primera regla de su prudencia el secreto de su casa y la ocultación de las cantidades que de cada especie de efectos encierra en ella, cuya máxima han observado los de España en esta Feria." The ownership requirement, Bernal has added, would have revealed the "detalles financieros de las operaciones con que ellos habían conseguido sus cargazones." Bernal, *Financiación,* 312.

74. Audiencia de Mexico, "Voto consultivo," 28 Jan. 1774, AGN, Consulado, 113–5, f. 44.

75. Since the Casa de Contratación, the colonial trade bureau at Cadiz, delegated the distribution of cargo space aboard *flotas* to the Cadiz *consulado,* "los poderosos venían a ser los dueños de todo el buque de los barcos . . . e impedían que los principiantes o de cortas facultades, pudiesen aprovechar de su industria." Tomás Murphy to Revillagigedo, Mexico, 1791, AGN, Consulado, 123–1, f. 240.

76. The following paragraph is based upon Whitaker, "Antonio de Ulloa," 155–94.

77. La Condamine, *Relation abrégée d'un voyage.*

78. Ulloa and Juan, *Relación histórica del viage a la América meridional.*

79. Whitaker, "Antonio de Ulloa," 174.

80. Whitaker, *Huancavelica Mercury Mine.*

81. Dermigny, *Cargaisons indiennes,* 1:37 nn. 36, 37.

82. Whitaker, "Antonio de Ulloa," 181–82.

83. Morineau, *Incroyables gazettes,* 415, proposes 19.6 million pesos; "Disertación sobre los abusos . . ." (1776), BRPal, Ayala XLIV, 2862, suggests 28–32 million.

84. Tomás Murphy to Revillagigedo, Mexico, 1791, AGN, Consulado, 123–1, f. 240v. As Juan Antonio de los Heros Fernández, a veteran of trade in the viceroyalty of Peru and director of Madrid's Cinco Gremios Mayores, commented: "Es notorio que a la publicación de una flota se atropellan los pretendientes por licencias. Siempre quedan quejosos. Aunque se compusiese de 20 navíos, habría quien todavía solicitase permiso . . . uno o dos navíos más sobre los que regularmente forman la expedición de flota en el dia." Heros Fernández, "Discursos sobre el comercio . . . ," 10–11.

85. Ulloa to Bucareli, Veracruz, 24 Dec. 1777, AGI, Ind. Gen., 1631.

86. Bucareli to Esquilache, Havana, 22 Jan. 1768, AGI, Ind. Gen., 1629. Three years later, he wrote Esquilache from Havana: "como toda la familia save lo que debemos a VE y no dejaría de demostrarlo con sus frecuentes avisos." AGI, Ind. Gen., 1629.

87. Ulloa, "Noticia i descripción de los países que median entre la ciudad i puerto

de Veracruz," AGI, Ind. Gen. 1631, ff. 146–233. We are indebted to the late Arthur P. Whitaker for this material.

88. Ulloa, "Noticia," f. 151.

89. Ibid., f. 166.

90. Ulloa to Bucareli, Veracruz, 22 Feb. 1777, AGI, Ind. Gen., 1631.

91. Ulloa, "Noticia," f. 155.

92. Ibid.

93. Ibid., f. 161.

94. Ulloa neglected to mention that rent gouging at Veracruz was repeated by house owners of Jalapa, "pués el precio en que los [flotistas] ceden por un año, suele superar al valor de la cassa." See also O'Crouley, *Description of the Kingdom of New Spain.*

95. Ulloa to Bucareli, Veracruz, 18 Mar. 1777, AGI, Ind. Gen., 1631. In a later letter to Bucareli, Ulloa indicated that his sympathies lay with the *comercio de España* who "sujetos por los convenios de comercio y por las reales resoluciones a residir en este pueblo mercaderías y encomenderos, y privados de poderlas trasladar a otras partes del reino para solicitar sus expendio, nos hallamos en la estrecha necesidad de esperar a que vengan a comprarlas." Real Díaz, *Ferias de Jalapa,* 108.

96. Letter to Domingo de Lardizábal, Jalapa, 18 Sept. 1777, AGI, Consulado, Copiador de cartas . . . Jalapa, 1777; Flotistas, "Representación," Jalapa, 29 Sept. 1778, in Real Díaz, *Ferias de Jalapa,* 106 n. 10.

97. Ulloa to Bucareli, Veracruz, 1 Oct. 1777, AGI, Ind. Gen., 1631.

98. Grimaldi to Aranda, Madrid, 4 Feb. 1777, in Franco, "Gardoqui," 141–42.

99. Ulloa to Bucareli, Veracruz, 17 Nov. 1777, AGI, Ind. Gen., 1631.

100. Ulloa to Bucareli, Veracruz, 12 Nov. and 24 Dec. 1777, AGI, Ind. Gen., 1631.

101. Ulloa to Bucareli, Veracruz, 8 and 12 Jan. 1778, AGI, Ind. Gen., 1631.

102. Ulloa to Bucareli, 7 Mar. and 22 May 1778, AGI, Ind. Gen., 1631. Ulloa subsequently filed a remarkably detailed report (preserved in AGSim) of his extended Atlantic crossing in the effort to elude interception by English warships.

103. Ulloa to Bucareli, Cadiz, 17 July 1778, AGI, Ind. Gen., 1631. See also Garner, "Exportación de circulante," 595, app. 3. Morineau assigns 19.6 million pesos to Ulloa's *flota* and calculates New Spain's peso exports in 1778 to have totaled 22.4 million, probably an underestimate (Morineau, *Incroyables gazettes,* 415, 417), although his figure is close to that reported officially, 22.08 million (AGS, DGR, 2a remesa [shipment] 568). The Consulado de Cadiz estimated the value of Ulloa's *flota* at 30 million pesos (AGI, Consulados, Libro de correspondencia, 85, f. 186).

104. Ulloa to Bucareli, San Ildefonso, 18 Aug. 1778, AGI, Ind. Gen., 1631.

105. Ibid.

106. Letter to Bucareli, Jalapa, 16 Oct. 1777, AGI, Consulados, Copiador de cartas . . . , Jalapa, 1777. In fact, in early September, the *flotistas* at Jalapa received a "mala notícia" suggesting the introduction of "Comercio libre de América en General," albeit perhaps limited to "ciertas reglas." There were rumors of "grande oposición," but the *flotistas*—correctly, in fact—were persuaded that New Spain might be excluded. Letter to Domingo Ignacio de Lardizábal, Jalapa, 4 Sept. 1777, AGI, Consulados, Copiador de cartas.

6. The Second Reglamento del Comercio Libre (1778)

EPIGRAPHS: "Copia del pliego entregado al . . . marqués de Sonora en . . . 1778," AHN, Estado, 3188[2]; José María Quirós, "Memoria de instituto . . . 1819," AGI, Mexico 2519, f. 5.

1. See Armytage, *Free Port System in the British West Indies,* and, for the French islands, Tarrade, *Commerce colonial de la France.*

2. On this point, see "Comercio," in Real Sociedad Económica de Madrid, *Memorias,* 2:21–50, esp. p. 37.

3. See Martínez Shaw's *Cataluña en la carrera de Indias.*

4. Gálvez, "Discurso y reflexiones de un vasallo," BRPal, Ayala 2816.

5. Gálvez, "Informe y reflexiones del visitador general," addressed to Prime Minister Grimaldi, Mexico, 14 June 1766, HSA, HC, 427/18.

6. Ibid.

7. Anonymous letter, 20 May 1778, BRAHM, Mata Linares, 68.

8. Campomanes, *Reflexiones sobre el comercio español a Indias,* 442; Campomanes, *Apéndice a la educación popular,* 1:148.

9. Armona, "Cartas . . ." (1773), HSA, HC, 330/263; R. de V., "Idea general del comercio de las Indias," in Florescano and Castillo, eds., *Controversia,* 1:33; AGI, Ind. Gen., 2409.

10. "Discurso sobre la libertad del comercio . . . ," in Real Sociedad Económica de Madrid, *Memorias,* 3:285.

11. BNMex, MS 1334, ff. 131v–132.

12. Junta de comercio, fábricas y agricultura de Cataluña, "Representación," Barcelona, 24 Apr. 1773, BMus, Add. MS 13976, ff. 139–51.

13. Anonymous, Cadiz, 1 Oct. 1776, AGI, Juzgado de arribadas, 134; Consulado de Cádiz to crown, 27 Mar. 1778, AGI, Consulados, Libro de correspondencia, 87, ff. 7–14v. Similar criticism is found in "Copia del pliego entregado al . . . Sonora . . . 1778," AHN, Estado, 3188[2]. Catalan crews were paid in *suertes,* or shares, rather than in monthly wages. Anonymous, 29 May 1778, BRAHM, Mata Linares, 68, f. 662.

14. "Informe," AGI, Ind. Gen., 2409; "Sobre el nuevo comercio de Indias. Dictamen," 12 May 1777, AGI, Estado, 86.

15. R. de V., "Idea general del comercio de las Indias," in Florescano and Castillo, eds., *Controversia,* 1:34.

16. Muñoz Pérez, "Publicación del reglamento de comercio libre," 640; Rodríguez Casado, "Comentarios al decreto y real instrucción de 1765," 100–135.

17. It has been viewed recently as a major step in Grimaldi's effort to salvage Esquilache's program for opening Spain's colonial exchanges to all major peninsular ports. Varela Marcos, "Primer reglamento para el comercio libre," 263.

18. Cf. Anon., "Ensayo apologético por el comercio libre . . . ," in Florescano and Castillo, eds., *Controversia,* 1:354.

19. "Observaciones sobre el sistema presente . . . ," which bears a covering title, "Copia del pliego entregado al . . . Marqués de Sonora en . . . 1778," AHN, Estado, 3188[2], ff. 8–11.

20. On Landázuri's career, see Bernard, *Secrétariat d'état et le conseil espagnol des Indes,* 127; Calderón Quijano, ed., *Virreyes de Nueva España,* 1:240–41; Landázuri, "Notícia de los minerales de oro y plata. . . de la Nueva España," BRPal. Ayala, 2834;

and Muñoz Pérez, "Publicación del reglamento de comercio libre de Indias de 1778," 640.

21. "Dictamen leído . . .," AGI, Estado, 86.

22. AHN, Ordenes militares, Santiago, 5040; Consulado de Cádiz to Larrarte, 7 May 1774, AGI, Consulados, Libro de correspondencia, 74, ff. 277v–278.

23. Real Díaz, *Ferias de Jalapa,* 110, and his observations cited in Calderón Quijano, ed., *Virreyes de Nueva España,* 2:17. Priestley, *Gálvez,* 367, describes him as the "protector of the commercial classes."

24. Muñoz Pérez, "Comercio de Indias bajo los Austrias," 9.

25. Letter, Jalapa, 4 Sept. 1777, to Domingo Ignacio de Lardizábal in Mexico City, AGI, Consulados, Libro de correspondencia, 74; Consejo de Indias, "Dictamen . . . ," AGI, Ind. Gen., 2409.

26. Manuel de Villalta, recently appointed *corregidor* of Abancay (Peru), wrote from Madrid to the "magnates del comercio" of the Cadiz *consulado* that he had seen a letter sent from Cadiz by José de Toro Zambrano to Colonial Secretary Gálvez supporting the extension of *comercio libre.* Conde de Villamar, Cadiz, letter to Gálvez, 11 Nov. 1778, cited by Muñoz Pérez, "Publicación del reglamento de comercio libre," 45.

27. The following paragraphs are based upon Landázuri's *informe* in AGI, Ind. Gen., 2409.

28. Substitution of ad valorem duties for the traditional *palmeo* cubic measurement would, he estimated, increase the duties on 400 *toneladas* of textiles from 665,600 to 1,119,700 *reales de vellon.* AGI, Ind. Gen., 2411, cited in Fontana et al., *Comercio libre,* 56 n. 7.

29. These statistics appear in the "Consulta original" of 1765, the position paper that was the basis of the *comercio libre* statute of 1765.

30. Calderón Quijano, ed., *Virreyes de Nueva España,* 1:241–42.

31. Priestley, *Gálvez,* 183, 204.

32. Hernández Palomo, *Aguardiente,* 75 n. 19.

33. Bernard, *Secrétariat d'état et le conseil espagnol des Indes,* 126–32.

34. The 1771 position seems ambiguous since he mentioned the advantages "que reportaría la supresión del sistema de flotas, aún vigente, para Nueva España." Muñoz Pérez, "Publicación del reglamento de comercio libre," 30.

35. Real Díaz, *Ferias de Jalapa,* 110. In February 1772, Landázuri had opined on the Consulado de México's petition that Madrid establish maximum tonnage for the next convoy. The government then requested data on annual consumption of imports, which the *consulado* neglected to supply. In December 1776, the *consulado* finally proposed one convoy every three years and put the maximum tonnage at 6,000 (4,000 in textiles); the Cadiz *consulado* upped this to 9,000 (4,500 in dry goods). Real Orden, 24 Apr. 1772, AGN, Consulado, 113, folder 5, ff. 40–41; AGN, AHH, 791-8; AGI, Consulados, Libro de correspondencia, 84, ff. 172v–176.

36. Many felt that the Consulado de Cádiz would look to "su interés particular" rather than that of the nation.

37. "Dictamen leído en consejo pleno," 12 May 1777, AGI, Estado, 86. On Landázuri's position in 1764 and 1771, see Muñoz Pérez, "Comercio de Indias bajo los Austrias," 26–27, 30.

38. In Mexico City, he had been linked to a group opposing the expulsion of the Jesuits. Calderón Quijano, ed., *Virreyes de Nueva España*, 1:327.

39. AGI, Ind. Gen., 2409.

40. *Títulos de Indias*, 302; Burkholder and Chandler, *From Impotence to Authority*, 173.

41. Consulado de Cádiz to crown, 27 Mar 1778, AGI, Consulados, Libro de correspondencia, 87, ff. 7–14v.

42. Morel-Fatio, *Études sur l'Espagne*, 138. Later, Gálvez appointed Magallón the presiding officer of a study group reviewing plans for intendancies in America. "Ynforme . . . intendencias," NYPub, Rich MS, para. 53.

43. Magallón's perspective was close to that of Campomanes, who in *Apéndice a la educación popular*, in what could only be a reference to Cadiz, observed: "El pueblo se cree libre en medio de la dominación de los factores y comisionistas extrangeros. Se contenta con que lo dejen vivir en sus métodos ordinarios de descanso y prefiere la opresión al trabajo."

44. "Testamento político," BNMad MS 11065, ff. 115v–157.

45. The *dictamen* represented the opinions of the seven *consejeros* who submitted written analyses, and of Contador General Landázuri, and the *consejo's* two *fiscales*. Of the seven *consejeros*, six opposed "libertad de comercio . . . a lo menos por aora."

46. In 1788, Campomanes felt that the colony of New Spain should not be conflated with other colonial areas in America. With only one major port on the Caribbean, Veracruz, he was convinced it was possible to estimate its annual import capacity on the basis of twenty-year statistics: "[L]a Nueva España es el único punto de las Indias, en que conviene tomar regla constante por ahora para el número de registros que devan ir y venir a Veracruz. "Apuntaciones," BRPal, Ayala, 2867, f. 41.

47. "Dictamen en pleno consejo," AGI, Ind. Gen., 86.

48. Levene, ed., *Documentos para la historia argentina*, 6:3–136.

49. Manuel Gijón, "Memoria . . . relativa al comercio de Indias," in Real Sociedad Económica de Madrid, *Memorias*, 3:258–59.

50. Junta de Gobierno to Soler, 26 Jan. 1803, AGI, Ind. Gen., 2819.

51. Great expectations rode on the commercial changes legislated in 1778. See, e.g., "Copia del pliego entregado al . . . marqués de Sonora en . . . 1778," AHN, Estado, 3188²: "El mayor consumo de géneros en Indias . . . por cuio motivo se abrirían nuevas minas, y consiguientemente vendrán maior cantidad de dinero a España: el aumento de las rentas reales . . . el fomento de la navegación, etc."

52. Concha to Francisco Pedro de Goyeneche, Burgos, 8 Mar. 1778, "Cartas y papeles sobre el comercio libre," AGI, Ind. Gen., 2409.

53. Consulado de Cádiz to SM, 27 Mar. 1778, AGI, Consulados, Libro de correspondencia, 87, ff. 7–14.

54. Miguel de Vallejo to Gálvez, Cadiz, Mar. 1778, "Cartas y papeles sobre el comercio libre," AGI, Ind. Gen., 2409.

55. Muñoz Pérez, "Publicación del reglamento de comercio libre," 655, 659. Few underestimated the pressure-group tactics of Cadiz. As Campomanes noted ("Apuntaciones," BRPal, Ayala, 2872), "no havía cuerpo visible que pudiese contrarrestar a la Universidad de Cargadores a Indias establecida en Cádiz, que mirava como un patrimonio suyo aquel tráfico." In 1765, Parayuelo had collaborated with Esquilache, who entrusted him with drafting *instrucciones* for officials leaving the metropole for

colonial posts. Esquilache also used him to bypass the Hacienda in an effort at fiscal efficiency. Eguía Ruíz, *Jesuitas,* 315; Béliardi to Choiseul-Praslin, 4 Nov. 1765, BNPar. MS Fonds Français, 10764, f. 402.

56. Concha to Francisco Pedro de Goyeneche, Burgos, 8 Mar. 1778, "Cartas y papeles sobre el comercio libre," AGI, Ind. Gen., 2409.

57. AHN, Ordenes, Carlos III, folder 58; Villamar, "Apuntes de un curioso. . . ." Cadiz, June 1778, AGI, Ind. Gen., 2409; Hamnett, *Politics and Trade in Southern Mexico,* 34–35. Villamar retired from business at Cadiz in the late 1770s, hence claimed his impartiality in matters of trade ("no me lleva la pasión del interés"). Villamar to Joseph de Toro Zambrano, Cadiz, 13 Feb. 1778, AGI, Ind. Gen., 2409.

58. Muñoz Pérez, "Publicación del reglamento de comercio libre," 659.

59. Aragon's royal society proceeded to offer a prize for the best essay on the advantages of comercio libre to its regional economy. Sempere y Guarinos, *Ensayo de una biblioteca española de los mejores escritores del reynado de Carlos III,* 143.

60. Muñoz Pérez, "Publicación del reglamento de comercio libre," 660–62, refers to Francisco Romá y Rosell, *Las sendas de la felicidad de España, y medios de hacerlas eficaces* (Madrid, 1768); Burkholder and Chandler, *From Impotence to Authority,* 178.

61. Carpenter, *Economic Bestsellers Before 1850.*

62. Consulado de Cádiz to Hacienda, 18 Dec. 1810, AGI, Consulados, Libro de correspondencia, 87.

63. Only the Real Orden of 23 Aug. 1796 permitted colonial residents to ship goods to peninsular ports in their own vessels. Villalobos, "Comercio extranjero a fines de la dominación española," 523; AGI, Ind. Gen., 2318.

64. Delgado i Ribas, "Modelo catalán dentro del sistema de libre comercio," in Fontana and Bernal, eds., *Comercio libre,* 56 and n. 8.

65. Ship inspections were far from perfunctory. As article 12 directed, "Verán . . . los Jueces de Arribadas si las embarcaciones están Marineras, y en disposición de navegar sin riesgo, no . . . sobrecargadas; Si llevan el velamen, xarcias . . . Si tienen los víveres y aguada."

66. Cf. AGI, Consulados, Libro de correspondencia, 87: "deben ser Españoles . . . mayores de 18 anos; libres de la patria potestad; o con permiso de sus padres; y los casados han de manifestar el consentimiento de sus mugeres" (Art. 13). Cargadores had to return within specified periods to render account of their "dependencias."

67. French observers were convinced that the 1778 decree was designed to end the "contrebande immense" of European products in the American colonies. Boyetet to Sartine, Madrid, 7 Dec. 1778, ANPar, AE, B I 794, f. 253.

68. A subsequent order (20 Feb. 1779) countersigned by Gálvez required customs personnel in colonial ports to examine "con sumo cuidado y exactitud" goods, especially those shipped from Cadiz, and to compare manifests (*registros*) against shipper's invoices (*facturas*). Levene, ed., *Documentos para la historia argentina,* 6:143–44.

69. In 1776, Ortiz de Landázuri calculated that the effect of bulk exit duties (*palmeo*) on luxury textile reexports was well under 1 percent but shot up to 80 percent under the 1778 Reglamento. Delgado i Ribas, "Model catalán dentro del sistema de libre comercio," in Fontana and Bernal, eds., *Comercio libre,* 56 and n. 7.

70. Ibid., 57–58 and n. 11. For example, in 1778, a Cadiz exporter insisted his cargo of imported textiles, dyed and printed at nearby Puerto Santa María, be duticd on

reexport as "national" goods (3 percent) rather than reexports (7 percent). Madrid intervened: Floridablanca, Gálvez and Sainz de Parayuelo overruled the *administrador general* of Cadiz's customs, Miguel de Vallejo, to classify the merchandise as "national." AGI, Ind. Gen., 2413.

71. Pedro de Rada in AGI, Ind. Gen., 2409; "Observaciones . . . Gálvez," AHN, 3188–5 n. 420. Cf. Ugartiria, "Carta segunda": in 1789, "los pintados que se fabrican en España son pocos, y no bastan aún para los consumos de la península." Nonetheless, despite the low output of Spain's manufactories, the tariff of 1778 still prohibited imports of textiles similar to those produced by the cottage industries championed by Campomanes. Delgado i Ribas, "Modelo catalán dentro del sistema de libre comercio," in Fontana and Bernal, eds., *Comercio libre,* 57 nn. 9–10.

72. Montesquieu, *De l'esprit des lois.*

73. Antonio Valdés to Consulado de la Coruña, San Lorenzo, 19 Oct. 1789, BRAHM, MS 6480, n. 12. Madrid officials were also disturbed by the large volume of unsold imports left by Ulloa's *flota.* Ignacio de Iriarte to Revillagigedo, BNMex, MS 1334, f. 219.

74. Francisco Montes, confidential to Múzquiz, Madrid, 21 Aug. 1782, "Expediente sobre la comisión dada al Tesorero General don Francisco Montes . . . ," AGI, Ind. Gen., 2311.

75. Real Orden, 22 Mar. 1779, quoted by Beleña, "Informe reservado," in Florescano and Castillo, eds., *Controversia,* 1:218.

76. Olson, *Rise and Decline of Nations.*

77. Cadiz merchants to the Regencia, 13 Dec. 1810, AGI, Ind. Gen., 2462.

78. Alvaro Florez Estrada credits Simón de Aragorri (marqués de Iranda) and Campomanes with having persuaded Gálvez to proceed with the two decrees of *comercio libre* in 1778. *Examen imparcial de las disensiones de la América con la España,* 207.

79. AHN, Estado, Junta de Estado, 23 June 1788, bk. 2, ff. 61v–62.

80. Varela Marcos, "Premier reglamento para el comercio libre," 267–68; Floridablanca to Múzquiz, 20 June 1778, AGI, Ind. Gen., 2413.

81. Gálvez, "Discurso y reflexiones de un vasallo," BRPal, Ayala 2816, f. 121.

82. Priestley, *Gálvez,* 235–36; Calderon Quijano, ed., *Virreyes de Nueva España,* 1:491 and passim. Gálvez himself knew that *registros sueltos* sent to Veracruz during wartime, 1740–48, had warned Mexico City's merchant community about making large purchases of imports. "Discurso y reflexiones de un vasallo," BRPal, Ayala 2816.

83. Larruga, *Memorias,* 4, pt. 1; Muñoz Perez, "Reglamento del comercio libre," 671 n. 11; letter to Consulado de Cádiz, Veracruz, 28 Dec. 1779, AGN, AHH, 129–10.

84. Grimaldi to Gálvez, 3 Dec. 1778, cited in Real Díaz, *Ferias de Jalapa,* 111 n.20.

85. Antonio Valdés to Consulado de La Coruña, BRAHM, 6480, no. 12.

86. Antúnez y Acevedo, *Memorias históricas,* 111.

87. "Observaciones sobre el sistema presente . . . ," AHN, Estado, 3188²; Calderón Quijano, ed., *Virreyes de Nueva España,* 2:70.

88. Fernán Nuñez to Gálvez, Lisbon, 12 Nov. 1778, in Muñoz Pérez, "Reglamento del comercio libre," 662–63.

89. Consulado de Cádiz to marqués del Real Thesoro, 24 Dec. 1773, AGI, Consulados, Libro de correspondencia, 84, ff. 172v–176; Consulado de México, "Repre-

sentación," Dec. 1776, AGN, AHH, 791–8, f. 54, and Real Orden, 24 Apr. 1772, to virrey de Mexico, AGN, Consulado, vol. 113, folder 5, ff. 40–41.

90. Consulado de México, "Expediente formado sobre licencia pedida a el Virrey . . . ," 20 Mar. 1777, AGN, AHH, 502–32.

91. Consulado de Cádiz, "Representación," 27 Mar. 1778, AGI, Consulados, Libro de correspondencia, 87, ff. 7–14v.

92. Cf. AGI, Consulados, Libro de correspondencia, 84, ff. 150–51, Domingo de Lardizábal, Jalapa, letter to viceroy, 16 Oct. 1777: "El miedo que ha derramado sobre los ánimos de todos, la voz . . . del establecimiento de un comercio libre para las Américas."

93. Vallejo to Gálvez, Cadiz, 1 Mar. 1778, "Cartas y papeles," AGI, Ind. Gen., 2409. For Vallejo's criticism of tradition-bound Cadiz merchants and their French collaborators, see also ANPar, AE, B I, 794, f. 281. Cf. José María Quirós, "Memoria de instituto, 1819," f. 7, the later recollection of the secretary of the Veracruz *consulado:* "Las corporaciones mercantiles y los sugetos acaudalados que negociaban con ellas vaticinaban . . . la ruina de la navegación y del comercio, la pérdida de las Américas, la aniquilación de las manufacturas y del cultivo peninsular y la decadencia de la Real Hacienda si se variaba el método de flotas." And see also Valentín Foronda, "Reflexiones sobre el comercio en tiempo de guerra . . ." (1800), BRAHM, Mata Linares, 68, f. 380.

94. Presidente, Casa de Contratación, Cadiz, 27 Nov. 1778, AGI, Ind. Gen., 2409.

95. Real Orden, 20 Feb. 1779, BRAHM, Mata Linares, 108.

96. Real Orden, 22 Mar. 1779; Beleña, "Informe reservado," in Florescano and Castillo, eds., *Controversia,* 1:217.

97. Concha to Francisco Pedro de Goyeneche, Burgos, 8 Mar. 1778, "Cartas y papeles sobre el comercio libre," AGI, Ind. Gen., 2409.

98. *Average Annual State Expenditure, 1775–78 and 1779–82*

(*reales de vellon,* 000's)

	Total	Defense
1775–78	505,870	339,966 (67%)
1779–82	691,860	433,982 (63%)
% change	37	28

Source: Tedde de Lorca, *Banco de San Carlos,* 35 table II-3.

99. Tedde de Lorca, *Banco de San Carlos,* 34.

100. Ibid., 38.

101. Ruíz Rivera, *Consulado de Cádiz,* 65–66.

102. The volume of French investment in *vales* suggests they managed funds placed at their disposal by investors in France. Tedde de Lorca, *Banco de San Carlos,* 42, table II-5.

103. Ibid., 45–46.

104. Ibid., 44.

105. Ibid., 46.

106. AGI, Ind Gen, 2311, 2313 A; AGI, Consulados, Libro de correspondencia 61, f. 54v; 62, ff. 131–131v; Anon., "Carta de un huevero de Fuencarral," 278; AHN, Con-

sejos 20214, f. 14; BNPar, MS Fonds Français, 10765, ff. 237–238v; BRAHM, Mata Linares, 6.

107. AGI, Mexico, 1250; AGI, Consulados, Libro de correspondencia 89, ff. 160–61; AHN, Estado, 2841, box 3; AGN, AHH, 635–38; Torales Pacheco, ed., *Compañía de comercio de . . . Yraeta,* 1:222 and n. 45, 243–44; Bernal, *Financiación,* 459.

108. Montes to Múzquiz, San Ildefonso, 16 Aug. 1782, confidential, "Expediente sobre la comisión dado al Tesorero General . . . ," AGI, Ind. Gen., 2311.

109. Múzquiz to Montes, San Ildefonso, 19 Aug. 1782, AGI, Ind. Gen., 2311.

110. Francisco Ignacio de Yraeta, letter, Sept. 1777, in Torales Pacheco, ed., *Compañía de comercio de . . . Yraeta,* 2:60.

111. Tedde de Lorca, "Política financiera y política comercial," in Anes Alvarez et al., eds., *Economía española al final del antiguo régimen,* 2:177–81.

112. Montes to Múzquiz, San Ildefonso, 21 Aug. 1782, "Expediente sobre la comisión . . . ," AGI, Ind. Gen., 2311.

113. Montes to Múzquiz, 7 Sept. 1782, AGI, Ind. Gen., 2311.

114. Montes to Landaburu, San Ildefonso, 23 Aug. 1782, AGI, Ind. Gen., 2311. In an aside, Montes added that he would have preferred to remind Múzquiz of the depressing effects of the recent "civil war" (i.e., the uprising of Tupac Amaru) upon business conditions in Peru and Santa Fe (Colombia) triggered by new colonial taxes and especially by property losses of "muchas casas ricas que tenían sus enlaces con las de Cádiz." He hoped for "otra ocasión en que puede hacerlo con oportunidad."

115. Conde de Villamar (Lorenzo Narciso Beyens y Huwin), confidential to Gálvez, Cadiz, 3 Sept. 1782, AGI, Ind. Gen., 2311. Montes's truncated version of the assembly discussion, omitting any reference to a possible repeal of *comercio libre,* is in Montes to Múzquiz, 7 Sept. 1782, ibid.

116. A few Spanish merchants at Cadiz purchased over 100,000 pesos' worth of *vales* each: Matías de Landaburu, Juan Antonio Giménez Pérez, conde de Prasca, and José de Llano y San Ginés. Tedde de Lorca, "Política financiera y política comercial en el reinado de Carlos III," 194, n. 87.

117. Villamar, confidential to Gálvez, Cadiz, 3 Sept. 1782, AGI, Ind. Gen., 2311. Gálvez acknowledged receipt of Villamar's confidential report on 10 September. Villamar had initiated his mercantile career in trading with Holland and England, followed by twenty-five years of colonial experience "navegando y haciendo expediciones a ellas," as he phrased it. He had no patience with bureaucratic mandarins in the Contratación at Cadiz. Villamar to Joseph de Toro Zambrano, Cadiz, 13 Feb. 1778, AGI, Ind. Gen., 2409.

118. Gálvez to Múzquiz, San Ildefonso, 14 Sept. 1782, AGI, Ind. Gen., 2311.

119. Francisco Viaña, "Memoria," 22 July 1814, AGI, Ind. Gen., 2463.

120. Valentín Foronda, "Reflexiones sobre el comercio en tiempo de guerra . . . ," BRAHM, Mata Linares, 68, f. 380.

121. Montes to Múzquiz, Madrid, 2 Mar. 1784, BRAHM, Mata Linares, vol.68, f. 188v. Francisco Viaña paraphrased this representation in more explicit terms decades later, capturing the essence of Montes's view: "es menester que se restablezca el método antiguo de flotas y en este restablecimiento me prometo auxilios bastantes para sostener las cargas de la Corona." Viaña, 22 July 1814, AGI, Ind. Gen., 2463.

7. The Aftermath in Spain

EPIGRAPHS: *EMDL*, Oct. 1788, 520; Hamilton, *War and Prices in Spain, 1651–1800*, 224–25.

1. *Coinage (Mexico) and Receipts (Spain)*
   (*pesos fuertes*)

	Coinage	Spain	% "Lost"
1767–68	187,579,451	103,889,652	44.6
1779–83	98,582,709	19,048,750	80.7

Source: BRAHM, Mutis, 5, n. 64, Real Sociedad Económica de Madrid, "Informe echo . . . sobre la Libertad de Comercio," (1779). Published in *EMDL,* beginning 22 Sept. 1788.

2. Real Sociedad Económica de Madrid, "Informe . . sobre libertad de comercio," BRAHM, Mutis 5, no. 64; Bourgoing, *Tableau de l'Espagne moderne,* 2:203–4.

3. *Reglamento y aranceles reales para el comercio libre de España a Indias . . . 1778* (Madrid, 1778), art. 21. Others placed the effective percentage increase—if changes in peso value were included—at between 35 and 53 percent. Real Sociedad Económica de Madrid, "Informe . . . sobre la libertad del comercio," BRAHM, Mutis 5, no. 64.

4. Real Sociedad Económica de Madrid, "Informe . . . sobre la libertad del comercio," BRAHM, Mutis 5, no. 64.

5. On the devaluation of colonial silver, see Burzio, *Ceca de la villa imperial de Potosí,* 43; Florescano, *Precios del maíz,* 80; and Uriortua, "Informe sobre la libertad del comercio," 449, who refers to the "alteración de la moneda."

6. Cf. Gregorio Parilla, Madrid, 12 July 1778, AHN, Estado 3208[2]: "Es constante que el comercio español está quasi perdido en los Reynos de Santa Fee, Perú y Nueva España . . . con las crecidas cantidades de ropas, y otros efectos que en ellos se introducen por las tres referidas naciones, Inglaterra, Francia, Holanda."

7. Cf. the comment of the businessman Manuel Francisco de la Torre, Cadiz, in "Algunas cartas de . . . 1788," AHN, Estado 2151[2], folder 122: "es moralmente imposible el arreglar y distribuir los envíos a los consumos, por ser una confusión y a proporción se experimentará por más arreglo que pongan nuevamente." New Spain's annual allotment of goods was made "sólo por las noticias particulares de la correspondencia privada del Virrey con [Gálvez]." Consejo de Indias, "Informe," 3 Oct. 1787, AGI, Mexico, 2505.

8. Cf. Tinoco Rubiales, "Capital y crédito en la Baja Andalucía durante la crisis del antiguo régimen," 3:287; Marichal, *Bancarrota del virreinato,* ch. 3.

9. Cf. BNMad. MS 19704[2]: "los Americanos hallan la ventaja de comprar de primera mano a las Naciones Europeas los géneros mismos de su industria que nosotros los llevamos; haciendo aquellas clandestinamente el comercio directo con la América, como lo estamos tocando." And see also "Informe" to Consejo de Indias, 3 Oct. 1787, AGI, Mexico, 2505.

10. "Reflexiones . . . al Consulado de Cádiz," BRPal, Ayala, MS 2851, no. 10, f. 308.

11. Real Díaz, *Ferias de Jalapa,* 112 n. 22.

12. *Precious Metals Exports, New Spain to All Spain and Cadiz, 1783–87*
   (*pesos fuertes*)

	To All Spain	To Cadiz
1783	12,933,692	12,933,692
1784	31,698,785	31,384,185
1785	10,871,226	10,216,226
1786	16,909,042	16,018,641
1787	13,224,927	12,073,370
Total	85,637,672	82,626,114 (96.5%)

Source: Adapted from Morineau, *Incroyables gazettes,* 432–33.

13. Real Sociedad Económica de Madrid, "Informe . . . sobre la libertad de comercio," BRAHM, Mutis 5, no. 64. The society estimated that by the end of 1784, Cadiz merchants had some 55.9 million pesos—40 million in receipts, plus another 15.9 in anticipated returns—available for reinvestment in colonial trade. Bernal calculates that Cadiz investors accounted for 55 percent of initial sales of the *vales.* Bernal, *Financiación,* 92.

14. Consulado de Sevilla, "Informe. . . sobre comercio libre," f. 265.

15. Fradera, "El Comerç america durant el segle XIX," 77. According to one calculation, an English smuggler at Jamaica might earn 90 percent profit on sales of *sempiternes;* the legally imported article at Veracruz might provide only 8.7. Consulado de Sevilla, "Informe. . . sobre comercio libre," ff. 285–86.

16. Even before the last war, between 1776 and 1778 Veracruz was the major destination of Spain's colonial trade, receiving 31.1 million pesos of imports, a high percentage of all Spanish exports to the colonies. "Demostraciones . . . ," AGI, Consulados, Acuerdos y Juntas, 1788.

17. Consulado de Cádiz to Gardoqui, 4 July 1794, AGI, Consulados, Libro de correspondencia, 49.

18. ANPar, AE, B I, 298 (12 Mar. 1790) notes: "les scèlles et les séquestres furent mis chez lui, et y sont encore sur ses comptoirs, ses magazins, ses livres et papiers, et effets . . . quelconques." Cf. the observations of the Cadiz *consulado* in a letter, Cadiz, 14 July 1786, AGI, Ind. Gen., 2312, apropos of "la situación en que está el comercio, con la repetición de . . . quiebras."

19. Licenciado Juan de Mora y Morales, Cadiz, 9 Dec. 1786, AGI, Consulados, Libro de correspondencia, 47.

20. Francisco de Valle, Juan Francisco de Vea Murguía, and Ruperto López García to Antonio Valdés, Cadiz, 31 Mar. 1789, AGI, Consulados, Libro de correspondencia, 47.

21. Ibid.

22. Antonio Pons y Cia., Bartolomé Lopetedi, vecinos y del comercio de . . . Cádiz, AGI, Ind. Gen., 2316.

23. Licenciado Juan de Mora y Morales, "Dictamen," Cadiz, 9 Dec. 1786, f. 264, AGI, Consulados, Libro de correspondencia, 47, ff. 265–66.

24. Ibid., f. 267.

25. Ibid., f. 267v.

26. Matheo Bernal, Madrid, 7 Oct. 1789, AGI, Ind. Gen., 2314.

27. Ibid.

28. Ibid.

29. Pedro del Puerto Vicario to Matheo Bernal, Veracruz, 7 Oct. 1789, AGI, Ind. Gen., 2314.

30. *Direction of Mathías Bernal's Exports, 1783–88*
    (*pesos fuertes*)

Veracruz	181,007	(61.6%)
Guatemala	12,373	(4.2%)
Lima	100,178	(34.1%)
Total	293,558	(100.0%)

Source: AGI, Ind. Gen., 2314, Bernal, Madrid,
14 Dec. 1789.

31. His son, Francisco de Frías, speculated in a variety of enterprises, purchasing cochineal at Veracruz, silk at Lima, and silver at San José del Parral in northern New Spain. Frías, *Informe jurídico,* 8.

32. Ibid., 3–18.

33. Consejo de Indias, "Dictamen," 4 Nov. 1788, AGI, Ind. Gen., 2316.

34. Thomas Ponze, Christobal Bulle, Francisco Vega, vezinos de Cádiz, Antonio Pons, Padre, Hijo y Sobrino, to Consejo de Indias, Cadiz, 25 Aug. 1788, AGI, Ind. Gen., 2316.

35. Ibid.

36. Ibid.

37. Licenciado Juan de Mora y Morales, Cadiz, 9 Dec. 1786, AGI, Consulados, Libro de correspondencia, 47, f. 265.

38. Antonio Flores, "Observaciones" (Salamanca, 1788), AGI, Consulados, Libro de correspondencia.

39. Miguel de Cervera, "Discurso . . . ," AHN, Estado, 2851, no. 112. A report ordered under Esquilache in 1761 indicated that the English earned "at least" 6 million pesos annually on direct (i.e., illegal) trade with Spanish colonies in and around the Caribbean. Christelow, "Contraband Trade Between Jamaica and the Spanish Main," 313.

40. In 1760 and again in 1766, Esquilache's ministry formulated new rules for handling national and foreign shipping entering Cadiz. Pérez Mesía, *Instrucción para el gobierno de la aduana de Cádiz.*

41. Christelow, "Contraband Trade Between Jamaica and the Spanish Main," 313 and nn. 8–9; "Mr . . . Thoughts on the American Trade," BMus Add. MS 32971, ff. 16–20v. Campomanes credited much of the success of English smuggling in the Caribbean to the activity of Jewish merchants there who spoke Spanish "perfectly." "Apuntaciones," f. 36.

42. Cervera, "Discurso," AHN, Estado, 2851, no. 112.

43. Consulado de Sevilla, "Informe . . . sobre comercio libre," f. 290.

44. Consejo de Indias, "Nota," 30 Oct. 1787, AGI, Mexico, 2505.

45. Southwell, "Proyecto," Madrid, 4 June 1788, AHN, Estado, 3188[1]; Southwell, letter, Aranjuez, 17 May 1787, AHN, Estado, 2839[2].

46. AHN, Estado, 3208, box 2.

47. AGN, AHH, 442–84:70 percent; Consulado de Sevilla, "Informe . . . sobre

comercio libre" (1788): 16 percent; Francisco Ignacio de Yraeta, "Informe," BNMex, MS 1334, f. 89v (1792): 27–35 percent.

48. Cf. Cole, "Trends in Eighteenth-Century Smuggling," 395–410; Ramsey, "Smugglers' Trade," 131–57; Jones, "Illicit Business," 17–38.

49. According to customs regulations, goods marked *tránsito* would not be inspected by the *vistas*. Bales and casks so designated would be listed on manifests as containing linens, woolens, and silks when in fact they held prohibited goods such as muslins, prints, and cottons. "Zelante Patricio" to Lerena, Cadiz, 1787 (AGSim, DGR, 2a remesa 448).

50. Múzquiz to Directores de Rentas Generales, Real Resolución, 18 Oct. 1779; *Correo mercantil de España y sus Indias,* 18 June 1804.

51. There was a precedent for such customs practice. In 1781, for instance, five prominent Cadiz merchants petitioned local authorities to permit the Cadiz customs simply to stamp and forward for export to the colonies, without inspection, long-warehoused English merchandise that may have been retained at the onset of war at sea. To the petition of Juan Francisco de Vea Murguía, Pedro de Landaeta, Miguel Vadillo, José de Llano y San Ginés, and Blas Ximénez, a local *junta* (which included the chief customs officer, Antonio Gálvez, the colonial secretary's brother) approved. AGI, Ind. Gen., 2420, 6 and 9 Dec. 1781.

52. Consulado de Cádiz to Antonio Valdés, 12 Feb. 1788, AGI, Consulados, Libro de correspondencia 47. Colonial Secretary Gálvez issued a special directive to customs officers to "reconocerse por menor los efectos y géneros contenidos en los fardos, caxas, y baúles de los cargazones particularmente en Cádiz." Real Orden, 8 Sept. 1786, in Levene, ed., *Documentos históricos argentinos,* 6:489–90.

53. Cf. Lerena to Mesía, Madrid, 15 Sept. 1785, AGSim, DGR, 2a remesa 452: "los muchos géneros que se introducen en América como manufacturados en España y falsificados con marcas de Barcelona y Valencia."

54. "Observaciones sobre los nuevos decretos . . . ," AHN, Estado, 3188[1]; Gardoqui to Godoy, Aranjuez, 12 May 1793, AHN, Estado, 4570. "On composait avec les fabricans de Cadiz qui prétoient leurs noms et leurs plombs," Mongélas, the French consul in Cadiz, reported (23 Jan. 1789, ANPar, AE, B I, 295). And to cite the interim administrator of the Cadiz customs in the late 1780s on transforming foreign into "national" products: "a la sombra [del número crecido de telares que se han establecido en Cádiz y sus inmediaciones] hacen los monopolios poniendoles los sellos de estas fábricas para que se tengan como nacionales. . . . Lo mismo sucede con os ilos." "Copia del informe del Sr. Ochando," AGSim, DGR, 2a remesa 452, ff. 1–5.

55. Lerena, "Paños extrangeros en América," Junta de Estado, 4 Aug. 1788, AHN, Estado, Libro 2d, f. 76.

56. Juan Marcolino, 14 Oct. 1786, AHN, Estado, 3200.

57. Manuel Francisco de la Torre del comercio de Valencia, Cadiz, 4 Jan. and 1 Mar. 1788, AHN, Estado, 2851[2]-12.

58. See Cabarrús, *Elogio del . . . conde de Gausa.*

59. Townsend, *Journey Through Spain,* 2:266; Ferrer del Rio, *Historia del reinado de Carlos III,* 4:133–38.

60. Léon de Arroyal, *Cartas económico-políticas.*

61. Real Orden, 11 Apr. 1782, AGSim, DGR, 2a remesa 451.

62. Manuel María de Heredia, confidential, Cadiz, 1785, AGSim, DGR, 2a remesa 451; Real Orden in Lerena to Mesía, 15 Sept. 1785, AGSim, DGR, 2a remesa 452.

63. Lerena to Mesía, "Instrucción reservada no. 1," 31 July 1785, AGSim, DGR, 2a remesa 451.

64. Poiret, Cadiz, 26 Aug. 1765, ANP, AE, B I 293.

65. Ibid.

66. Mesía to Lerena, Cadiz, 20 Sept. 1785, AGSim, DGR, 2a remesa 451.

67. Juan de Indart, "Primer reglamento para la aduana de Cádiz," AGSim, DGR, 2a remesa 450.

68. Ramsay, *English Overseas Trade,* 167.

69. Hoon, *Organization of the English Customs System,* 203–5, 212–13.

70. AGSim, DGR, 2a remesa 450.

71. Mesía, "Relación," Madrid, 20 Aug. 1789, AGSim, DGR, 2a remesa 451.

72. Ibid.

73. AGSim, DGR, 2a remesa 450. Mesía reported that exports were often assessed at a fraction of their real value, 16 percent in the case of a shipment of Spanish silks. This was, Mesía added, "una idea nada equívoca de la especulación superficial y poco cuidado con que se ha hecho hasta aqui el reconocimiento de géneros nacionales." Letter, Cadiz, 30 Apr. 1789, AGSim, DGR, 2a remesa 452.

74. "Algunas notícias dadas al Sr. Visitador . . . ," AGSim, DGR, 2a remesa 450.

75. Pérez Mesía, *Instrucción,* arts. 9–10, 15–17, 32, 43.

76. Mesía, "Relación," Madrid, 20 Aug. 1789, AGSim, DGR, 2a remesa 451. Málaga was a smugglers' paradise, where Cadiz merchants routinely shipped specie "con el único objeto de los . . . clandestinos embarques." "Zelante Patricio" to Lerena, Cadiz, 1787, AGSim, DGR, 2a remesa 448.

77. Mesía, "Relación," Madrid, 20 Aug. 1789, AGSim, DGR, 2a remesa 451.

78. "Zelante Patricio" to Pedro Lerena, Cadiz, 1787, AGSim, DGR, 2a remesa 448.

79. Anonymous, "En la superintendencia general hay notícias de varios puntos que necesitan providencias" (1788), AGSim, DGR, 2a remesa 452.

80. Martínez Shaw, *Cataluña en la carrera de Indias,* 202–3, 246, 251, 273–74, 282, 368–69. By lowering the price of French brandy in England, the Anglo-French commercial treaty of 1786 probably reinforced the interest of Catalan exporters in colonial sales. Anon., "Reflexiones sobre el comercio libre de América . . . un zeloso profesor del comercio. Año 1789," BMus Add. MS 13984, ff. 145–46.

81. Delgado i Ribas, "Modelo catalán dentro del sistema de libre comercio," in Fontana and Bernal, eds., *Comercio libre,* 55.

82. Martínez Shaw, *Cataluña,* 94, 96, 250. See also José María Oliva Melgar, "Reflexiones en torno al comercio libre de Barlovento: El caso catalán," 72–74.

83. Oliva Melgar, *Cataluña y el comercio privilegiado con América en el siglo XVIII,* 317; Fradera, "Una o varias crisis coloniales?" 98; Martínez Shaw, *Cataluña,* 281.

84. Vilar, *Catalogne,* 1:159; 2:483–84, 490, 503.

85. Oliva Melgar, *Cataluña,* 328.

86. Ibid., 141–47, 166–70.

87. Ibid., 326–28.

88. Ibid., 273–74 and n. 29, 275–76, 283–84. A propos of French flour imports, Oliva Melgar notes the paradox of Catalans importing for reexport "un producto agrario tradicional" of their province.

89. As Delgado i Ribas has argued, Madrid provided "una protección absoluta a las producciones de la industria popular" ("Modelo catalán dentro del sistema de comercio libre," in Fontana and Bernal, eds., *Comercio libre,* 57).

90. This has been advanced recently by Catalan historians. See, e.g., Fontana, "Introducción," in Anes Alvarez et al., eds., *Economía española al final del antiguo régimen,* 3:xxix–xxx, and esp. xxxii, n. 23.

91. Oliva Melgar, *Cataluña,* 284–85. During the 1770s, Madrid authorities complained repeatedly about the volume of foreign linen prints exported to the colonies under the category of "national" to take advantage of lower export duties. Levene, ed., *Documentos para la historia argentina,* 5:421–23.

92. Oliva Melgar, *Cataluña,* 76.

93. Ibid., 71.

94. Ibid., 150, 328.

95. Delgado i Ribas, "Modelo catalán dentro del sistema de comercio libre," in Fontana and Bernal, eds., *Comercio libre,* 61.

96. Delgado i Ribas, "Miratge del llivre comerç," 76.

97. Cf. Fontana, "Introduccion," in Anes Alvarez et al., eds., *Economía española al final del antiguo régimen,* 3:xxix–xxxi, and Tedde de Lorca, "Introducción," in ibid., 2:xxii–xxiii.

98. Delgado i Ribas, "Miratge del llivre comerç," 76–77; id., "Impacto de los crisis coloniales en la economía catalana," in *Economía española al final del antiguo regimen,* ed. Anes Alvarez et al., 3:108.

99. *Barcelona's Share in Spanish Exports/Reexports to the Colonies, 1784–86*
     (reales de vellon)

	Total	Barcelona
1784	434,808,580	14,387,241 (3.31%)
1785	767,249,787	26,962,926 (3.51%)
1786	435,282,872	27,066,493 (6.22%)
Total	1,637,341,239	68,416,660 (4.18%)

Source: Adapted from Vilar, *Catalogne,* 3:113–14.

100. Cited in Bitar Letayf, *Economistas españoles,* 206.

101. Anes Alvarez, *Antiguo régimen,* 188–89; Tinoco Rubiales, "Capital y crédito en la Baja Andalucía durante la crisis del Antiguo Régimen," 257 and n. 10; Marcelin Defourneaux, *Pablo de Olavide,* 147–51.

102. Arroyal, *Cartas económico-políticas,* 67.

103. Defourneaux, "Problème agraire en Andalousie au xviiie siècle," 48; García Sanz y Sanz Fernández, "Agricultura y ganadería," 54.

104. Anes Alvarez, *Antiguo régimen,* 190. See also Townsend, *Journey Through Spain,* 2:421.

105. Tithe receipts on wine in Sevilla's archdiocese rose 113 percent between 1765 and 1778, from 416,270 reales to 889,852, and one source estimated that the Spanish merchant marine expanded from 2,449 to 2,835 vessels between 1779 and 1787. AGI,

Ind. Gen., 2409 (Sevilla, 12 Dec 1778); Ferret, "Exposición histórica de las causas que más han influido en la decadencia de la marina española" (1813), MN, MS 444, f. 278v.

106. Consulado de Sevilla, "Informe . . . sobre comercio libre," f. 275.

107. Fontana, "Introducción," in Anes Alvarez et al., eds., *Economía española al final del antiguo régimen,* 3:xxviii–xxix; Tinoco Rubiales, "Capital y crédito en la Baja Andalucía," 258, 261.

108. Comment by Antonio García-Baquero Gonzalez quoted in Nadal and Tortella, eds., *Agricultura, comercio colonial y crecimiento económico,* 367–68.

109. Cf. Fontana, "Introducción" in Anes Alvarez et al., eds., *Economía española al final del antiguo régimen,* 3:xxvi and n.

110. Brown, "Anglo-Spanish Relations in America," 461–62; Calderón Quijano, ed., *Banco de San Carlos,* 15.

111. González Enciso, *Fábrica de Guadalajara,* 77–78; Tedde de Lorca, "Introducción" in Anes Alvarez et al., eds., *Economía española al final del antiguo régimen,* 2:xxxvi. In 1765, the French consul at Cadiz reported that Spanish merchants had misinvested the high earnings of colonial trade of 1745–63, the government's industrial incentives had failed, and that high labor costs and poor quality had made the woolens of Guadalajara and other state-subsidized manufacturies uncompetitive with those of Abbeville, Elboeuf, and Sedan. Puyabry to Choiseul-Praslin, "Mémoire," Cadiz, 19 Apr. 1765, AAE, M et D, Espagne, 32, n. 28. The criticism was hardly disinterested.

112. Pérez Moreda, "Población," in Artola, ed., *Enciclopedia de historia de España,* 1:385.

113. Bilbao and Fernández de Pinedo, "Artesanía e industria," in Artola, ed., *Enciclopedia de historia de España,* 1:146.

114. In 1779, the French commercial agent at Madrid, Abbé Béliardi, reported that the warehouses of the Cinco Gremios Mayores were overstocked with English woolens, while since about 1740, the number of looms at Segovia, Valencia, and Sevilla had fallen. "Mémoire pour l'Espagne," BNPar, MS Fonds Français, 10768.

115. From the contract between the state and the Cinco Gremios Mayores, 1757, in Miguel de Goyeneche, to viceroy, Mexico, 12 Dec. 1773, AGN, Consulado, 113, folder 5, f. 8v.

116. Francisco de Paula Sarmiento Fuentes de la Pradera, "Ynstrucciones para el bufete y mercancía arregladas a los comercios de la Europa" (1781), f. 49 (MS, John Carter Brown Library, Brown University).

117. From the contract of 1757 in Miguel de Goyeneche to viceroy, Mexico, 12 Dec. 1773, AGN, Consulado, 113, folder 5, ff. 7–7v.

118. Rodríguez López, *Laneras de Castilla,* 58–59.

119. "Reflexiones sobre la real orden de 20 de agosto de 1788 prohibiendo el embarco de paños extrangeros para Indias . . . ," AHN, Estado, 3188[1].

120. Letter, 1773, AGN, Consulado, 113, folder 5.

121. Miguel Vallejo, director, Reales Fábricas de Guadalajara, to Junta de Estado, Madrid, 16 June 1788, AHN, Consejo de Estado, bk. 2d, f. 53; Peuchet, *Dictionnaire de la géographie commerçante,* 3:227. Vallejo had been *administrador* of the Cadiz customs following service at Barcelona in the same capacity. The French commercial

agent at Madrid was convinced Vallejo was opposed to "tout ce qui est productions étrangères" (Boyetet, Madrid, 7 Dec. 1778, to Sartine, ANPar, AE, B I, ff. 250v–251).

122. Francisco Ignacio de Yraeta, Mexico, 1792, to Revillagigedo, BNMex, MS 1334, f. 190.

123. Poiret, Cadiz, 29 Aug. 1788. The Real Orden was dated 20 Aug. 1788. ANPar, AE, B I, f. 296. The measure had the support of Catalan merchants at Cadiz; at the time, Poiret reported the presence of French woolens there in the impressive amount of 10 million *livres tournois* (roughly 2 million pesos) worth.

124. "Reflexiones sobre la real orden de 20 de agosto de 1788 . . . ," AHN, Estado, 3188[1]. During his management of the plant, Eugenio Izquierdo, a skilled bureaucrat with many scientific interests, found a state of total confusion and that "every branch required reform." After a stormy two-year stint, he resigned. Townsend, *Journey Through Spain*, 2:270–72.

125. Junta de Estado, Madrid, 16 June 1788, AHN, Estado, bk. 2d, f. 53v.

126. The preamble of the Real Orden of 20 Sept. 1788 (countersigned by Hacienda Secretary Lerena) revealed Madrid's grasp of reality: since the colonies had received "muchos paños extrangeros con título de nacionales, subplantando a este fin las marcas, hay tal abundancia . . . que no puede darse salida a las crecidas cantidades que hay detenidas en las fábricas de Guadalajara, Segovia y otras del Reyno."

127. So insisted the Hacienda Secretary, Lerena. Junta de Estado, Madrid, 11 May 1789, AHN, Estado, bk. 3, ff. 20v–21.

128. The following paragraphs on Diez's activities at Soria are based upon Joseph Diez to Campomanes, Soria, 24 Nov. 1778, AHN, Estado, 3208, box 1.

129. For the "auténtico fracaso" of another textile enterprise, a cotton mill operating under initially far more favorable conditions, see the detailed monograph of Martín García, *Industria textil en Avila*.

130. La Force, *Development of the Spanish Textile Industry*, 145.

131. *EMDL,* Oct. 1788.

132. Acuerdo del Consulado, Cadiz, 5 Apr. 1788, AGI, Consulados, Libro de Juntas y Acuerdos.

133. García Herreros to Revillagigedo, Mexico, 1792, AGN, Consulado, 123, f. 44.

134. Tomás Izquierdo to Antonio Valdés, 1788, AGI, Mexico, 2505.

135. Floridablanca, "Memorial presentado al Rey Carlos III . . . ," 307–49.

136. Cf. ibid., 340: "las relaciones exactas de entradas y salidas de géneros extrangeros y nacionales por las aduanas . . . mandado formar en el presente ministerio."

137. *Spain's Exports to Its American Colonies, 1783–85*
    (*reales de vellon*)

	National	Reexports	Total
1783	68,754,081	65,163,144	133,917,225
1784	195,885,361	238,923,219	434,808,580
1785	337,266,601	429,982,185	767,248,786

Source: Gaceta de Madrid, 18 Apr. 1786.

138. Floridablanca, "Memorial presentado al Rey Carlos III . . . ," 336.

139. Ibid. 329, 337.

140. Ibid. 336.

141. Ibid. 337.

142. Ibid. 336.

143. Delgado i Ribas, "Miratge del lliuvre comerç," 75.

Spain's Exports to Its American Colonies, 1784–87
  (*reales de vellon*)

	(1)	(2)	(3)
1784	434,808,580	434,808,000	435,616,352
1785	767,248,786	767,249,000	457,675,683
1786	381,950,596	426,282,000	339,345,662
1787	320,069,500	320,070,000	258,725,291

Sources: (1) *Gaceta de Madrid* and Canga Arguelles, *Diccionario de hacienda;*
(2) Izard, "Comercio Libre," 302; (3) Fisher, *Commercial Relations,* 46.

144. "Estado que manifiesta el valor del comercio hecho a todas las Americas . . .
1776 a 1778" and "Demostraciones," AGI, Consulados, Acuerdos y Juntas, 1788.

145. Morineau, *Incroyables gazettes,* 438.

Spain's Precious Metals Receipts, 1783–87
  (pesos)

	Total	Cadiz	(from Veracruz)
1783	14,733,692	14,733,692	12,933,692
1784	42,188,597	38,197,396	31,698,785
1785	39,745,481	36,451,686	10,871,226
1786	32,690,462	28,440,117	16,909,042
1787	25,726,536	22,408,230	13,224,927

Source: Morineau, *Incroyables gazettes,* 431–32.

146. AGI, Ind. Gen., 2403.

147. Madrid was later convinced that Gálvez, using data sent from New Spain,
had simply overestimated New Spain's import capacity by one-third. Consejo de
Indias, "Informe," 3 Oct. 1788, AGI, Mexico, 2505.

148. According to Pedro Corbalán, *intendente* of Veracruz, the value of foreign
goods imported at that port dropped 46 percent between September 1787 (53,307,452
pesos) and September 1788 (28,873,467). AGI, Mexico, 2505.

149. Tinoco Rubiales, "Capital y crédito en la Baja Andalucía," 304–5 and nn. 52,
55. One of the firms, Galatoire, had financial ties to the Languedoc merchant
Gand, who spread the pain to correspondents at Amsterdam, Paris, Marseilles and
Montpelier.

150. Delgado i Ribas, "Miratge del lliuvre comerç," 76.

151. Guérard, "Rapport sur la législation politique qui régissait le commerce de
France avec l'Amérique Espagnole . . ." (1820), AAEPar, M et D, Espagne, 129, f. 315.

152. Note the behavior of the Gloria family of businessmen, noted by Tedde de
Lorca, "Introducción," in Anes Alvarez et al., eds., *Economía española al final del
antiguo régimen,* 2:xxx.

8. A Colonial Response to *Comercio Libre:* New Spain

EPIGRAPHS: *El Sol* (Mexico City), 17 June 1823; BRPal, Ayala, MS 2856, f. 208.

1. *Silver Coinage, Mexico City Mint, 1773–77 and 1783–87*
   (*pesos fuertes*)

	Coinage	Annual Average	% Change
1773	19,005,007		
1774	12,938,060		
1775	14,298,093		
1776	16,518,935		
1777	20,705,591		
Total	83,465,686	16,693,137	
1783	23,105,799		
1784	20,492,432		
1785	18,002,956		
1786	16,868,614		
1787	15,505,324		
Total	93,975,125	18,795,025	(+) 12.6

Source: Howe, *Mining Guild,* 457, app. A. These data virtually match those in BNMad, 13,210, F. 412, "Estado que manifiesta . . . acuñado . . . 1733 . . . 1818."

2. *Precious Metals Exports, Veracruz to Spain*
   (*pesos fuertes*)

1773–77		1783–87	
1773	24,727,736	1783	41,692,739
1774	3,942,893	1784	15,941,613
1775	12,677,402	1785	21,486,622
1776	8,253,809	1786	17,700,887
1777	8,182,758	1787	17,499,953
Total	57,784,598		114,321,814

Source: Adapted from "Colección de Estados," n. 16.

3. *Spain: Exports to the American Colonies*
   (*reales de vellon*)

1778	28,236,620
1783	71,453,420
1784	196,690,589
1785	213,016,298
1786	170,443,693
1787	116,799,803
Total	796,640,423
Average annual	132,773,403

Source: Adapted from Fisher, *Commercial Relations,* 46, table 6.

4. *Spain: Customs Collections on Colonial Trade, Imports and Exports*
   (*reales de vellon*)

1778	6,761,291
1788	55,456,949

Source: Bourgoing, *Tableau de l'Espagne moderne,* 2:202–3.

5. *New Spain: Revenues, 1765–77 and 1778–90*
   (*pesos fuertes*)

		% Change
1765–77	131,135,000	
1778–90	232,305,000	+77.1

Source: Foncerrada, *Exhortación,* 30–31.

6. Garner, "Long-term Silver Mining Trends," 904–5, 911, 914; id., "Exportaciones de circulante en el siglo xviii (1750–1810)," 569 n. 32; and id., "Further Considerations of Facts and Figures in Bourbon Mexico," 60.

7. Palerm, "Sobre la formación del sistema colonial," 104–5.

8. Salvucci, *Textiles and Capitalism in Mexico,* 18–20.

9. Elhuyar, *Memoria sobre el influyo de la minería,* 26. Richard Garner has encapsulated silver mining's role in the colonial economy in a few succinct paragraphs in "Exportaciones de circulante en el siglo xviii," 545–49, 588.

10. "En todos tiempos las naciones marítimas, manufactureras e industriosas apetecían y buscaban en America a estas porciones de metales para los fines de su economía interior, y de su comercio al Asia," a trio of Cuban planters and merchants, the conde de Santa María de Loreto, Francisco Laiseca, and Pedro Juan de Erice, noted in a communication to Capitan-General Someruelos in 1811. "Representación de la Junta Económica del Consulado," 7 Oct. 1811, AGN, Consulado, vol. 7, folder 16.

11. Miño Grijalva, "Circulación de mercancías," 47.

12. Humboldt, *Essai politique sur le royaume de la Nouvelle-Espagne,* 4:315, 322.

13. Garner, "Long-term Silver Mining Trends," 935; Quirós, "Memoria de instituto . . . 1803," AGN, AHH, 1869–2, para. 26.

14. Palerm, "Sobre la formación del sistema colonial," 96, 106.

15. Gálvez, "Discurso y reflexiones de un vasallo," BRPal, Ayala, 2816, ff. 110, 132–132v. For analysis, see Pérez Herrero, "Comienzos de la política reformista de Carlos III," 59 ff.

16. Gálvez, "Discurso y reflexiones de un vasallo," BRPal, Ayala, 2816, ff. 117, 130.

17. Ibid., ff. 131–131v.

18. Fabry, *Compendiosa demostración.*

19. Landázuri, "Noticia de los minerales de oro y plata. . . de la Nueva España," BRPal, Ayala, 2824; Navarro García, "Virrey Marqués de Croix," 240.

20. Landázuri, "Notícia de los minerales de oro y plata. . . de la Nueva España," BRPal. Ayala, 2834, ff. 142v, 143v, 153–153v, 155.

21. Ibid., ff. 153–154v, 158v–159.

22. Consulado de México, "Instruzión relativa a todos los puntos y negozios del Consulado para govierno de los deputados . . ." (1755). AGN, AHH, 635–8.

23. Those signing the "Instruzión" included Juan de Aristorena, Juan de Cas-

tañiza, Andrés Francisco de Quintela, Manuel de Aldaco, Augusto Alonso de Hortigoza, Augusto de Iglesias, and Joseph González Calderón.

24. Gamboa, *Commentaries,* 1:xxx. Both the *Comentarios* and the 1830 English edition of Gamboa's work, *Commentaries on the Mining Ordinances of New Spain,* will be cited.

25. Brading, *Miners and Merchants in Bourbon Mexico,* 120.

26. Gamboa, *Commentaries, 1:109.*

27. Ibid., 1:x.

28. Perhaps borrowing from J. A. Villaseñor y Sánchez's *Theatro americano.*

29. Gamboa, *Commentaries,* 1:xxv–xxvi.

30. Ibid., 1:xi.

31. Ibid., 1:xxv.

32. Gamboa, *Comentarios,* 247–48.

33. Cf. ibid., 55–56: "los flotistas . . . comisionistas, o Comerciantes de España, preocupandoles la facilidad de el rescate en los Minerales . . . que siempre . . . pagan a menos de la ley."

34. Gamboa, *Commentaries,* 1:240.

35. Ibid., 1:237.

36. Campomanes, *Reflexiones,* 435.

37. Ibid., 443–44.

38. Bakewell, *Silver Mining and Society in Colonial Mexico,* 171–73. In the seventeenth century, Mexico City merchants transferred 300,000 pesos to the metropole in payment for mercury; in 1709, Madrid again requested the Consulado de México, religious corporations, and private individuals to advance funds against the value of future shipments of 6,000 quintals. Fonseca and Urrutia, eds., *Historia general de Real Hacienda,* 1:320, and Lang, *Monopolio estatal del mercurio.*

39. Gamboa, *Comentarios,* 28–30; Fonseca and Urrutia, eds., *Historia general de Real Hacienda,* 1:309–11.

40. Gamboa, *Comentarios,* 31; Gálvez, "Discurso y reflexiones de un vasallo," BRPal, Ayala 2816; Gálvez, *Informe general . . . siendo visitador general . . . 1771,* 66. Complicating the state's mercury pricing policy was the need to supplement production from Spain's Almadén mines with Istrian supplies, which raised the cost substantially. Fonseca and Urrutia, eds., *Historia general de Real Hacienda,* 1:359.

41. Fonseca and Urrutia, eds., *Historia general de Real Hacienda,* 1:337–38, 345. Although prohibited by law, *mercaderes* and *aviadores* bought mercury in bulk and "lo menudeaban a precios excesivos, defraudando a los miserables." Colonial bureaucrats also castigated Indians ("demasiadamente inclinados al hurto") who in rebottling leaking mercury containers concealed mercury "en sus mismos cuerpos, bebiendoselo con otras razones de no menos consideración" (ibid.).

42. "Instrucción reservada que trajo . . . Amarillas recebida del . . . Julián de Arriaga," in *Instrucciones* (1873), 1:523–24.

43. Between 1736 and 1744, Madrid ordered the colonial mercury administration in Mexico City to ship between 200,000 and 400,000 pesos annually to Havana for tobacco purchases. Fonseca and Urrutia, eds., *Historia General de Real Hacienda,* 1:328. In 1779, Mexico City was directed to transfer 400,000 pesos for the same end. AGI, Mexico 1510. The state paid a price for its expensive mercury, since this stimulated refining of silver ores by smelting, which eased tax evasion and illegal exports.

Lerguinazával, "Thesoro de España," BRPal, Ayala, 2819, f. 33. Gálvez claimed that he managed to block illegal exports of 5 million pesos at the Jalapa fair of 1765, the equivalent of 13 percent of the coinage of that year. Gálvez, *Informe general*, 73–74. The *comercio de España* bought smuggled silver from *rescatadores* well under the market price. Gamboa, *Comentarios*, 55–56.

44. Cited in Navarro García, "Virrey Marqués de Croix," 241–42.

45. Gamboa, *Comentarios*, 54; Fonseca and Urrutia, eds., *Historia general de Real Hacienda*, 1:33–34; and Elhuyar, *Memoria sobre el influyo*, 53–54, which indicates that the state's action in 1723 was inspired by the increase of over 800,000 pesos in government silver taxes at Zacatecas in 1711–20 compared to those of the previous decade. Elhuyar, *Memoria sobre el influyo*.

46. *Memorial ajustado hecho en virtud de decreto de . . . la Real Junta de Comercio y Moneda*. Among those investigated were the silver bankers Francisco Valdivieso and Isidro Rodríguez de la Madrid.

47. Gamboa, *Comentarios*, 36, 94. Cf. García de Vera, *Relación y testimonio de los autos . . . sobre la erección de la Companía Real*. In 1741, Madrid granted Augustín Ramírez Ortuño a ten-year monopoly to supply New Spain with "todos los frutos de regular consumo." Under objection by the Consulado de Cádiz, the order of 24 July 1741 was suspended. Consulado de Cádiz to crown, 27 May 1778, AGI, Consulados, Libro de correspondencia, 87, ff. 7–14v.

48. One of the Colonial Office's directives guiding Gálvez's inquiry in New Spain concerned the supply and pricing of blasting powder (then farmed out to the private sector) so that the "public be supplied as economically as may be." Priestley, *Gálvez*, 409.

49. Brading, *Miners and Merchants*, 133.

50. Gálvez, *Informe general*, 64.

51. Ibid. 14, 75.

52. Ibid. 64–65, 71.

53. Ibid. 75–76.

54. On mineworkers' efforts in defense of their rights, see Ladd, *Making of a Strike*.

55. Gamboa, *Comentarios*, 246, 301. Cf. Humboldt, *Essai politique*, 4:36–37, which indicates that four decades later, working conditions in the mines were unchanged.

56. Gálvez, *Informe general*, 72, 246–47.

57. Beleña, "Informe reservado," in Florescano and Castillo, eds., *Controversia*, vol. 1; Priestley, *Gálvez*, 242 n. 10; Fonseca and Urrutia, eds., *Historia general de real Hacienda*, 1:40–41.

58. *Mercury Prices, 1762–66 to 1778–82*

Year	Price (peso/quintal)	Quintals Used
1762–66	82	35,755
1767–71	62	42,618
1772–77	62	53,810
1778–82	41	59,221

Sources: Priestley, *Gálvez*, 242, n. 10; Elhuyar, *Influjo*, 64, 66.

59. Consulado de México to *virrey,* 24 Nov. 1777, AGN, AHH, 791–8, f. 155v.

60. The order directed "mis delegados en los dominios de Indias anticipen las remesas del valor de azogue de Alemania que les está regulado y envían anualmente." AGSim, Secretaria y superintendencia de Hacienda, 316; Fonseca and Urrutia, eds., *Historia general de Real Hacienda,* 1:359. See also Dobado González, "Las minas de Almadén, el monopolio del azogue," 403–72.

61. Gálvez, *Informe general,* 70.

62. Francisco Xavier Machado y Fiesco, Gálvez's secretary in New Spain, was at Puebla when the Jesuits were expelled from New Spain, returning to Madrid as *contador general* of the Consejo de Indias; Antonio Porlier y de la Luz Dutari married a *criolla* from Tucumán (in modern Argentina). He returned to Madrid and the Consejo de Indias.

63. Howe, *Mining Guild of New Spain,* 38–39. Bucareli was instructed to include as *junta* members the official in charge of mercury distribution, the superintendent of the mint, a *fiscal* of the Audiencia, and treasury officials. His purpose was to exclude Mexico City *almaceneros.*

64. A concise biography of Velázquez de León is Moreno de los Arcos, "Apuntes biográficos de Joaquín Velázquez de León, 1732–1786," 41–75.

65. Howe, *Mining Guild,* 42–44.

66. Ibid. 50, 60–61. Valcárcel had on deposit at interest over 22,000 pesos with Manuel Aldaco, merchant, manager of a *banco de plata* (the Fagoagas'), and good friend of Gamboa. He was also director of New Spain's state-controlled mercury monopoly. Brading, *Miners and Merchants,* 179.

67. Howe, *Mining Guild,* 59–62, 94–95.

68. Ibid., 79, 134–35, 140.

69. Ibid., 82–83, 161–65, 169.

70. Ibid., 84–85, 93, 118–21, 127.

71. Ibid., 128–129, 140.

72. Ibid., 135.

73. Ibid., 128–35; Hamnett, *Politics and Trade in Southern Mexico,* 38–39; AHN, Estado 3156, 4194; Calderón Quijano, ed., *Virreyes de Nueva España,* 2:175; Rojas y Rocha, *Poema épico . . . conde de Gálvez* (Mexico City, 1785).

74. "Proyecto para mejorar todos los ramos de Hazienda," AGN, AHH, 635–2, f. 2; Howe, *Mining Guild,* 151–53.

75. Ibid., 93–98, 100.

76. Ibid., 164–65.

77. Ibid., 171.

78. Ibid., 64–67, and Brading, *Miners and Merchants,* 329.

79. Howe, *Mining Guild,* 271.

80. Brading, *Miners and Merchants,* 320.

81. The insurgent group complained that the outgoing *diputados* "pretendieron se declarase tocar al mas antiguo de ellos la propuesta de los nuevos sin que los electores tubiesen otra acción que la de elegir de los propuestos a los que les pareciesen más aptos." "Los electores de la minería de Guanajuato elegidos en la Junta General . . . 12 de Enero de este año . . . ," AGN, Consulado, vol. 9, folder 5.

82. Gálvez countersigned this decision on 30 Oct. 1783. AGN, Consulado, vol. 9, folder 5. In the interim the viceroy, on advice from the mercury administrator (Fer-

nando José Mangino) and the mining tribunal's Spanish superintendent-general (Juan Lucas de Lassaga), appointed Vicente Manuel de Sardaneta and Fernando de Miera as temporary deputies. The Audiencia de Mexico refused to involve itself in this thicket of powerful conflicting interests. AGN, Consulado, vol. 204, folder 10, f. 35.

83. The outcome of this election is unclear. Brading lists the two new *diputados* as *peninsulares* (Hernández Chico and Septién y Arce); Howe claims that one was peninsular (Septien y Arce) and the other *criollo* (Antonio Obregón, first conde de la Valenciana). Brading, *Miners and Merchants,* 330–31; Howe, *Mining Guild,* 227.

84. Brading, *Miners and Merchants,* 331.

85. Elhuyar, *Memorial sobre el influjo de la mineria.*

86. Morin, *Michoacán en la Nueva España,* 83; Van Young, "Age of Paradox," 69.

87. Cf. Beleña, "Informe reservado," in Florescano and Castillo, eds., *Controversia,* paras. 208–2. There was a financial interest, for the colonial state exported thousands of pesos annually from the state's mail monopoly (*renta del correo*).

88. Ibid., para. 205.

89. *Population of New Spain and Mexico City, 1743–1803*

	New Spain	Mexico City
1743	2,094,000	98,000 [1742]
1793	4,483,680	112,926 [1790]
1795	5,200,000	
1799	4,500,000	
1803	5,764,731	137,000

Sources: Florescano, *Precios del maíz,* 170, table 18; Lerner, "Población de la Nueva España," 328, 333, 342.

90. Sedano, "Noticias de Mexico . . . ," HSA, MS f. 98. Cf. AGI, Mexico, 2518: "saben la ninguna eficacia de los que se encargan de lo material de esta operación, y las inumerables personas que se ocultan para no ser empadronados."

91. Michoacán: Morin, *Michoacán,* 49; Rabell, *Los diezmos de San Luís de la Paz,* 73–74; Brading, *Haciendas and Ranchos in the Mexican Bajío,* 58; Guadalajara: Van Young, "A modo de conclusión: El siglo paradójico," 208.

92. Van Young, "Age of Paradox," 74; Brading, *Haciendas and Ranchos,* 58.

93. Morin, *Michoacán,* 59; Cook and Borah, *Essays in Population History,* 1:375.

94. Guanajuato's population jumped 134 percent between 1754 and 1803, which is hardly surprising given its economic importance. On the other hand, Valladolid's [Morelia] grew by only 50 percent between 1760 and 1803. Morin, *Michoacán,* 74. Van Young, "Age of Paradox," 66, sees a close link between expanding urban demand and the commercialization of agriculture.

95. Morin, *Michoacán,* 99–100 and 110–11, makes explicit the reciprocal relation, e.g., between the mining recession (roughly 1753–68) and agricultural production. For a comparable pattern elsewhere in the Bajío, see Rabell, *San Luís de la Paz,* 62, and Florescano, *Precios del maíz,* 189.

96. Anon., "Ensayo apologético por el comercio libre . . . ," in Florescano and Castillo, eds., *Controversia,* para 7.

97. Revillegigedo, "Carta reservada," 196.

98. Recent studies emphasize far more economic interregional exchange than has generally been thought. See Trabulse, ed., *Fluctuaciones económicas en Oaxaca,* 40.

99. Florescano, *Precios del maíz,* 95, 109, 188.

100. Licenses allocated to North American merchants for flour shipments to Havana in 1780 were a factor in the ultimate loss of this market to New Spain's producers. AGN, Consulado, vol. 49, 22 July 1806. The areas so affected in the jurisdiction of Puebla included Tesmelucan, Siénaga, Atlixco, Los Llanos, and Tepeaca. AGN, Bienes Nacionales, 1749–3. As Juan Antonio Yermo, a merchant and *hacendado,* put it, "como su extracción [flour's] es tan corta para las Yslas de Barlovento por que hay provedores de otras partes." Yermo, "Sobre todo género de agricultura en la Nueva España."

101. Consulado de México to *virrey,* 27 Aug. 1800, AGN, AHH 635–1.

102. Yermo, "Sobre todo género de agricultura en la Nueva España," ff. 82–132.

103. Howe, *Mining Guild,* 171.

104. The discussion of sugar in the colony is based upon Yermo, "Sobre todo género de agricultura en la Nueva España," ff. 9–18.

105. Junta de ciudadanos to viceroy [the conde de Gálvez], Mexico, 29 Nov. 1785, BNMex MS, vol. 1304, f. 36.

106. Yermo, "Sobre todo género de agricultura en la Nueva España," f. 34v. In the same vein, Viceroy Revillagigedo quoted Intendant Felipe Clere of Zacatecas, who described the "genial indolencia de [los Indios], sus inclinaciones viciosas, su abandono, desidia y la indispensable necesidad de compelerlos a que trabajen y vivan en sujeción y arreglo." Revillagigedo, "Dictamen sobre las intendencias," Mexico, 5 May 1791, in Jones, *Despotismo ilustrado y los intendentes de la Nueva España,* 325.

107. Van Young, "Age of Paradox," 75–76.

108. Florescano, *Precios del maíz,* 188–90, 193.

109. Van Young, "Age of Paradox," 69–70, and "A modo de conclusión," 213.

110. Cf. Morin, *Michoacán,* 77–78, 138.

111. Ringrose, "Carting in the Hispanic World," 30–51.

112. Manuel de Flon to Revillagigedo, Puebla, 12 May 1790, in Jones, *Despotismo ilustrado,* 287–88.

113. Bromley and Bromley, "Debate on Sunday Markets," 93.

114. Consulado de México to *virrey,* 11 Feb. 1774, AGN, AHH, 502–17, para. 46.

115. Austria, "Memoria de instituto, 1803," AGN, AHH, 1869–2, para. 35; Mora, *México y sus revoluciones,* 1:51–52.

116. It later proved to be a seedbed of revolutionary leaders like Morelos and Vicente Guerrero. Around 1810, Guerrero owned an extensive mule transport enterprise carrying goods between Acapulco and Taxco.

117. Benedict, "Hacienda management," 394. *Arrieros'* expenses included the cost of "costales, petates, caveceados de baúles y caxas, caveceados chicos de fierro y acero, lazos, ylos y echura de todo." AGN, Consulado, vol. 113, folder 13, f. 110. Juan López Cancelada mentions *chinchorreros,* presumably those with a small number of mules operating locally since "menos de 40 mulas no costea la empresa de camino real de puerto a puerto." *Ruina de la Nueva España,* 18; *El Observador* (Mexico), 5 May 1830.

118. "Inventario . . . Diego Fernández Peredo," Archivo de Notarías, Mexico, Francisco Calapiz, 1820, f. 149; Consulado de Veracruz, 4 Apr. 1810, AGN, Consulado, vol. 2, folder 16. Referring to the people in and around Jalapa, Antonio de Ulloa observed in 1776 that "El exercicio mas ordinario de estos Yndios es el de arrieros, pero proporcionandose a ello el tráfico continuo que hai con Veracruz, para

las ciudades y poblaciones de todo el reino." "Notícia i descripción," AGI, 1631. Years later, Intendant Flon found that the "gente de razon" of Izúcar "a ecepción de algunos pocos Artezanos, subsiste en el exercicio de arrieros." Flon to Consulado de Veracruz, 13 Jan. 1804, AGN, AHH, 917–3.

119. "Itinerario" (1804), BMus Add. MS 17557, f. 78. Cf. Gabriel Manuel de Yturbe e Yraeta and Leonardo Alvarez, "Declaración y protesto," Mexico, 27 May 1823, Archivo de Notarías, Mexico, Francisco Calapíz, 1823, f. 219: "con fecha . . . de ayer, les firmó el arriero D. Mauricio Aponte un conocimiento de 152 mil pesos colunarios del antiguo cuño Mejicano que en 76 cajones con la marca M. de a dos mil pesos cada uno." See also Arrangoiz, *México desde 1808,* 1:72; Consulado de México to *virrey,* 19 June 1767, AGN, AHH, 502–17.

120. Consulado de México, 5 May 1777, AGN, AHH, 791–8; Consulado de México, 19 June 1767, AGN, AHH, 502–17, f. 48.

121. Ortiz Vidales, *Arriería en Mexico,* 62.

122. Archivo del Ex-Ayuntamiento, Mexico, vol. 2000, folder 2 (1780).

123. Consulado de México to *virrey,* 6 Dec. 1773, AGN, AHH, 502–17.

124. Cf. Consulado de México to Virrey Bucareli, 7 Dec. 1775, AGN, AHH, 502–17: "las providencias dadas en las Aduanas sobre guías, tornaguías, obligación de responder el remitente por el arriero conductor, producción de facturas individuales y demás."

125. Consulado de México to *virrey,* 19 June 1767, AGN, AHH, 502–17, which notes that locating a priest in a rural parish was often difficult since "los más de los parajes están tan despoblados que si sus havitadores quieren oyr missa del día de precepto, necessitan caminar más de 10 leguas para lograrlo."

126. So declared the Consulado de México when farming the *alcabala* tax in 1735. Moñino and Campomanes, "Informe," AGI, Mexico, 1250, para. 27; Real Sociedad Económica de Madrid, "Informe . . sobre libertad de comercio," BRAHM, Mutis 5, no. 64.

127. Consulado de México to *virrey,* 19 June 1767, AGN, AHH, 502–17, ff. 51–51v.

128. Meek, *Exchange Media of Colonial Mexico.* Cf. Quirós, "Memoria de instituto . . . 1808," AGI, Mexico, 2997: "el aumento de 33 por ciento de la moneda sencilla a fuerte que antes se estimaba por cero, entra ahora como es debido en cuenta de las ganancias."

129. In 1772, the *consulado* had requested Madrid to "moderar y fixar el buque de éstas [flotas] para evitar los abusos y desórdenes que generalmente se han seguido hasta ahora de lo contrario." Real Orden, 24 Apr. 1772, in AGN, Consulado, vol. 113, folder 5, f. 40.

130. Castillo Negrete, "Dictamen" (1810), AGI, Mexico, 2516; Real Díaz, *Ferias,* 113, n. 22.

131. Consulado de Barcelona, "Informe sobre el comercio de America," *EMDL,* nos. 173–74 (1789).

132. Manuel Guiral, president of the Casa de Contratación at Cadiz in 1790, made clear that "la libertad recíproca concedida" by the reglamento of 1778 applied only to "frutos y efectos y no para la navegación." AGI, Ind. Gen., 2318.

133. Consulado de Sevilla, "Informe sobre . . . comercio libre," para. 30; Conde de Villamar to Gálvez, 16 Feb. 1779. "Cartas y papeles sobre el comercio libre," AGI, Ind. Gen., 2408. Cf. "Dictamen," 31 Jan. 1789, AGI, Mexico, 2505: "Si Alvarez y Frías

obtienen los registros para 4 buques que componen mas de 2000 toneladas, qué dexarán para los otros comerciantes?"

134. BRPal, Ayala, 2856, f. 208; Lorenzo Hernández de Alba to Audiencia de Mexico, BNMex MS, 1334, f. 233.

135. Cf. "Colección de estados de valores," BNMex., MS 1334, no. 15, f. 312.

136. AGN, Consulado, vol.113, folder 5, f. 40.

137. The Cadiz *consulado* estimated New Spain's annual import capacity based on annual coinage plus farm output sent to market, adjusted by estimates of "el consumo ordinario de que es capaz aquella parte de America," a method that was probably adopted by Gálvez's ministry. See Consulado de Cádiz, "Acuerdo," 5 Apr. 1787, AGI, Consulados, Libro de acuerdos.

138. *Distribution of* Toneladas *to Peninsular Ports, 1784*

Port	Toneladas
Cadiz	4,000
Sevilla	1,100
Málaga	1,500
Barcelona	1,000
Other	2,000
Total	9,600

Source: Real Días, *Ferias de Jalapa,* 113 n. 22.

139. La Mesa, "Minuta," 3 Oct. 1787, AGI, Mexico, 2505. One would like to know the sources of the viceroy's recommendations, whether from his staff or from Mexico City *almaceneros* via his staff.

140. Compañía de Filipinas, 1788, AHN, Estado 3208^1, no. 343.

141. Delgado i Ribas, "Impacto de las crises coloniales . . . ," in *Economía española al final del antiguo regimen,* ed. Anes Alvarez et al., 3:102–3.

142. Beleña to Viceroy Revillagigedo, 1792, AGN, Consulado, vol. 123, f. 111.

143. Brading, *Miners and Merchants,* 267 n. 3.

144. Cf. Anon., "Ensayo apologético por el comercio libre . . . ," in Florescano and Castillo, eds., *Controversia,* 1:314: "ay dobles o triplicadas tiendas o cajones que subdividen los grandes repuestos que antes habia entre 15 o 16 ricos."

145. Fonseca and Urrutia, eds., *Historia general de Real Hacienda,* 4:361.

146. Anonymous to the Consulado de Cádiz, Sevilla, 30 Nov. 1787, BNMad, MS 19704, f. 23.

147. Quirós, "Memoria de instituto . . . 1808," AGI, Mexico, 2997.

148. Tomás Murphy, "Representación a los señores presidente y vocales de la Junta de Govierno," 6 Dec. 1802, AGI, Mexico, 2510.

149. AGN, AHH, 502–17.

150. Consulado de México (Antonio Bassoco, Saenz de Santa María, and Rodrigo Sánchez), 2 July 1795, AGI, Mexico, 2995.

151. AGN, AHH, 635–2, f. 19v.

152. Beleña, "Informe reservado . . . ," in Florescano and Castillo, eds., *Controversia,* 1, paras. 145–46.

153. Claude Morin found that at the San Juan de los Lagos fair in 1792, sales reached one million pesos, the result of the operations of sixty *tiendas* displaying European and Asian imports. *Michoacán,* 155.

154. *Alcabala Receipts, 1770–77 and 1780–87*
(pesos)

1770–77		1780–87		(+/- %)
1770	1,639,273	1780	2,360,703	
1771	1,340,290	1781	3,466,503	
1772	1,282,462	1782	3,333,651	
1773	2,093,381	1783	3,229,178	
1774	1,688,245	1784	3,898,936	
1775	1,488,690	1785	4,038,828	
1776	1,367,466	1786	3,450,336	
1777	2,084,514	1787	3,708,630	
Total	12,959,321	Total	27,486,765	+112%

Source: "Colección de estados de valores de real hacienda," no. 12, "Valor entero en los 26 anos . . . 1765 . . . 1791." These are unadjusted receipts. On the need for a deflator, see Pérez Herrero, "Crecimiento novohispano," 84. This table appears in Florescana and Castillo, eds., *Controversia,* 1:374.

155. *Total Receipts, 1770–77 and 1780–87*
(pesos)

				(+/- %)
1770	9,694,583	1780	15,010,974	
1771	9,560,740	1781	18,091,639	
1772	10,805,532	1782	18,594,490	
1773	12,216,117	1783	19,579,718	
1774	11,116,638	1784	19,605,574	
1775	11,845,130	1785	18,770,056	
1776	12,588,292	1786	16,826,416	
1777	14,118,759	1787	17,983,448	
Total	91,945,791	Total	144,462,315	+57%
Av. An.	11,493,223	Av. An.	18,057,789	

Source: Adapted from "Colección de estados de valores de real hacienda," n. 11, f. 308.

156. *Coinage of Precious Metals, Mexico City Mint*
(pesos)

1770–77		1780–87		(+/- %)
1770	14,587,310	1780	17,514,263	
1771	13,353,432	1781	20,335,842	
1772	18,889,785	1782	17,580,490	
1773	20,237,325	1783	23,716,657	
1774	13,666,954	1784	21,037,374	
1775	15,032,193	1785	18,575,208	
1776	17,315,537	1786	17,257,104	
1777	21,524,805	1787	16,110,340	
Total	134,607,341	Total	152,127,278	
Av. An.	16,825,924	Av. An.	19,015,910	+13%

Source: Adapted from "Colección de estados de real hacienda," n. 10, f. 307.

157. Richard Garner, "Exportaciónes de circulante," 563.

158. *Specie Exports from Veracruz to Spain and the "Islas"*

	1766–78	1779–91	Total	% Increase
Government				
Spain	15,027,072	29,581,982	44,609,054	96.8
"Islas"[a]	36,259,528	78,846,705	115,106,233	117.4
Private	103,873,984	115,624,103	219,498,087	11.3
Total	155,160,584	224,052,790	379,213,374	44.4

Source: Adapted from "Colección de estados de valores de real hacienda," n. 16, f. 313. Note that an additional 45 million pesos (including 6 million smuggled) were shipped from Acapulco to Asia.

[a]"Islas" = mainly Cuba.

159. *Silver Transfers from Saint-Domingue to France, 1783–89*
(pesos)

1783	6,399,000	1787	1,411,800
1784	2,178,400	1788	1,154,480
1785	4,237,585	1789	960,000

Source: Morineau, *Incroyables gazettes,* 442 and n. 151.

160. Arroyal, *Cartas político-económicas* (1968), 160.

161. Revillagigedo to crown, Mar. 1796, AGI, Mexico, 2507.

162. See, e.g., Morineau, *Incroyables gazettes,* Garner, "Exportaciones de circulante," Perez Herrero, "Plata y libranzas," and Marichal, *Bancarrota del virreinato.*

163. Loss of the *alcabala* farm also affected the funding available for the *consulado*'s Madrid lobbyists. The *consulado*'s rococo argumentation in seeking in 1753 renewal of the administration of the *alcabala* contract (*asiento* or *cabezón*) is in Yuste, ed., *Comerciantes mexicanos en el siglo XVIII,* 112–32.

164. "Informe," BNMad, MS 19710. See also the perceptive observations of Pérez Herrero, *Plata y libranzas,* 199–200, 211.

165. Posada, "Dictamen del fiscal de Real Hacienda," in Florescano and Castillo, eds., *Controversia,* 1:264; Elhuyar, *Influjo,* 69.

166. Brading, *Miners and Merchants,* 100–102; Lavrín, "Law of *Consolidación*"; and Wobeser, *Crédito eclesiástica.* The origin, development and mechanisms of *libranzas* are meticulously and lucidly analyzed in Pérez Herrero, *Plata y libranzas,* ch. 9.

167. Consulado de México to crown, "Informe . . . sobre la situacion del comercio . . . ," in Florescano and Castillo, eds., *Controversia,* 1:77. Curiously, Gálvez had also proposed one annual fair at Jalapa in his "Informe y reflexiones del visitador general . . ." of 14 June 1766 to Grimaldi, HSA, MS 427/18.

9. Incorporating New Spain into *Comercio Libre* (1789)

EPIGRAPHS: Campomanes to Valdés, 3 Aug. 1788, AHN, Estado, 3208[1]; Consulado de Barcelona, "Informe sobre el comercio de America" (1788), EMDL, 30 Mar. 1789.

1. Floridablanca, "Memorial presentado al rey Carlos III," 336, where the effect of the critics of Cadiz on Floridablanca is evident in his allusion to the "lujo" and "desorden de los vicios adoptados por los comerciantes como si tuviesen las rentas fijas de los mas grandes señores." According to Delgado i Ribas, Floridablanca's support for *comercio libre* was inspired less by the prospect of an increase in customs receipts than by the possibility of drawing more merchants into colonial trade. Delgado i Ribas, "Modelo catalán dentro del sistema de comercio libre," in Fontana and Bernal, eds., *Comercio libre,* 58.

2. *BAE,* 59:278.

3. Floridablanca, "Memorial," 343; "Carta de un huevero," 279. For biographical details, see Antonio Valdés y Bazán, *Exposición documentada . . . a la Regencia.* Valdés was probably responsible for a secret circular to lay and religious figures in the colonies to forward reports on "qualquiera asunto, excesos, o personas empeñandome su Real palavra de que nunca se sabría . . . de lo que . . . informase a Su Magestad reservadamente." Haro, archbishop of Mexico, to Floridablanca, 26 June 1787, AHN, Estado, 2839.

4. "Dictamen," 31 Jan. 1787, AGI, Mexico, 2505.

5. Izquierdo to Antonio Valdés, Cadiz, 11 Mar. 1788, AGI, Mexico, 2505.

6. One member was Francisco Viana, the conde de Tepa, who supported further changes in colonial commercial policy; he joined the Consejo de Indias after years of colonial service, first at Manila and then Mexico City. It has been asserted that he was "en gran parte" responsible for "aquella libertad" [del comercio] pushed by Madrid authorities; if so, he was not alone. Whitaker, "Documents," 383.

7. Consejo de Indias, "Nota," 3 Oct. 1787, AGI, Mexico, 2505.

8. Real Orden, 19 Oct. 1787, AGI, Mexico, 2505. Recall the nature of data shortcomings: "sin datos, ni cálculos, y solo por las noticias particulares de la correspondencia privada del virrey con el Sr. Marqués de Sonora." Were these the observations of Landázuri *and* Viana? Later the Junta Suprema de Estado similarly advised Madrid's Real Sociedad Económica that it was difficult to provide statistical data on colonial trade prior to 1778 "por la poca exactitud y formalidad que había en las aduanas." Junta de Estado, 19 May 1788, AHN, Estado, bk. 2d, f. 32.

9. Ugartiria, "Carta . . . a un amigo," 954, 958.

10. "Real Orden, disponiendo sea libre para Nueva España y Caracas el comercio . . . ," 28 Feb. 1789, in Levene, ed., *Documentos para la historia argentina,* 6:393.

11. "Acuerdo del Consulado y Junta de examen," Cadiz, 5 Apr. 1788, AGI, Consulados, Acuerdos y Juntas (1788).

12. Consulado de Cádiz to *apoderado,* Nicolas Fernández Rivera, Cadiz, 4 Apr. 1788, AGI, Consulados, Libro de correspondencia, no. 47, ff. 313–131v.

13. "Acuerdo del Consulado y Junta de Examen," Cadiz, 5 Apr. 1788, AGI, Consulados, Acuerdos y Juntas, ff. 9, 11.

14. Ibid., ff. 20–21, 26.

15. Ibid., f. 40v.

16. Their language was explicit: "Todo lo combina prohivir a los Americanos que embíen a España sus caudales y frutos, para empleos de pura negociación, y que con arreglo a la Real Orden de 22 de Noviembre de 1745, solo tengan los Europeos la facultad de hazer primeras ventas en Yndias." AGI, Consulados, Libro de corre-

spondencia, no. 47, 5 Apr. 1788. Note that by *Americanos* was intended simply merchants residing in the colonies, whether criollos or peninsulares.

17. Consulado de Barcelona, "Informe sobre el comercio de América," 1014.

18. Ibid., 1014.

19. Ibid., 1015. Foreign countries paid a premium for Spain's colonial *pesos fuertes:* England, 38 percent, Holland, 41, and France, 33.

20. Ibid., 1017.

21. Ibid., 1022–24. The 6,000 tons were divided into 4,000 (spirits or *caldos*), 800 (manufactures), 700 (*artefactos naturales*), and 500 in *frutos.*

22. Ibid., 1047.

23. Ibid., 1043.

24. Ibid., 1045.

25. Ibid., 1043.

26. Ibid., 1050.

27. Ibid., 1024.

28. Vicente Basadre, "Memoria sobre fomentar en varios pueblos . . . la cría de gusanos de seda . . . ," Veracruz, 18 Jan. 1802, AGI, Mexico, 2996. Reaction in the colony of Chile was more vitriolic: "con una política áspera y un egoísmo inaúdito quiere ese [Barcelona] que se nos prive de todo recurso que no sean las destructoras minas, o los simples de la farmacia." Salas to Gardoqui, "Representación al ministro de hacienda . . . ," 10 Jan. 1796, in Cruchaga, *Estudios,* 6:157.

29. Consulado de Sevilla, "Informe . . . sobre comercio libre," f. 303v. The consulado's *prior* (Juan Manuel de Uriortua) and one *consul* (Manuel Joseph Guillén) called for a general assembly to nominate *consiliarios* to prepare the response to Valdés: Joaquín Cavaleri y Torres, marquéz de Moscoso, conde del Aguila, Manuel María del Valle, Matheo de Ureta, Manuel Antonio Tolesano, and Joseph Antonio Gómez, along with several others. The *informe* was drafted by Manuel María de Vera and Luis Bermudo Soriano. Tinoco Rubiales, "Consulado nuevo de Sevilla y el comercio libre," 107 n. 1.

30. Consulado de Sevilla, "Informe sobre . . . comercio libre," ff. 263v–266, 273v.

31. Ibid., f. 269v, which also observed that even under "regulated" trade before 1778, "a pesar de la limitación de toneladas, se dexava de cargar quanto se quería, ni se arreglaba el número de frutos o cantidad de alguna mercadería."

32. Ibid., ff. 271v–272.

33. Ibid., ff. 271v–272v, 274, 277. Apropos of Cadiz's advantage in storage of goods, see also "Reflexiones sobre el comercio de Nueva España, 1787," BRPal, Ayala, MS 2851: "esta ventaja no la puede tener ninguno de los otros puertos habilitados que tenga un comercio a las Yndias . . . no puede tener bastante extensión para que los extrangeros le manden enteros cargamentos de ropas de todas partes."

34. Consulado de Sevilla, "Informe sobre . . . comercio libre," ff. 277v, 279v–280. In his précis of the Sevilla *informe,* "Consulado nuevo de Sevilla," Tinoco Rubiales omitted the recommendation that Madrid suppress production of New Spain's *chinguirito.*

35. Consulado de Sevilla, "Informe sobre . . . comercio libre," ff. 269–269v, 281, 283.

36. Ibid., ff. 281–282, 285v.

37. Ibid., 288.

38. Consulado de México, "Informe. . . sobre la situación del comercio y de la economía de Nueva España (1788)," in Florescano and Castillo, eds., *Controversia,* 1:71–137 (the edition cited here); and "Cuadro de la situación económica novohispana en 1788," in *Documentos para la história económica de México,* ed. Chávez Orozco, vol. 2.

39. Consulado de México, "Informe" (1788).

40. Ibid.

41. Salvucci, *Textiles and Capitalism in Mexico,* esp. chs. 3, 5.

42. Consulado de México, "Informe" (1788).

43. Ibid., 73.

44. Ibid., 79–80.

45. The committee to draft the *consulado*'s response was created in typically oligarchical fashion by a small inner group (*junta particular*) of former elected officials of "reiterada experiencia en el tráfico" and endowed with the "más acreditada . . . inteligencia." This group then presented to a general assembly (*junta general*) a prechosen slate, which they claimed skirted the "multitude de opiniones [que] suele confundir aún los asuntos de menor dificultad." (Oligarchs invariably foresee the inefficiencies of participatory decision-making.) Later, the general assembly added other members knowledgeable in the "giro de España a Yndias para que no faltase una instrucción tan necesaria." (Note the one-way nature of colonial trade flows, the peninsular perspective of the Spanish transatlantic system.) To the first committee (Gabriel Gutiérrez de Terán, Pedro Antonio de Alles, Antonio de Bassoco, and Juan Antonio Yermo) were added Manuel García de Herreros, Gaspar Martín Vicario, Vicente Francisco Vidal, and Sebastián Heras Soto. Consulado de México to Antonio Valdés, 23 Feb. 1788, AGN, AHH, 442–12.

46. Consulado de México, "Informe" (1788), 120.

47. Ibid., 83.

48. Ibid., 82–102. Cadiz, Barcelona, and Mexico City emphasized that *alcabalas* and other duties levied on Veracruz's imports used as base prices those FOB at a peninsular port, supplemented by another 10–12 percent on arrival at the colonial port.

49. Ibid., 103–9. See also *Comerciantes mexicanos en el siglo XVIII,* ed. Yuste, document 11.

50. Consulado de México, "Informe" (1788), 111–12.

51. Ibid., 115–20.

52. Ibid., 122.

53. Ibid., 131–36.

54. "Razón de los puntos que se promovieron por . . . Consulado de México, y no se han determinado . . . ," AGN, AHH, 442–12. This précis indicates where the Mexico City merchant interests placed their lobbying emphases.

55. "Puntos que devilitan directamente al Comercio" and "Males generales," AGN, AHH, 442–12.

56. "Razón de los puntos," AGN, AHH, 442–12; Florescano and Castillo, eds., *Controversia,* 1:92.

57. Consulado de México, "Informe" (1788), 99.

58. Recall that when Cadiz proposed explicitly to concentrate all reexports to the colonies in its port, it provoked a tart objection from nearby Sevillan businessmen.

59. Compañía de Filipinas to Valdés, Madrid, 12 May 1788, AHN, Estado, 3208².

60. Real Sociedad Económica de Madrid, "Informe. . . sobre la libertad de comercio," BRAHM, Mutis 5, no. 64 (unfoliated). This is the version cited in the following paragraphs. It appeared in *EMDL,* no. 147 (22 Sept. 1788): 88–94; no. 148 (29 Sept. 1788): 104–12; no. 149 (6 Oct. 1788): 12–17; no. 150 (13 Oct. 1788): 33–38; no. 151 (20 Oct. 1788): 61–67; and no. 152 (27 Oct. 1788): 82–90.

61. In this connection, note that only a few issues earlier, *EMDL*'s editor had published Valentín Foronda's plea to support greater exports of agricultural and manufactured products "sin pagar ningun derchos, ni sufrir el menor examen" (3 Aug. 1788).

62. Uriortua, "Informe," *EMDL,* no. 152 (27 Oct. 1788): 89–90.

63. Uriortua [y Villanueva] was no friend of the Cadiz community, and it is unsurprising that his relations with that port deteriorated over the following decades. After being appointed *asesor* of the Ramo de Consolidación for the province of Cadiz, Uriortua was vehemently criticized by the Consulado de Cádiz. AAEPar, Espagne, CC 96, f. 96v; AGSim, Consejos, Hacienda, 281.

64. For example, a note from the Real Sociedad to Floridablanca and read to a meeting of the Junta de Estado in May 1788 called *comercio libre* an issue in which it would be mistaken to "confundirse la utilidad de la nación y su comercio con el interés particular de los comerciantes." It feared that Cadiz's stand-pat commercial interests might affect the ministry's decision on the role of New Spain in the transatlantic system. Real Sociedad Económica to Floridablanca, Junta de Estado, 19 May 1788, AHN, Estado, Junta de Estado, bk. 2 (1788), ff. 31v–32.

65. Anonymous letter to Manuel Francico de la Torre, Cadiz, 4 Jan. 1788, "Algunas cartas de D. Manuel de la Torre," AHN, Estado, 2851², no. 122.

66. Santander's merchants confined their observations to conditions in New Spain, presumably because they had good contacts with Mexico City's merchant community, to which they consigned merchandise, largely reexports. Like Cadiz and Barcelona, they traced a huge backlog of unsold imports in the colonial capital—they claimed it was 35 million pesos—to smuggling via Tampico and Veracruz from New Orleans and Havana, and to declining purchasing power following epidemic disease, poor harvests, and high mortality, as well as to overspeculation by some Cadiz merchants. Consulado de Santander, "Representación," 9 Nov. 1787, AGI, Mexico, 2505.

67. F.X.B., "Discurso primero," 276–77.

68. Ibid., 277. Note a comment from Cadiz: "es moralmente imposible el arreglar y distribuir los emvíos a los consumos, por ser una confusión los registros salen como se ha experimentado." AHN, Estado, 2851², no. 122.

69. F.X.B., "Discurso primero," 279.

70. F.X.B., "Discurso segundo," 9–11.

71. Ibid., 9. As an anonymous report from Cadiz in late 1787 put it: "Nuestras Yndias son colonias, que deben ser dependientes de la Metrópoli . . . ; Si se enriquecen demasiado . . . podrán algun día sacudir el yugo." "Reflexiones sobre el comercio de Nueva España, 1789," BRPal, Ayala, 2851.

72. F.X.B., "Discurso segundo," 11.

73. "[C]omo reina siempre la costumbre de pasarlos [cambios] a informe de

dicha Universidad [Cadiz] . . . o de algun parcial de ella; se confundían los unos con los otros, dexando siempre la enfermedad escondida; y así quedaban sepultados, las más bien concertadas ideas que se hallan en el Archivo de la Secretaría de Indias, por mantenerse siempre la citada Universidad el monopolio," Thomás Southwell commented in a note probably directed to his correspondent Campomanes. "Proyecto sencillo y concluiente para empezar con ahorro de dispendios, a corregir la decadencia que se experimenta en el comercio de esta Península con la Nueva España, Tierra Firme, y las Islas Nuestras en aquellas Mares," Madrid, 4 June 1788, AHN, Estado, 3188[1].

74. "Reflexiones en obsequio de la Real Orden de 19 de Octubre de 1787 . . . al Consulado de Cádiz," BRPal, Ayala, 2851, no. 10, f. 290v; Antonio Flores, "Observaciones," Salamanca, 5 May 1788, AGI, Consulados, Libro de correspondencia, 47, punto 30, reprinted in Florescano y Castillo, eds., *Controversia,* 1:139–64.

75. "Reflexiones . . . de la Real Orden," BRPal, Ayala, 2851, no. 10, ff. 298, 301.

76. Antonio Flores, "Observaciones," punto 5, nota, AGI, Consulados, Libro de correspondencia, 47.

77. "Proyecto para remediar las quiebras de los comerciantes. . . ." 20 June 1788, BRPal, Ayala, 2875, f. 16v.

78. Compañía de Filipinas to Antonio Valdés, Madrid, 12 May 1788, AHN, Estado, 3208[2].

79. "Proyecto para remediar las quiebras . . . ," 20 June 1788, BRPal, Ayala, 2875, ff. 37–39v.

80. Antonio Flores, "Observaciones," 5 May 1788, punto 1, nota, AGI, Consulados, Libre de correspondencia, no. 47.

81. Thomás Southwell, "Proyecto sencillo y concluyente . . . ," Madrid, 4 June 1788, AHN, Estado, 3188[1].

82. "Reflexiones . . . de la Real Orden," BRPal, Ayala, 2851, no. 10, f. 310.

83. Antonio Flores, "Observaciones," 5 May 1788, punto 7, nota, AGI, Consulados, Libro de correspondencia, no. 47.

84. "Apuntaciones sobre el comercio de las Indias," BRPal, Ayala, 2867, no. 1, f. 12. Campomanes cultivated commercial issues as an intense avocation, especially those associated with colonial trade, beginning, by his own admission in 1752, with a proposed "Historia completa de la marina, comercio y derecho náutico," and continued with his extended but (until recently) unpublished "Reflexiones sobre el comercio a Indias" (1762) and his widely read *Apéndice a la industria popular.* See Alvarez Requejo, *Campomanes,* 177–80; Campomanes, *Reflexiones sobre el comercio a Indias, 1762* edited with a thoughtful introduction by Vicente Llombart Rosa.

85. Campomanes, "Apuntaciones," BRPal, Ayala, 2867, no. 1, ff. 40, 42v.

86. Ibid., f. 19v.

87. Campomanes to Floridablanca, Madrid, 4 May 1788, and "Adición particular a las apuntaciones sobre el comercio de Indias que por ser reservadas se ponen a parte," AHN, Estado 3208[1]. He sent his "Adición" only to Floridablanca, since "por contener especies reservadas de Estado solo le dirijo a Vm. que sabrá hacer de él el uso que merece." Campomanes to Floridablanca, Madrid, 4 Aug. 1788, ibid.

88. Campomanes, "Copia de la carta escrita al . . . Valdés . . . en 3 de Agosto de 1788 remitiendole las apuntaciones sobre el comercio de Indias," AHN, Estado, 3208[1].

89. Campomanes, "Apuntaciones," f. 5.

90. Ibid., f. 2.

91. Ibid., f. 8. Cf. ibid. "los géneros que se venden al contado; quales es necesario fiar; y el modo de asegurar la paga a Plazos ciertos."

92. Ibid., ff. 14v–16.

93. Ibid., ff. 15v–16.

94. Ibid., f. 19.

95. Ibid., ff. 17–19.

96. Campomanes to Floridablanca, Madrid, 4 Agosto 1788, AHN, Estado, 3208[1].

97. Campomanes, "Apuntaciones," ff. 30v, 31v.

98. Campomanes, "Copia de la carta escrita al . . . Antonio Valdés por . . . en 3 de Agosto de 1788," AHN, Estado, 3208[1].

99. Campomanes, "Apuntaciones," f. 20.

100. Ibid., f. 41.

101. Ibid., f. 41.

102. Campomanes, "Adición (reservado)," in "Apuntaciones," f. 48v.

103. Ugartiria, "Carta . . . a un amigo," 953–59, and "Fin de la carta de D. J. Ugartiria . . . ," 963–71. "Ugartiria" covered methods of tax reduction and simplification in the metropole with limited reference to the colonies in America (953, 958). However, running the "Discurso" in two successive March issues set the stage for "Ugartiria's" letter devoted exclusively to analyzing the economic interdependence of metropole and colonies. See Ugartiria, "Carta segunda" (dated Madrid, 10 Feb. 1789).

104. Ugartiria, "Carta segunda," 989–90.

105. Ugartiria, "Fin de la carta," 965.

106. Ugartiria, "Carta . . . a un amigo," 958.

107. Ibid., 991.

108. *Peninsular Revenues*

(*reales de vellon*, ooo's)

	Ugartiria		Revised	
Peninsular	442,299	(58.3%)	267,299	(35.2%)
Colonial	317,000	(41.7%)	492,000	(64.8%)
Total	759,299	(100.0%)	759,299	(100.0%)

Source: Adapted from Ugartiria, "Carta," ff. 960–62.

109. "Ugartiria," "Carta . . . a un amigo," 955.

110. In mid February, Cadiz switched its position to urge that a 1788 prohibition on all reexports to the colonies be lifted for 1789. Consulado de Cádiz, "Representación," 13 Feb. 1789, AGI, Mexico, 2505.

111. Consejo de Indias, "Dictamen," 31 Jan. 1789, AGI, Mexico, 2505.

112. Floridablanca, "Dictamen," Madrid, 15 Feb. 1789, AGI, Mexico, 2505.

113. Junta Suprema de Estado, "Parecer," 16 Feb. 1789 (this order was signed by Eugenio de Llaguno); and "Parecer," 19 Feb. 1789, AGI, Mexico, 2505.

114. The basis for this judgment is the reproduction of the 1778 and 1789 documents in Levene, ed., *Documentos para la historia argentina*, 6:1–132, 393–94.

115. Tedde de Lorca, "Política financiera y política comercial," in Anes Alvarez et al., eds., *Economía española al final del antiguo régimen*, 2:216.

Customs Revenue from Spain's Colonies, 1787
　　(*reales de vellon,* 000's)

Duties on imports from Europe	47,250
Duties on imports from colonies	36,870
Duties on exports to Europe[a]	24,300
Duties on exports to colonies	22,050
Total Colonial Duties	130,470 (58.5%)
Total Duties	222,870 (100%)

Source: Adapted from AHN, Estado, 3208, box 2, "Examen analítico del producto que deberían tener las Aduanas exteriores del Reyno . . . 1787" (based on a model of what the appropriate duties on foreign and domestic products might yield but that in fact indicated how large a percentage of estimated duties was *not* collected).

[a]Presumably includes reexports?

10. The French Connection: Spanish Trade Policy and France

EPIGRAPHS: Masson de Plissay, AAEPar, M et D, France, 1990, f. 98v.; Floridablanca, "Memorial presentado al rey Carlos III" (1788).

1. Under the *convenio de Eminente,* French linens were dutied roughly 50 percent below those of Silesia and Switzerland. "Mémoire sur le commerce . . . ," ANPar, AE, B III, 334.

2. "Supplément," AAEPar, M et D, Espagne 209, f. 37.

3. Ozanam, "Colonie française de Cadiz au xviiie siècle, d'après un document inédit (1777)."

4. Choiseul to d'Aubeterre, 25 Dec. 1756, cited in Bourget, *Duc de Choiseul et l'alliance espagnole,* 7.

5. The tax on transfers abroad was 3 percent until 1768, then 4 percent for the following three years. Smugglers were paid 2.5 percent for their services. AAEPar, M et D, Espagne 20, no. 2.

6. Ch. Delacroix, Madrid, 3 floréal An 4 [23 April 1796], AAEPar, Espagne 18, suppl., ff. 19v–20v. On the incentives for smuggling pesos into France, see Mirabeau, *De la Banque d'Espagne,* 130.

7. Lecouteulx-Canteleu, "Mémoire," 6 vendémiaire An 5 [27 September 1796], AAEPar, M et D, Espagne 209, ff. 262–262v; Bourgoing, "Mémoires et observations sur le traité de Bâle," An 3 [1794–95], ANPar, AF, III, 61, dossier 245, pl. 4.

8. Dermigny, "Carte monétaire," 489–90 and n. 4.

9. Rambert, "France et la politique commerciale de l'Espagne au XVIIIe siècle," 269; AAEPar, M et D, Espagne, 207, n. 2.

10. Boislecomte, "Étude," AAEPar, M et D, Espagne, 97, f. 185v.

11. "Observations," ANPar, F 12, 644.

12. Dermigny, "Circuits d'argent," 250.

13. Vilar, *Oro y moneda en la historia,* 326. In the late 1760s, Arriquibar claimed that 60 percent of Spain's exports to Europe consisted of registered as well as smuggled gold and silver. Carrera Pujal, *Historia de la economía española,* 3:481–82.

14. Dermigny, "Circuits d'argent," 246–48. Of total profits of the Banco de San Carlos in 1784 (when the dividend was 6.21 percent), commissions on peso transfers were 58 percent. Boyetet, Madrid, May 1785, AAEPar, M et D, Espagne 209, f. 156.

15. Mirabeau, *De la Banque d'Espagne,* 18.

16. Mirabeau noted that French investors bought heavily into shares of the Banco de San Carlos, and that without "la spéculation des Parisiens sur les Actions de St. Charles, elles languiroient encore . . . dans les Portes-feuilles de la Banque. C'est notre argent qui fait aujourd'hui son fonds principal." *De la Banque d'Espagne,* 80. Dermigny also suggests that French financiers hoped to make Paris a center of international finance comparable to the Amsterdam and London centers. "Carte monétaire," 493.

17. Letters, Montlouis, 13 Jan. and 20 June 1785, ANPar, F 12 (1889).

18. Letter, Bayonne, 22 Aug. 1785, ANPar, F 12 (1889).

19. Letters, Bayonne, 22 Aug. 1785, and, Bordeaux, 24 May 1785, ANPar, F 12 (1889).

20. Charles Delacroix, 1796, AAEPar, CP, Espagne, 18, suppl., f. 20v.

21. ANPar, AE, B III, 335; Dermigny, "Circuits d'argent," 265.

Distribution of Silver Coinage, France, 1782–89

(livres tournois)

Pau	50,875,878	14.5%
Bayonne	76,904,889	22.0%
Toulouse	43,746,832	12.5%
Perpignan	35,279,622	10.1%
Total (all France)	350,002,630	100%

Source: Dermigny, "Carte monétaire," 481.

22. The orders were issued 22 July 1771. Béliardi, Madrid, 8 Aug. 1771, BNPar, MS Fonds Français, 10765, f. 251v.

23. AHN, Hacienda, 3781, B, no. 6; ANPar, B, I, 295.

24. In his *Souvenirs,* 2:320–21, Berryer, who knew the firm of Lecouteulx et Cie. well, describes it as "une maison antique, l'une des plus anciennes de la bourgeoisie de Paris" with headquarters (*maisons mères*) at both Rouen and Paris, and a branch at Cadiz.

25. Thomas Butler was charged with remitting 11 million *reales de vellon* (about 550,000 *pesos fuertes*) to Dhorman without license from the Banco de San Carlos. AHN, Hacienda, 3151.

26. A carefully researched yet uncritical study based on materials in the AHN is by Ortega Costa and García Osma, *Notícias de Cabarrús y de su procesamiento.*

27. Cf. Crouset, "England and France in the Eighteenth Century," 146, 150–51, and Braudel et al., *Histoire économique et sociale de la France,* 2:229–30.

28. *Mémoires et considérations sur le commerce et les finances d'Espagne,* 2:163; BNPar, MS Fonds Français, 10768, f. 203; Stein, *French Slave Trade in the Eighteenth Century,* 133–34.

Non-Spanish Textiles Reexported on Flotas to Veracruz, 1757–69

(*pesos fuertes* of 128 *quartos*)

Year	Total Exports	Ropa	% Ropa
1757	18,054,067	15,463,925	85.7
1760	24,057,510	20,696,150	86.0
1765	16,072,581	12,984,550	80.8
1769	13,097,075	11,299,275	86.3

Source: AAEPar, M et D, Espagne, 207, n. 2, "Mémoire sur les finances d'Espagne" (1771).

29. Braudel et el., *Histoire économique et sociale de la France,* 2:133–34.

30. Cf. Berrill, "International Trade and the Rate of Economic Growth," 354.

31. "Reflections . . . ," ANPar, AF, III, 57, dossier 224, pl. 35.

32. AAEPar, M et D, Espagne, 209, f. 254. In 1762, Béliardi claimed no French import at Cadiz could support a duty of 15 percent and compete in price. "Mémoire sur les traités . . . ," BNPar, MS Fonds Français, 10768, 33–39v.

33. Smith, *Wealth of Nations,* 319; Boyetet, Madrid, 26 Jan. 1777, ANPar, AE, B III, 334. J.-A.-C. Chaptal later claimed that rising Spanish import duties sharply reduced French linen and woolen exports to Spain. ANPar, AF, IV, 1610, pl. lvii. Pierre Léon detects a "long crisis" in France's traditional textile industries, woolen and linen, commencing sometime between 1750 and 1765, and spreading to Normandy, Brittany, Languedoc, and Picardy. "Structure du commerce extérieur et évolution industrielle de la France à la fin du XVIIIe siècle," 413–16.

34. Boyetet, Aranjuez, 2 July 1778, ANPar, AE, B I, 795, f. 165.

35. "Observations particulières . . . ," 11 Feb. 1780, AAEPar, CP, Espagne, suppl. 17. In 1787, Spain was the second largest importer (after Sénégal) of French linen and other manufactures. Léon, "Structure du commerce extérieur," 431–32.

36. ANPar, AE, B III, 371; Bairoch, *Révolution industrielle et sous-developement,* 334; Crouzet, "England and France," 153; Léon, "Structure du commerce extérieur," 418. Beginning about 1775, the total value of French exports to Spain fell from 52.2 million *livres* (1775) to 43.7 (1787–89).

37. Levain et al., "Contribution à l'état des mouvements de 'longue durée,'" 80.

38. "Mémoire des marchands de la Bourse de Montauban" (1716), ANPar, F 12, 1349.

39. Lévy-Leboyer, *Banques européennes et l'industrialisation internationale,* 121, n. 1; Bergeron, *Banquiers, négociants et manufacturiers,* 197–99. Markovitch, *Industries lainières,* 484, estimates that imported wools were between 15 and 20 percent of total raw wool consumption of French manufacturies. Aggregate figures obscure the importance of Spanish wools in fine cloth production at France's principal textile center, Elboeuf-Louviers, near Rouen. For example, Rouen's imports of Spanish wools rose 233 percent between 1730 and 1776. Braudel et al., *Histoire économique et sociale de la France,* 2:231.

40. AN, F 12, 1349. To ensure quality control, a royal *arrêt* (17 Dec. 1709) regulated the quality of wool, number of threads, etc., in French woolens destined for Spain and its colonies. The *arrêt* incorporated advice from Carcassonne's manufacturers and exporters.

41. "Extrait d'une lettre écrite d'Espagne" (1738), ANPar, F 12, 1349.

42. Ibid.; ANPar, AE, B I 792, ff. 77–78.

43. Kaplow, *Elboeuf During the Revolutionary Period,* 44, 46–47. Green and blue *sempiternes* and pink, blue, and white *bayetas* were exported to Veracruz, Havana, Caracas, and the west coast of South America. Swatches of these fabrics are in ANPar, F 12, 551–52.

44. "Essay sur diverses branches du commerce que la France fait à Cadiz," BNPar, MS Fonds Français, 10768, ff. 200v–208.

45. "Copie d'une lettre de M. Béhic Fils," 14 Jan. 1769, BNPar, MS Fonds Français, 10764, ff. 435v–436. Earlier, French imitators of English *bayetas* seeking a "gain sordid" were accused of cheapening their products destined for Spain and its colonies surreptitiously by lowering the raw wool content, ANPar, F 12, 1349.

46. Boyetet, 26 Jan. 1777, ANPar, AE, B III, 343, 373; Consulado de México, 1788, BRAHM, Mata Linares, 87.

47. J. Lenurbe, 1 Jan. 1777, ANPar, AE, B III, 373; Anglicanus, *Necessity and Policy of the Commercial Treaty with France,* 47–48.

48. Markovitch, *Industries lainières,* 473.

Woolen Output, Generalité of Rouen, 1780–89
(1789 = 100)

	Bolts	Index		Bolts	Index
1780	27,900	137	1785	35,300	137
1781	30,400	150	1786	35,100	137
1782	35,500	138	1787	38,500	150
1783	32,500	126	1788	30,900	120
1784	31,900	124	1789	25,700	100

Source: Markovitch, *Industries lainières,* 39.

49. The situation at Reims suggests the downward trend between 1780 and 1787–90.

Reims Woolen Industry, 1780–90

	1780	1787–90
Looms	4,750	3,120
Workers/dependents	40,000	20–30,000
Output (pieces)	76,000	67,000

Source: Clause, "Industrie lainière rémoise," 574–76.

50. Lévy-Leboyer, *Banques européennes,* 122–23; Henderson, "Anglo-French Commercial Treaty of 1786," 109.

51. Lévy-Leboyer, *Banques européennes,* 104 n. 38.

52. Lapeyre, *Famille de marchands: Les Ruiz,* 598, 600; Braudel et al., *Histoire économique et sociale de la France,* 2:549; AAEPar, M et D, Espagne, 79, f. 22.

53. Alvarez de Abreu, *Extracto historial,* vol. 1.

54. In the 1780s, most French linens exported to Spain were destined for colonial markets. "Observations particulières . . . ," 11 Feb. 1780, AAEPar, CP, Espagne, 17, suppl., f. 169. Cf. Dermigny, "Circuits d'argent," 244: "les toiles attirent l'argent, parce qu'elles sont transportées aux lieux mêmes d'où il vient."

55. In the 1760s, linens formed 75 percent of French merchandise sold at Cadiz. Béliardi, "Memoire pour l'Espagne," BNPar, MS Fonds Français, 10766, f. 108v; Dardel, *Navires et marchandises dans les ports de Rouen et du Havre,* 202, 565. If *toiles* also included *blancards,* then much in the category of *toile* exports from Rouen were indeed *blancards.*

56. ANPar, AF, III, 61, no. 245, pl. 2; Postlethwayt, *Universal Dictionary of Trade and Commerce.* In the second quarter of the eighteenth century, the Saint-Malo firm of Magon forwarded hundreds of bales of linens to Puerto Santa María on the bay of Cadiz, where it was easier than at Cadiz to smuggle goods aboard vessels loading for the American colonies.

57. Béliardi to Bertellet, 7 July 1764, BNPar, MS Fonds Français, 10768, f. 551v; "Mémoire . . . Pacte de Famille . . . ," BNPar, MS Fonds Français, 10766; "Essay . . . commerce . . . Cadiz," BNPar, MS Fonds Français, 10768, f. 215v; John, "War and the English Economy," 338.

58. Béliardi to Choiseul-Praslin, 12 Feb. 1766, BNPar, MS Fonds Français, 10764, f. 428v, and 10768, f. 199v; Dardel, *Navires et marchandises,* 202–6; "Copie d'une lettre de M. Béhic," BNPar, MS Fonds Français, 10764, ff. 437v–438.

59. Dardel, *Navires et marchandises,* 201–2, 565; Crouzet, "Wars, Blockade and Economic Change in Europe, 1792–1815," 571; ANPar, AF, III, 63, dossier 25; Béliardi, "Memoire pour l'Espagne," BNPar, MS Fonds Français, 10766, 108v.

60. ANPar, AE, B III, 344; "Observations particulières . . . ," 11 Feb. 1780, AAEPar, CP, Espagne, 17, suppl., ff. 168v–169.

61. "Mémoire sur le commerce de la France avec l'Espagne," ANPar, AE, B III, 334; "Conséquence pour la France de la conduite de l'Espagne," ANPar, K 107, no. 1.

62. "Mémoire sur la consommation des étoffes de la toilerie de Rouen," ANPar, F 12, 560; AAEPar, M et D, Espagne, 208, f. 198v.

63. Crouzet, "Wars, Blockade and Economic Change," 572, characterizes the French linen industry of the late eighteenth century as "archaic" and "doomed."

64. Prices current at Cadiz in 1788 covered woolens (*paños*) from Elboeuf, Sedan, Abbeville, and Louviers. "Nota de precios . . . Cádiz . . . ," Jan. 1788, AGI, Ind. Gen., 2318 B.

65. In a series of memoirs that Dupont de Nemours drafted to support the treaty, there is an underlying assumption: England's "industrie savante" and "machines ingénieuses" offered merely a temporary advantage that French manufacturers could overcome with lower labor costs, inventive skill and attention to fashion. AAEPar, Angleterre, 65, esp. mémoire 1, "Réflexions sur le bien qui peuvent se faire réciproquement la France et l'Angleterre," ff. 7, 12.

66. J. Lenurbe to Vergennes, Valencia, 1 Jan. 1787, ANPar, AE, B III, 373.

67. Boyetet, "Mémoire . . . à Vergennes," Mar. 1776, ANPar, AE, B III, 343, f. 29; "Précis des atteintes que l'Espagne a portées . . . contre les François," AAEPar, M et D, Espagne, 133, n. 40.

68. Investors at Paris, Beauvais, Orléans, Dijon, London, and Amsterdam placed funds with the Magon for investment in Spain's colonial trades. Dermigny, "Circuits d'argent," 338.

69. Carrière, "Renouveau espagnol et prêt à la grosse aventure . . . ," 236–37, 247. One such contract reads in part: "por los efectos vendidos a dos riesgos, a cargar en el Nao . . . a correr el riesgo de ida y de vuelta para Lima al premio de 45 por ciento." AHN, Consejos 21,377, pieza 4, f. 22.

70. Puyabry, Cadiz, to Choiseul-Praslin, 19 Apr. 1765, AAEPar, M et D, Espagne, 32, no. 28. He valued the cargo aboard the 1760 *flota* to Veracruz above 20 million pesos.

71. Dermigny, *Cargaisons indiennes,* 1:30, 37 n. 36.

72. Boyetet, S. Ildefonso, 27 Sept. 1779, ANPar, AE, B III, 334.

73. Boyetet, 2 May 1783, ANPar, AE, B III, 335.

74. Daladie, Bilbao, 27 June 1774, ANPar, AE, B 7, 436; Boyetet, "Observations sur le nouveau Règlement . . . ," Madrid, 16 Feb. 1778, ANPar, AE, B III, 334.

75. Apropos of a *génizaro* at Cadiz: "es hijo de Francés, y por consiguiente se puede rezelar mucho de los buenos deseos que aparenta." Antonio Gálvez, Cadiz, 1785, AGI, Ind. Gen., 2312.

76. Spanish merchants at Cadiz still concentrated on "toutes les commissions des marchandises que les fabriques étrangères fournissent à l'Amérique et que les

fortunes que ces commissions produisent resteront en Espagne." Béliardi to Boynes, 11 Nov. 1771, BNPar, MS Fonds Français, 10765, ff. 277v–278. Oddly, Múzquiz was considered by French resident merchants as their "secret protector." D'Ossun, Madrid, 3 Feb. 1772, ANPar, AE, B I, 792, f. 6.

77. D'Ossun, "Mémoire," ANPar, AE, B III, 343; Boyetet, Madrid, "Affaire de la cédule de 1767," ANPar, AE, B I, 793; Béliardi, "Mémoire sur la visite des maisons et . . . livres des négociants français," Madrid, 8 Mar. 1762, BNPar, MS Fonds Français, 10768, ff. 135v–136v.

78. Mongélas, Cadiz, 4 Oct. 1783, ANPar, AE, B III, 335.

79. AAEPar, M et D, Espagne, 32, f. 263.

80. ANPar, F 12, 619; Boyetet to Sartine, 8 June 1780, ANPar, AE, B I, 795, f. 72.

81. Boyetet, "Observations sur le nouveau Réglement." Madrid, 16 Feb. 1778, ANPar, AE, B III, 334, and "Extrait de la correspondance," AAEPar, CP, Espagne, 17, suppl., f. 58.

82. Boyetet was consul at St. Petersburg (1770), then chargé d'affaires representing the French colonial office at Madrid. He was later recalled to Paris as a *commissaire* charged with preparing a *balance du commerce* in 1785. (In 1632, the firm of Boyetet Frères operated at Cadiz.) Bonnassieux and Lelong, eds., *Conseil de Commerce,* xlii; Murphy, "Dupont de Nemours," 572; Girard, *Commerce français,* 550 n. 24.

83. "Mémoire sur le commerce . . . avec l'Espagne," AAEPar, M et D, Espagne, 209, f. 67.

84. Béliardi, "Réflexions. . . ." (1763), AAEPar, M et D, Espagne, 32, f. 219. Boyetet was confident that Gálvez held a "strong attachment" for France. "Analyse des contestations . . . ," ANPar, AE, B III, 339, f. 21.

85. The depth and overall quality of his reporting brought Boyetet reassignment to Paris as co-director of the Bureau du Balance du Commerce shared with economist Dupont de Nemours. Murphy, "Dupont de Nemours," 572–73.

86. Boyetet to Sartine, Madrid, 7 Dec. 1778, ANPar, AE, B I, 794, ff. 252–55.

87. Boyetet, San Ildefonso, 27 Sept. 1779, ANPar, AE, B III, 334.

88. The embryo of what decades later became the French continental system is also evident in a recommendation by Abbé Béliardi in 1762 that during the ongoing conflict, France joined by Spain, Portugal, and Italy agree to "cesser et . . . interdire à perpétuité tout commerce de quelque nature qu'il soit avec l'Angleterre." "Mémoire joint à la lettre de M. l'Abbé Béliardi," 18 Jan. 1762, ANPar, AE, B III, 436.

89. "Conséquences pour la France . . . de la conduite de l'Espagne relativement aux François et à leur commerce," ANPar, K 907, no. 13.

90. Boyetet, Madrid, 2 May 1782, ANPar, AE, B III, 335 n. 13.

91. Boyetet, Madrid, May 1785, AAEPar, M et D, Espagne, 209, ff. 158–59.

92. Fisher, *Commercial Relations Between Spain and Spanish America,* 92, app. A; Mongélas, Cadiz, 24 May 1786, ANPar, AE, B III, 344.

93. Mongélas, Cadiz, 7 Aug. 1787, ANPar, AE, B I, 295; Poiret, Cadiz, 29 Aug. 1788. ANPar, B I, 296.

94. AHN, Estado, 3188[1]; Faure, Perpignan, 25 Brumaire An 4 [17 November 1795], ANPar, AE, B III, 335.

95. Bills of lading were notorious for undervaluing precious metals loaded clan-

destinely in colonial ports, then unloaded at Cadiz "frauduleusement, ou que l'on fait passer dans l'étranger." Poiret, Cadiz, 19 Feb. 1785, ANPar, AE, B III, 335.

96. Sée, "Document . . . (1691–1752)," 983 n. 1; Poiret, Cadiz, 16 Nov. 1784, ANPar, AE, B I, 291; Puyabry, Cadiz, 1765, AAEPar, M et D, Espagne, 32, f. 372.

97. Mongélas, Cadiz, 17 Feb. 1778, ANPar, AE, B I, 284; Poiret, Cadiz, 13 Jan. 1786, ANPar, AE, B I, 294.

98. Poiret, Cadiz, 29 Feb. 1785, ANPar, AE, B III, 335.

99. Boyetet, Madrid, 19 Nov. 1778, ANPar, AE, B I, 795.

100. Poiret, Cadiz, 6 Dec. 1785, ANPar, AE, B I, 293.

101. Mongélas, Cadiz, 23 Jan. 1787, ANPar, AE, B I, 295. For details of falsifying imported stockings at Cadiz and elsewhere in Spain, see AGS, DGR, 2a remesa, 452.

102. Mongélas, Cadiz, 12 July 1786, ANPar, AE, B I, 294. Mongélas's estimate of revenue loss (about 50 percent) is lower than a more precise calculation by Spanish authorities in 1789 (68 percent). AHN, Estado, 3208, box 2, n. 3.

103. Poiret, Cadiz, 23 Aug. 1785, ANPar, AE, B I, 293; Antonio Gálvez to Lerena, Cadiz, June 1785, AGS, DGR, 2a remesa, 451.

104. Klaveren, "Fiscalism, Mercantilism and Corruption," 149.

105. This is illustrated by the effort of Múzquiz to compensate in part those French interests affected adversely by the unilateral abrogation of the Convenio de Eminente. "Mémoire sur le commerce de la France avec l'Espagne," ANPar, AE, B III, 334.

106. BN, Fonds Français, 13418, f. 175; Boyetet, "Mémoire . . . à Vergennes," Mar. 1776, ANPar, B III, 343.

107. "Conséquences pour la France de la conduite de l'Espagne," ANPar, K 907, no. 13, f. 4.

108. Rambert, "France et la politique commerciale de l'Espagne au XVIIIe siècle," 280–81.

109. Bourgoing, "Mémoires et observations . . . sur . . . Bâle," Gestion du Comité du Salut Public, an 3 [1794–95], ANPar, AF, III, 61, dossier 245, pl. 4.

110. Lecouteulx-Canteleu, "Mémoire," 8 Vendémiaire An 5 [30 September 1796], AAEPar, M et D, Espagne, 209, ff. 262–262v.

111. ANPar, AE, B III, 335.

112. J. Lenurbe to Vergennes, Valencia, 1 Jan. 1787, ANPar, AE, B III, 373.

113. Stein, *French Slave Trade in the Eighteenth Century*, 169.

114. AAEPar, M et D, Espagne, 32, f. 256.

115. Ibid., 209, f. 218v.

116. Boyetet, "Mémoire sur le commerce français en Espagne," 4 Aug. 1785, AAEPar, M et D, Espagne, 209, f. 166.

117. ANPar, AF, IV, 1610, pl. lvii; d'Ossun to Choiseul, Madrid, 19 Mar. 1767, AAEPar, CP, Espagne 568, f. 230; Mongélas to Vergennes, Cadiz, 1 May 1786, ANPar, AE, B III, 354.

118. "Mémoire touchant le commerce de France avec l'Espagne," ANPar, AE, B III, 335.

119. Boyetet, "Mémoire sur le commerce français en Espagne," AAEPar, M et D, Espagne, 209, f. 166v.

120. Cf. Taylor, "Noncapitalist Wealth and the Origin of the French Revolution."

121. "Projet d'instructions pour le Citoyen Barthélemy," ANPar, AF, II, 46, dossier 470, n. 9; "D'un traité de commerce avec l'Espagne," ANPar, AE, B III, 335.

122. Crouzet, "Wars, Blockade and Economic Change," 568.

11. Euphoria and Pessimism

EPIGRAPHS: Marías, *España posible en tiempos de Carlos III*, 87–88; Ruíz Martín, *Finanzas de la monarquía española en tiempos de Felipe IV*, 11.

1. Príncipe de Asturias, letter to conde de Aranda, Madrid, 13 July 1781, "Correspondencia del conde de Aranda con el Príncipe de Asturias, 1781–83," AHN, Estado, 2863, no. 4. Cf. Arroyal, *Cartas*, ed. Elorza, 67–68.

2. Defourneaux, *Pablo de Olavide ou l'afrancesado (1725–1803)*, ch 11.

3. On Masson, see Herr, *Eighteenth-Century Revolution in Spain*, 220.

4. Nicolas Masson de Morvilliers in *Encyclopédie méthodique*, ser. "Geographie moderne," 1:554–56. A former *alcalde mayor* in New Spain noted shortly afterward that he had read "la pintura que hizo de la Nueva España el atrevido M. Mason [*sic*]." Villaroel, *Enfermedades políticas que padecen la capital de esta Nueva España*, 438. On Villaroel's career in New Spain, see Borah, "Hipólito Villaroel," 505–14.

5. Herr, *Eighteenth-Century Revolution in Spain*, 222–24.

6. The *Gaceta*'s data was quickly reproduced in the *Encyclopédie, ou dictionnaire raisonné . . . Diderot et D'Alembert*, 2 (1786): 322–23.

7. As Floridablanca phrased it, "para que vean los Estrangeros que no está tan desierto como creen ellos." "Advertencia," in Congresso Histórico Nacional, *II Centenario del censo de Floridablanca*, 44. In point of fact, census data covering the Cantabrian area's crude birthrates, gender ratios at maturity, age at first marriage, and outmigration suggest the demographic profile of a poor, rural, subsistence-oriented society.

8. Floridablanca, "Memorial presentado al rey Carlos III y repetido a Carlos IV," *BAE* 59:321 (hereafter cited as Floridablanca, "Memorial"), which was soon republished in *SEV* 1 and later in English in Coxe, *Memoirs of the Kings of Spain of the House of Bourbon*, 1:325–407.

9. Floridablanca, "Memorial," 311, 317.

10. Campomanes to Antonio Valdés, Aug. 1788, in Stein and Stein, "Concepts and Realities of Spanish Economic Growth, 1759–1789," 118 n. 31; Tedde de Lorca, *Banco de San Carlos*.

11. Floridablanca, "Memorial," 335.

12. Ibid., 318. "Debilidad anterior" is clarified in his reference to the need to "libertar nuestro comercio y la autoridad de Vuestra Majestad . . . de las prisiones en que las había puesto el poder inglés en los precedentes siglos y tratados" (ibid.).

13. Ibid., 308–18.

14. Ibid., 329. Behind Floridablanca's support for the Banco de San Carlos was the hope of limiting the availability of foreign exchange in order to stimulate domestic production for colonial markets. Tedde de Lorca, *Banco de San Carlos*, 27–29 and nn. 66–68.

15. Floridablanca, along with Carrasco and Campomanes, was well aware of New Spain's commercial problems as early as 1760. Priestley, *Gálvez*, 392–93.

16. Ferrer del Rio, *Historia del reinado de Carlos III*, 253–54.

17. Floridablanca, "Memorial," 336–37. For a sharp critique of Floridablanca's "Memorial," see Bernardo Iriarte in BMus MS Egerton 379.

18. Guinard, *Presse espagnol de 1737 à 1791,* 26, 31–32, 37. The 1788 guidelines warned that the state would not tolerate criticism of the government or its agents, the honor of Spain, or the condition of the sciences and letters in Spain.

19. *SEV* I, "Prospecto."

20. *EMDL,* no. 154 (10 Nov. 1786). Guinard sees in the *Espíritu* the "voix de l'Espagne éclairée." *Presse espagnole,* 266, 271–72.

21. *EMDL,* no. 150 (13 Oct. 1788).

22. Cabarrús, *Elogio del . . . conde de Gausa;* id., "Discurso sobre la libertad del comercio . . ."; id., *Elogio de Carlos III.* Cabarrús shared Floridablanca's faith in the favorable effects of extending *comercio libre* of 1765 to all Spain's American colonies. In May 1788, the Real Sociedad Económica de Madrid appointed him to review the effects of the Reglamento of February 1778, which had included the Rio de la Plata in *comercio libre.* AHN, Estado, Libro 2d., ff. 31v–32. (Cabarrús was probably the leading agent of Paris bankers lending *à la grosse* to Cadiz exporters after 1778.)

23. Jovellanos, "Elogio de Carlos III," 314–15.

24. Cabarrús, *Elogio del . . . conde de Gausa,* 31.

25. Cabarrús, "Discurso sobre le libertad del comercio," 289, 292.

26. Cabarrús, *Elogio de Carlos III,* 41; "Discurso sobre la libertad del comercio," 286.

27. Cabarrús, "Discurso sobre la libertad del comercio," 292.

28. Cabarrús, *Elogio de Carlos III,* 11.

29. Cabarrús, *Elogio del . . . conde de Gausa,* 25, 45–46, 48–49.

30. Ibid., 55–56.

31. Cabarrús, *Elogio de Carlos III,* 41–42.

32. Ibid., 29.

33. Foronda, "Carta sobre el Banco Nacional de San Carlos."

34. Charles to Aranda, El Pardo, 19 Mar. 1781, AHN, Estado, 2863, no. 4.

35. Aranda to Charles, "Copias de la respuesta . . . sobre planta de govierno . . . ," Paris, AHN, Estado, 2869, no. 3.

36. This bleak view of the Spanish government led him to no radical recommendation, however. "No se trata de mudar la constitución, sino de mejorarla." Aranda to Charles, AHN, Estado, 2869, no. 3.

37. "Memorial secreta," BNMad, MS 13228. For the debate over the memorial's authencity and relevant bibliography, see Whitaker, "Pseudo-Aranda Memorial of 1783," 287–313, and Wright, "Aranda Memorial: Genuine or Forged?" 445–60.

38. See José Juan Cadalso, *Defensa de la nación española contra la carta persiana lxviii de Montesquieu;* Herr, *Eighteenth-Century Revolution in Spain,* 58.

39. Arroyal, *Cartas económicas-políticas,* ed. Caso González, carta 2a, 15, 60; and id., *Cartas económicas-políticas,* ed. Elorza, carta 3a, 134, 143–44.

40. Arroyal, *Cartas económicas-políticas, ed.* Caso González, pt. 2, carta 1a, p. 18.

41. Ibid., p. 177; Elorza, "Estudio preliminar," 20.

42. Ibid., carta 3a, p. 74. Pedro Polo de Alcocer, a bureaucrat close to Hacienda Secretary Lerena, had informed Lerena of Arroyal's critical views of government practices in covering deficits. Lerena invited him to put his ideas on paper, and the result was Arroyal's five letters written at Vara del Rey (Aragon), "una crítica exacta

para un ministro prudente" based on "papeles políticos y económicos" of Campillo, Ensenada, and Valparaíso. Ibid., carta 1a, p. 6, and carta 2a, p. 56.

43. Ibid., carta 4a, p. 84, and carta 5a, p. 117; Arroyal, *Cartas económicas-políticas,* ed. Elorza, 67–68.

44. Arroyal, *Cartas económicas-políticas,* ed. Caso González, carta 4a, p. 79.

45. Ibid., p. 84.

46. Caso González believes Arroyal forwarded a copy of the *Cartas* to Jovellanos (who amended and underlined his manuscript copy). Ibid., vi–viii.

47. Ibid., carta 4a, pp. 81, 84; Elorza, "Estudio preliminar," 14.

48. Arroyal, *Cartas económicas-políticas,* ed. Elorza, 27.

49. Stein and Stein, "Concepts and Realities of Spanish Economic Growth," 112–13.

50. Ibid., 111.

51. Ibid., 114–15.

Bibliography

Select Documents

Aranda, conde de. "Carta del . . . a D. Manuel de Roda, 9 abril 1766." AGSim, Gracia y Justicia, 1009.

———. "Copias de la respuesta . . . sobre planta de govierno. . . . Paris, 1781." AHN, Estado, 2869, no. 3.

Armona y Murga, Francisco Anselmo de. "Cartas." HSA 330/263.

———. "Catálogo." HSA, HC, 427/6.

Austria, José Donato de. "Memoria de instituto, 1803." AGN, AHH, 1869–2.

Béliardi, Abbé. "Mémoire pour l'Espagne." BNPar, MS Fonds Français, 10768.

Campomanes, Pedro Rodríguez. "Adición particular a las apuntaciones sobre el comercio de Indias que por ser reservadas se ponen a parte." AHN, Estado, 3208[1].

———. "Apuntaciones sobre el comercio de las Indias." BRPal, Ayala, 2867.

———. "El reyno de Galicia y Principado de Asturias . . . suplican. . . ." (1765). AHN, Estado, 3188[2].

Carvajal y Lancaster, José. "Testamento político." BNMad, MS 11065.

Cervera, Miguel de. "Discurso para acreditar el origen y decadencia del comercio de España con sus Américas y facilitar su aumento y perfección, 26 febrero 1765." AHN, Estado, 2851, no. 112.

"Colección de estados de valores de Real Hacienda que manifiestan su actual feliz situación para apoyo del 'Ensayo Apologético' sobre comercio libre." BNMex, MS 1334.

Consulado de México. "Informe . . . 31 mayo 1788." BNMex, MS 1304. See also under Articles below.

———. "Instruzión relativa a todos los puntos y negozios del consulado para govierno de los deputados." AGN, AHH, 635–8.

Consulado de Sevilla. "Informe sobre . . . comercio libre, 25 Junio 1788." BNMex, MS 1397, ff. 261–308.

"Consulta de una junta formada de SM por el marqués de los Llanos, Francisco Craywinckel, Simón de Aragorri, Pedro Goosens, Tomás de Landázuri, sobre el Proyecto de comercio de América. Acompaña un extracto de ella y otros documentos. Madrid, 14 febrero 1765." AHN, Estado, 2314.

"Copia del pliego entregado al . . . marqués de Sonora . . . 1778." AHN, Estado, 3188².

Crame, Agustín. "Discurso político sobre la necesidad de fomentar la Isla de Cuba." BRPal, Ayala, 2827.

"Derecho . . . segun los precios actuales, que son los mismos que se han pagado en Cádiz en el despacho de la última flota." BMus, Additional MS 13976.

"Dictamen leído, 12 mayo 1777." AGI, Estado, 86.

"Disertación sobre los abusos . . . " (1776). BRPal. Ayala, 2862.

Ferret, Zeferino. "Exposición histórica de las causas que más han influido en la decadencia de la marina española. . . 1813." MN, MS 444.

Foronda, Valentín. "Reflexiones sobre el comercio en tiempo de guerra, 1800." BRAHM, Mata Linares, 68.

Gálvez, José de. "Discurso y reflexiones de un vasallo sobre la decadencia de nuestras Indias españolas." BRPal, Ayala, 2816. Other copies in AGI, Estado, 86, and HSA.

———. "Informe y reflexiones del visitador general, Mexico, 14 junio 1766." HSA, HC, 427/18.

"Impugnación del comercio libre de América favoreciendo él de Cádiz." BRAHM, Mata Linares, vol. 6.

Landázuri, Tomás Ortiz de. "Noticia de los minerales de oro y plata que contienen las provincias del reyno de la Nueva España." Madrid, 1 Feb. 1764. BRPal, Ayala, 2824. Another copy, NYPub, Rich MS 9.

Lerguinazával, Manuel de. "Thesoro de España. Discurso sobre el comercio de España con sus Américas. 1764." BRPal, Ayala, 2819.

Llanos, marqués de los. "Papel . . . haciendo presentes. . . . " BRPal, Ayala, 2872.

"Mémoire sur le commerce. . . . " ANPar, AE, B III, 334.

[Anon.] "Observaciones sobre el sistema presente . . . 1778." AHN, Estado, 3188², ff. 8–11.

O'Reilly, Alejandro. "Descripción de la Isla de Cuba." BRPal, Ayala 2819.

Quirós, José María. "Memoria de instituto, 1803." AGN, AHH, 1869–2.

———. "Memoria de instituto, 1819." AGI, Mexico, 2519.

Real Sociedad Económica de Madrid. "Informe . . . sobre la libertad del comercio." BRAHM, Mutis, 5, no. 64.

Ribero, Juan Joseph del. "Méthodo fácil i conveniente de impedir los contrabandos." BRAHM, Mata Linares, 76.

Sarmiento de la Pradera, Francisco de Paula. "Yntroducciones para el bufete y mercancías arregladas a los comercios de la Europa, 1781." John Carter Brown Library, Providence, R.I.

Ulloa, Antonio de. "Noticia i descripción de los países . . . entre la ciudad i puerto de Veracruz. . . . " AGI, Ind. Gen., 1631.

Yermo, Juan Antonio. "Sobre todo género de agricultura en la Nueva España." 22 Apr. 1788. BNMex, MS 1304, ff. 82–132. Probably the same as "Informe dado . . . sobre el estado de todos los ramos de agricultura en Nueva España." BRPal, MS Ayala, 2875.

[Anon.] "Ynforme . . . intendencias." NYPub, Rich MS.

[Anon.] "Ydea general del comercio de Yndias, Tolosa de Guipúzcoa, 1 marzo 1776."

NYPub, MS Rich 19. Reprinted in *Controversia sobre la libertad de comercio en Nueva España,* ed. Florescano and Castillo, 1:23–68. Mexico, 1975.

Books

Acton, Harold M. M. *The Bourbons of Naples.* London, 1956.

Aguado Bleye, Pedro, and Cayetano Alcázar Molina. *Manual de historia de España.* 3 vols. Madrid, 1963–64.

Ajello, Rafaele, and Mario D'Addio, eds. *Bernardo Tanucci: statista, letterato, giurista.* Napoli, 1986.

Alvarado Gómez, Antonio Armando. *Comercio interno en la Nueva España. El abasto en la ciudad de Guanajuato, 1777–1810.* Mexico, 1995.

Alvarez de Abreu, Antonio. *Extracto historial del comercio entre Filipinas y Nueva España.* Edited by Carmen Yuste. 2 vols. Mexico, 1977.

Alvarez Requejo, Felipe. *El conde de Campomanes: Su obra histórica.* Oviedo, 1954.

Amador de los Rios, José. *Historia de la villa y corte de Madrid.* 4 vols. Madrid, 1860–64.

Anderson, Adam. *An Historical and Chronological Deduction of the Origins of Commerce.* 4 vols. London, 1801.

Anes Alvarez, Gonzalo. *Las crisis agrarias en la España moderna.* Madrid, 1970.

———. *El antiguo régimen: Los Borbones.* Madrid, 1975.

Anes Alvarez, Gonzalo, et al., eds. *La economía española al final del antiguo régimen.* Vol 1: *Agricultura;* vol. 2: *Manufacturas;* vol. 3: *Comercio y colonias;* vol. 4: *Instituciones.* Madrid, 1982.

Anglicanus. *The Necessity and Policy of the Commercial Treaty with France.* London, 1787.

Antuñano, Estevan de. *Pensamiento para un plan.* Puebla, 1834.

Antúnez y Acevedo, Rafael. *Memorias históricas sobre la legislación y gobierno del comercio de los españoles con sus colonias en las Indias occidentales.* Edited by Antonio García-Baquero Gonzalez. 1797. Reprint. Madrid, 1981.

Aragorri y Olavide, Simón de. *Reflexiones sobre el estado actual del comercio de España.* Madrid, 1761.

Archivo Histórico Nacional. Sala de Alcaldes de Casa y Corte, Archivo. *Catálogo por materias.* Madrid, n.d.

Armytage, Frances. *The Free-Port System in the British West Indies: A Study in Commercial Policy, 1766–1822.* London, 1953.

Arrangoiz y Berzábal, Francisco de Paula de. *México desde 1808 hasta 1867.* 4 vols. Mexico, 1871–72.

Arroyal, León de. *Cartas económicas-políticas al conde de Lerena.* Edited by Antonio Elorza. 1787. Reprint. Madrid, 1968.

———. *Cartas económicas-políticas al conde de Lerena.* Con la segunda parte inédita. Edited by J. Caso Gonzalez. Oviedo, 1971.

Artola, Miguel, ed. *Enciclopedia de historia de España.* 3 vols. Madrid, 1988–93.

Bairoch, Paul. *Révolution industrielle et sous-développement.* Paris, 1963.

Bakewell, Peter J. *Silver Mining and Society in Colonial Mexico: Zacatecas, 1546–1700.* Cambridge, 1971.

Baran, Paul. *The Political Economy of Growth.* New York, 1968.

Bergeron, L. *Banquiers, négociants et manufacturiers parisiens du Directoire à l'Empire.* Paris, 1978.

Bernal, Antonio-Miguel. *La financiación de la carrera de Indias (1492–1824): Dinero y crédito en el comercio colonial español con América.* Sevilla, 1992.

Bernard, Gildas. *Le secrétariat d'état et le conseil espagnol des Indes.* Geneva, 1972.

Berryer, Pierre-Nicolas, *Souvenirs de M. Berryer, doyen des avocats de Paris, de 1774 à 1838.* 2 vols. Paris, 1839.

Biblioteca de autores españoles, vols. 46, 59. Madrid, 1858, 1867.

Bitar Letayf, Marcelo. *Economistas españoles del siglo XVIII: Sus ideas sobre la libertad del comercio con Indias.* Madrid, 1968.

Bonnassieux, Louis J. P. M., and Eugene Lelong, eds. *Conseil de commerce et bureau de commerce (1700–1791): Inventaire analytique des procès-verbaux.* Paris, 1900.

Bourgoing, Jean-François. *Tableau de l'Espagne moderne.* 3 vols. 3d ed. Paris, 1803.

Bourguet, A. *Le duc de Choiseul et l'alliance espagnole.* Paris, 1906.

Brading, David A. *Miners and Merchants in Bourbon Mexico, 1763–1810.* Cambridge, 1971.

———. *Haciendas and Ranchos in the Mexican Bajio: Leon, 1700–1860.* Cambridge, 1978.

Braudel, Fernand, et al. *Histoire économique et sociale de la France.* 3 vols. Paris, 1970–76.

Burkholder, Mark A., and D. S. Chandler, *From Impotence to Authority: The Spanish Crown and the American Audiencias, 1687–1808.* Columbia, Miss., 1977.

Burzio, Humberto F. *La ceca de la villa imperial de Potosí y la moneda colonial.* Buenos Aires, 1945.

Bustos Rodríguez, M. *Los comerciantes de la carrera de Indias en el Cádiz del siglo XVIII (1713–1775).* Cadiz, 1995.

———. *Burguesía de negocios y capitalismo en Cádiz.: Los Colarte (1650–1750).* Sevilla, 1991.

Buttà, Giuseppe. *I Borboni di Nápoli al cospetto di due secoli.* 3 vols. 1877. Reprint. Bologna, 1965.

Cabarrús, Francisco. *Elogio del . . . conde de Gausa.* Madrid, 1786.

———. *Elogio de Carlos III.* Madrid, 1788.

Cadalso, José Juan. *Defensa de la nación española contra la carta persiana lxviii de Montesquieu.* Edited by Guy Mercadier. Toulouse, 1970.

Calderón Quijano, José Antonio. *El banco de San Carlos y las comunidades de Indios de Nueva España.* Sevilla, 1963.

———, ed. *Los virreyes de Nueva España (1759–1779).* 2 vols. Sevilla, 1967.

Campomanes, Pedro Rodríguez. *Disertaciones históricas del orden y caballería de los Templares.* Madrid, 1747.

———. *Memorial ajustado . . . sobre . . . los abastos de Madrid.* Madrid, 1768.

———. *Apéndice a la educación popular.* 3 parts, 4 vols. Madrid, 1775–77.

———. *Dictamen fiscal de expulsión de los Jesuitas de España (1766–1769).* Edited by Jorge Cejudo and Teófanes Egido. Madrid, 1972.

———. *Discurso sobre la industria popular.* Edited by John Rieder. Madrid, 1975.

———. *Reflexiones sobre el comercio español a Indias.* Edited by Vicente Llombart Rosa. Madrid, 1988.

Canga Arguelles, José. *Diccionario de hacienda con aplicación a España.* 2 vols. Madrid, 1833.

Cantillon, Richard. *Essai de la nature du commerce en général.* Boston, 1892.

Carpenter, Kenneth E., *Economic Bestsellers Before 1850.* Boston, 1975.

Carrera Pujal, Jaime. *Historia de la economía española.* 5 vols. Barcelona, 1943–47.

Cavignac, Jean. *Jean Pellet, commerçant de gros, 1694–1772. Contribution a l'étude du négoce bordelais du XVIIIe siècle.* Paris, 1967.

Chávez Orozco, Luís, ed. *Documentos para la historia económica de México.* 10 vols. Mexico, 1933–35.

Chorley, Patrick. *Oil, Silk and Enlightenment: Economic Problems in Eighteenth-Century Naples.* Naples, 1965.

Cipolla, Carlo M., ed. *The Fontana Economic History of Europe.* 6 vols. London, 1969–73.

Clarke, Edward. *Letters Concerning the Spanish Nation Written at Madrid During the Years 1760 and 1761.* London, 1763.

Cohn, Henry J., ed. *Government in Reformation Europe, 1520–1560.* London, 1971.

Coleman, D. C. *Revisions in Mercantilism.* London, 1969.

Congreso Histórico Nacional. *II Centenario del censo de Floridablanca.* Murcia, 1992.

Congreso Internacional. "El dos de mayo y sus precedentes." See Enciso Récio, Luís Miguel.

Congreso Internacional sobre Carlos III y la ilustración. *Actas.* 3 vols. Madrid, 1989.

Cook, Sherburne F., and W. W. Borah. *Essays in Population History. Mexico and the Caribbean.* 3 vols. Berkeley, Calif., 1971.

Cosío y Campillo, José del. See *Nuevo sistema de gobierno económico.*

Coxe, William. *Memoirs of the Kings of Spain of the House of Bourbon . . . to the Death of Charles III, 1700 to 1788.* 2d ed. 5 vols. London, 1815.

Cruchaga, Manuel. *Estudio sobre la organización económica y la hacienda pública de Chile.* In vols. 4–6 of *Obras.* 10 vols. Madrid, 1928–29.

Dahlgren, Erich W. *Les relations commerciales et maritimes entre la France et les côtes de l'océan Pacifique.* Paris, 1900.

Danvila y Collado, Manuel. *Reinado de Carlos III.* 6 vols. Madrid, 1893–96.

Dardel, P. *Navires et marchandises dans les ports de Rouen et du Havre au XVIIIe siècle.* Paris, 1963.

Defourneaux, Marcelin. *Pablo de Olavide ou l'afrancesado (1725–1803).* Paris, 1959.

Delgado, Josep M., et al. *El comerç entre Catalunya i América.* Barcelona, 1986.

Dermigny, L. *Cargaisons indiennes, Solier et Cie . . . 1781–1793.* Paris, 1959–60.

Dickson, Peter G. M. *The Financial Revolution in England: A Study in the Development of Public Credit, 1688–1756.* London, 1967.

Domínguez Bordona, Jesús. *Manuscritos de América. Catálogo de la Biblioteca de Palacio.* Vol. 9. Madrid, 1935.

Domínguez Ortiz, Antonio. *La sociedad española en el siglo XVII.* Madrid, 1955.

———. *Instituciones y sociedad en la España del siglo XVII.* Madrid, 1984.

———. *Instituciones y sociedad en la España de los Austrias.* Barcelona, 1985.

———. *El antiguo régimen: Los reyes católicos y los Austrias.* Barcelona, 1988.

Eguía Ruíz, Constancio. *Los Jesuitas y el motín de Esquilache.* Madrid, 1947.

El Colegio de México. Centro de estudios históricos. *Extremos de América: Homenaje a don Daniel Cosío Villegas.* Mexico, 1971.

Elhuyar, Fausto de. *Memoria sobre el influyo de la minería en la agricultura, industria, población y civilización de la Nueva España. 1825. Reprint.* Mexico, 1964.

Enciso Récio, Luís Miguel. *Prensa económica del XVIII: El "Correo mercantil de España y sus Indias."* Madrid, 1958.

———, ed. *Actas del Congreso Internacional, "El Dos de Mayo y sus Precedentes."* Madrid, 1992.

Encyclopédie méthodique, ou par ordre de matières. Ser. "Géographie moderne." 3 vols. Paris, 1783–87.

Encyclopédie, ou dictionnaire raisonné . . . par . . . Diderot et D'Alembert. 28 vols. Paris, 1754–72.

Estapé y Rodríguez, Fabián, ed. *Textos olvidados.* Madrid, 1973.

Fabry, José Antonio. *Compendiosa demostración de los crecidos adelantamientos . . . en el precio del azogue.* Mexico, 1743.

Fayard, Janine. *Les membres du Conseil de Castille à l'époque moderne (1621–1746).* Geneva, 1979.

Ferrer del Rio, Antonio. *Historia del reinado de Carlos III en España.* 4 vols. Madrid, 1856.

Fisher, John. *Commercial Relations Between Spain and Spanish America in the Era of Free Trade, 1778–1796.* Liverpool, 1985.

Florez Estrada, Alvaro. *Examen imparcial de las disensiones de la América con la España.* Cadiz, 1811.

Florescano, Enrique. *Precios del maíz y crisis agrícolas en Mexico (1708–1810): Ensayo sobre el movimiento de los precios y sus consecuencias económicas y sociales.* Mexico, 1969.

———, ed. *Ensayos sobre el desarrollo de México y América Latina (1500–1975).* Mexico, 1979.

Florescano, Enrique, and Fernando Castillo, eds. *Controversia sobre la libertad del comercio en Nueva España, 1776–1818.* 2 vols. Mexico, 1975.

Foncerrada y Ulibarri, José Cayetano. *Exhortación . . . a los habitantes de . . . Nueva España.* Mexico, 1810.

Fonseca, Fabián de, and Carlos Urrutia, eds. *Historia general de Real Hacienda.* 6 vols. Mexico, 1845.

Fontana i Lázaro, Josep. *La quiebra de la monarquía absoluta, 1814–1820: La crisis del antiguo régimen en España.* Espluegues de Llobregat, 1971.

———. *Crisis del antiguo régimen, 1800–1833.* 2d ed. Barcelona, 1983.

Fontana i Lázaro, Josep, and Antonio Miguel-Bernal, eds. *El comercio libre entre España y América (1765–1824).* Madrid, 1987.

Foronda, Valentín. *Miscelanea o colección de various discursos.* 1793. Reprint. Madrid, 1996.

Fortune, Stephen A. *Merchants and Jews: The Struggle for British West Indian Commerce, 1650–1750.* Gainesville, Fla., 1984.

Frías, Mariano Bernabé de. *Informe jurídico por . . . en los autos de culpable atraso. . . .* Madrid, 1790.

Gálvez, José de. *Informe general . . . siendo visitador general al virrey Bucarely y Ursúa . . . 1771.* Madrid, 1867.

Gamboa, Francisco Javier. *Comentarios a las ordenanzas de minas.* Madrid, 1761.

———. *Commentaries on the Mining Ordinances of New Spain.* 2 vols. London, 1830.

Gándara, Miguel Antonio de la. *Apuntes sobre el bien y el mal de España.* Edited by Jacinta Macías Delgado. Madrid, 1988.

Garofalo, Gaetano. *La monarchía borbónica a Napoli*. Rome, 1963.

Gárate Ojanguren, Montserrat. *Comercio ultramarino e ilustración: La Real Compañía de la Habana*. San Sebastián, 1993.

Garay, Martin de. *Manifiesto a la nación española*. Sevilla, 1809.

García-Baquero González, Antonio. *Andalucía y la carrera de Indias (1492–1824)*. Biblioteca de la cultura andaluza, Historia 52. Sevilla, 1986.

———, ed. *Cádiz, 1753, según las respuestas generales del catastro de Ensenada*. Cadiz, 1990.

García Caraffa, Alberto, and Arturo García Caraffa. *Enciclopedia heráldica y genealógica hispano-americana*. 88 vols. Madrid, 1952–63.

García del Prado, Joseph. *Compendio general de las contribuciones . . . deducidos del Real Proyecto de 5 de Abril . . . de 1720*. Cadiz, 1762.

García-Mauriño Mundi, M., *La pugna entre el consulado de Cádiz y los jenízaros por las exportaciones a Indias (1720–1765)*. Sevilla, 1999.

Garmendia Arruebarrena, J. *Tomás Ruiz de Apodaca, un comerciante alavés con Indias (1709–1767)*. Victoria, Spain, 1990.

Girard, Albert. *Le commerce français à Cadix et à Séville aux temps des Habsbourg: Contribution a l'étude du commerce étranger en Espagne*. Bordeaux, 1932.

Girón, Pedro. *Recuerdos, 1778–1837*. 3 vols. Pamplona, 1978–81.

Gómez-Centurión Jiménez, C., et al., eds. *La herencia de Borgoña: La hacienda de las reales casas durante el reinado de Felipe V*. Madrid, 1998.

González Enciso, Agustín. *Estado e industria en el siglo XVIII: la fábrica de Guadalajara*. Madrid, 1980.

Guerra y Sánchez, Ramiro, et al. *Historia de la nación cubana*. 10 vols. Havana, 1952.

———. *Manual de la historia de Cuba*. Havana, 1964.

Guía de fuentes para la historia de Ibero-América. The Hague, n.d.

Guinard, Paul-J. *La presse espagnole de 1737 à 1791: Formation et signification d'un genre*. Paris, 1973.

Hale, Edward E. *Franklin in France*. Boston, 1887.

Hamilton, Earl J. *War and Prices in Spain, 1651–1800*. Cambridge, Mass., 1947.

Hamnett, Brian. *Politics and Trade in Southern Mexico, 1750–1821*. Cambridge, 1971.

Hartz, Louis. *The Founding of New Societies in the History of the United States, Latin America, South Africa, Canada, and Australia*. New York, 1964.

Hartwell, R., ed. *Causes of the Industrial Revolution*. London, 1967.

Heredia Herrera, Antonia. *Inventario de los fondos de consulados (sección XII) del Archivo General de Indias*. Madrid, 1979.

Hernández Palomo, José Jesús. *El aguardiente de caña en México, 1724–1810*. Sevilla, 1974.

Herr, Richard. *The Eighteenth-Century Revolution in Spain*. Princeton, N.J., 1958.

Hoon, Elizabeth E. *The Organization of the English Customs System, 1696–1786*. London, 1938.

Howe, Walter. *The Mining Guild of New Spain and its Tribunal General, 1770–1821*. Cambridge, Mass., 1945.

Humboldt, Alexander von. *Essai politique sur le royaume de la Nouvelle-Espagne*. 5 vols. Paris, 1811.

Hussey, Roland D. *The Caracas Company, 1728–1784: A Study in the History of Spanish Monopolistic Trade*. Cambridge, Mass., 1934.

Instrucciones que los vireyes de Nueva España dejaron a sus sucesores. 2 vols. Mexico, 1873.

Instrucciones y memorias que dejaron los virreyes novohispanos. Edited by Ernesto de la Torre Villar. 2 vols. Mexico, 1991.

Jenkinson, Charles. *A Collection of the Treaties of Peace, Alliance and Commerce Between Great Britain and Other Powers.* 3 vols. 1785. Reprint. London, 1986.

Jones, Ricardo Rees. *El despotismo ilustrado y los intendentes de la Nueva España.* Mexico, 1979.

Kagan, Richard. *Students and Society in Early Modern Spain.* Baltimore, 1974.

Kamen, Henry. *The War of Succession in Spain, 1700–1715.* London, 1969.

———. *Spain, 1469–1714: A Society of Conflict.* New York, 1983.

Kaplow, J. *Elboeuf During the Revolutionary Period.* Baltimore, 1964.

Krebs Wilckens, Ricardo. *El pensamiento histórico, político y económico del conde de Campomanes.* Santiago de Chile, 1960.

Kuethe, Allan J. *Cuba, 1753–1815: Crown, Military and Society.* Knoxville, Tenn., 1986.

La Condamine, Charles-Marie de. *Relation abrégée d'un voyage fait dans l'intérieur de l'Amérique méridionale.* Paris, 1745.

Ladd, Doris M. *Making of a Strike: Mexican Silver Workers' Struggle in Real del Monte, 1766–1771.* Lincoln, Neb., 1988.

La Force, James C. *The Development of the Spanish Textile Industry, 1750–1800.* Berkeley, Calif., 1965.

Lafuente, Modesto. *Historia general de España.* 25 vols. Barcelona, 1887–91.

Lang, M. F. *El monopolio del mercurio en el México colonial, 1550–1710.* Mexico, 1977.

Lapeyre, H. *Une famille de marchands: Les Ruiz.* Paris, 1959.

Larruga, Eugenio. *Memorias políticas y económicas sobre los frutos, comercio, fábricas y minas de España.* 45 vols. Madrid, 1789–1800.

Levene, Ricardo, ed. *Documentos para la historia argentina.* Vol. 5: *Comercio de Indias: Antecedentes legales (1713–78).* Vol. 6: *Comercio de Indias: Comercio libre, 1778–1791.* Buenos Aires, 1915.

Lévy-Leboyer, Maurice. *Les banques européennes et l'industrialisation internationale dans la première moitié du XIXe siècle.* Paris, 1964.

Lizaso, Félix. *Libro jubilar de Emeterio S. Santovenia en su cincuentenario de escritor.* Havana, 1957.

Llombart Rosa, Vicente. *Campomanes, economista y político de Carlos III.* Madrid, 1992.

Lohmann-Villena, Guillermo. *El corregidor de Indios en el Perú bajo los Austrias.* Madrid, 1957.

López Cancelada, Juan. *Ruina de la Nueva España si se declara el comercio libre con los extrangeros.* Cadiz, 1811.

Lynch, John. *Spain Under the Hapsburgs.* 2 vols. New York, 1964.

———. *The Spanish American Revolutions, 1808–1826.* New York, 1983.

———. *Bourbon Spain, 1700–1808.* New York, 1989.

Manzano Manzano, Juan. *Notas a la recopilación de Indias. . . ilustradas . . . por Manuel Josef de Ayala.* Madrid, 1945.

Maravall, José Antonio. *Estado moderno y mentalidad social (siglos XV a XVII).* 2 vols. Madrid, 1972.

Marías, Julián. *La España posible en tiempos de Carlos III.* Madrid, 1963.

Marichal, Carlos. *La bancarrota del virreinato. Nueva España y las finanzas del imperio español, 1780–1810.* Mexico, 1999.

Markovitch, Tihomir J. *Industries lainières de Colbert à la révolution.* Geneva, 1976.

Martín García, Gonzalo. *La industria textil en Avila durante la etapa final del antiguo régimen: la Real Fábrica de Algodón.* Avila, 1989.

Martínez Salazar, Antonio. *Colección de memorias y noticias del gobierno general y político del Consejo de Castilla.* Madrid, 1764.

Martínez Shaw, Carlos. *Cataluña en la carrera de Indias, 1680–1756.* Barcelona, 1981.

Matilla Tascón, A. and Miguel Capella. *Los Cinco Gremios Mayores de Madrid. Estudio crítico-histórico.* Madrid, 1957.

Meek, Wilbur T. *The Exchange Media of Colonial Mexico.* New York, 1948.

Mélanges à la mémoire de Jean Sarrailh. 2 vols. Paris, 1966.

Mémoires et considérations sur le commerce et les finances d'Espagne. 2 vols. Amsterdam, 1761.

Memorial ajustado hecho en virtud de decreto de . . . la Real Junta de Comercio y Moneda contra Joseph Diego de Medina y Sarabia, thesorero de la casa de Moneda de México. . . . Mexico, 1734.

Mirabeau, Honoré-Gabriel de Riquetti, comte de. *De la Banque d'Espagne, dite de Saint-Charles.* Paris, 1785.

Mora, José Luís María. *México y sus revoluciones.* 2 vols. 1813. Reprint. Mexico, 1922.

Morel-Fatio, Alfred P. V. *Études sur l'Espagne.* 2 vols. Paris, 1906.

Moreno Fraginals, M. *El ingenio: El complejo económico social cubano del azúcar,* vol. 1: *1760–1864.* Havana, 1964.

———. *El ingenio: Complejo económico social cubano del azúcar.* 3 vols. Havana, 1978.

Morin, Claude. *Michoacán en la Nueva España del siglo XVIII: Crecimiento y desigualdad en una economía colonial.* Mexico, 1979.

Morineau, Michel. *Incroyables gazettes et fabuleux métaux: Les retours des trésors américains d'après les gazettes hollandaises (XVI–XVIIIe siècles).* Paris, 1985.

Mörner, Magnus. *The Political and Economic Activities of the Jesuits in the La Plata Region: The Hapsburg Era.* Stockholm, 1953.

Musset, Alain, and Thomas Calvo, eds. *Des Indes occidentales à l'Amérique Latine: À Jean-Pierre Berthe.* 2 vols. Paris, 1997.

Nadal, Jordi. *La población española: Siglos XVI a XX.* Barcelona, 1966.

Nadal, Jordi, and Gabriel Tortella, eds. *Agricultura, comercio colonial y crecimiento económico en la España contemporanea.* Barcelona, 1974.

Navarro Latorre, José. *Hace doscientos años. Estado actual de los problemas históricos del "Motín de Esquilache."* Madrid, 1966.

Noel, Charles Curtis. "Campomanes and the Secular Clergy in Spain, 1760–1780." Ph.D. diss., Princeton University, 1970.

Novísima recopilación de las leyes de España. 2d ed. Madrid, 1992.

Nuevo sistema de gobierno económico para la América con los males y daños que le causa el que hoy tiene de los que participa copiosamente España. Madrid, 1789.

O'Crouley, Pedro Alonso. *A Description of the Kingdom of New Spain.* Translated and edited by Seán Galvin. San Francisco, 1972.

Oliva Melgar, José María. *Cataluña y el comercio privilegiada con América en el siglo XVIII. La Real Compañía de Comercio de Barcelona a Indias.* Barcelona, 1982.

Olson, Mancur. *The Rise and Decline of Nations: Economic Growth, Stagflation and Social Rigidities*. New Haven, Conn., 1982.

Oñate, María del Carmen Lario. *La colonia mercantil británica e irlandesa en Cádiz a finales del siglo XVIII*. Cadiz, 2000.

Ortega Costa, Antonio, and Ana María García Osma. *Noticias de Cabarrús y su procesamiento*. Madrid, 1974.

Ortí y Brull, Vicente. *Doña María Manuela Pignatelli de Aragón y Gonzaga, duquesa de Villahermosa*. 2 vols. Madrid, 1896.

Ortiz Vidales, Salvador. *La arriería en México, estudio foclórico, costumbrista e histórico*. 2d ed. Mexico, 1941.

Ouweneel, Aryo, and Cristina Torales Pacheco, eds. *Empresarios, indios y estado: Perfil de la economía mexicana (siglo XVIII)*. Amsterdam, 1988.

Palacio Atard, Vicente. *El tercer pacto de familia*. Madrid, 1945.

Pares, Richard. *War and Trade in the West Indies*. Oxford, 1936.

Parry, John. *The Sale of Public Office in the Spanish Indies Under the Hapsburgs*. Berkeley, Calif., 1953.

———. *The Spanish Seaborne Empire*. New York, 1966.

Parry, John, and P. M. Sherlock. *Short History of the West Indies*. 2d ed. New York, 1966.

Pérez de la Riva, Juan, ed. *Documentos sobre la toma de Habana por los ingleses in 1762*. Havana, 1963.

Pérez Herrero, Pedro. *Plata y libranzas: La articulación comercial de México borbónico*. Mexico, 1988.

Pérez Mesía, Pedro. *Instrucción para el gobierno de la aduana de Cádiz*. Madrid, n.d. [1786?].

Peuchet, J. *Dictionnaire universel de la géographie commerçante*. 5 vols. Paris, An VII [1799–1800].

Pieper, Renate. *La Real Hacienda bajo Fernando VI y Carlos III (1753–1788)*. Madrid, 1992.

Postlethwayt, Malachy. *Universal Dictionary of Trade and Commerce*. London, 1766.

Priestley, Herbert I. *José de Gálvez*. Berkeley, Calif., 1916.

Rabell, Cecilia. *Los diezmos de San Luís de la Paz. Economía de una región del Bajío en el siglo XVIII*. Mexico, 1986.

Ramos, Hector R. Feliciano. *El contrabando inglés en el Caribe y el Golfo de México (1748–1778)*. Sevilla, 1990.

Ramos Gómez, Luís, ed. *Epoca, génesis, y texto de "Las noticias secretas de América."* 2 vols. Madrid, 1985.

Ramsay, G. D. *English Overseas Trade During the Centuries of Emergence: Studies in Some Modern Origins of the English-Speaking World*. London, 1957.

Raynal, Guillaume-Thomas-François. *Histoire philosophique et politique des établissements européens dans les deux Indes*. 10 vols. 2d ed. Paris, 1783–84.

Real Díaz, José Joaquin. *Las ferias de Jalapa*. Sevilla, 1959.

Real Sociedad Económica de Madrid. *Memorias*. 5 vols. Madrid, 1780–95.

Reglamento y aranceles reales para el comercio libre de España a Indias . . . 1778. Madrid, 1778.

Relación y testimonio de los autos . . . sobre la erección de la compañía real que ha solicitado instituir . . . aviadores de minas . . . en Perú. Lima, 1938.

Robertson, William. *The History of America.* 3 vols. 4th ed. London 1783.

Rodríguez Casado, Vicente. *La política y los políticos en el reinado de Carlos III.* Madrid, 1962.

Rodríguez López, Gabriel. *Laneras de Castilla en el siglo XVIII: Notas sociales de las fábricas de Segovia, Guadalajara y Béjar.* Madrid, 1947.

Rojas y Contreras, José, ed. *Historia del colegio viejo de San Bartolomé . . . por Francisco Ruiz de Vergara y Alava.* 2d ed. 2 vols. Madrid, 1766–70.

Romá y Rosell, Francisco. *Las sendas de la felicidad de España y medios de hacerlas eficaces.* Madrid, 1768.

Rousseau, François. *La règne de Charles III en Espagne (1759–1788).* 2 vols. Paris, 1907.

Ruiz Martín, Felipe. *Las finanzas de la monarquía española en tiempos de Felipe IV (1621–1665).* Madrid, 1990.

Ruiz Rivera, Julián B. *El consulado de Cádiz: Matrícula de comerciantes, 1730–1823.* Cadiz, 1988.

Sala Balust, Luis. *Visitas y reforma de los colegios mayores de Salamanca.* Valladolid, 1958.

Salvucci, Richard. *Textiles and Capitalism in Mexico: An Economic History of the Obrajes, 1539–1840.* Princeton, N.J., 1987.

Sánchez Gómez, Julio, et el. *La savia del imperio: Tres estudios de economía colonial.* Salamanca, 1997.

Schipa, Michelangelo. *Il regno di Napoli al tiempo di Carlo Borbone.* 2 vols. Milan, 1923.

Schumpeter, Joseph A. *History of Economic Analysis.* New York, 1961.

Seminario de Segovia sobre Agricultura e Ilustración en España. *Estructuras agrarias y reformismo ilustrado en la España del siglo XVIII.* Madrid, 1989.

Sempere y Guarinos, Juan. *Ensayo de una biblioteca española de los mejores escritores del reynado de Carlos III.* 6 vols. 1785–87. Reprint. Madrid, 1969.

Smith, Adam. *The Wealth of Nations.* Edited by E. Cannan. New York, 1937.

Sperling, John G. *The South Sea Company: An Historical Essay and Bibliographic Finding List.* Cambridge, Mass., 1962.

Stein, Ralph. *The French Slave Trade in the Eighteenth Century: An Old Regime Business.* Madison, Wisc., 1979.

Syrett, David, comp. *The Siege and Capture of Havana, 1762.* Publications of the Navy Records Society, 114. London, 1970.

Tarrade, Jean. *Le commerce colonial de la France de la fin du régime de l'exclusif de 1763 à 1789.* 2 vols. Paris, 1972.

Tedde de Lorca, Pedro. *El banco de San Carlos (1782–1829).* Madrid, 1988.

———, ed. *Comercio y colonias.* Vol. 3 of *La economía española al final del antiguo régimen,* ed. Gonzalo Anes Alvarez et al. Madrid, 1982.

Thomas, Hugh. *Cuba, the Pursuit of Freedom.* New York, 1991.

Titulos de Indias. Catalog XX del Archivo General de Simancas. Valladolid, 1954.

Torales Pacheco, María Cristina, et al., eds. *La compañía de comercio de Francisco Ignacio de Yraeta (1787–1797).* 2 vols. Mexico, 1985.

Tornero Tinajero, Pablo. *Crecimiento económico y transformaciones sociales: Esclavos, hacendados y comerciantes en la Cuba colonial (1760–1840).* Madrid, 1996.

Torres Ramírez, B., and José Hernández Palomo, eds. *Andalucía y América en el siglo XVIII: Actas de las IV Jornadas de Andalucía y América.* Escuela de estudios hispanoamericanos de Sevilla, 314. 2 vols. Sevilla, 1985.

Townsend, Joseph. *A Journey Through Spain in the Years 1786 and 1787.* 2d ed. London, 1792.

Trabulse, Elías, ed. *Fluctuaciones económicas en Oaxaca durante el siglo XVIII.* Mexico, 1979.

Ulloa, Antonio de, and Jorge Juan. *Relación histórica del viage a la América meridional.* 5 vols. Madrid, 1748.

———. *Noticias secretas de América. 1826. Reprint.* Buenos Aires, 1953.

Ulloa, Bernardo. *Restablecimiento de las fábricas, tráfico y comercio marítimo de España.* Edited by Juan Luís Castellano. 1740. Reprint. Madrid, 1982.

Uztáriz, Gerónimo. *Theórica y práctica de comercio y de marina.* Edited by Gabriel Franco. 1724. Reprint. Madrid, 1968.

Valdés y Bazán, Antonio. *Exposición documentada . . . a la Regencia del reyno el Baylío Fr. Don Antonio Valdés y Bazán.* Cadiz, 1813.

Vicens Vives, Jaime. *Aproximación a la historia de España.* 2d ed. Madrid, 1960.

Vilar, Pierre. *La Catalogne dans l'Espagne moderne: Recherches sur les fondements économiques des structures nationales.* 3 vols. Paris, 1962.

———. *Oro y moneda en la historia, 1450–1920.* Barcelona, 1965.

Villani, Pasquale. *Feudalitá, riforme, capitalismo agrario: Panorama di storia sociale italiana tra sette e ottocento.* Bari, 1967.

Villaroel, Hipólito. *Enfermedades políticas que padece la capital de esta Nueva España.* Mexico, 1979.

Villaseñor y Sánchez, J. A. *Theatro americano: Descripción general de los reynos y provincias de la Nueva España.* Mexico, 1746–48.

Voltes Bou, Pedro. *Carlos III y su tiempo.* Barcelona, 1964.

Ward, Bernardo. *Obra pía y eficaz, modo para remediar la miseria de la gente pobre de España.* Valencia, 1750.

———. *Proyecto económico en que se proponen varias providencias dirigidas a promover los intereses de España con los medios y fondos necesarios para su plantificación, escrito en . . . 1762.* Madrid, 1779.

Whitaker, Arthur P. *The Huancavelica Mercury Mine.* Cambridge, Mass., 1941.

Wobeser, Gisela von. *El crédito eclesiástico en la Nueva España, siglo XVIII.* Mexico, 1994.

Yuste, Carmen, ed. *Comerciantes mexicanos en el siglo XVIII: Selección de documentos e introducción.* Mexico, 1991.

Yuste López, Carmen, and Matilde Souto Mantecón, eds. *El comercio exterior de México, 1713–1850.* Mexico, 2000.

Articles

Anon. "Discurso sobre la libertad del comercio." In Real Sociedad Económica de Madrid, *Memorias,* 2:21–50. Madrid, 1780–95.

Anon. "Carta de un huevero de Fuencarral." *BAE* 59 (1867): 277–79.

Anon. "Ensayo apologético por el comercio libre. . . . " In *Controversia,* ed. Florescano and Castillo, 1:300–380. Mexico, 1975.

Anon. "Idea general del comercio de las Indias; Reino de Nueva España (1776) por R. de V." In *Controversia,* ed. Florescano and Castillo, 1:23–68. Mexico, 1975.

Andrien, K. J. "Economic Crisis, Taxes and the Quito Insurrection of 1765." *PP* 129 (1990): 104–31.

Anes Alvarez, Gonzalo. "Introducción." In *La economia española al final del antiguo régimen,* ed. id. et al., 1:xv–xlv. Madrid, 1982.

———. "Sociedad y economía." In Congreso internacional sobre Carlos III y la ilustración, *Actas,* 1:1–138. Madrid, 1989.

Beleña, Eusebio Ventura. "Informe reservado sobre el actual estado del comercio." In *Controversia,* ed. Florescano and Castillo, 1:183–234. Mexico, 1975.

Benedict, H. Bradley. "Hacienda Management." American Philosophical Society, *Proceedings* 123 (1979): 391–409.

Berrill, K. "International Trade and the Rate of Economic Growth." *EHR* 12 (1960): 351–59.

Bilbao, Luís María, and Emiliano Fernández de Pinedo. "Artesanía e industria." In *Enciclopedia de historia de España,* ed. Artola, 1:11–104. Madrid, 1988–93.

Borah, Woodrow W. "Hipólito Villaroel: Some Unanswered Questions." In *Des Indes occidentales à l'Amérique Latine,* ed. Musset and Calvo, 2:505–14. Paris, 1997.

Bromley, Rosemary O., and R. J. Bromley. "The Debate on Sunday Markets in Nineteenth-Century Ecuador." *JLAS* 7 (1975): 85–108.

Brown, Vera Lee. "Anglo-Spanish Relations in America in the Closing Years of the Colonial Era." *HAHR* 5 (1922): 325–483.

Cabarrús, Francisco. "Discurso sobre la libertad del comercio concedida . . . a la América meridional. 28 Febrero de 1778." In Real Sociedad Económica de Madrid, *Memorias,* 3:282–94. Madrid, 1780–95.

Campomanes, Pedro Rodríguez. "Alegación fiscal [Obispo de Cuenca]." *BAE* 59 (1867): 41–65.

———. "Dictamen de los fiscales sobre prohibición de capas largas y sombreros redondos. Madrid 4 Marzo 1766." In Eguía Ruiz, *Los jesuitas y el motín de Esquilache,* 349–59. Madrid, 1947.

Carrière, Charles. "Renouveau espagnol et prêt à la grosse aventure." *RHMC* 17 (1970): 221–52.

Christelow, Allan. "French Interest in the Spanish Empire during the Ministry of the duc de Choiseul." *HAHR* 21 (1941): 515–37.

———. "Contraband Trade Between Jamaica and the Spanish Main, and the Free-port Act of 1766." *HAHR* 22 (1942): 309–43.

Clause, Georges. "L'industrie lainière rémoise à l'époque napoléonienne." *RHMC* 17 (1970): 574–95.

Cole, W. A. "Trends in Eighteenth-Century Smuggling." *EHR* 10 (1958): 395–410.

Consulado de Barcelona. "Informe sobre el comercio de América." *EMDL,* no. 173 (23 Mar. 1789): 1013–26; no. 174 (30 Mar. 1789), 1040–53.

Consulado de México. "Informe . . . sobre la situación del comercio y de la economía de Nueva España (1788)." In *Controversia,* ed. Florescano and Castillo, 1:71–137. Mexico, 1975. See also "Extracto del informe hecho . . . por . . . Consulado de México," 31 May 1788, BNMex MS 1304, ff. 3–80, and a résumé in "Razón de los puntos que se promovieron por el . . . Consulado de México . . . en informe. . . . Mayo de 1788 . . . ," AGN, AHH, 442-12. First published by Luís Chávez Orozco in *Documentos para la historia económica de México* (Mexico, 1933–35).

Craywinckel, Francisco. "Papel útil y curioso de reflexiones . . . del marqués de Squilace . . . sobre el comercio de trigo." *SEV* 34 (1791): 131–50.

Crouzet, François. "Wars, Blockade and Economic Change in Europe, 1792–1815." *JEH* 24 (1964): 567–88.

———. "England and France in the Eighteenth Century. A Comparative Analysis of Two Economic Growths." In *Causes of the Industrial Revolution,* ed. Hartwell, 139–77. London, 1967.

Defourneaux, Marcelin. "Le problème agraire en Andalousie au XVIIIe siècle et les projets de réforme agraire." *RH* 81, no. 217 (1957): 42–57.

Delgado, Jaime. "El conde de Ricla, capitán-general de Cuba." *RHA* nos. 55–56 (1963): 41–138.

Delgado i Ribas, Josep M. "Floridablanca y el planteamiento de la política agraria de Carlos III." In Seminario de Segovia sobre Agricultura e Ilustración en España, *Estructuras agrarias y reformismo ilustrado en la España del siglo XVIII,* 639–61. Madrid, 1989.

———. "El impacto de las crisis coloniales en la economía catalana, 1787–1807." In *La economía española al final del antiguo regimen,* ed. Anes Alvarez et al., 3:1–98. Madrid, 1982.

———. "El miratge del llivre comerç." In *El comerç entre Catalunya i América. Segles XVIII i XIX,* ed. id. et al., 65–80. Barcelona, 1986.

———. "America." *HPE* nos. 108–9 (1987): 133–46.

———. "El modelo catalán dentro del sistema de libre comercio (1765–1820)." In *El comercio libre entre España y América, 1765–1724,* edited by Fontana and Bernal, 53–70. Madrid, 1987.

Dermigny, L. "Circuits d'argent et milieux d'affaires au XVIIIe siècle." *RH* 78 (1954): 239–78.

———. "Une carte monétaire de la France à la fin de l'ancien régime." *AESC* 10 (1955): 480–93.

Desdevises du Dézert, G. "La chambre des juges de l'hotel et la cour en 1745." *RHisp* 26 (1916): 1–51.

Dobado González, Rafael. "Las minas de Almadén, el monopolio del azogue y la producción de plata en Nueva España en el siglo XVIII." In *La savia del imperio: Tres estudios de economía colonial,* ed. Sánchez Gómez et al., 403–72. Salamanca, 1997.

Dornic, François. "Le commerce des français à Cadiz d'après les papiers d'Antoine Granjean (1752–1774)." *AESC* 9 (1954): 311–27.

Drain, M. "Carte agraire d'Andalousie." In *Mélanges de la Casa de Velázquez* 4 (1963): 371–86.

Elorza, Antonio. "Estudio preliminar." In Arroyal, *Cartas.* Madrid, 1968.

F.X.B. "Discurso primero sobre el comercio de América. *EMDL* no. 142 (1788): 276–79.

———. "Discurso segundo." *EMDL* no. 153 (3 Nov. 1788): 220–23.

Flores, Antonio. "Extracto del informe . . . por el Consulado de Cádiz sobre la situación del comercio entre España y las Indias con notas y observaciones formadas por. . . . " In *Controversia,* ed. Florescano and Castillo, 2:139–64. Mexico, 1975.

Fontana, Josep. "Introducción." In *La economía espanola al final del antiguo régimen*, ed. Anes Alvarez et al., 3:xi–xxxiv. Madrid, 1982.

Foronda, Valentín. "Carta sobre el Banco Nacional de San Carlos." In id., *Miscelánea, ó, Colección de varios discursos*. 1793. Reprint. Madrid, 1996.

Fradera, Josep M. "El comerç americà durant el segle XIX." In *El comerç entre Catalunya i América. Segles XVIII i XIX,* ed. Delgado i Ribas et al., 111–21. Barcelona, 1986.

———. "Una o varias crisis coloniales? A propósito del caso catalán." in *El "Comercio Libre" entre España y America,* ed. Fontana and Bernal, 95–106. Madrid, 1987.

Franco, José Luciano. "Diego de Gardoqui y las negociaciones entre España y Norteamerica, 1777–1790." In Félix Lizaso, *Libro jubilar de Emeterio S. Santovenia en su cincuentenario de escritor,* 139–65. Havana, 1957.

García-Baquero González, Antonio. "Aristócratas y mercaderes." In id., *Andalucía y la carrera de Indias (1492–1824).* Sevilla, 1986.

García Sanz, Angel, and Jesús Sanz Fernández. "Agricultura y ganadería." In *Enciclopedia de historia de España: Economía y sociedad,* ed. Artola, 1:11–109. Madrid, 1988–93.

Garner, Richard. "Exportaciones de circulante en el siglo xviii, 1750–1810." *HMex* 31 (1982): 545–88.

———. "Further Consideration of 'Facts and Figures in Bourbon Mexico.'" *BLAR* 6 (1987): 55–63.

———. "Long-term Silver Mining Trends in Spanish America: A Comparative Analysis of Peru and Mexico." *AHR* 93 (1988): 898–935.

Gijón, Manuel. "Memoria . . . relativa al comercio de Indias." In Real Sociedad Económica de Madrid, *Memorias,* 3:262–81. Madrid, 1780–95.

Glamann, Kristof. "Europe and Trade, 1500–1750." In *The Fontana Economic History of Europe,* ed. Carlo M. Cipolla, vol. 2: *The Sixteenth and Seventeenth Centuries,* 427–526. New York, 1974.

Henderson, W. O. "The Anglo-French Commercial Treaty of 1786." *EHR* 10 (1957–58): 104–12.

Heros Fernández, Juan Antonio de los. "Discursos sobre el comercio, las utilidades, beneficios, y opulencias que produce . . . y que es compatible el comercio con la primera nobleza." *SEV,* no. 26 (1790): 145–280; no. 27 (1790): 222.

Inglis, G. Douglas, and Allan J. Kuethe, "El consulado de Cádiz y el Reglamento de comercio libre de 1765." In *Andalucía y América en el siglo XVIII,* ed. Torres Ramírez and Hernández Palomo, 79–95. Sevilla, 1985.

Izard, Miguel. "Comercio libre, guerras coloniales y mercado americano." In *Agricultura, comercio colonial y crecimiento eonómico en la España contemporanea,* ed. Nadal and Tortella, 295–321. Barcelona, 1974.

John, A. H. "War and the English Economy, 1700–1763." *EHR* 7 (1955): 329–44.

Jones, E. T. "Illicit Business: Accounting for Smuggling in Mid-Sixteenth Century Bristol." *EHR* 54 (2001), 17–38.

Jovellanos, Gaspar. "Elogio de Carlos III." *BAE* 46 (1858): 311–17.

Klaveren, J. van. "Fiscalism, Mercantilism and Corruption." In *Revisions in Mercantilism,* ed. Coleman, 140–61. London, 1969.

Kuethe, Allan J., and Lowell Blaidsell. "French Influence and the Origin of Bourbon Colonial Reorganization." *HAHR* 71 (1991): 579–607.

Lavrín, Asunción. "The Execution of the Law of *Consolidación* in New Spain: Economic Aims and Results." *HAHR* 53 (1973): 27–49.

Léon, Pierre. "Structure du commerce extérieur et évolution industrielle de la France à la fin du XVIIIe siècle." In *Conjoncture économique, structures sociales: Hommage à Ernest Labrousse,* 407–32. Paris, 1974.

Lerner, Victoria. "Consideraciones sobre la población de la Nueva España (1793–1810)." *HMex* 17 (1968): 327–47.

Levain, J., J. Rougerie, and A. Strauss. "Contribution à l'état des mouvements de 'longue durée': La croissance de l'industrie lainière en France au XIXe siècle." In Institut d'histoire économique et sociale de l'université de Paris I, Recherches et Travaux, *Bulletin* no. 12 (1987): 59–96.

Macanaz, Melchor. "Auxilios para bien gobernar una monarquía católica. II." *SEV* 5 (1787): 233–36.

Martínez Shaw, Carlos. "Los orígenes de la industria algodonera catalana y el comercio colonial." In *Agricultura, comercio colonial y crecimiento económico en la España contemporanea,* ed. Nadal and Tortella, 243–67. Barcelona, 1974.

Masson de Morvilliers, Nicolas. "Espagne." In *Encyclopédie méthodique,* ser. "Géographie moderne," 1:554–68. Paris, 1783.

Mateo Dorado, Dolores. "La actividad de Carlos III durante el año 'sin rey' (1758–1759)." In Congreso internacional sobre Carlos III y la ilustración, *Actas,* 1:299–321. Madrid, 1989.

Miño Grijalva, Manuel. "La circulación de mercancías: Una referencia al caso textil latinoamericano (1750–1810)." In *Empresarios, indios y estado: Perfil de la economía mexicana (siglo XVIII),* ed. Ouweneel and Torales Pacheco, 45–58. Amsterdam, 1988.

Moñino, José, conde de Floridablanca. "Alegación del . . . contra el informe por el . . . Obispo de Cuenca, en 23 de mayo." *BAE* 59 (1867): 3–41.

———. "Memorial presentado al rey Carlos III y repetido a Carlos IV." *BAE* 59 (1867): 306–49.

Moreno de los Arcos, Roberto. "Apuntes biográficos de Joaquín Velázquez de León, 1732–1786." *HMex* 25 (1975): 41–75.

Moxó, Salvador de. "Un medievalista en el Consejo de Hacienda: D. Francisco, marqués de la Corona (1715–1791)." *AHDE* 29 (1959): 609–50.

Muñoz Pérez, José. "La publicación del Reglamento de Comercio Libre de Indias de 1778." *AEA* 4 (1947): 615–64.

———. "Los proyectos sobre España e Indias en el siglo XVIII: El proyectismo como género." *REP* 81 (1955): 169–95.

———. "El comercio de Indias bajo los Austrias y la crítica del proyectismo del XVIII." *AEA* 13 (1956): 85–103.

Muret, Pierre. "Les papiers de l'Abbé Béliardi et les relations commerciales de la France et de l'Espagne au milieu du XVIIIe siècle (1757–1770)." *RHMC* 4 (1902–3): 657–69.

Muro, Luís. "Revillagigedo y el comercio libre (1791–1792)." In *Extremos de América. Homenage a don Daniel Cosío Villegas,* 299–344. Mexico, 1971.

Murphy, O. T. "Dupont de Nemours and the Anglo-French Commercial Treaty of 1776." *EHR* 19 (1966): 569–80.

Navarro García, Luis. "El virrey marqués de Croix." In *Los virreyes de Nueva España en el reinado de Carlos III,* ed. Calderón Quijano, 1:161–381. Sevilla, 1967.

Oliva Melgar, José María. "Reflexiones en torno al comercio libre de Barlovento: el caso catalán." In *El "comercio libre" entre España y America,* ed. Fontana and Bernal, 71–94. Madrid, 1987.

Ozanam, D. "La colonie française de Cadiz au XVIIIe siècle, d'après un document inédit (1777)." In *Mélanges de la Casa de Velazquez* 4 (1968): 259–348.

Palerm, Angel. "Sobre la formación del sistema colonial: apuntes para una discusión." In *Ensayos sobre el desarrollo de México y América Latina (1500–1975),* ed. Florescano, 93–127. Mexico, 1979.

Pérez Herrero, Pedro. "Los comienzos de la política reformista de Carlos III." *CH Los complementarios/2* (1988): 53–70.

———. "El crecimiento económico novohispano durante el siglo XVIII." *Revista de História Económica* 7 (1989): 69–110.

Pérez Moreda, Vicente. "Población." In *Enciclopedia de historia de España,* ed. Artola, 1:345–431. Madrid, 1988–93.

Posada, Ramón. "Dictamen del fiscal de Real Hacienda (1792)." In *Controversia,* ed. Florescano and Castillo, 1:259–69. Mexico, 1975.

R. de V. See Anon., "Idea general." Mexico, 1975.

Rambert, G. "La France et la politique comerciale de l'Espagne au XVIIIe siècle." *RHMC* 6 (1959): 269–88.

Ramsay, G. D. "The Smugglers' Trade: A Neglected Aspect of English Commercial Development." Royal Historical Society, *Transactions* 2 (1952): 131–57.

Revillagigedo, segundo conde de. "Carta reservada." AGN, *Boletín* 1 (1930): 192–211.

Ringrose, David. "Carting in the Hispanic World: An Example of Divergent Development." *HAHR* 50 (1970): 30–51.

Rodríguez Casado, Vicente. "Comentarios al decreto y real instrucción de 1765." *AHDE* 13 (1936–41): 100–135.

Rodríguez Labandeira, José. "La política económica de los Borbones." In *La economía española al final del antiguo régimen,* ed. Anes Alvarez et al., 4:109–84. Madrid, 1982.

Ruiz Martín, Felipe. "La banca en España hasta 1782." In *El Banco de España, una historia económica,* 1–196. Madrid, 1970.

Saenz de Tejada Hermoso, Policarpo. "Memorial . . . sobre el comercio (16 de marzo 1776)." In Real Sociedad de Madrid, *Memorias,* 2:21–46. Madrid, 1780–95.

Saíz Milanés, Julián. "Orígenes y historia de los bienes y propios." In *Textos olvidados,* ed. Fabián Estapé y Rodríguez, 441–89. Madrid, 1973.

Sée, Henri. "Documents sur le commerce de Cadix (1691–1752)." *RHCF* 14 (1926): 465–520.

Stein, Stanley J., and Barbara H. Stein. "Concepts and Realities of Spanish Economic Growth, 1759–1789." *HI* 1 (1972): 103–19.

Taylor, George. "Noncapitalist Wealth and the Origin of the French Revolution." *AHR* 72 (1967): 469–96.

Tedde de Lorca, Pedro. "Introducción." In *La economía española al final del antiguo régimen,* ed. Anes Alvarez et al., 2:xi–lx. Madrid, 1982.

———. "El sector secundario." In *Enciclopedia de historia de España,* ed. Artola, 1:265–342. Madrid, 1988–93.

———. "Política financiera y política comercial en el reinado de Carlos III." In Congreso internacional sobre Carlos III y la ilustración, *Actas,* 2:139–217. Madrid, 1989.

Tinoco Rubiales, Santiago. "El consulado nuevo de Sevilla y el comercio libre: Un balance en 1787." In *El "comercio libre" entre España y America,* ed. Fontana and Bernal, 107–22. Madrid, 1987.

———. "Capital y crédito en la Baja Andalucía durante la crisis del antiguo régimen." In *La economía española al final del antiguo régimen,* ed. Anes Alvarez et al., 3:253–388. Madrid, 1982.

Ugartiria, J. "Carta . . . a un amigo suyo fuera de la corte, en que se incluye un Discurso económico-politico." *EMDL* no. 170 (2 Mar. 1789): 953–62.

———. "Fin de la carta de D. J. Ugartiria." *EMDL* no. 171 (9 Mar. 1789): 963–76.

———. "Carta segunda de . . . acerca del comercio a Indias." *EMDL* no. 172 (16 Mar. 1789): 987–98.

Uriortua y Villanueva, Francisco Xavier. "Informe sobre la libertad del comercio que por particular comisión de la Real Sociedad Económica de esta Corte. . . ." *EMDL* no. 147 (22 Sept. 1788): 88–94; 148 (29 Sept. 1788): 104–12; no. 149 (6 Oct. 1788): 132–37; no. 150 (13 Oct. 1788): 153–58; no. 151 (20 Oct. 1788): 181–87; no. 152 (27 Oct. 1788): 203–10.

Valladares, Antonio. "Prospecto." *SEV* 1 (1787).

Van Young, Eric. "A modo de conclusión: el siglo paradójico." In *Empresarios, indios y estado. Perfil de la economía mexicana (siglo XVIII),* ed. Ouweneel and Torales Pacheco, 206–31. Amsterdam, 1988.

———. "The Age of Paradox: Mexican Agriculture at the End of the Colonial Period, *1750–1810.*" In *The Economies of Mexico and Peru during the Late Colonial Period, 1760–1810,* ed. Nils Jacobsen and Hans-Jürgen Puhle, 64–90. Berlin, 1986.

Varela Marcos, Jesús. "El primer reglamento para el libre comercio con América: Su génesis y fracaso." *AEA* 46 (1989): 243–68.

Vilar, Pierre. "Structures de la société espagnole vers 1750: Quelques leçons du cadastre de la Ensenada." In *Mélanges à la memoire de Jean Sarrailh,* 2:425–47. Paris, 1966.

Villalobos, Sergio. "El comercio extranjero a fines de la dominación espanola." *JIS* 4 (1962): 517–44.

Whitaker, Arthur P., ed. "Documents relating to the Publication of the *Memorias históricas* of Antúnez y Acevedo." *HAHR* 10 (1930): 375–91.

———. "Antonio de Ulloa." *HAHR* 15 (1935): 155–94.

———. "The Pseudo-Aranda Memorial of 1783." *HAHR* 17 (1937): 287–313.

Wright, Almon R. "The Aranda Memorial: Genuine or Forged?" *HAHR* 18 (1938): 445–60.

Casas, conde de las (Luís de las Casas y Aragorri), 64

Castaños, Joseph, 148

Castille, 28. *See also* Consejo de Castilla

Castries, marquis de, 336

Catalans, 147, 161, 247, 258, 280, 349

Catalonia, 58, 208; competition of, 273–74; economic performance of, 204, 222, 275–76, 354; exports of, 144, 147–48, 154, 186, 190, 270–71, 273; imports of, 318; textile manufacturing in, 40, 204, 206, 328

catasto generale (national survey of wealth and income), 8

Catholic Church, 7, 32–36; and Charles III, 87; and Consejo de Hacienda, 46, 48; privileges of, 38, 46–47, 87, 346; property of, 46–48; as representative of papal interests, 4, 32; and Spain, 32–33; and state, 32, 46; and taxation, 4, 8, 45, 347

Catholic enlightenment, 115

Catholics, 32–34, 105, 338, 355

Catorce mining district, 224, 265

Cayla, Solier, Cabanes, Jugla et Cie (French Huguenot firm), 136, 323

censorship, 341–42, 344, 348

Central America, 11, 295

Cervera, Miguel de, 59–60, 196

Chaptal, J.-A.-C., 336, 417n33

Charles, Prince. *See* Charles IV

Charles II, 10, 229

Charles III: accession of, 3, 146, 306; anglophobic administration of, 23–24; and Aranda, 345; arrival in Spain of, 12, 19, 36, 83, 197, 305; and Caribbean, 49; and Catholic Church, 46, 87, 89, 96, 342; and civil servants, 26; and colonies, 12, 48–52, 107; and Consejo de Castilla, 366n88; *consulados* under, 260; and crisis of 1766, 85, 88–89, 99, 101, 114–15; death of, 218, 300, 355; era of, 197, 222, 226, 254, 266, 278, 306, 324, 344, 349, 352–54; and Esquilache, 6, 11, 29, 37–38, 69, 77, 82–83, 86, 89, 165; and Floridablanca, 25, 180, 267, 305, 338, 340,

345; and free trade, 343; and Gálvez, 180, 183; and Grimaldi, 25, 61; inner circle of, 112, 172; and Jesuits, 102, 106; memorial to, 218, 267–68, 270, 340–42, 409n1; and military, 56; ministers of, 30, 163, 322, 328, 331; in Naples, 3–11, 22–23; and parallel economy, 196; and periodicals, 341; policies of, 107, 111, 208–9, 343; privileged sectors under, 346; reforms of, 10–11, 24–25, 27, 29–30, 203, 229; reign of, 20, 170, 289, 338–39, 342, 349, 355; and Sarriá, 51; and textile manufacture, 216

Charles IV, 82, 115, 172, 239, 261, 304, 345; accession of, 10, 300–301, 311; and French alliance, 355

Chico, José Hernández, 242

Chile, 142, 162

Choiseul, Etienne François, duc de, 39, 53–54, 99–101, 362n4

Cinco Gremios Mayores, 34, 80, 200, 215; agents of, 146, 194, 211; and colonial trade, 20, 133–34, 286; and fall of Esquilache, 39, 64, 85, 88, 99, 101, 114; and Floridablanca, 176; and Second Reglamento, 164–65; and state finance, 184, 188

Cladera, Cristóval, 278, 300, 342

Clarke, Edward, 120

Colarte, Pedro, 16–18

Colbert, Jean-Baptiste, 160, 314, 342

Colegio Imperial de San Isidro, 102, 104

Colegio Seminario de San Telmo, 169

Colegio Viejo de San Bartolomé, 111

Colombia (Santa Fe), 166

Colonia del Sacramento, 21

colonialism, 277, 291; Spanish, 339, 343, 347

colonial trade: boom years of (1784, 1786), 273; crisis in Spanish, 11–24; and Esquilache's reforms, 37–68, 81–115; expansion and contraction (1783–87) in, 74, 188, 220, 272, 300; and First Reglamento, 69–80; and France, 305–37; incremental change

Mayorga, Martín de (viceroy), 242

Maza Alvarado, Gerónimo, 179

Meave, Ambrosio, 151

Medina Celi, duque de (Luís Fernández de Cordoba y Spínola), 84, 97, 103

mercaderes viandantes (traveling tradesmen), 140

merchant-banking houses, 175, 227, 307–8, 311, 322

merchant guilds, 18, 286

merchants, 4, 9, 29, 48, 353–54; Basque, 179, 229, 265; in Cadiz, 16, 19, 161, 219, 259, 292, 348; and colonial trade, 42, 292; in Consulado de Mexico, 146, 172; and Floridablanca, 178, 254–55; foreign, 15–16, 18, 20, 147, 157–58, 161, 163, 194, 221, 305, 353, 377n40; French, 15, 146, 176–78, 180, 192, 194, 221, 305, 321, 330, 333, 335; influence of, 183; investments of, 245; in Mexico City, 53, 61, 67, 127–29, 146, 179, 188, 211, 226, 229, 231, 241, 259, 265, 280–81, 289–90, 294, 297–98, 317, 353, 355, 412n66; and mining, 76, 228; *Montañés*, 241–42, 259–60, 265; in New Spain, 153, 255, 274, 281; and officers, 197; in Peru, 61; provincial, 258; resistance to free trade by, 183; and shipmasters, 333; small to medium-sized, 259, 261; Spanish, 153, 194, 280, 292, 297–98; Spanish-born sons of foreign (*genízaros*), 18–20, 296–97, 324; in Veracruz, 138. See also *almaceneros*

mercury: allocation of, 242, 402n63; efforts to locate, 240; export of, 170, 175, 193, 226; mining of, 136, 153, 284; payment for, 400nn38,43; supply and pricing of, 76, 227–28, 232–37, 353, 369n21, 400nn40,41

Mesía, Francisco Pérez, 200–203, 219, 301, 334, 393n73

Mexico, 13, 52, 56, 63, 76, 106; and Cadiz, 223; Comercio de, 127–35, 150, 188, 257; sugar in, 225, 247; suggested abandonment of, 346–47. *See also* Consulado de Mexico; New Spain

Mexico City, 35, 68, 72, 80, 108, 301, 312; Aduana (customs house) in, 252; Audiencia of, 242, 244; Basques in, 179, 229, 265; Consulado of, 149, 171; counterrevolution in, 254; decline of, 283; growth of, 244; and imports, 128; lobbying by, 172; merchants in, 53, 61, 67, 127–29, 146, 179, 188, 211, 226, 229, 231, 241, 259, 265, 280–81, 289–90, 294, 297–98, 317, 353, 355, 412n66; role of, 145; and Second Reglamento, 265; Spanish merchant oligarchs of, 280, 298; trade in, 119, 130; wage labor in, 249; workshops of, 277, 280

Mexico City mint, 177, 226, 234, 251, 288; annual coinage at, 263–64, 282, 299; output of, 223–24, 230, 261

military, 51, 56, 93; officers in, 29, 43, 49–50

mine owners, 240, 245; Creole, 237; and Gálvez, 239, 241, 243; problems of, 237–38, 266. *See also* Tribunal de Minería

mining, 78, 226, 233, 297; and *almaceneros*, 237–38; and merchants, 76, 228; mercury, 136, 153, 284; and taxes, 284. *See also* silver mining

mining districts, 52, 76, 78, 124; Catorce, 224, 265; Guanajuato, 224, 234–36, 239–40, 242–43, 245, 403n94; Pachuca/Real del Monte, 240–41; in Peru, 21–22, 136, 144, 224; Zacatecas, 153, 224, 234, 236, 265

Mirabeau, comte de (Honoré-Gabriel Riqueti), 308–9, 416n16

Misselden, Edward, 80

Molinillo, Francesco Fernández de, 76, 365n61

Mollinedo y La Cuadra, Nicolas (marqués de Los Llanos), 61, 63–67, 69–70, 78

Monarquía indiana (Torquemada), 251

Moñino, Francisco, 269

Moñino, José. *See* Floridablanca